This book is an analysis of thinking, remembering, and reminiscing according to ancient authors, and their medieval readers. The author argues that behind the various medieval methods of interpreting texts of the past lie two apparently incompatible theories of human knowledge and remembering, as well as two differing attitudes to matter and intellect.

This book comprises a series of studies taking as evidence of the past, ancient, scriptural and patristic texts, showing how these texts were understood by medieval readers and writers to be accounts of how people constructed narratives in order to give accounts of experience. These studies confirm that medieval and Renaissance understandings and uses of the past were not what is now generally understood by the past and its uses, but also that some modern understandings of the past and how it is remembered betray startling continuities with ancient and medieval theories.

Theories of remembering in the middle ages are shown to be in part about conceptual and linguistic signs, and in part about the reconstruction of narratives. Discussion extends to the nature of historical evidence, to the theories behind medieval historiography, and to various hypotheses relating physiological attributes of brain to intellectual processes of mind.

ANCIENT AND MEDIEVAL
MEMORIES

ANCIENT AND MEDIEVAL MEMORIES

Studies in the reconstruction
of the past

JANET COLEMAN

Reader in Ancient and Medieval Political Thought
Government Department, London School of
Economics and Political Science

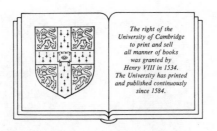

The right of the
University of Cambridge
to print and sell
all manner of books
was granted by
Henry VIII in 1534.
The University has printed
and published continuously
since 1584.

CAMBRIDGE UNIVERSITY PRESS

CAMBRIDGE   NEW YORK   PORT CHESTER
MELBOURNE   SYDNEY

Published by the Press Syndicate of the University of Cambridge
The Pitt Building, Trumpington Street, Cambridge, CB2 1RP
40 West 20th Street, New York, NY 10011–4211, USA
10 Stamford Road, Oakleigh, Melbourne 3166, Australia

© Cambridge University Press 1992

First published 1992

Printed in Great Britain at the University Press, Cambridge

A cataloguing in publication
record for this book is
available from the
British Library

Library of Congress cataloguing in publication data
Coleman, Janet.
Ancient and medieval memories: studies in the reconstruction of
the past / Janet Coleman.
p.   cm.
Includes index.
ISBN 0 521 41144 0
1. History, Ancient – Historiography. 2. Middle Ages –
Historiography. 3. Historiography. 4. Memory. 1. Title.
D13.C596 1991
930'.072 – dc20   90–27733 CIP
ISBN 0 521 41144 0 hardback

CE

To Gary and Shem

CONTENTS

PREFACE

Now that these studies have been written, I must, following Pascal, decide what should be put first. I must say something about what has been done here and why. Originally trained as a physical chemist, I was equally interested in the study of history and historical explanation. I turned out to be inadequate in both domains. Dissatisfied with theories of explanation in disciplines that were held to employ opposing methods of analysis of facts, I have not come up with some universally applicable method that is more satisfying. But in devoting myself to an interdisciplinary approach to the study of the middle ages, I have, over twenty years, reaffirmed my conviction that alien patterns of thought can be investigated to some degree of satisfaction, without my ever believing that the way medieval authors described their world was the way I described mine. It has never been clear to me that there is a single truth about living, that the world is indubitably one way for all of us or throughout history, except in trivial ways. With language one crosses and intersects other ways of describing how it is in the world for human experiencers without ever quite hitting on an expression which encapsulates how it really is for this one. Some expressions come close but only just: language is limited. I think it has always been thus. The otherness of thinking and living in the middle ages, as it is expressed in texts, is for me, in the first instance, simply a shift in discourse.

Perhaps more to the point, in having transplanted myself to a culture other than the one in which I was born and educated, I gradually became aware that my memories of dear ones, loves and acquaintances, seemed to recede and alter when I was out of the original setting in which I came to know them. More startlingly, I found they simply were not with me. I had not deliberately forgotten them; they simply were somehow edited out of my present, unsuited to present settings. And descriptions of my past were translated into another code which present friends used to describe their lives. My explanatory narratives became justifications of who I thought I had become, in a language that was mine but also theirs and in its sharing, somehow less mine. Instead of inducing a feeling of alienation, this reinterpretation of my experiences provided comfort and a shy kind of gratitude regarding the ease with which one learns conventional codes of self-expression. If I had reconstructed my personal past, not to lie about it in any conscious way but to communicate it coherently to others, could it be said that this is what various thinkers during the middle ages, concerned with issues of how the past is known and what the past means for someone who confronts it, were also doing? Here began my journey from the ancient Greek world through the Latin middle ages, to examine theories of memory and the consequent issue of how these memories were thought to be used by rememberers.

The great historian Maitland once reflected on the materials needed to reconstruct medieval history. For him they were records of the law and the courts, and he said one had to master an 'extremely formal system of pleading and procedure', 'a whole system of actions with repulsive names'. This is especially true of medieval philosophy and theology. Over the years I have attempted to master these 'repulsive names' and alien methods. In this book I have tried to give an account of some of the most prominent medieval theories and practices of remembering and reconstructing the past by examining the various ways in which texts (which were written in antiquity and which spoke to the future about the authors' present), were interpreted and understood during the middle ages. This book examines attitudes to and uses of the past through a study of texts written over a period of nearly 2,000 years. It is an attempt to construct a plausible account of earlier theories of remembering at a time when, for the most part, we hold that the past as past is irrecoverable and 'other' but that it can be known to some extent in its otherness if only through analogies that seem coherent to us.

As Collingwood put it, 'the past simply as past is wholly unknowable; it is the past as residually preserved in the present that is alone knowable'. In a certain sense, Thomas Aquinas in the thirteenth century knew this as well, and he and many of his contemporaries and successors were philosophically concerned to try to explain why the past as past was not only unknowable but in an important sense, trivial. Even those like William of Ockham, who argued that the past as past was knowable as such, and then developed complex psychological mechanisms to try to explain this 'fact', none the less believed that the past's importance, its significance, was only in and with respect to the present. Whether or not they could prove that men remembered exactly what was, they all argued that men make the past intelligible in the light of present circumstances. I use the term 'men' in its generic sense but meaning 'male' insofar as the medieval texts considered below do not explicitly include or exclude women from their discussions, taking mind's capacity for intellection to be sexually undifferentiated. There is no doubt, however, that for both Plato and Aristotle, on whose writings later medieval accounts depend, the characteristics of rational mind are explicitly male.

The bickering of philosophical sects are an amusement for the foolish; above these jarrings and creakings of the machine of thought there is a melody sung in unison by the spirits of the spheres, which are the great philosophers. This melody, *philosophia quaedam perennis*, is not a body of truth revealed once for all, but a living thought whose content, never discovered for the first time, is progressively determined and clarified by every genuine thinker.[1]

Furthermore, this book argues that behind the various medieval methods of interpreting texts of the past through an analysis of texts' language and the ways in which language signifies real experiences, lie not only two apparently incompatible theories of human knowledge, but also two differing attitudes to matter and intellect. It is a book that takes as evidence of the past, past texts, past accounts of how men constructed narratives about how it was for them to be in the world. And in locating what look like progressive and regressive lines of development in medieval arguments about the past, a past known through past texts confronted by medieval readers and writers, this book attempts to confirm two things. On the one hand, it argues that the medieval understanding of the past was in some outstandingly important ways not what we understand by the past. On the other, it also attempts to show that the modern sense of the past is, in fact, a very recent and even limited attitude and that it is not one subscribed to by all modern historians, nor by all of us all of the time.

The book is also an *indirect* attempt to reexamine ancient and medieval theories of remembering in order to evaluate whether modern psychological and neurophysiological theories of remembering have superseded past accounts as they affirm they have when they characterise earlier theories as belonging to a period of archaic mind and the childhood of civilisation now come to maturity. To my own astonishment, I have found that modern scientific accounts of the earlier theories of thinking and remembering are not only oversimplified and inaccurate.[2] The modern theories

---

[1] R. G. Collingwood, *Speculum Mentis or the Map of Knowledge* (Oxford, 1924), p. 13.

[2] For instance, they only provide Aristotle's imprint theory and not the nonphysiological side of his argument in the *De Anima*. Or they say things like: 'For Plato [sic] the formation and preservation of memory was likened to the imprint of a solid object in soft wax; when the wax hardened a trace was left behind. Using this example as an analogy, Plato held that experiences may similarly leave traces upon an impressionable mind. Memory traces are

which have replaced frequently misdescribed earlier theories, despite their experimental, scientific jargon, often are rather more unsophisticated than *some* medieval theories. This does not mean that any of the medieval theories more adequately 'saves the phenomena' than any of the modern ones. But I had not realised before embarking on this project that some of the most dominant current psychological theories of mind, learning, language and remembering, especially materialist theories of mind, have apparently unknowingly so narrowed the discussion of these perennial issues. They are working only with another set of analogies which often appear to me to be less fruitful than those of some earlier models, when they do not simply reproduce what some earlier thinkers themselves concluded, albeit in another language and narrative genre. In the final chapter I have attempted to give an overview of some modern theories of mind and remembering in order to take the account of ancient and medieval theories into the present. I leave it to the reader to determine how far we have come in these matters.

Theories of remembering in the middle ages turn out to be, in part, theories of signs, of language and the various ways in which language relates to thinking. Medieval theories of memory are, in part, theories of reconstruction. This is because learning to read and write depended for many centuries on late classical grammar and logic texts which effectively argued that things in the world, to which language referred and thinking referred, could not be 'touched' except through the mediation of linguistic or mental signs. Hence, the examination of a text which was a surviving fragment of the past in the present, could only be an examination of coherent ways of grammatically and logically speaking about experiences, rather than an examination of the events themselves. The nature of reliable evidence is at issue in medieval historiography and epistemology, intimately bound up with the nature of language and men's confidence in its conventionally established means to refer to and report nontextual evidence accurately. Physics and mathematics were taken to have their own ways of dealing with the world. Historical knowledge and understanding is of the world but only through language. Hence, they accepted the gospel testimony as the unembellished accounts of the eye-witness experiences of the evangelists, and sought no further verification of such accounts. But this, of course, is precisely what I am doing as an historian of ideas expressed in past texts: I cannot, through this examination, make any assertion about the extralinguistic reality or existence of what the

the records of past experience which occur as a result of learning.' John G. Seamon, *Memory and Cognition, An Introduction* (Oxford, 1980), p. 4. I discuss below how this is precisely not Plato's view but the view he rejects.

words and sentences refer to. Who knows whether what they said about their experiences accurately matched those experiences as experienced? But I am afraid I am in the same situation regarding any of my friends: we are using a conventional series of signs and constructions to turn private, sensual experiences into common counters.

But medieval theories of memory are not only theories of signs. They provide elaborate descriptions and hypotheses about the 'place' of thinking and remembering, and then relate physiological attributes to intellectual processes. We are still asking 'where in the brain are memories stored' and we still do not know.

In concluding this study with summaries of various competing contemporary neurophysiological and psychological theories of memory, I have meant only to indicate that the modern world is, in some important ways, reformulating issues and some answers, that were already at the heart of medieval discussions. Most of us remain unaware that modern science, some modern history and modern philosophy have inherited from the Renaissance a trivialisation of over 1,000 years of previous history. We have accepted that aspects of modernity began during the Renaissance and that preceding centuries were populated by men and women without historical perspective, without philosophical and logical insight, weighed down by an orthodoxy we have not, for the most part, even had the curiosity to examine before we reject it. Where thinkers in the Renaissance are believed to be like us, medieval thinkers, even when some concede they may be interesting, are not like us. But *neither* medieval nor Renaissance thinkers are like us. There is no argument in the following pages that we are simply repeating the middle ages. But there are important reasons why certain issues keep cropping up over the centuries in philosophical, theological and scientific circles, and one of these is that as a literate civilisation, we have constructed our pasts from inherited texts, taken what we see as relevant to our own situations while discarding the rest until the next generation picks up the threads dropped by its fathers. Certain kinds of questions, especially about thinking and remembering, do not seem to receive definitive answers at any time, and we repeat the analyses, moving backwards and forwards, in every generation.

This book was originally intended as a joint venture with Dr Burcht Pranger of the Theologische Faculteit of the University of Amsterdam. I have little doubt that had we collaborated it would have been very different. It would have been a more subtle, more beautifully and sensitively reconstructed memory of medieval rememberers. But events and experience led us in different directions. The resulting book is meant as a *semper memor* to our continuing friendship and common interests.

These pages have also, sadly, turned into a memorial to the most inspiring of my teachers, Professor Paul Vignaux (d. 1988), whose seminars at L'Ecole des Hautes Etudes, Paris, provided the setting and structure for my deepening acquaintance with fourteenth-century theology and philosophy. It was especially in cafés after class that M. Vignaux sat with this foreign student, and invited Duns Scotus and Ockham to join us, speaking through photocopied incunabula of the probable ordering of people's lives and thoughts. Because I have forgotten more than I can remember what I owe to M. Vignaux's inspiration, I have tried by writing these pages, to recapture that past through reminiscence. Vignaux's brilliance echoes only faintly, the traces have unwittingly been effaced, but they are the source of my continuing interest in the various medieval theories of remembering and knowing. I am all too aware that my past is only residually preserved in my present. And I also know that one learns only what one has it in one to learn, not what one's teachers have it in them to teach.

I should like to record my special thanks to Professor J. H. Burns, Dr Michael Clanchy, Professor Christopher Holdsworth, Mr Iain Hampsher-Monk, Professor David Luscombe, Professor Robert Markus, Dr Constant Mews, Professor Heiko Oberman, Dr Burcht Pranger, Professor Michael Wilks and to many others including my students at Exeter University and at the London School of Economics. I am grateful to these colleagues who read parts or all of this work in manuscript and offered their intellectual wit and inspiration so that this book might possess some virtue.

ABBREVIATIONS

AFH	*Archivum Franciscanum Historicum*
AHDLMA	*Archives d'histoire doctrinale et littéraire du moyen âge*
Archiv Gesch. Philos.	*Archiv für Geschichte der Philosophie*
BGPTMA	Beiträge zur Geschichte der Philosophie und Theologie des Mittelalters
CCEL	Corpus Christianorum Ecclesiasticorum Latinorum
Conf.	*Confessions*
CSEL	Corpus Scriptorum Ecclesiasticorum Latinorum
DA	*De Anima*
De Div. Qu.	*De Diversis Quaestionibus LXXXIII*
De Lib. Arb.	*De Libero Arbitrio*
De Ord.	*De Ordine*
DM	*De Memoria et Reminiscentia*
Ep.	*Epistolae*
Fin.	*De Finibus Bonorum et Malorum*
LI	*Logica Ingredientibus*, ed. B. Geyer, in *Peter Abelards philosophische Schriften*, BGPTMA, 21, vol. 1, 2, 3 (Münster in Westphalia, 1919–27)
LPNS	*Logica 'Nostrorum petitioni sociorum'*, ed. Geyer, BGPTMA, 21, vol. 4 (1933)
MGH	*Monumenta Germaniae Historica*
Nic. Ethics	*Nicomachean Ethics*
PG	J. P. Migne, ed., *Patrologia Graeca*
Phlb.	*Philebus*
Phil. Consolatio	*De Consolatione Philosophiae*
PL	J. P. Migne, ed., *Patrologiae Cursus Completus*, series Latina
Post. Anal.	*Posterior Analytics*
Prior Anal.	*Prior Analytics*

xix

List of abbreviations

REA	*Revue des Études Augustiniennes*
Rhet.	*Rhetoric*
RTAM	*Recherches de Théologie Ancienne et Médievale*
ST	*Summa Theologiae*
Sup. Periermenias	*Glossae super Periermenias*
Tht.	*Theaetetus*
TRHS	*Transactions of the Royal Historical Society*

PART I

THE CRITICAL TEXTS OF ANTIQUITY

INTRODUCTION

This book attempts, through a series of interrelated studies, to give an account of the range of views on memory and its uses during the middle ages. But we must begin with ancient Greek and Roman positions because these would be drawn upon, reinterpreted, even distorted by later, medieval rememberers in order that they might reach working hypotheses that served their own understanding of how men came to know their world and remember their pasts.

Medieval readers believed that the text itself was the self-sufficient object of inquiry and understanding, providing a timeless contribution to the truth of how it is to be a human knower and rememberer. For the most part, when medieval readers confronted ancient texts, they were not troubled by what for us appears to be a major methodological difficulty in understanding the meaning of past texts. Consequently, they rarely, if ever raised the issue of first having to know the social and economic context of a past text as the means of gaining access to its meaning and, so recovering the intentions of its author. Instead, they paid attention to a close analysis of the text, weighing it over and over again in order to elucidate what they took to be its timeless and universal meaning. Only gradually did they come to read a past text in the context of what they took to be the *linguistic* conventions of the time in which it was written. It is hoped that as the present reader confronts the accounts given of how and why attitudes to past texts changed during the medieval centuries, it will become clearer why a twentieth-century account of attitudes to memory and memorials must *try* to consider not only what medieval authors said but also the social, economic, legal and institutional reasons for their analyses taking the form they did. But this is precisely what most medieval readers never did themselves when they read the texts of antiquity. Consequently, the following treatment of the critical texts of antiquity attempts to present the classical arguments 'simply' as a-contextual, philosophical positions,

3

which later medieval readers thought to be relevant to questions about how human beings, at any moment of contingent history, learn about the world and then remember what they have learnt. There is no doubt, however, that I have chosen to highlight those aspects of classical discussions which, with hindsight, I know to have been of particular interest to medieval readers so that there is in what follows, an implicit skewing of classical positions towards their medieval future.

During the classical period of Greek thought, the question of what memory is was linked intimately with the problem of how we know what we know, and what the object of knowing essentially is. To know somehow also includes retaining over time information that is not necessarily continuously present to perception. To know implies a more stable and enduring grasp of what the something is than a momentary reception of its visible or audible characteristics affords us. And yet to understand what we believe we know requires that we forget the specificity of different things as they are individually perceived in order to generalise and abstract from details. The generation of meaning entails a destruction of the repleteness of the moment by moment experience of substantive living.

The Greeks were as concerned as we are, if not more so, about what appears to be the paradoxical requirement to forget in order to know. 'Just what are we remembering' and 'how does memory operate', consequently emerged as two primary issues for the Greeks in their search for an adequate theory of knowledge. To determine the contribution of the changing world of experience in men's lives, lives shored up by fixed opinions, beliefs, and stabilised by knowledge, was to become a major theme of the Greek philosophical enterprise. Two powerful, interrelated but contrasting theories emerged, that of Plato and Aristotle, that would dominate the western philosophical tradition. At the heart of each epistemology is an explanation of memory and beneath the surface of each is the fear of forgetting.

That we cannot speak of Plato's or Aristotle's understanding of memory without dealing with their wider epistemologies will become clear in what follows. With Plato, we find a theory of remembering that coincides with a theory of knowing. Aristotle, however, not only distinguishes memory from reminiscence but also treats memory and reminiscence as dependent activities made possible once we know something.

Chapter 1

PLATO

Plato on memory; his theory of mind, learning, recalling, knowing.
'Meno', 'Phaedrus', 'Republic'.

Plato's *Meno*,[1] a middle-period dialogue which is thought to report a conversation that took place in the newly restored democracy in Athens of 402 BC, sets out a theory of knowledge as recollection. The wealthy Meno raises the sophistic dilemma about knowledge, that one can never find out anything new so that either one knows it already and one has no need to find it out, or else one does not know and there is no means of recognising it when found. 'How will you look for something when you do not in the least know what it is? How on earth are you going to set up something you don't know as the object of your search? Even if you come right up against it, how will you know that what you have found is the thing you did not know?' (80 D). Socrates tries to answer this question of how it is possible to inquire into anything unknown by attempting to elucidate the nature of knowledge, inquiry and reality.[2] He propounds his theory that knowledge is recollection, rather than something imparted by teaching, basing it on the religious doctrine that the human soul is immortal. Instead of perishing at the body's death, the soul migrates elsewhere and is thereafter born in a new body. Its wanderings here and in the other world have exposed it to *all* there is to know: 'the soul is immortal and has been born many times and has seen all things both here and in the other world, it has learned everything that is' (81 C–D). It therefore follows that when a man recalls a single piece of knowledge he should be able to start from what he knows and be reminded of all the rest of knowledge latently stored in his mind. In ordinary language, Socrates says, we call this 'learning', but actually it is recollecting; 'for seeking and learning are in fact nothing but recollection' (81 C–D). The learning process is the activity of eliciting the knowledge that is already in the mind, recollecting it in order, which is the proper way

---

[1] Plato, *Protagoras and Meno*, trans. W. K. C. Guthrie (Harmondsworth, 1956). *Plato's Meno*, ed. R. S. Bluck (Cambridge, 1961), Greek text and introduction.

[2] In general, see J. M. Moravcsik, 'Understanding and knowledge in Plato's philosophy', *Neue Hefte für Philosophie*, 15–16 (1978), 53–69; S. Scolnicov, 'Three aspects of Plato's philosophy of learning and instruction', *Paideai*, Special Plato Issue (1976), 50–62.

5

to recollect (82 D), so that one possesses a knowledge of which one was hitherto unaware.

Socrates has evaded the either/or terms of the original dilemma that one either knows something or not, by recognising a process that starts from unconscious knowledge (which ought not to be taken as ignorance because at birth the mind is never completely blank), moves on to opinion or belief, and then on to the latter's conversion into knowledge. The object of cognition at the level of *doxa* (belief/opinion) or at the level of knowledge, is however, the same and unchanging. To know something in an imperfectly conscious, uncoordinated way through opinion, based either on inductive evidence, second-hand information, or trust, must be converted to knowledge by a repetition of a questioning process whereby one works out an explanation for understanding the reason why something is true so that it is firmly fixed in the mind. Reasoning out the cause as accomplished by dialectical question-and-answer over a long period of time is another name for recollection. This recollection process is awakened by skilful questioning. But what is the nature of the knowable? Plato treats this more fully in another middle dialogue, the *Phaedo*.[3]

Here, he asserts that the true objects of knowledge are Forms or Ideas, and these Forms are independent of the particular concrete things that embody them, or images of them, in the sensible world. All sensible things are in a perpetual flow of change so that there can be no knowledge of them. The true objects of knowledge are unchanging and stable. So what we know is not the concrete things around us but the objects of thought known by the mind when it withdraws from the senses to think by itself.[4]

Furthermore, in the *Theaetetus*,[5] Socrates says, against anyone who takes up the position of Protagoras (that man is the measure of all things and therefore, knowledge and perception are the same thing), that one ought not to suppose that in *remembering* what he has experienced, a man is having the same sort of experience (*pathos*) as he had when he was *experiencing* what he now remembers. Socrates wishes to show that memory is not knowledge of the remembered *things*; seeing is not knowing.[6] Indeed, the mind in itself is its own instrument for contemplating the

---

[3] *Phaedo*, trans. Hugh Tredennick, in *The Collected Dialogues of Plato including the Letters*, eds. E. Hamilton and H. Cairns (Bollingen ser. 71) (Princeton, New Jersey, 1973) pp. 40–98 (hereafter *Collected Dialogues*).

[4] G. E. R. Lloyd, *Magic, Reason and Experience, Studies in the Origins and Development of Greek Science*, (Cambridge, 1979); on the unreliability of the senses and observational methods in Plato, pp. 132–3. Only in the later dialogues does Plato point out that in perception it is the soul that grasps sense-objects *through* the senses. eg. *Tht.* 184b-c; *Phlb.* 33c ff.

[5] Trans. F. M. Cornford, in *Collected Dialogues*, pp. 845–919.

[6] *Tht.*, 163 D-164 B, pp. 869–870: Socrates: 'Suppose someone were to ask: "Is it possible for a man who has once come to know something and still preserve a memory of it, not to

common terms that apply to everything, for example, existence/ nonexistence, likeness/unlikeness, sameness/difference, unity and numbers in general. Thinking is discourse and judgement is a statement inwardly pronounced.

But what happens when someone judges falsely? Plato provides the following physiological analogy to show how some have thought false judgements come about, an analogy that would exert considerable influence not only on Aristotle[7] but on generations of medieval thinkers,[8] and which continues to be defended in certain twentieth-century schools of psychology and neurophysiology.[9]

Socrates asks Theaetetus to imagine for the sake of argument that the mind contains a block of wax which in this or that individual man may be larger or smaller, comparatively pure in some, murky in others, harder in some and softer in others. Some will possess a wax of just the right consistency. We might call this block of wax a gift from the Muses' mother, Memory. When we wish to remember something that we see, hear or conceive in our own minds, we hold this wax under the perception or ideas and imprint them on it, thereby stamping the impression as we do with a seal ring. What is imprinted we remember and know so long as the image remains. False judgements can occur when, for instance, I, who know Theaetetus and Theodorus and possess imprints of both like seal impressions in the waxen block, see you both at a distance indistinctly and am in a hurry to assign the proper imprint of each to the proper visual perception, like fitting a foot into its own footprint to effect a recognition, and then make the mistake of interchanging them. Therefore, in the field of objects both known and perceived, judgement can be false by bringing

know just that thing that he remembers at the moment when he remembers it?" This is, perhaps, rather a long-winded way of putting the question. I mean, can a man who has become acquainted with something and remembers it, not know it? ...' The conclusion is that a man who has come to know a thing and still remembers it, does not know it since he does not see it, *if* knowledge and perception are the same thing, which Socrates says they are not.

[7] See below, chapter 2.

[8] See below, ch. 15, on the *Prose Salernitan Questions* and on Arabic commentaries on Aristotle's *De Anima* and on ancient medical tracts.

[9] The literature is vast. See R. Edgley, 'Innate ideas', in *Knowledge and Necessity*, Royal Institute of Philosophy Lectures, vol. 3, 1968/9, (London, 1970), pp. 1–33, a critical discussion of among others N. Chomsky, 'Recent contributions to the theory of innate ideas', *Synthese*, 17 (1967), in contrast with various empiricist theories. Chomsky has said: 'The child who acquires a language ... knows a great deal more than he has learned', *Aspects of the Theory of Syntax* (Cambridge, Mass. 1965), pp. 32–3. Rationalism usually claims not only that we have ideas that are not derived from experience but that at least some of these ideas are ideas of reason or understanding. The ambiguity here centres on what precisely is innate: knowledge or a disposition of some sort? This would be recognised by Avicenna. See below, ch. 15

wrong imprints to match perceptions (191 D–6D). Socrates goes on to note that 'they' say when a man has in his mind a good thick slab of wax, smooth, kneaded to the right consistency, the impressions that come through the senses are stamped on the tables of the 'heart' – Homer's word hints at the mind's likeness to wax[10] – then the imprints are clear, deep enough to last. Such people are quick to learn and also have good memories and do not interchange the imprints of their perceptions but think truly. But those with muddy wax blocks which are over-soft or over-hard, are quick to learn (if their wax is soft) but forgetful; if their wax is hard they are slow to learn but retain. Impressions in soft wax are indistinct because they melt together and some become blurred. If they overlap through being crowded together into some wretched little narrow mind, they are still more indistinct. All these types of minds are likely to judge falsely.

Socrates, however, will reject this explanation that false judgement is simply a misfitting of thought to perception. Seeing is not knowing.

Plato separates the sensible from the thinkable, and through his interest in mathematics and geometry he shows that a system of truths obtains, truths which do not hold good of visible, tangible things of sense and whose proofs could not be demonstrated by reference to such things. Instead, mathematical and geometrical truths pertain to a supersensible world that is only accessible to intelligence. Material bodies only approximate the ideal objects of geometry and the latter are exempt from time and change. These eternal objects and necessary truths comprise reality and the real objects of thought are not found in the physical world, nor can they be extracted from it. Knowledge comes out of the mind itself and recollection is the process by which this knowledge is raised to awareness. Not only mathematical but also moral concepts, as the eternal objects of thought knowable without the senses, are recovered out of a memory latent in the soul. It is, then, the power of thought that pierces the surface of changeable appearance to disclose beyond it an objective, unchanging 'nature of things' knowable to mind alone. Knowledge is as much an eternal, immovable structure as is the nature of things. Plato's theory of recollection (*anamnesis*) is therefore based on a prior ontology.[11] There can be no knowledge of the natural world of material, concrete entities itself because the natural world is always in flux, coming to be and passing away. The world of experience leads only to opinion and belief, and when beliefs are false they can only be shown to be such through being shown *logically*

---

[10] *Iliad*, 2. 851; 16. 554.

[11] J. M. Moravcsik, 'Recollecting the theory of forms', in W. H. Werkmeister, ed., *Facets of Plato's Philosophy, Phronesis*, supplement 2 (Assen, 1976), pp. 1–20.

inconsistent with other beliefs accepted as more certain. True belief can be confirmed as knowledge, but this, once again, occurs only from repeated *logical* demonstrations of, for instance, how propositions necessarily follow from one another.[12] Opinion or true belief is converted into knowledge by repeated reflections on the *reasons* for something being the case. This work of repeated reflection binds a set of true beliefs into a coherent system and it is this repeated reflection which is recollection. Indeed, recollection of this kind is an endless process by which we move towards uncovering the whole, fixed, logical structure of truth by recovering it from our memories.[13]

In the *Meno* Socrates tries to demonstrate that an uneducated slave-boy can be shown to know implicitly geometric truths merely by being asked the right questions. He concludes: 'a man who does not know has in himself true opinions on a subject without having knowledge ... At present these opinions, being newly aroused, have a dream-like quality. But if the same questions are put to him on many occasions and in different ways, you can see that in the end he will have a knowledge of the subject as accurate as anybody's ... This knowledge will not come from teaching but from questioning. He will recover it for himself ... And the spontaneous recovery of knowledge that is in him is recollection' (85 C–D). The truth about reality has always been in our souls, and this demonstrates the soul's immortality. In effect, what the activity of recollection does is 'tether' true opinions, which are apt to run away from our minds, by repeated reflection. Knowledge, like right opinion, is acquired through the searching activity of recollection.

But let us note that it is only knowledge of a certain type that can thus be recovered. Historical knowledge in the sense of individual facts and events of human or natural history, is not contained in this inner consciousness or latent memory. Because particular facts are sensibly experienced and stored in what we might call a personal, individual, subjective memory, Plato does not consider this knowledge. Plato recognises that we have the capacity to preserve in the memory sensible instances but he says there is no *understanding* involved in this sense memory. Permanent, knowable reality, on the other hand, does not alter and it is immaterial. As such it is only accessible to pure thought. This means that Plato is talking of an impersonal memory of mankind.[14] Differences between individuals

---

[12] H.-P. Stahl, 'Beginnings of propositional logic in Plato', trans. Gertrud Weiler, in *Plato's Meno, Text and Essays*, ed. Malcolm Brown (New York, 1971), pp. 180–97.

[13] In general, see Jon Moline, *Plato's Theory of Understanding* (Madison, Wisc., 1981).

[14] F. M. Cornford, *Principium Sapientiae: The Origins of Greek Philosophical Thought* (Cambridge, 1952), chapter 4, part I, 'Anamnesis', pp. 45–61. Also in *Plato's Meno, Text and Essays*, ed. Brown, pp. 108–27; p. 120. This apparent dual memory, one related to

consist only in the degree to which knowledge has been elicited (or not) and made conscious (or not).

What has been put forward in the *Meno* and more explicitly in the *Phaedo* is the belief in the separateness of intelligence and objects known by it from the material world. This assumes the coherent logical necessity of the real and its truth, and represents a view of the sources of knowledge that is much older than the alternative medical-empirical doctrine that knowledge comes through the senses.[15] Aristotle was later to say that this Platonic theory of Forms or Ideas was a variety of the older Pythagoreanism on to which were grafted modifications by the Socratic influence.[16]

The end of the *Meno* returns to an issue raised in the beginning, whether virtue can be taught, by arguing that it probably cannot be taught, and therefore comes to man by means of a mysterious intuition, a divine dispensation achieved without thought and therefore, without knowledge. In the democracy of Athens during the fifth century, knowledge has not been a guide in practical public life; it is evident that virtuous public figures have been unable to impart their virtue to their sons although they must have desired to do so. Rather it appears to be

well-aimed conjecture which statesmen employ in upholding their countries' welfare. Their position in relation to knowledge is no different from that of prophets and tellers of oracles, who under divine inspiration utter many truths, but have no knowledge of what they are saying ... We are right therefore to give this title to the oracular priests and the prophets that I mentioned, and to poets of every description. Statesmen too, when by their speeches they get great things done yet know nothing of what they are saying, are to be considered as acting no less under divine influence, inspired and possessed by divinity. (99 D)

We shall have occasion to return to this divine intuitionism later on.[17]

Although the doctrine of knowledge as recollection has been set forth in the *Meno*, the dialogue ends as do many of the earlier dialogues, in an

perception, another related to thought, will later be interpreted by neo-Platonists and later medieval philosophers as indicative of a division between corporeal and intellectual faculties. Aristotle also proposes a 'lower' and 'higher' memory.

15 *Plato's Meno, Text and Essays*, ed. Brown, p. 127.

16 The mid sixth-century BC Pythagoras and his followers in Crotona, southern Italy, practised mathematics and studiously avoided literacy since writing was believed to be a source of error. They taught the doctrine of the transmigration of souls and their separability from body. Herodotus said Pythagoreans learned this doctrine in Egypt.

17 'So I soon made up my mind about the poets too: I decided that it was not wisdom that enabled them to write their poetry but a kind of instinct or inspiration such as you find in seers and prophets who deliver all their sublime messages without knowing in the least what they mean'. *Apology*, 21B–22E. For an extraordinary and controversial account relating ancient texts and modern psychological theories, see Julian Jaynes, *The Origin of Consciousness in the Breakdown of the Bicameral Mind* (Harmondsworth, 1982).

inconclusive manner, Socrates saying that we cannot really know how virtue is acquired unless we first examine the essential nature of virtue, and this has not been done here. Plato's *Republic* will pursue this issue not only to show that virtue is equivalent to knowledge, but also to set out the political consequences for individuals and the state where abstract truth is sought for its own sake by those naturally capable of what is, in effect, near absolute recollection of the Form or Idea of the Good. Society no longer need rely on divinely inspired well-aimed conjecture when the ideal state is established and ruled over by philosopher kings.

For Plato, then, all knowledge is latent in the mind and is never, strictly speaking, forgotten. The process of recollection merely elicits knowledge, raising it to consciousness. If anything is forgotten by thought, it is the changeable appearances of the concrete world of things of which there can be no knowledge, only opinion and belief. The *nature* of things, known to mind, is never lost to mind although it may remain implicit. The fixed, logical structure of truth is there to be recovered from our memories. The intricate tapestry of our inner experience is not derived out of mere matter, because consciousness and memory are not properties of the material. The Platonic process of recollection requires no explanation of how we interact with our environment precisely because the particularity of this world is forgotten in the recollective process. In discussing memory Plato forgets sense data as such and therefore implies that any conscious recollection is not the retrieval of images but rather of what, logically, must have been the essence of an earlier situation of which one was previously aware and then the reworking of these elements into a rational pattern. Reasoning out the explanation of what must have been is recollection. Aristotle will refer to this logical exercise of recollection as reminiscence, the conscious exercise of which need not rely on sense memory but which may end in remembering. But Aristotle denies the possibility and the desirability of editing out the world of particular experiences from our memories, thereby complicating the picture and opening up the discussion to what will later be seen as the insoluble paradoxes concerning the relation of intellect and brain, which endure to our own times. In effect, Plato is more assertive about the disjunction between thinking of our past experiences and the actual experiencing of them. The asserted disjunction is not, however, in the service of a theory of subjective, relativistic, creativity of thought. The presumed stability of being merely confirms the logical stability of reasoned recollection over and against a world of inconstant mutability. And by extension, concepts as classes of things exist in the mind, are prior to any sensual experience of an extramental individual belonging to a class, and are best raised to consciousness when the recollective mind is most removed from sensory stimulation. For Plato, one can never forget the essential formality of the world but in becoming conscious of that formality, one must forget its particularity, both temporal and material.

That the human memory is, for Plato, the means by which the rational part of the soul can be brought to a conscious reflection on the truths implicitly within it, is of some consequence in the wider and older Greek understanding of memory.[18] It is clear that Plato's *anamnesis* is not a mnemonic technique for recalling instances, places, things experienced. It is not a rhetorical art but a dialectical one, activated by appropriate questioning, 'mental midwifery', in which the logic of the world's structure is made plain. In fact, in the *Phaedrus*, Plato expresses a horror of those techniques like writing which will cause men to lose the true knowledge in their minds by encouraging them to lose their memories and to rely instead on letters or signs, external to the mind. Men, he says, will lose the ability to recall things that are within themselves when they use external letters.

The *Phaedrus*[19] relates how the Egyptian god Theuth, who invented number and calculation, geometry and astronomy, also discovered writing and thought he provided a recipe for memory and wisdom. When he brought his discovery to the ruler of Egypt, the god Thamus, he was warned that he had declared the very opposite of the true effect of writing.

If men learn this, it will implant forgetfulness in their souls; they will cease to exercise memory because they rely on that which is written, calling things to remembrance no longer from within themselves but by means of external marks. What you have discovered is a recipe not for memory but for reminder. And it is no true wisdom that you offer your disciples, but only its semblance, for by telling them of many things without teaching them, you will make them seem to know much, while for the most part they know nothing and as men filled, not with wisdom but with the conceit of wisdom, they will be a burden to their fellows.[20]

---

18 W. K. C. Guthrie, 'Plato's views on the nature of the soul', in G. Vlastos, ed., *Plato: A Collection of Critical Essays*, 2 vols. (New York, 1971), I, pp. 230–43.
19 Trans. R. Hackforth, in *Collected Dialogues*, pp. 475–525; p. 520, 275 A–B.
20 Colin Blakemore in *Mechanics of the Mind* (Cambridge, 1977) sounds a similar warning in another key when he says:
What we should be most afraid of, perhaps, is the fact that, since the invention of printing, magnetic tape and computer cards the Collective Mind has lost the vital ability to *forget*. A principal task for us lies in the organisation of knowledge for ready access. This problem is nowhere more acute than in science itself, where the sheer accumulation of facts threatens to impede rather than to assist the progress of new ideas ... Man might not go out with a bang of his own creation, nor freeze his race to death by stealing the energy resources of the earth. He might merely drown himself in a flood of information; society could collapse because it no longer comprehends its own cultural inheritance'

Plato's memory doctrine was very different from that other tradition, according to which the lyric poet Simonides of Ceos invented the mnemonic art of memory. This was a trivial technique which Plato scorned because it was sense-memory without understanding. Simonides taught one to arrange images of *things*:

> He inferred that persons desiring to train this faculty [of memory] must select places and form mental images of the things they wish to remember and store those images in the places, so that the order of the places will preserve the order of the things and the images of the things will denote the things themselves, and we shall employ the places and images respectively as a wax writing-tablet and the letters written on it.[21]

This technique would be influential in Latin rhetorical teaching throughout the middle ages and the Renaissance. But it was the Platonic recollection of immaterial Forms, what has come to be known as his Idealism, that would exert a much more fundamental influence on the Christian Latin west, largely through the writings of Augustine.

Plato's fear of literacy as no more than a faulty non-cognitive mnemonic 'device', is clarified if somewhat softened in the *Cratylus*,[22] where there is a discussion of the nature of words and their relation to reality. Cratylus argues that words refer naturally and necessarily to realities (383 A–B). Because names by nature have a truth, we are able to make true statements. Hermagoras on the other hand, argues that the truth of names is not at all automatic, otherwise one could not make false statements. He argues that the relationship between words and realities is purely conventional and arbitrary rather than logical (384 C–D). Socrates tries to settle the question by asserting that words do have a logical relationship to reality. Existing things have correlative signs and names and the relationship between a word and a thing is that of imitation. Verbal mimesis would not be possible if there were no natural resemblance between words and things (435 B–D). All words, however, have cognitive limitations (439 B–C). Seen as images, words are metaphysically a step removed from reality and they cannot therefore express what they refer to in a total manner. This is because words are not identical to things and their limitations increase when words imitate a-temporal, abstract forms. This, of course, depends on Plato's already elaborated transverbal criterion of truth which not only preexists writing but also language. Real objects of

---

(pp. 118–19). Also see Julian Jaynes, *The Origin of Consciousness in the Breakdown of the Bicameral Mind*, *passim*, and p. 208, 'The weakening of divine authority with writing'.

[21] As described by Cicero, *De Oratore*, II, lxxxvi. Translation used here is that of W. Sutton and H. Rackham, Loeb edition, pp. 351–4.

[22] Trans. B. Jowett, in *Collected Dialogues*, pp. 421–74.

thought are not to be found in the physical world and cannot be extracted from it. Knowledge comes out of the mind itself and is raised to consciousness by a process of recollection.[23] For Plato, a direct knowledge of real existence is not only possible but preferable to that achieved through the mediation of words and things. The soul and its objects of knowledge are eternal and unchanging; they may only be imperfectly known through verbal mimesis. Reality for Plato is both more than and other than linguistic and material.

For this reason the total reliance on written words as signs and on the circumstances of the material world to interpret and establish social convention, rather than on the immutable truths implicit in mind, will keep men in a state of forgetfulness so that they vacillate in a world of conflicting norms. The Socratic maxim, that the unexamined life is not worth living, was meant to serve as an injunction to examine and follow the 'inner voice' in mind rather than the changeable opinions of unreflective, memoryless men, most of whom are incapable of prophetic, divinely-inspired, unconscious intuitionism according to Plato. To know is, effectively, to remember; living must be a process of coming to know and therefore remembering what has always been true and worth uncovering. Plato was particularly pessimistic about the incapacities of most people, combined with their lack of interest, willingly to embark on the life-long task of remembering.

[23] For a thorough discussion of some of the dialogues that deal with recollection, see Carlo E. Huber, S. J., *Anamnesis bei Plato* (Pullacher philosophische Forschungen, VI) in *Kommission bei Max Hueber* (Munich, 1964).

Chapter 2

ARISTOTLE

*Aristotle on memory. The two-fold analysis of the soul; the relation
between the lower, physical and the higher, intellectual 'parts'. 'De
Anima' and 'De Memoria et Reminiscentia'; representative language and
the distinction between history and rhetoric.*

Memory, its physical structure, is an unsolved challenge. It is, perhaps, the
central question ... But theories about the nature of memory have still not really
progressed beyond the stage of description through analogy. Analogy has often
been a valuable step in the discussion of biological problems, but it is, of its
nature, constrained by the technological development of the time or the level of
scientific knowledge in other fields ... Even current models of memory dwell on
analogies with existing, artificial methods of storing information. Mental
memory has been compared with the electro-magnetic polarisation of ferrite
rings in the core memory of a computer, and with the 'distributed' image of a
hologram – a device that stores a record of a three-dimensional scene by
photographing the interference pattern produced by illuminating it with laser
light ... In any case, most theories of memory, whether couched in terms of
mere analogy, or even in terms of the storage of information in networks of real
nerve cells, concentrate on the manner in which events can cause changes in
physical structures. In other words, they are concerned with the *machinery* of
memory, not the *code* – the symbolic form in which the events are registered ...
Most theories of memory are, as it were, concerned with the question of ink and
paper and not with the much more fundamental issue of the grammar of
remembrance.

Colin Blakemore, Mechanics of the Mind (Cambridge, 1977), pp. 101–6.

Dear Reader,
We are about to observe how Aristotle was concerned both with the *machinery* of
memory *and* with the *code*, providing a physiological imprint theory as well as a
theory of intellectual reconstruction of the past, an iconic memory and a logical
reminiscence.

Author

Plato's student Aristotle was far more influenced by the medical-empirical
doctrine that knowledge comes through the senses. And he also gives a
larger role to the technique of memorising, recommending it for students
of dialectic. But there is much more than a mnemonic technique set out in

his *De Memoria et Reminiscentia*,[1] and in his *De Anima*[2] especially books II and III.

A wide range of things may be remembered according to Aristotle. The range extends from facts learned, contemplated, heard, seen; to objects of scientific and logical knowledge, that one did something the day before yesterday, a person, a name, the last member of a list of things; what one experienced and how much time elapsed since that experience, mathematical entities, abstract objects of thought, and the past. He distinguishes between the act of remembering at a particular time and a disposition or tendency to remember (*hexis* or *pathos*, a state or affection) which lasts over a period of time and is consequent on our perceiving, apprehending, experiencing or learning (*DM*, I, 449b 24–5, 451a 23–4, 451a 27–8). The disposition results from an imprint stamped into a bodily sense organ in a special way: there must be an object of perception and a sense organ capable of perceiving it. When one remembers, the *present* content of one's mind is an image which is a likeness or copy of the *past* thing remembered. This image is both similar to and somehow derived from the thing remembered, causally derived from the past *act of perception* (*DM*, I, 450a 25).[3] Remembering involves an image, an *eikon*, of the *thing remembered* and not some symbol of that thing. And it is not only remembering that requires images. Aristotle believes that all thinking uses images (*DM* I, 449b 31), so he is here very different from Plato for whom dialectical thinking transcends the need for images (*Republic*, 510B, 511C, 532A). For Plato, the objects of thought are not housed in the memory as they are for Aristotle; the Forms exist separate from the sensible, material, bodily world. But Aristotle believes very few things can exist separately from the sensible world and thought requires sensible vehicles which he refers to as the sensible forms of external things, which are somehow transferred to the perceiving sense organ. When perception is over, there is a further resulting image derived from the sensible form which provides a further

---

[1] Richard Sorabji, *Aristotle on Memory* (London, 1972), an English translation of the *De Memoria et Reminiscentia* and commentary. For an introductory analysis of Aristotle's mature theory of the soul in the setting of alternative contemporary Greek and modern theories, see *Aristotle, De Anima (On the Soul)*, trans. with intro. Hugh Lawson-Tancred (Harmondsworth, 1986). Also see the various essays in G. E. R. Lloyd and G. E. L. Owen, eds., *Aristotle on Mind and the Senses*, proceedings of the seventh symposium Aristotelicum (Cambridge, 1978). Generally, see J. Barnes, M. Schofield and R. Sorabji, eds., *Articles on Aristotle*, vol. 4 (London, 1979).

[2] Aristotle, *De Anima*, II, III, trans. with notes. D. W. Hamlyn (Oxford, 1968).

[3] 450a 25: '... one must think of the affection which is produced by means of perception in the soul and in that part of the body which contains the soul, as being like a sort of picture, the having of which we say is memory. For the change that occurs marks in a sort of imprint of the sense image, as people do who seal things with signet rings.' (Compare Plato's account in the *Theaetetus*.)

vehicle for remembering and thinking (*DM*, I, 450a 30–2). Both memory
and thinking require images. Aristotle therefore believes that the material
world can be known, the sensible forms and the memory images being
true likenesses without the materiality of the external object of sense or
experience (*DA*, II, 12, 424a 17f). In fact, he believes that one thinks of
certain magnitudes existing outside oneself by means of small scale
models created in one's mind whose proportions are accurate, where the
mental object is a miniature in relation to the object of perception (*DM*, II
452b 7–15). So too a memory image of a scene is a copy of that scene. He
seems to imply at times that one's memory image is a copy of one's
perception of that scene rather than of the objective scene itself, so that the
memory image agrees with the past *perceiving* of a past object of perception
(*DM*, I, 451a 4, 450a 31–2).[4] Although he describes the likeness or
imprint stamped into one as an imprint of one's sense image, he assumes
that the sense organs perceive accurately the objects of perception. This is
because he describes the sense organ as having a passive capacity to
become the imprint it receives. A memory image is thereafter produced
from the sense image by a further imprinting process. What makes it a
memory image rather than an image in the imagination is the simultaneous capacity to recognise a time lapse between the experience and its
recollection. It is not clear whether or not he means there is an image
representing a time lapse and an image representing the thing remembered.[5] Thus one who remembers *regards* his memory image as a copy of a

---

[4] *DM*, I, 450b 11f:
  But does one remember the affection or the thing from which it was produced? If the
  former, we would remember nothing absent, but if the latter, how is it that while perceiving
  the affection we remember the absent thing which we are not perceiving? And if it is like an
  imprint or drawing in us, why should the perception of this be the memory of a different
  thing rather than of the affection itself? ... One must conceive the image in us to be
  something in its own right and to be of another thing. Insofar as it is something in its own
  right, it is an object of contemplation or an image. But insofar as it is of another thing, it is a
  sort of copy and reminder.' (450b 20f)
  There is a problem in translating *aesthesis* which can mean sensation and perception. See
  I. Block, 'Truth and error in Aristotle's theory of sense perception', *Philosophical Quarterly*,
  11 (1961), 1–9.

[5] *DM*, I, 449b 24: 'Memory is not perception or conception but a state or affection
  connected with one of these when time has elapsed. There is no memory of the present at
  the present. But perception is of the present, prediction of the future, memory of the past.
  Therefore, all memory involves time. So only animals which perceive time remember, and
  they do so by means of that with which they perceive'. 449b 30f: '... it is not possible to
  think without an image ... But it is necessary that magnitude and change should be known
  by the same means as time [ie, spatialisation] and an image is an affection belonging to the
  common sense. [The latter is explained in the *De Anima*) ... knowledge of these is due to
  the primary perceptive part.' Also 450a 15f. In *Physics*, IV 10–14 (222a 10-b 7), Aristotle
  provides an extended treatment of time where he argues that 'now' is not part of time but a
  mathematical limit which marks a distinction of before and after movement.

past experience and one must 'say in one's soul or to oneself' that one has encountered this something before (*DM*, I, 449a 9f).[6] The link between one's present state of remembering and the past perception is a causal one, where the physical imprint connects the present image with the earlier perceptual act (*DM*, I, 449b 24). He does believe memory is of the past or what is past (*DM*, I, 449a 9). And the distinction between merely having an image in the imagination and having a memory image is that with the latter there is the correct judgement that one has encountered the memory image before (*DM*, I, 449b 24). This judgement is a temporal one and may be shared by certain animals which otherwise have neither higher capacities to judge nor intelligence. Hence, memory and imagination belong to the same part of the soul, the lowest, primary perceptual part most dependent on sense images.

The memory image can be called a physical trace imprinted in the surface of the 'mind'. But memory is not only a physiological process for Aristotle. He does, however, say that men with certain psychic surfaces, more or less fluid, have better or worse memories as a result of the imprint being more or less impressed and lasting. There is a way in which Aristotle may be interpreted to mean that sensation and remembering are basically physiological brain processes.[7] But this is not all he says, especially in the *De Anima*, as we shall see.

---

[6] He argues that the percipient does not acquire memory from the start; only when the affection has been produced within a person is there memory. There is a temporal distinction between the experience and one's memory of it and remembering does not occur until time has elapsed. A person remembers 'now' what he experienced earlier; he does not 'remember' now what he experienced 'now' (*DM*, II, 451a 23–25, 29–31). As Sorabji notes, Aristotle is arguing that since one can perceive a period as well as an instant, the present can be said to have duration, including experiences which one has just had, but these are not yet the objects of memory. This is to be contrasted with Augustine's view of the perception of the passage of time and its relation to remembering. See below. Where Aristotle says that one does not remember now what one experienced now, we can find parallels with Abelard's position. See below. S. Mansion, 'Soul and Life in the *De Anima*' in Lloyd and Owen, eds., *Aristotle on Mind and the Senses*, pp. 1–20, speaks of Aristotle as discussing the soul as the seat of consciousness. Also see C. H. Kahn, 'Sensation and consciousness in Aristotle's psychology', *Archiv Gesch. Philos.*, 18 (1966), especially pp. 44, 48 and 70. Schofield, 'Aristotle on the imagination', in *Aristotle on Mind and the Senses*, wishes to interpret phantasma not as a *mental* image but rather as a special sort of presentation that is a non-paradigmatic sensory presentation (p. 116).

[7] Certain Greek, Arab and Jewish doctors took over this physiological side of the argument. See below, chs. 12 and 15. G. E. R. Lloyd, 'The empirical basis of the physiology of the *Parva Naturalia*', in *Aristotle on Mind and the Senses*, pp. 215–39. In the *De Iuventute*, 469a 21f. Aristotle says organs of sight, hearing and smell are located in the brain but taste and touch extend to the heart which is the principle, *arche*, of all sensation. Lloyd argues that the role of observation and Aristotle's citations of zoological and anatomical data *corroborate* rather than test his own theories. Aristotle believes there are overwhelming *theoretical* reasons for holding the physiological opinions he holds (Lloyd, 'Empirical basis', p. 224). R. Sorabji,

Memory is not perception nor conception, but a state somehow connected with these when time has elapsed. There is no memory of the present at the present; we use the term perception to refer to what is present. Prediction is of the future, and memory is of the past so that unlike perception, memory involves a kind of consciousness of time lapsed, Aristotle describing this awareness in animals and man as a *perceptual* capacity (*DM*, I, 449b, 24f). Magnitude and change are also known by the same perceptual means. Memory in its own right, he says, belongs to the primary perceptive part of the soul. A memory can belong to thought, however, in virtue of what he calls an incidental association.[8]

We say that part of the body which contains the soul undergoes a kind of change in which the mark of the sense image imprint is akin to sealing things with signet rings. Hence, we say that men with poor memories are subject to much movement in their souls caused by some trouble or time of life, so that it is as though the seal were falling on running water (*DM*, I, 450a 32). Others seem to possess a kind of hardness and receive impressions poorly or not at all. This is true, according to Aristotle, of both the very young and the old. As we have seen, he is not unaware of the following problem: do we remember the imprint or the thing from which it was produced? How do we remember that which is now absent and which we are no longer perceiving? He attempts a solution by asserting that the imprint is *like* a figure drawn on a panel which *can be considered* both a figure and a copy, a figure in its own right and a copy of something else (*DM*, I, 450b 20–451a 16). Similarly *we must conceive* the image in us to be both something in its own right as well as of another thing. In its own right it is an object of contemplation; as a copy of something else it serves as a reminder of that something else. He assumes that sane people have adequate copies or reminders of past experiences unlike the insane who speak of their images as things that occurred which actually never occurred. Aristotle then goes on to distinguish reminiscing from remembering and we shall return to this later.

The *De Memoria* is part of a group of texts known as the *Parva Naturalia* and it is thought it was usually read as a continuation of his *De Anima*. All these texts hold that memory and other mental affections like dreaming are to be classed as perceptual powers and are attributes both of body and soul. He does not quite have a 'faculty' psychology such as would develop in later medieval accounts. Strictly speaking, animals and men do the

'Body and soul in Aristotle', *Philosophy*, 49 (1974), 68ff, argues cogently that mental acts as a distinct class of phenomena cannot be reduced merely to physiological processes.

[8] *DM*, I, 449b 30f: '... memory, even of objects of thought, is not without an image. So memory will belong to thought in virtue of an incidental association but in its own right to the primary perceptive part.'

perceiving, rather than a part of the soul or body doing the perceiving. As was noted above, memory belongs only incidentally to thought, so that one's ability to remember is never due to the fact that the thing remembered and the time lapse perceived are objects of thought. Rather, one remembers objects of perception because such objects are *imageable* and receivable by perception rather than by thought. A lack of a distinct 'faculty' theory of mind does not, however, mean that he does not see the soul as an interrelated set of powers. But such psychic powers are not spatially separated with a higher part existing separately from the lower part. The difference in powers seems to be largely definitional and reflects the way humans talk and think about psychology. So it is true to say that the image in the soul is also in the body, first because for Aristotle the soul is 'in' the body – indeed it is the form of the body, and the image is causally dependent on a sense organ's reception, but also because of his understanding of mental occurrences in general which, as he describes in the *De Anima*, are images and thus, in part, can be distinguished as physiological entities. And although he does not have a distinct notion of self-consciousness he does think that we can only remember when we are aware that we are so doing (*DM*, II, 452b 23f).

The *De Anima* gives a fuller account of how external reality strikes a human being, is experienced by us, is perceived and then conceived by the intellect through the images provided by the senses. He starts from the idea that in perception a sense organ is affected by things around us. The sense organ then receives the form of the object without its matter and he describes this process in a language of potentiality and actuality. The object actualises a potentiality which the organ has for receiving forms of objects so that the sense organ becomes what the object is. Before such perception the sense organ is only potentially what the object is actually. By using this potentiality–actuality terminology he is able to argue that perception is not a case of true alteration but rather a situation in which something becomes actualised from what it potentially is prior to being activated. The analogy used is of wax prior to receiving the imprint of the signet ring. Thus the activity of the object of perception and of the sense organ is one and the same, although what it is for them to be such is not the same: actual hearing takes place at the same time as the actual sounding of that which can be heard. But the activity of the object of perception and the activity of that which can perceive are both *in the perceiver* (*DA*, III, 2, 426a 8f). Hence scientific truths are *of* or *about* the natural world and not about the mental states of human beings. But the status of these scientific truths is, of necessity, a status defined by discourse and thought and not by natural things. There is a kind of realism here which believes that truth is one and the same for all sane thinking, speaking beings, but a realism limited by the rules of thinking and language; i.e. a realism circumscribed by what Aristotle takes 'being a man' to mean; hence his is an anthropocentric account. His discussion here is effectively in terms of those imageable features of the world which strike a human being as such.

People define the soul he says in two ways with reference to its distinguishing characteristics: perceiving and understanding. Aristotle says that they are not the same. (*DA*, III, 3, 427a 17f). He has much greater confidence in the accuracy of the soul's capacity to perceive its objects, but says it is possible to think falsely.[9] Perception is necessary and prior to all higher forms of mental activity such as imagining and thinking. Imagining is that in virtue of which we say that an image occurs to us and it often occurs when we do not perceive something distinctly and therefore, the image may be true or false (*DA*, III, 3, 428a 5f).

The most difficult section of the *De Anima* deals with that 'part' of the soul which knows and understands, which we have seen, is distinct from that which perceives. How, he asks, does thinking ever come about? (*DA*, III, 4, 429a 10f). Thinking can be said to be *analogous* to perceiving in that it too is essentially unaffected but moves from a potential to an actual thinking when the intellect becomes like its objects of thought.[10]

It is by the intellect that the soul thinks and judges, and its nature is that of potentiality. It is actually none of the existing things before it thinks (*DA*, III, 4, 429a 18f). The intellect is, therefore, a place of potential forms. What is specially interesting about the intellect is that it is distinct from the

---

[9] This confidence will be reversed by neo-Platonist interpretations and their influence on later medieval philosophy as we shall see. While Aristotle argues that the ultimate components of intellectual states are indivisible thoughts to which truth and falsity do not pertain, the compositions by the intellect into combinations *are* characterised by truth and falsity. Andreas Graeser, 'On Aristotle's framework of *sensibilia*', in *Aristotle on Mind and the Senses*, pp. 69–97, points out that Aristotle's *sensibilia* are not sense *data* (n. 37 p. 96). Falsity for Aristotle cannot occur except in connection with some kind of mental activity involving synthesis of terms (p. 86). In view of his theory of error and falsity in terms of what he thinks of as a synthesis of terms, it would seem possible to regard 'direct perception' as a mode of genuinely non-propositional perceiving that is not liable to the possibility of error (p. 87). Compare Ockham's intuitive cognition below. Malcolm Schofield, 'Aristotle on the imagination', in *Aristotle on Mind and the Senses*, pp. 99–140. Sense perception is a capacity in virtue of which we then judge so the imagining is a kind of interpretation which 'creates' images, imagination/ phantasia thereby being fallible. Schofield holds it to be a mistake to interpret phantasma as meaning 'mental image' since its meaning is 'what is presented', that is, a special kind of non-paradigmatic sensory presentation (p. 116), subject to the will. On the infallibility of intellection see Enrico Berti, 'The intellection of 'indivisibles' according to Aristotle, *DA*, III, 6', in *Aristotle on Mind and the Senses*, pp. 141–179.

[10] *DA*, III, 4, 429a 13f.

body, whereas sense perception is not independent of the body (*DA*, III, 4, 429a 29f). The intellect is potentially the objects of thought but is actually nothing before it thinks. Aristotle draws an analogy with a writing tablet on which nothing written as yet actually exists. Furthermore, the intellect is itself an object of thought; it can focus on objects of thought other than itself as well as on itself (*DA*, III, 4, 429b 29f).

Now, Aristotle refines his argument further. The intellect he has been discussing is of such a kind that it *becomes* all things. There is, however, another intellect which instead of being potential or passive, is actual and *produces* all things (*DA*, III, 5, 430a 10f). It is this intellect, the active or agent intellect as it will be called during the middle ages, which is distinct, unaffected, unmixed, essential activity and is immortal and eternal. The passive or potential intellect, however, is perishable (*DA*, III, 5, 430a 18f).

Since the soul never thinks without an image it is the gradual movement of sense images to imaginative images to memory images, each presumably as a 'copy' of the original extramental but imageable object of perception, that activates the various 'parts' of the soul to become what the object is. Thus he says that the soul is *in a way* all existing things and such existing things are either objects of perception or objects of thought. We are far from Plato when Aristotle defines knowledge as 'in a way the *objects* of knowledge' (*DA*, III, 8, 431b 20f); so too perception is the objects of perception. Since there is no actual thing which has a separate existence, be it a perceptual or an intellectual object, even the intellectual object is, he says, to be included among the forms, which are objects of perception. Abstractions and imprints of objects of perception must be part of the same continuum of perception and cognition. Aristotle asserts that unless one perceived things one would not learn or understand anything (*DA*, III, 8, 432a 3f). When one contemplates in the most abstract way one does so from an image. Images, he says, are like sense-perceptions except that they are without matter. At either end of the spectrum there is apparently no falsity; thinking of essences or universals (undivided objects) is always true and that which *produces* this undividedness is, in each case, the intellect. When thought is intuitive it is, according to Aristotle, always true. So too, as we have seen, sense perceptual images are also true. It is imagination which can be false or true and judgement consequent on imagination may be false or true (*DA*, III, 10, 433a 26). Thoughts are not themselves images but they cannot exist without images (*DA*, III, 8, 432a 3f). Furthermore, one can be deceived into believing that one is remembering when one is not, although when one exercises memory a person cannot fail to notice that he is doing so and remembering.

There is an attempt here to construct more of a coherent system than

Aristotle himself provides in these difficult passages of the *De Anima*. For the moment what appears to contrast so strongly with Plato's understanding of knowledge as recollection, is Aristotle's assumption that the world 'out there' which, in so far as it is imageable by us, can be known, is the *sine qua non* of all knowing and understanding. Like Plato but for different reasons, Aristotle does not need words to bridge the worlds of knower and known. But for Aristotle what we recognise as signs, like words, are sensible realities themselves and if they are ambiguous they are still accurate inferential tools about reality. Their ambiguity comes from men's abuse or misuse of signs (*De Sophisticis Elenchis*, I, 165a, *Rhet.* I, 1357a). In themselves, like images seen as copies of objects of perception, they do for the most part, correspond to objective reality in a satisfactory way for us.

We have seen that memory is placed in the perceptual part of the soul although its relationship to thought also exists, but, as Aristotle says, incidentally. There is, however, another kind of memory which he calls reminiscence or recollection and this is a much more intellectual endeavour as it was for Plato.

Recollection (*DM*, II, 451a 18f), is a sort of reasoning process, described as a search, starting from one's thinking of something rather than from one's perceiving it. It is a deliberate undertaking. It involves a succession of associated ideas. Recollection is the recovery of scientific knowledge, perception and the like, and memory need not precede the search. For instance, the conduct of a dialectical discussion where one treats of such issues as the greater, the less, the equal, the good, the beautiful, and so on, requires the recollection of relevant data. Somehow the man who recollects moves through his own agency from the first idea in a series to that which follows. It is a self-motivated search which does not require or depend on someone else, as does, according to Aristotle, learning and relearning (*DM*, II, 451b 6–18). Aristotle evidently disagrees with Plato's theory of knowledge as recollection because as we have seen 'learning' for Plato requires appropriate questions which cause to be elicited from the memory what one already knows, and Plato evidently believed that dialectical questioning could be performed by at least some people without the aid of someone else. Aristotle distinguishes the two activities of learning and recollecting, and it is the latter (which is not learning as it is for Plato) that is a deliberate, self-motivated, autonomous process of search. Although a successful recollective search culminates in remembering, it is different from remembering which requires sense images whereas recollection involves the association of *ideas*. Furthermore, recollection assumes there has been a gap during which knowledge is lost. Once again, he provides a partly physiological account to show that different people are good at recollecting from those good at remembering (*DM*, II, 453a 4f). Recollection is the more intellectual activity and is not shared by animals.

He establishes laws of association which are based on how we are reminded of a thing being something similar, opposite or neighbouring (*DM*, II, 451b 22f). The intellectual association is of '*things*' *imaged* which follow each other in some order, habitually.

He is adamant that when someone first learns or experiences something, he does not recover any memory since none preceded, *pace* Plato. But then, when someone wishes to recollect he seeks a starting point, and since '*things*' are related in succession and order, as in mathematics, so these are the more easily recollected. Nor is the recollecting person relearning; the principle by which people learn is different from that by which they recollect: he says, people recollect when a principle is within them over and above the principle by which they learn. So that what appears to be required in this process is the presence within one of a power to excite physiological changes in some kind of order of succession, and the recollector thereafter moves himself from change to change, one 'thing' imaged to another (*DM*, II, 451b 29f). People are therefore thought to recollect, he says, starting from places, and from such a starting point they associate to a succession of other things until they achieve the terminus of their search (*DM*, II, 452a 12). But note that a recollection process is a sort of reasoning since one *reasons* that one formerly saw or heard or had some experience, so that the search is a deliberative one.[11]

Despite his evident often outspoken differences with Plato, it seems that Aristotle's recollection bears some similarities to Plato's dialectical reasoning or recollection. In exercising scientific knowledge, for instance, Aristotle says one works out a conclusion, deriving it syllogistically from premises. Such an activity is not remembering but recollecting. Because recollection is the process of finding the next or neighbouring item in a series it derives from the habit of *thinking* of 'things' in a certain order. This habit is like nature and produces in man alone a kind of second nature to think of B after A. Frequent exercise creates nature, but it is based on our ability to recognise some *similarity* between things imaged and ordered. Unlike Plato, however, Aristotle will not conflate first time learning with any kind of memory, and he further makes it clear that one could not even perform this deliberate recollective search amongst associated ideas if one previously had no sense experience of the world. In fact,

---

11 *De Memoria*, II, 453a f: '... recollecting is a sort of reasoning for in recollecting a man reasons that he formerly saw or heard or had some such experience, and recollecting is a sort of search. This kind of search is an attribute only of those animals which also have a deliberating part; for deliberation is a sort of reasoning.'

the very ability to move associatively from one thing imaged to another in a recollective search, has something to do with the physiology of body; he even defines recollection as a search in something bodily for an image (*DM*, II, 453a 14f). Melancholic people who appear to have certain physiological psychic qualities (fluid around the perceptive region) are moved most by images and they find themselves recollecting all the time without being in control. They get upset because the fluid around their perceptive regions, once moved, is not easily stopped until what is sought returns and thereafter, the movement takes a straight course, and presumably only then a straight course of successions can be followed. This kind of temperament seems to produce people who are continuously associating or recollecting. What affects the recollective mind is 'affections' or images of a specific sort, like names, tunes and sayings (*not* sense images) after one such has come to be on someone's lips, i.e. *after* one has learned it (*DM*, II, 453a 26f). Thereafter, even without wishing it, it comes to us to sing it or say it again.

Now this alteration between physiological and logical explanation of recollection, as with memory, previously, is characteristic of Aristotle's approach to these issues, and of course, it has been a source of confusion for later readers and commentators.

Because there is a difference between men who are naturally retentive and those who are not, Aristotle advises that repetition can check the disruption of imprints. Artifice can help to supply the retentiveness needed for recollection and it extends the period of time in which a man may deliberately recollect. This is especially useful in dialectical debate where one remembers patterns of an argument memorised, classifying these according to numbers. The difficult mnemonic technique of midpoints described in the *De Memoria* has given rise to a host of differing interpretations (*DM*, II, 452a 17f). None the less, recollection by means of starting with the midpoint of a series of associated ideas or images was meant to be more useful for dialectical debate than for rhetoric (*Topics*, VIII).

What must always be kept in mind is that for Aristotle the soul is the material cause of our knowing anything; but it is also the formal cause of our living and perceiving. The distinction between form and matter is, for him, a relative one. The soul is a form and is the actuality (*entelechy*) of the body, but it depends for its existence on the body. Remembering and recollecting, therefore, are never wholly disembodied psychic activities.

Furthermore, his hierarchical arrangement of the 'parts' of the soul, whilst raising numerous problems, requires that anything which has intellect must also have perception and self-nutrition. The world is for him external to ourselves and the self which is implied by the outside being in relation to 'us' 'inside' is none the less accessible. This inside self is not to be confused with personal identity although the accessibility of 'outside' has little to do with itself; it is, in the case of man, man's natural potentiality to become the objects of his perception actually, a capacity for actualisation in all of us which can take place only because of something 'external'. The capacity or tendency (*hexis*) to perceive, sensually, is born with us; it is not learned. Perception requires external objects which are particular and as such imageable by the sense organs which produce sense images.

But then there is the more problematic issue of the objects of knowledge, which are universals and, as he says, 'somehow in the soul itself'. This problem was already forecast when he spoke of sense-perception consisting in sense organs receiving the form of the object of perception without its matter. Sense is a capacity of the sense organ and the latter can only be affected if its object is of the relevant form. He gives a largely physical account of hearing, touching, seeing etc., all of which require intervening media (water, air) between the sense organ and its object. But the intellect has no specific organ so that its reception of form without matter is not a purely physical or physiological doctrine. He is seen to vacillate in the *De Anima* on the issue of whether all things or only pure forms or essences are the objects of intellect, and the process of form reception by intellect remains mysterious.[12] But in so far as he suggests that it is our intellect that judges essences, intellect is not completely distinct from the senses and he has already said that the intellect is dependent on the senses for its existence. The argument is that mathematical entities exist only in abstraction from physical things but have no independent existence. Thus depending on the nature of its object, our intellect is concerned in different ways according to the extent and degree to which its objects are separable from matter. There is the most abstract of intellect's activities, which is contemplation, an exercise in pure thought, and here we cannot interpret its activity in the same physical terms applied to sense perception. This appears to be the problem of the 'other' intellect, the active intellect which is entirely actual and distinct from anything material. Some philosophers during the middle ages would interpret the process of the intellect receiving the form from its objects which do have matter as one of abstracting species from phantasms. Aristotle does not speak in these terms, although Augustine will. The extent of confusion, which is not simply a result of his terse exposition of passive and active intellectual roles, would lead to more systematic

[12] See D. W. Hamlyn, notes to *DA*, III, 4, p. 135, in Aristotle's *De Anima*, II, III.

attempts throughout late antiquity and the middle ages to elucidate the problems of how men know, in the present and about the past. But then they would argue in ways Aristotle never did, for Aristotle never ascribed to humanity a *disembodied* existence in the form of an active intellect. Furthermore, it is important in all this to recognise that Aristotle's active intellect is always thinking and is eternal. But since men do forget and therefore do not think about what they have forgotten it cannot be the active intellect that is responsible for psychic functions like remembering and forgetting. In treating the problem of how intelligising or intuitive thinking can be explained, Aristotle asserts that love, hatred, memory, discursive thinking are not activities of the active intellect (which is impassible so that its activity is not bound up with the body) (*DA*, III, 4, 429a 18–29), but are activities of the composite man, of intellect, soul and body (*DA*, I, 4, 408a 30–b 24). In assuming a double intelligence, it is the lower part, the passive or potential intellect that is 'changeable' and possesses memory. He denies that active intellect remembers (*DA*, III, 5, 430a 23), and therefore seems to mean that the survival of higher, active intelligence after life implies that there is no survival of the former life. That there is no place for memory in his theory of *Nous*, except incidentally, gave rise to numerous discussions in the second century AD related to the soul's immortality.

The passive or potential intellect then, which can perish and is responsible for ordinary psychic functions, apparently rules over memory and recollection. Whether the active intellect has any distinct role to play in remembering and recollecting, apart from the assertion that the passive intellect is dependent on the active intellect for thinking of any kind, remains unclear. This lack of clarity would provide much scholastic thought its scope for creativity in epistemological analysis.

It is important that we draw from the above Aristotle's confidence in the soul's capacities to perceive and know the past as a perceptual and intellectual experience. Objects of perception and objects of thought are imageable. This is part of a larger interest that Aristotle displays in many of his other writings on ethics, politics, language and the logic of argument, common discourse and its relation to our experiences. He seems generally interested in the extent to which humans are passive and receptive towards the world and the relation this has to human action and to being to some extent self-moving and self-determining. The *De Anima* gives us some insight into his notion of human action and his notion of humans as self-moving animals causally related to the world of phenomena, that is, to experiences and appearances as they strike human beings. Aristotle, we saw, said that recollection by means of starting deliberately

27

with the midpoint of a series of associated ideas was more useful for dialectical debate than for rhetoric. What bearing, we might ask, has his understanding of men's sensual experience of the world through representative images on what he has to say about ordinary discourse?[13] Do we, in common discourse, say things which are at variance with the phenomena, at variance with our experience or appearances? Because Aristotle believes men are naturally rational and political[14] and they manifest these characteristics through reasoned speech, the community of thinking and acting and experiencing men rests on a sharing of discourse. Hence, his writings on rhetoric, which show it to be a discipline ranked between demonstrative science and sophistry, point to the role of rational persuasion through speeches as fundamental to the political life of men. Is there a way in which our accounts of the present and past can remain faithful to ordinary experience and thereby preserve appearances?

When Aristotle speaks of the 'phenomena', he usually seems to mean 'what we commonly believe', the appearances to us, and as such, the phenomena are sufficient witness to the truth.[15] Truth for Aristotle is not far from the path of human experience; it is not contrasted with appearances but rather is in the common opinion and perceptions of the way things are for us. Meaning is immanent in things as they are experienced and interpreted by us; meaning is not transcendent over and above things and us. So that what we say about what we commonly believe about our experiences and phenomena has a truth. And because the phenomena, the things we experience, are not belief-free facts, they are set down through our linguistic usage and the way we think. For Aristotle there is no sharp distinction between perception data 'out there' and communal belief, and, consequently, throughout his scientific works, conceptual and linguistic usages are prominent. There is a focus throughout on the notion of appearances and experiences of human observers and how human beings might define or speak about such things. Unlike Plato, then, Aristotle has an anthropocentric conception of truth and when he speaks of ethical truth, he attaches it to a general argument that denies our beliefs are linked to objects that are altogether independent of and more stable than human thought and language. Hence his interest in rhetoric.

[13] Larry Arnhart, *Aristotle on Political Reasoning, A Commentary on the 'Rhetoric'* (Dekalb, Illinois, 1981).
[14] *Politics*, I, 1253a 5–18.
[15] Martha C. Nussbaum, *The Fragility of Goodness, Luck and Ethics in Greek Tragedy and Philosophy* (Cambridge, 1986), pp. 240–63. Also G. E. L. Owen, 'Tithenai ta phainomena', in S. Mansion, ed., *Aristote et les problèmes de méthode* (Louvain, 1961), pp. 83–103, also reprinted in J. Barnes, M. Schofield, R. Sorabji, eds., *Articles on Aristotle* (London, 1975), I, pp. 113–26.

Rhetorical persuasion is not sufficient to make men virtuous. Rather, the rhetorician appeals to that part of the soul that can be persuaded by reason after men have been effectively habituated by the laws of a community, laws which compel rather than persuade. Rhetorical persuasion is most effective where it draws not on complex scientific demonstration but on the common opinions of men, opinions which have probable but not necessary validity. According to Aristotle, reputable opinions usually manifest some partial understanding of the truth prior to any refinements that may issue from proper philosophic, demonstrative examination of opinion. Rhetoric is subordinate to demonstrative reasoning but in the public space of politics, it is sufficient as a means by which to make oneself clear to fellow citizens who experience their world, perceive it, think about it, discuss it and remember it.

In practical living we move in a continuum from the confused mass of appearances to an intellectual ordering and an ability to give an account of present and past experiences. We must experience the world before we think and talk about it. Hence any logical argument must be brought back to the phenomena to preserve them, where we can, as true. Experts in logic, in scientific demonstration, help to refine arguments and define scientifically, and thereby produce more general theories which give accounts of what is commonly believed of individual experiences. That we can state the nature of the phenomena is evidence of Aristotle's belief in language's capacity adequately to signify experiences which relate to extramental and extralinguistic occurrences in the world. Where natural science experts should be able to validate claims to understanding by giving systematic logical demonstrations, common speech does not require such stringent proofs. In our discourse on moral action, past and present, we do not demand a deductive system so formally and explicitly set out.[16]

The subject matters of rhetoric, ethics and politics, therefore, share in their concern for the regularities of human actions past and present, a subject matter about which Aristotle believes there cannot be absolute certainty but only probability. But probabilities presuppose, rationally, a natural regularity in things which is experienced as such. Rhetorical enthymemes are, therefore, taken to be true syllogisms but where the premises and conclusions are based on probably certain common opinions, often with one of these premises implicit and to be supplied by the

---

[16] Generally see the discussions in M. Schofield and M. Nussbaum, eds., *Language and Logos, Studies in Ancient Greek Philosophy presented to G. E. L. Owen* (Cambridge, 1982), and M. Nussbaum, ed., *Logic, Science and Dialectic: Collected Papers on Ancient Greek Philosophy* (London, 1986).

listener. Since Aristotle believes that truth exists in all signs and that ambiguity comes only from men's misuse of signs,[17] we have here a parallel with his epistemological theory of the presumed accuracy of representation of sense experience in the soul. The consequence is that verbal representation can accurately signify the world we experience and a trained rhetorician is concerned to proffer probable truths without going through the kind of demonstration that would be required to confirm these truths scientifically. Were he to do the latter he would be aiming over the heads of his audience. Since the rhetorical enthymeme moves an audience not only by probable or plausible reasons but also by appealing to the emotions, rhetoric is that public skill that best communicates to composite men, men whose practical intellects are irrevocably tied to their corporeal existence and experience, men with sense memories and the rational capacity to recollect voluntarily, activities that are never wholly disembodied psychic activities. Even in his interpretation of rhetoric, Aristotle's argument can be seen to be governed by epistemological considerations.

Rhetoric can be misused or used with good intentions. Unlike Plato, Aristotle argues that the common political opinions of men are not mere illusions but precisely where one begins in the search for probable truth by means of true as opposed to sophistic rhetoric. Therefore, he takes rhetoric to be a counterpart of dialectic (*Rhet.*, I, I, 1351a 1–11), sharing in the universality of the latter and concerned with reasoning as such. (*Rhet.*, 4, 1359b 12–17). A man of experience knows particulars and preserves them in sense memory; but when he also knows the general principles involved he can give an *account* of his activity and engage in recollection or reminiscence (*Post. Anal.* 99b 26–100b 18). The rhetorical skill rests on a knowledge of causes that underpins the collection of experiences one may have and hence a true rhetorician understands why he is successful. Although a dialectician reasons from common opinions that are axiomatic in a logical and consistent manner (e.g., the principle of noncontradiction), he cannot produce scientific demonstrations. His purpose is to raise difficulties on either side of a question. So too a true rhetorician with good and just intentions is engaged in creating a kind of discourse that ultimately leads to the discovery of probable truth, based on a kind of reasoning, through enthymemes, that is related to ordinary men's experience, to the common things known by all. Although rhetoric may be misused, it need not be; although you may be able to argue both sides of a case rhetorically, you should not thereby seek to convince men of what is wrong.

[17] *Prior Anal.* 70a38. T. H. Irwin, 'Aristotle's concept of signification', in Schofield and Nussbaum, eds., *Language and Logos*.

That Aristotle makes the claim that truth and justice are usually stronger in speech than falsity indicates his reliance on the character of common opinions based as they are on the general reliability of our sense experience of the world and thinking. Imagination and judgement may go astray but they can be corrected, especially in the public space where collective rational judgement can best be made to reflect common sense wisdom and prudence. He says explicitly that common opinions, especially of those thought to be wise, do bear a likeness to the truth (*Rhet.*, I, I, 1355a 13–17). And among those things men find credible are those things which are, or those which are probable.

A certain kind of oration known as the forensic or judicial pertains to the past and its plausibility. Common opinion even about the past is not, because Aristotle believes it cannot be, completely malleable. 'Men have a natural appetite for truth and generally attain it. It therefore follows that he who is apt in judging truth will also be apt in conjecturing what is probable' (*Rhet.* I, I). And it is the well-habituated man who thinks about what is true. As he notes in the *Nicomachean Ethics*, 'we first set the "phenomena"[18] before us, review the difficulties, and then go on to prove if possible, the truth of common opinions about the beliefs held about experiences. Having solved the difficulties and preserved the common opinion we shall have sufficiently proved the case' (*Nic. Ethics*, VII, 1145b 1–7).[19]

The proper use of rhetoric, therefore, both maintains the common opinion where it can and agrees with the 'phenomena', the beliefs we hold of experience. Rhetorical skill eliminates the distortion of a self-interested perspective in grasping the probable or plausible truth of a situation in which contingent human activity is involved and is to be judged. Aristotle assumes, as we have seen, that there is a correspondence between logic and objective reality; since events in the world may be characterised as necessary, possible or contingent, so too syllogisms of all kinds, including the enthymeme, have these corresponding features (*Prior Anal.*, 25a 1–3, 29b 29–30a 14). The premises of enthymemes are usually probable (*Rhet.*, I, 1357b 21–25, and reference to *Prior Anal.*, 70a 2–10), based on men's common experiences and the soul's capacity to represent them in order that men may think and give accounts.

Aristotle distinguishes three types of oratory: epideictic (demonstrative), deliberative and forensic (judicial). When the hearer of an oration is to judge of that which is past, it is appropriate that the orator speak in the

---

[18] These are not belief-free facts but our interpretations and beliefs as expressed in linguistic usage.
[19] Martha Nussbaum, *The Fragility of Goodness*, chapter 8, pp. 240ff, especially p. 244.

forensic terms of accusation and defence. At the end of Book I of the *Rhetoric*, Aristotle examines the motives of injustice, including the dispositions of those who suffer it and those who act unjustly. And he proceeds to outline seven causes of human action (1368b 27–1369b 17) in order to account for the motives of unjust actors.

For our purposes what is most significant is his analysis of rational desire as a motive for action which he identifies with a calculatory, prudential reason (*logismos*). It is therefore distinguished from *Nous* which is the capacity of the rational soul to grasp invariable first principles or form universals. *Nous* enables us to see the fundamental role played by principles in the structure of a theory, but we implicitly grasp these principles through our experiences first before we understand them as distinct principles. The first principles of deductive science are not grasped by autonomous acts of intellect divorced from experience.[20] And as we shall see, medieval Aristotelians like Aquinas and Ockham understood this well. Practical reason, however, concerns variable things and therefore is a kind of prudential reasoning. Aristotle links it to the kind of prudential knowledge, *phronesis*, that in the world of practical activity is elevated above theoretical wisdom or *sophia*. Practical reason can be a motivating cause of human action because it is connected with desire. *Nous* cannot cause human action; indeed 'thinking by itself moves nothing' (*DA*, III, 432b 8–433b 31). In the *De Anima*, III, 10, 433a–b, Aristotle had argued that both intellect and desire motivate men to action, 'and the intellect in question is that which reasons for a purpose and has to do with action and which is distinct in its end from the contemplative intellect'.[21] Since it is the object of desire that is the point of departure for action, then that intellect which refers back to sense experience, through images in imagination and memory, is the practical kind of intellect with which anyone interested in judging past actions must be concerned. Prudential reason as a kind of practical, rational calculation, aims at the expedient or the apparently pleasant (*Rhet.*, I, 1369b 18–33). And because the rhetorician appeals to men through persuasive speech, he must be aware of cognitive rather than merely sensual pleasures, because speech appeals to men's minds through mental images rather than to their bodies. The rhetorician rouses the cognitive side of the passions through words and thereby incites physiological side effects. This is not to say that Aristotle argues for a

[20] *Ibid.*, p. 251. J. Lesher, 'The role of *Nous* in Aristotle's *Posterior Analytics*', *Phronesis*, 18 (1973), 44–68. Miles Burnyeat, 'Aristotle on understanding knowledge', in E. Berti, ed., *Aristotle on Science: 'The Posterior Analytics'*, Proceedings of the Eighth Symposium Aristotelicum (Padua, 1981), pp. 97–139.

[21] Once again the contrast between the passive intellect which embraces those aspects of thinking which in men are most connected with mortality, and the active intellect.

causation of the physical by the mental, but rather that one can *describe* desire materially as a physiological process and also formally as a cause of action. Furthermore, pleasure is defined as a movement of the soul and therefore requires some cognitive awareness beyond the mere having of a sensual experience. Even the most base and basic of natural appetites have psychic components for Aristotle.[22]

Bearing in mind his analysis of sensation, imagination and sense memory, as discussed earlier, he notes in the *Rhetoric*, I, c.11 that pleasure consists in the sensation of an emotion. Imagination is a kind of cognition where images of sense impressions can be maintained after the experience of sensation. Here in the *Rhetoric* he only says that memory and hope are attended by a kind of imagination of the object of memory and hope. Thus where there is sensation, pleasure attends our memories or hopes. Those who remember, experience pleasure since there is sensation through imagination (I, 1370a 28–32). There is pleasure both in present sensation and in memory with reference to past time (I, 1370b 9–11).

The rhetorical understanding *that* pleasure of direct sensation and pleasures of the imagination and memory are linked, parallels what we have seen Aristotle to have said in his analysis of *how* we think through images of experiences, as set forth in the *De Anima* and the *De Memoria*. In the psychological works he was concerned to show how imagination is also essential to higher intellectual activity since even theoretical cognition requires images. But his *Rhetoric* does not explain the hows and whys of our psychic responses to the world we inhabit; it merely confirms that the rhetorical skill need only draw upon common opinion through the enthymeme and examples of what has happened before, to persuade men of a plausible position without proving demonstratively its truths or falsities. Therefore, the epistemological underpinning of his analysis of rhetorical persuasion remains largely mute. That this was the case had important repercussions on the limited scope of later discussions of memory.

Future generations in Rome of the orators would enthusiastically empha-sise the wonders of memory and techniques for its improvement without seeking to understand its relation either to a satisfactory theory of know-

---

22 Nussbaum, *The Fragility of Goodness*, p. 244: 'There is, in fact, no case for crediting Aristotle with anything like the Baconian picture of science based on theory-neutral observation. He was not concerned in his talk of experience or how the world 'appears' to separate off one privileged group of observations and to call them the 'uninterpreted' or 'hard' data. Such a bounding-off of a part of the data of experience as 'hard' or 'theory-free' was, in fact, unknown to any early Greek scientist ... we find in Aristotle as in his predecessors, a loose and inconclusive notion of 'experience' or the way(s) a human

ledge or to the establishment of truth. Even where Cicero would be concerned to go beyond the current platitudes concerning memory, he would be shackled to a rhetorical tradition which provided no serious explanations of how memory operated or, indeed, what it was. As a consequence, he would turn the 'problem of memory' into an unproblematic skill best practised by orators concerned to plunder the past for present polemical purposes. For Cicero, it was the orator's role to be the memory of a people and elicit from the chaos of lived life an immortal and universal message.

By conflating the orator with the historian Cicero would transform Aristotle's distinction between the poet and the historian. In the *Poetics*, VI,[23] Aristotle said it was not the poet's province to relate such things as have actually happened but such as might have happened, such as are possible, according either to probable or necessary consequences. Herodotus as an historian related what had been: he was no poet. Poetry is the more philosophical skill according to Aristotle, dealing with general truth. History, however, deals only with the particular. In what manner, for example, a person of a certain character *might* speak or act, probably or necessarily – is general. What Alcibiades did or what happened to him – is particular. The poet, therefore, is a maker of fables imitating actions. But history, in dealing with the particular in the order of its happening, has no dramatic form so that an historian's record is as chaotic as life. Its universal truth is missing from its written account and therefore, the historical record is valid for one time and place only. It is the poet who, like the rhetorician, draws out the probable, universal lessons from a succession of discontinuous events. This is not the historian's task. As we will see, Cicero's concern for history is well-ensconced in the province of oratory. In contrast, for Aristotle, the historian serves as a people's sense memory, the poet as the creator of its plausible fictions, the dialectician as a people's deliberative reminiscer.

RECAPITULATION

We have observed that for Plato learning *is* recollection, an active process of eliciting knowledge already in the mind and bringing it to our awareness. The object of knowledge is unchanging and stable. It is always there to be recollected and the process of recollection is a conversion of

observer sees or 'takes' the world, using his cognitive faculties (all of which Aristotle calls '*kritika*' – concerned with making distinctions).' I am convinced that this analysis is correct. It is certainly what Ockham takes Aristotle to mean. See below. But see also G. E. L. Owen, 'Tithenai ta phainomena', in *Articles on Aristotle*, I, pp. 113–26.

23 Aristotle, *De arte poetica* (Oxford, 1958). See c. 9, 1451b, 'on history'.

what is known imperfectly and unconsciously through a logical questioning, a reasoning out of the cause of why something is true. And what we come to recognise as true objects of knowledge are Forms that are independent of those particular concrete things in the world of experience which embody them. What we know and recollect are objects of thought rather than concrete things around us. To remember an experience is not the same as to have the experience. The sensible is separated from the thinkable. Recollection is the process by which knowledge, which comes out of the mind itself, is raised to awareness through a repeated reflection on the reasons for something being the case. That which is to be recollected and known is a fixed, logically necessary structure of the truth that is already implicit in our memories. But not all men have the will to recover this truth. Only those few capable of and desirous of developing a philosophical examination of truth for its own sake will achieve a near absolute recollection of the Form of the Good. An ideal state would be ruled over by the recollecting philosopher-king who does not retrieve images but the essence or nature of an earlier situation. Indeed, his recollective mind best achieves a knowledge of the Forms or natures of things when *removed* from sensory stimulation. A mnemonic technique for recalling individual instances, places, things experienced or words, is for Plato, trivial if not dangerous, because it is a kind of memory device without understanding. Although words are signs and names of existing things, all words have cognitive limitations and are incapable of expressing their referents totally. The truth that is to be recollected preexists and transcends language. Men who rely on a memory for words remain in a state of forgetfulness so that they dwell in a realm of fluctuating opinions and ethical norms.

We have observed that for Aristotle, in contrast with Plato, we must perceive, apprehend, experience or learn something *before* we can remember it. Our sense organs need to be affected by things around us. And our capacity to perceive is born with us. When we remember, the present content of our mind is an image which is a copy of a past thing, the image being similar to and derived from our past act of perceiving something. When we perceive, our sense organs receive the form of an object without its matter, the sense organ becoming what the object is, just as wax is imprinted by a signet ring. Remembering, like all psychic activities, is iconic: after perception there results an image derived from the sensible form in our sense organs, a sense image that is itself caused by an external object of sense or experience. Once we perceive something there is, as it were, stamped into our memories an imprint of our sense image, now accompanied by a recognition on our parts that a time lapse has occurred between our past perceiving and our present remembering. The physical imprint connects the present memory image with the earlier perceptual act. Both a memory image and an image in the imagination (which has no accompanying temporal judgement) belong to the primary *perceptual* part of the soul which is dependent on sense images of an exterior world, there to be experienced and 'imaged'. Although Aristotle speaks of memory as a physiological process of imprinting on psychic surfaces, and therefore he says that memory belongs to the primary perceptive part of the soul, he also says memory belongs to the thinking part of the soul through an incidental association. But one's ability to remember is due to the thing remembered and the time lapse perceived being objects of perception rather than objects of thought. Indeed, to think at all depends on first having perceived and sensually experienced the world. The soul's capacity to perceive and to conceive or understand are not the same for Aristotle. But perception is a prior necessity to any higher kind of mental activity. Men are not disembodied minds but are composite beings, their souls are the forms of their bodies.

Thinking is *analogous* to perceiving in that just as perception is the actualising of a potential of a sense organ to receive forms of objects in order for it to become what its object is, so too the intellect is actualised when it is actually thinking of its objects, becoming like its objects of thought. This intellect is potential or passive having the capacity to become the objects of thoughts when actually thinking. The soul never thinks without an image and is in a way all existing things which are either objects of perception or objects of thought. And unless one first perceived things, one would not learn, think, understand or remember anything.

Like animals, men remember. But men have the unique capacity to recollect. Recollection or reminiscence is a reasoning process, deliberately undertaken, through an association of ideas. Recollection starts from one's thinking of something rather than from one's perceiving it. Self-motivated recollection starts with an idea and according to certain laws of association, which remind one of something similar, opposite or neighbouring, one proceeds in succession and order to find something once known but now lost. Reminiscence is a reasoning process through an association of ideas where one reasons that one formerly had some experience. Successful reminiscence culminates in remembering but it is different from remembering which requires sense images. Recollection is a thinking process whereby one works out a conclusion, deriving it syllogistically from logical premises. It derives from the habit of thinking of things in a certain order, a habit that produces in men a second nature of thinking of B after A. Hence, reminiscence is useful in a dialectical debate where one requires the recollection of relevant data. And although there are some people who are physiologically better disposed to successful reminiscence, recollection is itself a logical technique of association and is intimately related to the logic of argument in common discourse. The human community of human experiencers and rememberers shares discourse. So that even when we speak without supporting our statements with rigorous logical demonstrations, we say things about our present and past experiences which have a truth. We commonly share a discourse that expresses how the world is for experiencers and thinkers. Hence, we can be persuaded by rhetoric when it gives a plausible account of present and past experiences. Words signify the world we experience and know adequately enough, that is, with sufficient probability for us to accept the account given without further proof. And when rhetoric is not misused it gives an account of those things men commonly find credible about the present as it is and the past as it probably was, without further proof. So that when a rhetorician asks us to judge of that which is past he appeals to our practical reason which governs our capacity to reminisce through laws of association, a process which itself refers back to our sense experiences through images in the imagination and memory. Aristotle believes that pleasure, which consists in the sensation of an emotion, attends remembering, and rhetoricians are aware of inducing pleasure by inducing remembering.

But the rhetorician speaks in terms of what probably happened or of what is possible. He is not concerned to relate what actually did happen. This is the job of the historian who deals only with particular events in the order of their happening. An orator does something more than present a chaotic record of lived life. He provides a more general account of the probable and therefore, more universal lessons to be drawn from past experiences. The orator unites a community of individual rememberers by integrating them into the collectively accepted plausible fictions of their common past. His job is effectively to edit out the uniqueness of past experiences remembered and to forge in its place a general truth in which all men share. The rhetorician-*cum*-poet, a creator of plausible fictions, is a moraliser who draws a timeless and universal message from a plausible past. The historian, a recorder of sensually experienced events, has no such message. In the end, then, a sense memory of the past must be and always is replaced by an interpreted and more general, logically meaningful fiction about the past, expressed through the sharing of a common discourse by polis-living men. But Aristotle believes that this plausible fiction would never be accepted if men did not first experience the world and remember it as a consequence of having perceived it. Any old fiction would not suffice to convince men of what their remembered past meant.

The Romans, however, appear to have had little interest in the epistemological reasons behind rhetorical success. This lack of interest would have enormous consequences for a western understanding of memory and its uses. And yet memory was of great interest to Romans. What, we now ask, did they take memory's role to be?

Chapter 3

CICERO

The Roman tradition: rhetorical 'ars memoria' and Cicero, the anonymous 'Ad Herennium libri IV', Quintilian. The trivial mnemonic memory tradition; the rhetorical uses of memory and history

As we have seen, Plato and Aristotle had a great deal to say about memory and most of their discussions related memory to theories of knowing and being. But it was the technique of memorising by impressing 'places' (*loci*) and 'images (*imagines*) on memory, the art of mnemotechnics, that was passed on to orators in Rome and thence to the European rhetorical tradition. Before the age of printing a trained memory was, of course, vitally important. In his *De Oratore*,[1] Cicero tells the story of how Simonides of Ceos had trained his memory by place images which enabled him to recall who was where at a banquet which ended in tragedy: after Simonides had departed, the roof fell in and crushed all the guests. And Cicero speaks of memory as one of the five parts of rhetoric. Whereas Aristotle the philosopher sees rhetoric as subordinate to logic or dialectic, Cicero the politician and public orator reverses their superiority: demonstration is for him ancillary to persuasion. He seems unaware of Aristotle's discussion of imagination and memory beyond what little is said explicitly in Aristotle's rhetorical and logical works.

Two other descriptions of this art of memory, both in Latin treatises on rhetoric, have come down to us: the anonymous *Ad Herennium Libri IV* (contemporary with Cicero but wrongly attributed to him in the middle ages) and Quintilian's *Institutio Oratoria*. The emphasis was always on a means by which a rhetorician could improve his memory, enabling him to deliver long speeches from memory without error. Frances Yates has summed up the system as it appears in Quintilian in the following way:

In order to form a series of places in memory, he says, a building is to be remembered, as spacious and varied a one as possible, the forecourt, the living room, bedrooms, and parlours, not omitting statues and other ornaments with

[1] M. Tulli Ciceronis, *Libri de oratore tres*, ed. A. S. Wilkins (Scriptorum Classicorum Bibliotheca Oxoniensis, Oxford, 1902–3), vol. I, book II, § 86, ll. 351–5. Cicero, *On Oratory and Orators*, trans. J. S. Watson (London, 1855). See Frances A. Yates, *The Art of Memory* (1966; Harmondsworth, 1969), from which derives the following account of the Latin sources for the *ars memoria*.

39

which the rooms are decorated. The images by which the speech is to be remembered – as an example of these Quintilian says one may use an anchor or a weapon – are then placed in imagination on the places which have been memorised in the building. This done, as soon as the memory of the facts requires to be revived, all these places are visited in turn and the various deposits demanded of their custodians. We have to think of the ancient orator as moving in imagination through his memory building *whilst* he is making his speech, drawing from the memorised places the images he has placed on them. The method ensures that the points are remembered in the right order, since the order is fixed by the sequence of places in the building. Quintilian's examples of the anchor and the weapon as images suggest that he had in mind a speech which dealt at one point with naval matters (the anchor), at another with military operations (the weapon). There is no doubt that this method will work for anyone who is prepared to labour seriously at these mnemonic gymnastics.[2]

The *Ad Herennium*, the only full treatise on the subject in Latin to be preserved, speaks of the memory as 'that treasure-house of inventions and the custodian of all parts of rhetoric'. The author distinguishes between natural memory and that achieved by artifice. But his interest is in the latter, the artificial memory. And every *Ars memorativa* treatise in the western tradition discusses the memory for things and words in ways that repeat the plan of this text-book on places and rules for images. We are told that nature is not aroused by common, banal events, but is moved by something new and striking. If art is to imitate nature, then an art of memory must choose striking, 'memorable' images that can adhere longest in memory. We must seek active images of exceptional beauty or ugliness, ornament them in some singular way, and we shall remember them more readily. And thereafter we must repeatedly run through all the original places in order to refresh the images.

There are rules for images of things and rules for images of words. A memory for things relies on images that remind one of an argument or situation; a memory for words relies on finding images that recall every single word in proper order. This method is not altogether dissimilar to Aristotle's recollective technique devised for dialecticians, where Aristotle is concerned with remembering the successive points in an argument or in searching for something already learnt but temporarily forgotten. We recall that he suggests finding a starting point and then proceeding, because of the habit of thinking in an ordered succession, to things associated as similar, opposite or neighbouring. His associative process relies on 'things' imaged which follow habitually in some order. He seems less concerned with the technique aiding one to remember words.

[2] Yates, *The Art of Memory*, p. 19.

The *Ad Herennium* is more specific about a technique for remembering words through images. If one wishes to acquire a memory for words, one begins in the same way as for acquiring a memory for things. One memorises places which hold images, such places being well-lit, and striking, dramatic images are placed within. But then the procedure becomes complicated. A line of verse, for instance, is remembered by creating a vivid scene which may have almost nothing to do with the verse's meaning but which may call to mind a noun used therein but in a more striking context. And one also uses sound resemblances to the notion suggested in the striking image (but not in the verse itself). Furthermore, one must memorise the line of verse and then represent the words by means of images. Thus one memorises whole poems and debates first in the manner with which we would be familiar – by heart – and then one confirms this memorisation by setting up places as cues at strategic intervals. Another method mentioned is said to have been elaborated by the Greeks, where images are listed in a kind of short-hand set of symbols. This seems closer to Aristotle's mid-point theory. There is no doubt that the author of the *Ad Herennium* thinks that a memory for words is a much more difficult skill to acquire than that for things.

Cicero's *De Oratore* presents these rules for an art of memory in condensed form, apparently assuming that the reader would know the text-book account of works like the *Ad Herennium*. He decides as well that a memory for things is more useful to the orator (and easier to acquire). He is more concerned to grasp general ideas by means of images and their order by means of places. What is striking in these Roman examples is the greater interest in the practical employment of a memory technique than in the epistemological foundations for its success. Plato was apparently correct when he said that these memory 'devices' were akin to sense memory lacking understanding. Yates amusingly recalls the ancient (and subsequent) complaint against this art of memory, when she notes that inert or lazy or unskilled people who used the art were using all these places and images 'only to bury under a heap of rubble whatever little one does remember naturally'. This was Plato's fear in the *Phaedrus*. But as Yates notes, Cicero was a believer in this art and 'he evidently had by nature a fantastically acute visual memory'.[3] And yet he had much more to say about the memory than a discussion of this technique implies.

Although Cicero is nowhere so subtle and elaborate in his various discussions of psychic faculties as his Greek forebears, he does attempt in his rhetorical writings to discuss memory in a serious way. His primary interest, as with the Stoic tradition which inspired him, is in the practice of

---

[3] *Ibid.*, p. 35.

virtuous behaviour. So that in the *De Inventione*, II, 53, 159–60, he defines virtue as a habit of mind in harmony with reason and the order of nature. Virtue has four parts, prudence, justice, fortitude and temperance. Prudence is the knowledge of what is good, bad, or neither, and it too has parts: memory, intelligence and foresight (*memoria, intellegentia, providentia*). 'Memory is the faculty by which the mind recalls what has happened. Intelligence or understanding is the faculty by which it ascertains what is. Foresight is the faculty by which it is seen that something is going to occur before it does'. Aristotle's trilogy had been, as we saw, *perception* of the present, *prediction* of the future and *memory* of the past. That there is a great difference between perception being of what is present and intelligence/understanding being of what is present, indicates the divergence from the more physiological Aristotelian tradition in Rome of the orators and a greater emphasis on rhetorical acts of judgement, on understanding the probable natures of things, than on sense experience of particulars. Aristotle's medical-empirical doctrine that knowledge comes through the senses was already modified by those later Stoics more influenced by the Platonic tradition of the dominance of mind over matter, essential stability over particular things in flux. As an orator, Cicero knew well those aspects of Aristotle's rhetoric that would enable him to transmit Aristotle's sign theory, from the *De Sophisticis Elenchis*, the *Rhetoric*, and the *Prior Analytics*, without, however, sharing Aristotle's interest in the relationship between signification and epistemology's wider issues.[4] It will become clear that Cicero's interest is in arguing the case for what seems likely to have occurred in the past rather than discovering what did actually happen.

In his early work, the *De Inventione*, I, 29, 36, Cicero defines what is meant by probability. That is probable which for the most part usually comes about or which is a part of ordinary men's opinions, or which contains in itself some resemblance, either to what usually happens or to men's opinions, *whether the resemblance is true or false*. He says that resemblance is seen mostly in contraries and in analogies. Arguments of this kind are sometimes rigorous and sometimes only plausible. A probable argument then, deals with what is thought usually to occur or with what men ordinarily believe. Those who judge of a probability are present auditors. Probable arguments are judged against present thought and opinion and not against factual evidence. Indeed, a statement is credible which is supported by the opinion of the listener without corroborating evidence.

[4] Marcia Colish, *The Mirror of Language, A Study in the Medieval Theory of Knowledge* (New Haven, 1968) for a good discussion of Cicero's role in transmitting the Aristotelian theory of signs without an interest in epistemology.

He says that all probability used in argument is either a sign or it is something credible, or it is a point on which judgement has been given, or something which affords an opportunity of comparison (*De Inventione*, I, 30, 48). A sign is something apprehended by one of the senses indicating something that *seems* to follow *logically* as a result of it; the sign may have occurred before the event, or in immediate connection with it, or have followed after it, and yet needs further evidence and corroboration, eg. blood (as a sign of murder), flight, pallor, dust etc. When a probable statement is taken to be a sign it needs further supporting evidence, but when a probable statement is simply credible, it needs only the assenting opinion of the auditor without further evidence. The nature of evidence and corroborative support is not discussed. Probability in argument can also be a point on which judgement has been given, judgement being defined as the approval of an act by the assent or authority or judicial decision of a person. Judgement can be supported by religious sanction, by the common approval and practice of ordinary men or by a special act of approval. The epistemological and cognitive basis of approval, assent, opinion, common practice is not discussed by the orator.

Cicero appears to be drawing on Aristotle's *Rhetoric* (1357b 21–5) where Aristotle distinguishes between a probability and a sign. A probability is a generally accepted premise; that which people know as mainly happening or not, being or not, is a probability. A sign is a demonstrative premise necessarily or generally accepted; that which exists with something else or that which happens before or after something else happens, is a sign of something having happened or being. The first – probability – is a general principle as to the probability that something happens or not based on commonsense experience. But the second, the sign, which is a demonstrative premise, is something that by its own existence signifies the occurrence of that with, after or before which it exists or occurs; the sign's own character has a relationship to something unknown and contingent.

What is important here is Cicero's emphasis on signs as sensually perceived and then his rapid shift into a kind of logical inference. This ties in with his interest in memory as one of the parts of prudence. Aristotle described memory as an aspect of the perceptual part of the soul; it belongs to thought only incidentally. But Cicero discusses memory only in terms of the practical intellect's sphere of ethics and it is therefore closer to Aristotle's rhetorical discussion of the practical reason's reference to sense experience through images in the imagination and memory. For the Aristotelian rhetorician, it is such reference to common sense experience, made through plausible arguments, which enables a prudential and probable evaluation of past actions to be had, without requiring any

43

discussion of the epistemological underpinning of why true rhetoric persuades.

In the *De Inventione*, Cicero discusses two methods of *argumentatio*. All argumentation, he says, is carried out *per inductionem aut per ratiocinationem*. But induction and deduction are for Cicero rhetorical rather than logical kinds of reasoning. Induction is a form of argument (*inductio est oratio*) which leads the person with whom one speaks to assent to certain undisputed things. Thereafter one wins approval of a doubtful proposition because the latter resembles those things to which he has assented (*De Inventione*, I, 31, 51). One introduces a statement as a basis for analogy, the truth of which must be granted. The statement to be proved by induction must then resemble the previous indisputable statement. The interlocutor must not understand (*ne intellegat*) what is the aim of those first examples or to what conclusions they will lead. Cicero believes this argumentation by analogy describes the Socratic method.

Then there is deduction (*ratiocinatio*) or syllogistic reasoning which, Cicero says, is the Aristotelian practice. But here we are not presented with the Aristotelian dialectical syllogism but rather with a rhetorical modification. As Cicero presents syllogism, it is a form of *oratio* which draws a *probable* conclusion from the thing being considered. When the probable conclusion is set forth and recognised by itself, it proves itself by its own force and reasoning (I, 34, 57). Indeed, there is no point in requiring proof or demonstration of a premise which contains a plain statement which must be granted by everyone. A proof is a thing separate from a premise (I, 36, 63). Cicero effectively confuses Aristotle's distinction between dialectic (the logical/dialectical art of demonstrative proof, using the syllogism) and rhetoric (the art of persuasion using the enthymeme – a syllogism with one of the premises implicit). Because the logical syllogism deals with established facts (if . . . then) and the rhetorical enthymeme deals with decisions about actions in which there are alternative possibilities regarding the contingent nature of actions, Cicero places greater importance on the latter, calls it syllogistic reasoning, and favours it in the practical art of persuasion for the active, prudential, good life lived in public space. Eclectically Platonist, Stoic and Aristotelian, Cicero is confident that signs, including words, have the capacity to be accurate tokens of what is taken to be the present meaning of the things they represent without proving anything about the being of the things they point to.

Cicero then outlines the five parts of an argument by what he calls deductive or syllogistic reasoning, but which is actually a rhetorical adaptation of syllogistic reasoning, using the rhetorical enthymeme. The

44

major premise (*propositio*) briefly sets forth the principle from which springs the force and meaning of the syllogism; *the proof* (*approbatio*) by which the brief statement of the major premise is supported by reasons and made plainer and more plausible (*probabilius et apertius*); the *minor premise* (*assumptio*) in which is premised the point which on the basis of the major premise is pertinent to proving the case; *the proof* (*assumptionis approbatio*) of the minor premise by which what has been premised is established by reasons; *the conclusion* (*complexio*) in which there is stated briefly what is proved by the whole deduction.

The following is Cicero's example in practice of a deductive argument:

It is right, gentlemen of the jury, to relate all laws to the advantage of the state and to interpret them with an eye to the public good and not according to their literal expression. For such was the uprightness and wisdom of our ancestors that in framing laws they had no object in view except the safety and welfare of the state. They did not themselves intend to write a law which would prove harmful, and they knew that if they did pass such a law, it would be repealed when the defect was recognised. For no one wishes laws to be upheld merely for their own sake, but for the sake of the state, because everyone believes that the state is best governed when administered according to law. All written laws ought, then, to be interpreted in relation to the object for which laws ought to be observed: that is, since we are servants to the community, let us interpret laws with an eye to the advantage and profit of the community. For as it is right to think that the art of medicine produces nothing except what looks to the health of the body, since it is for this purpose that medicine was founded, so we should believe that nothing comes from the laws except what conduces to the welfare of the state, since the laws were made for this purpose. Therefore in this trial, also, cease to search the letter of the law and rather, as is just, examine the law in relation to the public welfare. What was more useful to Thebes than the defeat of Sparta? ... But certainly this point has been examined and established beyond a doubt, that no law has been passed except for the good of the state ... (*De Inventione*, I, 37, 68–9)

This theory and practice of argument and language has important consequences. Cicero was frequently concerned to retell Roman history and to use past examples of virtue as *exempla* so that the behaviour of contemporary men might repeat the successes of the past. But this could only be done because Cicero believed that the appropriate use of signs, that is, language, could mirror accurately contemporary opinions about the *meaning of* the events described rather than the events themselves. Cicero's faith in a correspondence between an event's universal meaning and its rhetorical description provided a confidence in the capacities of texts and speeches to impart an already interpreted, meaningful, universal and timeless reality, a confidence which Plato did not share. It could, however, be elicited from Aristotle's *Rhetoric*, the art of which is essentially a mode of probabilistic reasoning without the rigour of apodictic, demonstrative proof. As we have seen, for Aristotle, reasoning is through enthymemes whose aim is to persuade (rather than to instruct or compel) by being premised on opinion (which is neither absolutely true nor false): an enthymematic inference is characterised by its probability falling between necessity and random chance. Enthymemes have probable rather than necessary validity. Aristotle's principle that one should demand only that degree of certitude that is appropriate to the subject matter under discussion means that like ethics and politics, rhetoric, being concerned with human action, can only treat of the probable regularities in human activity rather than with absolute certainty. And that is what interested Cicero. But rhetorical arguments for Aristotle are not sufficient to make men virtuous. Cicero, on the contrary, in raising rhetorical persuasion above dialectic, believed that rhetoric *was* the key to human virtue. Implicit in his rhetorical enthusiasm is his belief that the *meaning* of the event experienced is sufficiently equivalent to its meaningful description, how it is understood, that the description warrants a degree of faith in its accuracy similar to that inspired not by the mere perception or experience of the event itself, but by its meaning, what men believe to be the case now and for all time. Here we have the essence of the Roman rhetorical tradition's interest in Aristotle: a concern to elicit from Aristotle's submerged epistemology in his rhetorical theory, the view that the world can be known essentially and meaningfully and that signs, if not abused, can correspond not to some historically specific 'objective reality' but to the way that reality is understood by men throughout time. Although Cicero, like Aristotle and Plato, observes that signs and words may be ambiguous, he not only draws no epistemological conclusions from this, but affirms that the rhetor should take advantage of ambiguity and multiple meanings. This is not meant to confuse but to illuminate. His discussion of *ænigma* as a species of metaphor, a figure of speech, implies that the varieties of speech and discourse help to bring the objects of knowledge signified by words to a heightened consciousness.[5]

Cicero, unlike Aristotle, believed the good rhetorician could both persuade *and* instruct. And for this reason Cicero believed it was the orator's voice, skilled in the art of rhetoric, that should recommend history by showing history to be 'the witness of time, the light of truth, the life of the memory, the messenger of antiquity' and therefore an immortal guide to virtuous behaviour' (*Historia vero testis temporum, lux veritatis, vita memoriae, magistra vitae, nuntia vetustatis, qua voce alia nisi oratoris immortalitati commendatur?*) (*De Oratore*, II, 9, 36, and 12, 51). But what kind of

5 Colish, *The Mirror of Language*, p. 16.

46

history is this? And what does it tell us about Cicero's implicit understanding of how we remember and what it means to remember the past? History as recalled by the orator was that reservoir of multiplied experiences which *readers* and *listeners* could learn and make their own *without* having the experiences themselves, in order to repeat past successes. It was not argument, demonstration or experience but rhetoric which showed history to be the great teacher of life. *Historia magistra vitae.* The rhetorically trained historian, interested in probable arguments and imitable examples drawn from an unproblematic past, would replace the philosopher in ancient Rome.

Aristotle's historian who records, uninterpreted, the chaotic facts of life is replaced by the poet-orator who speaks in terms of contemporary plausibilities, possibilities, and thereby elicits a didactic message from the past to teach a present generation to imitate what is taken to be the essential meaning of an ancestral past. The orator reads pattern into a past to show that the past has a lesson to be learnt. The reconstructed past persuades and instructs in the present; Cicero does not enquire into the past as it was, but emphasises the past in terms of what he takes to be its universal meaning for and in the present. Indeed, in teaching philosophy Latin and thereby conferring Roman citizenship on her (*Fin.*, 3, 40) Cicero transformed her character. If in his late manifesto of his rhetorical ideals, the *De Oratore*, Cicero used the Platonic dialogue form, it was to display the oratorical Aristotelian format where opinions expressed are those already held. For Cicero, thought could not be separated from speech, nor could philosophy be separated from rhetoric. Oratorical eloquence was no mere knack but the offspring of the accomplishments of prudent and learned men, men who are none the less concerned with common usage and the custom and language of all men. He insists that not only does the orator need to be able carefully to construct words, but all the emotions of the mind which nature has given to man must be known intimately by him (*De Oratore*, I, 5). This means that the whole of antiquity and a multitude of examples not only must be, but *can* be kept in the memory of the orator. 'What can I say of that repository for all things, the memory which, unless it be made the keeper of the matter and words *that are the fruits of thought and invention*, all the talents of the orator, we see, though they be of the highest degree of excellence, will be of no avail?' (I, 5; emphasis added). Cicero's rhetorical memory keeps the fruits of thought and invention, not sense data or its remnant impressions but meaningful understanding and interpretation of these. It is this power of rhetoric which has assembled mankind into one place and brought them from wild and savage life to the present humane and civilised state of society (I, 8). Graceful diction is insufficient. Beneath it must lie the matter, clear and intelligible to the speaker, for words must have knowledge and meaning contained in them (I, 12). The true wisdom of the orator consists in his knowledge of the nature of mankind and all the passions of humanity and those causes by which our minds are either impelled or restrained. The orator needs not a knowledge of facts but of universal human psychology (I, 12). He must be instructed in all liberal knowledge by making enquiries of those skilled in various arts and sciences and then speaking about these arts with greater eloquence than any of their professional practitioners. The orator learns from verbal descriptions rather than from doing (I, 16). And that is how we learn from him.

But can true eloquence be taught? Ultimately, no. It is nature and genius in the first place which contribute most aid to speaking, rather than skill and method. One must possess a natural talent based on certain lively powers in the mind and understanding which may be acute to invent, fertile to explain and adorn and strong and retentive to remember. These powers, we are told, are not acquired by art but are natural gifts and indeed there are men who are so eminently adorned with these gifts of nature that they seem not to have been born like other men but moulded by some divinity (I, 25). But if this is the case, then what of the techniques of the artificial memory? It is true that certain proficient orators employ certain rules which assist them in remembering, but 'I consider that with regard to all precepts the case is this, not that orators adhering to them have obtained distinction in eloquence, but that certain persons have noticed what men of eloquence practised of their own accord and formed rules accordingly, so that eloquence has not sprung from art but art from eloquence' (I, 32). Cicero's mouthpiece, Crassus, does believe that the artificial *ars memoria* is of some use to the orator but primarily to that kind of orator who has a memory and understanding that is somehow divine.

The divine memory shall be discussed later insofar as he clarifies its nature in his *Tusculan Disputations*. But what is of significance here is that the orator's insight is trained on language rather than on nonverbal experience so that what he tells us about the past and how it is to be remembered has nothing to do with the particularity of past events but rather with the timeless exegesis of texts. Writing, we are told, is the best and most excellent modeller and teacher of oratory, since all the arguments relating to the subject on which we write, whether they are suggested by art or by a certain power of genius and understanding, will present themselves and occur to us while we examine and contemplate it in the full light of our intellect (I, 33). And the rhetorical intellect is concerned with what appear to be plausibilities and probabilities. If we study the civil law, as a good orator should, we shall find there in the Twelve Tables and the developments thereafter, the general principles of civil government, and that virtue has always been and still is above all things desirable since honest, just and conscientious industry has been and continues to be ennobled with honours, rewards and distinctions. And we shall also see that the vices and frauds of mankind are and always have been punished with fines, ignominy, imprisonment, banishment, death. Indeed we are taught the universal principles to hold our appetites in subjection, restrain our passions, defend our property and keep our thoughts, eyes and hands from that of others! (I, 44).

It is the orator who exhorts to virtue, reclaims from vice, reproves the bad and praises the good. It is his voice that commits history – the evidence of time, the light of truth, the life of memory – to immortality (II, 8). And what sort of orator is required to write history? Not the (Aristotelian) sort who compiles annals and preserves the singular memories of public events, dates, persons, places. That kind of 'historian' is 'not an embellisher of facts but a mere narrator' (*ceteri non exornatores rerum, sed tantum modo narrationes fuerunt*) (II, 12). The true historian speaks of great affairs, such as are worthy of remembrance (*quoniam in rebus magnis memoriaque dignis consilia primum*). He does not lie. He sets forth all the causes of actions whether arising from accident, wisdom or temerity and he sets forth not only acts but the characters of those who performed them, especially when such actors are of eminent reputation and dignity (II, 15). He interprets, he understands, he does not simply report. And his aim is to influence the understandings of those who listen to him with some power of deciding on public or private matters (II, 16). He need only present 'facts' that are probable, clear and concise. What changes in every age is the peculiar style of speaking but not the message (II, 23).

When an orator examines the nature of his cause, he finds it is never obscure with regard to information about 'whether a thing has been done or not' or 'of what nature it is' or 'what name it should receive'. Natural good sense tells him 'what constitutes the cause' without which there would be no controversy. He gives the following extraordinary example:

Opimius slew Gracchus: what constitutes the cause? That he slew him for the good of the republic, when he had called the people to arms, in consequence of a decree of the senate. Set this point aside and there will be no question for trial. But Decius denies that such a deed could be authorised contrary to the laws. The point therefore to be tried will be, whether Opinius had authority to do so from the decree of the senate, for the good of the commonwealth. These matters are indeed

49

clear and may be settled by common sense. But it remains to be considered what arguments, relative to the point for trial, ought to be advanced, as well by the accuser as by him who has undertaken the defence.

Cicero tells us that there is no obscurity here, since it is by natural good sense that we affirm not merely that Opimius slew Gracchus but that he did so for the good of the republic in consequence of a senatorial decree. It is also by common sense that we know that if Opimius had the authority from the senate, it was for the good of the commonwealth. Everyone not only agrees as to what happened but also about the intentions behind the act. The orator's skill is simply to select what arguments are to be advanced by either side in the trial over whether such an act could be authorised contrary to the laws. What if Opimius slew Gracchus because he was an ambitious man of envy? What if he were paid by some faction to get rid of Gracchus for the good of the faction and not that of the commonwealth? It appears that commonsense tells us that this could not be the case: common opinion does not believe these alternatives. Indeed, we are told that the person of Opimius and Decius has nothing to do with the common arguments of the orator since we are discussing whether he seems deserving of punishment who has slain a citizen under a decree of the senate for the preservation of his country, when such a deed was not permitted by the laws. The point that falls under the dispute is not to be considered with reference to the parties of the suit. We are only to deal with the general question and whatever is said for or against the defendant must of necessity be abstracted from the occasion and individual and referred to the general notions of things and questions of the kind (II, 31). The general question being addressed is whether a senatorial decree may be acted upon if the deed authorised by the senate is against the law. An historical act is transformed by the nature of the legal language of a trial which asks the more general question, by what authority is the act performed? A good orator does not describe the merit or demerit of the persons involved, nor the peculiar situation of the times: the multitude of causes is to be dreaded for it is infinite if they are referred to persons: so many men, so many causes. But if they are referred to general questions, they are so limited and few, that studious orators of good memory and judgement ought to have them digested in their minds, and learned by heart. The good orator does not deal with particular occasions or names but with affairs and events of a general kind (II, 32).

And it is clearly this kind of legal trial lawyer, concerned with general principles rather than with particularities, who is being recommended to us as the ideal historian, the nation's professional rememberer. Just as the civil law must be set forth arranged under general heads so too must the historical record (II, 33). 'It is now understood that all matters which admit of doubt are to be decided, not with reference to individuals, who are innumerable, or to occasions, which are infinitely various, but to general considerations and the nature of things' (II, 34). And we are told that this method of discourse is none other than Aristotle's (II, 36).

The orator's purpose is not directed towards how truth may be discovered but how it may be judged. His mode of speaking is to be adapted to the ear of the multitude, to fascinate their minds, and to prove matters that are not weighed in the scales of the goldsmith but in the balance of popular opinion (II, 38). The orator must get his hearers on his side so that he may move them more by impulse and excitement of the mind than by judgement or reflection. 'For mankind make far more determinations through hatred, or love, or desire, or anger, or grief, or joy, or hope, or fear, or error, or some other affection of mind, than from regard to truth or any settled maxim or principle of right, or judicial form or adherence to the laws' (II, 42). And it is best, and most convincing if the orator feels these emotions in himself which he is trying to arouse in others.

Hence the technical art of memory serves the eloquent orator in a particular way: it not only allows him to remember selectively but also to forget. Themistocles the Athenian is honoured in the *De Oratore*, not for wishing to learn a technique that would enable him to keep in mind everything he had ever learnt; it was much more desirable, he believed, 'to be enabled to forget what he did not wish to remember than to remember whatever he had once heard or seen' (II, 74). But other orators may not be possessed of such great intellectual powers and therefore require some method by which to order what they remember. And what they remember is already interpreted information, thought, opinion, discourse. Memory techniques organise language and thoughts through imaginative representations.

Those things are the most strongly fixed in our minds, which are communicated to them and imprinted upon them by the senses; that of all the senses that of seeing is the most acute; and that, accordingly, those things are most easily retained in our minds which we have received from the hearing or the understanding, if they are also recommended to the imagination by means of the mental eye; so that a kind of form, resemblance and representation might denote invisible objects and such as are in their nature withdrawn from the cognisance of the sight, in such a manner that what we are scarcely capable of comprehending by thought we may retain as it were by the aid of the visual faculty. By these imaginary forms and objects, as by all those that come under our corporeal vision, our memory is admonished and excited; but some place for them must be imagined; as bodily shape cannot be conceived without a place for it ... we must fancy many plain distinct places at moderate distances, and such symbols as are impressive, striking, and well-marked so that they may present themselves to the mind and act upon it with the greatest quickness. This faculty of artificial memory practice will afford, from which proceeds habit, as well as the derivation of similar words converted and altered in cases, or transferred from particulars to generals, and the idea of an entire sentence from the symbol of a single word after the manner and method of any skillful painter who distinguishes spaces by the variety of what he depicts ...

The memory of things is the proper business of the orator; this we may be enabled to impress on ourselves by the creation of imaginary figures, aptly arranged, to represent particular heads, so that we may recollect thoughts by images and their order by place ... A memory cannot be entirely formed by this practice if there is none given by nature; yet certainly, if there is latent natural faculty, it may be called forth. (II, 87–8)

What we have here is a somewhat confused, traditional account of how we recall what we sensually experience. Aware of the importance of sense data Cicero rapidly shifts into a discussion of imaginative and mental imagery. Mental images adequately resemble what we have perceived as well as what we have understood. The memory deals with imaginary forms and objects as well as objects of sensation. And then we imagine distinct places and organise all these images in them so that mind may act on them. There is no discussion of the nature of imaginative resemblances and their relation to that which they represent; and there is no discussion of the possibility of imagination being false. But then orators never deal with truth or falsehood. They deal only with probabilities and plausibilities as these seem likely to their auditors. And they deal with a selective choice amongst that which is to be remembered in order to serve a predetermined case. Orators remember what is deemed worthy of remembrance. Rome of the orators tells us about an ideological use of memory and not what memory is. Ought we to worry that such men were the self-appointed guardians of history?

Cicero's oratorical use of memory is supplemented by what Quintilian, the educator had to say in his *Institutio Oratoria*. Here he describes the old story of how Simonides invented the art of memory.[6]

This achievement of Simonides appears to have given rise to the observation that it is an assistance to the memory if places are stamped upon the mind, which anyone can believe from experiment. For when we return to a place after a considerable absence, we do not merely recognise the place itself but remember things that we did there, and recall the persons whom we met and even the unuttered thoughts which passed through our minds when we were there before. Thus, in most cases, *art originates from experiment.*

---

6 Yates's slightly modified translations from the Loeb edition have been used.

Places are chosen, and marked with the utmost possible variety, as a spacious house divided into a number of rooms. Everything of note therein is diligently *imprinted on the mind*, in order that *thought* may be able to run through all the parts without let or hindrance. The first task is to secure that there shall be no difficulty in running through these, for that memory must be most firmly fixed which helps another memory. Then what has been written down or thought of, is noted by a sign to remind of it. This sign may be drawn from a whole 'thing', as navigation or warfare, or from some 'word'; for what is slipping from memory is recovered by the admonition of a single word ... These signs are then arranged as follows. The first notion is placed, as it were, in the forecourt; the second, let us say in the atrium, the remainder are placed in order all round the impluvium and committed not only to bedrooms and parlours but even to statues and the like. This done, when it is required to revive the memory, one begins from the first place to run through all, demanding what has been entrusted to them of which one will be reminded by the image ... What I have spoken of as being done in a house can also be done in public buildings, or on a long journey, or in going through a city with pictures. Or we can imagine such places for ourselves. We require, therefore places, either real or imaginary, and images or simulacra which must be invented. Images are as words by which we note the things we have to learn, so that as Cicero says, 'we use places as wax and images as letters.' (xi, ii, 17–22; emphasis added)

Quintilian has less confidence that this method will enable one to recall a whole series of connected words. Some words, e.g. conjunctions, cannot be represented by any likeness, he insists. And such a technique if applied to remembering whole speeches will impede the flow of our own connected speech by requiring that we constantly look back at separate forms for each individual word. Quintilian's technique is a descriptive and enabling one but it explains nothing about imprinting and thought running over imprints.

Quintilian's reference to Cicero as an expert in the art of memory leads us to seek further in the latter's writings for a greater expansion of the notion of memory beyond its application to oratory. For Cicero was not only a practised advocate and orator but an active statesman in troubled republican Rome. And he linked his political activity with his philosophical beliefs. He was an admirer of Greek philosophy, much of which he associated with Plato, who 'crushed him with the weight of his authority'. During that period of enforced retirement from public life and to comfort himself in distress, he was able to reflect on various philosophical doctrines. He composed, among other works, the *Tusculan Disputations* (45 BC).[7] This does not claim to be an original work; it consists in many cases of judicious extracts or borrowings from Greek authoritative texts to hand.

---

[7] Cicero, *Tusculan Disputations* with an English translation, J. E. King (Loeb Classical Library) (London, 1971).

But Cicero was responsible for the illustrations taken from Roman history and literature, and anxious to redeem the reputation of Roman culture from the reproach of having neglected philosophy. He set to making Greek philosophy accessible in Roman form and language. He provides a survey of the history of philosophy (probably derived from Posidonius) and when he reaches Plato, the apogee of the discipline is seen to have been achieved. Aside from the logical, dialectical and rhetorical writings of Aristotle, Cicero does not appear to be otherwise well acquainted with him. He then speaks of the post-Aristotelian schools of Stoicism.

Cicero himself belonged to that New Academy school which, under Philo, aimed at bringing the teachings of Stoicism and Plato's Academy closer together. Stoicism saw the role of philosophy as a training ground for practical virtue. Accepting Aristotle's logic, Stoics elaborated a theory of knowledge which, like Aristotle's, began with sense perceptions. These gave rise to memory, repeated acts of which produced experience. Experience then gave rise to conceptions and thereafter to knowledge. So too, much of Stoic physics derives from Aristotle, to which is added an adaptation of earlier Ionian philosophy to bolster their doctrine of the unity of all being. Cicero may have rejected Stoic fatalism and pantheism but it is clear in his later works, and as he grew older, that he was drawn to them and especially to their teaching on virtue as the sole end of human life expressed as a detailed doctrine of duties. This suited what might be called the Roman spirit of the time. Stoic tenets were well adapted to the purposes of oratory and eloquence especially during the mid–first century BC when a mongrel philosophy produced its most eloquent exponent. Cicero claims to sip the best of every school often to the extent of blatant inconsistency. But his aim in the *Tusculan Disputations* is to offer the general reader advice on how to cope with death, endure pain, alleviate distress and other psychic disorders and finally, to argue for the sufficiency of virtue for the happy life. And so he chooses advice from the various schools of philosophy whose texts he had near at hand. In Book I Cicero offers us his views on the memory, by way of reflections on the nature of the soul, and this is a part-New Academy, part-Platonic exegesis of available and current philosophical beliefs.

Cicero is speaking of the various theories concerning the nature of the soul:

On the other hand, if the soul, as we regard it, belongs to the four classes of elements of which all things are said to consist, it consists of kindled air, as I see is the view which most commends itself to Panaetius [the Stoic] and such a soul necessarily strives to reach higher regions ... If it survives unadulterated and unchanged in substance, it is of necessity carried away so rapidly as to pierce and part asunder all this atmosphere of ours, in which clouds, storms and winds collect because of the moisture and mist produced by evaporation from the earth. When the soul has passed this tract and reaches to and recognizes a substance resembling its own, it stops amongst the fires which are formed of rarefied air and the modified glow of the sun and ceases to make higher ascent ... And as it is the fires of the flesh in our bodies which commonly enkindle us to almost all desires, and the flame is heightened by envy of all who possess what we desire to possess, assuredly we shall be happy when we have left our bodies behind and are free from all desirings and envyings: and as happens now when the burden of care is relaxed we feel the wish for an object of our observation and attention, this will happen much more freely then, and we shall devote our whole being to study and examination, because nature has planted in our minds an insatiable longing to see truth ... For the beauty of that vision even here on earth called into being that philosophy 'of sires and grandsires' as Theophrastus terms it, which was first kindled by longing for knowledge ... what, pray, do we think the panorama will be like when we shall be free to embrace the whole earth in our survey ...? We do not even now distinguish with our eyes the things we see; *for there is no perception in the body*, but, as is taught not only by natural philosophers but also by the experts of medicine, who have seen the proofs openly disclosed, there are, as it were, passages bored from the seat of the soul to eye and ear and nose ... *it is the soul which both sees and hears and not those parts of us which serve as windows to the soul*, and yet the mind can perceive nothing through them, unless it is active and attentive. What of the fact that by using the same mind we have perception of things so utterly unlike as colour, taste, heat, smell, sound? These the soul would never have ascertained by its five messengers, unless it had been sole court of appeal and only judge of everything. Moreover, surely objects of far greater purity and transparency will be discovered when the day comes on which the mind is free and has reached its natural home. For in our present state, although the apertures which, as has been said, are open from the body to the soul, have been fashioned by nature with cunning workmanship, yet they are in a manner fenced in with a compound of earthy particles; when, however, *there shall be soul and nothing else, no physical barrier will hinder its perception of the true nature of everything*. (I, xix–xx, pp. 52–57; emphasis added)

Cicero is happy to accept the view of Plato that the soul is immortal and its nature is separable from the body and mounts aloft. His companion astonishingly says: 'I prefer, before heaven, to go astray with Plato, your reverence for whom I know, and admiration for whom I learn from your lips, rather than hold true views with his opponents [sic]'. And Cicero replies: 'well done. I should not myself be unwilling to go astray with that same thinker.'

Cicero continues: 'and yet no reason really suggests itself to my mind why the belief of Pythagoras and Plato should not be true. For though

Plato produced no reasoned proof – note the tribute I pay the man – he would crush me by the mere weight of his authority'[8] (I, xxi, pp. 58–9).

Thus Cicero says there is no reason for thinking the immortality of the soul is incredible, and one must understand the concept of the soul without the body. He notes it is easier to understand the soul when it has quitted the body. He has more difficulty with the notion of the soul embodied 'in a home that is not its own', that is, with the Aristotelian and Stoic positions.[9]

'It is a point of the utmost importance to realize that the soul sees by means of the soul alone, and surely this is the meaning of Apollo's maxim advising that each one should know himself.' This cannot mean, he says, that we should know our own limbs, our shape, and indeed, Cicero distinguishes between 'self' and 'body'. 'Our selves are not our bodies, and in speaking as I do to you, I am not speaking to your body.' Thus 'know thyself' means 'know thy soul'. He then cites Plato's *Phaedrus* and *The Republic* where it is said that 'that which is always in motion is eternal, and that which is self-moving is the source of all other movement.' It appears likely that this 'property as self-moved, eternal motion has been bestowed on souls and is their peculiar essence and character'.

Now, one of the characteristics of soul is memory which is unlimited. Plato we are told, calls this recollection of a previous life, and he proves this in the *Meno*. In addition, Socrates on the very last day of his life argued that knowledge is remembrance:

Indeed in no other way was it possible for us to possess from childhood such a number of important ideas, innate and as it were impressed on our souls and called *ennoiai*, unless the soul, before it had entered the body, had been active in acquiring knowledge. And since there is no true existence in any sensible object, as Plato everywhere argues – for he thinks that nothing that has a beginning and an

---

[8] A rhetorical topos to confirm further the willingness of the orator to be persuaded by authority, if not plausibility, over and above demonstrative proof and empirical evidence. This passage indeed reads like an ironic reversal of Aristotle's famous statement in *Nicomachean Ethics*, I, 6 (1096a 12–17): 'This inquiry is an uphill task since men who are dear to us have introduced the Forms. But it would seem to be better, in fact to be necessary, to uproot even what is one's own for the sake of preserving the truth – both as a general principle and because we are philosophers. For when both the people and the truth are dear to us, it is fitting to put the truth first.' Indeed the beloved Plato himself said (*Republic*, X, 595): 'Yet the love and respect I've always had from a boy for Homer makes me hesitate – for I think he's the original master and guide of all the great tragic poets. But one must not respect an individual more than the truth.'

[9] For Stoics the human soul is a fragment of *pneuma*, that is, immanent divinity in all things and the human soul is born of segmentation of the paternal *pneuma* from which a part is transmitted in the semen of life. Stoicism therefore teaches material traducianism. As Seneca said, the soul is nothing other than a parcel of divinity plunged into the body of man. *Epistolae ad Lucilium*, 66, 12.

ending exists, and only that exists which is always constant to its nature; this he calls [idea] and we 'idea' – the soul in the prison-house of the body could not have apprehended ideas; it brought the knowledge with it: consequently our feeling of wonder at the extent of our knowledge is removed. Yet the soul, when suddenly shifted into such an unaccustomed and disordered dwelling-place [the body], does not clearly see ideas, but when it has composed and recovered itself it apprehends them by remembrance. Thus, according to Plato, learning is nothing but recollecting. (I, xxiv, pp. 66/7–68/9).

What Cicero has done here, as he attempts throughout the *Tusculan Disputations*, is to summarise from Plato's writings the theory of the soul's immortality, by the plausibility of which he finds himself persuaded. He does not seem to know or understand the epistemological or ontological foundation for Plato's theory of recollection. This lack of understanding is made clear when Cicero takes the discussion of memory further. He asks – 'what is it that enables us to remember, or what character has it, or what is its origin?' He says he is not inquiring into the powers of those who possessed great memories, evidently by means of mnemotechnical devices. Rather, he wants to know about the memory of the average man, especially of those engaged in some higher branch of study and art, and who have estimable memories. He decides this quality of the memory is not of the heart, blood, or brain. He does not know, and 'is not ashamed to admit it', whether the memory is of breath or fire, but he does affirm that it is divine. His language here is not especially Platonic and he provides no analysis whatever of the doctrine of the forms (apart from mentioning the ideas as impressed in the soul before birth [above]). He does not seem to understand what these ideas or forms are *before* they are impressed in the soul. It is ridiculous, he says, to think that there is in the soul a sort of roominess into which the things we remember can be poured as if into a kind of vessel. And he finds it incomprehensible to assume that like wax the soul has marks impressed upon it and that memory consists of the traces of things registered in the mind. Effectively he reiterates the arguments of *Theaetetus* and rejects them as did Plato. 'What can be the traces of words, of actual objects, what further could be the enormous space adequate to the representation of such a mass of material?' (I, xxv, pp. 70/1–72/3).

Cicero pauses however at this question-mark. He provides no resolution to the problem of what the memory is. And then he changes tack by asking the question about the soul's powers of investigation, discovery and contrivance. He runs through all the great first moments in the history of civilisation when someone first united the scattered human units into a body and joined them in social life, when someone first named and defined by means of written characters all the endless variety of vocal sounds; when someone first marked down the course of the stars. All of these were instances of divine genius to Cicero. Plato held philosophy to be a *gift* of the Gods; Cicero would rather hold it to be a discovery of the gods. (This is an ambiguous phrase which only assumes clarity when he later implies his meaning is *man's* discovery of the gods because of man's divine genius.)

'A power able to bring about such a number of important results is to my mind wholly divine. For what is the memory of facts and words? what further is discovery? Assuredly nothing can be comprehended even in God of greater value than this' (I, xxvi, pp. 74/5–76/7). Instead of attributing human feelings to the gods as did Homer, it would have been better, argues Cicero, had he attributed divine attributes to man; and these are activity, wisdom, discovery, memory. In the elements themselves there is nothing to possess the power of memory, thought, reflection, nothing capable of retaining the past or foreseeing the future and grasping the present; these capacities are divine, and their source is God, but they are in man.

'And indeed god Himself who is comprehended by us, can be comprehended in no other way save as a mind unfettered and free, severed from all perishable matter, conscious of all and moving all and self-endowed with perpetual motion. *Of such sort and of the same nature is the human mind.*' (I, xxvii, pp. 76/7–78/9; emphasis added).

Where is the place of this divine power of mind, for Cicero? He believes it to be in the head. He distinguishes it from the place of the soul – 'which is in you' – but he says he will explain this at another time. When he does so he argues that were one to hold, as one might, that the soul is mortal, then because destruction at death is so complete, there is no sensation in the soul and the soul is nowhere. But this is presented only as a plausible argument rather than as his own belief. Cicero prefers to see the memory as a divine power of the mind which is somehow distinct from the immortal soul. And he leaves the issue there.

Cicero may have wished to redeem the Roman reputation from the charge of displaying no interest in philosophy, but it is by now clear that he has given us very little of either of the two great Greek epistemologies that were founded on differing ontologies in which memory played its part. He passed on in his rhetorical works the tradition of mnemotechnics but he has no serious discussion of what memory is and how it works. Evidently, as he stated in the *Tusculan Disputations*, he found the notion of the soul as a vessel containing the infinite number of possible memories, and the notion of the soul being imprinted like wax with memory traces, equally incomprehensible. And he provided no other hypothesis.

What he did provide for future generations was a veneration for the orator's task in discovering and preserving the immortal and imitable aspects of past history. He proclaimed the orator to be possessed of a duty: to maintain the life of the collective memory through recalling the exemplary nature of the past, for *plena exemplorum est historia* (*De Divinatione*, I, 50). This recollection was unproblematic; its capacity to convince depended not on an investigation of evidence, not on 'wie es eigentlich gewesen', in Ranke's terms, but on the rhetorical plausibility of present arguments whose basis lay in unreflective common opinion.[10] Cicero is truly father of History as it would be understood in the West[11] until the period of the Enlightenment, and in some cases, beyond.

We shall have another occasion to discuss the Ciceronian attitude to the past and to the uses of memory when we come to analyse historical writing in the twelfth century and then during the Renaissance. But the Roman rhetorical legacy would not stand alone as an influence during the high middle ages and the Renaissance. Epistemological theories with their roots in the philosophy of Greek antiquity would come to play an even more dramatic role in medieval and Renaissance discussions of memory and thereby influence men's attitudes to the past: how it may be known and then used.

[10] '... deberi hoc a me tantis hominum ingeniis putari, ut, cum etiam nunc vivam illorum memoriam teneremus, hac immortalem redderem, si possem' (*De Oratore*, II, 2, 8).

[11] There were Latin writers who would distinguish between history and rhetoric, e.g. Lucian of Samosata during the reign of Marcus Aurelius, where he says the historian's brief is to write the truth and not an historical novel full of fantastic stories claiming accuracy. An historian of current affairs must understand public affairs and must desire to imitate the ancient writers, mainly Herodotus and Thucydides. But here too there is very little concern for finding substantiating evidence for an account of events. See J. A. S. Evans, 'The attitudes of the secular historians of the age of Justinian towards the classical past', *Traditio*, 32 (1976), 353–8.

Chapter 4

PLINY AND THE ROMAN NATURALISTS ON MEMORY: BORGES'S *FUNES THE MEMORIOUS*

The problem of the memory and how it operated remained one of amazement for Romans of the first centuries after Christ. That extraordinary encyclopedia of exceptional events, Pliny's *Historia Naturalis*,[1] which has much in common with a *Guinness Book of Records*, or even more so with a *Ripley's Believe It or Not*, devotes Book VII to exceptional endurances, exceptional transmissions of sound, exceptional sight and strength evidenced throughout the history of mankind. Chapter 24 speaks of memory, another exceptional faculty brought to its height by certain exceptional men of the past:

As to memory, the boon most necessary for life, it is not easy to say who most excelled in it, so many men have gained renown for it. King Cyrus could give their names to all the soldiers in his army. Lucius Scipio knew the names of the whole Roman people, King Pyrrhus's envoy Cineas knew those of the Senate and knighthood at Rome the day after his arrival [280 BC]. Mithridates who as king of twenty-two races gave judgements in as many languages, in an assembly addressing each race in turn without an interpreter. A person in Greece named Charmadas recited the contents of any volumes in libraries that anyone asked him to quote, just as if he were reading them. Finally, a *memoria technica* was constructed, which was invented by the lyric poet Simonides and perfected by Metrodorus of Scepsis, enabling anything heard to be repeated in the identical words. Also no other human faculty is equally fragile: injuries from and even apprehensions of, diseases and accident may affect in some cases a single field of memory and in others the whole. A man has been known when struck by a stone to forget how to read and write but nothing else. One who fell from a very high roof forgot his mother and his relatives and friends, and when ill forgot his servants also; the orator Messala Corvinus forgot his own name. Similarly tentative and hesitating lapses of memory often occur when the body even when uninjured is in repose; also the gradual approach of sleep curtails the memory and makes the unoccupied mind wonder where it is.

[1] Pliny, *The Historia Naturalis*, text and translation H. Rackham (Loeb Classical Library); *Plinius Secundus, C.* (Pliny the Elder), *Naturalis Historia*, ed. L. Jahn and C. Mayhoff, 5 vols. (Leipzig, 1892–1909).

60

It is significant that Pliny calls the memory the boon most important for life, and then rehearses exceptional examples of its capacities in very many men. Clearly he is speaking of those who have learned mnemotechnical devices for recalling without understanding. But he goes on to record other amazing characteristics of this important faculty, its fragility, its susceptibility to illness and blows, its weakening upon repose and sleep, without any reference to what memory is and why it can be made to act as it does. The prodigious memory is simply an amazing technique acquired by some; others lose even the average function of memory through illness or injury. All of us lose it somewhat when we fall asleep.

The ancient Roman sensibility stopped short to marvel at these feats without questioning how and why.

Let us digress for a moment and consider Funes the Memorious, 'recalled' in 1942 by Borges, who drew appropriate conclusions about this kind of remembering.[2]

With evident good faith Funes marveled that such things (as were to be found in the lists of exceptional rememberers in Pliny) should be considered marvelous. He told me that previous to the rainy afternoon when the blue-tinted horse threw him, he had been – like any Christian – blind, deafmute, somnambulistic, memoryless ... On falling from the horse he lost consciousness; when he recovered it, the present was almost intolerable it was so rich and bright; the same was true of the most ancient and most trivial memories ... And now, his perception and his memory were infallible ... These recollections were not simple; each visual image was linked to muscular sensations, thermal sensations, etc. He could reconstruct all his dreams, all his fancies. He told me: I have more memories in myself alone than all men have had since the world was a world. And again: my dreams are like your vigils. And again, toward dawn: my memory, sir, is like a garbage disposal ... In effect, Funes not only remembered every leaf on every tree of every wood, but even every one of the times he had perceived or imagined it. He determined to reduce all his past experience to some seventy thousand recollections, which he could later define numerically. Two considerations dissuaded him: the thought that the task was interminable and the thought that it was useless.[3]

But Borges goes on to say that he suspects that this prodigious memory rendered Funes incapable of thought. 'To think is to forget a difference, to generalise, to abstract. In the overly replete world of Funes there were nothing but details, almost contiguous details.'[4]

The world is much richer in its infinite particularities than the few generalisations we are able to make about it in language: it is also

---

[2] Jorge Luis Borges, 'Funes, the Memorious' (1942), in *Ficciones*, ed. Anthony Kerrigan (New York, 1962).
[3] *Ibid.*, pp. 112–13.   [4] *Ibid.*, p. 115.

meaningless in its repleteness without interpretation so that between the uniqueness of our experiences and the signs we use to represent this, there is a space of which Funes was now unaware. The discrepancy between experience and the succinctness of language is overcome for Borges only by forgetting, leaving things out, in order to create meaning. Plato had also seen this as essential. In our own century, the distinguished Russian psychologist Alexander Luria described, in what he called a biographical novel, a similarly remarkable man, a mnemonist whose capacities to remember facts and numbers in minute detail, even many years after his initial experience, led Luria to speak of him as in some sense mentally ill. Here was a man whose greatest difficulty was in forgetting endless trivia.[5] Total recall is a disaster for any but mnemonic rememberers whose naive realism makes them indifferent to the consequences of their technique, not least the over-congested mind incapable of seeing overall purposes, narratives or plots. Funes's garbage-disposal type memory, possibly organised numerically or by place-systems, like that of Luria's mnemonist, is an uncomprehending memory, divine in its capaciousness though it may be. But the memory on which thinking relies must somehow depend on its opposite, forgetting, and the truth – that we all live by leaving behind – was to inspire second- and third-century philosophers to reevaluate their inheritance from the Greeks. Thereafter, Christian theology, directed by Augustine's neo-Platonist psychological insights, would indeed lead, as Borges noted, to the most important sense in which all Christians are memoryless.

The problems raised by both Plato and Aristotle concerning the various operations of the soul were not to be buried, despite the rhetoricians. They were actively taken up in the second- and third-century revival of Platonism and consequently the problem of memory with its relationship to the immortality of the soul became a live issue for the pagan, neo-Platonist Plotinus (d. 270). Cicero had wanted to know about the memory of the average man. Plotinus, three centuries later, provided something of an answer.

[5] A. R. Luria, *The Mind of a Mnemonist* (New York, 1968). Also see Oliver Sacks, *The Man Who Mistook His Wife For a Hat* (London, 1985) especially the preface.

Chapter 5

PLOTINUS AND THE EARLY
NEO-PLATONISTS ON MEMORY AND MIND

In a book on ancient and medieval memories, why should we spend time on Plotinus? Firstly, it must be said that his *Enneads* would greatly influence the thought of St Augustine, that most important of Church Fathers whose views on virtually everything would dominate the medieval, Renaissance and Reformation worlds. But Plotinus also greatly influenced the mystical, neo-Platonist tradition of the high middle ages as we shall see. His thought was revived amongst certain twelfth-century thinkers who would propound one of the most powerful psychological theories concerning memory in relation to knowledge, a theory that would profoundly influence the practical ways certain men not only thought about but also lived their lives. Plotinus is a difficult thinker. But for us he represents a distinct and influential manner of discussing the relation of the human soul to the cosmos and human memory in relation to knowing that was prominent during the third century AD. He also represents the manner in which the Platonic and Aristotelian legacy was to be synthesised and used by philosophers and theologians who were later to be concerned to graft onto the classical inheritance other, specifically Christian, insights during the first centuries of the development of the Church.

In what follows, I present those aspects of Plotinus's thought that enable us to see where memory eventually fits into his system. In becoming familiar with the Plotinian argument we enter a thought world that would be shared by later, learned medieval thinkers, and we thereby come to share their language and perspective. As we shall see, there is much in the writings of St Augustine that will seem obscure without a prior knowledge of Plotinus, not least Augustine's resolution of difficulties in the Plotinian explanation of memory and its human significance.

Plotinus is considered the last great philosopher of antiquity and one of the founders of neo-Platonism. He was an Egyptian Greek who taught in Rome, dying there in AD 270. Although he was an heir to the great ancient

63

philosophies of Plato, Aristotle and the Stoics, the dominant influence on him was Platonism. Plato, he believed, possessed the whole truth. Plotinus did not proclaim himself a commentator on the writings of either Plato or Aristotle, but saw himself only as an exponent of Plato's philosophy. Aside from his intimate acquaintance with Plato's writings, however, he was also familiar with what scholars call the middle Platonists of the second and third centuries,[1] whose works have now perished. These eclectic Platonists clearly influenced his understanding of Plato, as did his immediate predecessor Numenius of Apamea. In fact, in his own life time Plotinus's Greek colleagues accused him of plagiarising Numenius. His writings also conceal much latent Stoicism and Aristotelianism and he certainly dealt with the problems they bequeathed to posterity, but in a Platonising manner. Undoubtedly his system is not an explicit one, but throughout his works and especially in the *Six Enneads*,[2] he treats two major problems: that of the soul, its actuality, its states and its experiences; and that of the world (cosmos), its objects and their rational explanation. The memory is an important constituent of his system.

According to Plotinus, Divinity is a graded triad of three hypostases or 'persons'. The One, or First Existent is completely unknowable; the Divine Mind is the first thinker and thought; and the All-Soul, the third hypostasis, is the first and only principle of life. We shall primarily be concerned with the second and third hypostases, Divine Mind and the All-Soul, and these require further elaboration here. The Divine Mind is otherwise called Real-Being, the Universal First Intelligence, and it is the act or offspring and image of the First or One which is unknowable.

[1] 'Middle Platonism' is usually applied to revived Platonism of the Roman imperial period before Plotinus; and 'neo-Platonism' to Platonism from Plotinus onwards, without a breach of continuity between them. See J. Dillon, *The Middle Platonists* (London, 1977).

[2] I have used *Plotinus, The Enneads*, translated by Stephen Mackenna, revised by B. S. Page, with introduction by Paul Henry, S. J., 4th rev. edn (London, 1969); with reference to the Henry and Schwyzer edition, *Plotini Opera* I–III (Paris and Brussels, 1959 and 1973). Also see P. Henry, *Plotin et l'Occident* (Paris, 1934); Cornelia de Vogel, 'Plotinus' image of man, its relationship to Plato as well as to later neo-Platonism', in *Images of Man in Ancient and Medieval Thought. Studia G. Verbeke* ... (Louvain, 1976), pp. 147–68. The most useful literature for what follows has been: *The Cambridge History of Later Greek and Early Mediaeval Philosophy*, ed. A. H. Armstrong (Cambridge, 1967); E. R. Dodds, *Pagan and Christian in a World of Anxiety* (Cambridge, 1965); H. J. Blumenthal, 'Plotinus in later Platonism', in *Neoplatonism and Early Christian Thought, Essays in Honour of A. H. Armstrong*, ed., H. J. Blumenthal and R. A. Markus, (London, 1981), pp. 212–22; H. J. Blumenthal, *Plotinus' Psychology* (The Hague, 1971); A. H. Armstrong, 'Form, individual and person in Plotinus', *Dionysius*, 1 (Halifax, Nova Scotia, 1977) 49–68; H. J. Blumenthal and A. C. Lloyd, eds., *Soul and the Structure of Being in Late Neoplatonism: Syrianus, Proclus and Simplicius* (Liverpool, 1982); R. Arnou, *Le désir de Dieu dans la philosophie de Plotin* (Paris, 1921); Cornelia de Vogel, 'The concept of personality in Greek and Christian thought', in *Studies in Philosophy and the History of Philosophy* (Washington DC, 1963), II, pp. 20–60; Gerard J. P. O'Daly, *Plotinus' Philosophy of the Self* (Shannon, 1973).

Divine Mind, as first thinker and first thought, is a mediation of the Unknowable One and as such is identified as the Intellectual-Principle.

The third hypostasis of divinity is the All-Soul. It is an eternal emanation and image of the second hypostasis, the Intellectual-Principle. Characteristic of the All-Soul are two Acts: one in upward contemplation of the One, and downward 'generation' towards that which is lower.[3] This All-Soul contains all the souls there are in the cosmos including the human, and thus it is particularised for the space of the mortal life of man, accepting the limitations this implies. Furthermore, in man there are three phases of the All-Soul: there is the Intellective Soul, otherwise referred to as, and identical with, the intuitive, the intellectual, intelligent Soul and the intellectual principle of Soul. Its characteristics are its impassibility and its being all but completely untouched by matter. It is separate from the body. For a man to live by this Intellective Soul, is to live as a God.

But then there is the second phase of the All-Soul in man: that of the Reasoning Soul, and this corresponds to the normal nature of man. It is separable from the body but is not separated. It acts through discursive reasoning, arriving at imperfect True Knowing by means of logic and doubt. It also has a lower action which acquaints it with surface or sense-knowing and opinion based on this. It is this second phase of the human soul which possesses as powers Will, Intellectual-Imagination and Intellectual-Memory. These are distinct from an even lower Imagination and Memory which belong to the Third phase of the All-Soul in man: unreasoning soul. This is the principle of Animal-life where the soul is conjoined with body, and possesses faculties of sense, imagination and sense memory. Man, for Plotinus, is somehow divine and the philosophical life must aim at restoring the proper relationship with the divine All through an understanding of this divinity. As part of that All, man may come to union with his transcendent source, the One or Good. 'The philosophic life merely obeys the ordinance of the God who bade us know ourselves' (p. 259).[4]

Ennead, IV, 3 takes us on a journey which begins with that general instinct to seek and learn the nature of the soul, that instrument with which we search, and tries to satisfy our longing to possess ourselves of the vision of the Intellectual-Principle, the second hypostasis of divinity. Plotinus first argues that his position is not that alternative Platonist

---

[3] Plotinus maintained that some part of our mind remained permanently in the Intelligible, usually within the second hypostasis itself and was, therefore, permanently active. *Enneads*, IV, 8.8. 1–3. This was admittedly unorthodox and was rejected by later neo-Platonists who said the soul descends as a whole. See Blumenthal in *Neoplatonism and Early Christian Thought*, pp. 213–15.

[4] All page references refer to the Mackenna translation.

position which states that the human soul is a mere segment of the All-Soul.

'The Soul is not a thing of quantity; we are not to conceive of the All-Soul as some standard "ten" with particular souls as its constituent units' (p. 261). Clearly, soul is not subject to parts in the manner of magnitudes; the particular soul is part of the All-Soul only in the sense that the latter bestows itself on all living things. 'Even difference of function, as in eyes and ears, cannot warrant the assertion of distinct parts concerned in each separate act; all is met by the notion of one identical thing, but a thing in which a distinct power operates in each separate function. Thus all the powers are present either in seeing or in hearing but different organs are concerned. The varying impressions received are *our* various *responses* to Ideal-Forms that can be taken in a variety of modes' (p. 262). Because perception demands a common gathering place – the soul – each organ with its distinct function interprets its experience in its own way, but judgement on these is vested in a unifying principle, the soul. Furthermore, 'each soul is permanently a unity, a self, and yet all are, in their total, one being' (p. 264). Now our relation to the Supreme is variable: some of us are capable of becoming Uniate whilst others strive and almost attain this state; a third is much less able: it is a matter of the degrees or powers of the Soul by which our temperament is determined, the first degree dominant in one person and so on (p. 265). The soul's total being latently holds within it the scheme of reason, its rationalising power.

'As we know, the Reason-Principle carried in animal seed, fashions and shapes living beings into so many universes in the small. For whatsoever touches soul is moulded to the nature of soul's own Real-Being' (p. 269); soul produces only what represents its powers. 'Soul has *the distinction of possessing at once an action of conscious attention within itself, and an action towards the outer*. It has thus the function of giving life to all that does not live by prior right and the life it gives is commensurate with its own; living in reason it communicates reason to the body' (pp. 269–70; emphasis added). Thus every particular entity is linked to that Divine Being in whose likeness it is made and insofar as it is alive, its reason is an activity of its soul.

All that is Divine Intellect will rest eternally above, and could never fall from its sphere but, poised entire in its own high place, will communicate to things here through the channel of Soul. Soul in virtue of neighbourhood is more closely modelled upon the Idea uttered by the Divine Intellect, and thus is able to produce order in the movement of the lower realm, one phase [the World-Soul] maintaining the unvarying march [of the cosmic circuit], the other [the Soul of the Individual] adapting itself to times and seasons. (p. 270)

66

To indicate that the diversity of conditions in our world is determined by individual responsibility, Plotinus provides a summary of Plato's doctrine of the cycle of the soul's embodiments (metempsychosis) found in the Myth of Er of *The Republic*.

The souls peering forth from the Intellectual Realm descend first to the heavens and there put on a body [but they are not *in* body as an object is in space]; this becomes at once the medium by which as they reach out more and more towards magnitude [physical extension] they proceed to bodies progressively more earthy. Some even plunge from heaven to the very lowest of corporeal forms; others pass, stage by stage, too feeble to lift towards the higher burden they carry, weighed downwards among them, by their heaviness and forgetfulness. As for the difference among them, these are due to variation in the bodies entered, or to the accidents of life, or to upbringing, or to inherent peculiarities of temperament, or to all these influences together, or to specific combinations of them. (p. 273)

There are some souls however who continue, whilst below, to live according to the code which is woven out of the Reason-Principle ruling the Cosmos and which is consonant with those of higher existences. Misfortunes are not laid up in the master-facts of the universe, he says. They are either deserved or accidental. The reason may elude us and we can only accept accidental hardship as precise in the distribution of what is due whilst we are ignorant of the higher scheme, but we know that this higher scheme cannot proceed without God and justice (p. 274).

Although we speak of souls as reasoning, Plotinus sees this activity as primarily appropriate after the soul's descent and embodiment. For reasoning is the act of the soul fallen into perplexity, distracted with cares, diminished in strength; the need of deliberation goes with the less self-sufficing intelligence; 'craftsmen faced by a difficulty stop to consider; where there is no problem their art works on by its own forthright power' (p. 275).

But then he asserts that there are two modes of reasoning; one is an enduring activity flowing uninterruptedly from the Intellectual-Principle; it is a reflection of the Principle itself. Ours, however, is a deliberation of doubt and difficulty which does not always have happy issue. At any rate, reasoning and the act of intellect are not vested in the body and their task is not accomplished by means of the body which in fact is detrimental to any thinking on which it is allowed to intrude (p. 276).

He rejects the notion of the soul as truly *in* body as in a containing space, as well as Aristotle's doctrine of the soul as form in matter where they are inseparable. Rather, Plotinus says soul is that which engenders the form residing in matter (p. 277). But he thinks that the reason we none the less speak of the soul being *in* body is because the soul is not seen and the body is, and so its existence is inferred. The precise mode of the soul's presence in the body is elusive. But we do know that a living body is illuminated by soul, and each organ and member participates in soul after some manner peculiar to itself (p. 279). The functionally fit organs serve as vehicles of the soul-faculty under which the function is performed. But the soul's faculty is of universal scope. We can, however, speak of various soul-faculties as 'responsible' for certain functioning organs.

The faculty presiding over sensation and impulse, for instance, is vested in the sensitive and representative soul: 'it operates by drawing upon the Reason-Principle immediately above itself; downward it is in contact with an inferior of its own' (p. 279). He then runs through the views of the ancients who sought the seat of the soul in the sensitive part of the brain. Indeed, he believes there must be a linking between body, or that point most receptive of body's activity, and the reasoning act which is utterly isolated from body but which is in contact with something which is a form of soul (and not merely vegetative or quasi-corporeal forms), appropriating perceptions originating in the Reason-Principle.[5]

In asking where souls go when they leave the body, Plotinus also asks whether, when they have left, they retain memory of their lives (IV, 3, 25 [p. 281]). Thus we come to his discussion of memory. What is a remembering principle? (He says he does not mean, at least for the moment, what memory is, but in what order of beings it can occur.) What characteristics are present where memory exists?

A memory has to do with something brought into ken from without, something learned or something experienced. The Memory-Principle therefore, cannot belong to such beings as are immune from experience and time. *No memory* can therefore be ascribed to any divine being or to the Authentic Existent or the Intellectual-Principle (the first and second hypostases of divinity). These are intangibly immune and time does not approach them. They possess eternity centred around Being; they know

---

[5] It is this linking of body and reason, the demarcation between those faculties involved with the body and those which are not, which would engage later neo-Platonists and medieval philosophers alike. As Blumenthal has shown, most neo-Platonists worked with an Aristotelian-type arrangement of the soul and posited a demarcation somewhere in the area of imagination, *phantasia*, which is actuated by sense-impressions or messages from them and therefore, is associated with body. But imagination also provides a dematerialised form of information for rational thought to judge. In reverse, imagination transmits the operations of intellect downwards thereby linking the upper and lower soul. Plotinus specifically has the imaginative faculty associated with the upper soul. He preserves the upper soul's freedom from sense data and affection by positing another imaginative faculty associated with lower soul, thereby doubling the faculty, as we shall see. Blumenthal, *Plotinus's Psychology*, pp. 90ff. He would also double the Intellect, positing a rational and a super-rational intellect, with which later neo-Platonists disagreed.

nothing of past and sequent; all is an unbroken state of identity, not receptive of change. Such divine being has intuition rather than memory.

But in the human being, he asks, in which of the constituents of our nature is memory vested? If in the Soul, then in what power or part; if in the third phase, the Animate Soul supposed to be the seat of sensation, then by what mode is it present? And may we ascribe sensation and intellectual acts to one and the same agent or do we imply two distinct principles (p. 282), two different phases of the human soul? Because sensation depends on soul and body together, sensation itself can be considered to have a double nature: the Soul feels and the body works as its tool, passively, whilst Soul is active, reading such impressions as are made upon the body or discerned by means of the body, judging as a result of bodily experiences (IV, 3, 26 [p. 282]). But although sensation is a shared task, *memory is not a shared task of body and soul*. The Soul has from the first taken over the impression either to retain it or reject it. The *act* of remembering then, though grounded in sensation, is an *act of the Soul*. And when we regard matters learned and not merely felt, it is the soul alone that is involved. He rejects the Aristotelian language where soul is a mere potentiality in the animate whole. Nor are the imprints magnitudes; they are not of a corporeal, physiological nature; and there is no resemblance to seal impressions, no stamping of a resistant matter. The process is entirely of the intellect though *exercised upon* things of sense; there is no need of body or bodily quality as a means of such imprinting. Thus Aristotle's whole scheme in its physiological aspects is rejected. A further autonomy of the soul is asserted: only the Soul can remember its own movements, its desires and frustrations of desire; the body can have nothing to tell about things which never approached it and the Soul cannot use the body as a means to the remembrance of what the body by its nature cannot know.

There are then two orders of fact in the process of sense perception: an order in which the body is a means but all culminates in Soul, and an order which is of the Soul alone. Plotinus is so concerned to eliminate the physiological side of Aristotle's explanation of the functioning of the primary perceptive soul, that he adds – 'Actually, memory is impeded by the body and addition of many sensible experiences often brings forgetfulness; with thinning and clearing away, memory will often revive. The Soul is a stability and the shifting and fleeting thing which body is can be cause only of its forgetting not of its remembering.' Memory is therefore exclusively a fact of Soul.

Memory is of the Soul we envisage as the more divine by which we are human, and it is also of that which springs from the All (p. 283). Each of these represents personal memories and shared memories respectively. This extends Plato's description of the soul's memory of its recent embodied personal history, and that more general, shared memory of disembodied, pre-natal souls which see all there is to know (and subsequently, to remember). Plotinus explains the personal and general, shared memory as follows: the Soul which still drags a burden will tell of all the man did and felt; but upon death there will appear, as time passes, memories of the lives lived before, some of the events of the most recent life being dismissed as trivial. It will eventually come to forgetfulness of many things that were mere accretion. Once free and alone, what will it have to remember? The answer depends on our discovering in what faculty of the Soul memory resides (p. 284).

On the one hand he asks why must the seat of our intellectual action be also the seat of our remembrance of that action? And on the other hand, why should the principle by which we perceive be the principle by which we remember? The process must be that where there is to be memory of a sense perception, this perception must then become a mere *presentment* to the image-grasping power; for in this imaging faculty the perception culminates; even when the impression passes away the vision remains present to the imagination (p. 285). So that by the very fact of harbouring the presentment of an object that has disappeared, the imagination is, at once, the seat of memory; where the persistence of the image is brief, the memory is poor; people of powerful memory are those in whom the image-holding power is firmer, not easily allowing the record to be jostled out of its grip. Remembrance, therefore, is vested in the imaging faculty; and memory deals with images. 'Its differing quality or degree from man to man we would explain by difference or similarity in the strength of the individual powers, by conduct like or unlike, by bodily conditions present or absent, producing change and disorder or not' (p. 286). Thus, Plotinus describes the first of two kinds of memory – that of sense–objects, which belongs to imagination (*Enneads*, IV, 3, 29).

But if the imaging power of the Soul is the seat of remembered sense-perception, do the memories of mental acts also fall under the imaging faculty? (IV, 3, 30). If every mental act is accompanied by an image we may well believe that this image, fixed and like a picture of thought, would explain how we remember the object of knowledge once entertained. But if there is no such necessary image (as Plato asserted) another solution must be sought. Plotinus then describes the second kind of memory – of intellectual conceptions which belong to reason (IV, 3, 30). He does not wish to accept Aristotle's assertion that both remembering and thinking require images. So that he offers the astonishing suggestion that perhaps the second kind of memory would be the reception, into the image-making faculty, of the *verbal formula* which accompanies the mental conception: this mental conception – an indivisible thing, and one that never rises to the exterior of consciousness – lies unknown below; but the verbal formula serves as a revealer, as the bridge between the concept and the image-taking faculty, and exhibits the concept as in a mirror; the apprehension of the verbal formula by the image-taking faculty would thus constitute the enduring presence of the concept; words are the means by which ideas rise to consciousness and would be our memory of the concept (p. 286). Verbal formulae, language, thus serves as a mirror of concepts for Plotinus. Augustine would make much of this.

Thus far Plotinus has argued that memory is only appropriate to beings which experience in time. Memory is an *act* of the human soul; it is a process of intellect *exercised upon* things of sense. In fact, memory is impeded by the body. The latter is, if anything, the cause of forgetting. Thus memory is not shared by body and soul but is a fact of soul alone. The memory of sense perception depends on the perception becoming a mere presentment to the faculty that grasps images – the imagination, which therefore is the seat of memory. Where one remembers mental activities which do not have attendant images, what is taken into the imagination is the verbal formula which accompanies the unconscious mental conception. The verbal formula, language, is a bridge between the concept and the image-making faculty, exhibiting the concept as in a mirror.

Now, we know that the Soul is unfailingly intent upon intellection; and only when it acts upon the image-making faculty does its intellection become a human perception, so that intellection is one thing, the perception of an intellection is another. We are continuously intuitive but we are not unbrokenly aware. The reason is that the recipient in us receives from 'both sides', absorbing not merely intellections but also sense-perceptions. This must mean then, that there are two phases of the Soul, one acting on sense perceptions and another on concepts.

Now if there *are* two phases of the Soul and each possesses memory, and memory is vested in the imaging faculty, there must be two such imaging faculties. This might be suitable when the two Souls stand apart; but when they are at one in us, in which Soul is memory vested? (IV, 3, 31 [p. 286]). If each Soul phase has its own imaging faculty then the images must in all cases be duplicated, since we cannot think that one faculty deals only with intellectual objects and the other with objects of sense; this implies the coexistence in man of two life-principles utterly unrelated. What then is the difference between the Souls? The answer is that, when the two Souls chime each with each, the two imaging faculties no longer stand apart; and the union is dominated by the imaging faculty of the *higher soul*, and thus the image perceived is as one; the less powerful is like a shadow attending upon the dominant, like a minor light merging into a greater (p. 287). In such conditions we would be dominated by memories of mental acts, conceptions, and memories of sense perception would fade through being conceptualised.[6] Indeed, Plotinus, like Plato, believes we seek to leave behind sense experiences and their memories.

The higher soul must desire to come to a happy forgetfulness of all that has reached it through the lower ... the more urgent the intention towards the supreme, the more extensive will be the Soul's forgetfulness unless when the entire living has, even here, been such that memory has nothing but the noblest to deal with. In this world all is best when human interests have been held aloof. We may truly say that the good soul is the forgetful. It flees multiplicity; it seeks to escape the unbounded by drawing all to unity, for only thus is it free from entanglement, light-footed, self-conducted. (IV, 4, I [p. 287])

Therefore the Soul's discourse, its memories, in the Intellectual Realm when it has at last won its way to that Essence, will be in contemplation of that order; of things of earth it will know nothing; it will not even remember an act of philosophic virtue. When we seize anything in the direct intellectual act there is room for nothing else than to know and contemplate the object. And, at this stage of contemplation, *the subject is not included in the act of knowing.*[7] Thus once purely in the Intellectual, no one of us can have any memory of our experience here. All intellection is timeless and hence there is no memory here. *All is presence*, and it is this towards which the human soul aims.[8]

Plotinus' description of what is, in effect, the escape from memory through the contemplative vision, was to be fundamental to the Christian Latin tradition of mystical contemplation. As we shall see, ten centuries of the middle ages, though knowing nothing of his *Enneads*, would be dependent on the thought he expressed here through its fundamental influence on Porphyry, Augustine and the pseudo-Dionysius. In contem-

---

[6] This is important and would be exceedingly influential for later medieval thought. On monastic remembering and on St Bernard's understanding of memory, see below, ch. 11.

[7] This was to be of great importance to Augustine. See below, ch. 6.

[8] Also see *Enneads*, V, 4, 7–14: on the knowing hypostases and that which is beyond. The man who knows himself is double, one knowing the nature of the reasoning which belongs to soul, and one up above this man, who knows himself according to Intellect because he has become that intellect; and by that Intellect he thinks himself again, not any longer as man, but having become altogether other and snatching himself up into the higher world, drawing up only the better part of soul, which alone is able to be winged for intellection, with which someone there keeps by him what he sees.

plative intellection there would not even be memory of the personality, no thought that the contemplator is the self – (Socrates, for example) – or that it is Intellect or Soul. In contemplative vision, he says, we are not at the time aware of our own personality; we are in possession of ourselves but the activity is towards the object of vision with which the thinker becomes identified; he has made himself over as matter to be shaped; he takes ideal form under the action of the vision while remaining, potentially, himself. He is actively himself when he has intellection of nothing (p. 289). He is empty of all.

There is then, such a thing as possessing more powerfully *without* consciousness than in full knowledge for Plotinus; with full awareness the possession is of something quite distinct from the self; unconscious possession runs very close to identity with its object. Plotinus then asks the question that would be fundamental to Augustine's self analysis in the *Confessions*: Augustine asked how he had a memory of God within himself? Is this power which determines memory also the principle by which the Supreme becomes effective in us? And Plotinus provides Augustine with a response that would hardly require alteration in the latter's Christian scheme. Plotinus argues that at any time when we have *not* been in direct vision of that sphere, memory is the source of its activity within us; when we *have* possessed that vision, its presence is due to the principle by which we enjoyed it:

this principle awakens where it wakens, and it alone has vision in that order, for this is no matter to be brought to us by way of analogy, or by syllogistic reasoning whose grounds lie elsewhere; the power which we possess of discoursing upon the Intellectual Being, so far as such discourse is here possible, is vested in that principle which alone is capable of their contemplation . . .

Memory, by this account, can only begin *after* the Soul has left the higher spheres. We shall need to recall this passage to discuss Augustine's experience with Monica – when mother and son transcended their speech about God, and, after their contemplative vision, fell back to the 'noise of their mouths where words begin and end'. Those who descend from the Intellectual will recall their memories (of former times). But the lapse of time will have utterly obliterated much of what was formerly present to them. This will become the image for the Fall: the fall of man into time and into memory. And so long as souls which have fallen into time and the cosmos have not touched the lowest region where non-being begins, Plotinus believes there is nothing to prevent them rising again (p. 291). Souls that change their state have memory which deals with what has come and gone. Reminiscence is for souls that have lost the continuous vision (IV, 4, 7 [p. 292]) and their quest, inspired by their memory of that higher state, seeks a return to that condition in which self and its memory will once again be lost.

Plotinus takes up again the relation between sense perception and the working of memory here below. He argues that it is not essential that everything seen should be laid up in the mind; clearly, when the object is of no importance, or of no personal concern, the sensitive faculty, stimulated by the differences in the objects present to vision, acts without accompaniment of the will and is alone in entertaining the impression.

The emphasis on the will's direction of the soul's attention radically influenced Augustine as we shall see. At these times, when the will is not operating in conjunction with perception, the Soul does not take into its deeper recesses such differences as do not meet any of its needs. But there is another, now deliberate, *lack* of retained sense experiences, and this must occur, above all, when the Soul's act is directed towards another, higher order; then it must utterly *reject* the memory of such things, things over and done now, and not even taken into knowledge when they were present (p. 293). Even in ordinary circumstances purely accidental circumstances need not be present to the imaging faculty and if they do so appear, they need not be retained or even observed, and in fact the impression of any such circumstance does not entail awareness. It is common knowledge Plotinus says, that when the understanding has no reason to foresee any departure from the normal, it will no longer expect and so observe detail; in a process unfailingly repeated without variation, attention to the unvarying detail is idleness (p. 293).[9]

Plotinus observes, as did Aristotle, that our mental acts fall into a series according to the succession of our needs, being not self-determined but guided by the variations of the external: we change to meet every incident as each fresh need arises and as the external impinges in its successive things and events. Because various organs and their various governing principles operate in us there is a variety in the images formed upon the representative faculty; these images do not issue from one internal centre but, by difference of origin and of acting-point, dependent on outside sense objects (stimuli), they bring compulsion to bear upon the movements and efficiencies of the self. For instance, when the desiring faculty is stirred, there is a presentment of the object – a sort of sensation in announcement and in picture, of the experience – calling us to follow and to attain; the personality, whether it resists or follows and procures, is necessarily thrown out of equilibrium. And thus we successively respond

[9] This can be compared with modern theories of attention and remembering. See, for instance, R. C. Schank, *Dynamic Memory* (London, 1986).

to our different needs. However, variations of *judgement* do not affect that which is the very highest in us. The doubt and change of standard by which we judge belong to the Soul-phase in contact with the body; the right reason of that highest Soul-phase in us is, however, weaker by being given over to inhabit this mingled mass of soul-body. Our existence is like being amid the tumult of a public meeting where the best adviser (our highest reason) often fails to dominate, and assent goes to the roughest of the brawlers and roarers (p. 300). But then who are we? With what Soul-phase should we identify ourselves?

'Us, the true human being', that is, personality, for Plotinus, is the higher Soul. It is not the container body. And yet the modified [ensouled] body is not alien but attached to our nature – our higher self, and is a concern for us for that reason (p. 301).[10]

Plotinus has thus far left unanswered by what means the image-making faculty responds either to sense-perceptions or to intellectual objects. He has rejected the notion of imprinting the sense-organs, the imagination and the memory as wax receives the imprint of the signet ring (IV, 4 23 [p. 306]). Instead, he declares there is a third something, an intermediate that accepts the impressions of shape and the like. He says that this intermediate must be able to assume the modifications of the material object so as to be an exact reproduction of its states, and it must be of the one elemental-stuff; it thus will exhibit the condition which the higher principle is to perceive; and the condition must be such as to preserve *something* of the originating object and yet not be identical with it; the essential vehicle of knowledge is an intermediary which, as it stands between the Soul and the originating object, will similarly, present a condition midway between the two spheres of sense and the intellectual, linking the extremes, receiving from one side to exhibit to the other, in virtue of being able to assimilate itself to each.[11] As an instrument by which something is to receive knowledge, it cannot be identical with either the knower or the known, but it must be *apt to likeness* with both – akin to the external object by its power of being affected, and to the internal, the knower, by the fact that the modification it takes becomes a Form (p. 306). This is not a rephrasing of the non-physiological side of Aristotle's argument: that Soul has the potential to become actually its object of intellection/perception. Aristotle had argued that there is no actual

10 See A. H. Armstrong, 'Form, individual and person in Plotinus' *Dionysius*, I, (Halifax, Nova Scotia, 1977), especially pp. 59 ff.
11 Twelfth-century Cistercians would be much exercised with the nature of the 'intermediate' between sense and intellect. See below, chapter 12, where we discuss the intermediate between lower and higher soul, an intermediate third vehicle as a *vis corporeus* or a *vis sensualis*.

change in perception or conception, but an actualisation of potentiality, knower becoming the known.[12] Plotinus does, however, agree with Aristotle that bodily organs *are* necessary to sense-perception; but Aristotle would not accept his disembodied soul, which according to Plotinus, when entirely freed of body can apprehend nothing in the order of sense. What then is this intermediate vehicle which is neither knower nor known but which reproduces the conditions of the material object and is yet not identical with it? The intermediate, third something receiving from one side to exhibit to the other is never adequately explained. And yet Plotinus goes on to argue further against the Aristotelian hypothesis. Perceptions are not imprints; they are not to be thought of as seal-impressions on soul or mind; accepting this statement, there is one theory of memory which must be definitely rejected – Aristotle's. Memory is not to be explained as the retaining of information in virtue of the lingering of an impression which in fact was never made; so he tells us that if we study what occurs in the case of the most vivid form of perception, that is, sight, we can transfer our results to the other cases and so solve our problem.

In any perception we attain by sight, the object is *grasped* there where it lies in the direct line of vision; it is there that *we* attack *it*; there, then, the perception is formed; the *mind looks outward*; this is ample proof that it has taken and yet takes no inner imprint and does not see in virtue of some mark made upon *it* like that of the ring on the wax; it need not look outward at all if, even as it looked, it already held the image of the object, seeing by virtue of an impression made upon itself. It includes with the object the interval, for it tells at what distance the vision takes place. Further, if to see is to accept imprints of the objects of our vision, we can never see these objects themselves and we see only vestiges they leave within us, shadows, and the things themselves would be very different from our vision of them. So Aristotle has not proved his empirical assumption that we see what is out there accurately and adequately through like images or copies imprinted. Sight can only deal with an object *not* inset but *outlying*. But then what is the process? (IV, 6, 2 [p. 339]). Plotinus argues that the mind affirms something not contained within it; this is precisely the characteristic of a power to act. And the very condition of the mind being able to exercise discrimination upon what it is to see and hear is not that these objects be equally impressions made upon it; on the contrary, there must be no impressions, nothing to which the mind is passive; there can be only acts of that in which the objects become known.

---

[12] There is no room for an Aristotelian potentiality in Plotinus's intelligible world where everything is purely actual. Plotinus, however, has great difficulty in keeping potentiality out of his discussion of the intelligible world altogether.

Our tendency is to think (wrongly) of faculties submitting to their environment, though in reality the faculty is the master not the victim (p. 339).

Furthermore, Plotinus rejects the theory that vision (or any sense experience) *requires* the modification of an intervenient substance, like air (IV, 5, 4 [p. 333]). In hearing, air simply takes the impression as a kind of articulated stroke which may be compared to letters traced upon it by the object causing the sound; however, vision and hearing do not depend on the transmission of impressions of any kind made upon the air (IV, 5, 3 [p. 330]). Rather, it belongs to the faculty and the soul-essence, to read the impressions thus appearing before it, as they reach the point at which they become matter of its knowledge. All sensation phenomena arise, according to Plotinus, through what he calls 'a certain co-sensitiveness inherent in a living whole' of which object and perceiver are united (IV, 5, 5 [p. 334]). Indeed, perception of every kind seems to depend on the fact that the universe is a living whole sympathetic to itself: that it is so appears from the universal participation in power from member to member (IV, 5, 3 [p. 331]). Perception is by active sympathy. Sensations and judgements are mental acts and belong to an order apart from the experiences upon which they are exercised. But then what is the third, intermediate something described above? This lack of clarity would cause Augustine to express ignorance when trying to answer how external things become inward perceptions.

Then Plotinus turns to knowledge of objects of intellection. This knowing is not in any such degree attended by impact or impression: objects of intellection come forward, on the contrary, as from within, unlike the sense-objects known as from without; they have even more emphatically the character of Acts, in the stricter sense, for their origin is in the Soul and every concept of the Intellectual order is the Soul about its Act (p. 339). Now we need not be surprised that the Soul or mind, having taken no imprint, yet achieves perception even of what it in no way contains. The Soul is in its essential nature the Reason-Principle of all things and is the primal Reason-Principle of the entire realm of sense. Thus it deals with both orders. Of the Intellectual, the Soul is said to have intuition by memory upon approach, for it knows objects of intellection by a certain natural identity with them; this is clearly Plato's ideas or forms, recollected but indwelling. Thus the Soul's knowledge of objects of intellection is attained by possessing its objects of thought; they are its natural vision; they are the mind itself in a more radiant mode and mind rises from its duller pitch to that greater brilliance in a sort of awakening, a progress from its latency to its Act (p. 340).

On the other hand, to the sense order the Soul or mind stands in a similar nearness and to such things it gives *a radiance 'out' of its own store* and, as it were, elaborates them to visibility; and whenever it puts out its strength in the direction of what has once been present in it, it sees that object as present still, and the more intent its effort the more durable is the presence. This is why, it is agreed, children are better at remembering. Their attention or mental 'radiance' is still limited and not scattered. Is Plotinus here implying a kind of illuminationism? The sense objects are only perceived when the *mind* reaches out to them, illuminates them? Mind looking outward is evidently the active process by which sense perception is acknowledged or not. And memory is a similar act of radiance towards objects previously present to mind.

He continues his anti-Aristotelian onslaught less in relation to perception and more regarding the retaining of perceptions. If memory were a matter of seal-impressions retained, he argues, the multiplicity of objects would have no weakening effect on the memory, as we know they do. And we would have no need of thinking back to revive remembering; nor would we be subject to forgetting and recalling; all would lie engraved within and forever.

The very fact that we train ourselves to remember shows that what we get by the process is a strengthening of the mind – how else can it be explained that we forget a thing heard once or twice but remember what is often repeated, and that we recall a long time afterwards what at first hearing we failed to hold? All these considerations testify to an evocation of that faculty of the Soul or mind in which remembrance is vested; the mind is strengthened, either generally or to this particular purpose. Let us observe that memory follows upon *attention*; those who have memorised much by dint of their training in the use of leading indications (suggestive words and the like) reach the point of being easily able to retain without such aid; must we not conclude that the basis of memory is the Soul-power, its very act, brought to full strength? (p. 341). This seems to fill the lacuna left by Aristotle in his ambiguous discussion of the active or agent intellect. Plotinus insists that the other explanation of memory, that is, Aristotle's, which put memory within the realm of the passive intellect in control of the primary perceptive part of the Soul, implied that impression is something received passively. If this were so, he says, then the strongest memory would go with the least active nature. He insists that what happens is actually the reverse; in no pursuit do technical exercises tend to make a man less the master of his acts and states. It is significant that in the old, the senses are dulled and so is the memory. Sensation and memory then, are not passivity but active power. The reason this active power of mind does not come at once to the recollection of its unchanging objects is that it needs to be poised and prepared for the task. Quick memory does not, in general, go with quick wit – they are not under the same mental faculty. In general, Soul is activity and not receptivity, as is evident from its lack of extension (its immateriality) (p. 341). And here Plotinus ends his discussion of perception and memory.

This is a powerful and elaborate analysis of mind, its operations and its aspirations. But it is a disappointment in the final analysis, since his ambiguous explanation of the memory process raises so many fundamental problems. Plotinus may well have raised all the relevant objections to Aristotle's theory, but what of his own argument that memory is the soul's activity, its power, brought to full strength, a kind of illuminationism where mind shines its radiance out of itself onto what it decides or wills to perceive, where object and perceiver are part of one sympathetic cosmos? To what extent is this any more helpful? And what *is* that 'third, intermediate something' between knower and known, rememberer and remembered? There is no doubt that we have been treating one of the most sophisticated of theories of memory thus far encountered in the ancient world. It would vastly influence later neo-Platonists and especially twelfth-century Latin thinkers. But if Plotinus is 'the last great philosopher of antiquity' then antiquity appears to have provided no more completely satisfactory solution to the problem of memory's nature, its actuality, and even its purpose, than that which he provided. Otherwise we are left with the relatively trivial mnemotechnics of the rhetoricians. Perhaps ironically, Plotinus's views on *forgetfulness* were to be the reason for his being remembered through the Latin Christian mystical tradition of more than thirteen centuries.

Plotinus's pupil Porphyry, a Greek from Tyre, published his master's work and attempted to make a coherent, almost text-book systematic presentation of his predecessor's views. These were published at the beginning of the fourth century just when Christianity was emerging as a tolerated sect and would soon become the official religion of the Roman Empire. Porphyry had himself been attached to Christianity but late in life he wrote a tract against the Christians for which he was later to be best remembered. He has been called, however, the first systematic theologian in the history of thought, and merely to have organised Plotinus's undisciplined but brilliant arguments of his fifty-four treatises into the six *Enneads* warrants a reputation that is nobler than the one he has received. It was Porphyry's Plotinus, together with his other works, including his commentary on Aristotle's *Categories*, to which much of subsequent medieval philosophy would owe its greatest debt.

Chapter 6

AUGUSTINE: THE EARLY WORKS

For the truths which the intellect apprehends directly in the world of full and unimpeded light have something less profound, less necessary than those which life communicates to us against our will in an impression which is material because it enters us through the senses but yet has a spiritual meaning which is possible for us to extract.

M. Proust, *Remembrance of Things Past: Time Regained.*

Related things are things remembered and for a creator, certainly for a Spanish creator of the twentieth century, remembered things are not things seen, therefore they are not things known. And so then always and always Picasso commenced his attempt to express not things felt, not things remembered, not established relations but things which are there, really everything a human being can know at each moment of his existence and not an assembling of all his experiences.

Gertrude Stein, *Picasso* (London, 1939), p. 35.

During the mid-fourth century, the African professor of rhetoric, Marius Victorinus joined the Christian church; he also translated Plotinus and other neo-Platonists into Latin. This excited the fashionable Platonist circles in Milan, where Augustine had gone to pursue his rhetorical career. Already much of the current Platonism was of a Christian variety, Bishop Ambrose drawing on the insights of pagan philosophy and adapting them in his sermons. With Victorinus's translations of Plotinus and other neo-Platonic writings – translations that were provided by a man known to have died as a Christian – Christian Platonism received an incalculable boost.[1] Plato's philosophy, thought to be reconciled with that of Aristotle, had suddenly emerged as the one true, synthetic system of thought which naturally merged with Christianity.[2] Augustine entered this

---

[1] Pierre Hadot, *Porphyre et Victorinus* (Paris, 1968); P. Hadot, ed., *Marius Victorinus: traités théologiques sur la trinité* (Sources Chrétiennes, 68) (Paris, 1960), introduction, pp. 7–76.

[2] Neo-Platonists' overriding conviction was that all serious philosophers (Platonists and Aristotelians) were really trying to say the same thing. H. J. Blumenthal, 'Neo-Platonic elements in the *De Anima* commentaries', *Phronesis*, 21 (1976), and 'Plotinus in later

80

movement of Latin-speaking amateur philosophers, and in his *Confessions* he tells us, with disappointing vagueness, that he read these Platonist works.[3] We can only attempt to reconstruct with difficulty what books these were, but his own writings disclose close parallels with the writings of Plotinus in their Latin translation. In the *City of God*, he presents Plotinus as a great impersonal mind 'drawing out the hidden meaning of Plato'. Analysis of Augustine's writings shows that his reading of this notoriously difficult author was an extremely intense endeavour, so thorough in fact, that Plotinus's ideas were completely absorbed and then transformed by him. It has been argued in the light of recent research that Plotinus and Porphyry were grafted almost imperceptibly into Augustine's writings as the ever present foundation of this thought. And in making these masters his own he was able to elaborate their thought in different terms and in different directions. This is especially true of Augustine's attitude to memory. In general, perhaps the most striking use and inversion of Plotinus's thought can be shown by comparing that passage of the *Confessions* which is directly inspired by the *First Ennead*. Here the parallelism of movement, ideas and vocabulary is particularly close and constant. The words of Plotinus (*Enneads*, I 6.9) are: 'Now call up all your confidence; you need a guide no longer; strain and see.' And Augustine writes: 'Being admonished by all this to return to myself, I entered into my own depths with You as guide; and I was able to do it because You were my helper. I entered, and with the eye of my soul such as it was, I saw Your unchangeable light shining over that same eye of my soul, over my mind.' (*Conf.*, VII, x). Here, it is said, lies the distance between neo-Platonic and Christian mysticism, in that last moment of contemplation; the one autonomous, the other wholly reliant on God's guidance.[4]

Augustine's powerful prose, in both the *Confessions* and in his magisterial *De Trinitate*, conceals an eclectic and synthetic mastery of much of the logical, rhetorical, epistemological and ontological material that comprised the ancient understanding of the importance of memory. Augustine's is an uncanny sensitivity to the problem of the memory and its unsatisfactory resolution amongst the ancients.

Augustine began his career as an orator and became a professor of

Platonism' in *Neoplatonism and Early Christian Thought: Essays in Honour of A. H. Armstrong* (London, 1981), pp. 212–22.
[3] E. TeSelle, 'Porphyry and Augustine', *Augustinian Studies*, 5 (1974), pp. 113–47. E. L. Fortin, 'Saint Augustin et la doctrine néo-platonicienne de l'âme', in *Augustinus Magister* (Paris, 1954), III, pp. 371–80; *Confessions*, VIII, ii.
[4] See the introduction by Paul Henry to *Plotinus: The Enneads*, trans. Stephen Mackenna (London, 1969), p. lxix. In general, see Peter Brown, *Augustine of Hippo, A Biography* (London, 1967), and for a comparative discussion of Plotinus and Augustine, pp. 91ff.

rhetoric. It is, therefore, probably not surprising that his theory of cognition depended so extensively on language.[5] In his *Soliloquies* he speaks of an internal dialogue or conversation with the self in which objects of knowledge are the participants, brought to consciousness through speech.[6] The problem of knowledge was for him the problem of language as a system of signs. He elaborated his linguistic epistemology in the *De Magistro* and the *De Doctrina Christiana*, and when in the *Confessions* he came to discuss the possibility of intellectual contact with God, he would show how man's redemption through Christ the Word depended on a dynamic relationship between language and objective truth. Recalling the Plotinian insight that the memory of verbal formulae accompanies the implicit mental conception, words serving as bridges and mirrors to exhibit the concept, thus constituting its enduring presence in the mind, we can see a parallel in Augustine's understanding of how the Incarnation of the Word enabled man's faculty of redeemed speech to become a mirror through which men may know God in this life. Through the redeemed human word which could take on Divinity, man and the world could be brought back to God.

In the *De Magistro*,[7] Augustine repeats the assurance of Aristotle and Cicero that signs or words are not inferior to what they signify. Words as a kind of sign, adapt most readily to the task of showing the true nature of realities. The real significance of words is so absolute that someone may speak the truth without knowing it. When one speaks falsely it is through one's own abuse of words. Language operates in two ways; as commemorative and as indicative. What it commemorates and indicates is a knowledge that God provides, so that language is a tool that enables us to look for realities. When we speak we either know what the words signify or we do not. There is, then, cognitive reality behind words. If we know what the words signify we are recalling an implicitly known truth. This is recollection rather than learning. If we do not know what words signify then we do not even recall. But we may be inspired by our ignorance to inquire and this will lead to further recollection. We are of course hearing the echoes of Plato's doctrine of knowledge as recollection.[8] It is clearly the commemorative function of speech that is most important for the Christian, for through prayer and the reading of Scripture, man's memory is stimulated. Prayer hardly conveys information to God who knows all; rather prayer

---

5 Marcia Colish, *The Mirror of Language, A Study in the Medieval Theory of Knowledge* (New Haven, 1968), pp. 19–81, for an extended discussion of Augustine's language.
6 See the discussion of Plotinus above and *Enneads*, trans. Mackenna, IV, 3, 30, p. 286.
7 *De Magistro*, XI, 36 and I, 2.
8 He confirms this in *Confessions*, VIII, ii: 'in the Platonists, God and His Word are everywhere implied'.

helps to remind man by enabling him to recall from his memory the reality of God whom he addresses. The anteriority of the knowledge of God in man, stored away in his memory, is the *sine qua non* of the believer. And he is aided by his memory of this anterior knowledge when he reads and studies the Bible. For Augustine believes that a reader who has no anterior faith, and therefore no knowledge and memory of God within his mind, cannot understand any meaning in the sacred page.[9] Christ the Word acts as a prior, interior teacher and only thereafter can he be further elicited and remembered by human words.

Augustine believes that the vast majority of men require large quantities of human speech to orient them towards God, in effect to stimulate their memories. There is, however, a small minority of men, not unlike Plotinus's few who are closer to the sphere of the Divine Intellect, who do not need to rely on sensory stimulation provided by the sound and sight of words. They naturally perceive intellectual entities the more readily and may acquire faith through that inward divine speech achieved through personal meditation.

The reading of Scripture requires an exegetical technique according to Augustine because understanding the Bible requires that a reader recognise facts, events and words as signifying divine realities. The sign does not teach us anything. Rather it causes us to think of something beyond the impression the word as sign makes on our senses. In the *De Doctrina Christiana*[10] he runs through the three kinds of sign – natural, conventional and linguistic – arguing that natural and conventional signs may be described verbally, but words cannot, with equal success, be described by other signs. What is most striking in his argument here is that all signification can ultimately be reduced to verbal signification.[11] And like Cicero he argues in favour of the multiple meanings engaged by figurative and metaphorical language to illuminate the truth. There is then a two-fold exegetical method described, one which accepts the literal signifying capacity of a word and the other which opens up the word's multiple referents. In the light of the latter, the *signum translatum*, episodes in the Bible concerning, for instance, the story of Abraham and Isaac, or an object like the lamb, may be read as referring not only to themselves, literally, but also as symbolic objects of the passion of Christ.

---

[9] But it is also clear that anyone who seeks God 'in the good things that are seen' can find God. He cites Scripture, *Confessions*, VIII, i: 'Certainly *all men are vain in whom there is not the knowledge of God and who cannot, by these good things that are seen, find Him that is*. Now I was no longer in that sort of vanity; I had gone beyond it and in the testimony of the whole creation I had found You, our Creator, and Your Word who is with You …'.

[10] *De Doctrina Christiana*, CSEL, 80, I and II.

[11] Of course, this recalls the beginning of John's Gospel: 'In principio erat verbum'.

Augustine has largely taken over Aristotle's doctrine of signs as it was transmitted through the works of Cicero. But whereas Aristotle did not require words to bridge the realms of objects of knowledge and knower, Augustine developed a theory of signification which required the verbal sign as the necessary medium for knowing and understanding. Man must come to God through a linguistic rejuvenation, and his theory of cognition through speech required an active participation of the memory. The transient, sensory medium of language must stimulate that faculty of memory which is essential to sustained cognition. The word, human and divine, with all its characteristic capacity to signify literally and metaphorically, is retained in the mind's memory and points beyond itself. As we shall see, Augustine argues that mind created its actual knowledge from the content of memory, and this creation of knowledge involves the mind's symbol-making activity, its creation of a *verbum*, a word or sign as the vehicle of meaning.

Augustine distinguishes gradations in the mind and in its knowledge. This results from the hierarchical ordering of the mind's objects rather than from real distinctions in the soul or mind's processes involved in knowing its objects. The mind or soul, then, is a unity but it has two classes of objects: on the one hand the mind perceives through the bodily senses; on the other it perceives by itself its own immaterial objects of knowledge. Just as Aristotle drew the analogy between the process involved in our knowledge of the intelligible world and that involved in knowledge of the sensible world, so too Augustine says our knowledge is analogous to sight; understanding is the same thing for mind as seeing is for the bodily senses (*De Ord.*, II, 3, 10).[12] He offers the same problematic division between truths known via sense experience and truths known independently of the senses. But whereas Aristotle affirmed that even the most abstract conceptualisation somehow depended on sense experience, Augustine argues, along with Plotinus, for what is, in effect, an autonomous life of mind. He uses the well-tried example of mathematical and logical propositions which are, for him, indubitable truths, necessary, unchanging, and as with Plato, they are not proved by reference to sense experience. Indeed, truths known thus independently of the senses are known with a superior clarity and certainty independent of the body and even over and above what sense experience might suggest to the contrary. But the way we know is held to be analogous to the way we sense (*De Lib. Arb.*, II, 8, 21).[13]

In his *De Quantitate Animae* (23.41), he defines sensation as the mind's

---

[12] *De Ordine*, ed. W. M. Green, CCSL 29 (Turnhout, 1970).
[13] *De Lib. Arb.*, CSEL, 74, II, 8, 21.

awareness of the body's experience.[14] He offers a physiological account of sight which differs from Aristotle's and seems to be a physiological rendering of Plotinus's illuminationism – for vision is described as taking place in virtue of an emission from the eyes which impinges on the object of perception. Later, in the *De Trinitate*, he will describe sensation in terms of Aristotelian imprints or impressions, although he will never quite adopt the physiological side of Aristotle's argument where the soul has impressionable surfaces. But he comes close to this by using the wax and signet ring analogy. He will, in the end, affirm in the *De Genesi ad Litteram* (XII, 16, 33) that the body cannot act on mind, so the very process by which sense perception is taken inwards and conceptualised, the mind's ability to register sensations, is affirmed to be miraculous. Like Aristotle and Plotinus he asserts that the soul is not spatially diffused in the body but he is closer to the latter when he describes the soul's presence in the whole body as a kind of vital act of attention.

Augustine gradually refined his theory of cognition and in the commentary on Genesis, *De Genesi ad Litteram* (XII, 6.15–7.16), a later rethinking of his earlier views on mind and its activity as found in his *Confessions* and the *De Trinitate*, he distinguishes three kinds of vision: corporeal sight, spiritual sight and intellectual sight. Never will there be Aristotle's primary perceptive part of the soul under consideration. The epistemology which emerges in this later work is a blend of Augustine's scriptural understanding of *spiritus* and his neo-Platonically inspired psychology. What results is a trichotomy of *corpus*, *mens/intellectus*, with an intermediate *spiritus*, each with its own *visio*. The spiritual *visio* is an intermediary between the intellectual and the corporeal, not being itself corporeal but similar to corporeal things (XII, 24.51). It is reminiscent of Plotinus's third, intermediary something, as Porphyry presented it.[15] Augustine will argue that mind is involved in both seeing and imagining, and what is before the mind is not the physical objects themselves but their copies or likenesses. But here he does not share Aristotle's confidence in the truth of sense perception. Rather mind 'sees' what is of the same nature as itself, an image that is created by mind out of its own substance. Aristotle would agree but also affirm that the soul's representation was an adequate likeness of its referent. For Augustine, the only way we know that we actually see rather than imagine, is through a conscious awareness and attention that some bodily modification has accompanied the experience

---

[14] *De Quantitate Animae*, 23.41, *PL* 32.

[15] Porphyry's *tria genera visionum*, in P. Hadot, *Porphyre et Victorinus*, I, pp. 178–206 and 234ff. R. A. Markus, 'The Eclipse of a neo-Platonic theme: Augustine and Gregory the Great on visions and prophecies', in *Neoplatonism and Early Christian Thought*, pp. 204–11.

of sight. Our willing, conscious attention plays a vital role in Augustine's account of sensory awareness, and this is because of the central role allotted to deliberate direction of the mind's gaze towards its chosen portion of its field of vision. Here, towards the end of Augustine's life is a modified Plotinian act of mind to explain sensory awareness, and an implicit rejection of Aristotle's passive, potential intellect.[16]

Augustine extends the analogy of sight and intellection by including believing in the category of thought, seeing it as an inescapable process of thinking. Then, in contrasting believing with seeing, he distinguishes between what we know as a result of having learned it from others and to which we have assented by having accepted their testimony, and what we know through our own experience. True belief is in a sense blind though rational, its object remains obscure, and in this sense it is inferior to understanding acquired from direct experience. But it is the prolegomenon to such understanding and as such is an aspect of human existence. We have here the relationship between rhetorical plausibility and common opinion based on lived experience in its unreflective mode. Belief on the authority of others is a necessary condition of human life in the family and society, a Ciceronian view that is in direct contrast to Plotinus's view that man is fundamentally isolated and not a political animal. Augustine adopts the earlier Platonic, Aristotelian and Ciceronian concept of man as requiring society and adds to it the notion that the search for and return to God necessarily requires this social context. But the acceptance of belief on the basis of authority is not arbitrary so that one is responsible for assenting to true or false beliefs.

The classification of beliefs outlined in the *De Diversis Quaestionibus LXXXIII*, 48 and in his *Epistle*, 147, 6–8, provides an alternative view of his epistemology and these texts incidentally divulge an attitude to the past and present which would be fully developed in the *Confessions* and the *De Trinitate*. There are three classes of *credibilia*. Firstly, there are those which can only be believed and never understood. Here, he places historical truth.[17] Credal statements, for instance, concerning particular historical events, like the resurrection of Christ, shall never be accessible to philosophical reflection since they lie outside the realm of abstract truths. Secondly, there are those where belief implies understanding, and here are placed mathematical and logical reasoning. Thirdly, there are

[16] On the Porphyrian and Plotinian background, see E. L. Fortin, 'Saint Augustin et la doctrine néo-platonicienne de l'âme', *Augustinus Magister* (Paris, 1954), III, pp. 371–80. J. Pépin, 'Une nouvelle source de S. Augustin: le *zētēma* de Porphyre sur l'union de l'âme et du corps', *REA* 66 (1964), pp. 53–107.

[17] *De Div. Qu. LXXXIII*, 48, *PL* 40. See R. A. Markus, 'Augustine', in *The Cambridge History of Later Greek and Early Medieval Philosophy* (Cambridge, 1967), p. 345.

those which must first be believed and subsequently may be understood. Here are placed truths about God which believers will one day understand if they live according to revealed divine rules of the scriptural commandments.

That historical truth can only be believed and never understood, that particular historical events are effectively matters of intuited belief and never of knowledge, precisely because they are particular rather than abstract and universal, is a statement in line with the Aristotelian distinction between the historical and the rhetorical or poetical. But for Augustine this means that authoritative biblical history, which is the only history that matters, stands in the uninvestigable realm of the assent of faith. This view will have important consequences for the medieval understanding of history, how one interprets it and writes it.

It is evident that belief structures all aspects of our lives so that Augustine sees the need as did Plato, to establish a dominant role for the power of thought in order that it may break through the surface of appearance and habit, disclosing beyond it the objective, eternal, immovable structure of the nature of things, of man and of history, knowable to mind alone. Therefore, Augustine will contrast belief as a lower kind of thinking, with understanding as a result of reasoning, and he will thus arrange a hierarchy in the objects of thought that runs from a knowledge of temporal things (*scientia*) to a knowledge of eternal objects of thought (contemplation). Like Plotinus's soul-phases, there is a higher and lower reason, the higher focusing on eternal objects, the lower on corporeal entities and temporal activities. There is no doubt that Augustine thinks along Platonist lines, especially when he thinks of intellectual vision, for it is in the intellectual realm divorced from all sense experience, that moral and philosophical truths reside, an intelligible world of ideas consonant with those of the divine mind. That this is also compatible with Cicero's Platonism, with which Augustine, the classical rhetor, was intimately familiar, cannot be doubted.[18] But the Christian Augustine went further and said that moral and philosophical truths, divorced from sense experience, are the manifestations of God's interior presence in the mind of man, where Christ dwells in the human soul as the word of God, illuminated as the intelligible *verbum mentis*. The immortality and immateriality of the soul require for Augustine, as for Plato, Plotinus and Cicero, that rational knowledge does not enter the mind from outside; it is, in some way, present to it. And yet because as a Christian, Augustine must reject the Platonist metempsychosis or cycle of rebirths of the soul, he qualifies his assertion of the soul's immateriality and immortality by

---

[18] But as he says of the distinguished rhetor and translator Victorinus, 'there had been no salvation in the Rhetoric he had taught' (*Conf.* VII, ii).

insisting on a sense in which the soul is subject to mutability. Like all created beings, the soul does suffer change, sin, and repentance, and in so far as man's self is identified with embodied soul, the soul has an empirical history that is never divorced or aloof from the vicissitudes of life. This must be true even of that aspect of the soul most concerned to contemplate eternal truths, in contemplation. In this life man will never be capable of a sustained contemplation of eternal, unchanging objects of thought.

What effect do Augustine's various (and evolving) analyses of cognition from sense objects to intelligible objects have on his understanding of the role of memory? In *Epistle*, 7.1, 1–2,[19] an early letter to a friend, Nebridius, Augustine answered his question on memory by showing the inadequacy of the common sense notion of remembering. Normally, he says, people think memory refers to past experiences. But some knowledge is not derived from past experiences, nor known through the senses. Thus, memory does not necessarily refer to the past and it need not involve images derived from past sense experience. But when one undergoes such experiences, traces (*species*) are left in the memory, and mind moves into action deliberately by focusing its attention on these traces and recalling them; furthermore, mind can use these traces in constructive imagination. Augustine was thereafter to sift through the various theories of the memory process, weighing the evidence to support theories for physiological imprinting on a passive, potential receptor against a kind of active reading by the soul of what is within itself and independent of past sense experience.

His two works, the 'autobiographical' *Confessions* and his *De Trinitate* present his eclectic and magisterial synthesis of the most subtle aspects of the antique memory with the requirements of a Christian ontology and theology. This synthesis would, as we have said, be modified in his later *De Genesi ad Litteram* but his earlier treatments would greatly influence later medieval discussion which sought inspiration from what was taken to be Augustine's authoritative pronouncements, with little evident concern for the evolution of his thought on the matter.

In Book 8, xi of the *Confessions*, Augustine relates that turning point in his life when he heard a child's voice calling from a nearby house 'Take up and read', and he interpreted this child's game as a divine command to open his book of Scripture. There he read that passage on which his eyes first fell: 'Not in rioting and drunkenness, not in chambering and impurities, not in contention and envy, but put ye on the Lord Jesus Christ and

[19] *Ep.* 7.1, 1–2., *PL*, 33. 68. Also *Epistolae*, ed. A. Goldbacher, CSEL, 34, 44, 57, 58 (Vienna, 1895–1911).

88

make not provision for the flesh and its concupiscences' (Romans XIII, 13). In that instant he was converted to Christianity. He was now thirty-two, a successful rhetorical career already established, and behind him many years of seeking a satisfying philosophy to sustain his life. He had tried Manicheism and neo-Platonism. Now he was set free from the burden of teaching rhetoric, free from Manicheism, but would never be entirely free from neo-Platonism. Not long after, his mother's life was nearing its end and one day, sitting in a house in Ostia on the Tiber, they fell to talking about what the eternal life of the saints could be like:

But with the mouth of our heart, we panted for the high waters of Your fountain, the fountain of the life which is with You: that being sprinkled from that fountain according to our capacity, we might in some sense meditate upon so great a matter.[20] ... Rising as our love flamed upward towards that Self-same, we passed in review the various levels of bodily things, up to the heavens themselves, whence sun and moon and stars shine upon this earth. And higher still we soared, thinking in our minds and speaking and marvelling at Your works: and so we came to our own souls, and went beyond them to come at last to that region of richness unending, where You feed Israel forever with the food of truth: and there life is that Wisdom by which all things are made, both the things that have been and the things that are yet to be. But this Wisdom itself is not made; it is as it has ever been and so it shall be forever: indeed 'has ever been' and 'shall be forever' have no place in it, but it simply is, for it is eternal: whereas 'to have been' and 'to be going to be' are not eternal. And while we were thus talking of His Wisdom and panting for it, with all the effort of our heart *we did for one instant attain to touch it; then sighing, and leaving the first fruits of our spirit bound to it, we returned to the sound of our own tongue, in which a word has both beginning and ending.*'[21]

That moment in which the soul did not think of self but mounted beyond itself and in that silence heard the Word of God, that moment of divine speech which Augustine describes as spoken not by any tongue of flesh nor the voice of an angel nor the sound of thunder nor in the darkness of a parable, that moment constituted the reaching forth, the flash of mind in which eternal Wisdom was touched. If this could continue and all other visions taken away, so that total absorption in inward joys should be eternally what that one moment of understanding was, then this continuous inward vision of the divine word would be the experience of those who have risen, and been released from the body. But its continuity is not to be had in this life.[22]

[20] *The Confessions*, trans. F. J. Sheed (London, 1944) is the translation used here. *Confessiones*, ed. P. Knöll, CSEL, 33 (Vienna, 1896).
[21] *Conf.*, IX, x, emphasis added.
[22] He asks in *Conf.*, VIII, iii:
What is it in the soul that makes it delight more to have found or regained the things it

The memory of this contemplative moment fuels the last books of the *Confessions* where he analyses the nature of memory and time as part of his methodology of knowledge of God. By looking within and focusing on the memory, we recognise that our knowledge of God is a truth learned at a particular moment, and since that time when it was learned it has been stored in the memory. Such stored knowledge is then made accessible to the mind's attention. He distinguishes his own position, that knowledge of God is learned in time, from that of Plato for whom truth preexists in the mind from eternity and is made present through dialectically stimulated recollection. This must mean that for Augustine some men have never learned of God and therefore cannot recall him.[23] He explains this on the level of daily experience:

One man merely sees the world while another not only sees but interrogates it. Now the world does not change its speech, its outward appearance which speaks so as to appear differently to the two men. And yet to one it says nothing and to the other it gives all the answers. Those who have the answers have seen the world and compared its voice as it comes through their sense with the truth that is within them. (x, vi).

Men are provided by God with the various senses with respective places and functions. 'But I, the one soul, act by these' (x, vii). Augustine is concerned to mount beyond the animal senses. In so mounting he moves beyond this power of his nature to come to 'the fields and vast palaces of memory where are stored the innumerable images of material things brought to it by the senses'.[24] But the images of material things brought to memory by the senses are not alone in the memory faculty, for 'there is stored in the memory the thoughts we think by adding or taking from or otherwise modifying the things that sense has made contact with, as well as all other things that have been entrusted to and laid up in memory'. Only forgetfulness is not here, 'swallowed in its grave.'

Memory is a chaotic storage place of images and it requires the active turning of the mind to it, 'to bring forth what I want'. Memory is a deliberate, willed activity, an active search on the part of mind, not unlike Aristotle's recollective process. Augustine has here moved quickly from sense images to mind's activity:

loves than if it had always had them? ... Note too that men procure the actual pleasures of human life by way of pain ... What does it mean that this part of creation thus alternates between need felt and need met, between discord and harmony? Is this their mode of being, this what Thou didst give them? ... Thou dost never depart from us, yet with difficulty do we return to Thee.

23 Hence, his doctrine of grace.   24 *Conf.*, x, viii.

And some things are produced immediately, some take longer as if they had to be brought out from some more secret place of storage; some pour out in a heap, and while we are actually wanting and looking for something quite different, they hurl themselves upon us in masses as though to say: 'may it not be we that you want?' I brush them from the face of my memory with the hand of my heart until at last the thing I want is brought to light as from some hidden place. (x, viii)

Now some things are produced from memory easily and in the right order and then things that come first are followed by the next. This, Augustine says, is what happens when one says something by heart.

Augustine's memory has the capacity to store things in categories although they entered the memory through different gates, as it were. Light and colours for instance, sounds and scents come in through the sense organs. These diverse experiences are stored in 'the vast recesses, the hidden and unsearchable caverns of memory ... to be available and brought to light when need arises.' But it is not the objects of sense that have entered. Only the images of the things perceived by the senses are present in the memory for thought to remember them. Precisely how these images were formed Augustine does not know.[25]

'And even though we know by which senses they were brought in and laid up in the memory, who can tell how these images were formed?' Aristotle's physiological imprints, and Plotinus's 'third something' or the soul's radiation outward, as yet, provide no satisfactory answer for Augustine. And yet once the images are there, mind does all. All these images of colour, and sounds are stored inside him, 'in the huge court of my memory'. It is here that he meets himself, recalls himself, 'what I have done, when and where, and in what state of mind I was when I did it'. And not only does the memory store all those experiences he remembers to have had himself, but also those told him by others. This is important because Augustine is using the memory as a storage place not only for images of personal experience but for information held on faith, believed on the authority of others. Consequently, from this truly vast store he says he can thereafter weave into the past endless *new* likenesses of things either experienced by himself or believed on the strength of things experienced, inferring, in other words, a rhetorical category of the plausible 'must have been' on the basis of factual experiences recalled through their likenesses. And the 'must have been' or probable inference is based not only on his own recollected experience but also on that of others. On the basis of all these he can picture actions and events and hopes for the future. On all of these he can meditate 'as if they were present'. But the

---

[25] But see the later *De Genesi ad Litteram* and the spiritual, intermediary *visio*.

images, however formed, must be there now, in the present, for without them 'I could not so much as speak of the things.' Clearly Augustine is referring to recollection in the Platonic sense of the true logical inference as much as to Aristotle's reminiscent, self-motivated rational search amongst ideas when he weaves new likenesses of things. Sense memory, whatever its role and however it may influence cognitive higher memory, remains a paradox for him. It also appears that Augustine believes conscious thought precedes speech whereas for Plotinus unconscious thought is made conscious through speech.

And although memory is where one meets oneself through recalling what one has experienced, Augustine does not believe he can totally grasp all that he is. The mind, he says, is not large enough to contain itself. But how can this be? He phrases this question in yet another way. When one speaks of mountains, the sea, the stars, one does not see them with one's eyes. 'Yet I could not have spoken of them unless these mountains and waves and rivers and stars which I have seen and the ocean of which I have heard, had been inwardly present to my sight.' These things are in his memory and they possess the 'same vast spaces between them as if I saw them outside me'. 'When I saw them with my eyes I did not by seeing them swallow them into me, nor are they themselves present in me but only their images, and I know by what sense of my body each one of them was impressed upon my mind.' Once again, Augustine does not know how these images are made, but here he does assume their accuracy as signs of external experience. He also alludes to the necessity of having had experience of the world in order to recall it, and know it, and he will say more about this in the *De Trinitate* with important consequences for the understanding of texts. He leaves the problem of how images are formed and how they bring with them accurate spatial dimension, and turns to other stored entities in the memory.

Not only are there images of experiences and images of things told us by others stored in the memory. In the memory are all the things we have learned of the liberal sciences and have not forgotten. Now these are not stored as images but 'as the things themselves'. 'For what grammar is or the art of disputation ... whatever I know of such matters is in my memory not as though I retained the image and left the thing outside, or as though it had sounded in my mind then passed away.' Indeed, sense images 'are seized with marvelous speed and stored away marvelously' but grammar, logic and the like are in the mind themselves. Questions concerning logical categories may be phrased in verbal signs and pass through the air with a certain noise when spoken. But the things themselves to which they refer are not grasped by a bodily sense. They are only 'seen' by the mind, and what the memory stored was not their images but categorical, logical truths themselves. Once again, Augustine halts. 'But how they got into me it is for them to tell if they can.' Surely they have not entered by 'the doorways of my body'. 'Very well then, whence and how did they get into my memory? I do not know.' All he knows is that when he learned logical, grammatical truths he recognised them, in his own mind. Plato's slave-boy of the *Meno* comes to mind here. Augustine concludes that 'they must have been in my mind even before I learned them, though they were not in my memory' (x, x). At first Augustine does not appear to want to go the whole way with Plato, for whom eternal ideas or forms were latently in the memory there to be recollected and brought to conscious knowledge through the appropriate dialectical methodology. But when Augustine asks how it came about that when he heard logical truths spoken he recognised them and said: 'It is so, it is true', he concludes: they must have been in his memory already, although this does not imply their eternal or pre-natal presence, 'but so far back, thrust away as it were in such remote recesses, that unless they had been drawn forth by some other man's teaching, I might perhaps never have managed to think of them at all' (x, x).

He summarises what he has so far discovered:

Thus we find that to learn those things which do not come into us as images by the senses, but which we know within ourselves without images and as they actually are, is in reality only to take things that the memory already contained, but scattered and unarranged, and by *thinking* bringing them together, and by close attention have them placed within reach in that same memory so that things which had formerly lain there scattered and not considered, now come easily and familiarly to us.[26]

Thus all those things we are said to have learned and know are, in effect, already in the memory but in a chaotic manner. Thinking organises and orders them. Aristotle had said that the reminiscent search relied on having learned things habitually in succession and order, so that once one got a starting point one could locate the object of one's search through following laws of association, these reminding us of a thing being similar, opposite or neighbouring. Although the Aristotelian recollective process is, like Augustine's, a sort of reasoning process, an association of ideas, a search starting from one's thinking of something rather than from one's perceiving it, for Aristotle the things sought, as in mathematics, are already related in succession and order. Not so for Augustine in the *Confessions*. The order is provided by the mind, out of the randomness and

---

[26] *Conf.*, x, xi.

dispersion of the memory storehouse. Indeed, Augustine argues that the word *cogito* (I think) has the same relation to *cogo* (I put together) as *agito* to *ago* and *factito* to *facio*. Cogitation is the mind's putting things together, which are otherwise dispersed (x, xi).

Furthermore, the memory contains all those principles and laws of numbers and dimensions. These have not been impressed on the memory by a bodily sense. Numerical principles have no sense dimensions. 'I have heard the sounds of the words by which they are expressed when we discuss them but the sounds are not the same as the truths themselves.' The sounds may be in Greek or Latin but that to which they refer is unique in itself. 'I have seen the lines drawn by architects, some of them as fine as a spider's web; but the truths are different, they are not the images of such things as the eye of my body has shown me. To know them is to recognise them interiorly without any concept of any kind of body whatsoever' (x, xii). Basic numbers by which we count, whatever we call them, alone really are. This interior recognition relies, as Augustine argues later in the *De Genesi ad Litteram*, on the mind seeing what is of the same nature as itself, an image created by the mind out of its own substance. Thus, even when the memory stores feelings, they are not in the mode in which the mind has them when it is experiencing them sensually but in a different mode, proper to the power of memory.[27] Thus mental feelings, stored in memory are not present with their attendant emotions, for he asserts, the mind is one thing, the body another. The mind and memory, however, are not two different things. In fact, we call the memory 'mind' (x, xiv). The memory is like the mind's stomach, 'a ridiculous image perhaps, but some sort of resemblance there is'. (x, xiv). When we speak of sorrow or fear we do not, in the mere naming of these emotions, feel sorrow or fear, and yet we could not speak meaningfully in this way unless stored in our memories was not only the sound of their names 'according to images impressed upon it by the senses of the body [!] but also the notions of the things themselves', notions not received through our sense organs. It is mind which is aware of sense experiences and notions and mind commits them to the memory store. But conscious mind is only an aspect of the mind which includes the memory, so that it often happens that the memory 'of itself' commits experiences to retention without mind doing so, or being aware – his sole reference to a passive sense memory.

Augustine has moved Aristotle's memory from the primary perceptive part of the soul to a station somewhat higher in the psyche, as did Plato and the neo-Platonists, largely because he wishes to ensure that memory is for the most part a deliberate act of thinking. And yet he is still confused

[27] Plato's *Theaetetus*, where perception is not knowledge, comes to mind here.

and keeps returning to the issue of how images are made. Whether we remember sense experience as well as notions by images or not, 'it is not easy to say' (x, xv). When one names memory one recognises what one is naming and this recognition can only be in the memory itself. Likewise, one can name forgetfulness and know what one means by the word. But how can one recognise the thing itself unless one remembered it? Here is the dilemma of the *Meno*: 'How will you look for something when you do not in the least know what it is?' Augustine cries in anguish: 'Who can analyse this, or understand how it can be? Assuredly lord, I toil with this, toil within myself ... the power of memory in me I do not understand, though without memory I could not even name myself.' Augustine simply does not understand the mechanism of forgetfulness although he knows that he remembers forgetfulness and by it what we remember is effaced. Rejecting the Aristotelian physiological imprint theory, he can offer no other answer, and Plotinus's 'third intermediary something' is of little help here. What is so impressive in this powerful prose is Augustine's recognition of the antique dilemma and all the complexities of the processes of remembering and forgetting.

Augustine acknowledges the miraculous powers of memory and he has been at some pains to describe what they are. How they are caused and how they operate are different matters again. But he has drawn together the threads of antiquity to weave a multicoloured fabric that is more revealing of the nature of the issues at stake than perhaps anyone we have thus far examined. Plotinus was more sure of his systematic description of a sympathetic cosmos than Augustine seems to be of his own. But like Plotinus, Augustine aims towards a transcendence of this thing which is himself, his mind, his memory: 'I shall mount beyond this my power of memory ... to come to You, O lovely light ... I must pass beyond memory to come to Him who separated me from the four-footed beasts and made me wiser than the birds of the air ... and where shall I find You?' (x, xvii).

When something is not before our eyes but is present to memory, it is there through the image that is held within. It is this image we seek when we try to recall what is lost to sight. When it has been found we recognise it by the image that is in us. It was lost to the eyes but not to memory. Is God in the memory for him to be retrieved? Is happiness, which is sought by all men but not possessed, something they remember, or is it forgotten but at the same time one is aware that one has forgotten something? Is there a natural appetite to learn of happiness as something utterly unknown, or is it somehow known and preserved obscured in the memory? Have we then at some time in the past been happy, individually or through Adam, and now know that we have lost this but remember enough to know what we have lost? Happiness for Augustine is probably known to all, and the thing itself, signified by the word, does actually lie somehow in the memory (x, xx).[28] But it lies in the memory not as one remembers bodies, or numbers, or rhetorical eloquence. Where, or when, Augustine asks, had he any experience of happiness that he should remember, love and long for it again? His answer recalls us to that primal experience he had when speaking with his mother. 'I find nothing concerning Thee but what I have remembered from the time I first learned of Thee, and from that time I have never forgotten Thee' (x, xxiv). And the manner in which God rests in his memory is not akin to images of corporeal things. Nor is the innermost self, where God is. God was not in his memory before Augustine learned of him and he did this by finding God above himself. 'Where did I find You to learn of You, save in Yourself, above myself' (x, xxvi). And this transcendent experience behind him, Augustine seeks to reacquire it, by continence, fasting, bodily subjection, and prayer (x, xxx).

If one knows God by remembering him, by recalling that one has learned at some moment of his eternal presence, then there is clearly a problem of the nature of time which Augustine must try to explain. Time is created by God as man is created who operates in time and uses tensed language to express successions of moments. But what is time?[29] Does past time and future time have an existence? How can the past and future 'be'? If the present were all there is and there were no flow of present into past, then there would be no time at all but eternity. Time-present *is* only in so far as it tends towards not-being, time-past. And God who is not created but who creates time, is without time in eternity. Thus to ask the question, 'what was God doing before the creation' must be a non-question. God cannot be in time before he created time; his 'years' abide in one act of abiding, in an eternal present. And yet for man, time which has existence does so only as it tends towards not being, towards the past, so that the notion of temporal duration, when we speak of a long or short time, is not a measurement of time. Time is a kind of extendedness of mind itself. The present is an instantaneous moment, fleeing from being

---

[28] Compare *De Trinitate*, XIV, xv, 21, the way in which man correctly remembers himself *after* having received God's spirit and is inwardly instructed.
[29] Gerard J. P. O'Daly, 'Augustine on the Measurement of Time: Some Comparisons with Aristotelian and Stoic texts', in *Neoplatonism and Early Christian Thought*, pp. 171–9: 'Although Augustine says he is inquiring into the nature of time itself, asking "to what do temporal terms refer" – *quid autem familiarius et notius in loquendo commemoramus quam tempus? ... quid est ergo tempus?* (*Conf.*, XI, 14.17) – he does not give an answer nor a definition of time. The problem is rather how we measure time rather than what it is' (p. 171). Also see Richard Sorabji, *Time, Creation and the Continuum: Theories in Antiquity and the Early Middle Ages* (London, 1983).

future to being past so that it has no extent of duration at all.[30] When we compare periods of time, some being longer than others, we are measuring our awareness.[31] Grammatical time present, future and past exist only in so far as we *mentally* see these. If the future and past were to exist other than in mind we would have to ask where they are. 'Wherever they are they are not as future or past but present … wherever they are and whatever they are, they are only as present' (XI, xviii). Only what is present exists.

When we relate the past truly [note that Augustine thinks this is possible, presumably at the level of true opinion and belief rather than knowledge, if we are speaking of the particularity of the past] it is not the things themselves that are brought forth from our memory – for these have passed away: but words conceived from the images of the things: for the things stamped their prints upon the mind [! – have we got a physiological impression theory here?] as they passed through it by way of the senses. Thus for example, my boyhood, which no longer exists, is in time past, which no longer exists; but the likeness of my boyhood, when I recall it and talk of it, I look upon in time present because it is still present in my memory. (XI, xviii)

Thus future and past have no existence, and despite grammatical, customary use there are not really three times of past, present and future.[32] Rather there is a present of things past, a present of things present and a present of things future because these temporal entities exist in mind and nowhere else. Memory therefore is the present of things past. And we measure the presentness of past, present and future as a measurement of the extendedness of mind itself. Temporal duration is in the mind and of the mind.[33] And when, turning to poetry, one measures the length of syllables, short and long, one is measuring not the syllables but something which remains engraved in the memory.

[30] O'Daly discusses Augustine's erroneous conclusion that 'now' is a point or part of time albeit without duration ('Augustine on the Measurement of Time' p. 172).

[31] Julian Jaynes argues in *The Origin of Consciousness in the Breakdown of the Bicameral Mind* (Harmondsworth, 1982), that today's psychological experiments demonstrate that conscious memory is not a storing up of sensory images as is sometimes thought. Remembering consciously asks what must have been there and therefore starts with ideas and reasoning and proceeds to the reworking of these elements into rational or plausible patterns (p. 28). So too, things that in the physical-behavioural world do not have a spatial quality are made, by conscious mind to have such, and this is referred to as spatialization, time being the obvious example. Time's spatial properties are by analog (p. 60).

[32] *Tempora* means both 'times' and 'tenses'. That Augustine believes time is measured in mind, *in te, anime meus, tempora metior*, is akin to Stoic teachings and even possibly, to Aristotle's *Physics*, 223a 21–9.

[33] O'Daly argues that according to Augustine, our ability to make temporal measurements is prior to and independent of, an observed physical movement; therefore Augustine is speaking of a 'time sense' independent of experienced physical change ('Augustine on the Measurement of Time', p. 175).

Not only is this a radical theory of the subjectivity of time but, curiously, for the first time, we see Augustine implying that memory images are engraved, in the Aristotlelian mode, in the memory. We shall meet this again in the *De Trinitate*. Most importantly, Augustine argues that we cannot give the length of a process while it is going on, but only after it has ceased or we have arbitrarily ceased to observe it.[34] Therefore, it is not processes themselves that we measure but 'something in the memory' that is, the *affectio* or likeness which remains after perceptions.

'It is in you, O my mind, that I measure time... what I measure is the impress produced in you by things as they pass and abiding in you when they have passed: and it is present. I do not measure the things themselves whose passage produced the impress: it is the impress that I measure when I measure things' (XI, xxvii). It is the mind itself that expects (in terms of the future), attends (in terms of the present) and remembers (in terms of the past). A long past, he says, is merely a long memory of the past (XI, xxviii).

Now, this theory of mental time gives rise to some extraordinary views about how we interpret texts about the past, how we trust them to speak the truth, and how we make them our own. In Book XII of the *Confessions*, Augustine treats of true exegesis of texts and asks:

What harm is it to me if I think the writer of Scripture had one meaning, someone else thinks he had another? All of us who read are trying to grasp the meaning of the man we are reading: and given that we *believe* him a speaker of the truth, we should obviously not think that he was saying something that we know or think to be false. While therefore each one of us is trying to understand in the sacred writings what the writer meant by them, what harm if one accepts a meaning which You, light of all true minds, show him to be in itself a true meaning even if the author we are reading did not actually mean that by it: since his meaning also, though different from mine is true.

Augustine proceeds to provide various true ways of interpreting 'In the beginning God made heaven and earth'. First of all, we are dealing with that class of *credibilia* which can only be believed and never understood, like the historical truth of the resurrection which is not accessible to philosophical reflection and demonstrative proof. But when a narrative is constructed with a beginning, middle and end, the narrative does not merely (if at all) assert the facts, but rather constructs a more universal context based on probability and common sense plausibility. Thus we accept the scriptural author's narrative as true, not only in intention but in terms of meaning. We cannot *know* it to be true. Aristotle's rhetorical

---

[34] Compare and contrast Aristotle, *De Memoria* 451a 23–5, 29–31.

theory, as taken up by Cicero, already argued that this was the case when an orator argued from common opinion, via the enthymeme, to probable or plausible truth. A well-intentioned and true orator was not in the business of persuading men of lies and to evil. In interpretation of a scriptural passage, disagreement may arise when something is related by those messengers whom we hold to be reporting truly. On the one hand, the events described may not be true in themselves although the narrator describes them truly. On the other hand, a scriptural author may be interpreted in various ways as to his meaning. Different meanings are extracted from texts by different enquirers. So it is possible that when Moses said 'in the beginning', he meant 'in the beginning of creation', and when he said 'heaven and earth', he had in mind not spiritual or corporeal nature that was already perfected and formed but inchoate and unformed nature. We must recall that for Augustine there is an antecedent truth which is expressed and understood by words. This antecedent truth can have several true meanings and therefore several true interpretations.[35] Augustine says he can see that whatever Moses meant by 'in the beginning God created heaven and earth' the meaning would be a true one. But precisely which meaning he had in mind when he wrote the words Augustine cannot so clearly see. And yet whatever was in Moses's, the author's, mind when he wrote, Augustine argues that what he saw in his mind was true and he wrote it truly. 'Let no one then go on bothering me with such words as: "Moses did not mean what you say, he meant what I say".' Some see these words as 'a thick-leaved orchard in which they see fruit hidden and they flutter about it with joy and gaze upon it chattering and eat of the fruit'. Thus true statements are open to figurative interpretation which is also true.[36]

When one man says to me: 'Moses meant what I think' and another 'not at all, he meant what I think' it seems to me the truly religious thing to say is: why should he not have meant both if both are true and if in the same words some should see a third and fourth and any other number of true meanings, why should we not

---

[35] Compare *De Genesi ad Litteram* where Augustine describes the essential constituent of prophecy, by which he means true interpretation. This occurs in the highest kind of *visio*, the mind's understanding of the material presented to it by sense-knowledge or imagination. As Markus points, out, the prophet is such by virtue of a special quality of his understanding or judgement and not in virtue of the material on which his judgement is exercised. Thus, it is Joseph who is a prophet because he understood (truly interpreted) Pharoah's dream and not Pharoah who had the vision. R. A. Markus, 'The Eclipse of a Neoplatonic Theme: Augustine and Gregory the Great on Visions and Prophecies, in *Neoplatonism and Early Christian Thought*, pp. 204–11; p. 206. This is the contrast between Aristotle's historian (Pharoah) and the true orator or poet (Joseph).

[36] Note what a good Ciceronian Augustine is. On the positive qualities of ambiguity and ænigma, see above, p. 46.

believe that Moses saw them all, since by him the one God tempered sacred scripture to the minds of many who should see truths in it yet not all the same truths. (XI, xxxi).

We have here the inspiration and licence for the elaborate metaphorical interpretation of Scripture that would reveal its truths, all divine and meaningful, to men of the middle ages trained in rhetorical and exegetical textual analysis, where true words were none other than signs of the *verbum mentis*. Rhetorical truth is not a reporting of historical facts.

Augustine's epistemology, then, requires the active participation of the memory, a memory whose treasures are revealed through the transient sensory medium of language. In the present, memory works to distinguish, on the one hand, present and future from past; but it does so by performing its function in the now, a moment in which the mind's attention is focused on its images and it extends itself to comprehend times past, present and future. The truth of the past is the same truth of the present and will be so for the future, since truth itself has no temporal dimensions. How we interpret events of the past, especially those *taken to be* true descriptions of true events, is by the same method employed to interpret the present's truth. Mind then deals in temporal modes with an antecedent static truth so that what one might take as history, is in terms of its meaning, not historical at all but ever present and ever relevant. The real distinction between time past and present is in the empirical stamp, on mind, of events sensed, stamped as imprints, and imaged for the mind's attention. In so far as any past experience has meaning, its meaning is in the present grasped by the mind's gaze. Whatever the pastness of the past is, it *is* only in the present and the meaning itself has no temporal modes despite the ambiguities of grammar. There is a sense, then, in which Augustine the Roman orator has destroyed the past as meaningfully distinct from the now, and made all Christians paradoxically memoryless.[37] Only in this way can sacred Scripture be seen to have true meanings for and in the forever present for men seeking an enduring message. There is no distinct historical Christ here. Verbal signs truly mirror an eternal, unchanging truth, and it is through words that a believer is transformed in Christ to a translinguistic vision of God.

[37] Not only does Augustine *not* subject those events taken to be true descriptions of true events to further demonstration; he provides a Christianisation of Cicero's true orator who draws out eternal *exempla* from the historical record which is never checked for evidential accuracy.

Chapter 7

AUGUSTINE'S *DE TRINITATE*

Augustine's *De Trinitate*[1] divides into two parts, the second (books 8–15) centring on the human soul's psychological experiences. Here he turns to the human soul in order to try to penetrate into the mystery of this soul being the image of God which he knows through revelation: Genesis i, 26, where it says God made man in his image. He attempts to unite the two kinds of knowledge available to man, that derived from the exterior world and that which resides in one's mind. In the process of perception where exterior sense objects are perceived, the sense does not come from the perceived body or object but from the body of the subject, the perceiver, endowed with sensation and life. Perception through this sensing body is performed by the soul in a manner proper to it and which Augustine describes as a mysterious manner of knowing (*quodam miro modo contemperatur*) (xi, ii, 3). But it is the object perceived which engenders vision, the object 'informs' the subject's senses but it cannot do this alone; it requires a perceiver. Sensation would be totally impossible if there were not produced in the sense organ some similitude of the perceived sense object, (*aliqua similitudo conspecti corporis*) (xi, ii, 3). He now confirms the Aristotelian mode of sense perception by drawing upon the analogy of seal and wax, the form of the seal remaining in the wax after the seal is removed. So too the form in the sense organ is the image of the object perceived. The mind gazes on this form (xi, ii, 3). Once the physically perceived object is removed from view there remains in the memory a similitude towards which the will can turn the soul's regard in order to be informed of what is exterior. There is, then, a trinity in the awareness of the exterior world by means of sense organs and sense images; this trinity

[1] Augustine probably wrote the *De Trinitate* with some intervals, between 399–419. See Michael Schmaus, *Die psychologische Trinitätslehre des hl. Augustinus*, (Münster, 1927). Thomas Fay, '*Imago Dei*: Augustine's Metaphysics of Man', *Antonianum*, 2–3 (1974), pp. 173–97. The edition used here is *De Trinitate*, ed. Bénédictine, t.2, les images (*De Trinitate*, viii–xv), in *Oeuvres de Saint Augustin*, 16 (Bruges, 1955), Latin text with French trans. P. Agaesse S. J., notes in collaboration with J. Moingt, S. J.

is made up of the memory, the interior vision and the will which unites the memory image with the interior vision. This union (*coactus*) is what we call thought (*cogitatio*). Replacing the form of the body, exteriorly perceived by the sense organ, is the memory which preserves the form; in place of the vision which was produced from outside when the sense organ was informed by the sensible body is an interior vision which is similar. The memory image preserved in the memory faculty then informs the soul's gaze and by this means one is able to think about absent objects of perception. The role of the will is that of consciously attending to the sense experience so that once informed by the sense image it turns the soul's gaze to the memory store. The soul then evokes the memory image and there is produced in thought an image that is like the memory image. Only reflection on this process permits us to distinguish these different forms, of the object which informs the sense organ and the similitude engendered which produces vision, since the union of these differing images or similitudes is so narrow that without the help of conscious reflection one would think they were but one reality.

There is a similar process operating when we imagine. Here the soul thinks of the form of an object already seen. The elements which constitute this vision are on the one hand the image of the body retained by the memory and on the other hand, that which issues from the memory and is formed in the soul's gaze which evokes the remembrance. There are, then, two phenomena here which can be separated only by rational judgement and reflection. When thought is occupied elsewhere the memory image is still in the memory awaiting evocation (xi, iii, 6). If the interior regard of the person who evokes the memory image were not informed by this reality which rests in the memory faculty, the thought vision could not be produced. However, the union of these two is so narrow and intimate, the image preserved in the memory and the expression which forms in the interior regard of him who evokes the memory, are so alike, that they appear to be one and the same.[2]

Therefore, what the extended exterior body is to the senses, the image of that body present to the memory is to the soul's interior gaze. Likewise, what the sensible vision is to the corporeal form imprinted in the sense organ, the vision of thought is to the corporeal image fixed in the memory and imprinted in the soul's gaze. The role of the will is that of conscious attention, uniting the object perceived and the vision of it, although the

---

[2] ... quia simillimae sunt ... cum autem cogitantis acies aversa inde fuerit atque in quod in memoria cernebatur destiterit intueri, nihil formae quae impressa erat in eadem acie remanebit atque inde formabitur quo rursus conversa fuerit ut alia cogitatio fiat: manet tamen illud quod reliquit in memoria, quo rursus cum id recordamur convertatur, et conversa formetur, atque unum cum eo fiat unde formatur. (pp. 176–9)

elements of this process are diverse and distinct. And yet the diverse images are not naturally distinct because they are of the same substance, all of them interior, and so the soul operates with and on its own (XI, iii, 6).

As we move inwards, we find a second trinity, but it too, though at a greater distance, finds its point of departure in the sensible world. Here it is no longer the exterior body or object which informs the corporeal sense organ, but the memory which informs the soul's regard once there is fixed within the memory the form of the body exteriorly perceived. This form (species)[3] immanent in the memory faculty, tells us that it somehow engenders that form produced in the imagination of the thinking subject. The form existed in the memory before we thought of it, just as the perceived body existed in space before we perceived it. When thought evokes the form conserved in the memory, the memory form is reproduced in the soul's sight: thus, the form produced as the last stage in recollection is in some way engendered by that which is held in the memory. But then Augustine describes something unusual which recalls Plotinus's act of mind. He says that the memory form or image and the thought image do not share a true filiation. The regard of thought which is informed by the memory when we evoke something by thinking of it, does not proceed from the form of what we recall having seen or experienced. But it is true that it would be impossible to recall these things if we had not experienced them. However, the interior regard which is informed by the phenomenon of recollection, already existed, actively, before we saw the object of perception, before there was engraved on our memory the image of this object. Rejecting the concept of a passive intellect at the mercy of the exterior world by which it becomes actually what it is potentially through its objects of perception, Augustine, like Plato and Plotinus, affirms the active nature of mind's thought, a nature that is already actualised and prepared to think on exterior objects. Aristotle's elusive active intellect has been given a more fully explained role in perception, to the exclusion of the potential intellect (XI, viii, 11).

Now the will can only operate if the memory image exists at least partially in the memory faculty. Total forgetfulness prevents the will from activating recall, since there is nothing to recall. Augustine, then, gives an example of Aristotelian recollection or reminiscence.

For example if I wish to recall what I ate yesterday at dinner, I must already remember that I ate; or if this memory escapes me, I at least remember some circumstance connected with the hour of dining. In default of even this I recall at least the day, yesterday, and that part of the day at which habitually I dine or at the very least, what it is to dine.

[3] ' ... illam speciem quae in memoria est' (XI, vii, 11).

Thus the will to recall proceeds from images contained in the memory to which are added those images which are the expressions of the memory image in the mind's vision which produced the evocation of the memory. In other words, the will proceeds from the linking between the thing we recall and the vision which issues from the memory image in thought when we evoke the memory. The will, linking these two elements, presupposes a third element which is somehow in the neighbourhood and in close proximity to that which evokes the memory we seek (XI, vii, 12). Aristotle's recollective laws of association were based on being reminded of something being similar, opposite or neighbouring, association being of things imaged which follow habitually in some order.

Remembering, therefore, involves trinities of representation. Although we preserve memories of corporeal forms according to the various capacities of our sense organs and the intensity of experiences, all these visions of representation have their origins in these realities present in the memory, which, thereafter, are multiplied and diversified by thought. But there is a considerable hazard involved in the mind working in this way. Since the forms of real objects are sensible and material, the soul can make an error since it can form an image other than that which we remember from experience, substituting for the fidelity of the memory image the play of representation (*non recordandi fide, sed cogitandi varietate formatur*) (XI, viii, 13). This implies that the aspect of mind dealing with external reality, though capable of rendering accurate and adequate copies of perceived objects, is not altogether 'at home' with such objects of knowledge and not infallible in the realm of imaging truly the exterior truth beyond itself. Augustine will later place the blame for false representations at the door of the will. However, he affirms that in the wholly interior intuitive realm of knowing the mind sees an inviolable truth that is divorced from the exterior realm of change and appearance. Here it does not go wrong because it judges against eternal reasons. Thus we move to the other kind of knowledge.

Augustine argues that when we ask ourselves what the mind (*mens*) of man is, we do not come to know its generic nature by seeing a number of human minds before us, seeing with our fleshly eyes various characteristics which we then synthesize together to create a composite picture. Rather, we acquire a specific, generic knowledge of the human soul through having an intuition of the inviolable truth according to which we then define perfectly, in so far as we are able, not what the soul of such and such a man is, but what it must be according to eternal reasons. In sense perception we start from corporeal images of the sense organs, emptied into the memory, and thence we are able to form imaginary representations; we can even create images of things we have never seen. These imaginary representations may or may not be images of reality. But if this is the process by which we form images it is according to a completely different set of rules which are immutable and which transcend our minds that we pronounce judgement on these images. We judge images, approving or disapproving of them according to an interior right reason. Cognition and understanding operate according to fixed and unchanging rules which transcend the mind, and enable us to judge the truth of things. This judgement of truth shines forth and affirms itself over and above sensible images, and must never be confused with the veiled world of material images. The material object is reported by the sense organ and passed into the memory as an image, an imaginary representation. But seeing by means of the spirit and according to which one judges of the image's beauty, or by which one corrects the image if it is displeasing, is a very different activity. Even corporeal things are judged according to an eternal truth possessed by the rational soul as an intuition. The corporeal imagination, the corporeal vision of corporeal things, is quite different from that apprehension by pure intellect 'above the eye of the spirit' of laws and ineffable reasons pertaining to the beauty of things (IX, vi, 9 and 10). 'In this eternal truth, according to which have been created all temporal things, we see, with the gaze of the soul, that form which serves as a model for our very being, a model of all we do corporeally or interiorly, when we act according to true and right reason. Thanks to this eternal truth as form, we have in us a true knowledge of things engendered like the word, in an interior diction.[4] This word remains immanent within us and we use sensible words and signs to provoke a similar word in the mind of another when we communicate. When we approve or disapprove of the actions of others it is not by means of some corporeal action or word; Augustine affirms that there is nothing that we do voluntarily which we have not previously said in our hearts (IX, vii, 12).

The 'word' comprising syllables which is pronounced and thought of occupies a certain space in time. But the 'interior word' which is impressed in the soul with every object of knowledge so long as the memory is able to express it, is yet another sense of the 'word'. And finally, the 'word' is taken to be that which indicates the soul's accommodation to what it has conceived; then mind is what it conceives. It is according to this last meaning that we must interpret the word of the apostle when he said: 'No one says Lord Jesus except in the Spirit that is in him' (I Cor. xii, 3). This last word is knowledge united with love (IX, x, 15).

When we represent a body or object of perception by means of a

---

[4] ' ... et dicendo intus gignimus' (IX, vii, 12; pp. 96–7).

sensible word or sign, there is, as has been said, a certain similitude of this body produced in the mind. This image is present in the memory faculty. And this mental image is superior to the corporeal form, *pertaining as it does to a superior nature*, a living substance, mind.[5] So too a knowledge of God renders us better than we were before we knew him, especially when this knowledge provokes the love it merits, and is, as a word or sign, a similitude of God. Of course this word in the mind as similitude of God is inferior to God himself, pertaining as it does to an inferior nature, the created mind. Augustine concludes that when the soul knows itself, when separated from body, its knowledge is the soul's word and is perfectly equal and adequate to itself. This exemplifies Augustine's linguistic epistemology, the soul's very knowledge of itself being adequately signified by its word. The word as adequate signifier of what the knower knows and what the knower is in himself displays a one to one correspondence between being and idea, where the sign is wholly adequately identical to the signified. That the word can be so identical to the thing takes us far from the Platonic insistence that words never wholly adequately render the signified. Although words do bear a logical relationship to reality for Plato, all words as signs have cognitive limitations. Words as images are metaphysically a step removed from Platonic reality and they cannot express their referents totally and adequately.

But the word in the interior mind is not adequate to God as he is. Augustine affirms that no sign is perfectly known if the referent for which it is a sign is not wholly known (x, i, 2).[6] But then how can one love what one does not fully know? The soul, he explains, is inspired by an ideal it has not yet attained, and this is the spur to inquiring after the sense of words we do not yet know. This notion plays on the distinction between the soul's view of the ideal in the light of an interior, intuitive truth, and its desire to realise this ideal in itself. For instance, ideally one sees the great good of being able to understand all languages of the world and the more one hopes to be able to accomplish a universal command of languages, the greater one's fervour and love for this ideal not yet attained. Recognising the impossibility of the task, men tend to study their maternal language in its entirety. Even here, an ideal touches his heart, an ideal he somehow knows intuitively to which he applies his thought. Thus, it is by the light of

---

[5] ' ... melior est tamen imaginatio corporis in animo quam illa species corporis, in quantum haec in meliore natura est, id est, in substantia vitali, sicuti animus est' (IX, xi, 16; pp. 104–5).

[6] 'Quia vero non solum esse vocem, sed et signum esse jam novit perfecte id nosse vult. Neque ullum perfecte signum noscitur, nisi cujus rei signum sit cognoscatur' (x, i, 2; pp. 116–17).

this ideal, discovered within himself, that he discovers the price, the value of a meeting of minds through an understanding of words heard and spoken. Knowledge of the ideal stimulates love in the search to discover the word that is not yet known (X, i, 2).

The soul's knowledge of itself is a memory of itself. In order to remember itself it must be alive. And its memory is related to its understanding although Augustine finds it difficult to distinguish the soul's memory of itself from its understanding of itself. What one remembers and understands is linked to a moral quality, what one desires or wills. Thus, when we evaluate the mind of man we speak not only of the natural powers of a man's memory, his understanding and his will. We also examine the knowledge acquired by his memory and understanding as a result of the force of his will. And further we look to how the will was employed, the degree to which a man's free will has influenced him to seek to remember certain things and know certain things in order to go beyond the mere possession of knowing in its own right (X, x, 13). In the end, the soul seeks not only to know and understand itself but to reach beyond itself and to know God. And here Augustine adopts the Plotinian notion of knowing that which is beyond oneself by means of a forgetting what is past, one's bodily experience of the world, and holding one's mind in a kind of tense attention towards what is yet to come. Perfection in this life is none other than forgetting what went before in order that one may extend oneself, by means of a tension in one's very being, towards the next stage upwards, that which is yet to come. This straining to the future by means of forgetting the particularity of the past, comprises the abstract unity of contemplation of that ideal which is beyond mind (IX, i, 1).[7] One achieves that forgetting of self which Augustine sought in the *Confessions*: the transcendence by means of memory of his very memory.

Falling back to the realm in which the memory is the measure of self, and an aspect of self is related to changeable, sensible experience in the world, Augustine summarises the process of mind creating four forms, running from that form of the perceived body, to the form produced in the sense organ of the perceiving subject, from which is produced the form in the interior gaze of the perceiver who has represented within his memory the object of perception.[8] He says that in effect there are two visions, the

---

7 '... unum autem, quae retro oblitus, in ea quae ante sunt extentus, secundum intentionem sequor ad palmam supernae vocationis Dei in Christo Jesu ... Perfectionem in hac vita dicit, non aliud quam ea quae retro sunt oblivisci, et in ea quae ante sunt extendi secundum intentionem (IX, i, 1; pp. 72–5). This would have immense influence on St Bernard, see below, ch. 11.

8 IX, xi, 16, and IX, x, 15.

vision of the perceiver and that of the representer.[9] It is only in speaking of mind as a representer that one then goes on to speak of similitudes in memory towards which the interior mind is turned. In effect, he argues that there are two modes of describing man and they are analogous: one in which man is a sentient body, the other in which he is a perceiving *mind* engaged in verbal mimesis at all levels. Because it is clear that the exterior world is only experienced in so far as there is a mind to perceive and know, man is, ultimately, his mind.

At every stage in which there is a form requiring transformation in order to be received ultimately by the soul's interior vision, there is a linking third something which serves as an element in the union between what he calls the quasi-engendering extreme and the quasi-engendered extreme: this is the will, and it supplies Augustine's solution to the Plotinian third something which was so obscure (XI, ix, 16). In providing a role for the will as this linking third something, Augustine explains why it may be that our representations may be false, despite our remembering only that which we have perceived, and our representing only that which we remember. The will, in uniting these separate realities and thereby informing the gaze of the interior soul of the memory representation, acts by wandering about pursuing its fancy amongst the memories hidden in the memory faculty. The will can only search amongst the memories stored, but it may sometimes select aspects of one memory and those of another, so that all the aspects when assembled in a single vision, form as it were, an artificial whole, a whole which does not exist as such outside of mind. This is how he explains our ability to think of a black swan without ever having seen one (XI, x, 17).

The striking aspect of this theory is that will determines whether or not mind accurately reflects empirical experiences. It is not only that man's self is an interpreting mind, and reads itself as a text is read, in the autonomy of its disembodiment. In displaying the will as a potential distorting capacity which can render mind helpless because of the will's antecedent role in choosing what the interior vision will interpret, the will further isolates thinking from empirical experience. Of course, it need not do this and when the will operates correctly it relays memory images which are accurate similitudes of the exterior world to the interior gaze. But the consequences of a distorting will are enormous for the writing of and interpreting of historical narrative when we cannot assume, on the one

---

[9] IX, vi, 9 (*mentis duplex notitia*), but also see the *De Genesi ad Litteram* for the three *visiones* (corporeal, spiritual, intellectual). This dual notion in the *De Trinitate* of a perceiving and a representing vision will be of fundamental importance for twelfth-century theories of the soul. See below, for example, William of St Thierry.

hand, the intentions of an author to be true, and on the other, our own exegetical skills to be unimpaired. Only with Scripture can one have faith in the true intention of its author and the true meanings revealed in the texts. It is not then surprising to find Augustine worried about the truth of narratives where the experiences therein related are not our own. And it is also not surprising to find that true, reliable history, at least in terms of authorial veracity, can only be scriptural history. There is no other kind of history that man need believe.

Take the situation where we believe the truth of certain facts on the basis of a faith in the testimony of others. We therefore construct mental representations on the basis of the narrative offered by others rather than from our own experiences. We have no recourse to our own memories of experiences here but only to what we have heard tell, and we represent to ourselves the corporeal forms suggested to us by the narrative's words and the sounds of these words. Augustine says that even when we are thus representing what we have not ourselves experienced, the capacity of our own memories is never exceeded. This is because we cannot even understand the narrator in the first instance if the things of which he speaks, assuming that this is the first time we hear of them, do not correspond to a generic memory we already possess. Someone who, for example, speaks to me in his narrative of a mountain stripped of its forests and planted with olive trees, is speaking to someone who has in his memory images of mountains, forests, olive trees. Supposing that I have forgotten all these memory images. If this were the case, I would understand absolutely nothing of the narrative; I could not represent to myself what he told me.[10] 'Thus whoever represents to himself material objects, whether he creates in himself the image of some object, or he hears or reads a narrative of past things or one of things to come, must have recourse to his own memory in order to find there the measure and rule of all the forms he represents to himself' (XI, viii, 14). If I have never seen a certain colour, tasted a certain taste, heard a certain sound, Augustine says it will be absolutely impossible for me to represent them in my mind to myself. Now if the representation of a material object depends on perception, because the memory of the material object presupposes its having been perceived, it is memory which is the measure of the representation, just as the material object is the measure of perception (XI, viii, 14).[11] Surely Augustine is saying here that to understand someone

---

[10] ' ... quas si oblitus essem, quid diceret, omnino nescirem, et ideo narrationem illam cogitare non possem' (XI, viii, 14; pp. 200–1).

[11] 'At si propterea nemo aliquid corporeale cogitat nisi quod sensit, quia nemo meminit corporale aliquid nisi quod sensit, sicut in corporibus sentiendi, sic in memoria est cogitandi modus. Sensus enim accipit speciem ab eo corpore quod sentimus, et a sensu memoria, a memoria vero acies cogitantis' (XI, viii, 14; pp. 200–1).

else's past, were he to tell it to you, requires analogous experiences of your own for you to understand him. Furthermore, those analogous experiences must be remembered by you before you can understand him. This is, implicitly, one of the most important and influential statements about the nature of historical understanding ever to have been uttered. It provides an extraordinary insight into the interpretation of ancient narratives during the middle ages when men's own experiences of their world were at such variance with those of ancient Greece and Rome as to result necessarily in two distorting exegetical modes: one was simply to ignore what could not be seen as analogous to one's own experiences and therefore, not in one's memory. The other was to reinterpret a narrative, scriptural or from classical antiquity, with one's own memory as the measure, and hence to endow a text with entirely new meaning if it were to possess any at all. It also provides an interesting interpretation of, if not license for, forgery.

We have already spoken of the possible distorting role of the will. Augustine notes that the will can turn the memory away from the senses and fix its attention elsewhere by preventing it from focusing on objects that are present. This can easily be demonstrated, he says, by the example of a conversation, during the course of which, we realise that we have not heard a question posed because our attention was elsewhere. But it is quite wrong to say we had not heard the question. We did indeed hear but our memories did not get involved, and the words simply slid past our ears as a result of the will distracting the memory elsewhere. Ordinarily the will would have caused the sounds to be engraved in the memory. What we should say in such instances is not that we had not heard, but rather that we had not retained. The will is, then, responsible for focusing mind on objects of perception and knowledge. In effect, Augustine is saying that we only perceive, understand and learn what we wish to perceive, learn or understand! And we can experience the same phenomenon when we are reading. Only when the will's attention is fixed on the words can memory pay attention and represent images to mind (XI, viii, 15).

In what has been called that realm in which memory is the measure of self, as self is related to sensible experience, the will undoubtedly is that active aspect of mind which focuses memory and image representation on a select field. The will therefore determines how we respond to and cope with our personal experiences and our private histories. It is also the will, however, which, in bearing the responsibility for turning the soul's gaze away from the memory, thereby prevents self-representation (XI, viii, 15).[12] The will can obliterate the self. Although it is true that Augustine is

12 'Jam porro ab e quod in memoria est, animi aciem velle avertere, nihil est aliud quam non inde cogitare, (XI, viii, 15; pp. 204–5).

concerned to show the soul as an interrelated trinity comprising memory, understanding and will – the three moments in cognition, he has burdened the will alone with the greatest power: to bring man back to God, in the final resort, by getting him to forget himself.

In his mature work, the *De Genesi ad Litteram*, Augustine rethought his previous views on mind's activity and many of his final ideas on the soul took shape. Here he enumerates three kinds of seeing: *corporale, spirituale* and *intellectuale* in the light of his rereading neo-Platonic sources. Noting the ambiguities to be found in biblical passages where *spiritus* is used, he chooses to draw upon I Cor. xiv, 14–15 because there is a clear distinction between *spiritus* and *mens* (xii, 7.18–8.19). As Markus has shown, Augustine's *City of God*, x, ix, 2 had pointed to Porphyry's distinction derived from Plotinus, between that 'intellectualis pars animae' by which 'rerum intelligibilium percipitur veritas, nullas habentium similitudines corporum' and that other 'spiritualis pars animae qua corporalium rerum capiuntur imagines'. The epistemology which emerges is a blend of Augustine's scriptural understanding of *spiritus* with this neo-Platonically inspired psychology. By 'dematerialising' Porphyry's concept of *spiritus*, Augustine produces three *partes animae*: the *corpus*, an intermediary *spiritus*, and a *mens/intellectus*, each possessing its characteristic mode of seeing (*visio*). He says (xii, 24–5):

I think that spiritual *visio* can suitably be taken as a kind of intermediary between the intellectual and the corporeal without absurdity. For in my view, that which, though not itself corporeal, is similar to corporeal things, can appropriately be called an intermediary between that which really is corporeal and that which neither is corporeal nor similar to corporeal things [i.e. *mens*].[13]

The problem of a bridge between the corporeal and the intellectual would come to be one of the central issues in twelfth-century discussions on the soul. Augustine's theory of sense-knowledge, imagination and understanding based on what begins as a two-fold way of seeing (in the *De Trinitate*, xi, ix, 16) and develops into a three-fold vision,[14] will be one of the keys to interpreting monastic and early scholastic theories of the soul, and therefore, one of the keys to medieval remembrance.

---

13 R. A. Markus, 'The eclipse of a neoplatonic theme: Augustine and Gregory the Great on visions and prophecies', in *Neoplatonism and Early Christian Thought*, p. 205. The *De Genesi ad Litteram*, CSEL, 28, was Augustine's fourth attempt at commenting as literally as possible on the first chapters of Genesis, finished when he was sixty-one years old.
14 The two visions: perceiver and representer linked by will. In John J. O'Meara, 'The neo-Platonism of St Augustine', in Dominic J. O'Meara, ed., *Neoplatonism and Christian Thought* (New York: Albany, 1982), pp. 34–44, there is a good discussion of Augustine's dependence on Plotinus and Porphyry in the *De Genesi ad Litteram* as well as on the adaptation of the Plotinian doctrine of the One as beyond the sensible and rational and even intellectual perception so that Augustine affirms that God is better known in *not* being known (p. 40).

PART II

THE PRACTICE OF MEMORY DURING THE PERIOD OF TRANSITION FROM CLASSICAL ANTIQUITY TO THE CHRISTIAN MONASTIC CENTURIES

INTRODUCTION

Now that we have become somewhat familiar with the various strands of the complex arguments put forward by some of the key writers of the ancient and early Christian traditions concerning knowing and remembering, the reader might wish to pause and reflect on the essential continuity of this tradition. The reader should be aware that we have been examining through exegesis a repertory of texts that would serve as a legacy to the *later* medieval and early modern centuries and to which later writers would return in order to get their bearings on the problems of memory.

But in part II we must adopt another method to investigate what, during the early middle ages, was discovered about memory. This is because the ancient legacy of texts would recede into the background, indeed be purposely forgotten by men who in an extraordinary way were determined to create their future in a manner that recalled very little of their past. Today, it is not uncommon to hear the sighs of those distressed by how little a younger generation knows about even a recent past; and if memory is inspired at all, it adopts the nostalgic, utopian pose contrasting the bad new present with the purportedly good old days. But what if the past were to be viewed as the bad old days? What if the turmoil of the present were seen as caused directly by those bad old days and their values? Should men's energies be concentrated on those texts whose principles praised those aspects of a culture that were distinctly unworthy of remembrance? If all the things of the world are doomed to perish, why recall them?

To give an account of those centuries during which the ancient world was transformed into its medieval successor is to give an account of the conditions and reflections upon them by contemporaries, which led to a very different attitude to memory from the ones we have already examined. Because we are bereft of major texts on memory for this period, we must look elsewhere to gain some understanding of the practical deployment of memory which replaced any wide-scale theorising about the workings of mind. Textual exegesis must be replaced by a cultural history which examines writings from diverse quarters whose centres of focus were not on the mechanics of how mind recalls the past but rather on the practicalities of how that past might be transformed and reconstructed to produce a future that bore little resemblance to its past.

We begin with an account of how and why ancient memories were forgotten during the fifth–seventh centuries and then, we reminisce about the development of the monastic practice of memorialisation which produced an edifying 'remembrance of things past' but only *sub specie aeternitatis*. If secular learning had concerned itself with memories, Christian learning would set the past aside in an attempt to lead the soul above itself and thus to suggest to all Christians the gracious virtue of the forgetfulness of self.

Chapter 8

THE EARLY MONASTIC PRACTICE OF MEMORY: GREGORY THE GREAT: BENEDICT AND HIS RULE

All of the methods so far described deal with factors influencing individual observers. They help to show what occurs when a person makes use of some new material which he meets, assimilating it and later reproducing it in his own characteristic manner. Already it is clear, however, that several factors influencing the individual observer are social in origin and character. For example, many of the transformations which took place as a result of repeated reproduction of prose passages were directly due to the influence of social conventions and beliefs current in the group to which the individual subject belonged. In the actual remembering of daily life the importance of these social factors is greatly intensified. The form which a rumour, or a story, or a decorative design finally assumes within a given social group is the work of many different successive social reactions. Elements of culture, or cultural complexes, pass from person to person within a group, or from group to group, and eventually reaching a thoroughly conventionalised form, may take an established place in the general mass of culture possessed by a specific group. Whether we deal with an institution, a mode of conduct, a story, or an artform, the conventionalised product varies from group to group, so that it may come to be the very characteristic we use when we wish most sharply to differentiate one social group from another. In this way, cultural characters which have a common origin may come to have apparently the most diverse forms.

F. C. Bartlett, *Remembering, A Study in Experimental and Social Psychology* (Cambridge, 1932), p. 118.

It is frequently argued by historians of the late Roman Empire that the period from the fourth to the seventh centuries, in important ways, is a recognisably whole period. Men worked on an unbroken ancient legacy and the intellectual, social, political and economic transformations of this period should not be seen as the prelude to the nadir of the middle ages. Rather, they should be seen as contributing to enduring structures: the codes of Roman law, the hierarchy of the Catholic Church, the idea of a Christian empire, the monastery. Instead of this period being considered the prolegomenon of disintegration where men increasingly led the lives of sheltered souls hiding from a crumbling world, the world that was created from the fourth to the seventh centuries was a product of new men who ensured through their own experiences the sudden flooding of the inner life into enduring social forms, and this is what distinguishes the period from the earlier classical world.[1]

During the fourth century the main strength of Christianity was in the lower and middle classes of the towns, manual workers, clerks, shopkeepers and merchants. Gradually, Christianity conquered the hinterland. From the emperorship of Constantine onwards, higher civilian offices carried senatorial rank and were open to men of humble background to produce a vastly inflated senatorial order. Barristers got the posts previously offered to men of a liberal education: rhetoric was despised and young men of ambition went instead to the law schools. Those who were not from the old aristocratic families in the senatorial order were frequently Christians. A nobility of service was created and thereby the conditions for the increasing social mobility of Christians which continued into the sixth and seventh centuries.[2] Christianity had seeped upwards from the lower middle classes to create a court aristocracy of *parvenus*.[3] The boundary between Christianity and paganism that once divided the court and the traditional aristocracy had disappeared. Both Church and State harnessed this social mobility of talents to their own advantage.

From the fourth century onwards, university rhetoricians were increasingly held in suspicion. This would, of course, have serious consequences for the transmission of rhetoric's theory of mnemonic remembrance. The study of rhetors in later Roman history is a study of intense and insoluble rivalries between Christians and pagans, where rhetors were accused of pagan sorcery by those who believed their memories had been damaged so that they could no longer recall their mastery of classical literature. Most of the great rhetoricians of the fourth through sixth centuries remained pagans, feeling a tie with their Hellenic heritage. But they were a dying

[1] Peter Brown, 'Sorcery, demons and the rise of Christianity: from late antiquity into the middle ages', in *Religion and Society in the Age of St Augustine* (London, 1972), pp. 119–46; also see introduction, p. 13. Judith Herrin, *The Formation of Christendom* (Oxford, 1987) for an excellent and detailed survey of this period, east and west.

[2] A. H. M. Jones, 'The social background of the struggle between paganism and Christianity', in A. Momigliano, ed., *The Conflict Between Paganism and Christianity in the Fourth Century* (Oxford, 1963), pp. 17–37.

[3] Frank D. Gilliard, 'The senators of sixth-century Gaul', *Speculum*, 54 (1979), pp. 685–97, discusses Gregory of Tours's pride in his ancestry which, in effect, cannot be traced back very far, and the wide use of Gregory's word *senator* to mean rich as well as old Roman families now in Gaul. Also see Peter Brown, *Relics and Social Status in the Age of Gregory of Tours*, The Stenton Lecture (1976) (University of Reading, 1977). 'A court aristocracy of parvenus' is Brown's phrase, *Religion and Society*, p. 123. Robin Lane Fox, *Pagans and Christians* (Harmondsworth, 1986), pp. 265 ff.

breed. Athens, the leading sixth-century university town in the East, was still strongly pagan in tone until the Christian emperor Justinian made his move and expelled the philosophers. He issued a decree prohibiting pagans from holding positions in public education. Although the pagan legacy lingered on, it was those familiar with the law who acquired the positions previously occupied by men of a liberal, rhetorical education.[4] An anti-rhetorical sentiment coupled with the arrival of the barbarian world, led to a situation in which the voices of Rome's orators were gradually silenced. The artificial memory of the rhetorical tradition would find little role to play in the ensuing culture. Where classical oratory survived, it did so at relatively minor courts.[5]

Although the classical syllabus continued to be taught and studied, some of the more overtly pagan elements were either removed or 'harmonised' with Christian teachings. And by the sixth century the Christian west, largely incapable of studying Greek thought in the original, learned the modified ancient syllabus in Latin translation. The extraordinary sixth-century scholar, Boethius, was exceptional not only in being able to read Greek philosophy in the original but in his interest in it. Through his translations of and commentaries on part of the Aristotelian corpus, the medieval west would have preserved the ancient Greek interest in logic.[6] But in general, by the later sixth century in Italy, the principle of a sound (pagan) classical education as the best preparation for a Christian life no longer survived 'in the restricted and narrow culture' of the times.

Augustine had died (*c.* 430) as the Vandals invaded North Africa and during the sixth century the Lombards succeeded in fragmenting the imperial province of Italy. The existence of the Roman Church was threatened. The aristocrat, administrator, teacher and scholar who ascended the throne of St Peter as Pope Gregory I, the Great (590–604, b.*c.* 540) embodied the contradictions implicit in the ancient world becoming a medieval world, for Gregory was both a Roman and a

---

[4] Jones 'The social background', p. 30. In general, see Pierre Riché, *Education et culture dans l'occident barbare, VIe–VIIIe s.* (rev. edn Paris, 1973). Also Brown, 'Sorcery, demons and the rise of Christianity', pp. 119–46; p. 129.

[5] Averil Cameron, ed., *'In laudem Iustini minoris' by Corripus (566–67)* (London, 1976), and Herrin, *The Formation of Christendom*, p. 83.

[6] Pierre Courcelle, *Late Latin Writers and their Greek Sources* (Cambridge, Mass., 1969), pp. 274–318. J. Shiel, 'Boethius' commentaries on Aristotle', *Medieval and Renaissance Studies*, 4 (1958), pp. 217–44; Henry Chadwick, *Boethius, The Consolations of Music, Logic, Theology and Philosophy* (Oxford, 1981); Margaret Gibson, ed., *Boethius* (Oxford, 1981). I discuss aspects of the Boethian legacy below, ch. 12. Averil Cameron, 'The last days of the Academy at Athens', *Proceedings of the Cambridge Philological Society*, 196 (1969), pp. 7–29. Herrin, *The Formation of Christendom*, p. 86.

Christian and was the first monk to attain the papal throne.[7] Not only did he stand at the junction between late antiquity and the middle ages, but he linked old and new Rome. Just as he looked forward to a medieval world in which monasteries would serve as stable centres of a life divorced from the flux inherent in a fragmented political order, a world in which a monarchical papacy would eventually emerge as a unifying, structuring and ethical force in western Christian society; so too he looked back on a vanishing imperial order, discipline and unity which had all too briefly united Roman Church and Empire.

Gregory would express many of the characteristics of the changed cultural climate of western Christianity that Augustine himself at the end of his life, had begun to witness.[8] Such changes would help to establish an attitude to memory which was very different from its ancient, classical predecessors.

With the arrival in the west of the exiled Athanasius (*c.* 335) and the publication of Latin versions of the 'lives' of eastern monastic athletes like St Anthony,[9] popular literature about monasticism, as well as an interest in astrology, magic and the supernatural, became widespread. Educated Christians became interested in miracle stories and by the end of Augustine's own life, he too would adopt an attitude of belief in the miraculous which would be fully expressed in book 22 of the *City of God*.[10] A blend of serious philosophical thinking and a love of the miraculous became typical of much writing of the period addressed to cultivated men in the increasingly dark times of the early fifth century. In Augustine's case, a belief in

---

[7] Jeffrey Richards, *Consul of God, The Life and Times of Gregory the Great* (London, 1980), and review by R. A. Markus in *History*, 65 (1980), pp. 450–60. Claude Dagens, *Saint Grégoire le Grand: structure et expérience Chrétiennes* (Paris, 1977), and review by R. A. Markus, in *Journal of Ecclesiastical History*, 29 (1978), pp. 203–5. R. Gillet, ''Spiritualité' et place du moine dans L'Eglise selon Saint Grégoire le Grand', *Théologie de la vie monastique* (Paris, 1961), pp. 323–52.

[8] Brown, 'Society, demons and the rise of Christianity', pp. 119–46; See the various contributions in A. Momigliano, ed., *The Conflict between Paganism and Christianity in the Fourth Century*. T. S. Brown, *Gentlemen and Officers* (London, 1984), pp. 21–37, on the collapse of the Roman education system and the cessation of the Senate.

[9] *Vita Antonii*, translated into Latin by Evagrius of Antioch from Athanasius' original Greek, H. Hoppenbrouwers, ed., *La plus ancienne version latine de la vie de Saint Antoine par S. Athanase*, text and study (Latinitas Christianorum Primaeva, 14) (Nijmegen, 1960). Also Hippolyte Delehaye, *Les passions des martyrs et les genres littéraires*, (Subsidia hagiographica, 13b), 2nd rev edn (Brussels, 1966).

[10] *De civitate Dei*, Book XXII, chapter 8, written in 427. Augustine came to see 'modern miracles' as supports to faith. Peter Brown, *Augustine of Hippo: A Biography* (London, 1967), p. 415, and Brown, 'Society, demons and the rise of Christianity', pp. 119–46. It is important to realise that from now onwards 'factual history' would include the literal recording of events including the miraculous. Gregory the Great and Bede would hold to the definition of history as a narrative of 'literal' deeds and words, events reported 'secundum litteram' including the miracles of saints.

miracles was tempered by his biblical and typological outlook, a concern to see miracles as the outcome of an inwardly holy life. This attitude would be inherited by Gregory the Great.[11] Increasingly, emphasis was to be placed on the miraculous works of *living* men rather than on the miraculous deeds of the dead in the *past*. The *Vita S. Martini* by Sulpicius Severus (*c.* 393–97),[12] a hagiographical account of Martin, bishop of Tours, with an obvious debt to the eastern monastic *topoi* found in Athanasius's *Vita S. Antonii*, was read by circles of cultivated Latin-speaking people in the Mediterranean region, consisting of small monastic groups, secular clergy and educated laymen who remained the audience for the writings of Gregory the Great in the sixth century.[13] That they ceased to be interested in the historical past and sought instead edification from texts that painted pictures of *current* heroic sanctity, interpreted as *gestae sub specie aeternitatis*, and in the light of biblical typology, led to a radical alteration in the way memory would play a role in men's lives.

We are dealing with politically chaotic times. The administrative centre of the Empire had earlier, in the fourth century, moved to Constantinople and in the sixth century the last Latin-speaking emperor Justinian attempted to restore the barbarian-dominated western province of Italy to a united eastern Empire. Frankish Gaul, Anglo-Saxon England, most of Visigothic Spain barely felt the restoration of imperial rule in the west. Italy itself, and Rome in particular, became something of an historic backwater, removed from the mainstream of imperial strategy centred in Byzantium and now linked to Ravenna – the sole imperial administrative centre in the west. The sixth-century nightmare of plague, famine, war and death induced a belief that the world's end was at hand as the imperial reconquest of Ostrogothic Italy brought with it a collapse of the Roman senatorial aristocracy and wholesale massacre and plunder, carried out by Gothic kings fighting the imperial machine from the east. The Roman organised education system collapsed and the Senate ceased to function. The new provincial administration that emerged, centred at Ravenna, was a consciously anti-Roman feature of Justinian's policy. The most famous buildings in Rome were deserted and left to decay. When Gregory became pope he observed that he had taken charge of an old and shattered ship. His was a strong sense of the transitory nature of this world and its

---

11 Joan M. Petersen, *The Dialogues of Gregory the Great in Their Late Antique Cultural Background*, Pontifical Institute of Mediæval Studies, Studies and Texts, 69 (Toronto, 1984), p. 94. This attitude would also be inherited by Bede. See Roger Ray, 'Bede's *Vera lex historiae*', *Speculum*, 55 (1980) pp. 1–21, esp. p. 13.
12 Sulpicius Severus, *Vita S. Martini, Vie de Saint Martin*, ed. and trans. J. Fontaine, 3 vols., Sources Chrétiennes, 133–35 (Paris, 1967–9).
13 Petersen, *Dialogues of Gregory the Great*, pp. 103–4.

history which could only be regarded as an imperfect mirror through which to catch glimpses of the next. There was no virtue in remembering the past or even the present in and of itself.

It is likely that Gregory had been elected pope because he was a church deacon and administrator, a revered and eminent Roman who had the ear of Emperor Maurice, dating back to his six-year stay in Constantinople.[14] But he was also one of a trio of major monastic figures of the sixth century, following Benedict of Nursia and Cassiodorus of Vivarium. In those troubled times their enthusiasm for monasticism mirrored the wider concern on the part of many to flee from the world. They fostered one of the two strains of early fourth-century Egyptian monasticism, that of the cenobitic life of a community devoted to life and work in common. Monasticism had arrived from the east in the mid-fourth century and was firmly established a century later, in Italy, in both cenobitic and eremitic forms.[15] Gradually the monks formed a potential rival power structure to that of the ordered secular clerical hierarchy. With hindsight, this was, in part, Gregory's achievement although it was not his explicit intention.[16] But early in the sixth century the monastic movement was unconcerned with power beyond its own foundations. And as we shall see, the monastic attitude to memory was unique, unconcerned as it was with men's collective and personal pasts.

The western monasticism that flourished only in part under the inspiration of Gregory's older contemporary Benedict of Nursia, in general adhered to Benedict's prophecy that Rome would gradually and inevitably dissolve through natural disasters. Following the reinstatement of imperial rule in Italy the Lombards struck and by the third quarter of the sixth century they had effectively gained control of half of Italy. Italy was a

[14] His writings, and in particular, his correspondence suggest Gregory had received a legal training. He was *praefectus urbi* of Rome for an unknown period. Paul Meyvaert, 'Gregory the Great and the theme of authority', *Spode House Review*, (1966), pp. 3–12; p. 4. Judith Herrin argues that had Gregory been born in Ravenna, he possibly would have pursued a civilian career longer, 'but in Rome there was hardly a satisfying career to pursue' (*The Formation of Christendom*, p. 151). His mother and aunts had embraced the monastic life, albeit temporarily, and did not resist his plans to convert the family home into a monastery; Joan M. Petersen '*Homo omnino Latinus*? The theological and cultural background of Pope Gregory the Great', *Speculum*, 62 (1987), pp. 529–51.

[15] A. Momigliano, 'Cassiodorus and the Italian culture of his time' *Proceedings of the British Academy*, 41 (1955), pp. 207–45; Peter Brown, 'Eastern and western Christianity in Late Antiquity: a parting of the ways', *Studies in Church History*, 13 (1976), pp. 1–24; W. Owen Chadwick, *John Cassian: A Study in Primitive Monasticism*, 2nd edn (Cambridge, 1968); W. Owen Chadwick, ed., *Western Asceticism* (London, 1958).

[16] Robert A. Markus, 'Gregory the Great's *rector* and his Genesis', in *Colloques internationaux du CNRS. Grégoire le Grand* (Paris, 1986), pp. 137–46. F. Prinz, *Askese und Kultur: vor und frühbenediktinisches Mönchtum an der Wiege Europas* (Munich, 1980), p. 19.

mixture of Roman Christians, Arian Christians and pagans, and the general mood was epitomised in Gregory's letter to the clergy of Milan:

Behold, all the things of this world, which we used to hear from the Bible were doomed to perish, we see now destroyed. Cities are overthrown, fortresses are razed, churches are destroyed; and no tiller of the ground inhabits our land any more. Among the few of us who are left the sword of man rages without cease along with the calamities which smite us from above. Thus we see before our very eyes the evils which we long ago heard should come upon the world ... *In the passing away of all things we ought to take thought how all that we have loved was nothing.* View therefore with anxious heart the approaching day of the eternal judge ...'[17]

If all was doomed to perish, why remember it? Gregory was not alone in thinking of the imminent end of the world. The concern for the responsibilities of the church waiting for the return of Christ and the arrival of His kingdom were paralleled by the monastic concern for elaborating a structured life that would not only reject the values of the fragmented, secular world, but would lead to sharing a life beyond history as men stood at the threshold of the last things. The true Christian life now meant the search for God through a truly spiritual existence, beginning with conversion and followed by adopting a life-style of humility, setting aside acquired worldly knowledge. Worldly knowledge was not worth recalling; indeed it was to be studiously forgotten. Secular learning was inferior to the Bible and the Church Fathers and the learning in these texts was meant to lead to that contemplation which carries the soul above itself. With this attitude, Gregory 'looks forward' to the monastic medieval world with its active concern to forget the world's and one's own past.[18]

---

[17] *Ep.*, III, 29, *Registrum epistolarum*, M. G. H. Epp. I (i), ed. P. Ewald; I (2) and II, ed. L. M. Hartmann (Berlin, 1887–93). S. Mazzarino, 'The judgements of God as an historical category', in *The End of the Ancient World* (London, 1966), pp. 58–76; Jeffrey Richards, *Consul of God*, p. 53; C. Dagens, 'La fin des temps et l'église selon Grégoire le Grand', *Recherches de science religieuse*, 58 (1970), pp. 273–88. This appears to follow the pre-Christian classical Latin *ubi sunt* tradition, modified by Christianity. Compare Statius's poem on Glaucias in *Silvae*, II, 1, ed. J. H. Mozley (London, 1928): 'All that has had beginning fears its end. We are all doomed, doomed ...'

[18] Gregory's subordination of knowledge to the service of the church is highlighted in his disapproval of Bishop Desiderius of Vienne's interest in classical rhetoric. *Ep.*, XI, 34. V. Paronetto, 'Gregorio Magno e la cultura classica', *Studium*, 74 (fasc.5) (1978), pp. 665–80; N. Scivoletto, 'I limiti dell' "ars grammatica" in Gregorio Magno', *Giornale Italiano di Filologia*, 17 (1964), pp. 210–38. But Gregory's own writings, either in oratorical style or in content were not simple. He has, in the past, been unjustly maligned because of his supposed antagonism to secular learning. For a rectification of this view, see Henri de Lubac, 'La 'barbarie' de S. Grégoire', in *Exégèse Médiévale*, II, i (Paris, 1961), pp. 52–77. In his preface to his *Moralia*, Gregory did say that he spurned the grammatical rules of Donatus and would not seek to avoid 'barbarisms'. Experts, however, assure us

It is clear that in his *Moralia on Job*,[19] addressed to the monks of his household, Gregory is proffering an image of the monastery filled with the converted as the still point of contemplation divorced from the flux of chaotic political history. At the same time, he speaks of a mission by a few of the converted to the as yet unconverted pagans of the far-flung Roman empire. They in turn will convert others of their own kind, leading all the world eventually into the monastic enclosure where they will remember nothing of their pagan past. Is this a political attitude to the barbarian world that encircled Rome or a millenarian missionary zeal, an understanding of which is unlocked exclusively through a spiritual interpretation of his words? Surely it is both, and as such would serve as a model for the future. Gregory believed that although the apostles had experienced some success in preaching in Judea, the multitude of the Jewish reprobate rejected the Christian message so that it is now the case that only after the Gentiles will believe that the Jews will follow (*Moralia*, xxx, ix, para. 32). 'For when the Jews behold the Gentiles converted to God by the labour of preachers they will blush at least at the folly of their own disbelief and at the sentences in Scripture which say that the Truth was known to the Gentiles before it would be known to the Jews.' Gregory's hopes, millenarian in tone and content, for the eventual conversion of the Jews, can only be realised through the prior conversion of the barbarians by their own, preceded by a few exceptional monks from his own *familia*. The majority of the converted remain enclosed in the monastery.[20] Eventually, the whole world will be converted to this form of life and join the memoryless (*Moralia*, xxx, ix, para. 32, and xviii, xxxvii, para. 58).

This was the distinctively Gregorian attitude that Gregory shared with other Christian Romans of his own day who ensured through their own experiences the sudden flooding of the inner life into enduring social forms.[21]

that they can discover no barbarisms in his own writings. See Paul Meyvaert, 'Bede and Gregory the Great', *Jarrow Lecture*, 7 (1964), pp. 1–26, p. 14, although especially in the *Dialogues*, where Gregory sets down edifying stories told him orally by contemporaries, one sees numerous sixth-century modifications of classical latinity.

[19] Gregory the Great, *Moralia in Job*, xxx, xii, in *PL* 76, 530. Paul Meyvaert, 'Diversity within unity, a Gregorian theme', *The Heythrop Journal*, 4 (1963), pp. 141–62, reprinted in *Benedict, Gregory, Bede and Others* (Variorum reprints, London, 1977). For another interpretation, see R. A. Markus, 'Gregory the Great and a papal missionary strategy', in G. C. Cumming, ed., *The Mission of the Church and the Propagation of the Faith*, Studies in Church History, 6 (Cambridge, 1970), pp. 29–38.

[20] Claude Dagens, *Saint Grégoire le Grand, culture et expérience chrétiennes* (Paris, 1977), pp. 251–3. In general, see the magisterial work of Christine Mohrmann, *Etudes sur le latin des Chrétiens*, Edizioni di Storia e Letteratura, 65, 87, 103, 143 (Rome, 1958–77).

[21] Paul Meyvaert, 'Gregory the Great and the theme of authority', *Spode House Review* 3 (1966) pp. 3–12, reprinted in his *Benedict, Gregory, Bede and Others*. Meyvaert discusses

Gregory seems to have been influenced by the Alexandrian school of biblical exegesis where the allegorical took precedence over the historical,[22] so that Scripture was the starting point for contemplation. The great biblical ascetics, Elijah, Elisha and John the Baptist were seen to be precursors of those who founded monasticism as was clear in Athanasius's *Vita S. Antonii*. Like other hagiographers who selectively remembered the past, Gregory was not concerned to achieve historical accuracy but to retell inspiring stories to members of his own circle who wished to hear about the miracles of Italian holy men of their own times.[23] It has plausibly been suggested that especially in his *Dialogues* Gregory aimed to tell stories that would act as substitutes for the *passiones* of the martyrs in a nominally Christian society in dark times, where opportunities for martyrdom were now nonexistent.[24] In Christian Rome one might die through violence but no longer because of one's faith. But because he was not intent on dwelling on the past, he gives virtually no information about martyrs of former ages. Rather, he wished to show that there were holy men in Italy in comparatively recent times and currently, modern martyrs and confessors, appropriate to the situation in which the sixth-century church found itself. Such martyrs were *occulti* rather than public, their sacrifice was a monastic one accompanied by miraculous works. Monks were the new successors of the ancient martyrs, their lives seen as edifying because they were unlikely people through whom God carried out his purposes. Gregory will extract these men's stories from his memory:

Gregorius: 'Nonnumquam vero ad augmentum mei doloris adiungitur, quod quorumdam vita, qui praesens saeculum tota mente reliquerunt, mihi ad memoriam revocatur ... '[25]

the conclusion of Gregory's *magnum opus*, the *Moralia on Job*, where Gregory says that in scrutinising his own motives for writing, he knows his gifts are from God but there is also a furtive desire for human praise that has crept in. He, therefore, confesses to his monastic brethren: 'It seems worthwhile to me openly to avow to fraternal ears all that I find reprehensible within myself. By open confession I have not hidden my secret feelings. My writings manifest the gifts which God has given me, my humble confession lays bare my own wounds.' (*Moralia*, xxxv, xlix). The monastic sense of authority, not as *dominium* but as humble service, combined with the image of the monk as a *martyr occultus*, a confessor, would greatly influence the monastic *topoi* employed by later writers.

[22] Paul Meyvaert, 'A new edition of Gregory the Great's commentaries on the *Canticle* and I Kings', *Journal of Theological Studies*, ns 19 (1968), pp. 215–25, reprinted in *Benedict, Gregory, Bede and Others*. Meyvaert notes that despite Gregory referring scathingly to the heretic Origen, he owes a great debt to this Alexandrian, more than he may have liked us to believe (p. 220).

[23] W. F. Bolton, 'The supra-historical sense in the *Dialogues* of Gregory the Great', *Aevum*, 33 (1959), pp. 206–13. Petersen, *Dialogues of Gregory the Great*, pp. 17–18, 20, 66.

[24] Petersen, *Dialogues of Gregory the Great*, pp. xvi–xvii, 73–5.

[25] *Dialogues*, I, prol 2, 14–15, in A. de Vogüé, ed. *Les Dialogues de Grégoire le Grand*, 3 vols, Sources chrétiennes, 251, 265, 266, with trans. P. Antin, (Paris, 1978–80).

But his memory makes no claims to historical accuracy. That remembering need not be historically accurate would serve as an immensely influential presupposition for other monastic rememberers. Instead of remembering events and experiences as they actually were, Gregory takes over unverified and unverifiable traditional stories and recasts these in a literary form. He uses anonymous informants to introduce certain types of stories and names other informants who provided him with suitable material. Or he says he personally recollects a story. Giving coherent form to a local, oral tradition, he often goes beyond this and creates a literary work. His evidence seems to have reached him orally through friends and acquaintances who travelled the Roman roads, many of whom were employees in the papal administrative service, monks, persons living in or near Rome including exiles from territories now held by the Lombards and therefore no longer in imperial hands. The element of hearsay is overwhelming. Such oral testimony is not necessarily unreliable but this is not the point.[26] Gregory was concerned to offer beliefs strongly held rather than unimpeachable proofs for his narratives. What is important is the spiritual lesson that may be drawn from such stories for the lives of contemporary holy men were to be interpreted *spiritualiter* rather than as one-off biographies.

The evocation of exemplary stories from one's own memory or that of others does not appear to have been a practice limited to the *illiterati* of the countryside but was common amongst Gregory's own circle of monks, secular clergy and educated laymen who comprised the congregations of Roman churches. Behind the general, a-historical claim to edification lay Gregory's more didactic motive: to restore the troubled spirits of Italian Christians during a period of floods, plagues and Lombard invasions at the end of the sixth century. The events he narrated about the present or recent past were to be understood as similar to situations recorded or prophesied in Scripture. And his extensive knowledge of the Bible which came from the daily *lectio divina* of the codex assigned to him in his early years in the monastery of St Andrew, forged a typological mind that led him to rely on his memory in creating a narrative from hearsay materials, based on a biblical type, a cast of mind which he shared with numerous other authors of the miraculous and the holy throughout the Mediterranean region.[27] The capacity to perform miracles was a *topos* of late antique and early medieval *vitae* of holy men – *whether or not the miracles ever happened was immaterial.*

This is not a genre of writing to be explained exclusively in the terms of

---

[26] Petersen, *Dialogues of Gregory the Great*, pp. 14–15.   [27] *Ibid.*, p. 49.

a social and economic analysis of these dark times,[28] but also should be seen as a consequence of a cast of mind that found literary and spiritual models in eastern monastic literature as it appeared in the west from the fourth century and thereafter. And in Gregory's portrait of Benedict, the new type of Christian sanctity is portrayed – the *martyr occultus* as monk. Here, all the *topoi* relevant to this increasingly popular kind of hagiographical literature display themselves so that they reveal the influence of Cassian's Latin writings, amongst others on Egyptian monasticism, as the type for its Italian counterpart. A patently hagiographical *topos* appears in Gregory's *Dialogues*, II, where he tells us that Benedict had originally come to Rome to study the liberal arts, had been appalled by the worldliness of his fellow students, and had withdrawn from the world to become a hermit.[29] Gregory's memory of Benedict is not to be tested against the facts. What he remembers of Benedict's purpose and experience is meant to be exemplary, inspiring, and imitable by others. Gregory believed it to be true as, indeed, we must. And so we are told that when Benedict was invited to become abbot of an already existing community of monks, they found him too strict, and he once again retired to the life of a hermit. Again he attracted disciples and founded twelve monasteries including the one at Subiaco where he first lived: thereafter, he went to Monte Cassino to found another community which he ruled until his death (*c.* 545). This last community was probably the beneficiary of his Rule, written in colloquial Latin 'for beginners'.

Benedict's Rule prescribes a systematisation and codification of all aspects of monastic life. This is what will concern us here as we try to understand the mechanisms by which a community of men is taught how to forget the world and remember only those aspects of a symbolic life that will lead them to God. There is no theory of memory here along ancient models. Instead, there is a practice which emphasises the new monastic obsession with *oblivio* on the one hand and *semper memor* on the other.

Benedict's Rule was only to spread to northern Italy, Gaul and England in the late seventh and early eighth centuries. It was not in general use in Italy of the sixth century.[30] If Benedictinism can only be asserted universally of the monastic movement throughout Europe during the ninth and

---

[28] Sofia Boesch Gajano, 'La littérature hagiographique comme source de l'histoire éthnique, sociale et économique de l'occident européen entre l'antiquité et moyen âge', *XX Congrès International des Sciences Historiques* (Bucharest, 1980), pp. 177–81.

[29] A. de Vogüé, 'Bénoit, modèle de vie spirituelle d'aprés le deuxième livre des Dialogues de saint Grégoire', *Collectanea Cisterciensia*, 38 (1976), pp. 147–57.

[30] Paul Meyvaert, 'Problems concerning the 'autograph' manuscript of St Benedict's Rule', *Revue Bénédictine*, 69 (1959), pp. 3–21, and 'Towards a history of the textual transmission of the Regula S. Benedicti', *Scriptorium*, 17 (1963), pp. 83–110. Both reprinted in *Benedict, Gregory, Bede and Others*.

tenth centuries, none the less many of its early characteristics define those elements of communal monastic living which provide an insight into how monks used their memories in ways that were consciously different both from that obtaining in the world beyond the monastic walls and from the ancient theory and practice of remembering.

It now appears that Benedict used an earlier Rule called The Rule of the Master, written in the early sixth century, possibly in southern France.[31] He also drew upon the Rules of Cassian, Augustine and the Egyptian Fathers. Fundamental to his synthesis was the simple life style focused around a regime of work, prayer and study. He is silent as to whether his monastery had a scriptorium as is thought was common in other monasteries of the time. We know that in general throughout the sixth century, in both monasteries and the church, there was a growing interest in the preservation and interpretation of biblical manuscripts and the works of the Church Fathers. Benedict's silence here fosters in us a sense that he was less concerned with preserving the memory of ancient and patristic learning than in living a life characterised by an unlearned wisdom, even forgetfulness.[32]

His contemporary Cassiodorus, on the other hand, was explicitly concerned in his *Institutiones*[33] to urge the study of the liberal arts and the preservation of the great works of the past. He, too, stressed the importance of manual labour for monks but placed the work of the manuscript copyist highest as that labour that pleased him most. It was the scriptorium at his country home-turned-monastery, Vivarium, that produced translations from the Greek historians Socrates, Sozomen, Theodoret, Josephus and copied the exegetical works of Origen, Clement of Alexandria and John Chrysostom.[34] The works of western Latin writers, Boethius, Ambrose, Augustine, Cassian and Jerome were collected and copied, as were commentaries on the Psalms and the Pauline Epistles. He compiled

---

31 *La Règle du Maître*, ed. and trans. A. de Vogüé, 2 vols., Sources chrétiennes, 105–106 (Paris, 1964).

32 Gregory in *Dialogues*, II, prol. 2, pp. 126–7, refers to Benedict as 'scienter nescius et sapienter indoctus'. Also see Christine Mohrmann, 'La latinité de Saint Benoît, (étude linguistique sur la tradition manuscrite de la Règle)', *Revue Bénédictine*, 62 (1952), pp. 108–39, reprinted in *Etudes sur le latin des Chrétiens* (Rome, 1958), pp. 403–35.

33 *Cassiodori Senatoris Institutiones Divinae*, 26.30, ed. R. A. B. Mynors (Oxford, 1937); A. van de Vyver, 'Cassiodore et son oeuvre', *Speculum*, 6 (1931), pp. 244–92; A. van de Vyver, 'Les *Institutiones* de Cassiodore et sa fondation à Vivarium', *Revue Bénédictine*, 63 (1941), pp. 59–88; Pierre Courcelle, *Late Latin Writers and Their Greek Sources* (Cambridge, Mass., 1969), pp. 331–409; M. L. W. Laistner, *The Intellectual Heritage of the Early Middle Ages* (Ithaca, New York, 1957), pp. 22–39; A. Momigliano, 'Cassiodorus and the Italian culture of his time', *Proceedings of the British Academy*, 41 (1955), pp. 218–45.

34 He selected passages from eastern continuations of Eusebius's *Ecclesiastical History*.

a medical corpus from Greek texts with a sixth-century Greek commentary that would come to be important in the eleventh-century revival of medical studies at Salerno. But these literary achievements did not survive Cassiodorus's death. Justinian's reconquest of Italy destroyed his project of setting up a Christian university. His library was dispersed. And only through his own writings, his *Institutiones*, his treatise on orthography, his *De Anima*,[35] did he eventually come to play a role in European monasticism in the long term. It is significant that in the section on rhetoric in the *Institutiones*, his encyclopedia of the liberal arts, he makes no mention of the memory devices so dear to ancient Roman oratory. And in the *De Anima* all he says about the memory, following Augustine's *Confessions*, x, 8, is that it is the preserving store of experiences from which we draw, as required, *when we meditate*. Cassiodorus's familiarity with classical literature like that of Boethius, was exceptional in his own day. Greek had already become a thing of the past, as had an interest in secular learning.

If Cassiodorus remembered almost nothing of the ancient discourse on memory, Benedict's monastic routine would recall even less.

When Benedict accepted the task of organising community life early in the sixth century, he appears to have felt the need of some code of law with a definite *horarium* for the Divine Office, for study and manual labour, for discipline of punishments when the monastic code was breached. In one sense, Benedict's enterprise was a kind of political theory, focused on the practical reality of men coming together to live a near perfect and holy life in community, a life that differed dramatically from that of the secular Roman citizen. It appears that he composed his Rule 'for beginners' as he went along through the years, completing it *c.* 530–40.[36] But the chapters

---

[35] *Liber Magni Aurelii Cassiordori Senatoris De Anima*, ed. and introd. James W. Halporn, CCSL, 96 (Turnhout, 1973), Cap. vii, 'de virtutibus eius moralibus', p. 549:
Tertia, memoria, cum res inspectae atque deliberatae in animi penetrabilibus fida commendatione reponuntur ut, quasi in quodam conceptaculo, suscipiamus quae frequenti meditatione conbibimus. Vestiaria nostra, cum fuerint plena, nihil capiunt; hoc thesaurarium non gravatur requirit. [Compare Cicero], Tetigimus supradictas partes quasi harmoniam tricordem; tali enim numero delectatur anima; ipso noscitur guadere divinitas.

[36] *Benedicti Regula*, ed. R. Hanslik, CSEL, 75, 2nd edn (Vienna, 1977). See the extensive criticisms of this edition in Paul Meyvaert, 'Towards a History of the Textual Transmission of the *Regula S. Benedicti*'. *La Règle de Saint Benoît*, ed. A. de Vogüé, trans. J. de Neufville, 6 vols., SC 181–86 (Paris 1971–2), vol. 7 (Paris 1977); *The Rule of St. Benedict*, in Latin and English, ed. and trans. J. McCann (London, 1969); see Philibert Schmitz, *Histoire de l'Ordre de saint Benoît*, 7 vols. (Maredsous, 1942–56). Compare the interesting discussion of Augustine's understanding of monasticism where 'la fonction sociologique de l'amour' is realised and one assumes, through *conversio* to the monastic vocation, a new social identity, in R. A. Markus, 'Vie monastique et ascétisme chez Saint Augustin', *Atti, Congresso internazionale su S. Agostino nel XVI centenario della conversione* (Rome, 1987), pp. 199–225.

which describe the substance and ritual of the Divine Office hang together as though enjoying an independent existence and it is thought that this portion of the Rule is the most primitive.

The precepts of the master, described in the Prologue of the Rule, speak of 'freely accepting and faithfully fulfilling the instructions of a loving father, that by the labour of obedience thou mayest return to him from whom thou hast strayed by the sloth of disobedience'. Should we wish to dwell 'in the tabernacle of his kingdom' we must run there with good deeds. If we wish to escape the pains of hell and reach eternal life, then we must hasten to do now what may profit us for eternity. A monk is therefore concerned with his own salvation and the duties he must fulfil to achieve this. He has no concern for those outside this 'school for the Lord's service'. Never abandoning the monastic Rule and persevering in its teachings in the monastery until death, the monk will share by patience in Christ's sufferings so that he may deserve to be a partaker in Christ's kingdom (Prologue).

It is not only the ten commandments that must be obeyed within the monastic walls. Chapter 4 lengthens the list of 'good works' with injunctions to deny oneself in order to follow Christ, to chastise the body, not to seek soft living, to love fasting, and to avoid worldly conduct. Patience, love of one's enemies, humility, the ability to attribute to God and not to self whatever good one sees in oneself, and yet to recognise that evil is one's own doing, and to keep death always before one's eyes, are further ideal characteristics of the new monastic man. The tools of the spiritual craft of monasticism enable men to hate their own will and to keep constant guard over their own and others' actions, for nothing is private here. God sees one everywhere. The monastery is the workshop where these tools are employed in an enclosed and stable community. Clearly, what is broken down here is man's pride in his achievements, a pride in seeing himself as unique and a self-mover. This sense of self must be replaced by the first degree of humility which is obedience without delay. There is no living by one's own will here, no obeying one's own desires and passions. Rather, the individual 'walks by another's judgement and orders' and desires to have an abbot to judge him and to order him (chapter 5). Obedience given to superiors is obedience given to God. The humility and sobriety enjoined is of such a serious kind that Benedict felt it necessary to warn monks 'not to speak vain words or such as move to laughter; not to love much or violent laughter'. The concentration on the road to salvation is all-consuming and not individually undertaken but achieved through communal obedience where the fear of God is ever present before the monk's eyes. This he never forgets.

And what he remembers is not the past or events in the extramural world. Rather he remembers the commandments of God and how hell will burn for their sins those who despise God. The monk's memory is filled only with the images of the eternal life which is prepared for those that fear God. God must always be present in his thought and he must 'say constantly in his heart': 'Then shall I be spotless before him if I shall have kept myself from my iniquity' (chapter 7). The *semper memor* of the Rule must become a habit (*habitus*), achieved through a technique, an artificial nature that is the very monastic life itself, a created monument.[37]

Scripture is read as forbidding us to do our will and the second degree of humility is 'that a man love not his own will, nor delight in fulfilling his own desires'. He accomplishes this not only by constantly observing himself but also by confessing to his abbot 'any evil thoughts that enter his heart and any secret sins that he has committed'. This is the fifth degree of humility. In all activities he is to evaluate himself as worthy of the meanest and worst of everything and he is to know that he is a bad and unworthy workman. The seventh degree of humility enjoins him not only in his speech to declare himself lower and of less account than all others, but to believe it in his heart of hearts. Silence abounds and obedience abounds. In fact a kind of sorrow abounds, that man is so recalcitrant and so poor a specimen as to be unworthy of God's attention. There is nothing to laugh at here, and indeed the tenth degree of humility is that the monk be not ready and prompt to laughter for it is written 'the fool lifteth up his voice in laughter'. His intense humility must be expressed inwardly and outwardly. The monk, when working, praying, sitting, walking, must bow his head and his eyes are to be downcast, pondering always the guilt of his sins and considering that he is about to be brought before the dread judgement seat of God. This is the twelfth degree of humility. Only when all these degrees of humility have been climbed will the monk have achieved that perfect love of God which casts out all fear. Only then will the above injunctions have become habit, performed naturally and now without fear. One begins one's obedience through fear and ends with habitual love. One obliterates one's will and one's memory of the outer world, and one's past.

Groups of men capable of putting these injunctions into practice so that they become habit, have truly transformed their personalities and made themselves unfit indeed to live in the world for which they have no concern. What is of course striking, is that so many people sought to change their characters in this way, to refocus their lives, and to live according to the strictest of constantly observed rules that inverted

---

[37] Burcht Pranger, 'La langue, corps de la théologie médiévale', in *Le Roman, le récit et le savoir*, eds. H. Hillenaar and E. van der Starre (Groningen, 1986), pp. 50–67.

behaviour they knew in the outside world. It is not irrelevant that some of the monks who had requested Benedict's guidance found him so harsh as to attempt several times to poison him. So far as we are able, we must examine the ways in which these injunctions for beginners in the school of the Lord's service were put into practice. Certainly, the theory of such a renovation of the human personality is extraordinary, perhaps all the more so because it was not in general seen as overly strict or even bizarre in a late Roman context.

Beginning with chapter eight, there run eleven chapters that deal in detail with the ritual of the Divine Office. If what we observed earlier was a series of injunctions to humility and obedience to cover, in some general way, the daily personal crises confronted by the monk, these later chapters tell us much more precisely how time was spent throughout the day and night, and across the seasons as the community organised itself around stipulated prayers. The liturgical day and night consist of eight sessions, the Night Office (nocturns) of Matins, followed by Lauds at dawn, Prime, Terce, Sext, None, Vespers and Compline. David of the Psalms (118) is taken as the model for praying seven times a day, to which is added the eighth, at night.[38]

Benedict is precise about the order in which the psalms are to be said (chapter 18) and once the prayer cycle is arranged, the remaining psalms are equally distributed among the seven Night Offices of the week, giving twelve psalms to each night. Only here does he say that if such an arrangement of these extra psalms is displeasing to anyone, they may be otherwise arranged. But they must be certain that the whole psalter of 150 psalms is chanted every week and begun again every Sunday at Matins. There is also time for private prayer which is usually 'short and pure' 'unless it chance to be prolonged by the impulse and inspiration of divine grace' (chapter 26).

All of this comprises, undoubtedly, a very full day of communal prayer, much of which is expected to be memorised and much of it will eventually be memorised, especially the psalms, as one proceeds to move through the liturgical year. Thus occupied in liturgical celebration, the monks hear and read texts over and over so that they acquire a familiarity which not only leads to memorisation, but also to the situation in which the seasons, the very time of day is identified and recognised by texts chanted. One need not be sensitive physically to changes in the season and weather. The liturgy would tell a monk where he was in the year. Substituting art for

---

[38] G. Dorival, 'Les heures de la prière (à propos du psaume 118:164)', in *Annales de Bretagne et des Pays de l'Ouest (Anjou, Maine, Touraine)*, 83 (1976) = *Actes du colloque: Le Temps et l'Histoire*, Université Francois-Rabelais, Tours, (1975), pp. 281–90.

nature, art becomes nature by habit, and the mental space of members of a monastic community is transformed by a collective memory and collectively perceived, artificially created duration.

Augustine had said that time was an extension of mind. Indeed it seems, following the work of Halbwachs,[39] that when there are several groups of men, each group with customarily established regimes, then different time schemes operate for these groups. The traditional division of temporal duration accords with the course of nature, but from one group to another, the divisions of time are not only not the same but do not have the same meaning. There is no unique exterior calendar to which different groups refer although a group with its own established temporal regime can, if it is in contact with others, live according to several time scales, which are determined by competing currents of thought. And it is in a shared group time scheme that men fix the place of at least a part of their memories.

In such conditions the same event can affect several men in the same way because they share a collective manner of interpretation dependent on their shared time scheme. The length of time is not equivalent to a series of successive events if we understand that the events divide up the time but do not fill it. For instance, when we remember, we run through time intervals that are more or less long in duration, but with a speed that varies not only from group to group but from individual member of the group to individual member. Furthermore, when we recall our pasts, we do not follow the order of all the successive happenings but only a selection of images determined by a time scale operating interiorly. And it is according to this time scheme which is also that of the group to which we belong, that we seek to recall or reconstruct the memory. This collective time is the foundation of one's memories. This collective time serves as a continuous milieu enabling us to find yesterday in today.

That time can appear to remain somehow immobile and unchanging during a period of extended duration results from a group's experience of itself as unchanging in structure and purpose, where the same routine, the same objects drawing members' attention do not vary. And what consti-

---

[39] Maurice Halbwachs, 'La mémoire collective et le temps', *Cahiers internationaux de Sociologie*, 2 (1947), pp. 3–31; also M. Halbwachs, *Les Cadres Sociaux de la Mémoire* (Paris, 1952) published posthumously. Professor Halbwachs died on 16 March, 1945, in Buchenwald; Otto Gerhard Oexle, 'Liturgische memoria und historische Erinnerung: zur Frage nach dem Gruppenbewusstsein und dem Wissen der eigenen Geschichte in den mittelalterlichen Gilden', in *Tradition als historische Kraft, Festschrift für Karl Hauck*, ed. Norbert Kamp and Joachim Wollasch (Berlin, 1982), pp. 323–40. Also see Arnold Angenendt, 'Theologie und Liturgie der mittelalterlichen Totan-Memoria', in *Memoria, der geschichtliche Zeugniswert des liturgischen Gedenkens im Mittelalter*, ed. K. Schmid and J. Wollasch, Bestandteil des Quelenwerkes, Societas et fraternitas, (Munich, 1984), pp. 79–199, esp. chapter 3.3: 'Das kumulative Gedenken', pp. 179–85.

tutes a group with a shared collective time is a shared interest, an order of ideas and preoccupations which, of course, reflect the individual personalities of members but which are also general enough and even impersonal enough to enable the individual to see them as bearing on himself. What unites all the individuals is the perception on the part of each member that the general ideas which sustain the group also sustain the individual. A group's shared time scheme induces the perception, on the part of the individual, of the similitude that unites everyone. A group's collective time induces a perception of a continuous tradition – whether or not one exists – against which individual experiences are measured and interpreted.

And group time gives rise to group memory, shared or individual experiences in a shared temporal context, which comes to replace memories of experiences had within another time scheme no longer operating.

It would seem that someone who has left the time scheme of the secular world and enters a monastery with a rigorous temporal organisation of day, night, season, no longer can recall his past as easily as he once did because the time scheme necessary to bring forth the memory has been totally altered and replaced. When he does recall his pre-monastic past he alters it by reinterpreting it in the new light of monastic ethics in a new time scheme. The so-called permanence of social time is therefore relative. A society that has evolved extensively but not across the board, that is, where some groups live in more 'primitive' ways than others, is a society which possesses mutually exclusive time schemes. The society can be seen to decompose into a multiplicity of groups each operating according to its own time.

If time is some immobile mental frame particular to a group, then events succeed in this time. For those who do not, as monks do not, participate in several time schemes but only in one, then they share a view of the past which is unique to them. The aim of monastic life through its ritual is, in part, to destroy the situation obtaining in the secular world where there are as many irreducible, different times as there are individual consciences owing to individuals participating in numerous groups with differing time schemes. The secular world produces individuals with competing collective time schemes. The monastery produces men with, in effect, a time scheme closed off from all else and peculiar to itself and the needs of its own traditions. If memory has its source and its content in the thought of the diverse groups to which secular man is attached, then the monk's memory has its source and content in the thought of his enclosed and singular group. Beyond the movement of the collective social time of the monastery there is nothing.

A day so structured and time so filled, ensures that before the monk's mind is the presence of God and his works as described in Scripture. After several years of such an experience the monk would be a walking thesaurus of biblical history expressed in words shared by the whole community. One's own sense of self as unique would be humbled through daily focusing on one's faults, faults shared by fallen man but seen as worse in oneself. Gradually the habit of selflessness would develop and with wilful behaviour and consciousness behind one, the monk would be, as Augustine and Plotinus sought to encourage, a man without a personal memory. His memory would be filled anew with God. To what extent this personal obliteration is possible is perhaps a question for psychologists. But the ideal now set in practice was the creation of a man whose personal past was relegated to oblivion, and he lived only for the future.[40] His memory

---

[40] In the wide ranging and richly annotated article by Friedrich Ohly, 'Bemerkungen eines philologen zur Memoria' in *Memoria, der geschichtliche Zeugniswert des liturgischen Gedenkens im Mittelalter*, ed. K. Schmid and J. Wollasch (Munich, 1984), there is ample evidence that monastic memory lists of dead and living brethren refer to specific names and request prayers incorporated into local liturgies not only *in memoriam* but also as reminders of future divine service to be rendered by a religious house. Noble families also were to be remembered by name to perpetuate the family memory. The complete anonymity of the monk was not yet achieved nor, evidently, desired. But note how sarcophagal representations of those to be remembered depict aspects of the dead man's life in conformity with that of Christ's. On the significance of the monastic *liber vitae*, see especially pp. 31–2. Perhaps most important, the concern was not to recall the monk's past life amongst his brethren but rather his name served as a reminder to God that he might be inscribed in God's book of the living just as he is inscribed in the monastic *liber vitae*. He is therefore to be entered into God's eternal memory and thus these memorials for the dead are future-orientated:
Die Form des Paradigmengebetes, das Gott seine vergangenem Erhöhungen der Frommen vorhält, hat den Sinn der Erinnerung Gottes an die in seinem Wesen liegende Aufgabe der gnädigen Erhörung. Der Name, den wir tragen, dient allen, die von uns wissen, zum Gedächtnis unserer Identität. Die Eintragung des Namens im Gedenkbuch soll seiner Träger garantieren, dass Gott sich seiner also eben der Person erinnert, deren auch die Brüder in der Fürbitte gedenken ... Die Einschreibung der Namen zur Ermöglichung der Fürbitte im Gedächtnis der Gebetsgemeinschaft bürgle als Gewahr für die verwandlung dieses Klosterlebens in das himmlische ... (pp. 31–2)
Also see the study by Arnold Angenendt, 'Theologie und Liturgie der mittelalterlichen Toten-Memoria', in this same volume, pp. 79–199. A further attempt at securing more collective thought was achieved by the twelfth-century Cictercians. The extraordinary belief that God can remember and forget has been treated by Christel Meier, 'Vergessen, Erinnern, Gedächtnis im Gott-Mensch-Bezug', in *Verbum et Signum. Festschrift für Friedrich Ohly*, ed. Hans Fromm, Wolfgang Harms and Uwe Ruberg, vol. I (Munich, 1975), pp. 143–94. On *memento* and *oblivisci* of God, following Augustine, see pp. 150 ff. Hence, the need to remind God through the liturgical monastic *commemoratio*. Also as Gerd Tellenbach emphasizes, in 'Die historische Dimension der liturgischen Commemoratio im Mittelalter' in *Memoria*, ed. Schmid and Wollasch, pp. 200–14: 'Gewiss werden in die Diptychen, die Libri memoriales, Sakramentare, Messbucher und Nekrologien Namen geschrieben, *aber die Träger und ihre Lebensgeschichten sind grosstenteils in normalen Fristen vergessen*' (p. 203; emphasis added).

faculty was now only a storehouse of divine texts, completely given over to the *verbum mentis* which could take him, if only momentarily, to unity with God.

The last stage of contemplative unity may indeed be a mystical leap, but it is sought for by every monk who voluntarily places himself in an environment in which the group's time will transform his memory of himself and, therefore, who he is. Ideally, this renovated temperament cannot find a place for secular history or even the liberal arts of antiquity.

But this attitude did not last. Gradually the world would impinge on these men who had fled from it, and finally make of the monastery not only the school for the Lord's prayer, but in calmer times, the schoolroom of society beyond its walls. Monasteries would become the memory store house of the European past.

The future of Benedictine monasticism was neither imagined nor sought after by either Gregory or Benedict himself. But what would survive the vagaries of the future would be the indifference to historical accuracy and verifiability on the part of monastic rememberers. The object of their memories was something quite different from 'the past'.

Chapter 9

BEDE, MONASTIC *GRAMMATICA* AND REMINISCENCE

...the human accomplishment of lengthy verbatim recall arises as an adaptation to written text and does not arise in cultural settings where text is unknown. The assumption that nonliterate cultures encourage lengthy verbatim recall is the mistaken projection by literates of text-dependent frames of reference. Lengthy verbatim recall (LVR) is a large-scale unit of language performance, namely, the recall with complete word-for-word fidelity of a sequence of 50 words or longer. The criterion is strict. The words and their sequence must be verbatim correct. A close paraphrase does not meet the criterion, nor does recall which is 'almost' word for word ... My interest in the relations between LVR and text arose from curiosity about a belief that nonliterate cultures encourage feats of work-for-word remembering. The belief runs like this. In the days when no-one could read or write, there were people with such extraordinary memory that they could give word-for-word recitals of sagas, stories, ballads, family histories. The words were written, not in books but in living memory and were passed by word of mouth from person to person and from generation to generation ... I met the belief when I was a school-boy and I accepted it unthinkingly. Years later, I read Bartlett (1932) and became involved in experiments where people listen to stories and try to recall them. In such experiments there is not much word-for-word recall ... Do nonliterate cultures really contain people with exceptional word-for-word memory? If so, how does the culture, which has no written records, recognise word-for-word remembering? Likewise, how do literate outside observers recognise word-for-word remembering unless they have mechanical recording devices? Is the belief just wrong? ... Oral narrations about the past are understood in terms of written history. Storytelling is understood in terms of written literature. The very term 'oral literature' shows the bias, as does the use of the word 'text' in reference to oral performances. Thus, literates bring a textual frame of reference to their perceptions and descriptions ... The other source of misunderstanding is verbatim insensitivity. Even when trying, people are not reliably good at judging whether two oral performances, heard at separate times, are verbatim the same or not. Further, under the conditions of every-day life, people are disposed to deal with verbalised material in terms of what they take to be its meaning rather than in terms of its precise wording.

Ian M. L. Hunter, 'Lengthy verbatim recall: the roll of text', in *Progress in the Psychology of Language*, ed. A. Ellis (London, 1985), pp. 207–35.

137

On another occasion, Sir David asked; 'Macaulay, do you know your Popes?' 'No', was the answer; 'I always get wrong among the Innocents'. 'But can you say your Archbishops of Canterbury?' 'Any fool', said Macaulay, 'could say his Archbishops of Canterbury backwards,' and thereupon he went off at score, drawing breath only once in order to remark about the oddity of there having been an Archbishop Sancroft and an Archbishop Bancroft'.

G. O. Trevelyan, *The Life and Letters of Lord Macaulay* (1876; Oxford, 1978), pp. 142–3.

Chapter 48 of Benedict's Rule states that monks must be occupied at stipulated hours in manual labour and again at other hours in sacred reading. Between the celebration of the liturgical hours the monk is to participate in *lectio divina*. The words *legere* and *meditari* in a monastic context explain one of the most characteristic features of monastic literature, the phenomenon of textual reminiscence.[1] From Easter to 14 September, monks are to spend at least four hours daily confronting sacred texts in addition to those which they chant, often from memory, during the Divine Office. From September to Lent monks are to spend the first two hours reading and then, after the meal, they are to apply themselves to reading or studying the psalms. During Lent, monks are to read in the morning for three hours after which they work. During this period they receive a book from the library which they are to read through *consecutively*. And at meals there is always to be reading by one so appointed; the meal is had in silence and in listening.

Reading in antiquity as in the medieval monastery was done with eyes and lips, a murmuring of what was seen so that one heard as well as saw the 'voices of the text'.[2] This acoustical reading is very close to *meditatio*. Among the texts gathered by Martène (*PL* 66: 413–14) one find *meditatio* used as a synonym for reading, study, singing the psalms in private as well as for contemplation. *Meditari* could mean 'to say the psalter'. Secular and scriptural meanings intertwine so that to meditate is to think or reflect on something with an intent to do it. It is a prefiguring in the mind, a desiring of something for which one prepares oneself in advance. In translating the Hebrew *hagam* the Vulgate used the term *meditari* to mean reciting to oneself by murmuring and learning the pronouncements by heart, so that the mouth meditates wisdom.[3] Pronouncing sacred words is an exercise in memory.

So too for the ancients, to meditate was to read a text and to learn it by

[1] Jean Leclercq, *The Love of Learning and the Desire for God, A Study of Monastic Culture*, trans. C. Misrahi, 2nd rev. edn (London, 1978), pp. 19–22 and *passim*. This gives a comprehensive and sensitive analysis of the monastic life in the middle ages.

[2] J. Balogh, '"Voces paginarum". Beiträge zur Geschichte des lauten Lesens und Schreibens', *Philologus*, (1927), pp. 83–202.

[3] Leclercq, *The Love of Learning*, p. 21.

heart. But specifically in the monastic context, the purpose of committing sacred texts to memory through meditation was not in order to achieve abstract knowledge but to achieve a foretaste of an anticipated eschatological order, that of heaven. Reading, meditating and memorising served a contemplative culture. Celestial realities are the object of monastic meditations day and night, and meditation is less an intellectual activity than an experience in the monastic setting.[4]

Monks generally acquired their education individually under the guidance of an abbot through reading the Bible and the Church Fathers within the liturgical context of the monastic day. This kind of education places greater emphasis on reading, indeed, reciting texts, than on discussion. It presupposes, in Benedict's time, a group of men who may not be highly literate, but who speak and understand their native tongue: Latin. This binds them closely to the language of the Vulgate and to that of patristic commentaries no matter how relatively uneducated or unsophisticated sixth-century Italian monks may have been. For such men, elementary grammar was taken to be the first stage of general culture since it instructed the student in how to write, read, understand and prove (according to Quintilian). Grammar at a more sophisticated level constituted a logical analysis of the categories of understanding and opened up methodically the correct manner to treat the texts of the great authors of the past. But in Benedict's time, this grammatical methodology had been of the most elementary kind and was not aimed at reading the great authors of antiquity or at writing in their style. Grammar's function in a society that concentrated on written sacred texts, in a language men could understand, rather than on oral discussion, was to provide a means of learning the Bible or at least the psalms by heart.[5]

But by the eighth century, especially in Gaul and Anglo-Saxon England, there was a revival in monasteries of philosophical studies founded on the revival of the *ars grammatica* of antiquity. Monks began to write textbooks on grammar, logic and Scripture. This combination of

---

[4] Carol Heitz, *Recherches sur les rapports entre architecture et liturgie à l'époque Carolingienne* (Paris, 1963). On the later liturgical 'memorial' aspects of cathedral architecture, see Friedrich Ohly, 'Die Kathedrale als Zeitenraum. Zum Dom zu Siena', in *Schriften zur mittelalterlichen Bedeutungsforschung* (Darmstadt, 1977), pp. 171–273, especially the chapter 'Die Zeitenraum und das liturgische Zeitengedächtnis', pp. 254–67.

[5] Leclercq, *The Love of Learning* pp. 3, 9, 23, 53. On the development of monastic grammar, see below and on its links with philosophical and theological issues, see below, chapter 12. Here, one can say that monastic literacy served the combined needs of both auditory and visual minds, in effect, *reversing* the development of abstract thinking that comes from learning the symbols of phonetic events. What might be called an earlier form of thinking (in evolutionary terms) is emphasised in the monastic milieu, a form of thinking that uses writing or signs as pictures of visual events, where such signs serve as mnemonic devices to release information already possessed.

interests was typical of the scholarly generation of especially the late eighth–early ninth centuries as a whole, monks and clerics, where literary culture was understood to begin with an understanding of grammatical and logical doctrines of antiquity which then were to be brought into a relation with theology. For them, there was much more to *grammatica* than the elementary text-book by Donatus. The degree to which Bede in the early eighth century revived the patristic conception of the *disciplinae* in which the *ars grammatica* occupied a central position, illustrates this new development in monastic milieux.[6] But this revival of *grammatica* is not always well understood. Was it a key to unlocking the pastness of the past, the key to an historical examination of other times the way we today understand the term 'historical'? Not at all. Bede provides a case study of the way the monastery would employ grammar to serve the end of remembering the eternal truths of Scripture. His enterprise would serve as a model for later monastic rememberers who were proficient in the grammatical arts of antiquity.

We must recognise that the old Graeco-Roman learning, the seven liberal arts, some knowledge of Roman law, all came to Canterbury not with the Gregorian mission to the Anglo-Saxons at the beginning of the seventh century, but in 669 with Theodore of Tarsus, a Greek-speaking monk originally from Asia Minor, and Hadrian, originally from Africa and thereafter abbot of a monastery near Naples. As Archbishop of Canterbury, Theodore set up a school for his monks. The only surviving written monuments to his teaching comprise his Penitential and some commentaries on Scripture. It has been argued that these works and especially the scriptural commentaries, link the biblical exegesis of the later patristic period, via Gregory the Great's writings, with the later seventh century, a tradition that Bede would maintain.[7]

The early seventh-century mission of Gregory the Great to convert the Anglo-Saxon peoples to Catholicism appears to have been carried out almost entirely free of the world of Graeco-Roman written learning.

---

[6] Martin Irvine, 'Bede the grammarian and the scope of grammatical studies in eighth-century Northumbria', *Anglo-Saxon England*, 15 (1986), ed., Peter Clemoes, Simon Keynes, and Michael Lapidge *et al.*, pp. 15–44. Also Vivien Law, *The Insular Latin Grammarians* (Woodbridge and Totowa, New Jersey, 1982).

[7] In general, see Margaret Deanesly, *The Pre-Conquest Church in England*, 2nd edn (London, 1963); Peter Hunter Blair, 'The letters of Pope Boniface V and the mission of Paulinus to Northumbria', in Peter Clemoes and Kathleen Hughes, eds., *England Before the Conquest, studies presented to Dorothy Whitelock* (Cambridge, 1971), pp. 5–13; Michael Lapidge, 'The school of Theodore and Hadrian', *Anglo-Saxon England* 15 (1986), pp. 45–72: Peter Hunter Blair, 'Whitby as a centre of learning in the seventh century', in *Learning and Literature in Anglo-Saxon England; Studies Presented to Peter Clemoes on the Occasion of his Sixty-Fifth Birthday*, ed. Michael Lapidge and Helmut Gneuss (Cambridge, 1985), pp. 3–32.

Those monks from Gregory's *familia* who were sent to evangelise the Anglo-Saxons, converted and trained Anglo-Saxon youths in the monastery of St Augustine's, Canterbury, and these men in turn preached in the vernacular to convert their fellows. Whatever the success of the original Gregorian mission, fanning out from Canterbury, as we can view it with hindsight, by the 650s and 60s the English Church's fortunes were at a low point, the mission had nearly petered out, and parts of the country had lapsed back into paganism. By the mid seventh century, there were very few who were even aware of Gregory's mission. Bede in the following century provides us with some clues as to the minimal consideration given to patristic, exegetical texts, even those by Gregory himself, in the period after the Gregorian mission until his own times. He says in his prologue to the *XXX quaestiones in regum librum*,[8] that he wishes to be seen as a populariser because the volumes of the Church Fathers are large, only possessed by the few rich and read only by the equally few learned. He sees his task as collecting from the books of the Fathers whatever can instruct the untrained reader. Indeed, Bede's vocation was that of the enclosed scholarly monk rather than the missionary to the unlettered. He was concerned with novice monastic pupils, untrained readers.

Elsewhere, he says that he plans to take into account 'the inertia of our nation, the English, which not long ago, that is in the time of pope Gregory, received the seed of faith and cherished it only lukewarmly so far as reading is concerned'. Hence, he will elucidate the meaning of patristic texts at his disposal and compress their arguments. 'For plain brevity is usually fixed better in the memory than lengthy disputation'.[9] Young monks and novices, untrained readers, required help in first learning to read Latin and then in interpretation of texts. How might this best be done? And what does this tell us about the monastic remembrance of things past as such past events were inscribed in past texts?

The general scholarly view is that Bede's library at Monkwearmouth and Jarrow, with its intimate ties to Theodore and Hadrian's Canterbury held no rhetorical manual other than Isidore of Seville's *Etymologies* book II, and possibly Cassiodorus's *Institutiones*. Benedict Biscop and Ceolfrid, however, zealously collected grammars rather than works by rhetoricians. On their book-buying ventures to Rome they would have discovered, no doubt, that Christians stayed clear of the *rhetorici*.[10] But *grammatica*

---

[8] CCSL, 119, p. 293.

[9] Sister M. Thomas Aquinas Carroll, *The Venerable Bede, His Spiritual Writings*, (Washington, D.C., 1946) cited in Paul Meyvaert, 'Bede and Gregory the Great' *Jarrow Lecture* VII (1964), pp. 1–26, reprinted in *Benedict, Gregory Bede and Others* (Variorum reprints, London, 1977), p. 15.

[10] But see Roger Ray, 'Bede's *Vera lex historiae*', *Speculum*, 55 (1980), pp. 1–21, who believes

according to the patristic interpretation, consisted in a comprehensive art of letters and was devoted to literacy, the interpretation of texts, writing and the scribal arts. Grammar would maintain and promote a Christian monastic paideia comprising Scripture, Christian literature and liturgy.[11]

For Jerome, Augustine, Cassiodorus and Isidore, the value of grammar was in its service to literary exegesis. For the *litteratus*, grammar provided topics of discourse and an exegetical agenda well beyond the requirements of pedagogical literacy.[12] Augustine had said that grammar was the study of letters (*litterae*) and is the *custos historiae*, the guardian of the *writings* which constitute tradition.[13] Grammar asserts the systematic principles of language.[14]

In Bede's day, this more sophisticated understanding of grammar's role in monastic circles is confirmed by the preface to a commentary on Donatus's *Ars Minor*, known as the *Anonymous ad Cuimnanum*, compiled or composed c. 700 in an Insular centre.[15] *Grammatica* is treated here as the central discipline of the monastic life, providing access to *autores catholici*. Patristic sources are cited to support the value of grammar as an *ars animi*, dealing with textual study. The two main branches of grammar are defined as *scientia interpretandi* and *ratio recte scribendi et loquendi*. One had to learn to write and speak correctly but the overriding purpose of such skills was to enable one to interpret *timeless* authoritative texts.

When Bede came to write his *De Orthographia*, he excerpted passages from grammatical treatises by Caper and Agroecius and Virgilius Maro Grammaticus. He rearranged their grammatical *idiomata* and provided examples drawn from patristic and biblical texts. He used Virgil and other pagan authorities along with verses from the Psalms and passages from

Bede's preface to the *Historia Ecclesiastica* owes much to Jerome's *Adversus Helvidium* where the rhetorical doctrine of probability lies behind Jerome's words, and that Bede had enough rhetorical sophistication to understand Jerome. See especially p. 9. He argues that the recent critical edition of Bede's *De Orthographia, de schematibus et tropis*, and his *De arte metrica* show he consulted at first hand more than twenty grammarians and grammars. 'If in all their apparent zeal to multiply grammars Benedict Biscop and Ceolfried, the great builders of the abbey library, bothered to collect from all their travels to the continent, not one rhetor other than Isidore, one certainly wonders why'. My explanation is that the *rhetorici* were linked with the pagan occult and shunned in fifth-seventh-century Rome. At any rate the major doctrinal issues on the reliability of scriptural history came from Augustine and Gregory – no need for rhetorical theories here other than theirs.

11 See Irvine, 'Bede the Grammarian', p. 17.
12 *Ibid.*, p. 18: 'It meant the knowledge of texts instituted by the traditions of the literate class'.
13 Augustine, *De musica*, II, i, l, *PL* 32, 1099.
14 Augustine, *Soliloquia*, II, xi, 19, *PL* 32, 894.
15 To be edited by Bernhard Bishcoff and Burkhard Taeger, noted in Irvine, 'Bede the Grammarian', p. 17 n. 7.

Gregory's *Moralia*. These ancient authors from different periods do not provide representations of differences, indicating how things were 'other' in the past. Rather, all are sources for *latinitas*, but where pagan, are neutralised of non-Christian values.[16] And Bede justified the studying of classical metres and figures of speech by saying that not only are they used by Christian writers but that their very source is in the language of Scripture. As in the *Anonymous ad Cuimnanum* Bede authenticated classical metres and poetic forms by insisting that they derive ultimately from the Bible! The primary function of grammatical studies in the monastic milieu was, for Bede, not a means of access to the historical past but the means by which one might interpret 'those letters which have eternal life'.[17] In his preface to the *De Schematibus et tropis*, he says: 'The Greeks boast that they invented these figures and tropes. But my beloved son, that you and all who wish to read this work may know that Holy Scripture surpasses all other writings not only in its authority (because it is divine) or in its usefulness (because it leads to eternal life) but both in its antiquity and in its own expression, I have decided to demonstrate by collecting examples from Scripture itself so that teachers of secular eloquence are able to present none of these schemes and tropes which did not first appear in Scripture'.[18] Grammar, then, is a tool which confirms universality rather than particularity.

Hence, it is not surprising to find Bede giving definitions from Donatus followed by examples from Scripture with the approriate exegesis. For Bede all the sciences of discourse may be subsumed under grammar because it is grammar that serves as the primary vehicle to divine wisdom. Classical texts are valued for their latinity but ultimately superseded. Classical texts are not in themselves interesting as evidence of the uniqueness of past occurrences. That branch of grammar concerned with interpretation shows all texts from whatever time and by whatever author, to be saying the same general thing.

Bede was not, of course, a native Latin speaker. Anglo-Latin, when written by the learned in monasteries, was almost totally an exercise in

---

16 Irvine, 'Bede the Grammarian', p. 31. 'Bede could take from the classical poets everything but the pagan content' (p. 33).
17 *De arte metrica* ed. C. B. Kendall, in Charles W. Jones and C. B. Kendall, eds., *Bedae Venerabilis Opera, pars 1, opera didascalica*, CCSL, 123 A (Turnhout, 1975), p. 141. Also see Robert M. Palmer, 'Bede as a text-book writer: a study of his *De arte metrica*', *Speculum*, 34 (1959), pp. 573–84. Also Paul Meyvaert, 'Bede the Scholar', in *Famulus Christi. Essays in Commemoration of the Thirteenth Centenary of the Birth of the Venerable Bede*, ed. Gerald Bonner (London, 1976), pp. 40–69.
18 Ed. Kendall, in *Bedae Venerablilis Opera*, I, pp. 142–3, cited by Irvine, 'Bede the Grammarian', p. 35 n. 48.

construing the texts of a language that was not spoken.[19] They compiled and used elaborate glossaries when they wrote in Latin.[20] Students in monasteries that were established in regions where Latin, even in its evolved 'vulgar' form, was not the native language, were intensively engaged in memorising metrically fixed formulae in order to use them when called upon to compose texts of their own. The proficient, like Bede, and the unskilled, alike, struggled to express themselves in an unfamiliar medium with an inherent thought-pattern that was not theirs: Latin. That is a very modern thing to say.

Bede was not in the position that the Latin-speaking Gregory of Tours found himself in, that is, needing to apologise for the disappearance of quantitative verse and the purer grammar of an older, more venerable Latin in his own writings. And where Gregory the Great may have used impure, sixth-century forms, he none the less spoke and wrote in a vernacular Latin of great eloquence. Nor is it surprising that Gregory the Great showed no real interest in textual matters as such and had no theory of textual criticism or emendation.[21] Bede, however, was supremely conscious of such issues. This is because men like Bede had to learn Latin from books and from imitating the Roman models found in the libraries of Canterbury and Wearmouth/Jarrow. Men like Bede who learned their Latin from books used the memorised metrical or conceptual formulae as a shorthand to sustain an orthodoxy that was expressed in an alien language. It is in this light that we must see Bede's sophisticated concern for grammar as a discipline in the aid of literary and especially biblical exegesis of texts written in a hieratic, indeed, *eternal*, rather than native, medium.

Grammar became the central discipline of the monastic life from at least the eighth century onwards because it alone could provide access for non-native speakers to Catholic authors and Scripture. Grammar provided a systematic network of presuppositions that provided the basis for a literate monastic community whose *raison d'être* was the living of an exegesis made possible by the rules of grammatical discourse. The monastic interest in grammar therefore paralleled the monastic concern expressed in more overtly spiritual writings: instead of grammar aiding a

---

[19] See Michael Lapidge, 'Aldhelm's Latin poetry and Old English verse', *Comparative Literature*, 31 (1979), pp. 209–31.
[20] Michael Lapidge, 'The School of Theodore and Hadrian', *Anglo-Saxon England*, 15 (1986), pp. 45–72, esp. pp. 58–60. Also W. M. Lindsay, *The Corpus, Epinal, Erfurt and Leiden Glossaries* (Oxford, 1921); Joseph D. Pheifer, *Old English Glosses in the Epinal-Erfurt Glossary* (Oxford, 1974); J. H. Hessels, ed., *A Late Eighth-Century Latin-Anglo-Saxon Glossary Preserved in the Library of the Leiden University* (Cambridge, 1906).
[21] Paul Meyvaert, 'Bede the Scholar', in *Famulus Christi*, especially pp. 47–9.

recovery of the past, it was meant to teach a way to reach heaven through latinity. Grammar was seen to facilitate the ascent to heaven by making possible the reading of Scripture and the Fathers, whose truths had no historical dimension whatsoever.

And grammatical study in the monastery led to its further uses in the liturgical cult. The benedictions of the Divine Office, the responses and antiphons were cadenced and ornamented in accord with the laws of metre. These were often no more than memory devices. Existing chant was interpolated with elaborate and lengthy *melismata* sung on one of the vowels of the text. Such musical embellishments and extensions of a vowel, at first on the last syllable of *Alleluia*, swelled to such tremendous proportions that this musical interpolation, or trope, became difficult to remember. So the long *melisma* had a few simple words added to the liturgical text in order that the melismatic meolody could be more easily recalled. These textual additions to the liturgy in turn became more formal and elaborate and eventually became a wholly new member of the chant known as the Prose or Sequence. They were to be treated eventually as independent poetic compositions and set to hymn-like melodies. Gradually, every part of the liturgy came to be troped.[22]

Therefore, the precise art of grammar came to be, in monastic circles, a collection of rules serving written expression and aiding in the ascent to heaven. The monastery of the eighth and ninth centuries, and thereafter, confirmed Augustine's statement in his *De Ordine*, II, xii, 37, 'that everything which does not deserve to pass into oblivion and has been trusted to writing belongs necessarily to the province of grammar'.[23] But it was precisely the judgement of what was worthy of oblivion and what of remembrance that lies at the heart of memory's significance in the monastic milieu.

We shall return to discuss the practical deployment of the monastic judgement concerning what was worthy of remembrance when we deal specifically with monastic historiography. But we cannot understand the presuppositions behind the writing of monastic history if we do not first emphasise that the application of grammar to Scripture developed into a specially monastic preoccupation. Because the majority of biblical exege-

---

[22] P. M. Gy, 'Les tropes dans l'histoire de la liturgie et de la théologie, in G.Iversen, ed., *Research in Tropes* (Stockholm, 1983). Also Helmut Hucke, 'Die Cheironomie und die Entstehung der Neumenschrift', *Musikforschung*, 32 (1979), pp. 1–16; Michel Huglo, 'La chironomie médiévale', *Revue de Musicologie*, I, 49 (1963), pp. 155–71, on singing from memory.

[23] Also see Leclercq, *The Love of Learning*, p. 59. Augustine, *De Ordine*, II, xii, 37: 'Sed quia ipso nomine profiteri se litteras clamat, unde etiam latine litteratura dicitur, factum est ut quidquid dignum memoria litteris mandaretur, ad eam necessario pertineret' (*PL* 32. 1012).

sis from the eighth to the early thirteenth centuries comes from the monastic context, it is the monastic preoccupation with grammar in the service of meditation and prayer that can tell us something about the role of memory as they understood it.[24]

Monastic *lectio divina* is specifically oriented towards the reading monk's benefit who meditates on the text in order to come to an experience of the desire for heaven. When he pronounces the text by murmuring the words, he involves more than his visual memory of the written words. He engages a physical, muscular process, his memory recalls the sensation of the words pronounced and heard. Meditation consists in focusing one's attention on this exercise in memorisation, so that the sacred text is inscribed in the soul, a soul that is 'located' in every part of one's body. Rumination, the repeated mastication of divine words as spiritual nutrition follows the Augustinian notion that the memory is the stomach of the soul where the divine words are chewed to release their flavour. One tastes or savours the words with the *palatum cordis*. Now, this understanding of the experience of *lectio* and *meditatio* had significant consequences for the monastic understanding of psychology.[25] Furthermore, the nature of the soul was intimately linked with grammatical interests since, following Augustine, the structure of language is a key source of theological understanding.

This is illustrated in the ninth-century debate between the monk Ratramnus of Corbie with an unknown student of the Irishman Macarius over an interpretation of a passage in Augustine's *De Quantitate Animae* (xxxii, 69).[26] Ratramnus interprets rhetoric's understanding of the soul as a species to which all individual souls belong. Ratramnus is concerned to argue that universals do not exist really and the only way we understand universals is through particular things. Genera and species are thought-formations in the mind and do not consist in concrete existing things. He argues that things are distinct from that which signifies them, that is, diverse existing things are signified by words. Every verbal sign is a mental thing formed by conceptions; so too a mental concept, had by means of thought, is a sign of the thing. We know that images or forms of existing things are perceived through the corporeal senses and the soul through its memory hides them away and in the end, signifies them by words. The variety of things can only be known as a process and not all at the same time. Now genus and species exist in thought and do not subsist in or through some exterior substance. The images of things perceived through

24 See below, chapter 12, on the relation between grammar and metaphysics.
25 Leclercq, *The Love of Learning*, p. 90.
26 Ratramnus of Corbie, *Liber de Anima ad Odonem Bellovacensem*, ed. D. C. Lambot OSB, Analecta Mediaevalia Namurcensia, 2 (Namur/Lille, 1951), P. Delhaye, *Une controverse sur l'âme universelle au ix^e s.* (Nauwelaerts, Louvain, 1950).

the corporeal senses are images formed in the mind and thereafter create conceptions in the soul and these are called the images of the things perceived. However, the things perceived are singular, existing things. But they are imagined by universals which are genera and species rather then existing individuals. These universals are in the mind as images and are brought out in words, clothed as nouns or verbs. For this reason an utterance, *oratio*, is divided into three parts: either it is the essence of all existing things; or it is their concept perceived in the mind; or lastly, it is the word which explains their nature. Those things which are singular and are in things through subsistence, are in the mind through the imagination, and in words through pronunciation. But universals are not in things through subsistence. They are in thought alone through the operations of intelligence and they are then clothed in words. In the vocally uttered words they truly are, and are outside by means of enunciation; but they are in the mind by means of concepts.[27]

This means that when we remember we are not remembering individuals themselves but rather the interior, universal concept which points to the individual thing. We do not have direct access to singular existing individuals when we think or remember. We have access only to essences, concepts or signs which refer to individuals. Images or forms of existing things are hidden in our memories. Our memories are filled with signs which are either concepts or words which refer to past things but which themselves – as mental or verbal constructions – are present.

[27] *Liber de Anima*:
... quoniam res quae sunt distant ab his quae (eas significant) hoc est, existentia rerum diversa consistit a vocabulis quibus res significantur. Omne namque vocabulum signum est rei mentis conceptione formatae; sicut quoque mentis conceptio per cogitationem signum est rei consistentis. Deinde imagines sive formae rerum existentium per corporis sensus percipiuntur, et animo per memoriam reconduntur: ad extremum per verba significantur. Sic ergo fit ut simul esse nequeant, nulla sub intercapedine, nulloque tempore, quae tanta varietate differre cognoscuntur. (p.112)
Denique iam superius monstratum est quod genera seu species in cogitatione per intelligentiam subsistentiam habeant, nec sint in aliqua re per substantiam extrinsecus. Etenim primum necesse est, res quae sunt subsistere suis formis suisque qualitatibus. Harum rerum imagines, dum per sensus corporis perceptae in mente formantur, fiunt quaedam conceptiones animorum, quae dicuntur imagines rerum perceptarum: quae cum de singulis existentibus particulariter formantur, dicuntur individua; cum vero de universalibus imaginantur, genera sunt vel species. Quae tamen dum in mente solummodo versantur, nec in vocem proferuntur, imagines sunt tantummodo rerum existentium: ut vero proferantur in vocem, vestiantur necesse est nominibus aut verbis. Ita trifariam dividitur oratio, id est, dum aut rerum existentium essentiam aut conceptiones earum mente perceptarum, aut verborum explicat naturas. Igitur illa quae sunt singularia, et in rebus sunt per subsistentiam, et in mente per imaginationem, et in voce per pronunciationem. At quae sunt universalia, non in tantummodo per intelligentiam, quae vestiuntur voce per verba. In voce vero quae sunt, et foris sunt per annunciationem, et in mente per conceptionem ... (p. 131).

Ratramnus's view that universals only exist in the mind was hotly disputed at the time and subsequently. What is interesting here is the belief that universals, as mental images of things, are brought out again as percussive utterances, things in themselves. In addition, the *oratio* is a *verbum mentis*, a concept perceived interiorly by mind. And it is also indicative and explanatory of the nature of the thing signified. Words then for Ratramnus not only have the indicative and commemorative function that Augustine gave to them. Like Augustine (*De Trinitate* IX, x, 15), Ratramnus also stresses the vocal utterance as a noise in itself, an aspect of language to which monks would be peculiarly sensitive as they murmured their way through the Divine Office and their readings.

In practice, the threefold nature of *oratio* helps to impregnate the words of Scripture in the mind so that verbal echoes excite the memory to such a degree that a mere allusion to one word of Scripture will spontaneously cause to be evoked whole quotations often from elsewhere in Scripture. Leclercq has described these words as 'hooks' which catch hold of one or several others which then become linked together and make up the fabric of the monk's associative thoughts.[28] And if he is writing, his whole exposé of Scripture will be dominated by this wide-ranging reminiscence. Consequently, it is often difficult to determine if a monk is quoting older versions of Scripture or modifying them.[29] Most frequently he would be quoting from memory by means of hook words which then group themselves together in the mind and under the pen:

The mere fact of hearing certain words which happen to be similar in sound to certain other words, sets up a kind of chain reaction of associations which will bring together words that have no more than a chance connection, purely external, with one another. But since the word or passage which contains this word comes to mind, why not comment on it here?[30]

It is not surprising that monastic authors do not always seem to compose after a logical pattern; rather, they follow a psychological plan of verbal and aural association which leads to digressions. There is no mnemotechnics of the antique variety here. Nor is there the Aristotelian logical and

---

28 Leclercq, *The Love of Learning*, pp. 91–2.
29 Joan Petersen, *The Dialogues of Gregory the Great in their Late Antique Cultural Background* (Toronto, 1984), noted a similar process of reminiscence by Gregory: 'Gregory was almost certainly relying on his recollection of the text of the Bible – the notion of verifying quotations or comparing one version of a quote with another would be alien to him'. His attempts at longer quotations from Kings ii, 4, Kings iv, 27 (*Dialogues*, 2.21, vol. 2, pp. 200–1) consist 'of a mixture of the Vulgate and the Vetus Italica'. The sentence structure is from the V.I. but the two main verbs are from the Vulgate. This suggests he was quoting from memory (p. 32).
30 Leclercq, *The Love of Learning*, p. 92.

dialectical association of 'naturally' successive words or events. Monastic rumination and reminiscence is almost wildly imaginative in comparison to these earlier techniques.

The active association of heard and seen words enabled monks to 'make present' through images, all the details provided by Scriptural texts. They advised a renunciation of carnal images in order to substitute holy images, whose power of suggestion ran beyond the requirements of logical thought that demanded clarity and precision first.[31] Language was to be used to encourage an association of experiences rather than to inform with knowledge. As Leclercq has made clear, the monastic memory 'fashioned wholly by the Bible and nurtured entirely by biblical words and the images they evoke, causes them to express themselves spontaneously in a biblical vocabulary. Reminiscences are not quotations, elements of phrases borrowed from another. They are the words of the person using them; they belong to him.'[32]

The phenomenon of monastic reminiscence reached its high point with St Bernard's biblical exegesis. Later, we shall observe Bernards' memory operating as a living concordance where he explains one verse by another in which the same word occurs. His knowledge of the Bible was so extraordinary that he was able, through having learnt the texts by heart, to supply spontaneously a text or word corresponding to a situation described in the text under consideration and which explained each separate word. But Bernard's perfection of monastic reminiscence was of a piece with the monastic tradition as a whole.

Within that tradition, it appears that monks relatively rarely used the written concordance for the Bible that was to hand. This would be the practice of scholasticism. However, there were in monastic circles certain books like lexicons where the meaning of words was given, collections of *nomina sacra* explaining the etymology of place names and names of persons, as well as philological repertories.[33] Monks seem to have assimilated these and referred to them from memory. They derived further etymologies through reminiscence when the sound of one word evoked another. These remembered lexical authorities set limits to verbal interpretation so that it was never entirely arbitrary. Some monks relied on the writings of ancient naturalists to explain the names of animals and stones and plants and they found these collected in bestiaries and lapidaries. But unlike what would become a method of composition amongst scholastics, the scissors-and-paste manner of writing, monks appear to have relied more extensively on their associative memories.

As a consequence of this mental attitude to Scripture as a mirror to be

[31] *Ibid.*, p. 93.   [32] *Ibid.*, p. 94.   [33] *Ibid.*, p. 96.

reproduced, Leclercq has argued that monastic exegesis is literal because of the importance it gives to words. Grammar is applied to them and because of the auditory memory of them, reminiscences follow. It is literal because of the use of repertories which explain words. Monks interpreted Scripture by Scripture itself, the letter by the letter.[34] And the vast influence of Augustine made monastic exegesis a mystical enterprise because Scripture was not a source of knowledge about the past so much as a means to salvation based on the communication of the word of God to man. This literal methodology of biblical exegesis interprets the Old Testament as a prefiguration of the New and not as an historical document. The Bible has mainly a figurative meaning and is never purely historical. In fact, the use of the monk's memory in recalling passages requires that past events are made present to elucidate universal and eternal religious problems rather than historical ones. There is a real sense in which monks had no conception of the past as we would understand it.[35] Or perhaps it is better to say that the past in and of itself held no interest for them. In fact, to say that they had no *sense* of the past is, technically, wrong. They had a *sense* of the past but no *understanding* of pastness. This will become clear once we have the opportunity to examine the monastic attitude to the soul in which a strict divorce is defined between the corporeal senses and mind's understanding. What we must emphasise here is that the object of a monastic commentary on Scripture

[34] *Ibid.*, p. 99.
[35] What they meant by 'history' is discussed more fully below, ch. 14. Here, let us note that history as we understand it is impossible without the spatialisation of time that is characteristic of consciousness. If a technique is developed, as in monasteries, by which to lose this consciousness, then there is also a loss of the spatialisation of time and history collapses into a 'present'. We shall discuss the twelfth-century 'renaissance' below, chapter 14. Let us note here, in anticipation, what Chrysogonus Waddell has argued in 'The Reform of the Liturgy from a Renaissance Perspective', in *Renaissance and Renewal in the Twelfth Century*, ed. Robert Benson, Giles Constable, Carol Lanham (1982; Oxford, 1985), pp. 88–109. Whatever the liturgical reforms, liturgy like history and the reading of scriptures continued to emphasise the transtemporal aspects of texts. There was no return to antiquity as antique; rather, where Plato was cited he was taken to be Moses talking Attic, his *eros* was equated with the New Testament's *agape* as it was understood in the twelfth century. It was not to Classical Greece and Rome that *homo medievalis* looked for regeneration. Classical antiquity had nothing of substance to offer twelfth-century liturgical reform. Where antiquity made a contribution it was at a superficial level, that is, ancient rhetoric, literary excellence, beauty, ideas, examples of moral excellence and virtue were all translated. Where the twelfth-century 'reforms' appear to have gone back to classical antiquity they actually went back to what they took to be early Christian Rome (summarising pp. 91–2). 'Our twelfth-century liturgist simply did not have available the tools of philology and archaeology which the later Renaissance was to provide as a means for situating liturgical rites and formularies in their proper and original cultural milieu' (p. 92). As we shall argue below, they also had no interest in developing such tools.

is to elucidate God's eternal relationship with each soul and Christ's presence in it. The aim is to use the words of Scripture as God's word to induce a spiritual union of the monk with God. Meditation on Scripture induces the recollection of God, that experience sought by Augustine, to find God in his memory and thence to surpass his memory to come to God. The monastic exegesis seeks not to instruct the mind but to recall from the memory store the presence of God dwelling therein. He is always there, present, and must be remembered.

This concern to touch the heart rather than the intellect was achieved, interestingly, without the aid of Augustine's neo-Platonic forebears and without knowledge of the pseudo-Dionysian tradition. In the ninth century John Scotus Eriugena translated and commented on these pseudo-Dionysian works but they were to have little effect on the monastic tradition until the twelfth century. Rather, it is a meditation on the texts of the Fathers, Augustine in particular, as well as Augustine through Gregory the Great, that would inspire the practical implementation of the monastic art of memory.

Monastic literary genres from the eighth to the twelfth centuries barely evolved. The proliferation of monastic texts aimed at embellishing other texts. And it was especially the elaboration of the liturgy, which must have taxed their already extended memories, that serves as a mirror of this contemplative community whose aim is to absorb texts in praise of God and in God's own words in order to induce a forgetfulness of self.

From the perspective of an examination of the natural limits of monastic remembrance, the story of Cluny's evolution from the tenth to the twelfth centuries is instructive.[36] Having been founded in the tenth century and riding the crest of a wave of monastic reformism, Cluniac Benedictinism set to spreading a new, purified monasticism throughout its radiating institutions. Several generations of extraordinary abbots ruled over the mother and daughter houses, creating an aristocratic dynasty of abbatial inheritance. Surrounded by non-monastic communities which took on the burdens of monastic work, Cluniac monks found themselves free from labour and able to devote themselves to the liturgical office and prayer. The Office was prolonged and choral prayers were added to occupy the whole

---

[36] Raffaello Morghen, 'Monastic Reform and Cluniac Spirituality' (1958), in Noreen Hunt, ed., *Cluniac Monasticism in the Central Middle Ages* (London, 1971), pp. 11–28, translated from 'Riforma monastica e spiritualità cluniacense' in *Spiritualitá Cluniacense*, Convegni del Centro di Studi sulla spiritualitá medievale, 1958 (Todi, 1960), pp. 33–56; in Hunt, see p. 19. Also Marvin B. Becker, *Medieval Italy, Constraints and Creativity* (Bloomington, 1981) especially chs 1 and 2. Also Joachim Wollasch, *Mönchtum des Mittelalters zwischen Kirche und Welt*, Münstersche Mittelalter-Schriften, 7 (Munich, 1973), esp. pp. 145–56.

or at least most of the day. Eventually, it would be judged that this liturgical elaboration had gone too far and had overloaded the monastic memory. The Customaries of Cluny from the end of the eleventh century speak of the chanting of 215 psalms daily and the attendance at two conventual masses, possibly three, along with processions, litanies and other public prayers![37] There was, however, time for private prayer as well, for reading and studying, and work in the scriptorium. A monk could receive a dispensation from the liturgical round if he had other necessary tasks to perform. But in general, by the time of abbot Peter the Venerable (1150s), the Cluniac was engaged in a near heroic practice of the liturgy in a continuous manner, whose prolixity of psalmody was to inspire criticism from outside as well as from Peter the Venerable himself.

Our purpose here is to examine briefly Peter the Venerable's practical response to what some claimed was an overburdening of the monastic memory. Thereafter, we must look at the more radical reform of Benedictinism by the new Order of Cistercians for it is amongst the latter that we see the elaboration of a technique of remembering, as formulated by St Bernard, that would clarify the distinctiveness of remembering within the monastic enclosure.

It must be said at the outset that although other non-Cluniac foundations differed in nuances of their day, comparing customaries shows that from the tenth and eleventh centuries, monasticism offered a life that was essentially the same everywhere.[38] The length of the Cluniac liturgy was not longer than sources for customaries of the eleventh-century liturgy elsewhere indicate.[39] The long liturgy was simply suitable to the

---

[37] G. de Valous, *Le monachisme clunisien des origines au XVe siècle* (Ligugé-Paris, 1935, re-éd. 1968) – a study of the coutumiers; Robert Folz, 'Pierre le Vénérable et la liturgie', in *Pierre Abélard, Pierre le Vénérable, les courants philosophiques, littéraires et artistiques en occident au milieu du XIIe s.*, colloque international, Abbaye de Cluny, 1972 (Paris, 1975), pp. 143–64; p. 151; Jean Leclercq, 'Pour une histoire de la vie de Cluny' (I), *Revue d'Histoire Ecclésiastique*, 57 (1962), pp. 385–408; (II), pp. 783–812. Leclercq here reevaluates the so-called opposition between Cluny and Gorze, partly with reference to K. Hallinger, *Gorze-Kluny*, Studia Anselmiana, 22–5, 2 vols. (Rome, 1950–1). Also a discussion of the different *consuetudines*.

[38] The term 'Cluniac' was often used for any black Benedictine monk in the later middle ages and there is a problem when one speaks of Cluny in determining the meaning of 'Cluniac'. See Giles Constable, *Cluniac Studies*, Variorum reprints (London, 1980), introduction. One speaks of the spread of the Cluniac order in the sense not of a juridical union but of a loose confederation of monasteries some of which followed a way of life that was more or less parallel to that of Cluny. Constable notes that Cluniac customaries were freely adapted at other houses. Also see G. Constable, 'Monastic legislation at Cluny in the eleventh and twelfth centuries', *Proceedings of the Fourth International Congress of Medieval Canon Law*, Toronto, 1972; (Vatican City, 1976), pp. 151–61.

[39] Giles Constable, 'The monastic policy of Peter the Venerable', in *Pierre Abélard, Pierre le Vénérable*, pp. 119–38; p. 128.

devotional ideals and needs of contemplative monks. But was it? By the end of the eleventh century there were already signs of dissatisfaction. These increased in the twelfth century and Peter the Venerable recognised that many monks were now finding the multiplicity and tedium of the additions to the liturgy 'burdensome and hateful'.

Peter had said that the monk's life was a laborious leisure, *negotiosum otium*:

If the spirit [*animus*] is occupied in prayer, reading, psalmody [*orando, legendo, psallendo*] and other good activities of this genre, then the Rule is followed to perfection since in living in this way it is evident that the monk is not lazy but is a true labourer [*non otiosus sed negotiosus*].[40]

What had once been an alteration of work in the fields with that in the choir had, however, evolved into a liturgical labour and one which seemed to strain the memory beyond endurance. And so it has been argued that Peter the Venerable was put on his guard and interested in liturgical reform well before criticism of the lengthy liturgy from outside, notably from the new Order of Cistercians. He therefore promulgated *Statutes* for Cluny (1146/7) which objected to the excessive display in the processions and additions to the Office. He tried, against considerable resistance from some quarters within the Order, to vary the hymns, making the texts match the ceremonies. He aimed at eliminating the monotony and senseless repetition that some monks had found so burdensome.

But it was one thing to alter custom by practice, another to alter customs by written law.[41] The constitutional uniformity at Cluny did not necessarily imply for everyone a uniformity of daily life. There were men who probably lived outside the written customs, but to inscribe these alterations in written texts as Peter attempted to do, created difficulties for the monastic temperament. And yet one Cluniac author noted that monks in the new Order of Cistercians were able to sleep all night because they had pruned the liturgy. The Cluniacs, however, 'were exhausted by prolonged chants and almost varicose from standing in the choir' and therefore needed a rest after Matins.[42] Some rethinking was needed.

It is not clear whether Peter the Venerable's *Statutes* aimed to restore the old Cluniac liturgy in line with the Benedictine Rule or are to be interpreted as his desire, under outside pressure, to move with the times and purify and simplify the Office. Evidence that his interests were

[40] *Epistle*, I, 28, *PL* 189, 129.
[41] See the comments to Constable's paper in *Pierre Abélard, Pierre le Vénérable*, by A. Bredero, p. 141.
[42] A. Wilmart, 'Une riposte de l'ancien monachisme au manifeste de Saint Bernard', *Revue Bénédictine*, 46 (1934), pp. 296–344; pp. 334–5, possibly by Hugh of Reading.

stimulated by the internal needs of the Order comes from *Statute* I, where it seems he is less interested in shortening the liturgy than in reestablishing its meaningfulness to the monks.[43] Peter seems to have been sensitive to the psychological requirements of a monk's natural memory. And so he regulated pauses in the chanting of the regular hours, thereby establishing a mean between the relatively rapid mode of chanting that was coming into fashion with the vast number of texts to cover, and the very slow, older pace with pauses of two or three 'Our Fathers'. A very fast pace of chant would prevent the desired meditation on words and meaning, turning the liturgy into a mechanical recitation of tedious texts.

Peter the Venerable's problems at Cluny appear to be a microcosm of the problems common to twelfth-century Benedictine monasticism in general. Imprisoned in a liturgical tradition and weighed down by its customs and accretions, Cluny was, at the same time, becoming more responsive to a new society, increasing its charity to the outside world and, through Peter the Venerable himself, was made more sensitive to a world in which an urban-based scholasticism was beginning to flourish alongside a blossoming lay spirituality. Monasticism was becoming increasingly aware of the competing time schemes in which competing memories operated. The new Order of Cistercians would, in particular, take on board all these competing time schemes and competing memories by showing their members how to *blanch* the memory of men's personal pasts within the monastic Jerusalem.

---

[43] Constable, in *Pierre Abélard, Pierre le Vénérable*, p. 130.

Chapter 10

MONASTIC MEMORY IN SERVICE OF OBLIVION

INTRODUCTION

The ninth-century monastic revival of the study of ancient grammatical and logical texts in the service of elucidating scriptural meaning and enriching theology, led to the development of a methodology to investigate the *meaning* of those elements of sacred history held on faith. Events of sacred history, as *credibilia*, were not to be further investigated to determine whether Scripture recorded such memories accurately. Grammatical and logical studies of the *words* of Scripture enabled monks to argue coherently about Christian belief and it was words from Scripture, representing the atemporal, exemplary, universal experiences of mankind rather than personal experiences that they were remembering.

From the eleventh century onwards we have texts once again that can be analysed exegetically in order to determine the role of memory in the monastic milieu as members of this milieu drew together some of the threads of the antique memory tradition, especially as these were discussed in the writings of St Augustine. Ancient memory as discussed in texts and medieval memory as exercised in practice were forged together to produce practical discussions like that of St Anselm and St Bernard. They saw themselves as expounding methods by which the practitioner might transcend the memory of sacred text and the memory of lived life, to achieve the forgetfulness of self in the contemplation of God. The memory store house was a varied collection of paving stones on the path to the kind of knowledge that is atemporal, eternally present, a knowledge that requires for its achievement the forgetting of all those paving stones, all the constituents of the past which comprised the material, experienced world of a man's private past and personality. If memory and understanding require likenesses or images which represent their objects to the soul, the aim of the monastic meditator is to use such images as signs or 'speakings' to attain what is ultimately ineffable and unimageable.

Thoughts formed from memorial images are the representing words or images of the objects of thought. But both conventional language and mental language are incomplete, oblique signifiers of reality. And the monk seeks to transcend all human understanding of what he remembers, knowing however, that he can only do so by means of remembering himself and then meditating on himself as an image of a higher Being which has no image. The final end which the monastic memory was meant to serve was oblivion. But we are focusing on the means to that end, the understanding of monastic memory and its uses. If we ask, what happened to the private man with a personal, even unique past, we must answer that in theory at least, and to some extent in practice, he was forgotten. He was not judged worthy of remembrance by the monastic rememberer who saw individualism as a limitation. That which *was* judged worthy of monastic remembrance was the ideal in the individual, the exemplary, atemporal and universal aspect of a past experience, the useful for the present, the converted past. And St Bernard, in particular, appears to have discovered a method of reminiscence that worked!

But such practical methodologies employed to achieve an understanding of sacred texts which monks remembered and thereafter meditated upon, were founded on a wider anthropology of the soul and its powers. Here a discussion of the classification of the soul's powers derived from Boethian sources which defined three methods for investigating objects of knowledge. The sixth-century Christian Boethius had provided Latin translations and commentaries upon Aristotle's logical works and, most notably, he employed Aristotelian categories in a theological discussion of the trinity. Boethius's logical approach to theological issues was thereafter cited in a variety of later monastic treatises on the soul and its cognitive powers. The ancient legacy of a grammatical and logical approach to certain philosophical issues, like the nature of universals, was thereby kept alive in monastic circles. In this way the role of language as signifying that which we perceive and that which exists, as Aristotle had discussed it in his *Categories* and *De Interpretatione*, enabled monks – whose education had been devoted to grammar and logic in order to read and interpret sacred texts – to raise wider metaphysical questions concerning what there is to be known, and thereafter how the soul knows what there is and remembers it. We shall observe how monks combined an Aristotelian logic with a Platonist ontology to arrive at a division, indeed a conflict between reason and sensuality, a divorce between flesh and spirit. Out of a grammatical and logical education came an anthropology of the soul that was supplemented by ideas found not only in revived and translated Greek neo-Platonist sources, but also as found in the recent translations of

Greco-Arabic medical writings. A sensual memory and an intellectual memory along with their respective objects, would come to be elaborated in the twelfth century in a distinctive way. And this in turn would be integrated back into a peculiarly monastic manner in which the sensual, visible world, literally expressed in a sacred text, could be transformed metaphorically so that God might be remembered and known through his words. The exterior man and his memory would be contrasted with and superseded by the interior man and his powers of reminiscence. The Boethian Aristotle would be read by Augustinian eyes. What, they asked, was the nature of the connection between body and soul, the memory of sensed and transient experience and the memory of immutable truth? Is there an unbreachable disjunction between sense memory and cognitive memory? Yes.

ANSELM

At the Benedictine monastery of Bec-Hellouin in Normandy, Anselm of Aosta (b. 1033) became abbot in 1078. He would, in 1093 become archbishop of Canterbury. Despite heavy administrative duties which these positions involve, he found time to write a series of treatises for the instruction of members of his communities, treatises in which the study of logic and grammar as pursued in the monastic milieu were employed in the service of rationally proving what the monk held on faith. We have already mentioned how, from the ninth century onwards, the ancient logical or dialectical tradition had been enriched, in monastic circles as elsewhere, by its contact with theology. The propaedeutic study of grammar and logic was not seen, especially by Anselm, to rival Christian faith but rather to serve as approved methodologies, either to investigate key events in Christian history – why God became man, or how one might meditate on supreme Being. Anselm himself wrote no exegesis of holy texts.

Many of the ancient logical treatises of Aristotle (his *Categories*, his *De Interpretatione*, Porphyry's introductory study of the *Categories* – the *Isagoge* – along with the pseudo-Augustinian *Categoriae Decem*) had survived, and some had been commented upon by the Christian Boethius in the sixth century. Boethius had also provided translations of Aristotelian logic into Latin, had glossed these, and also had composed short monographs on certain technical aspects of logic.[1] These texts provided monks with the means to analyse holy texts and argue coherently about matters of faith.

---

[1] We shall have more to say about this below, chapter 12, especially on the availability of Boethius's translations in the eleventh and twelfth centuries and the evidence for their use.

157

But logical coherence was less important than truths exposed in Scripture and the Fathers, and in Anselm's writings the use of logic is always contained within a framework imposed by his unquestioned theological aims. His first major treatise, the *Monologion*, is meant as a meditation on certain theological truths without using scriptural authority, in which his simplified discussion of rational necessity would prove and clarify the conclusion from which he starts.[2] Although there are evident echoes of Boethius's second commentary on Aristotle's *De Interpretatione* when Anselm distinguishes between written and spoken signs, heard and contemplated in the mind, it is to Augustine's theory of language that Anselm specifically resorts.[3] And he advises the reader in his preface that before he reads his work he should look at Augustine's *De Trinitate* to understand Anselm's intention. In the *Monologion* (1076), he wishes to investigate and dispute with himself by means of reflection alone, *sola cogitatione*. The subject of the treatise is the nature of conceptual and verbal expression of pre-existent objects of knowledge, the highest of which is the Supreme Being. It is overwhelmingly Augustinian and distinctively monastic in its meditative preoccupations. There is not only a logical development of the argument but a specifically monastic play of verbal associations which lead him from one issue to the next and beyond the text. And it provides a key example of the monastic understanding of signification and expression as these relate to the workings of memory. Anselm seems to have in his memory the arguments presented by Augustine in the *De Trinitate*, and he meditates freely on what is drawn forth from his own memory according to his own, rather than Augustine's, order of associations.

Anselm begins by reflecting that all men seek to enjoy those things they consider good, and that they have the capacity now and again to turn their mind's eye to investigate the source of these goods. By reasoned judgement alone, men can advance to the matters of which they are unreasonably ignorant. We begin by acknowledging that there is a great variety of goods perceived through the senses or distinguished through the mind. Are we then to believe that there is one thing through which all good things are good or that different goods are good through different things?

---

[2] *Anselmi Opera Omnia*, vol. 1, *Monologion*, ed. F. S. Schmitt (Rome, and Edinburgh, 1938–68); Also *Obras completas de San Anselmo*, 2 vols. ed. P. Julian Alameda OSB (Madrid, 1952–3): Anselm of Canterbury, *Monologion, Proslogion, Debate with Gaunilo, Meditation on Human Redemption*, vol. 1, ed. and trans. Jasper Hopkins and Herbert Richardson (New York, 1974). Anselm is aware that he is writing for a reading audience rather than a listening one. See Brian Stock, *The Implications of Literacy: Written Language and Models of Interpretation in the Eleventh and Twelfth Centuries* (Princeton, New Jersey, 1983), pp. 333ff.

[3] See chapter 2, 'St. Anselm', in Marcia Colish, *The Mirror of Language, A Study in the Medieval Theory of Knowledge* (New Haven, 1968).

Adopting the Platonist Augustinian position, Anselm concludes that all good things are good with respect to something which is understood to be identical in these various goods. From there one assents to the fact that there is a Nature which exists through itself and which is the highest of all existing things. Through this Nature all that is, exists. Reason teaches that that which exists through itself and through which all other things exist is the highest of all existences. Likewise, one reasons that this Nature not only exists *per se* but also *ex se*, through itself and from itself. This Supreme Nature or Being existing through and by itself produced from nothing the great complexities of things, and these are harmonious in their diversity. But there is a problem about how something can be caused from nothing. Anselm reasons that before the creation of all the diverse things made from nothing, they were *not* nothing in the divine mind, in the thought (*ratio*) of their Maker. Indeed, the Maker's thought (*ratio*) is an expression of all things. What then is the form of things which in the Maker's thought preceded the creation of things? It is a conceptual expression (*locutio*) of things, but by mental or conceptual expression Anselm says he does not mean the divine *locutio* is a thinking of words which are significative of things. Rather, the divine *locutio* is a viewing mentally with the keenness of thought the things themselves which either already exist or else shall exist. There is then, for Anselm as for Augustine, an antecedent existent, the thing in itself which is equivalent to its divine expression, prior to any word that might signify it.

In ordinary usage Anselm says we can speak of a single object in three different ways. Either we can employ signs which are perceived by the bodily senses; or we can think, imperceptibly to ourselves, these same signs which are perceptible outside us; or we can, inwardly and mentally, speak of the objects themselves by imagining them or by understanding their definitions. He provides the example of speaking of a man when one signifies him by the name 'man' (the first use of bodily perceived signs); or one thinks this name silently (the second, imperceptible use of the same sign outside us); or lastly, one speaks of a man when one's mind beholds him in an image of his body or by means of his definition, i.e. conceiving him universally as a rational mortal animal. Now, these different kinds of 'speaking' of objects of knowledge are to be found in the words of all races. But only the universal conception, the last inward, mental 'speaking' through image or definition, is a natural sign which is the same for all races.[4] All other words have been formulated on account of these natural

---

[4] *Monologion*, ch. 10:
Hae vero tres loquendi varietates singulae verbis sui generis constant. Sed illius quam tertiam et ultimam posui, locutionis verba, cum de rebus non ignoratis sunt, naturalia sunt,

words, these mental concepts. These natural words are, furthermore, truer the more they resemble and the more they expressly signify the objects for which they are words. These natural words, or inward mental images, are more similar to the object for which they are used as words or signifiers in the mind, than any uttered word or thought utterance. Natural words bear a likeness to their objects in the acuteness of the mind as it conceives the object itself. No expression of anything more closely approximates an object than that which is present in natural words and in no one's thought can there be anything else which is so similar to an object, whether already existing or going to exist. Now, if this is true of the human mind's word, then in the case of the Supreme Being its expression of its objects of thought can be seen to have existed before these very objects were created, in order that they might be made through it and once made, known through it. The Supreme Being of Substance spoke within itself all creatures before it created them, and according to its own inmost expression. Only in part can man conceive in his own mind, imaginatively, his creations or any material object. Human mental conceptions derive only from those images or material objects already experienced; for instance, a man can form the concept of the image of some kind of animal which has never existed but he does so only by putting together parts which he remembers from his experience of other objects. These he draws from his memory which stores things known from elsewhere. Therefore, the things made through a craftsman's expression would not exist unless they were something more than what they are through his expression. They have prior being which they owe to the Supreme Being or Substance.[5]

Now, we are capable of considering a rational mind whose nature, quality and quantity is perceived by no bodily sense; indeed we can understand that a rational mind which is subject to the bodily senses

et apud omnes gentes sunt eadem. Et quoniam alia omnia verba propter haec sunt inventa, ubi ista sunt, nullum aliud verbum est necessarium ad rem cognoscendam.
[5] *Monologion,* ch. 11:
Faber vero penitus nec mente potest aliquid corporeum imaginando concipere, nisi id quod aut totem simul aut per partes ex aliquibus rebus aliquo modo iam didicit, nec opus mente conceptum perficere, si desit aut materia aut aliquid sine quo opus praecognitatum fieri non possit .... nequaquam tamen hoc facere valet, nisi componendo in eo partes quas ex rebus alias cognitis in memoria attraxit. Quare in hoc differunt ad invicem illae creatrice substantia et in fabro suorum operum faciendorum intimae locutiones, quod illa nec assumpta nec adiuta aliunde, sed prima et sola causa sufficere potuit suo artifici ad suum opus perficiendum, isto vero nec prima, nec sola nec sufficiens est ad suum incipiendum. Quapropter ea quae per illam creata sunt, omnino non sunt aliquid quod non sunt per illam; quae vero fiunt per istam, penitus non essent, nisi essent aliquid quod non sunt per ipsam.
Compare Abelard, below, ch. 13.

would be an inferior mind. And a mind divorced from bodily senses is, as is the Supreme Being, without beginning or end. It exists in every place and at every time and yet in no place and no time; it is present but not contained; it did not exist in the past nor in the temporal present which we experience, nor will it exist in the future. The Supreme Being cannot be subject to the distinguishing properties and temporal modes of finite and mutable things.[6] Likewise, one might say that the intellect is there in the soul where rationality is. 'There' and 'Where' are spatial terms. But the soul does not contain something within spatial limits, nor is the intellect or rationality contained.[7] Language applied to material entities becomes inaccurate when applied to abstract concepts; that mode of verbal expression that uses spoken, grammatical words as signs, is cognitively incomplete. The truest signifiers are mental concepts or images, natural words. But even these in man's mind are limited when compared with the Supreme Spirit's expression (*locutio*). The Spirit's expression is equivalent to its understanding. For what else is it for this Spirit to speak a thing than for it to understand it? Unlike man, the Supreme Spirit never fails to express what it understands, for its nature is its understanding. The Spirit's expression is, indeed, one word through which all things have been made. This word is not, as in man, the likeness of created things. This word is true existence itself.[8] Created things, however, are likenesses of this true existence. And all the words by which we mentally speak of objects, that is, by which we think them, are likenesses and images of those objects for which they are words. Anselm believes that these likenesses and images in the mind, natural words, are true *in proportion* to the exactness with which they imitate the thing whose likenesses they are.[9] But that Word by which all things were spoken and through which all things were made is not a likeness of its creation. It is, rather, their simple

---

[6] *Monologion*, ch. 22:
Quomodo quoque non est impudentis imprudentiae dicere quod summae veritatis aut locus circumscribat quantitatem aut tempus mediatur diuturnitatem, quae nullam penitus localis vel temporalis distentionis magnitudinem suscipit vel parvitatem?

[7] *Monologion*, ch. 23: 'Nam cum *ibi* et *ubi* localia verba sint, non tamen locali circumscriptione aut anima continet aliquid, aut intellectus vel rationalitas continentur'.

[8] *Monologion*, ch. 31:
Sic quippe verbum summae veritatis, quod et ipsum est summa veritas, nullum augmentum vel detrimentum sentiet secundum hoc quod magis vel minus creaturis sit simile; sed potius necesse erit omne quod creatum est tanto magis esse et tanto esse praestantius, quanto similius est illi quod summe est et summe magnum est ... Non est itaque dubium quod omnis essentia eo ipso magis est, et praestantior est, quo similior est illi essentiae, quae summe est et summe praestat.

[9] *Monologion*, ch. 31: 'Unde necesse est non idem verbum secundum rerum creatarum similitudinem magis vel minus esse verum, sed omnem creatam naturam eo altiori gradu essentiae dignitatisque consistere, quo magis illi propinquare videtur'.

existence. In created things, however, there is not a simple, absolute existence but a meagre imitation of true existence. Thus, every created nature consists of a degree of existence, the higher the degree the more the created nature approximates the Word.

We have seen that for man, every word by which an object is mentally spoken, is a likeness of that object. But then how can the divine word be a word at all if it is not a likeness of its created things? Every word, says Anselm, or every mental image is a word or image of something and had there never been a creature there would have been no word or image of a creature.[10] This may explain the human mind's word but what does it tell us of the Word that is the *locutio* of the Supreme Being? Anselm pushes forward by defining the Supreme Spirit as eternal and as a consequence of its eternity it eternally remembers and understands itself. This is analogous, he says, to the way the rational mind of man remembers itself. But it is better to say that the Supreme Spirit remembers and understands itself according to no likeness but rather principally, and the rational mind remembers and understands itself in a way that is similar but not identical to the Spirit's remembering and self understanding.[11] The Supreme Spirit understands itself eternally and so speaks itself eternally. Whether or not this Spirit is thought of as having creatures or not, its coeternal Word must be with itself. And when it is thought of as having creatures, it speaks itself and its creation by means of one word.

Again, let us consider the way the human rational mind understands itself by thinking itself. It has a mental image of the mind, or rather, the mind's thought of itself is its own image formed according to the likeness of the mind and formed, as it were, from an impression of the mind.[12] This mind then tries as best it can to formulate, either through the sensory imagination or through reason, the mental likeness of whatever thing it desires to think. Now the more truly it formulates this likeness, the more truly it thinks the object. We can notice this especially when the mind thinks of something other than itself – say, a material object. When I think of a man whom I know and who is absent, the sharpness of my thought is focused on the image of him which I contracted into my memory through the vision of my eyes. This mental image is a word or likeness of the man

---

[10] *Monologion*, ch. 32: 'Nempe omne verbum, alicuius rei verbum est. Denique si nunquam creatura esset, nullum eius esset verbum'.

[11] *Monologion*, ch. 32: 'Ergo summus ille Spiritus sicut est aeternus, ita aeterne sui memor est et intelligit se ad similitudinem mentis rationalis; immo non ad ullius similitudinem sed ille principaliter et mens rationalis ad eius similitudinem'.

[12] *Monologion*, ch. 33: 'Nam nulla ratione negari potest, cum mens rationalis seipsam cogitando intelligit imaginem ipsius nasci in sua cogitatione; immo ipsam cogitationem sui esse suam imaginem ad eius similitudinem tamquam ex eius impressione formatam'.

whom I speak of by thinking of him.[13] Anselm has wholeheartedly adopted
Augustine's linguistic espistemology here but in an even more explicit
manner, for perception, remembering and even understanding are
matters of 'speaking', *locutiones*. If we then consider what happens when
the mind understands itself by thinking itself, we (analogously) see that it
has an image of itself begotten from itself as a thought of itself. This image
is formed after the likeness of itself, formed from its own impression of
itself. As in the *De Trinitate*, where Augustine noted that the different
images or forms of perception, imagination, memory, and conceptualisation could only be distinguished by reasoned judgement, because otherwise they appeared so close to one another as to be indistinguishable, so
too Anselm says that it is only through reason that the mind can distinguish itself from its own images. This image of the mind of and to itself is,
he says, a word or likeness of the mind.[14] Likewise, the Supreme Wisdom
begets its own consubstantial likeness, its word. In this sense, its word can
be called its own image, and likeness. But it speaks its creatures not with a
word or image of creatures.[15]

Thus, the Word of the Supreme Being, Spirit, or Wisdom speaks its
creatures as their principal existence; the human mind, however speaks its
mental concepts including its understanding of the Supreme Being, only
in mental, natural words which are more or less likenesses of what is,
ultimately, ineffable. Human knowledge cannot comprehend how the
Supreme Spirit speaks and knows created things. Indeed, created substances exist in themselves very differently from the way they exist in our
knowledge where only their likenesses exist rather than their own being.[16]
Anselm has not gone beyond Augustine. Both thinkers believe that human
words are validated and controlled by objective realities which they are
designed to express and it is clear in Anselm that natural words are not
adequate to that reality because they express only in mental images
without including the objective being of reality. Anselm seems here to

---

[13] *Monologion*, ch. 33:
Cum enim cogito notum mihi hominem absentem, formatur acies cogitationis meae in
talem imaginem eius, qualem illam per visum oculorum in memoriam attraxi. Quae imago
in cogitatione verbum est eiusdem hominis quem cogitando dico. Habet igitur mens
rationalis, cum se cogitando intelligit secum imaginem suam ex se natam, id est,
cogitationem sui ad suam similitudinem quasi sua impressione formatam; quamvis ipsa se
a sua imagine non nisi ratione sola separare possit. Quae imago eius verbum eius est.

[14] *Monologion*, ch. 33.

[15] For a discussion of the image/resemblance theme, see below, chapter 12, and R. Javelet,
Image et ressemblance du xiie s., de S. Anselme à Alain de Lille (Paris, 1967).

[16] *Monologion*, ch. 36: 'Nam nulli dubium creatas substantias multo aliter esse in seipsis
quam in nostra scientia. In seipsis namque sunt per ipsam summam essentiam; in nostra
vero scientia, non sunt earum essentiae, sed earum similitudines.'

imply that mental words are subjective signifiers for the species man who may only come to know, in part, the nature of the signified.

In chapter 48 Anselm picks up the thread of Augustine's arguments in the *De Trinitate*[17] where the Father is referred to as memory, just as the Son is referred to as understanding. And how, he asks, is the Son the understanding of memory, as well as the memory of the Father and the memory of memory? He is recalling Book xv, the last summarising book of that huge work where Augustine speaks of the Father as memory, the Son as understanding and the Spirit as will or love. What are we to believe about the memory? Since we cannot deny that Supreme Wisdom remembers itself, it is appropriate that as the Son is referred to as the Word, so the Father is referred to as memory, for, says Anselm, the word seems to be born from memory. This we may observe more clearly in regard to our own minds. Words, then, especially natural words, are not arbitrary counters but implicit in man's memory. This is not meant to refer to the Augustinian mystical experience when he heard the word of God after he had forgotten himself. Rather, Anselm refers here to an extended notion of the word as signifier taken here as the interior concept. He asserts in this rational meditation which is not meant to pursue the mystic leap into forgetfulness, that although the human mind does not always think of itself it does always remember itself. But when it thinks of itself the word or image of itself is begotten from memory. To think of a thing which we remember is 'to speak' this thing mentally. This thought, formed from the memory and in the thing's likeness is the word or image of the object of thought. By analogy the coeternal Word is begotten from the eternal memory. What begins to be apparent here is that Anselm, like Augustine, is trying to understand the nature of the Supreme Being by a rational analogy with the operations of the human mind. He is not seeking a means by which the human mind unites with the divine mind because he thinks it cannot be sought and attained. Rather, both 'minds' have memories and so each in its own way is a parent of its word. The Supreme Spirit is not, however, in its own memory as one thing is in another, and as is the case with those remembrances which exist in the human mind's memory, where they exist in such a way that they are not our memory itself. Rather, the Supreme Spirit remembers itself so that it *is* its memory whilst the Son is the understanding and wisdom of the paternal memory. The Son is the memory remembering the Father who is memory; Christ is therefore memory begotten from memory.

Anselm presses on to say that the Supreme Spirit loves itself because it remembers and understands itself. It cannot love without remembering;

[17] Augustine, *De Trinitate*, xv, 7.12.

love proceeds from its remembering and understanding. This is instructive, by analogy, of how the monk meditating on his scriptural memory and his mastication of the text in his mind's stomach, his memory, comes to an understanding of what he remembers and thence proceeds to love what is in his memory. But for man the analogy stops short. We often say many things which do not express things precisely as they are. We signify obliquely that which we either cannot or else do not want to express properly.[18] Furthermore, we see a thing not as the object itself but by means of its likeness or image as when we see someone's face in a mirror. The human mind says and yet does not say one and the same thing; we do and do not see one and the same object. We speak and see obliquely. Not only is language as utterance incomplete. Mental language is also incomplete. We do not speak and see in accordance with the respective reality. Anselm says that when he thinks of the meanings of his words, he more readily conceives of what he observes in created things than of that Being which he knows, by faith, to transcend all human understanding. By their respective significations these words form in his mind, something much less than, indeed, he says, something far different from, that towards which his mind, by means of these inadequate meanings, tries to advance in order to understand the ineffable. And yet through this rational apprehension we do understand truly but always obliquely. While it is only the rational mind that can mount an investigation of the divine Nature, it only approximates to it through oblique likenesses. And it is only because we know that the rational mind most nearly approximates to the Supreme Nature through a likeness of natural being, that the rational mind focuses on studying itself. The human mind then is the mirror and image of the Supreme Being and only by beholding itself as an image can it come to know what it cannot see face to face. And the mind beholds itself by remembering itself, then understanding itself and finally loving itself. The monk then must meditate on himself as an image of that higher Being which exists as an ineffable trinity of memory, understanding and love. This generic self-focus is a distinctive characteristic of monastic spirituality and contrasts with the spirituality that would emerge amongst Augustinian canons, mendicants and various lay groups in the twelfth century.

Anselm ends this treatise not only with the encouragement that one know oneself in order to come obliquely to God; but with the rational

18 *Monologion*, ch. 65:
Saepe namque multa dicimus quae proprie sicut sunt non exprimimus, sed per aliud significamus id quod proprie aut nolumus aut non possumus depromere; ut cum per ænigmata loquimur. Et saepe vidimus aliquid non proprie quemadmodum res ipsa est, sed per aliquam similitudinem aut imaginem; et cum vultum alicuius consideramus in speculo.

conclusion that rational creatures ought to desire nothing so much as to express the image impressed on the mind as a natural ability.[19] The expression of the natural mental word is the expression of man's remembered history, less his own personal history than the species' history as recorded in sacred history. Monastic self-expression as a voluntary effect of the image that is impressed on the rational mind as a natural ability, logically takes the literary form of the text, that is, the letter, the meditation, the sermon, the history, in words remembered not from personal experience but from universal experience as expressed and memorised in Scripture and the Fathers. We shall see how this attitude to expressed memory has a special role to play in monastic historical writing.

Anselm's general ideas on theology and religious knowledge clearly derive from Augustine's verbal theory of signs. In many of his other writings Anselm works in the verbal medium of logical argument seeing as one of his major epistemological concerns the theological problem of speaking about God.[20] Like others in the late eleventh century he sought to explain logical relationships in terms of grammatical relationships and he shows himself fully in command of the Augustinian understanding of the function, possibilities and limitations of cognition through words. In his *De Veritate*[21] he speaks of an intrinsic, natural truth in speech. This *veritas enuntiationis*, this natural significative function of a statement signifying truly what a speaker means pertains to all statements even when they are not factually accurate.[22] Augustine also had argued for the true intention of a speaker whose statement none the less may be factually inaccurate.[23] But when a statement is both factually accurate and expresses a speaker's intentions, then the combination of fact and intention constitutes rectitude, the correct relation between the sign and the thing signified. Anselm and Augustine are both concerned to underline that there is a rectitude antecedent to signification; a mode of being and truth that is independent of signs. Antecedent realities are expressed by words with rectitude but in their own terms, without altering or delimiting the objects of knowledge. Therefore, the *Monologion* and the later *Proslogion* provide a method which elucidates the proper attitude by which a technique using words about God can be true and necessary,

---

[19] *Monologion*, ch. 68.
[20] Gillian R. Evans, *Anselm and Talking about God* (Oxford, 1978); D. P. Henry, *The Logic of St. Anselm* (Oxford, 1967).
[21] *De Veritate* in *Anselmi Opera Omnia*, ed. Schmitt, I, xiii, p. 198.
[22] Crucial to Anselm's understanding of meaning is not only what a speaker means but the contrast between signifying *per se* and *per aliud*.
[23] Abelard will also argue for the true intention of a thinker or speaker whose statement might none the less not refer to factual existence. See below, ch. 13.

even though a statement about God is never totally adequate to its subject. Although Anselm, as we have seen, drew on the Augustinian analogy of the formation of concepts in the human mind to explain how created things had an existence in the mind of the Maker before they were made visible, Anselm depreciates the similarities between the operation of man's interior *locutiones* and God's. Man requires materials or images drawn from external sources to formulate his thoughts whereas God is completely original and there is no distinction between his thought and his expression. Because of the identity of the Creator and His *verbum mentis*, man has great difficulty in trying to speak of either. Anselm is therefore forced to shift his focus to human psychology and human cognition because only an understanding of the human process of knowing can provide an oblique understanding of the divine. Thus in all his works the words *ratio, cogitare*, and *intelligere* play important parts.[24]

Specifically in the *Monologion*, he uses *intelligere* to mean *mente dicere*; *cogitatio* is equivalent to *verbum rei ad eius similitudinem ex memoria formata*. *Cogitare* is the creative activity, the generative activity by which the mind proffers its mental word interiorly and constructs a concept. *Cogitare* is a stage in the mind where we have representations or images either of perceived things or absent things reported to ourselves in order to conceive them according to the image registered and stored in the memory. *Intelligere* however, is oriented differently, in that it implies a confrontation between mind and external reality. *Cogitare* then applies to pure thought and it is the word he most frequently uses in his more speculative or doctrinal works. In his correspondence, on the other hand, Anselm uses *intelligere* where the mind is in contact with exterior reality, measuring it and rendering the exterior inward; this is especially true of situations in daily life where one seeks to understand the thought or feelings of others.

The *ratio* of the soul is an activity proper to the mind as is *cogitatio*, but like the *intellectus, ratio* is only exercised through a reference to exterior reality. It judges and validates the truth of acquired knowledge, engendering conviction in the person who uses it. *Ratio* also is used in an objective sense designating the basis of one's conviction, the proof which entails persuasion of some truth, necessarily. *Ratio* is not affected by another source of truth for man, which is faith through divine revelation. Rather, the activity of *ratio* penetrates the reality offered by God which is accepted unconditionally and then is investigated logically. All these mental capaci-

24 Pierre Michaud-Quantin and Michel Lemoine, *Etudes sur le vocabulaire philosophique du Moyen Age* (Rome, 1970), c.viii: 'Notes sur le vocabulaire psychologique de Saint Anselme' (reprinted from *Spicilegium beccense I. Congrès international du ix* centenaire de l'arrivée d'Anselme au Bec* (Le Bec-Hellouin and Paris, 1959)), pp. 151–62. This article is by Michaud-Quantin.

ties are placed in the service of a faith seeking understanding. And as one might expect in a monastic milieu, *memoria* is characterised by its presence in the mind, that which in the act of intelligence seizes the reality immediately offered as image or similitude, be it an image of an existent exterior reality or of one now absent. Memory's activity is in the present regarding images or words interior to mind and Anselm is hardly concerned with the temporal mode of the object imaged. As with Augustine, for Anselm memory is a mental activity in the present rather than of the past. Neither thinker was interested in proving truths concerning faith to man who did not start with the assent of faith. The purpose of monastic meditation, in particular, is to ruminate on memorised truths, seeking to understand them better, for they are already in the memory. Meditation is therefore an activation of an already filled memory. Anselmian meditation is an expression of memory. It is interesting to note that Anselm believes, as did Aristotle, that all thinking is through images, Anselm referring to these images as words. Evidently he has shifted Augustine's linguistic epistemology into a wholly monastic environment of memorised texts and meditated memories, a communication to the self from the self,[25] to be investigated logically.

Texts in the monastic environment are memoranda, aids to the recreation of the experiential process that links man and God through Christ, but where *scriptum verbis* is distinguished from the *verbum Dei*. Texts stimulate man to explore the *limits* of what he can know with certainty, but obliquely, concerning divine truth,[26] and these limits are, for Anselm, open to the logical analysis of signification. Therefore, Anselm's use of linguistic logic shows him to be straddling what would later become the great divide between monastic and scholastic mentalities. He linked a scholastic textual exegesis with a monastic *collatio*. The methodological split would widen in the twelfth century, but we see in Anselm the use of a new method of analysing the logic of language still serving the monastic purpose.

[25] In a private communication, 20 November 1985, Dr Burcht Pranger notes that 'the problem with the *Monologion* is that in spite of its richness, it is rather "abstract". The other works like the *Proslogion* and *Cur deus homo* offer even more opportunities for the application of images. *Cur deus homo*, for example, is a perfect specimen of the way man's memory is trained, purified and developed by means of "forgetting" the focus point of all memory: Christ. In the *Proslogion* man has forgotten himself and in line with monastic memory methods talks and thinks himself back into the vision of himself and God.'

[26] See Brian Stock, *The Implications of Literacy*, pp. 361–2.

Chapter 11

CISTERCIAN 'BLANCHED' MEMORY AND ST BERNARD: THE ASSOCIATIVE, TEXTUAL MEMORY AND THE PURIFIED PAST

Remember thee!
Ay, thou poor ghost, while memory holds a seat
In this distracted globe. Remember thee!
Yea, from the table of my memory
I'll wipe away all trivial fond records,
All saws of books, all forms, all pressures past,
That youth and observation copied there,
And thy commandment all alone shall live
Within the book and volume of my brain
Unmixed with baser matter, – yes by heaven!

Shakespeare, *Hamlet* I.5

Benedictine monasticism was enlivened, enriched, re-thought by the Cistercians in the twelfth century. Much more than the black monks, these white monks set out to live a life detached from contemporary social and economic developments. In theory and practice, early Cistercian abbeys remained self-contained units divorced from ecclesiastical, political–feudal ties, with a unanimity of observance. Theoretically at least, they possessed a clear and detailed uniform code throughout the Order according to which departure from the expressed norm could be corrected by the frequent visitations of abbots. They consciously divested themselves of the accretions of customs to which they believed black monks had needlessly and excessively succumbed. They saw as their primary task the organisation of a self-contained common life for their monastic family centred round labour, reading and prayer, Therefore, they radically shortened the Cluniac liturgy. In the early days, contact with commerce and trade was almost nil. They set themselves up in forests and severed themselves from the manorial system, living meagrely, dressing in course cloth, testifying to their civil and feudal independence which was as complete as their independence of the material world. Originally they had no direct relations with the crown, had no tenants and no jurisdictional

169

rights. Only by the middle of the twelfth century and under St Bernard's influence did they actively seek to submit to their bishop and deny exemptions. However, within a few decades Cîteaux was on its way to fully privileged status, financially and jurisdictionally, episcopal authority being limited through popes granting the Order immunities.[1]

This new monastic Order only recruited adults whose entire lives would totally change under the regime of austerity, hard labour, silence and absolute uniformity which prevailed. Cistercian recruits came in middle life often from successful worldly or ecclesiastical careers. Some had previously been troubadours. Such men posed new and radical problems for St Bernard who took upon himself the extraordinary task of restructuring these men's memories. Bernard would inspire others to see the nature of this new problem: in the thirteenth century, Stephen of Salley (Sawley) wrote a *Speculum novitii* in which he alludes precisely to the need to transform these memories of former worldly living.[2] It was Bernard's genius to have elaborated, especially in his sermons to his community, a method whose psychological acuity won him many hearts and minds.

Returning to the original three divisions of the day as set out by St Benedict, early Cistercian legislation rearranged the Cluniac *horarium* so that during the winter they laboured in the fields between Chapter (following Mass and Terce) and dinner: in the summertime, they either laboured after Chapter which followed Prime, continuing until Terce and Mass; or they laboured after their rest preceding None, making up nearly six hours of work. Harvest time demanded further arrangements.[3] This amount of agricultural labour required that they severely prune the accretions to the canonical office so that their chant was not only shorter but far less ceremonial than that of black monks. And they dropped the second Mass. It is often thought that relations between Cluniacs and Cistercians were strained from the beginning, and certainly by the 1120s.[4]

---

[1] L. J. Lekai, *The Cistercians: Ideals and Reality* (Kent State University Press, 1977), pp. 65–8. Also J. Bouton and J. van Damme, eds., *Les plus anciens textes de Cîteaux: sources, textes et notes historiques*, in *Cîteaux: Commentarii Cistercienses*, Studia et Documenta, II (Achel, 1974).

[2] Edmund Mikkers, ed., 'Un *speculum novitii* inédit d'Etienne de Salley', *Collectanea Ordinis Cisterciensis*, Ref. 8 (1946), p. 45.

[3] Lekai, *The Cistercians*, on the *horarium*, pp. 364–5. Also David Knowles, 'The primitive Cistercian documents', in *Great Historical Enterprises: Problems in Monastic History*, (London, 1963), pp. 197–222.

[4] For a detailed discussion of the enmity between Benedictines and Cistercians one reads the chronicles of William of Malmesbury, *Gesta regum Anglorum* (1122–3) Rolls series 90, Stubbs ed., 2 vols (London, 1889), II, pp. 380–5, and of Orderic Vitalis, *Historia Ecclesiastica* (c. 1133), ed. M. Chibnall (Oxford, 1973), IV, pp. 312–27. Both of these authors were Benedictines. As Lekai and others have pointed out, the problem between Cîteaux and Cluny resulted largely from Cîteaux's geographical proximity to Cluny. 'In Burgundy the

Stephen Harding had thought the Ambrosian hymns of Milan were the authentic compositions of Ambrose and he brought them to Cîteaux where the brethren were to sing only these. Abelard and Cluniacs[5] criticised the Cistercians for abandoning the traditional hymns sung by the whole church. Furthermore, the Cistercians went back to the earlier antiphoner of Metz which they believed to be Gregorian and which was distinctive for its lack of trills (*quilismas*) and they changed the texts and melodies in order to avoid repetitions. By 1134, Bernard was placed in charge of further reforms of the antiphonary, especially suppressing long vocalisations (*jubilus* and *cauda*). He desired that Cistercian chant be 'quite solemn, nothing lascivious or rustic. Its sweetness should not be frivolous, pleasing the ear only that it might move the heart.'[6]

Cistercians also vastly simplified the work of their *scriptoria*, often eliminating artistic copying and illumination of manuscripts.[7] As we shall see, it was the vivid images of the mind rather than corporeal images,[8] that

advocacy of eremitical discipline within a monastic community was taken as a challenge to the mode of life accepted everywhere in the heartland of the Cluniac "empire". The founding fathers of Cîteaux were forced at the outset into a defensive posture. The most effective tactic against the accusation that they were introducing unwelcome novelties was to hold up the Rule as a shield'. (Lekai, *The Cistercians*, p. 23). The debate flared up in 1124 when Bernard attacked Cluny in his widely distributed *Apologia ad Guillelmum*. Also see André Wilmart, 'Une riposte de l'ancien monachisme au manifeste de Saint Bernard', *Revue Bénédictine*, 46 (1934), pp. 296–344. Also David Knowles, 'Cistercians and Cluniacs', in *The Historian and Character* (Cambridge 1963), pp. 50–75.

5 I use the term 'Cluniacs' to refer to the older Benedictine orders that were often loosely connected with Cluny. For a discussion of the terminology, see Giles Constable, *Cluniac Studies*, Variorum reprints (London, 1980), introduction. Also Giles Constable, 'Monastic legislation at Cluny in the eleventh and twelfth centuries', *Proceedings of the Fourth International Congress of Medieval Canon Law*, Toronto, 1972 (Vatican City, 1976), pp. 151–62; p. 153. Even contemporaries were in doubt as to who was and who was not a Cluniac and the term was used loosely. Abelard's criticism in a letter to St Bernard is in *PL* 182, 610–11. For a more modern edition of St Bernard's works now see *Opera Sancti Bernardi*, ed. J. Leclercq, C. H. Talbot, H. M. Rochais, *Epistolae*, 1–180 in vol. 7 (Rome, 1974), and *Epistolae*, 181–310 plus *Epistolae extra corpus*, 311–547 in vol. 8 (Rome, 1977).

6 *Ep.*, 398, *PL* 610–11; *Opera* VIII, p. 378. In general, Bede Lackner SOCist, 'The liturgy of early Cîteaux', in *Studies in Medieval Cistercian History presented to Jeremiah F. O'Sullivan* (Spencer, Mass. 1971), pp. 1–34; p. 16.

7 From the *Summa Cartae Caritatis*, X: 'The books that must not be dissimilar: the missal, the Gospel book, book of epistles, book of collects, gradual, antiphonary, book of hymns, psalter, lectionary, Rule and calendar of saints shall be used everywhere in one and the same way' (Translation in Louis J. Lekai, *The Cistercians, Ideals and Reality*, Appendix, p. 448). The 'charter of charity' is not now believed to have been the fruit of the earliest abbatial conventions but rather came into being after decades of evolution. Although the text was initiated by Stephen Harding, the exact nature of the as yet undiscovered primitive text, its date and the extent of its amplifications, are contested (Lekai, *The Cistercians*, p. 22). Final features of the charter are dated at *c*. 1165–90. For all extant texts, see *Textes*, ed. Bouton and van Damme (1974).

8 *Summa Cartae Caritatis*, XXVI: 'We may not have sculptures anywhere; we may have paintings, but only on crosses; and we may have crosses made only of wood'. Lekai, *The*

would lead these new monks onwards from *lectio* to *contemplatio*. Although the chronology of Cistercian regulations is still confused, it appears that the writing of books came to be forbidden by statute in that no member could write a book without the permission of the general chapter; hagiographic works were not, however, prohibited. Bernard, a prolific writer, often at the request of others and somewhat against his will, mainly wrote letters and sermons; the former he considered substitutes for speaking face to face. In a letter (89) to Ogier, canon of Mont-Saint-Eloi near Arras, he described the mental turmoil he experienced when writing, whereby several phrases jostled for expression at the same time and a number of different senses and ideas presented themselves in a shifting pattern. He stressed how when one was apart from friends, one had to compose what one wanted to say laboriously, and this was different from the ease with which one conversed face to face. The books or tracts that comprise almost half his corpus were composed extraordinarily for special occasions at the request of others. Bernard preferred to speak.

Only towards the end of the twelfth century did such contrived 'illiteracy' begin to alter rapidly,[9] and indeed the library at Clairvaux became one of the richest of all medieval libraries now extant.[10] By the thirteenth century, the revised Antiphoner and Gradual, in which were excised many of the *jubila* of the alleluias, began to give way to more secular fashions. If the purity of the experiment was relatively brief,[11] its ideal of a uniformity of disciplinary and liturgical custom with identical service books for the whole community, maintained by a yearly visit by the

Cistercians, Appendix, p. 450). After Abbot Stephen Langton's death the general Chapter adopted the norms as set out in Bernard's *Apologia*, reaffirming the requirements of the *Exordium parvum*, prohibiting illuminated initials and the use of colours in manuscripts, banning fine bindings and costly decoration of codices. Stained glass windows were also forbidden as were figurative carvings and murals in both churches and monasteries (Lekai, *The Cistercians*, p. 264).

9 Lekai, *The Cistercians* p. 30: 'Instead of purely customary relationships, however, the Cistercian constitution based itself on a carefully worded written law', influenced by the revival of Roman law with its influence, in turn, on ecclesiastical and civil legislation. For the whole *Consuetudines*, see *Nomasticon Cisterciense*, ed., J. Paris and H. Séjalon (Solesmes, 1892), including the *Ecclesiastica officia; Instituta Generalis Capituli* and the *Usus conversorum*. Lekai argues that the formulation of basic principles and norms of life at early Cîteaux as well as the nucleus of the Charter of Charity *preceded* the General Chapters, and the consultative annual conventions of abbots did *not* claim legislative authority. Prior to 1180 they passed no laws. See Louis J. Lekai, 'Ideals and reality in early Cistercian life and legislation', in *Cistercian Ideals and Reality*, ed. John R. Sommerfeldt (Kalamazoo, Michigan, 1978), pp. 4–29; p. 15.

10 Jean Leclercq, *Etudes sur Saint Bernard et le texte de ses écrits*, Analecta sacri ordinis Cisterciensis, IX (Rome, 1953), p. 192.

11 Lekai, 'Ideals and reality', in Sommerfeldt, ed., *Cistercian Ideals and Reality*, notes that the revisionist view is that the downward slide in ideals was noticeable as early as at Bernard's death in 1154.

abbot of the founding house,[12] tells us some interesting things about the direction in which the monastic mentality moved as it culminated in Bernard's attempt to transform other men's minds on the analogy with his own.[13] Clairvaux was for him a Jerusalem joined to that which is in heaven, imitating the life above and sharing spiritual kinship with it (*Ep.*, 64). This was not an original image in monastic circles, but it would take on a special meaning when expressed by Bernard.

Bernard had a past that required transformation. We are told in William of St Thierry's *Vita Prima* that Bernard's mother, who was of a distinguished family related to the dukes of Burgundy, desired that her favourite son be educated. He was sent to a grammar school at St Vorles at Chatillon-sur-Seine, about which we otherwise know nothing. How far his education proceeded in the logical textbooks current in his day, we do not know. But he evidently had a firm foundation in grammar, rhetoric and the development of literary skills which he mastered sufficiently to enable so fine a scholar as John of Salisbury to speak of his preaching and writing style as superb:

Abbas enim, quod ex operibus patet, praedicator erat egregius, ut ei post beatum Gregorium neminem censeam conferendum, singulariter eleganti pollebat stilo, ... Non memini me legisse auctorem qui poeticum illud tanta felicitate fuerit assecutus.[14]

He knew his Latin poets and composed verses of his own. Berengarius, a supporter of Abelard, would later recall in his *Apologeticus* for Peter Abelard that Bernard had written in his youth secular tunes and profane melodies. He asked: 'is it not stamped into your memory deeply that you always strove to outdo your brothers in rhymed verse competitions by means of your facility for inventions? Now you use this ability to compose fictions and fooleries in the service of God'.[15] Bernard's rhetorical ability would be turned, as Augustine's was turned, to convert men to God. For Bernard, the conversion would be more specifically to the monastic life, but he would first have to experience the transition from secular to holy

---

[12] It is well known that evidence for such visitations is rare.
[13] Bernard's *Apologia*, says Lekai, is the best proof that after a quarter century many Cistercians had come to believe that, in the words of an unnamed monk quoted by Bernard, they were 'the only ones with any virtue, holier than everyone else, and the only monks who lived according to the Rule; as far as [they] were concerned, other monks were simply transgressors' Sommerfeldt, ed., *Cistercian Ideals and Reality*, p. 24. Peter the Venerable of Cluny would respond to Bernard, but the debate continued for decades producing nearly a dozen still extant pamphlets.
[14] John of Salisbury, *Historia Pontificalis*, ed. M. Chibnall (Edinburgh, 1956; reprinted with corrections Oxford, 1986), chapter 11.
[15] *PL* 178, 1857.

learning himself. After his mother's death his family encouraged him to pursue his studies and enter the schools rather than the monastery. Instead, he decided abruptly, with thirty companions, many of whom were relatives, to do his monastic novitiate under Stephen Harding at Cîteaux. He had recalled his mother's wishes that he become a monk and he sought a harder life than that offered at Cluny. At the age of twenty-five in 1115, he was offered the abbacy of Clairvaux, and remained its abbot for nearly forty years.

The influence of the writings of Augustine was immense in monastic circles as we have seen. Monastic biblical exegesis consciously followed the method and substance of Augustine, as the monk Rupert of Deutz affirmed when he commented on John's Gospel. Saying that he follows Augustine, he notes that he has been inspired by the Holy Spirit to delight in what he reads and to expound it: 'illa me causa impulit, *quia memor fui Dei et delectatus sum*'.[16]

Drawing on Augustine's *De Trinitate* (x, 11–12, and xiv, 8), he speaks of seeking God through the mirror of his works in which a three-fold image is shown, alluding to Augustine's mental trinity of memory, interior vision, and will, and ultimately to the memory representing the Father where the Son is understanding. Likewise, the converted Hermannus Judaeus, influenced by Rupert, speaks in his Little Book on his Conversion of having chewed over the matter in the stomach of his memory.[17]

Monastic discussion of the moment of perception of truth, in which the process of truth is made plain in the innermost mind, relied on Augustine's exposition. All this is commonplace. But what is of greatest importance in Augustine's influence, was his method of reading scriptural texts a-temporally. Leclercq has rightly argued that 'practically the whole Bible is a book of images' having at least two meanings:

Whatever may be the precise signification – about which there was never any unanimity – to be given to words such as symbol, allegory, typology, or parable, it is certain that, since, through the history of a given people and in connection with it, the main concern was to narrate the history of universal salvation, any image first conjured up something different from what it actually designated. This ability to interpret everything symbolically was greatly developed in the monastic milieu of the high middle ages and doubtless also among clerics and, though probably to a lesser extent, among the laymen'.[18]

---

[16] *Ep., Nuncupatoria, PL* 169, 201–3.
[17] *De Conversione Sua* (Hermannus Judaeus), ed. G. Niemeyer, *MGH*, Quellen, 4 (Weimar, 1963).
[18] Jean Leclercq, *Monks and Love in Twelfth-Century France* (Oxford, 1979), p. 34.

The cloister, in which a closed and regulated living tradition was structured by the divine office and public and private reading, assured that biblical texts were constantly heard and memorised along with the spiritual interpretations of the Fathers. Such a regulated life ensured that a limited number of images invoked a maximum number of symbols which evoked common 'realities'.

In the early Cistercian *Ecclesiastica Officia* (*c.* 71)[19] silence was imposed, *except* for those learning antiphons, hymns and the content of the Gradual. For such monks it was permitted that they ask other brethren to hear them as they practised reciting what they had memorised. They were forbidden to ask questions, except concerning the length of the syllables and accentuation in reciting. Men with private histories, of love, sex, marriage, knightly warfare, involvement in the world, memorised biblical texts which were detailed and symbolic concerning human and divine relationships, but which mentioned love only as a means of spiritual union of God with his people. On the basis of these spiritualised experiences, men with private pasts learned to evoke from the store house of their altered memories texts and symbols whose literal sense was perhaps sensual, but whose overriding meanings were allegorised so that they were able to think of and derive pleasure from quite different realities of which the biblical images were symbols.

The Cistercian liturgy, renovated by 1147 under the guidance of Bernard, placed even greater emphasis than did others on lyrical antiphons which were inspired by the Song of Songs, a series of highly erotic poems whose literal meanings were, none the less, virtually never expounded as such. If the Song of Songs was interpreted allegorically by all commentators (except for one northern French rabbi of the thirteenth century), then its entry into the divine office lectionary, and the Cistercian increase in new antiphons taken from the Song, led to nuptial and erotic events being frequently on monks' lips. But they recalled spiritual symbolism where the bridegroom is Christ and the bride, the church. Bernard was to go further and associate the bride and bridegroom with the relationship between God and the human soul. This allegorisation of sensual fact for men with elaborated sensual past histories and experiences attempted to edit out empirical fact by replacing visual and literal images with ideas. Bernard is eloquent on just how this is achieved in his sermon, *De Conversione*, as we shall see. Geoffrey of Auxerre, who had

---

[19] The *Ecclesiastica Officia*, *c.* before 1154; the earliest draft is dated 1130. See Bede Lackner, 'Early Cistercian Life as described by the *Ecclesiastica officia*', in Sommerfeldt, ed., *Cistercian Ideals and Reality*, pp. 62–79. The texts are in *Textes*, ed. Bouton and van Damme. Also *PL* 166, 1446.

been won over by Bernard's preaching 'on conversion' to Paris scholars in 1140, wrote a commentary on the Song of Songs in which, as Leclercq noted, he praises the bride in nothing but symbols. 'There is not a single visual image ... all we have is ideas, hardly any images, or even none at all ... What could easily have become the most realistic description [of love-making under an apple tree] is the one which is least imagined and even the least "seen". Nothing is eroticized ...'[20]

Cistercian authors are not reticent about how this may be achieved. Another of Bernard's 'catches', for he was said to be a fisher of souls and caught many fish whenever he preached, was William of St Thierry. In his *Golden Epistle*, written for the Carthusians of Mont-Dieu, William stresses the importance of the regular habit of reading *consistently* a single work until it is mastered. What he means by mastering a work is the concentration on an author until his very habit of expression becomes so familiar as to become one's own, it having entered into the reader's mind. David's Psalms he says, must be read so that the experiences out of which they were written are made the personal experiences of the reader. This can only be done if the text's words are committed to memory daily so that one can ruminate on this text without it being before one's eyes.[21]

As Augustine had said, one would not understand an author if the experiences he described were not somehow analogous to one's own. But thereafter, if one memorises the author's experiences and his language in describing them, one comes to store in one's own memory the textual images, the reflection on which by *higher mind*, de-temporalises and universalises the images. The final significance of such experiences is provided by the interpretation of higher mind, measured against unchanging truths.

Like Augustine, Bernard believed man to be a social animal, requiring a community setting for him to come to know his inner self. But the monastic experience further emphasised the communal personality of the monk, where the brethren not only lived as one, but where each individual was seeking freedom from the limitations of his private past and his individuality. As in the Benedictine Rule, the role of the abbot is to ensure the destruction of the individual will in his monks, the abbot representing the common observance over and against personal judgement. Bernard was a master in teaching the means of converting private memories into communal, universal ones and he did so by drawing on sensual and

---

[20] Leclercq, *Monks and Love*, p. 56. The famous Cistercian hymn, *Dulcis Jesu Memoria*, is a good example of a great affective poem almost entirely devoid of precise images. Text in *The Oxford Book of Medieval Latin Verse*, ed., F. J. Raby (Oxford, 1959), pp. 347–53.

[21] *Ad fratres de Monte Dei*, I, xxxi, 120–2; *PL* 184, 327D.

military experiences of his individual converts to show the higher, spiritual meaning in all of these individual experiences. The individual must be surpassed and transformed. He knew that whatever the origins of his mature monks, most of them continued to maintain some interest in the literature of chivalry and courtly love, along with remnants of their own personal memories of adventures as knights-at-arms.

Thus it is no matter for astonishment that the aggressive images conveyed by such literature should be a mine of associations and potential motivation. This is possibly why St Bernard at the beginning of his long and splendid exposition of the Song of Songs insistently compares monastic life and asceticism to military service and the community to a militia doing battle for the king.[22]

These images were not only chivalric but also biblical and patristic and therefore, suitable to the monastic mentality.[23] And Bernard's parables often took the form of romances in which the story of God's love unfolds by means of images and metaphors of feudal life and chivalric institutions. As Leclercq says:

we may easily imagine the interest that the monks as ex-knights gave to such parables; perhaps there was a certain tension too, as nostalgia alternated with whimsical joy and delighted amusement at finding again in spiritual theology, in the Bible and even in God himself, qualities and attributes explicable in terms of symbols and images from a way of life still so fresh in their memories.[24]

Bernard evoked these chivalric and romance images from his own memory of his pre-monastic experiences to draw the minds of his similarly formed monks away from the world of literal experience. And he did so because his memory was flooded with biblical images that served to transform personal experience by the activity of higher mind's understanding. The operation of his memory was like a living concordance where he was able to explain one verse by another in which the same word occurs. Clearly, he had memorised much of the Bible.

The Bible called 'St Bernard's Bible' exists in a manuscript of Clairvaux library (2 volumes, now conserved at Troyes, 458) with marginal notes. It is a highly ornate manuscript with beautiful writing and it is believed to have been a gift, not produced at Clairvaux, but a precious item which Bernard used in common with his monks. But the notes, few as they are,

---

[22] Leclercq, *Monks and Love*, pp. 90–1.
[23] See the Prologue (2–3) to the Benedictine Rule: 'Ad te ergo nunc mihi sermo distinguitur, quisquis abrenuntians propriis voluntatibus, Domino Christi vero regi militaturus oboedientiae fortissima atque praeclara arma sumis'.
[24] Leclercq, *Monks and Love*, p. 92.

are not now believed to be Bernard's. Bernard is known to have written more often on wax tablets when he was inspired. The pages of the Song of Songs appear to have been often handled and the lessons are numbered for conventual lectures, the liturgy, or refectory readings.

If 'Bernard's Bible' tells us nothing of his manner of working and thinking, we must turn to contemporary testimonies, hagiographical though they often are. And we can learn something from the redactions of Bernard's works themselves. His sermons come down to us often in two forms where we cannot be certain as to which was anterior, the brief or the more extended form. The sermon *de conversione ad clericos*, exists in an abbreviated form.[25]

The brief version is not merely an abridgement of the longer version. It is believed that the longer and shorter sermons represent two redactions of the same sermon and a comparison of the two texts suggests that the brief text is a *reportatio* of the sermon as it was spoken; the long text, a literary reshaping which develops from the 'oral style' of the original. The addition in the longer version is not so much on conversion but a tract on the unfortunate morals of contemporary clergy. The longer version looks to Leclercq like an attempt to rework the sermon into a kind of treatise, *De Moribus clericorum*. As with the case of the sermons on the psalm *Qui Habitat*, the manuscript tradition can help us to understand how Bernard's oral preaching, when set down in literary style, underwent not a progressive corruption of an original text which was originally perfect, but rather, a progressive re-using of the same text for different audiences and diverse purposes.[26]

We shall never know precisely how Bernard preached, but we can learn something about how he did so in certain cases. Although most of his sermons have been preserved, his oral sermons were never written down; on the other hand, his written sermons may not have been preached. The sermons written down were not written by Bernard himself, according to Bernard's own testimony and that of two of the devoted recorders of his words – Nicholas of Clairvaux and Geoffrey of Auxerre. In 'destructuring' some of the written sermons one can see the repeated use of certain formulae and re-employed themes. And certain sermons can be dated by the reference to liturgical texts appropriate to the time of year on which Bernard then provides a commentary. The *De Conversione* is a case in point where the textual references to Christmastide show how Bernard's

---

[25] MS. Engelberg 34, *Analecta monastica*, I, pp. 124–35. Text in *Opera Sancti Bernardi*, IV pp. 61–7, introduction.
[26] Leclercq, *Recueil d'Etudes* (Rome, 1966), pp. 75–6.

mental categories and language were stamped with the Bible and the prevailing liturgical season and readings.[27]

His oral style varied according to his auditors. His written styles vary not only according to genre but according to the means by which his notaries took down what he said. He preached to the people in vernacular, but addressed his monks in Latin. But even when he spoke in Latin to his monks, some of whom were certainly not cultivated latinists, he appears to have used a Latin that was close in grammar and vocabulary to that of the vernacular.[28] He was, however, a master of skilled rhetoric, capable of addressing the learned clergy in a high style that would be appreciated. Geoffrey of Auxerre called him *litteratus apud eruditos*. But his brief sermons and his parables show a more familiar, less artificial Bernard. If we wish to know how he taught we must look here and at the testimony of his notaries, rather than at his great literary sermons. In the former, his commentaries on the Bible with reference to monastic life are flooded with a language of sensual experience, of smells, tastes, colours, of picturesque, familiar and homely images. He would begin with the familiar and draw one on to the inner mind's understanding so that the familiar was left behind.[29] His commentaries on the Song of Songs were not addressed to the intellect but to the heart, experience, senses. He sought by means of a passionate language to foster the *sense* of heavenly life. The personal nature of his sermons on the Song of Songs was meant to relate to the monastic experience, assuming a claustral, perfect, even celestial life amongst his auditors, inspiring reminiscence which would culminate in that final reminiscence, lost to fallen man but made possible for the monk. Practised in the *ars grammatica*, he used literary fiction as did Augustine, to render through artistic rather than natural means, a way to express the truth; this could be done more easily through memorised, and therefore spontaneously evoked, rhetorical devices which lead on to concording verbal reminiscences.

St Gregory the Great had said that to dissemble (*fingere*) was the same thing as to compose (*componere*). The composition of monastic history and the recollection of biblical history was an edifying experience in which

---

[27] 'Isaiah ix, 6 (vigils for Christmas and antiphon of Lauds and introit of the third mass on Christmas day; Isaiah xl, 5 (third reading at vigils for Christmas); hymn *Hostis Herodies* of the feast of Epiphany; Wisdom xviii, 15, used in antiphon *Omnipotens* of office of the fourth Sunday of advent and in the Sunday office within the octave of Christmas and in the introit of the mass *Dum medium silentium* of the same day. See the introduction to Bernard's *Sermons on Conversion*, trans. Marie-Bernard Said OSB (Kalamazoo, Michigan, 1981). See Leclercq, *Etudes*, pp. 185–201, for context.

[28] Christine Mohrmann, *Etudes sur le latin des Chrétiens* (Rome, 1961), 3 vols. Also G. R. Evans, *The Mind of St Bernard of Clairvaux* (Oxford, 1983), pp. 104ff.

[29] Leclercq, *Etudes*, pp. 73–80.

there was no interest in the past for its own sake. The religious implications of events and the recollection of events in a saint's life were
considered only from the standpoint of their religious, a-temporal implications. Bernard would be primarily concerned to evoke the ideal in the
individual in order that a past experience could be remembered only as an
exemplum, made comprehensible and useful to men in an environment
radically different from that in which the experience had its origins.
Bernard believed that until man comes back to God through a graduated
climb from the sensual to higher understanding, he wanders in a realm of
unlikeness, a *regio dissimilitudinis*, and is in exile.[30] The passage from
dissimilitude to similitude was, for Bernard, an epistemological process
which began in the senses and transcended them, replacing bodily feelings
not with intellection but with a tasting in and of the mind. The most
perfect way to convert the past and all that was and is exterior and
sensually perceived, was, for Bernard, to become a monk. Conversion for
Bernard is to choose the monastic cloister, to flock to the city of refuge,
the monastery, where one can do penance for the past.[31]

In the first of his sermons on the Song of Songs, Bernard begins by
reflecting on how one speaks to someone who has chosen the cloister and
the Rule: 'to you my brothers I must say something different from what I
say to others, to those in the world, or in any case, I must say it in a
different way'. He would prepare what he had to say to his monks in his
mind or by writing on wax tablets where, as Arnaud de Bonneval said, he
restored to the wax the sweetness of the honey deposited by bees:
'Dictabat vir Dei, et non-numquam scribebat in tabulis cereis, mella
restituens, et quidem gratiora prioribus, non patiebatur perire inspirata
sibi divinitus.'[32]

But to those who were clerics rather than monks, he had to be more
explicit, outlining an epistemology which they could understand without
having had the monastic experience. He draws dramatically on Augustine's method but reinterprets his themes in a new key. Bernard delivered

---

[30] R. Javelet, *Images et ressemblance au XIIᵉ siècle de S.Anselme à Alain de Lille* (Paris, 1967).
Also P. Courcelle, '"Tradition néo-Platonicienne et traditions chrétiennes de la "region
de dissemblance"', *AHDLMA*, 24 (1957), pp. 5–33. Augustine, *Confesssions*, VII, x;
When first I knew Thee, Thou didst lift me up so that I might see that there was
something to see, but that I was not yet the man to see it. And Thou didst beat back the
weakness of my gaze, blazing upon me too strongly, and I was shaken with love and dread.
And I knew that I was far from Thee in the *region of unlikeness*, as if I heard Thy voice from
on high: "I am the food of grown men: grow and you shall eat Me. And you shall not
change Me into yourself as bodily food, but into Me you shall be changed" (Trans. Sheed,
p. 113).
[31] *De Conversione*, 37.
[32] *Vita Prima*, II, viii, 51; *PL*, 185, 298; Also Leclercq, *Etudes*, p. 185.

his sermon 'on conversion' in Paris to students sometime in 1139–40, probably during Advent. This text tells us how important Bernard thought the memory to be and he goes far beyond Augustine's teaching to make his distinctively monastic point.

For Bernard, all past events are to be censured. The memory stores up in its secret recesses the remembrance of past evil deeds, either our own or those of others. For Bernard, man's memory is stained. It can only be purified by living the word which forgives sins. Augustine's treasure house of memory has become a sewer for Bernard. The belly of Bernard's memory is congested with filth. The soul has to make reparation with the senses which have been the cause and occasion of sin. And it must do so while man is alive because after death there is no sense and no body. So we must set to work now through the spiritual custody of the senses. The senses have been the doors through which death, sin and vice have seeped into our souls. But even when we recognise this, our will does not always follow our reason. Hence the attraction of the monastery. Monastic life eliminates self-will; it ensures that one is forbidden to do one's own will. The soul, protected in the monastery, seeks to purify the memory. But even when the outward temptations have been eliminated by moving into the cloister, the memory remains so tainted that the source of evil is still within the soul. The heart of the struggle then, is to purify the memory from its stains; it must be blanched.

The first step is to listen to the inner voice of God speaking to you (*De Conversione* I, 2). We have no difficulty in hearing God's voice; the difficulty is rather in stopping our ears from hearing it. Bernard speaks of God's voice as mighty and also as a beam of light which informs men of their transgressions and illuminates things hidden in darkness. Like Augustine, he argues that the substance of the soul is spiritual and single in nature, seemingly devoid of distinctions in its senses and yet it sees and hears. The beam of God's light opens the book of our conscience so that the wretched sequence of our lives passes in review. God's beam of light unfolds the sad events of our history and enlightens our reason. Our memory has been set before the eyes of our soul. Both memory and reason are not so much faculties of the soul, he says, but the very soul itself, as observer and observed. The soul as memory is dragged before its own assizes to be judged by its own thought (II, 3). Augustine, we recall, had described how the interior vision was turned on the memory to illuminate what was stored, emphasising the activity of inner perception guided by the will, to search in the treasure house of memory. Reason then judged what it found there, but for Augustine, not all in the memory had entered by the gates of the senses.

181

Bernard insists he does not know what is in each individual memory to be recalled; our own reason detects individually what is there to censure, judge and sentence. And he cites, as did Augustine when he asked 'how does anyone know what I say to be true', the same biblical phrase that no one knows what is in a man, except the spirit of the man which is in him.[33] He continues to describe how in each individual, the memory is a cesspool of sensuality. He makes no mention of it also housing principles which are eternal and measured against immutable truths.

Even though all the itching of evil pleasure quickly passes and any charm of sensual satisfaction is short-lived, still it *stamps* on the memory certain bitter marks; it leaves filthy traces. Into that reservoir, as into a sewer, all these disgusting and dirty thoughts drain off. The stomach now endures bitterness ... wretched man! my stomach aches! How could the stomach of my memory not ache, when it is crammed with so much filth?

Going well beyond Augustine by narrowing the memory to that store house not of personal identity but of sensual gratification, Bernard says that our flesh is the corruptible garment with which we are clothed – asserting thereby that personality, the self, is the soul enshrouded by a garment to be doffed if only one knew how (III,4). This worldly and sensual garment prevents the soul from knowing itself, from remembering itself. 'Is it any wonder that the soul should feel her own wounds so little when she has forgotten who she is and is inwardly estranged from herself?' (IV,5).[34]

The soul will only come to herself after death has closed all those physical doors by which she used to go out seeking the figure of this world which passes away ...[35] But it will be a sorry homecoming, for though she repents she will not be able to do penance because where there is no body, there is no activity and no satisfaction either. (IV, 6).

So we must come to ourselves before physical death or we shall be left with a soul that mirrors the state of the body, its crimes eternally punished but never purged.

Extending Augustine's image of perceptions entering through bodily windows, Bernard more dramatically says that it is through the person's windows that death has entered, consisting in wantonness of eyes, itching of ears, the urges for gratifying touch, taste and smell. Because a man who is so tied to his sensuality is still 'carnal', he has greater difficulty recognising his spiritual vices which are the more serious. He will be less afflicted by his pride and jealousy than by the memory of the more

---

33 *Conf.* X, iii.   34 Compare Petrarch below, chapter 23.
35 Compare Cicero, *Tusculan Disputations*, I, xix–xx and see above, chapter 3.

notorious and sensual deeds he has performed (IV, 7). The remedy is 'to close the windows, lock the doors, block up the openings carefully and then, when fresh filth has ceased to flow, you can clean out the old' (VI, 8). Yet the strict new decrees of a monastic lifestyle which 'close the windows and lock the doors' by removing temptations, will cause the senses and the will to rebel, and Bernard runs through a series of superbly theatrical outbursts voiced by the various senses (VI, 9). In the long run, sensual distress enlightens the reason, enabling it to recognise how difficult it is to achieve one's intentions to 'close the windows'. The reason sees the memory clogged with dirty things, says Bernard, and it sees more and more bilge still flowing in. It seems incapable of closing the windows thrown wide open to death. The will, though ailing, still spreads the infection of her festering wounds. The soul recognises that it is contaminated and that this contamination springs from its own body, from itself. The poison is something in the soul, as the memory which is tainted, and as the very will which is perverse. The soul, says Bernard, is nothing but reason, memory and will; but in its ailing state, its reason is greatly reduced. It discovers how foul and fetid is the memory and that the will is sick (VI, 11).

This is a reworking of Augustine to an extraordinary and personal degree; for where Augustine blamed the will, Bernard blames both the will and the memory.[36] Bernard's claustral version of Augustine's epistemology locks out all the advantages of the senses as the true but temporary means towards higher meaning. For Bernard, the sensual images are all frivolous; he asks 'what use are they to the soul? ... a curious man is an empty man, curiosity bringing frivolous, vain, fleeting consolation, proved by the transitoriness of these pleasures' (VI, 14). Where Augustine insisted that sensual experiences were often required for knowledge and understanding, Bernard has focused entirely on that other prong of the Augustinian argument that asserted the autonomous realm of truths already in thought, the realm of similitudes with the divine word in one's interior

---

36 It is as though Bernard's understanding of the faculties of the soul places memory in the lower soul, without creating its doublet, the higher memory in which immutable truths are housed as well. E. von Ivánka argues that in effect, Bernard's schematic structure of the soul varies incessantly. 'Ce flottement de formules– qui ne désignent jamais des facultés distinctes de l'âme mais seulement des états différents, des attitudes diverses', distinguishing only the two 'arms' of the soul: knowledge and love. Unlike Bernard's contemporaries, there is a general absence of Greek elements of the soul in Bernard's writings. See E. von Ivánka, 'L'union à dieu, la structure de l'âme selon S. Bernard', *Analecta sacri ordinis Cisterciensis*, 9 (1953) = *S. Bernard Théologien*, Actes du congrès de Dijon, 1953, pp. 202–8; pp. 206–7. It must also be noted that Augustine's clear but complex structure of the soul is very eclectically employed by Bernard for his own purposes. Clearly he was not ignorant of Greek arguments nor of Augustine's, but used these as he required them without a slavish adherence to either.

vision. Bernard, likewise, tells his audience of Parisian scholars that the reason suggests inwardly to the will all these and similar things, more insistently *as it is perfectly instructed by the light of the Spirit* (XI, 22). But reason's suggestions to the will may be insufficient for the will may be deaf or callous. In what follows, Bernard outlines precisely how the soul may be enticed: promised spiritual delights are expressed in sensual language, the language of love, of gardens, refreshment, sweet odours and tastes. He treats the soul as a sensing organ but capable only of spiritual pleasure: thus, he tells his auditors that spiritual delights will include eating the bread of angels, discovering a paradise of pleasure planted by the Lord; the soul shall discover a flowering and thoroughly lovely garden, a place of refreshment (XII, 24). 'You must not suppose this paradise of inner pleasure is some material place' he warns. 'You enter this garden not on foot but by deeply-felt affections' (XIII, 25). From romance poetry and the poetry of Scripture (the Song of Songs), rather than from patristic theories of intellection, Bernard depicts earthly beauties of an enchanting copse of trees, but then says it is *not this* that will be seen *but* a garden of spiritual virtues, an enclosed garden with a sealed fountain flowing out into the four streams of paradise. 'There too the most splendid lillies bloom and as these flowers appear, the voice of the turtle dove is also heard'. He is associating one scriptural text with another, a courtly image with its biblical, spiritual similitude. Perfumes and aromatic oils abound. And 'in the midst of the garden is the tree of life, the apple tree mentioned in the Song ...' (XIII, 25). 'There one's nostrils inhale the exquisite scent of hope, of a rich field which the Lord has blessed.'

Bernard is not describing the heavenly Jerusalem. He is telling Parisian clerks that the mind's craving for the satisfaction of its spiritual senses is available here on earth in that other Jerusalem, the monastery. He says: 'But these are not yet the rewards of eternal life but only the wages paid for military service; they have nothing to do with the future promise made to the Church, but concern rather her present due'. The tastes, smells and sights of the monastic Jerusalem are not held out as mystic leaps but as the rewards of a psychological conversion, of a purged memory. That other vision is ineffable and Bernard says: 'do not hope to hear me sing the praises of all that. That is revealed through the spirit alone, and you will consult books to no avail.' The monastic delights must be experienced. You can taste it in the monastery and unless you taste it, you shall not see it. Bernard is, in effect, telling these Parisian scholars that they have chosen not quite the right way. For learning, he says, does not teach the wisdom he has been describing, but God's anointing teaches it; not science but conscience grasps it. And the sewer of the memory must be purged before this can be experienced (XIII,25).

Once the will has been turned and the body subdued to service, a third and very serious step remains to be taken; and Bernard describes just how the memory is to be purified and the bilge water drawn off. This may seem impossible. To any reader of Augustine, to cut one's life out of one's memory would be to destroy one's very self. Precisely.

Bernard responds to the question: 'how am I going to cut my life out of my memory?' by reminding us that 'the dark ink has drenched my cheap, flimsy parchment. By what *technique* can I blot it out? It is useless for me to attempt to rub it out: the skin will be torn before the wretched characters have been effaced. Forgetfulness might perhaps efface the memory if, for example, I were touched in the head and did not remember what I had done' (recall Pliny). 'But to leave my memory intact and yet wash away its blotches, what penknife can I use?' Bernard answers that the only 'penknife' is that living and effective word, sharper than a two-edged sword, and that word says: 'your sins *are* forgiven you'.

Bernard does not believe he has devised a technique of memory purgation. Rather he says it is God who speaks to him through the word of Scripture, for God devised the whole way of discipline, giving it to Jacob and to Israel, and afterwards he appeared on earth and lived among men. Bernard interpreted St Benedict's Rule not as an innovative human scheme, a technique, but God's discipline already exposed in Scripture. The technique offered in the monastery is no less God's discipline. Christ's forbearance wipes away sin, 'not by cutting it out of the memory, but by leaving in the memory what was there causing discolouration, *and blanches it thoroughly*'.

When Augustine said that he turned his interior vision towards his memory he could recall past sorrow without feeling any of the attendant emotions. Bernard says that when God, the word of forgiveness, blanches the memory, we then may remember many sins which we know to have been committed by ourselves or by others, but only our own sins stain our memories. But if the word takes away damnation, fear, confusion, then God's forbearance takes all these and our sins away so that they no longer harm us. Instead, they work together for our good, reminding us to offer devout thanks to him who has remitted them (XV,28). Once again, Bernard is not speaking of the promise or even the hope of remission. He who tastes of the spiritual paradise he has described, experiences that merciful remission of sins. And once you have begun the process by groaning for penance, remembering to drench your bed with weeping, the peace eventually, gradually comes. The peace of a purged memory and a denial of self will, leads not to a focus on oneself as unique, but on the contrary, towards one's neighbours (XVI, 29). And when one has acted in one's life according to the similitude of divine remission of sins, thereby forgiving the trespasses of others, restoring what you have fraudulently taken, giving alms, then 'not only is the reason enlightened and the will straightened, but the memory too is cleansed so that you may now call upon the Lord and hear his voice say: blessed are the pure in heart for they shall see God' (XVI, 29). Bernard is not describing what those eternal disembodied souls of the saved will experience but, rather, the vision at the end of the monastic discipline. He cites the apostle John: We are now God's children. It does not yet appear what we shall be, but we know that when he appears we shall be like him, for we shall see him as he is (I John iii,2). The transference of an earthly to a heavenly city of God, one Jerusalem for another, each united with the other through a spiritual similitude and kinship, is not the abrupt moment of self-transcendence described by Augustine as a rare, even momentary ineffable self-forgetting, from which one would fall back to the words of one's mouth, falling back into personal, private memory. Bernard's monk seems to have trained himself to an habitual loss of self, distinguished by a purged memory and a capacity for remembering only the universal experiences of the sensual delights of Scripture. Augustine had decided upon a course of fasting and prayer in order to re-experience a mystic unity with God. Bernard's monk cannot quite be described as experiencing a 'perpetual' mystic leap. Rather, he has converted his psychology so that no leap is required; the process is a graduated progression. Bernard says 'let no one imagine he is cleaned up right away, once he has emptied out the bilge water of his memory'. Perhaps not right away, but Bernard is assuring his audience that it does happen, one day, and in this life, within the cloister. Converted souls thereafter dwell in a perpetual communion with God, hearing his voice inwardly, that is, hearing his word through the words of Scripture memorised (XVII, 30).

Linguistically, Bernard has worked a transformation in the future tense. Augustine may have said that there was only a present of things future, with tenses existing artificially in grammar. But Bernard actually transformed a tensed grammar into a vehicle that gave much greater weight to a converted present. The past and future for Bernard seem quite extraordinarily flattened into a present that is only initially internally distinguished by a graduated progression towards a foreseeable and attainable goal. The past is to be purged, censured; the future is, in effect, to be realised as a similitude through discipline. The monastic method of scriptural exegesis, of reminiscent, near random associations of texts through verbal concords, along with allegorical interpretation of these texts, was so thoroughly absorbed by Bernard that it seems to have rendered his own extraordinary psychology tenseless, even when he still followed the rules of the artificial *ars grammatica* which prescribed the use of tenses. The penknife required to excise the blotches stained into one's memory *is* the word: 'your sins *are* forgiven', rather than, your sins shall be forgiven!

Augustine never believed that any monastery, any church, would succeed in being a coherent city of God on earth. The members of that true city could only be pilgrims, unique in their election to salvation. No true commonwealth could exist cohesively within history. Bernard's monastic ideal, however, *is* the city of refuge. With this sermon *De Conversione* Bernard convinced Geoffrey of Auxerre to take refuge with him.

If secular clerks needed reminding that their memories were sewers, monks did not, at least not to the same degree or in the same way. So that it is in his writing meant exclusively for his monastic community, writings that often had an oral origin but whose written transformation is our only recourse to his method, that we may observe Bernard exercising his concording, associative memory and inspiring his brethren to do so with him.

At the beginning of Sermon 54 on the Song of Songs, Bernard says that he will give a different interpretation from that offered yesterday. He says he need not repeat his first interpretation because he is certain his monks have not forgotten it so quickly. But if some parts have been forgotten, 'scripta sunt ut dicta sunt, et excepta stylo, sicut et sermones ceteri' – 'it has been written down as it was preached except for the style, just as have been written the other sermons'. Leclercq has argued convincingly that Bernard's notaries did not take down his orally delivered sermons while they were being delivered, word for word. The twelfth century had lost the Tironian notation that permitted a kind of stenography in antiquity, and no system of abbreviations existed which permitted the exact transcription of a delivered talk. The *Brevis Commentatio in Cantica*, once doubted as a genuine work of Bernard, is now thought to provide a true echo of Bernard's teaching, probably less elaborate than his actual oral style but far less literary and digressive than his written sermons. A close study of the written sermons shows a mixture of passages, some more theologically nuanced than others and thought unlikely to have been presented orally in this form. Other passages still have the sound of the spoken word.

Sermon 22, 'On the four ointments of the bridegroom and the four cardinal virtues', allows us to examine if not the sound of his spoken word, at least something of the way his mind progressed as he commented on the verse. He begins by saying that

if the ointments of the bride are as precious as you have heard them portrayed, then how much more exquisite are the ointments of the bridegroom. Some of you may want to say – stop praising these gifts and explain them. But no, I make no such promise. For believe, me, I have not as yet decided whether I ought to express all the thoughts that suggest themselves.

Bernard then goes on to give his opinion that the bridegroom has a plentiful stock of perfumes and ointments. And their odours are the better sensed 'the more one is assimilated to him by a virtuous life and an upright will.' The soul's sensitivity is intensified to receive the fragrance of Christ's perfumes. One senses them with the nose of the soul rather than with the corporeal senses. 'In matters of this kind', he says, 'understanding can follow only where experience leads.' He is not referring to those whose senses have become subtle to the tastes and smells of the world. Rather, he says he will titillate the senses of the soul by drawing from 'public sources':

I shall even pay myself a mild compliment in this matter, for no small effort and fatigue are involved in going out day by day to draw waters from the *open* streams of Scripture and provide the needs of each of you, so that without exerting yourselves you may have at hand spiritual waters for every occasion, for washing, for drinking, for cooking of foods.

You understand what it is to draw water, to cook food, but this is transformed by the word of God, Scripture, because 'the word of God can cook the raw reflections of the sensual man, giving them a spiritual meaning that feeds the mind rather than the belly'.

Not all of Bernard's auditors in the monastery were learned men, or even men who had achieved a spiritual ascesis. Far from disapproving of those who have purer minds and who are therefore able to grasp sublimer truths less actively linked, even in images, with the senses, Bernard says he admires them, congratulates them. But he is speaking to 'simpler souls' and so his doctrine must be simpler. He wishes that his monks were indeed without need for this scriptural exegesis which draws them on from sense to understanding. 'How I wish that all had the gift of teaching: I should be rid of the need to preach these sermons! It is a burden I should like to transfer to another, or rather, I should prefer that none of you would need to exercise it, that all would be taught by God [interiorly] and should have leisure to contemplate God's beauty.' But this gift does not come at the beginning. A monk must have the Scripture in his own mind so that he need not hear Bernard's exposition or even read the text. He would then be able to mount beyond the images of the words to their spiritual significance.[37] But, Bernard says, 'I am a man and describe God to men according to the human form that he adopted in order to reveal himself with the maximum of esteem and love; I present him as attractive rather than sublime, as God's appointed servant and not as a remote deity.'[38] Thus, he offers what he has received from a common source, Scripture, the Song of Songs, for the common good.

Bernard proceeds by insisting that every person is free to pursue the thoughts and experiences, however sublime and exquisite, that are his by special insight on the meaning of the bridegroom's ointments. His own method is to take up a set of issues that are evoked by scriptural texts on the four streams of wisdom, righteousness, holiness and redemption, which he says may be considered either as water or as perfume. The Church was devoid of the power to run in the odour of her Solomon until Christ appeared. Although in the beginning was the word, the shepherds only began to run when Christ's human birth was announced. Before that, while the word remained solely with God, they did not, they could not, stir.

Bernard then goes on to treat rhetorical objections: 'but you will say – I cannot see how he could have brought redemption to the angels'; he treats of a four-fold anointing with the oil of gladness; and returns to the theme of 'perceiving' the fragrance by asking:

what excuse can anyone have for not running in the fragrance of your perfumes except that the fragrance has not reached him? the gospel has been spread, so that he who fails to perceive this life-giving fragrance that permeates all places must be either dead or corrupt ...

But all of us do not run with equal passion in the fragrance of all the perfumes – some are more eager for the study of wisdom, others concentrate on works of penance, others reflect on the memory of his Passion.

[37] As Dr Burcht Pranger, Theologische Faculteit, University of Amsterdam, has said in a private communication, 'memorising is turned into a collective, social event or rather, structure. The very structure of collective memory provides the opportunity for endless variations as a prolongation, so to speak, of memory. Hence, the fundamentally open character of the text as a result of the almost materialistic way in which it is structured'. I owe much of the inspiration for this chapter in particular, to numerous discussions with Dr Pranger whose insights into Bernard's method and meaning are, to my mind, unrivalled.

[38] Dr Pranger also points out that there is a complexity and subtlety in Bernard's notion of 'audience'. In reality his monastic audience consisted of simple minds not capable of appreciating the subtleties of high rhetorical style. But one knows that Bernard was also writing for *litterati* both within and outside the monastery. His starting point is in matter, *caro* and memory. But at the same time the monk is supposed to be *expertus* as Bernard indicates at the beginning of the first sermon on the Song of Songs, *expertus* in the monastic experience. And it is insufficient to take Bernard's remarks on the reactions of

Bernard wishes that his monks reflect on and enjoy the fragrance of *all* the four ointments, of wisdom, righteousness, holiness and redemption, but not in a manner that arouses a curiosity concerning the manner in which they are made or the number of ingredients they contain. Such a knowledge is infinite, eternal, unique and inexplicable. 'The wise of the world have multiplied arguments about these four virtues to no purpose.' Only those who have been imbued with Christ's teaching have had their sins pardoned through mercy, who follow his disciplined way of life and who are patient, and from no other source, can anyone strive to acquire Christ's virtues. Bernard has slowly shifted from the spiritual odours of the bridegroom to a monastic analysis of the four cardinal virtues. Interwoven with the verse from the Song of Songs are verbal associations to other scriptural passages, Bernard moving in ever-widening concentric circles of exegesis until he ends by linking the four ointments of the bridegroom with the four cardinal virtues.

Bernard was not a natural logician in the mould of Anselm although some have thought him to have been in control of much of the same basic technical skills.[39] But Bernard's skills issued from the grammatical and rhetorical education he received rather than from anything more than an amateur knowledge of the new methods of speculative logic just then emerging from the urban schools. Much of his method owes most to Augustine supplemented by the monastic experience of scriptural reminiscence, an experience that exercised the soul's senses more than its intellect. He had no love of philosophers who tried to elucidate divine mysteries through rational arguments. He said, when he was forced to confront the great dialectician Abelard at Sens, that he was a mere child in such matters (*Ep.*,189) and had been called out into the public arena of disputation, to a dialectical joust, when he was hardly prepared. In fact, his lack of preparation is shown when, on his own testimony, he says that the night before his public confrontation with Abelard, he simply extracted *capituli* from Abelard's works; at the meeting before various bishops and scholastics, he simply did what he did to Scripture, commented on these extracted chapter headings out of context. This is what he knew how to do, but scriptural words were never out of context for him. Abelard's method of analysing Scripture was not only deeply unfamiliar to Bernard but he also saw it as an unfortunate development which would not lead to the kind of conversion he saw necessary for men. And even had he wished to employ the highly technical aids to interpreting textual inconsistencies in

his monks literally since at the same time they are part of the overall rhetorical self-presentation of Bernard at the moment, e.g. at the arrival of guests.
[39] Evans, *The Mind of St Bernard of Clairvaux*, p. 92.

Scripture, much of the material available to the next generation (for example, Peter the Chanter) was simply not yet accessible to him. When he addressed himself to scriptural inconsistencies, as in his *Sententiae*, III, 31, where he compares Paul's statement (Philippians i, 23–4) 'I *long to be* ... with Christ', and Christ's own words in Matthew xxviii, 20: 'I *am* with you until the end of the world', Bernard called upon the teaching of Augustine. He explains that in one sense we *are* with Christ in this world, through contemplation, but in the next we *are to be* with him in a different way, in actual presence. 'Thus both texts speak the truth.' Augustine, we recall, had treated exactly this issue in his *Confessions* and arrived at the same conclusion: 'the truly religious thing to say is – why should he (Moses) not have meant both if both are true'.[40]

This is not a simplified theory of signification as found in the work of the early logical schools' *disputatio* (*pace* Evans). Nor can we assert that Bernard had an up-to-date theory of logical fallacies, nor any theory at all, when he speaks of the 'fallacy of life'.[41]

Bernard plays with the words *fallacia vitae* rather than discusses any technical difficulties in resolving fallacies. His concern with words was always practical, illustrated in his preaching, and one might say he studiously ignored any discussion of the technical principles of disputation because he did not see these as having any role to play in his monastic epistemology. He discouraged disputation for its own sake (sermon *De Conversione* and Sermon 22), and adhered far more closely to Augustine when he mentioned in his *In Laudibus Virginis Matris*, IV 11,[42] that 'if something is said after the Fathers which is not against the Fathers, I do not think it ought to displease the Fathers or anyone'.[43]

Bernard was first and foremost a monastic preacher whose goal was to inspire his monks to *meditatio* and then *contemplatio* in the protective refuge of the monastic Jerusalem. He was concerned to live an experience of God and to share it with his brethren. His eighty-six sermons on the Song of Songs, begun in 1135 and still unfinished at his death, stand as the supreme example of his monastic method which cauterised the memory and yet stimulated it by replacing private memorials with scriptural reminiscences, which he saw as the very discipline of a converted life. In this sense, he was the last great spokesman of many monastic generations.

---

40 Augustine, *Confessions*, XI, xxxi. See above, ch. 6.
41 *Sermones Diversi*, I, *Opera*, VI, i, pp. 73, 3–7; See Evans, *The Mind of St Bernard of Clairvaux*, pp. 94–6.
42 *Opera*, IV, p. 58, 5–9.
43 William of St Thierry said of Bernard's exposition that it was imbued with the Fathers. See his *Vita Prima*, I, iv; *PL* 185, 241.

Chapter 12

TWELFTH-CENTURY CISTERCIANS: THE BOETHIAN LEGACY AND THE PHYSIOLOGICAL ISSUES IN GRECO–ARABIC MEDICAL WRITINGS

... the anatomist is primarily concerned with the study of the brain as the material substratum of mental processes. No more than the physiologist is he able to suggest how the physico-chemical phenomenon associated with the passage of nervous impulses from one part of the brain to another can be translated into a mental experience.

> W. E. Le Gros Clark, 'The structure of the brain and the process of thinking', *The Physical Basis of Mind*, ed. P. Laslett (Oxford, 1950), p. 24.

It matters a great deal whether mind is regarded as something which is distinct from and which animates the body – or whether the word is thought of as a generic term to cover such processes as feeling, thinking, remembering, perceiving and so on. If mind is conceived of as something which interacts with body – or as some parallel manifestation to body – the scientist may be misled into trying to solve problems which may prove unreal, e.g., I'm not convinced about the validity of the proposition, raised by Professor Le Gros Clark, that some parts of the brain have the special function of transforming measurable electrical impulses into consciousness ... If mind is a verbal cloak for processes of perceiving, abstracting, reasoning – how far can these processes be explained in physical terms? ... But because we humans use symbolic language our own memory also works independently of immediate environmental control. No one knows the physical basis of this particularly human capacity.

> S. Zuckerman, 'The mechanism of thought: the mind and the calculating machine', in *The Physical Basis of Mind*, ed. Laslett, pp. 25–8.

At the centre of Bernard's theological interests was the theme of the human soul and its longing for God. His interest in a theological anthropology reinforced the more widespread concern to construct a human psychology based on a classification of the soul's powers that developed during the twelfth century in non-Cistercian circles. Initially, however, the centre of interest (as expressed by disciples of Anselm of Laon) lay in the question of man's moral activity within the rather simplified framework of a battle between flesh and spirit, categorised under the name of two faculties: reason and sensuality. Each led either to good or evil through the mediating operation of the free will. But when problems were posed that were not specifically moral, authors had recourse to a list of four cognitive faculties as found in the sixth-century author Boethius: sense, imagination, reason and intelligence, the last being transcendent and somehow separated from the other three.[1] Boethius had little to say about the operations of memory which he subsumed under imagination.[2]

We have not previously elaborated on the importance of Boethius's writings and translations because the memory was of little consequence to him, especially in his theological treatises known later as the *opuscula sacra* of the monastic schools: *De Trinitate*, *De Hebdomadibus*, *Contra Eutychen et Nestorium*. Boethius had proposed three correlative methodologies for investigating the objects of knowledge based on his division of speculative science into physics, mathematics and theology. Physics deals with motion and is not abstract or separable, being concerned with forms of bodies together with their constituent matter. We investigate it *rationabiliter*. Mathematics neither deals with motion nor is it abstract, since it investigates forms of bodies apart from matter, although forms cannot really be separated from bodies; thus the mathematical concepts are systematical (*disciplinaliter*). Theology does not deal with motion and is abstract and separable. We investigate theology using intellectual concepts (*in divinis intellectualiter*). He says we deal with each speculative science in terms of its objects, as they actually are. 'Thus in theology we should not be diverted to play with imaginations but rather apprehend that form *which is pure form and no image*, which is very being and the source of being. All being is dependent on form.'[3]

Boethius's *opuscula sacra* served as teaching texts in the Carolingian schools at Aachen and at Tours. It was his logical approach to theology that attracted great interest. As standard texts in monastic libraries into the twelfth century, they were cited seriously in various treatises on the soul.[4] Scotus Eriugena and his intellectual heirs, the masters of Auxerre, Haimo, Heiric and Remigius, also used these Boethian texts. Eventually the commentaries on the *opuscula* from Auxerre became practical guides to

---

[1] In general, see the magisterial study by O. Lottin, *Psychologie et morale aux xiie et xiiie siècles*, 6 vols. (Gembloux, 1928–60). Also, P. Michaud-Quantin, 'La classification des puissances de l'âme au xiie s.', *Revue de moyen-âge latin*, 5 (1949) pp. 15–34. Boethius, *De Trinitate*, II, PL 64, 1250. See also Boethius, *The Theological Tractates with an English Translation*, H. F. Steward, E. K. Rand and S. J. Tester (Loeb editions, 74) (London, 1978), pp. 8–13.

[2] See below, chapter 13.

[3] *De Trinitate*, II, Loeb edn, pp. 8–11. The sources for Boethius's theological treatises are Augustine and Proclus. See Luca Obertello, *Severino Boezio: La Consolazione della Filosofia: gli Opuscoli Teologici* (Milan, 1979).

[4] For example, Ratramnus's *De Anima ad Odonem*, written *c.* 865. See above, pp. 146–8.

terminology and were used elsewhere alongside the *logica vetus*, serving as the only means of keeping theological issues alive within a curriculum that was largely devoted to grammar and logic.[5] As these works became theological set texts, the Boethian vocabulary set the boundaries of many discussions of the soul's cognitive capacities.[6] It is here in Boethius's writing that one sees the tension between an Aristotelian logic and a Platonic ontology at odds, a tension that would increase into the thirteenth century when more of Aristotle's works became available in Latin translation. By the thirteenth century, the *opuscula* appear to have been dropped as set texts in the universities. They were replaced by far more subtle and elaborate cognitive theories as we shall see. But it is of some interest to review aspects of the earlier monastic curriculum in greater depth, in order to see how the initial interest in grammatical and logical texts of antiquity came to inspire an interest in certain philosophical problems that would dominate all later discussions: of universals, of essence, and of categories. The focus was, therefore, more on imagination and its images than on the memory.

Not only was Boethius's *opuscula sacra* an important influence on early medieval thought about logic, but even Augustine's *De Trinitate* was mined as an important source for a discussion of categories. The late fourth-century pseudo-Augustinian *Categoriae Decem*, the most widespread text used to study the categories was, in fact, a summary of Aristotle's *Categories* with commentaries and glosses which added much that was of interest to early medieval thinkers. Here, Aristotle was taken to be concerned with a discussion of things that are perceived and such things arise from what exists; furthermore one could not discuss them without the aid of language. But if Aristotle's interest was taken to be in that which is signified rather than in that which signifies, the *Categoriae Decem* adds considerably to discussions of purely linguistic points.[7]

These additions were of special importance, as we should expect, in later milieux that were largely interested in teaching reading and writing according to classical grammatical and syntactical rules.

Aristotle's first category is Substance or Essence by which he means 'the composite individual': for him, substance is neither said *of* a subject nor is it *in* a subject. Substance is not separable. However, this was used

---

5 Margaret Gibson, 'The *opuscula sacra* in the Middle Ages., in *Boethius: His Life, Thought and Influences*, ed. Margaret Gibson (Oxford, 1981), p. 222.

6 Gibson, 'The *opuscula sacra*', p. 220. N. Häring, *Commentaries on Boethius by Thierry of Chartres and his School*, Studies and Texts, 20 (Toronto, 1971); N. Häring, *The Commentary on Boethius by Gilbert of Poitiers*, Studies and Texts, 13 (Toronto, 1966).

7 John Marenbon, *From the Circle of Alcuin to the School of Auxerre; logic, theology and philosophy in the early Middle Ages* (Cambridge, 1981), pp. 21 ff.

as a basis for medieval metaphysical speculation, one interpretation going so far as to state that substance meant 'an uniquely differentiated *substrate* to which *accidents* were *added*'. Boethius provided an interpretation of Aristotle's *Categories* that shifted the meaning further into a Platonic mode. Concerned to stress that Aristotle was interested in the names of things, not as words that were subject to grammatical rules, but only insofar as they denoted objects, Boethius was reflecting on Aristotle's belief that things in the world can be known as they are and that words are true symbols of extralinguistic items. But even where Porphyry's *Isagoge* (c. 272–305) – his Introduction to the *Categories* – treats Aristotle as dealing with the *nature* of things, the early medievals seem to have had difficulty with Aristotle's understanding of this nature whereby form and matter were inseparable. Cicero had, as we have seen, already emphasised the dichotomy between body and soul. With further help from Boethius and the neo-Platonist circle which influenced him (for example, Ammonius [440–520] was his teacher), early medieval thinkers turned Aristotle's notion of a composite nature into a Platonic dualism of matter versus spirit, each with distinct characteristics.[8] It is this tradition that continued into the early twelfth-century conflict between reason and sensuality.

During the ninth and tenth centuries, Substance came to be treated either as a *genus generalissimum* with no superior genus, as in Boethius's translation and commentary on Porphyry[9] or it came to be treated as a substrate sustaining those accidents which comprised the world of appearances. Early monastic authors were relying on a Platonic theory of universals. Although Boethius attempted to assert the primacy of individuals over universals, the latter having no real existence, his own Platonic ontology surfaced in the *opuscula*. Here, he argued that concrete

---

[8] The story is more complicated. From the early fourth to the sixth centuries, writings that were both pagan and Christian dealt with an anthropology that would influence twelfth-century writers. It has been argued that although Plotinus dramatically influenced Augustine, the treatise of Porphyry (now lost) on the *Return of the Soul* – see fragments in J. Bidez, *Vie de Porphyre le Philosophe néo-platonicienne* (Gand, 1913) – was of possibly greater influence. Those texts that survived into the twelfth century included Chalcidius's *Commentary on Plato's Timaeus* (early fourth century), Martiannus Capella's *The Marriage of Mercury and Philology* and the *Commentary on the Dream of Scipio* by Macrobius, all of which provided an eclectic use of neo-Platonism prior to Boethius. It should also be noted that it was Porphyry who reinstated the categories in Platonic philosophy where they had already found a place among the Middle Platonists who adopted them but perhaps without a full consideration of the implications. See J. Dillon, *The Middle Platonists* (London, 1977), pp. 276ff. Also see the entry by Sten Ebbesen, 'Ancient scholastic logic as the source of medieval scholastic logic', in *The Cambridge History of Later Medieval Philosophy*, eds., N. Kretzmann, A. Kenny and Jan Pinborg (Cambridge, 1982), pp. 101–27; p. 106.
[9] *PL* 64, 42, 103.

individuals owe their existence as specific things to their *forms*. When he distinguishes between form and matter he says that he is not really speaking of forms but of images of the true forms which exist outside matter. 'For from these forms which are outside matter have come those forms which are in matter and produce a body. We misname the entities that reside in bodies when we call them forms since they are mere images, for they only resemble those forms which are not incorporate in matter.'[10] *Nam ceteras quae in corporibus sunt abutimur formas vocantes, dum imagines sint. Adsimulantur enim formis his quae non sunt in materia constitutae.*

Furthermore, in running through the ten categories which can be universally predicated of all things, Boethius employs a negative theology in arguing that 'it is otherwise, of course, with God',[11] the categories applicable to man being either inadequate or inapplicable to God who is not a subject at all. The stark contrast between terms applied to created nature and those inadequately or inappropriately applied to God would be, along with a form-matter dualism, the Boethian legacy in monastic circles and beyond. The progress from grammar and predication to a speaking about God as a trinity in one God in the Boethian texts, set the agenda for all those following the traditional grammar education and pursuing it in a theological context.

Boethius had said that he was inspired to write his *De Trinitate* by the seeds sown in his mind by Augustine's writings.[12] Books v–vii of Augustine's *De Trinitate* were crucial to Boethius's interests in applying the Aristotelian categories to a theological discussion of the trinity. When Alcuin(?) came to write the *Dicta albini de imagine dei* (before 791, Munich passages, vii)[13] he too used Augustine's *De Trinitate* for his own purposes, to elaborate on the place of images in Christian worship. This was, doubtless, a response to the ongoing iconoclast controversy between eastern and western churches.[14] The Munich passages (Munich clm

---

[10] *De Trinitate*, Loeb edn, 74, pp. 12–13.   [11] *Ibid.*, IV, Loeb edn, pp. 20–1.

[12] *Ibid.*, prologue, Loeb edn, 74, pp. 4–5.

[13] Marenbon, *From the Circle of Alcuin*, p. 44.

[14] Pope Hadrian commissioned a Latin translation of the Greek *acta* of the seventh oecumenical council of 787. It was made in Rome, 788–9 and sent on to the Frankish court. Here was defined what was to be the correct Christian approach to holy images. Iconoclasm was deemed heretical and penitent iconoclasts received back into the Church. The reaction of Carolingian scholars, against the imperially dominated 'oecumenical' council and against Hadrian's own acceptance of the decisions of this eastern synod, was expressed in the *Libri Carolini* which defined an independent Frankish theology. See Ann Freeman, 'Carolingian Orthodoxy and the Fate of the *Libri Carolini*', *Viator*, 16 (1985), pp. 65–108. It is debated whether or not Alcuin took a large proportion of responsibility for this work since he was away in York during 790–3. See Luitpold Wallach, *Diplomatic Studies in Latin and Greek Documents from the Carolingian Age* (Ithaca and London, 1977), collected studies, especially pp. 43–287. The Frankish intellectuals did not admit that

6407) in which one finds the *Dicta albini* may be divided according to subject matter: on the trinity, the demonstration of God's existence, on the ten categories, and exercises in syllogistic method. While the divided subject matter tells us what interested Carolingian intellectuals besides grammar and logic, the reliance on Augustine helped to focus a contemporary theological and political controversy, that of iconoclasm, sharpening their thinking on the nature of images and more specifically on the meaning of Genesis i, 26: 'faciamus hominem ad imaginem et similitudinem nostram'. The *Dicta albini* included Augustine's teaching from which Alcuin adopted the parallel between the persons of the trinity and the human mind's *intellectus, voluntas* and *memoria*. Alcuin differs from Augustine, however, in contrasting the two terms of the Genesis text: *imago* and *similitudo*. For Augustine, it was not open to man to attain a likeness to God by good behaviour as it is for Alcuin. Alcuin is primarily concerned with the *distinction* between an innate image of God in man and man's capacity to attain a likeness to God. Here, Alcuin seems to be drawing on the fifth-century Platonist Claudianus Mamertus's *De statu animae*.[15] For Claudianus and for Alcuin, there is a distinction between the trinitarian image that man has imprinted in him by nature, and the divine resemblance or similitude he acquires by his own merits, that is, by the operation of free will and grace. Only similitude is voluntary.

Alcuin's borrowing of Augustine's image of the trinity excludes much of the complex psychological discussion surrounding it. But he does note that the *image* of God is had in the memory whereas something other is meant by similitude. He argues that just as God the Father, God the Son and God the Holy Spirit are not three gods but one God having three persons, so too we speak of an *anima intellectus*, an *anima voluntas* and an *anima memoria*, not as three souls in one body but as one soul having three *dignitates*.[16] The more one loves the creator, the more is he intellectually known and held in the memory. But it is insufficient to possess an intellectual knowledge of God without it being had *in amore ejus voluntas*. Therefore, each dignity of the soul strengthens the other, memory added

icon veneration posed a serious problem but they proposed a *via media* between the two extremes of iconoclasm and iconophilism. They insisted, as had Gregory the Great, on the pedagogic function of images in faith but no veneration of the profane, unconsecrated materials of images. And where icons may be used as a means of instructing the laity the scenes depicted were to be correctly identified in writing, 'since words are superior to images'. *Libri Carolini*, 2.13, *PL* 98, 999–1248; *Libri Carolini sive Caroli Magni capitulare de imaginibus*, in *Concilia aevi Karolini*, MGH Legum sectio 3, III supplement II (Hannover and Leipzig, 1924), p. 30. For the general background, see Judith Herrin, *The Formation of Christendom* (Oxford, 1987), pp. 389–439.

[15] *PL* 53, 699–777; also ed. G. Engelbrecht, CSEL, 11 (Vienna, 1885).
[16] This is a pseudo-Augustinian idea to be found in Cassiodorus and others.

to will and intellect. The similitude with God, on the other hand, has to do with morality. He who has more virtues is properly or strictly closer to God, *tanto proprius est Deo et majorem sui conditoris gerit similitudinem....*[17]

This interest in the image of God in man on the one hand and man's similitude with God on the other, would persist in twelfth-century, largely Cistercian but also Benedictine, Cluniac circles.

The Platonising tendences of earlier monastic works based on the Boethian tradition were supplemented, especially in the twelfth century, by renewed interest in Eriugena's translations of the pseudo-Dionysius, Maximus Confessor and Gregory of Nyssa, and by what has been called Eriugena's 'attempted marriage of Plotinus and the Gospel'.[18] As a result they placed particular emphasis on the *divorce* between flesh and spirit, body and soul, reason and intelligence, intelligence and God. Such post-lapsarian dualism could only be restored to unity by God's grace. This *divortiumque animi et sensus* dominated twelfth-century accounts. The difficult pseudo-Dionysian writings did not speculate on the part of the soul by which man may eventually unite with divinity. But late fifth- and sixth-century neo-Platonist philosophers, writing commentaries on Aristotle's *De Anima* had sharpened the Aristotelian account into one which separated the irrational from the rational soul. This strict dichotomy was not present in Aristotle's account (*De Anima*, III, 4) where, as we have seen, he moves in a more ambiguous way, using the language of potentiality and actuality, from discussing imagination to a discussion of thought. He argues that thinking is akin to perceiving and that it is reasonable to suppose the intellect should not be mixed with body. The faculty of sense perception is not independent of body whereas intellect is distinct. 'And yet perceiving is like mere assertion and thought; when something is pleasant or painful, the soul pursues or avoids it, as it were asserting or denying it. To the thinking soul, images serve as sense perceptions ... hence the soul never thinks without an image' (*De Anima* III, 7).

Much more so than Aristotle, the neo-Platonists John Philoponus,

---

[17] 'Dicta albini super illud Geneseos: faciamus hominem ad imaginem et similitudinem nostram' (*PL*, 100, 565–8).

[18] Jean Déchanet, *Guillaume de Saint-Thierry aux sources d'une pensée* (Paris, 1978), p. 27. The ignorance of Greek in the fifth-century Roman church had caused Pope Gelasius (492–96) to call upon the translation efforts of an eastern monk Dionysius exiguus (= pseudo-Dionysius) who translated eastern hagiographical works as well as Gregory of Nyssa's *On the Condition of Man*. Such translation efforts were directed towards matters of Christian theology rather than ancient learning. See Herrin, *The Formation of Christendom*, p. 86. For an excellent discussion of twelfth-century Platonism and its sources, see Tullio Gregory, 'The Platonic inheritance', in *A History of Twelfth-Century Western Philosophy*, ed. Peter Dronke (Cambridge, 1988), pp. 54–80.

Stephanus of Alexandria and Simplicius were preoccupied with allocating the soul's faculties and activities to higher and lower sections. The neo-Platonist distinction between the rational soul and sensation was based on the Platonic model of the soul *using* the body as a tool or instrument, and they assumed in their commentaries on Aristotle that he must be speaking in terms of a detachable soul. Believing in a harmony between Aristotle and Plato the neo-Platonists provided the material for an enduring tension between Aristotelian logic and Platonic ontology already evident in Boethius's works.[19]

It is not clear to what extent these Greek neo-Platonists were known in the twelfth century beyond Eriugena's translations of pseudo-Dionysius, Maximus, Gregory of Nyssa[20] and Boethius's exposition of some of their doctrine, for example, of separation or abstraction. A certain knowledge of Plotinus seems likely. But the views of the Greek neo-Platonists would surface in the writings of Arabic philosophers who used the neo-Platonised Greek tradition to affirm a harmony between Plato and Aristotle, and Arabic writings would seriously influence thirteenth-century Latin theologians for whom many more such texts had become available in translation. What is significant for the twelfth century is the neo-Platonist emphasis on the separation between sense and reason, lower and higher mind. By contrast, what was required for a more sophisticated understanding of the memory was an anthropology in which memory could lead on progressively and continuously to higher mind and therefore, a theory that linked rather than divorced sense and interpretation in a continuum. In other words, what was required was another look at Aristotle where the soul is the form of the body. Boethian and neo-Platonist interpretations had to be moved into the background by the neo-Aristotelianism of the thirteenth-century scholastics. As we shall see, Abelard would show signs of moving in this direction already in the twelfth century.

During the twelfth century, Chartrains like Thierry and Clarembald of Arras faithfully reproduced the Boethian list of four cognitive faculties. Only in his *Commentary on the Timaeus* did William of Conches add to these four the powers of *ingenium*, memory and opinion, showing the influence of Latin rhetorical theory as well as following the newly trans-

---

[19] Henry Blumenthal, 'Neo-Platonic interpretations of Aristotle, on *Phantasia*', *Review of Metaphysics*, 31 (1977), pp. 251–2. Also Henry Blumenthal, 'John Philoponus and Stephanus of Alexandria: two neo-Platonic Christian commentators on Aristotle', in Dominic J. O'Meara, ed., *Neoplatonism and Christian Thought* (Albany, New York, 1982), pp. 54–63; pp. 55–6. H. Blumenthal, 'Neo-Platonic elements in the *De Anima* commentaries', *Phronesis*, 21 (1976), pp. 72–83.
[20] See J. T. Muckle, 'The doctrine of St. Gregory of Nyssa on Man as the image of God', *Mediaeval Studies*, 7 (1945), pp. 55–84.

lated works of Arabic physicians.[21] But he did so in a general manner that provided little opening for a discussion of the soul's higher powers.[22] In his *Dragmaticon* William of Conches provided a philosophical synthetic analysis of medical and Boethian theories. Gradually, however, Cistercian authors in the twelfth century also began to be preoccupied with a number of physiological issues taken from Greco-Arabic medical writings in translation. We shall observe how they combine this physiological psychology with theology.

The *Isagoge ad Tegni Galeni* of Honein ben Ishaq (otherwise known as Johannitius), the *Canon of Medicine* of Avicenna and the *Pantegni* of Hali ben Abbas (cited under the name of the translator, Constantinus Africanus) were of enormous importance.[23] Each set out three 'lives' located in three different organs. Natural life is attached to the liver, animal life is attached to the brain and spiritual life is attached to the heart. This growing emphasis on a physiological understanding of sense memory in particular would serve to reinforce the dichotomy between sense and intellect. Indeed it is an instructive precursor of the awkward and more modern distinctions between brain and mind.

Natural life is said to include faculties which minister to others: that is, appetitive, retentive, digestive and expulsive, and those faculties which are served by others: nutrition, growth and reproduction. Except for external sense organs, the functions of the animal life are localised in the *ventriculi* of the brain but in man the reason that is considered properly human is also located here. This inventory comes from Arab physicians who were disciples of Galen and were influenced by certain aspects of Aristotle's *De Anima*. It is important to point out that these *phisici* usually omitted any discussion of the higher faculties.[24]

The gradual appearance of such physiological doctrines in the writings of Cistercians shows them to be concerned with an understanding of human psychology as an introduction to the science of spiritual life. In the works of William of St Thierry in particular, one finds in effect two

---

[21] See E. Ruth Harvey, *The Inward Wits; Psychological Theory in the Middle Ages and the Renaissance* (London, 1975) for a general survey.

[22] P. Michaud-Quantin, 'La classification des puissances de l'âme au xiie siècle', *Revue de moyen-âge latin*, 5 (1949), pp. 15–34; p. 17. Also P. Michaud-Quantin, 'Une division "augustinienne" des puissances de l'âme au moyen-âge', *Revue des Etudes Augustiniennes*, 3 (1957), pp. 235–48.

[23] E. Ruth Harvey, *The Inward Wits*, p. 13. A complete version of the *Pantegni* was translated by Stephen the Philosopher, 1127, called *Regales dispositio*. On Avicenna's *Canon*, pp. 21 ff., translated by Gerard of Cremona (d. 1187); also Avicenna's philosophical encyclopedia *al-Shifā'*, partly translated by Gundissalinus including his *De Anima* or *VI Naturalium*. More will be said of these works below.

[24] But see the discussion of the physician Isaac Israeli, below, ch. 15.

competing classifications, one depending on the medical tradition onto which is superimposed the classification of Augustine and Boethius.[25] Although William of St Thierry[26] was, like Bernard, a somewhat conservative thinker, dependent on Augustine, his view of human nature relied on an anthropology that was not Augustinian. It is not clear whether he could read Greek, but his writings include Greek words, and there was an overwhelming influence on his thought by certain Greek Fathers, namely Origen, Claudianus Mamertus, Gregory of Nyssa and Plotinus. He is thought to have trained at the school of Laon.[27] Despite his inclusion of aspects of the Greco–Arabic medical tradition drawing on Aristotle, William was more extensively influenced by neo-Platonists, in part through his reading of the works of Scotus Eriugena.. The twelfth century was something of a golden age for Eriugena's works, especially his *De divisione naturae* (*Periphyseon*) although his name was never cited because it was thought he was to be read with caution, having favoured Greek interpretations over those of the Latin Fathers.

William spent fifteen years as the abbot of the Benedictine monastery of St Thierry at Reims before he became a Cistercian. He was a compulsive reader, familiarising himself with the thought, style and literary habits of Augustine, Ambrose and Gregory the Great. But his eclecticism led him beyond these authors to Origen, possibly at the same time that his friend Bernard found Origen of interest. When the two friends were ill together at Clairvaux, they are thought to have read Origen's *Homilies on the Song of Songs* from whence the nuptial spirituality of both William and Bernard issued. William's reading of Eriugena further influenced his style, vocabulary and syntax, especially regarding his exposition of the soul's itinerary towards God.

In the *Enigma Fidei*,[28] he speaks of three factors by which men know: (1) the *corporeus sensus*, things discerned by the senses; (2) the *animus*, represented by thought; (3) *in mente*, through a seizure, a spiritual 'intellection' of the object.[29] His trilogy of cognition is therefore *sensus*,

---

[25] *Physica corporis et animae*, PL 180, 695–726. There is a partial French translation in J. Déchanet, *Oeuvres choisies de Guillaume de Saint-Thierry* (Paris, 1943).

[26] J. Déchanet, *Guillaume de Saint-Thierry, aux sources d'une pensée*, ch. 2, p. 31. Also see David N. Bell, *The Image and Likeness*, Cistercian studies, 78 (Kalamazoo, Michigan, 1974).

[27] Valerie J. Flint, 'The school of Laon: a reconsideration', *Recherches des théologie ancienne et médiévale*, 43 (1976), pp. 89–110. On the links between Laon and Cîteaux, I. P. Sheldon-Williams, 'Eriugena and Cîteaux', *Studia monastica* 19 (1977), pp. 76–92. Also J. Conteni, *The Cathedral School of Laon from c. 850–c. 1000* (Munich, 1978).

[28] PL 180, 397–440.

[29] It has been argued that in the *Enigma Fidei* not a single eastern source can be found. William of St Thierry's discussion of man's vision of God is based, rather, on his reading of Augustine's *Epistle* 147. John D. Anderson, 'The Use of Greek sources by William of

animus, mens.[30] God is known by man at each level; God is like a light (see Bernard above)[31] which enables us to see all things, but he is not a visible radiation but rather invisible and ineffable and none the less intelligible. Our corporeal soul 'touches while our *animus* 'represents' and our *mens* or intelligence 'contemplates', the latter in a manner completely different from the way we see bodies.'[32] For William, like Augustine, sensible knowledge is a consequence of the Fall. If Adam had not fallen he would have known God and truth directly. But since original sin, we have to pass through a deceptive world of the senses and reasoning and we have to work at disengaging the idea of God from the metaphors of biblical texts and from the vast panorama of the visible world. The garden of Scripture is offered first to our senses but we can only know God through his words.[33] This is the first stage by which monks attempt to reach God.

Given the monastic context so infused with the grammar and logic of scriptural texts, it is not surprising to find in William of St Thierry a sense in which all of creation is a book to be read. But for William, God is not physical or corporeal beauty. Rather there is between him and all created things a region of dissemblance,[34] a disparity. 'Non enim corpora pulchritudine aut molis magnitudine superat, sed dissimilitudine ac disparitate naturae' (*Enigma Fidei*, 405 b). Furthermore, in the human intellect, *mens*, there are tangible realities without any similitude with bodies or corporeal forms. These realities, as Augustine too had outlined, are given us naturally, and it is here that resides the idea of God in us. If intellectual realities reside in us such as justice, wisdom, love, none the less, God is ineffable, his divinity surpassing the possibilities of common language. 'Excedit supereminentia divinitatis omnem communis eloqui facultatem' (*Enigma Fidei*, 411 c). And we see a repeat of the earlier monastic neo-Platonism in which the 'quantity' of things is predicated 'accidentally'

St. Thierry especially in the *Enigma Fidei*, in M. Basil Pennington, ed., *One Yet Two: Monastic Tradition East and West*, Cistercian studies, 29 (Kalamazoo, Michigan, 1976), pp. 242–53. Anderson also denies that the *Enigma Fidei* discloses pseudo-Dionysian elements; rather it is a 'western' theological statement even though Greek words are used. But see the works of Déchanet who argues for a more pervasive Greek influence. J. Déchanet, *Aux Sources de la spiritualité de Guillaume de Saint Thierry* (Bruges, 1940). William used Rufinus' unstrict translation of Origen. William wrote his *Exposition on Romans* at Signy along with other works which rely on Latin translations of Greek sources.

30 *Enigma Fidei, PL* 180, 404d–405a.
31 See Plotinus, *Ennead*, V, 3, 49: 'This light [of Intellect], shining in the soul, illumines it: that is, makes it intelligent; that is, makes it like itself, the light above ... One must believe one has seen, when the soul suddenly takes light; for this light is from Him and He is it'.
32 See Augustine, *De Trinitate*, IX, vi, 10–11.
33 Augustine, *De Trinitate*, IX, vi–vii. See discussion above, ch. 7.
34 E. Gilson, '*Regio dissimilitudinis* de Platon à Saint Bernard de Clairvaux', *Mediaeval Studies*, 9 (1947). Also E. Gilson, *The Mystical Theology of St Bernard* (London, 1940), p. 45.

of realities, where this quantity is transposed, *translata*, by reason to the divine plane. Words are only instruments by which one attains God who is above language. 'Suscipienda sunt [verba] sicut ad inveniendum Deum divina quaedam instrumenta ... sed tamen rerum notitiam quarum signa sunt, minime impleta' (*Enigma Fidei*, 427 a). Drawing on the monastic experience, William affirms that since words cannot express the incomprehensible trinity, silence is the best way of honouring God. As for Eriugena and Augustine so for William, at the highest point of *mens* is situated the seizure of truth,[35] the theophanies which leave behind the imagery of sensible knowledge. The savoury experiences of the earlier phases of knowing are left behind in the intellectual vision which is an effect of grace. And for William as for Augustine, Eriugena, as well as for Alcuin in the *Dicta albini*, this 'seizure' is an affair of love and of the heart. The Holy Spirit illuminates conscience with love.

William's *De physica corporis et animae*,[36] written *c.* 1125, also took up some of the themes of Gregory of Nyssa. William, in fact, describes this work as a compilation of interesting textual extracts from others, although he does not cite the name of Greek authorities. The sources of the section on *physica corporis* (Book I) have been identified as Empedocles, Hippocrates, Constantinus Africanus (Hali ben Abbas), Nemesius, Avicenna, and Isidore of Seville. Here he enumerates the natural, animal and spiritual faculties or powers; then the senses and voluntary movement. In the brain there resides in addition to reason, the imagination and the memory which animals also possess. But imagination and memory are perfect only in rational animals. In fact, he says that animals have neither memory nor imagination in any meaningful way. Human imagination is located in the front, larger lobe with sensation. Memory and movement are located in the rear lobe. Between them is the reason and discernment in the middle lobe. Reason, imagination and memory act of themselves whilst animal power, that is, sensation, works through the five senses (*De physica*, I, 6). William believes one can learn much about the exterior man from philosophers and scientists, but when we turn to study the interior man we must consider what the Fathers learned from God and taught to men.

---

35 On the *apex mentis* and its Greek sources, see E. von Ivánka, '*Apex mentis*, Wanderung und Wandlung eines stoïschen Terminus', *Zeitschrift für katholische Theologie*, 72 (1950), pp. 129–72; also E. von Ivánka, 'Byzantinische Theologumena und hellenische Philosophumena im Zizterziensisch-bernardischen Denken', in *Proceedings* of the St. Bernard conference (Mainz, 1953).

36 *PL* 180, 695–726. Now see the translation in *Three Treatises on Man, A Cistercian Anthropology*, ed. Bernard McGinn, Cistercian publications, 24 (Kalamazoo, Michigan, 1977), pp. 101–52.

The second book, *De physica animae* opens with twenty-eight extracts from Gregory of Nyssa's *On the formation of man*.[37] He knew Gregory through Eriugena's translation. Then he moves on to a discussion of the nature of the soul where he mainly draws on Claudianus Mamertus's *De statu animae*. William mentions the inorganic faculties here: the rational, the irascible, the concupiscent, and the image of God in man which includes a spiritual memory, intelligence and will.[38] He closes with a section on the degrees of the soul's greatness derived from chapter 33 of Augustine's *De Quantitate Animae*.[39]

Combining information from Gregory of Nyssa and the works available of Greco-Arabic physicans, William speaks of the three generating organs of life: the brain, heart and liver. He is interested in locating the *anima* which animates the diverse organs of the exterior man (I, 4). Gregory of Nyssa had emphasised that the human soul, that which pertains to the interior man, is a simple spiritual substance rather than material, and that it is formed by the image of God in a manner very similar to its model. It is present in the body as God is present in the world. Man's *animus* is an intelligent soul, whereas the *animus* of animals lacks this intelligence. But the human soul's singularity does not appear at first, according to William. As a result of original sin, he believes we are born like animals and only later, after long and great labour, is the image of God manifested in us. He notes that the spirit of man is far different from the sensual manner in which animal life is animated. Man is governed not by the senses but by reason which rules and judges the senses. Reason, as queen in her castle, recognises the servants bringing in familiar and unfamiliar things through the gates of the senses and reason puts each in its place of knowledge, distinguishing each by its kind, its cognates and its class and giving each room in the memory. Therefore reason recognises general categories, universals. The intellectual soul is something other than sensation, being simple and noncomposite, although it *reaches outwards* in the various operations of the senses (II, 3). The union of the intellectual soul with the individual bodily parts is through *a mysterious power*, ineffable and beyond our comprehension. The incorporeal intellectual soul, having no speech of its own, is satisfied to express its thoughts through the bodily senses (II, 4). Quite extraordinarily, William adds that were we unable to communicate with one another through speech or writing, which compresses sounds of letters into characters made by our hands in writing, we could not be rational. The soul expresses its activity through speech and has its own 'pens' to record perceptions in the memory (II, 4). This means that the animal memory of Book I must be replaced by the spiritual memory.

[37] *PG* 44, 62–256.   [38] *PL* 53, 722–3.   [39] *PL* 32, 1074–6.

Man arrives at a kind of perfection only by travelling through the region in which he exercises the material and animal powers of his soul. What is ultimately sought is the image of God in man by which is meant the union of body and soul. And yet the divine image which is an imprint in us we only known as a similitude of the trinity. Man only has a natural affinity with God, rather than an identity. Therefore one speaks of man's royalty in the world, his power to dominate nature, because of his ability to *reflect* the transcendent reality of God's sovereign powers. But the image does not imitate its exemplar regarding God's divine nature and the incomprehensibility of his essence (II, 5).

It has been argued that the key to William's spirituality is the distinction he makes between the divine image man has by nature and the divine resemblance or similitude he acquires by his merits, commanding reason and choosing what is useful.[40] Spiritual life is the passage from the state of possessing the imprinted image to the actualisation of powers and energies which make the soul a deified similitude of the trinity. Here William drew on Claudianus Mamertus's *De statu animae* which was well known at Clairvaux during Bernard's lifetime. In fact, Nicholas of Clairvaux referred to Claudianus as a 'new Augustine for us'.[41] We have also seen that the *Dicta albini* drew on Claudianus, and much of William's own argument, indeed his words, can be compared with those of Alcuin, as found in the Munich passages.[42] William speaks of contemplating God by a proportionate resemblance to God. The approach to God is through a resemblance that is as exact as possible for those distinguished from him by dissemblance caused by sin. The rational soul is impelled by love towards that which is above it in order to fix itself to its exemplar.[43] The goal is a 'unitas cum Deo vel similitudo ad Deum'.

Just as the body's life is controlled by the powers in the liver, heart and brain so the virtues control and preserve the life of the spirit (II, 8). The soul therefore has both animal and spiritual senses. The interior senses are heightened by the virtues (II, 9). The unity of body and spirit comes through the invisible bridges of the senses '*in a marvelous way*'. The soul, then, is 'in' the body just as God is 'in' the world. Although the soul does not move locally, it does move through desire, but not in place nor time. The soul, then, is the mean between God and the body. The soul recognises in some way in itself the image of its Creator, seeing him as an illuminating light and itself as the light able to be illumined. When the soul thinks, what it is thinking of is wholly in the mind and the whole of what it

---

[40] Déchanet, *Guillaume de Saint Thierry* (1978), p. 103.   [41] *Ibid.*, p. 113.
[42] See below, n. 45.
[43] Déchanet, *Guillaume de Saint Thierry* (1978), p. 104.

remembers at any moment it thinks of wholly at the moment. It wills to think and remember, that is, it loves to have a mind and thought. And if the whole of each, all at the same time, loves, thinks or remembers itself, the three together will be no greater than the whole mind recalling or the whole thought thinking or the whole love loving. Rational thought and love *are* the man, made to the image of his Author, though not created his equal (II, 11).

William draws on Augustine's *De Quantitate Animae* in describing how the soul gives life to and administers the body. The first stage is common to all things living; the second, the senses, is possessed by animals and man. The third stage is that of memory. But he is careful to say: do not think of memory as recalling things brought into the soul through the senses, for animals can do this as well; rather, think of memory as the recollection and signs of numberless things committed to memory and retained there, i.e. the skills of craftsmen and agriculture, letters, words, pictures, paintings, languages, songs, musical skills etc. Included here are present conjectures of the past and future. All these are completely human. Most of this is, of course, Aristotle's recollection as seen through Augustinian eyes. Thereafter, we move to a purgative obedience to the authority and precepts of the wise, the soul's ascent beyond the material, its recognition of its own greatness and the leap towards union with God through contemplation, which becomes direct, static and finally the vision of God (II, 14).

In his early work, the *De natura et dignitate amoris*,[44] William discussed the genesis of divine love in man.

When the divine trinity created man in his image, it formed in him a certain similitude of sovereign nature destined to reflect the three persons. Thanks to this initial resemblance and in virtue of the principle which wishes that like is naturally drawn to like, the new inhabitant of the world is attached to his principle, and if he wishes, he is thus attached unfailingly. Despite all the distractions and seductions exercised on him by a multiplicity of sensual creatures, the individual never separates from the creator and sovereign trinity ... Having thus projected on the face of the newly formed man the breath of life, (the breath being a spiritual or intellectual force, or it may be considered the vital power otherwise called the animal part of the soul), the sovereign trinity then places at the summit of the human being the force of memory. Through the power of memory the goodness and power of the creator is always present in the spirit. Immediately the memory engenders from itself the reason; then memory and reason combine to produce the will. Therefore the memory possesses and contains in it the terminus towards

---

[44] *PL* 184, 379–408. Written as an early work when William was still a Benedictine abbot. Déchanet, *Guillaume de Saint Thierry* (1978), p. 107. Déchanet, ed., *Oeuvres choisies*, pp. 151–213. Also see M. M. Davy, *Deux traités de l'amour de Dieu* (Paris, 1953).

which it must tend. The reason knows that it must move in this direction; the will impels itself there. These three soul faculties are in one sense a single thing but nevertheless three principles of efficacy as in the sovereign trinity with one substance but three persons.

William then draws the parallel of the Father who engenders, the Son who is engendered and the Holy Spirit which proceeds from one to the other, with the reason which is engendered from memory, and the will which proceeds from memory and reason. In this way the rational soul that is given to man is attached to God.[45]

In his later works William mentions the memory, reason and will but only in passing. The influence of Augustine appears to have been redirec-

---

[45] *PL* 184, 382b–d. Compare the *Dicta albini* below, *PL* 100, 565–8 (also see Marenbon, *Circle of Alcuin*, Appendix, pp. 159–61):
... sed etiam quod ad imaginem et similitudinem suam ipse creator omnium eum creavit, quod nulli alii ex creaturis donavit. Quae imago diligentius ex interioris hominis nobilitate est consideranda. Primo quidem, ut, sicuti Deus unus semper ubique totus est, omnia vivificans, movens et gubernans, sicut apostolus confirmat ... (Actus XVII, 28); sic (et) anima in suo corpore ubique tota viget, vivificans illud, movens et gubernans. Nec enim in majoribus corporis sui membris major et in minoribus minor; sed in minimis tota et in maximis tota. (Claudianus Mamertus, *De Statu Animae*, III, 2). Et haec est imago unitatis Dei omnipotentis, quam anima habet in se. Quae quoque quandam sanctae trinitatis habet imaginem. Primo, in eo quia sicut Deus est, vivit et sapit; ita anima secundum suum modum est, vivit et sapit. Est quoque et alia trinitas in ea, quae ad imaginem sui conditoris, perfectae quidem et summae trinitatis, quae (est) in patre, et filio et spiritu sancto condita est. Et licet unius sit illa naturae, tres (tamen) in se dignitates habet, id est, intellectum, voluntatem et memoriam. Quod idem, licet aliis verbis in Evangelio designatur, dum dicitur: Diligis Dominum Deum tuum ex toto corde tuo, et ex tota anima tua, et ex tota menta tua (Matthæus, 37); id est, ex toto intellectu, et ex tota voluntate et ex tota memoria. Jam sicut ex Patre generatur voluntas, et ex his item ambobus procedit memoria, sicut facile (a quolibet) intelligi potest. Nec enim anima perfecta potest esse sine his tribus, nec horum trium unum aliquod, quantum ad suam pertinet beatitudinem, sine aliis duobus integrum constat. Et sicut Deus Pater, Deus Filius, Deus Spiritus Sanctus est, non tamen tres dii sunt, sed unus Deus tres habens personas; ita et anima intellectus, anima voluntas, anima memoria; non tamen animae tres in uno corpore, sed una anima tres habens dignitates; atque in his tribus ejus imaginem mirabiliter gerit in sua natura noster interior homo; ex quibus quasi excellentioribus animae dignitatibus jubemur diligere conditorem, ut quantum intelligatur, diligatur; et quantum diligatur semper in memoria habeatur. Nec solus sufficit de eo intellectus, nisi fiat in amore ejus voluntas; immo nec haec duo sufficiunt nisi memoria addatur, qua semper in mente intelligentis et diligentis maneat Deus: ut sicut nullum potest esse momentum, quo homo (non) utatur, vel fruatur Dei bonitate et misericordia; ita nullum debeat esse momentum, quo praesentem eum non habeat in memoria. Et haec de imagine habeto
Hoc vero de similitudine aliqua intelligere, quae in moribus cernenda est; ut sicut Deus Creator, qui hominem ad similitudinem suam creavit, est charitas, est bonus et justus ... Quas virtutes, quanto plus quisque in seipso habet, tanto proprius est Deo, et majorem sui conditoris gerit similitudinem.
In the *De dignitate humane conditionis*, School of Alcuin but circulating under the name of Augustine or Ambrose, one finds the same text, *PL* 17, 1105–18A, especially 1018A where *moribus* is read (wrongly) as *minoribus*.

ted by his reading of the Greek Fathers, and especially Plotinus, whom he never cites.

William understands the soul to have, in effect, two memories, one which is somehow corporeal and shared with animals. The other is that which God places at the very summit of the human being. It is a recollective power, and an active force by which God's goodness is always present to *mens*, and it also has the capacity to engender reason. It works along with reason to produce the will. If the image of God in man's memory originally has ontological status (as in the *Dicta albini*, Munich fragment), then William ends by emphasising that the moral resemblance must be the fruit of the virtuous activity of mind. The absence of a theory or of a systematic presentation of his reflections owes much to his eclectic use of sources and to the monastic associative reminiscence of the texts which inspired him.

A rather different, far more Augustinian method is demonstrated in the *De Anima* of the English Cistercian Aelred of Rievaulx.[46] He too, however, maintained a distinction between the image of God in man which is never completely destroyed, and the similitude which issues from the soul's capacity to attain a likeness to God under the influence of its exemplar. His *De Anima* (*c.* 1167) was written for his community at Rievaulx during his final illness when his health was undermined by arthritis. At the end of his life he lived apart from his order in a small hut adjacent to the monastery's infirmary, and he sat before the fire reading Augustine's *Confessions*.

The *De Anima* takes the form of a dialogue between Aelred and one of his monks, John, rather than a 'de physica'. At Rievaulx, Aelred continued the practice of spontaneous and informal dialogues with his monks that he had instituted when a novice master.[47] Like other Cistercian authors of the twelfth century, Aelred grafts aspects of Augustine's psychological analysis on to the questions of the soul's resemblance to God and the nature of the image. As we saw, in general, this doctrine argued that since God is ineffable a knowledge of the divine nature can only come to man indirectly through the imprints he perceives of it in creation, especially

---

[46] Aelred of Rievaulx, *De Anima*, Latin text, ed. C. H. Talbot, in *Medieval and Renaissance Studies*, supplement 1 (London, 1952). Also see A. Hoste and C. H. Talbot, eds., *Aelredi Rievallensis, Opera Omnia, 1: opera ascetica*, CC, continuatio medievalis, 1 (Turnhout, 1971). C. H. Talbot, trans. and introduction, *Aelred of Rievaulx, Dialogue on the Soul*, Cistercian publications, 22 (Kalamazoo, Michigan, 1981), based on the text in the *Patrologia Latina*.

[47] Walter Daniel, *Vita*, ed. M. Powicke, p. 40. See C. H. Talbot, trans., *Dialogue on the Soul*, introduction.

through contemplating his own human nature. The closest resemblance the soul has to God is in its trinity of faculties: intellect, memory and will, and the existence of the memory indicates the coexistence of the intellect and will. Because Adam had not made proper use of these three faculties, fallen man finds himself in a region of dissimilitude where the original likeness to God is obscured. The object of the monastic life is the restoration of the proper use of man's three faculties by which he may attain, through the concentration of memory, intellect and will, a focused concentration on God as the soul's object. Only through a spiritual assimilation to the trinity can the soul assume a divine resemblance and become something near to its perfection. For Aelred, such perfection consists in remembering without forgetfulness (inspired by the *semper memor* of the *Rule*), knowing without error, and loving without satiety.[48]

By following Augustine, Aelred is much more interested in the connection between body and soul, sense and intellect. He seems to have written his tract independently of William of St Thierry's *De natura corporis et animae*, and he adds to what he finds in the writings of Augustine, aspects of Aristotle's arguments from the *De Anima*, II, I, as well as taking up, but to inconclusive ends, aspects of earlier arguments which tried to solve the problem of the nature of the soul's manner of uniting with the body. He has something of a physiological argument in Book I (reminiscent of the *Timaeus*) when he says that the body, which is composed of gross elements of earth and water, can unite with the soul through the medium containing the elements of fire and air.[49] This medium he calls the *sensualis vis*, and it combines qualities that are common to both body and spirit. Just as the two natures of Christ united through the medium of soul to form one person, so too the two substantial principles of the human person are united *through the medium of sense*, the *sensualis vis*. This power is the most interesting one discussed by Aelred but he makes little of it. His understanding of the *vis sensualis* has some affinity to Plotinus's affirmation of a co-sensitiveness inherent in the living world which unites the object and the perceiver. It is also akin to the Plotinian intermediate, third something, accepting modifications of the material object as a likeness to it and yet exhibiting the condition which the higher principle is to perceive. It stands between soul and object, between sense and intellectual. As we mentioned above, Augustine in the *De Genesi ad Litteram* spoke of the corporeal, the intermediary spiritual and the highest intellectual visions.

Above the *vis sensualis* one finds the *ratio* comprising memory, intellect

---

48 Talbot, trans., *Dialogue*, introduction p. 10.
49 See Plato's *Timaeus*, 32, the composition of the world by means of its four elementary constituents: earth, air, fire and water.

and will, to be understood as the one substance of the soul itself. This is treated in Book II. Lacking a highly detailed anatomical study he none the less provides a fair amount of compressed information on the inferior faculties that are dominated by reason, stressing the importance of the link between reason and sense through memory. But he too seems untroubled by the lack of a specific manner in which unity between a sensible and an intellectual memory is achieved. He is still dominated by the dualism of body and mind. And he appears to be at the mercy of the information provided by the Arabic medical texts available which had nothing to say about the higher faculties.

He responds in a traditional way to the twelfth-century problem concerning how the many acts of sensible apprehension could be reconciled with the uniqueness of the soul's substance, by arguing that the soul is an incorporeal substance with three faculties that are separated neither in function nor in thought. The soul's faculties are not accidents. Reason, memory and will are three 'words' which denote one substance, following Augustine. Aelred avoids speculation and emphasises instead more traditional preoccupations with questions of creation and the origin of the soul that link him, some believe, with the school of Laon.[50] But he draws upon certain physiological doctrines found also in Greco-Arabic medical texts, namely the *vis sensualis*, which serves as an intermediary between body and soul, and he argues that the five senses play a cognitive role, the *vis sensualis* including the imagination and memory. Therefore, the memory is for him not only a faculty of knowledge but also one of activity corresponding to a habit. But this memory is still spoken of as an inferior activity of the soul. For an understanding of higher mind, when spiritual memory acts in conjunction with intellect and will, Aelred draws on the traditional theological argument to avoid saying that an animal's soul could be receptive to God's word.

Book I begins in Augustinian fashion when Aelred says to John:

You think that you cannot have an idea of anything unless you use corporeal images which you have either perceived with your sense or built up in your imagination. Just as when you think of a man you have seen, you set up his image before you, so when you try to think of 'life' you look for its image and believe there is no substance unless it has a certain form in the memory. In wishing to think of 'life' you look for its image in your mind and because you do not find it you are disturbed. And yet without using any form or corporeal image you think of many things which are more important than bodies. For when you think of the virtues

---

[50] Valerie J. Flint, 'The school of Laon: a reconsideration' *RTAM*, 43 (1976), pp. 89–110. Also I. P. Sheldon-Williams, 'Eriugena and Cîteaux', *Studia Monastica*, 19 (1977), pp. 76–92.

you do not gaze upon the image of any of them. When you consider and turn over in your mind [*mens*] what light, what knowledge, what consolation, what grace wisdom bestows on human minds, how much are you moved, how much do you desire to enjoy a share of it, being stimulated to this by sacred scripture ... Therefore what you think of and desire without any corporeal image is greater than and superior to any body.[51]

When animals seek to satisfy bodily needs and affections, these are implanted and impressed on their soul by habit, the sense and affection, so that they become part of the memory. But whereas in animals it is acute sense that enables them to live, in man it is rational judgement. The senses do nothing other than present images of those things they have seen and heard and impress them on the memory. We think of the thing according to the image of it that we see. The senses, however, are no help in understanding and reflecting on concepts like justice. In fact, bodily senses can be a distraction to this kind of reflection; thinking is done by the soul (I, 48). The soul is constituted by memory, reason and will as its very substance. They can only be separated from one another in thought (see Augustine). And although each may seem to possess individual powers they are unable to act separately, for memory can do nothing without the reason and will. We all share the same rational nature but some use it well and others ill (I, 56). Now, whatever is perceived by the senses is presented to the memory. On all of them reason passes judgement and the will consents. And man from birth had a rational soul as soon as his body began to live. The rational soul cannot exist in the body without the senses, and it is through the *vis sensualis*, possessed by the body through the elements of air and fire that it can unite with the coarser body made up of the unresponsive elements of earth and water. This power of sense, the *vis sensualis*, is so subtle and so akin to spirit that it is almost a spirit and is called spirit of life (*vis spiritualis*). The word of God could only be united with flesh through the medium of that subtle nature, the rational spirit.[52]

Therefore, sense may be thought of as something midway between flesh and soul. Because of its nature which is akin and nearer to spirit, it has in some way a capacity for holding the soul and is like a glue by which the soul is joined to the body and held in the body. It is this subtle power of

---

[51] Talbot trans., *Dialogue*, introduction, p. 41. Page references in the text below refer to the Talbot translation. This is a striking parallel with Plato's *Theaetetus* where Socrates disputes the definition of knowledge as perception by objecting: 'If I see and then shut my eyes and remember what I saw, I still know it but am not perceiving it.' Knowledge is therefore, not perception. See above, ch. 1.

[52] See Augustine *De Genesi ad Litteram*, XII, and the discussion above, ch. 7, of his *De Trinitate*.

sense, *vis sensualis*, which is capable of receiving a power of a higher order, flowing invisibly and incorporeally from the love of the father and mother, and then it lies preserved in the seed until it passes into the nature of the soul. Only the intellect can discern this invisible and immaterial force in the seed of the body (I, 62).

But the soul exercises in itself no activity through the senses, says Aelred, and John is confused. How can that be, he asks, when the soul can think of nothing corporeal which has not had its image brought in by the senses? Aelred answers that when the senses have brought it in, 'do you not think about it with your eyes closed?' If so, then whatever the soul does within itself, it does without the assistance of any of the senses (I, 69).

In Book II, Aelred addresses the problem of what the soul can achieve by itself through the memory, reason and will and without the assistance of the senses. Drawing on Augustine's *Confessions*, X, viii, 14 he says that the memory is like a vast hall containing almost countless treasures, namely the images of different bodily objects which have been carried into it by the senses. In the memory are stored and separately labelled all those things that have been borne through its doors by ears, eyes, mouth, nostrils, touch. All these things the memory receives and to the mind seeking out now one, now another, the memory presents each one in turn by means of its own particular image (*De Anima*, II, 71–2). Certain things come so readily to hand that they present themselves to the thinker immediately, but some, even when other things are being sought for, thrust themselves forward and are brushed aside only with difficulty. Some things are hidden beneath such a deep layer of objects that they can be retrieved from their dark recesses only with great mental effort. Others make their appearance, whenever they are required, in perfect order. In the memory the heavens, the earth, the sea and all the creatures that can be perceived in them are present to the reflective mind. Only those things that forgetfulness has buried in its tomb are removed from its sight. But we must note that images of bodily things are not themselves bodies.

The memory image, according to Aelred, cannot be greater than the thing, the memory, on which it is impressed. He draws an anology with images reflected in a mirror and the memory as a kind of mirror. He asks John:

How do you remember the vast size of London, Westminster Abbey, the Thames, St Paul's? You remember these because you have seen images of them in your memory. But does London appear smaller in your memory than it did to your eyes? We must admit that your memory and consequently your soul is greater than London; since the image of London is impressed on one's memory and no image can exceed the size of the thing on which it is impressed, then the soul is greater than the world, not in material size but in spiritual nature ... Thus in my memory I have at hand all the information I can gather excepting the things I have forgotten. Unless I could see them all in my memory with their vast spaces, just as I see them outside me, I should be unable to speak about the heavens or the sea or the stars or the mountains or about anything else that I have actually seen or heard others describing. (*De Anima*, ii, 73–5)

He continues his Augustinian discussion of memory by passing to the soul's higher power which is concerned with 'real things'. And here is the science of measurement, disputation, rules and different arts, virtues of prudence, fortitude, justice, all in the soul not in the guise of images but in their true selves. Such noncorporeal sciences did not enter the soul from outside; mathematical demonstrations, for instance, are in your mind all the time, even when you failed to notice them. They reside in the deepest recesses of memory and when realised they have not been brought in from outside but are implanted by nature. More familiar with the requirements of demonstrative and logical proof than this Augustinian discussion implies, he closes the explanation of memory housing by nature 'real things' that have not entered through sensual experience, in the following way: he says, all this appears to have Augustine's approval, '*but because there is difficulty in providing a convincing proof for it, let us move forward to the discussion of other things*' (ii, 77; emphasis added).

At last we come to that supreme quality of memory that overrides all else, its capacity to receive God. From the moment that man knows God, God begins to dwell in his memory and as often as man brings God to mind, he finds him there. God dwells in all memories but only those who glorify him and have him in their memories in love, have survived (ii, 77). Furthermore, the memory cannot be treated independently because it so depends on reason that it would be able to retain, distinguish, judge nothing except images conveyed to it through the senses. Thus, memory shorn of reason does not go beyond the power of an irrational soul. And without reason the memory would be unable to make anything connect or hang together. Memory signifies that power by which the soul recalls things and by which it links up sequences of events, connecting those that follow to those that have gone before and those of the future to those of the past. Reason distinguishes between all these and passes judgement on them approving one as true, another as false, just or unjust, happy or unfortunate. The will's function is to consent. When united to reason it is the free will. Unlike Bernard who argued that both memory and will can be blamed for man's misdemeanours, Aelred follows Augustine and says that no weakness of the sense, no defect of the reason or memory can make a man evil.

Aelred therefore has a clear understanding of sense memory as a short-term dwelling place for images conveyed to it through the senses and seems not to distinguish sharply between it and the imagination. When we speak of memory in man, however, we must always link it to reason if we wish to explain retention, judgement, the recollection of things which can then be linked sequentially. Cognitive memory, therefore, contrasts with sense memory. Sense memory is meaningless. This is important when we consider that Aelred did more than write a treatise on the soul; he also wrote historical works and was one of the promoters of the historical revival in twelfth-century monasteries. His understanding of the memory as a faculty that recalls sequences of events and with the help of reason links these together truly or falsely, tells us what he self-consciously took his own historical enterprise to be as it depended on the operations of higher mind. Sensually perceived facts were meaningless as they were endowed with meaning only when man's judgement established their veracity or false-hood, based not on an examination of evidence but on logical argument. The trinity of memory, intellect and will, independent of corporeal images provided meaning and understanding and the historical enterprise could therefore only be carried out by men with rational souls imprinted with the divine image.[53] The primary function of memory was to recall rational souls to a divine similitude through contemplation of scriptural remi-niscences or historical events endowed with higher universal meaning.

In the final book, III, Aelred enumerates in Boethian and Augustinian fashion the four powers of cognition: sensual perception, the comparison of images impressed on the senses which then recreate by imagination further images; the rational capacity to discern truth from falsehood, and finally the intellectual power which transcends all earthly images and attains the source of truth. We recall that the Boethian list comprised sense, imagination, reason and intelligence. Aelred says that it is the imaginative power that keeps man bound to the world, both when awake and asleep. And he has an interesting discussion of the nature of dreams. So long as body and soul are joined, our sense organs receive corporeal images. In the rational soul there is a sensory power, an imaginative power, a rational power and an intellectual power. Since the soul pays attention all day to the bodily senses, the images of these corporeal objects are deeply impressed on the soul and are with great difficulty erased. Thus, even when the senses are dulled in sleep the soul is occupied with images that the senses have impressed on it while awake. *Aelred would*

---

[53] See J. T. Muckle, 'The doctrine of St. Gregory of Nyssa on Man as the image of God', *Mediaeval Studies*, 7 (1945), pp. 55–84. For the rhetorical and logical importance of this kind of history, see the discussion below, ch. 14, on John of Salisbury.

prefer that these images be erased. Even when the mind is awake and trying to concentrate, it has difficulty, he says, in driving away, even for a single moment, the 'frippery of corporeal images' and in attaining a fleeting glimpse of intellectual purity' (III, 117). Here, then, we see the influence of Bernard and the whole Cistercian monastic discipline. Aelred's initial interest in the connecting *vis sensualis* is transformed by a stronger opposition between mind and senses.

Another Cistercian of English origins, Isaac of Stella, wrote an *Epistola de Anima* (*c.* 1162).[54] Isaac is thought to have been the abbot of the abbey of Notre Dame des Châteliers on the island of Ré a few miles off the French coast near the port of La Rochelle. He studied in the schools before 1130 and was greatly influenced by the Chartrains William of Conches and Thierry, and by the school of St Victor, especially Hugh. Having entered the Cistercian order after a career in the schools, his various writings testify to the wide range of sources to which he was exposed. His *Epistola de Anima* is addressed to the monk Alcher of Clairvaux, skilled in *physica*, who had asked him to provide a treatise on the soul which did not base itself on the givens of Scripture or the Fathers. Isaac says he will concentrate on the *natura et vires* of the soul.

For Isaac, the human soul essentially is comprised of two parts, one cognitive and the other affective. The words he uses are *sensus* and *affectus*. The *sensus* is equated with the soul's *ratio*. Addressing the familiar problem of the image of God in man, Isaac asserts that the image is in the highest point of the soul, the *mens* or *intelligentia*. The *imago* is to be taken as the generalised intellectual power of the soul's *sensus* (*ratio*) and the *similitude* is to be understood as the generalised volitional power of the soul's *affectus*.[55] And as with Augustine and Alcuin, Isaac says that the *ratio* which is a property or function of the soul is not really distinct from the soul. He then proceeds to distinguish between the *naturalia* identified with the soul, and the *accidentalia*, which are not. *Accidentalia* are virtues including the four cardinals, while the *naturalia* are powers (*vires*) or faculties for which we are given two lists: *ratio, ingenium, memoria* (also to be found in the *Ysagoge in theologiam* of the 'School' of Abelard, *c.* 1140), and *rationabilitas, concupiscibilitas* and *irascibilitas*.[56]

---

[54] PL 194, 1875–90. Also see Bernard McGinn, *The Golden Chain, A Study in the Theological Anthropology of Isaac of Stella* (Washington, D.C., 1972). B. McGinn, introduction and translation in *Three Treatises on Man: A Cistercian Anthropology* (Kalamazoo, Michigan, 1977): 'A letter on the soul' by Isaac of Stella, pp. 153–78 with a useful introduction pp. 47–63. Also see Anselm Hoste, ed., *Isaac de L'Etoile: sermons*, I, 69–81 (Paris, 1967) and with Gaston Salet, ed., *Sermons*, SC 130 (Paris, 1967).
[55] McGinn, *The Golden Chain*, pp. 116–17.   [56] PL 194 (IV) 1877B.

The accidental virtues descend from a divine source and they enable man to ascend the ladder of being to his essential source. The faculties however, are considered as prime substance and are the substantial being of the soul. Both the *naturalia* and the *accidentalia* are mutually required for the existence of each other.[57] Through reasonableness, *rationabilitas*, the soul is of such a nature as to be illumined to know something either below itself or above itself, or in itself or besides itself.[58] From *rationabilitas* arises the power of knowledge variously named *ratio, memoria* and *ingenium*. These are distinct in the soul because of the division of time into present, past and future. Where *ingenium* searches out unknown matters, *ratio* judges the things found and memory preserves matters *already judged*[59] and presents things to be further determined. Memory, therefore, brings back what it has hidden. The hidden word, expressed exteriorly by the mouth, is only gradually drawn out of the memory and formed in the mouth of the mind. For God, however, nothing is past, present or future, but eternally present in the Word, the act of mind which simultaneously thinks and speaks. For God, the whole of every act of knowing is called neither memory, nor *ingenium*, but the Word. For the human soul, however, there are multiple powers of knowledge dependent on time (VII).

Furthermore, the soul can also move affectively through *concupiscibilitas* and *irascibilitas*. Thus the two fundamental powers of the soul consist in *sensus* and *affectus*: 'de rationabilitate igitur omnis oritur anime sensus, de aliis vero omnis affectus' (V, 1878 D).[60] The journey back to God must therefore be taken in a two-fold manner, using *sensus* and *affectus*, paralleling *cognoscere* and *diligere*, for he says: 'The journey must be undertaken as it were on the two feet of reason and affective power. By means of the first it proceeds from the letter to the spirit; by means of the second, from vice to virtue' (*Migrandum vero quasi pedibus duobus, sensu et affectu, altero de littera ad spiritum, altero vero di vitio ad virtutem*).[61]

Isaac outlines a five-fold ascent of *rationabilitas*, which is the essence of the soul, to God. He says there is sense knowledge, imagination, reason, discernment and understanding. These proprerties are distinguished by various activities but there is only one rational essence and one soul. The terms he uses are: *sensus corporeus, imaginatio, ratio, intellectus* and *intelligentia*. The *sensus corporeus* perceives bodies; the *imaginatio* perceives likenesses of bodies; the *ratio* perceives dimensions or forms of bodies, like universal concepts, whose existence depends on their being realised in

---

[57] McGinn, *The Golden Chain*, p. 143; also *Sermo* IX, ed. Hoste, p. 130.
[58] *PL* 194 (v) 1878 C.
[59] See below: Avicenna on *estimativa* and memory, ch. 15.   [60] *PL* 194 (v) 1878 D.
[61] *Sermo* X, ed. Hoste, p. 220; McGinn, *The Golden Chain*, p. 152; *PL* 194, 1723 B.

physical bodies: the *intellectus* perceives created spirits of men and angels; and lastly, the *intelligentia* perceives immediately and beholds the incorporeal nature of God.[62] The object of *imaginatio* is the *similitudines corporum* or *phantasiae*[63] which are nearly corporeal (*fere corporeum*), and these may be studied in Boethian fashion, by the *scientia naturalis*. Isaac links corresponding elements to these objects and to the objects of imagination he associates the element fire (XII).[64]

Following in the Augustinian and Plotinian tradition, Isaac understands the operation of the *sensus corporeus*, not as a passive power which is actualised by impressions from exterior bodies as did Aristotle. Rather, he sees the *sensus corporeus* as an active power of the soul which is directed towards perceiving those corporeal forms of present bodily realities: 'Est igitur sensus ea anime vis qua rerum corporearum corporeas formas percipit et presentes'.[65] The only manner in which the *sensus corporeus* is itself corporeal is that its objects do not surpass the level of bodies. Augustine, in the *De Quantitate Animae* had also held that sensation is the soul's awareness of modifications made on the body.[66]

Imaginatio is, for Isaac, that aspect of *rationabilitas* directed to matter that is nearest to the purely spiritual realm. *Imaginatio* is, therefore, somehow on the borderline between the physical and the spiritual. It is the power of the soul which perceives absent corporeal forms of bodily things, just as sensation perceives real bodies through their present qualities. *Imaginatio* arises out of the *sensus*, it is linked to the *sensus*, and never has an incorporeal object. Rather, its object is *spiritus corporeus* or *spiritus pecoris* or *spiritus vitalis* or *sensualitas carnis*, that is, the material principle of life which man shares with all animals.[67]

Imagination perceives likenesses and images of real bodies; it is at a certain distance from bodily things but not yet incorporeal. Isaac's faculties reach downward, never upwards to more immaterial objects (XI). With respect to the imagination, the phantasms arise from below into the imagination and such phantasms are *similitudines et imagines* of real bodies. Thus, the *imaginatio* is still corporeal and he intends that the corporeal and the spiritual can never cross the unalterable line that divides them.

---

[62] *PL* 194 (IX), 1880 C.   [63] *PL* 194, 1888B.

[64] Compare the discussion of Cicero's *Tusculan Disputations* on the linking of the elements with aspects of the soul, above, ch. 3.

[65] *PL* 194 (X), 1880 D.

[66] Augustine, *De Quantitate Animae*, I, 21–30; *De Trinitate*, XI, 1–3 and *De Genesi ad Litteram*, XII.

[67] Compare Constabulinus = Costa ben Luca, d. 935, *The Difference of the Spirit and the Soul*, ed. S. Barach in *Excerpta ex libris Alfredi* (Innsbruck, 1878), translated into Latin by John of Spain in Toledo *c.* 1150. Also see discussion in McGinn, *Three Treatises*, introduction, pp. 22 ff.

Isaac, however, is concerned to show that the opposition of matter and spirit is none the less *somehow* linked and joined in a continuum. He uses a recurrent image of a continuous golden chain of being throughout nature to God. And thus, he affirms that the highest point of corporeal nature and the lowest point of spiritual nature are so similar that they can be joined in a personal union but without a confusion of their natures (XI): '... in quibus sine naturarum confusione personali tamen unione'. The soul which is truly spirit and not body, and the flesh which is truly body and not spirit, are united in their extremities, that is, in the imaginative faculty which is almost body and in the flesh's faculty of sensation which is almost spirit.

We have already seen that Aelred also affirmed that the *vis sensualis* was so subtle and so akin to spirit that it is almost a spirit and is called the *vis spiritualis*. It is somewhere midway between body and soul and because its nature is akin and nearer to spirit, it has a capacity for holding the soul like glue to the body. For Isaac, the union without confusion of natures of God and man in the person of Christ becomes the all-important analogy for the union of body and soul in man. This union occurs at the two extreme points of the material and spiritual spheres of being. The *phantasticum animae* which is almost corporeal and the *sensualitas carnis* which is almost spiritual, are thus somehow united. It is thought that this description is a variation of Hugh of St Victor's unity *in medium* approach to the problem in his *De unione corporis et spiritus.*[68]

In all this, Isaac, far more elaborately than Aelred, was attempting to correct the Platonic and Boethian disjunction between body and soul. But the *sensualitas carnis* (*spiritus corporeus*) remains distinct from the soul and is the source of animal life. The enduring force of the Platonist tradition maintains its hold on Isaac; never does he allow the Aristotelian principle of the soul being the form of the body to emerge. Instead, *imaginatio* must always be described as on the edge of the corporeal and it has no capacity to transcend the level of corporeal similitudes at which it operates (XIV).[69] And just as phantasms rise up from below into the imagination, so theophanies descend from above into the understanding (XXII).

Isaac sees no contradiction between his theory of sense knowledge and his theory of the knowledge of reason (XV). When he speaks of the *ratio*, the next level of the soul's ascent, and refers to the soul's *sensus*, he is speaking of the capacity for active perception of forms of corporeal things

---

[68] *PL* 177, 285–94; McGinn, *The Golden Chain*, p. 161. Also compare Hugh of St Victor, *De Sacramentis*, II,i, ii (*PL* 176, 408–9), and Hugh's *De unione corporis et spiritus*, *PL* 177, 285–94. I discuss the conjunction of the external and internal senses according to Avicenna below, ch. 15.

[69] McGinn, *The Golden Chain*, p. 170.

where the *sensus* is now a spiritual power. Sensations for the soul are *intelligible* impressions. Isaac says that reason abstracts from the body those things which are found in the body, but by a contemplative reflection rather than through any activity. 'Abstrahit enim a corpore que fundatur in corpore non actione sed consideratione' (xv).[70] Whilst his generalised understanding of abstraction sounds Aristotelian, reason abstracting the universal concept from a body, there is no Aristotelian abstracting from impressions of sense knowledge made on the passive intellect to produce intelligible phantasms which then become universal concepts. Instead of a continuum of impressions starting from outside bodies and their effects on the senses, Isaac provides an *analogous* and *parallel* operation of the soul where sensations are intelligible impressions. There is then, a radical break between the lower stages of his epistemological ladder where *corpora* are perceived and the higher stages of knowing. There is a symbolic or anagogic relation between the operations of lower mind and higher mind but no true natural continuum. The phantasms in the imagination have no capacity to ascend into the reason.[71] This means that the highest of the stages of inferior reason directed at bodies and leading to *scientia*, is split off from the next stage which is that of the superior reason, the gaze of the soul directed to true realities unsullied by any connection with matter.[72] For all of Isaac's fascination with the unity of the universe through mediating terms and concatenations, he maintains the Boethian and Platonist divergent realms of being.

Thus, when he speaks of the highest aspect of the soul, the *intelligentia*, he says it is that power of the soul which immediately suggests or stands in for (*supponere*) God just as (by analogy only) the *phantasticum anime* suggests the body, or as the *sensualitas carnis* suggests the lowest part of the soul: 'ea vis anime est que immediate *supponitur* deo, sicut phantasticum anime supponitur corpori vel sicut sensualitas carnis *supponitur* infimo anime' (xxiii).[73] There remains a series of disjunctions between body, soul and God, united only analogously. These disjunctions are a result of sin and only Christ fulfils in himself the perfect unity of body, soul and God. There is very little importance given to the memory subsequent to the workings of the *imaginatio* as it somehow links itself with higher mind, despite attempt to include information from the Greco-Arabic medical writings in which the animal faculties are categorised according to the three ventricles of the brain: imagination, reason and memory. Corporeal similitudes in imagination and memory have no capacity to ascend into the soul's reason.

[70] *PL* 194 (xv) 1884 A.   [71] *PL* 194, 1888 B; McGinn, *The Golden Chain*, p. 173.
[72] McGinn, *The Golden Chain*, p. 174.   [73] *PL* 194 (xxiii), 1888 B.

The depth of Isaac's knowledge of Plato's *Timaeus*, Chalcidius's *Commentary* on the *Timaeus*, Macrobius's *Commentary on the Dream of Scipio* and the works of Boethius, was shared with Chartrains like Thierry, William of Conches and Clarenbald of Arras. He also drew on the newly available Greco-Arabic medical writings as did the Chartrains. His knowledge of Aristotle does not go beyond the Boethian Aristotle of the *Categories* and the commentaries on Porphyry's *Isagoge*. His Platonism was heightened by the pseudo-Dionysian popularisations of Hugh of St Victor, and the Eriugenean tradition of the school of Laon. And whilst he influenced a slightly later work, the *De Spiritu et Anima*, once thought to be by Alcher of Clairvaux, but which survived in the later twelfth and thirteenth centuries as a work of Augustine, his analysis remained within the Cistercian programme of seeking a monastic means of return to God, divorcing sense from intellect.

The *De Spiritu et Anima*,[74] compiled *c.* 1170 and falsely attributed to Augustine, played a more important role in the history of medieval thought than did Isaac's *Epistola ad quemdam familiarem suum de anima*. But recent analysis has shown this work to be a string of excerpts from Augustine, Cassiodorus, Isidore of Seville, Alcuin, Anselm, Bernard, Hugh of St Victor and Isaac of Stella. Here as is common to earlier glosses on Plato's *Timaeus* we find a notable image, comparable to the more well-known organic formulation of the state by John of Salisbury. For our author, the soul is a city (*civitas*) which is counselled by its intellectual faculties and defended by its knights – the reason, whose army consists in *concupiscentia* fighting for justice. The labourers and *rustici* who do the heavy work are the sensual faculties.[75]

The *De Spiritu et Anima* appears to be the first attempt to study on its own the purely sensual psychology as present in animals. This will increasingly be the focus of texts in the thirteenth century. We are told that animals operate by the senses, the imagination and the memory to which is added a kind of providence which permits them, without intellectual judgement, to acquire what is advantageous to them.[76] This

---

[74] *PL* 40, 799–832, listed under the works of Augustine. See McGinn, *Three Treatises*, introduction, pp. 63–74, and translation by E. Leiva and Sister Benedicta Ward, pp. 179–288.

[75] *PL* 40 (XXXVII) 807. Compare this with the organic metaphor of the *civitas/respublica* in John of Salisbury's *Policraticus*. Compare also with William of Conches' commentary on the *Timaeus*. See P. E. Dutton, *Illustre civitatis et populi exemplum*: Plato's *Timaeus* and the transmission from Calcidius to the end of the twelfth century of a tripartite scheme of society', *Mediaeval Studies*, 45 (1983), pp. 79–119; text, p. 98 nn. 69–70.

[76] Aristotle discussed this in the *Historia Animalium*. See the discussion on *estimativa* below, ch. 15. There are numerous parallels with the works of Thierry of Chartres and

emphasis on animal sensual psychology derives from Arabic writers and in particular from Avicenna. But in this compendium of information on the soul, as in Isaac's more coherent work, it proved impossible to speak of human motivation without reference to man's link with divinity and therefore, one sees again, the uneasy combination of natural science and theology operating side by side.

For the Cistercian (?) author or compiler of this compendium of texts, the memory houses incorporeal similitudes of corporeal objects, images to which the mind's eye wilfully returns in order to think on them.

Thus the face of man is to us externally visible, but it is also visible to our memory where its image is preserved, an image which in itself is incorporeal but certainly body-like. Just as the beauty of the world is available to us exteriorly, so too its image is in our memory as an incorporeal similitude to which we return when we think of the world's beauty with shut eyes. Therefore what a corporeal object in space is to the bodily senses, the object's likeness in the memory is to the highest power of the soul, the *acies animi*.[77]

The mind's vision is called *intelligentia*; the mind's taste is wisdom. Like Isaac, this author distinguishes between the rational powers and the affections of the soul. *Imaginatio* is the lowest rung of ascension to a combined *intellectus in intelligentia* and the affective love of *sapientia*.[78] But sense and imagination cannot ascend to the level of reason. What is sought is an experience of higher mind, a combination of contemplation and spiritual delectation.[79]

The *sensus*, as for Isaac, is a power of the soul to perceive the present forms of corporeal bodies; the imagination perceives such forms of absent bodies. But the *sensus* perceives the forms in the material, the imagination perceives them *extra materiam*. Hence the things seen by the spirit, which is a certain power of the soul that is inferior to mind, are not corporeal. They are only similar to corporeal realities. Imagination has its origins in the senses, and just as the eyes of the *carnalis anima* sees many things, so the imagination conceives many phantasms. In contrast with what Aelred

---

Clarembald of Arras who emphasise a natural order proceeding from the formation of heavenly bodies down to animals on earth.

[77] *PL* 40 (x) 786. Translation in McGinn, *Three Treatises*, p. 193:
Facies siquidem hominis et nobis forinsecus nota est, et in memoria nostra habet imaginem suam, incorporalem quidem, sed corpori similem ... ad quam recurrimus cum clausis oculis eam cogitamus. Quod enim est ad corporis sensum aliquod corpus in loco, hoc est ad animi aciem similitudo corporis in memoria; et quod est intentio voluntatis ad corpus visum visionemque copulandam, hoc est eadem intentio voluntatis ad copulandam imaginem corporis, quae est in memoria et visione cogitantis.

[78] *PL* 40(XII): 'Mentis visio est intelligentia; gustus, sapientia est'.

[79] '...illa contemplatur, ista delectatur. Per intelligentiam utique ipsam veritatem intelligit, per sapientiam diligit ...'

said, this author believes that the soul *never* goes outside itself to exterior things but rather, pictures them within itself through its own reflexive activity. It has within itself latitude, longitude and height.[80] The reason (*ratio*) is that power of the soul which perceives the different forms, both *propria et accidentia*, incorporeally but which are not found apart from bodies, *non extra corpora*. And it does so by abstracting from bodies through reflection, *consideratione non actione*.[81] All those incorporeal attributes not found apart from bodies, none the less subsist only in reason. Thus the nature (*natura*) by which body is a body, is not itself a body. Whatever the senses perceive through sense knowledge the imagination represents through similitudes, the *cognitio* forms, the *ingenium* investigates, the *ratio* judges, the memory delivers up, the *intellectus* defines or separates, and the *intelligentia* comprehends. *Intelligentia* is the soul's power which immediately perceives invisible things. One is led then to meditation or contemplation.[82]

This compendium incorporates the various traditions we have thus far observed in earlier Cistercian authors, drawing them together in separate chapters so that the medical and theological information stand side by side. Drawing indirectly on the Greco-Arabic medical tradition, probably as found in William of St Thierry's *De Physica Corporis et Animae* but surprisingly close to Avicenna's interpretation, we learn that the *vis animalis* is located in the brain, from where it gives rise to the five corporeal senses. The three ventricles of the brain comprise an anterior part which directs all the senses; the posterior part which directs movements, and the median, third part which is rational. One can refer to these powers as much as of the soul as of the body: they are of the body when considered physiologically and of the soul when considered in relation to higher reason.[83] In the first part of the brain the *vis animalis* is called *phantastica*, or imagination, because the similitudes of corporeal things and images or phantasms are contained here. In the median part of the brain one examines and judges that which is represented through images. In the *ultima pars* of the brain we have memory because here we have the memories judged by reason.[84] Thus the memory is located in the posterior part of the brain and we recall that according to this division of the soul into powers located in liver, heart and brain, spiritual understanding which sees *incorporeal truths* is located in the heart. Memory is a lower part

---

[80] *PL* 40 (XI) 787. McGinn, *Three Treatises*, translation, p. 195.   [81] *PL* 40, 787.
[82] *Ibid.*
[83] '...istae vires tam animae quam corporis dici possunt, quia ab anima in corpore fiunt, nec sine utroque fieri possunt'.
[84] *PL* 40 (XXII) 795. McGinn, *Three Treatises*, introduction p. 32 for parallels with William of St Thierry, part I. Also compare with William of Conches, *De Philosophia Mundi, PL* 172.

of mind because it is attached to corporeal objects of cognition, but we see that memories in the third ventricle are already 'processed', having been rationally judged.

Like Aelred, Isaac and especially William of Conches (*Dragmaticon Philosophiae*), the author of the *De Spiritu et Anima* provides a physiological analysis of cognition linking the various elements of which corporeal objects are made with cognitive faculties. This tradition, heavily influenced by Chalcidius's translation and commentary on Plato's *Timaeus*, would continue into the thirteenth century and the discussion here is one of the most interesting and developed parts of this treatise. Since the human body is made up of the four elements, the flesh and bones possess most of the element earth to attain their solidity. Water is in the humours and air in the lungs. But the seat of iron is in the heart and when tempered by air these elements ascend to the brain. In such purified form, the eyes, ears and corporeal senses are put in contact with exterior forms. What touches the senses in the anterior sensual part of the brain is then transferred to the posterior motor part of the brain and diffuses through the whole body. But the author believes that in this kind of corporeal vision, the soul can be mistaken whereas in intellectual vision, the soul never errs for if something is not true, the intellect does not understand it (xxiv). Like Isaac, this author has a congruence theory by which objects of like elemental matters are perceived by sense and imaginative faculties which deal with these elements.[85] But what comes through the senses to the sensing and imaginative capacities of the brain does not ascend to the reason.[86] Once these elements are in purified form, within the imagination (*ab anteriori parte capitis*), they are moved to the median part where the rational soul is excited to judge them. In animals, the phantasms do not transcend the *cella phantastica*: but, he adds, that in humans the phantasms *purior fit* and are brought into contact with the rational and incorporeal substance of the soul. Then the imagination's phantasm is a likeness of the body.

He seems to wish to include an Augustinian explanation, as in the *De Genesi ad Litteram*, of how the soul becomes what it perceives and knows, but is unsure of the mechanics. Therefore he says that it is certain that there is in us some spiritual nature where *either* the likeness of corporeal things is formed *or* where these likenesses are imprinted ready-formed

---

[85] 'Porro ipsa vis ignea, quae exterius formata sensus dicitur, eadem formata per ipsa sensum instrumenta, per quae egreditur et in quibus formatur, natura operante introrsum ad cellam phantasticum usque retrahitur et reducitur, atque imaginatio efficitur.'
[86] '... sensus vero et imaginatio ad rationem non ascendunt, sed infra remanentes eam, aliquatenus deducere possunt, et quasi a longe quaedam ostendere, ad quae non possunt pervenire' (*PL* 40, 788).

(*ubi corporalium rerum similitudines aut formantur, aut formatae ingeruntur*). This occurs when, in the present, something is touched by a corporeal sense and the continuation of the object's similitude is formed in the spirit and stored in the memory. Likewise this happens when we think of (*cogitamus*) known or unknown absent objects and a spiritual discernment is thereafter formed, (*sive cum absentia jam nota vel quae non novimus cogitamus, ut inde formetur quidam spiritualis intellectus*).[87] Sometimes through an illness, as occurs to the delirious who run high fevers, the images of corporeal things can be so firmly impressed (*exprimuntur*) on the spirit that we think it was the body's senses perceiving other bodies, rather than only the images of bodies. Then things that are not before our eyes are perceived as though present, things which do not exist at all, coming to seem to be present. Thus, the author believes that only through some *vis morbi* are we subject to contriving things in our mind which either do not exist at all or which are not known to exist. Normal imagination, however, does correspond through similitudes, to sensed experience.

Corporeal things and their similitudes, the senses and the images fixed in the memory, all belong to the exterior man since they are messengers to the soul (*nuntii animae*) of the things that are outside.[88] Lower memory is therefore attached to this world of sensed experience. But thereafter the author defines an autonomous aspect of soul, theoretically independent of sense experience. He says that what is even more present to the mind is mind itself, mind seeing itself in itself through an interior presence not dependent on similitudes but on the present truth.[89] And yet the mind is so bound to corporeal things that the mind cannot detach itself from such images even when it desires to see itself alone. The attachment to its phantasms of corporeal images deforms the mind. And the author seems to invoke Bernard's consideration of how mind might purge itself of the filth of this life in order that when the soul leaves the body at death it will carry nothing corporeal with it.[90] It is the imagination which acts as a bridge between the corporeal and the spiritual for this author and hence, it is the imagination, when under the influence of reason, that allows man to leave the filth of this life. At one extreme the imagination is a corporeal spirit, whilst at the other it is something rational which informs the bodily nature and is in contact with rational nature (XXXIII).[91]

[87] *PL* 40, 796.   [88] *PL* 40 (XXXII) 801.
[89] *PL* 40, 801: 'Mens ergo cui nihil se ipsa praesentius est, quadam interiori non simulata, sed vera praesentia, videt se in se'.
[90] *PL* 40, 801–2.
[91] *PL* 40 (XXXIII) 803: '... nihil enim in corpore altius, vel spirituali naturae vicinius esse potest, quam id ubi post sensum vel supra sensum vis imaginandi concipitur, quod quidem in tantum sublime est, ut quidquid supra illud est, aliud non sit quam ratio.'

Higher reason, *ratio*, is what distinguishes us from animals with which we share sense and imagination. When we speak of man then, we are speaking of a being endowed with an intellectual spirit and man's memory 'simply' records images. The ability to judge these belongs to a distinctly human *ratio* located in the middle part of the brain.

Concerned to include all aspects of the tradition in this *summa*, including what looks like an increasingly close reading of Aristotle through Avicenna, the author says that the soul's *potentiae* are *rationalitas, concupiscibilitas* and *irascibilitas*. Its *vires* include *sensus, imaginatio, ratio, memoria, intellectus* and *intelligentia*. But he adds that we can call the *potentiae, vires* and the *vires, potentiae.*[92] He draws on the doctrine of Isaac and Hugh of St Victor that body and soul are united through extremes, that is 'in phantastico animae, quod corpus non est, sed simile corpori, et sensualitate carnis, quae fere spiritus est, quia sine anima fieri non potest'. This unification of the nearly spiritual and the nearly carnal occurs, however, without the confusion of the respective natures of either. This marvellous association of body and spirit, 'mira societas carnis et animae, spiritus vitae et limi terrae', is achieved through an *imitation* of reason in the senses and memory (XIV).

For this author the memory is inserted between the imagination and reason but it clearly is, as for Aristotle and, as we shall see, for Avicenna, a faculty to be categorised in lower mind in contact with corporeal objects. In the whole body, one finds an *imitation* of the spiritual life rather than a continuum from corporeal to spiritual cognition. 'In his omnibus corporea vita spiritualem vitam imitatur.'[93] The *sensualitas carnis* and the *phantasticum spiritus* comprise the midpoint between body and soul: 'Convenientissima autem media sunt carnis et animae, sensualitas carnis, quae maxime ignis est, et phantasticum spiritus, qui igneus vigor dicitur.'[94]

Shifting to the Augustinian understanding of the soul as the whole of *homo interior*, the author leaves behind the physiological understanding of imagination and memory and now speaks of *memoria etiam mens est*; 'omnium rerum thesaurus et custos est memoria, nec enarrari potest, tam grandis est ejus perplexitas et anima ipsa est.[95] Mens autem vocata est, quod emineat in anima, vel quod meminerit.' And we next find the Carolingian parallel of the divine trinity with *anima intellectus, anima voluntas* and *anima memoria.*[96] This memory operates in conjunction with reason: 'Memoria etiam consors et cooperatrix est rationis, quoniam sine

---

[92] *PL* 40 (XIII) 789.   [93] *PL* 40, 790.   [94] *Ibid.*
[95] *PL* 40 (XXXIV) 803. 'Memory is the treasurehouse of all things nor can one speak of it sufficiently for it is great in its perplextity and it is the very soul. Moreover, it is called mind.'
[96] *PL* 40, 805–6.

ea ratio nec ad incognita procedere, nec cognitorum scientiam retinere potest. Memoria est vis animae accepta retinens, praeterita repetens, elapsa recolligens.'[97] Through memory we revisit the past, but we cannot understand the past without reason (xxviii). Placed between God and the body, the soul moves through time by remembering the forgotten, learning the unknown and willing what had been denied (xv). Since memory is mind, we say that those who have lost their memory have also lost their mind. The memory as the treasury and guardian of all things can never be completely unfurled so great is its intricacy. The interior man's intellectual soul is identical with memory.[98]

As a treatise comprising excerpts, the *De Spiritu et Anima* lacks coherence as its dips into various traditions. It even suggests that the ordering of the material in this tract has taken into account that man's memory is dull and, rejoicing in brevity, might indeed find the author's summary reduction of ancient doctrines useful in order to commit them to memory (*quod memoriae commendetur*)![99] But the 'author' is perhaps most concerned to locate texts and repeat what we have seen elsewhere, especially in Cistercian writings: that man is by nature double: 'una interior, quae est ipse homo, quoniam mens unius cujusque est ipse; altera exterior id est corpus'. He says he disagrees with those who posit *two souls*, a sensual one which is the source of animation in man, and a rational one, the supposed source of knowledge. Instead, he argues that one indivisible soul exists of itself through discernment and it endows the body with animation through the senses. Before the human body receives such a soul it merely vegetates, irrationally.[100] But the life of the soul is two-fold, living in the flesh and in God. Hence, there are two kinds of sense knowledge in man, an exterior sense knowledge and an interior sense knowledge. Each has its own proper object, either a contemplation of divine things or a reflection on human, corporeal things.[101] His real interest, then, is in the vestige of the trinitarian image *in mente* which therefore shifts interest to higher mind unsullied by the body, and so to theological doctrine. The soul's eye is the mind, exempt from all bodily stains and the gaze of the mind is called reason.[102]

Only later, during the thirteenth century, would human psychology and the role of memory be treated with respect to the realm of nature alone. A closer link would be established between the memory of the lower part of mind that is in contact with the body and exterior reality, and higher mind.

[97] *PL* 40, 808.
[98] *PL* 40, 803. 'Mens autem vocata est quod emineat in anima, vel quod meminerit'.
[99] *PL* 40, 811.   [100] See (ix), McGinn, *Three Treatises*, translation pp. 190–1.
[101] *Ibid.*, p. 191.
[102] *Ibid.*, p. 192.

This could not be achieved either through the more coherent efforts of Isaac of Stella in particular, or through the Cistercian influence in general. Indeed, the founding of a house for the Cistercians at the University of Paris during the thirteenth century did not produce any major Cistercian theologians: their understanding of psychology and of the role of memory would prove to be retrograde in the light of the new speculation of the schools. But this tract would, in the 1230s and early 1240s, be connected with the beginnings of Franciscan theology, providing a centre for the continuation of a neo-Platonic and Augustinian current in the teeth of a developing Aristotelianism.

PART III

THE BEGINNINGS OF THE SCHOLASTIC
UNDERSTANDING OF MEMORY

INTRODUCTION

Memory cannot be treated separately from a more inclusive theory of knowing. There appears to be a tendency in some but not all modern discussions to try to extract remembering from other operations of mind. Personally, I do not believe this should be pursued if we are ever to give a satisfactory account of what memory is for us and how it works. At any rate, it must by now be clear that ancient and medieval theories of memory are intricately linked to an epistemology. And we now are in a position to discuss one of the most sophisticated theories of knowing and remembering to have emerged from the medieval concern to describe how man uses language to understand both the present and the past: that of Peter Abelard. Even if the ancients and medievals located memory in one of the temporal lobes of the brain (the medieval version of Penfield's experiments), its function could not be dealt with meaningfully without informing memory with reason. Perhaps what is most startling in the writings of Abelard is his ability to elucidate knowing and remembering primarily by means of an analysis of the logic of language and how it works. Meaning is generated by the mind's activities through the use of signs or universals, be they images, words or ideas. Mind's present active attention enables us to consider the past through words and images, so that the past is given meaning, without which attention it has none.

Abelard's theory of knowing and remembering through language serves as the most coherent attack we have so far encountered not only on the realism of his own times, but on the realism of many present day psychological theories of knowing and remembering as described by Weisberg and referred to in our final chapter. The scholarly literature on Abelard points to numerous problems in his analyses and it is not surprising that modern philosophers, interested in logic and language, have sought to refine many of his insights. These corrections and modifications cannot detain us here. Instead we must try to present as coherently as possible the

231

role that language and its logic played in Abelard's discussion of human knowing and remembering. Furthermore, Abelard is an excellent example of how a linguistically based theory of knowing and remembering necessarily gives rise to specific proposals concerning how men understand past history through reading and understanding texts written in and about the past. With Abelard we see one of the first attempts to constitute what we today might recognise as a theory of historical understanding.

Chapter 13

ABELARD

Knowing, remembering, language, and interpreting past texts. The new linguistic logic of memory. Mind, language and external reality.

Since some readers may be dismayed by the stress I have put on so animistic a concept as 'attention' it may be well to review its basis once more. If we allow several figures to appear at once, the number of possible input configurations is so very large that a wholly parallel mechanism, giving a different output for each of them, is inconceivable. To cope with this difficulty, even a mechanical recognition system must have some way to select *portions* of the incoming information for detailed analysis. This immediately implies the existence of two levels of analysis: the preattentive mechanisms, which form segregated objects and help to direct further processing, and the act of focal attention, which makes more sophisticated analyses of the chosen object. The observation that even a competent automaton would require processes of figure-formation and attention lets us understand why they have appeared, explicitly or implicitly, in so many psychological theories ... The notion that perception is basically a constructive act rather than a receptive or simply analytic one is quite old. It goes back at least to Brentano's 'Act Psychology' and Bergson's 'Creative Synthesis' and was eloquently advanced by William James (1890) ... the mechanisms of visual imagination are continuous with those of visual perception – a fact which strongly implies that all perceiving is a constructive process.

Ulric Neisser, *Cognitive Psychology* (New York, 1967), pp. 94–5.

During the twelfth century a countervailing wind was already blowing which, by the thirteenth century, would sweep the monastic understanding of memory from the centre of philosophical and theological concerns. The students and masters of those urban schools which gave rise to the universities in the thirteenth century came to place increasing emphasis on Aristotelian logic and dialectic in the arts curriculum.[1] They called themselves, and were called, the *via moderna* in contrast with the *via antiqua*.[2] But highly skilled dialecticians like Peter Abelard did not confine

---

[1] See G. L. Bursill–Hall, *Speculative Grammars of the Middle Ages* (The Hague and Paris, 1971); Jan Pinborg, *Die Entwicklung der Sprachtheorie im Mittelalter*, BGPTMA, 42, vol. 2 (Münster, 1967).

[2] Elisabeth Gössmann, *Antiqui und Moderni im Mittelalter* (Paderborn, 1974).

themselves to logic; they drew upon the rules of dialectic in an analysis of theological issues,[3] just as monastic grammarians applied grammatical analysis to matters of faith. William of St Thierry and Bernard feared the consequences of the applications of school dialectic and they were roused to attempt to silence the new development. It is said that where Bernard had addressed the heart, Abelard was addressing the intellect, opening up the mysteries of faith to the scrutiny of rational dispute. Partly because of Abelard's poor reception with those church authorities who were so indelibly influenced by Bernard, but largely because of the increasing influx of translations into Latin of more of the works of Aristotle, from Greek and Arabic along with translations of Arabic commentators, it has sometimes been thought that Abelard's original insights remained unexplored beyond the generation after his own. None the less, it is clear that despite the belief of some of his contemporaries that Abelard was subject to error, his thought was a major and continuing stimulus to future debate. Indeed, we shall see some of the same conclusions to which Abelard came surface in the writings of Aquinas. And aspects of Isaac of Stella's *Epistola de Anima* (XIII–XVI) show the influence of Abelard's 'School'.

Abelard addressed many of the epistemological concerns of his age as we have already examined them amongst the Cistercians, but he dealt with the same issues as did other dialecticians, by means of insights taken more explicitly from semantic logic. Aside from the evidence provided by his logical writings we have had, until recently, little notion of what epistemological theories Abelard held, so it is to the logical writings that we must, in the first instance, turn. But now the *Tractatus de Intellectibus* is judged to be one of his works and we shall examine it in conjunction with his logical writings.[4] In the long run the universities would have available a more comprehensive and systematic philosophy on which to build a sophisticated epistemology in which memory would play a considerable role. In the short term, Abelard's logic and his application of logical dialectic to theological matters reveal important new developments, not least in the manner in which the past was to be regarded through its texts. He was not alone in this for, as we shall see, twelfth-century historians, influenced by

---

[3] See Abelard's justification of dialectic in the service of theological discussions of the trinity in his *Theologia Christiana*, III, ed. E. M. Buytaert, *Petri Abaelardi Opera Theologica*, CCCM, 12 (Turnhout, 1969). For a discussion of Abelard's influence and his 'school', see D. E. Luscombe, *The School of Peter Abelard* (Cambridge, 1970), pp. 4–5 f; and D. E. Luscombe, 'Peter Abelard', in *A History of Twelfth-Century Western Philosophy*, ed. P. Dronke (Cambridge, 1988), pp. 279–307.

[4] Abelard, *Tractatus de Intellectibus*, in Urban Ulivi, ed. and introduction, *La psicologia di Abelardo e il tractatus de intellectibus* (Rome, 1976). Also see Jean Jolivet, *Arts du language et théologie chez Abélard*, Etudes de philosophie médiévale, 57 (Paris, 1969), appendix, 'Mode de connaissance'.

the revived ancient disciplines of grammar, logic and rhetoric would also treat the significance of historical documents of the past and establish practical ways of using and writing about the remembered past. Indirectly through his concerns with linguistic meaning and directly through his application of logical analysis to matters of faith, Abelard provided a significant alteration of the monastic position in explaining the relation between meaning and remembering.

In his *Logica Ingredientibus*[5] as in his *Dialectica*[6], Abelard provided elaborate glosses on the then standard logical works used in the emergent schools: Porphyry's *Isagoge*, Aristotle's *Categories*, the *Perihermenias* (*De Interpretatione*), and Boethius's translations and commentaries on these works. Abelard was, therefore, drawing mainly on the works of the *logica vetus*.[7] But he gives some evidence of being acquainted with the content of some of the works of the new logic as they were being made available in translations: Aristotle's *Prior Analytics*, the *Sophistical Refutations*, etc.[8] Just as the cloister set up its demands for Bernard, so too for Abelard, the classroom with its questions and disputes set up its demands. Hence, Abelard understood logic or dialectic as an art whose aim was to distinguish between valid and invalid arguments. It was an *ars disserendi*. The scope of logic, therefore, inquires into the use of speech to elucidate meaning. But logic is not epistemology. In fact, logic is neither a theory about how we think nor does it inquire into the nature of things. It is a discipline lying somewhere in between – a discipline that is, none the less, a part of philosophy and therefore it is not an autonomous *ars*.[9] Indeed, his theory of terms was strongly influenced by non-logical positions which

---

5 B. Geyer, ed. *Peter Abelards philosophische Schriften*, BGPTMA, 21, 4 vols. (Münster in Westfalia, 1919–33) and Mario dal Prà, ed., *Pietro Abelardo, Scritti filosofici* (Rome, 1954). The *Logica Ingredientibus* comprises extended glosses on Porphyry's *Isagoge*, on Aristotle's *Categories*, the *De Interpretatione* and other glosses on Boethius's *De Differentiis, Topicis* and the *De divisionibus*, including discussions *de syllogismo, categorico, topica*.
6 *Petrus Abaelardus, Dialectica, First Complete Edition of the Parisian Manuscript*, ed. L. M. De Rijk, 2nd rev. edn (Assen, 1970). Constant Mews dates this before 1117–21. See C. Mews, 'On dating the works of Peter Abelard', *AHDLMA*, 52 (1985), pp. 73–134.
7 N. Kretzmann, 'The culmination of the old logic in Peter Abelard', in *Renaissance and Renewal in the Twelfth Century*, eds. R. L. Benson, G. Constable, C. D. Lanham (Oxford, 1982; 1985) pp. 488–511. See the interesting discussion on Boethius's interpretation of Aristotle's *De Interpretatione* and Abelard's understanding in Brian Stock, *The Implications of Literacy, Written Language and Models of Interpretation in the Eleventh and Twelfth Centuries* (Princeton, 1983), chapter 4, section 2, pp., 366 ff.
8 Mews thinks Abelard did not know the new logic, but there are numerous parallels with issues raised by Aristotle in Abelard's writings and it is evident that John of Salisbury, in *Metalogicon*, II, 10, does use the *Prior Analytics*, the *Sophistici Elenchi* etc. to serve the same points concerning universals and common names, how and why they are used, that Abelard also highlighted.
9 See the introductory discussion of this in De Rijk, ed., *Dialectica*, pp. xxiii ff.

grew out of his concern to distinguish the domain of logic from that of grammar and rhetoric, leading him to associate logic with metaphysics and psychology. Like many of his contemporaries he saw the focus of logic to be in the first instance a problem about predication but centrally related to the philosophical problem of universals.[10] In discussing linguistic logic one had to speak about mental conceptions. Therefore, in his *Commentary on Porphyry* where he treated universals, he described the activity of knowing mind, tracing the passage from sensation to intellection.[11] At the beginning of his *Gloss on the Perihermenias* one finds a full analysis of this process.

As Boethius had noted in his *Commentary* on Aristotle's *De Interpretatione*,[12] but modifying the Aristotelian original, things are conceived by the intellect, the words signify these mental conceptions or intellections, and therefore the intellect has conceptions of objective reality and things as these are signified by words. For Boethius, things precede and give rise to mental conceptions so that understanding must proceed from things because it is from things that the significance of words arises. But it is the *mental awareness* of things that endows words with meaning.[13] This observation would be central to Abelard's linguistic logic.

In addition, Aristotle defines the universal in his *De Interpretatione*[14] as 'that which is naturally suited to being predicated of more than one thing'. The universal therefore involves a grammatical concept since language is the necessary condition for predications. Whether universals have to do only with words or with things as well, was the question Abelard asked. He answered that we can ascribe universality only to words and not to things.[15]

As a logician Abelard denied the direct relation between logical operations and reality. Here, he was unlike logical realists or logical Platonists who took concepts, propositions and logical operations to be referring directly to reality. As a logical nominalist,[16] although not as

---

[10] See John of Salisbury, *Metalogicon*, II, 19–20, for a discussion of how important the problem of universals had become by mid century. Also see Martin M. Tweedale, *Abailard on Universals* (Amsterdam, 1976) for an excellent study of this difficult subject.

[11] *Sup. Porphyr*, II in *LI*, pp. 20–1.

[12] Boethius, *Commentaria in librum Aristotelis Peri ermeneias*, ed. C. Meiser, vol. 2 part I (1880), Book I, p. 20: 'Tribus his totus orandi ordo perficitur: rebus, intellectibus, vocibus. Res enim ab intellectu concipitur, vox vero conceptiones animi intellectusque significat, ipsi vero intellectus et concipiunt subiectas res et significantur a vocibus ...'

[13] My emphasis. See Stock, *Implications of Literacy*, p. 369.

[14] *De Interpretatione*, VII, 17a 39–40.

[15] *Logica Ingredientibus* IX, 16. 17. Also see Kretzmann in *Renaissance and Renewal*, p. 491.

[16] John of Salisbury, *Metalogicon*, II, 10, says that after he studied with Abelard at Mount Ste. Geneviève, the latter departed 'all too soon' and John thereafter became a disciple of Master Alberic (of Paris) who was a most bitter opponent of the Nominalist sect. Some

extreme as his older contemporary Roscelinus, Abelard spoke of logic as an *ars sermocinalis*, that is, the art of the use of language where the *term* is the object of analysis, not as a sound or physical entity, but as the bearer of meaning.[17] This meaning is imposed upon the term by human choice in the establishment of linguistic conventions. Boethius had also said that *res* and *intellectus* are by nature, whereas words change according to man's cultural context (*positio*).

The position maintained by logical nominalism is that only that which can be common to many so as to be predicable of many, are signs.[18] Therefore 'Man' is a universal, a sign for what is common to many men.[19] Nominalist logic, as a study of signs, verbal or otherwise, argues that signs or common names such as 'universal', 'genus', 'true', 'category', denote *signs* and not the things signs are of. According to Abelard a term signifies something or it can signify itself; propositions either refer to an idea about things or a proposition has the sense of a statement where the statement is not a thing. A term is capable of being applied to, or can be predicated of, a group of individuals because of these individuals' sharing a common nature or *status*, and this *status* is not 'in' things but is abstracted by the human mind from a set of similar individuals.[20] The *sermo* signifies a common nature of individual things and is a purely human application or imposition whose own character is therefore unreal because it is not a separable thing but a universal name, a signifier.[21]

Early on Abelard ascribed universality to *voces* or utterances, that is, to sounds produced by the speech organs, as well as to linguistic entities, *sermones* and *vocabula*. And he argued that whatever is universal must be

current scholars question the use of the term 'nominalist' but it is clear that the word was used to describe that school of logical thought opposed to the realists. Also see De Rijk, ed., *Dialectica*, introduction, p. xcv, on logical nominalism which does not exclude philosophical realism, p. xcvii.

[17] But even when one speaks *de speculationibus, hoc est intellectibus*, Abelard says he regards the various distinctions between *sensus, imaginatio, existimatio, scientia* and *ratio* to be part of *doctrina sermonum. Tractatus de Intellectibus*, ed. Ulivi, pp. 102–27; p. 103.

[18] Abelard, *Sup. Porphyr.*, in *LI*, pp. 7–8.

[19] For Abelard, universals are not limited as a class to nouns and adjectives but include verbs.

[20] Et nulla est natura quae indifferenter subsistat; sed quaelibet res, ubicumque est, personaliter discreta est, atque una numero reperitur. Corporea quippe substantia in hoc corpore, quid est aliud quam hoc corpus, vel humana natura in hoc homine, hoc est in Socrate, quid aliud est quam ipse? Nihil utique aliud, sed idem penitus essentialiter. (*Tractatus de Intellectibus*, p. 119)

Also *De Intellectibus*, pp. 123–4: 'Solet frequenter quaeri de significatione atque intellectu universalium vocum, quas res videlicet significare habeant, aut quae res in eis intelligantur; ut cum audio hoc nomen homo, quod pluribus commune est rebus, ad quas aequaliter se habet, quam rem in ipso intelligam quaeritur ... [et sequitur].'

[21] *Sup. Porphyr.*, in *LI*, p. 15.

meaningful, must bear meaning, so that the *sermo* is a more complex expression whereas the *vocabulum* or word is a noncomplex expression. In the later *Logica 'nostrorum petitioni sociorum'*[22] Abelard redefined his terminology. Here, he argued that universality is attributed neither to things nor to utterances (*voces*). Only expressions (*sermones*) may be universal or singular.[23] The utterance (*vox*) was a creation of nature, whereas the formation of expressions (*sermones*) owed everything to their establishment by men.[24] And in virtue of their formation, these expressions, as universals, are predicable of many. But neither utterances nor things are in any way universal, even if it is agreed that all expressions are also utterances.[25]

At what point then, does meaning arise when one utters a meaningful proposition? Abelard says that a single understanding is gathered from many different words. The significance of one word is not usually clear until the whole sentence is expressed. Signification is therefore a product of the *hearer's understanding mind* once the ordering of verbal sounds is produced according to language's conventions.[26] In explaining the use of words, Abelard investigates only in a general way the properties of things which the mind uses words to signify. A logician does not investigate the nature of things themselves – this is the realm of physics; but rather, he investigates those properties of things which the mind understands through words which signify such properties.[27] Therefore, he believes that

---

[22] The *LNPS* is dated 1121–24; Mews places it after the *Dialectica*. It is an elaborated gloss on Porphyry's *Isagoge*.

[23] Geyer argued that Abelard redefined a universal as a *sermo* rather than a *vox* to distinguish himself from Roscelinus with whom he was engaged in controversy, *LNPS*, pp. 599–600.

[24] 'Quid enim aliud est nativitas sermonum sive nominum quam hominum institutio? Hoc enim quod est nomen sive sermo, ex hominum institutione constrahit.' *LNPS*, p. 522.

[25] *LNPS*, p. 522. A generation later, John of Salisbury would say that universals like genera and species are not word concepts (*sermones*) but intellections, concepts of mind. See *Metalogicon*, II, 20. Concepts of mind, what scholastics later call the *species intelligibiles*, are prior in the epistemological process of abstraction to word concepts/*sermones* which are *signa expressa*.

[26] *Dialectica*, pp. 67–8; 'Oportet itaque voces quoque ipsas coniungi ac quodammodo uniri continua prolatione, ut unus sit earum intellectus ac compositus ... Nec minus quidem oratio dici non possunt prolatie a diversis dictiones, sed casu potius ab his proferri videntur, quorum intellectus diversi poterant iudicari.'

[27] Hoc autem logicae disciplinae proprium relinquitur, ut scilicet vocum impositiones pensando quantum una quaque proponatur oratione sive dictione discutiat. Physicae vero proprium est inquirere utrum rei natura consentiat enuntiati, utrum ita sese, ut dicitur, rerum proprietas habeat vel non. Est autem alterius consideratio alteri necessaria. Ut enim logicae discipulis appareat quid in singulis intelligendum sit vocabulis, prius rerum proprietas est investiganda. Sed cum ab his rerum natura non pro se sed pro vocum impositione requiritur, tota eorum intentio referenda est ad logicam. Cum autem rerum natura percontata fuerit, vocum significatio secundum rerum proprietates distinguenda est, prius quidem in singulis dictionibus, deinde in orationibus, quae ex dictionibus iunguntur et ex ipsis suos sensus sortiuntur. Neque enim absque partium discretione composita perfectio cognosci potest. (*Dialectica*, pp. 286–7)

Aristotle's doctrine of categories is basically semantic rather than ontological in the first instance, that is, Aristotle is not interested in how things 'are' but rather how *language* signifies the properties of things, according to Abelard. In the *Logica Ingredientibus* he says:

> But I think that this separation of the [10] categories occurs more on account of the signification of utterances than on account of the nature of things. For if Aristotle had paid attention to the nature of things there would not have appeared any reason for his not having more or fewer categories. If we look at the signification of common names [*nomina*, which include adjectives] we can see that he considered ten names in which begin the significations of all other common names, generic and specific, and therefore he put them over the others as though they were naturally first and contained nobler things, because they were more universal.[28]

Abelard believes Aristotle's semantic logic deals not with reality but with *expressions about* reality.

Now, it is clear for Abelard that universal words like man, animal, genus, species, are possible because the things each word applies to exist somehow.[29] The prior existence of that of which universal common names are predicated is a necessary condition for language. But it is the expressions of language, propositions and not any of the things to which they refer that are to be called universals. Things subsist as discrete individuals in the world, so that the meaning of universal words must be based on the fact that these individuals agree in some common nature. But this nature is not a separable thing that we can point to saying, 'this is what we are signifying'. It seems clear that Abelard is concerned with predication based on a psychology of signification and only in a secondary way, with ontology. But in the *De Intellectibus*, he argues that sensation is the necessary prerequisite for knowledge: 'tota humana notitia a sensibus surgit'.[30]

Although meaning is imposed on terms by human choice, language is not an arbitrary and completely autonomous set of rules for Abelard, but

---

[28] *LI*, pp. 116–17. See Tweedale, *Abailard on Universals*, pp. 93–4.

[29] Kretzmann discusses the problems with the earlier theory in the *LI*, in *Renaissance and Renewal*, pp. 501–2. He cites (p. 497) *Dialectica*, p. 131, 4–6 to demonstrate how for Abelard a thing's existence is not considered one of its characteristics, essential or accidental. The verb 'is' which is a peculiar sort of common name, is or has been predicated or imposed on all things in accordance with their *essentia*. 'Is' names everything (i.e. what is not, is nothing) and determines its substantial existence. In the *Tractatus de Intellectibus*, p. 115, Abelard says the following: 'Sanus autem intellectus Aristoteles [in the *Categories*] in eodem rerum similitudines appellat, hoc est ita concipientes ut rei status sese habet, veluti cum hominem intelligo ... singuli intellectus, quia cum statu rerum concordant, sani sunt.' This is a sensitive reading of Aristotle.

[30] *Tractatus de Intellectibus*, p. 119.

for reasons that are somewhat different from Anselm's view. By means of Boethius's *Commentary* on Aristotle's *Perihermenias*, Abelard follows Aristotle's belief that the truth of a proposition depends on the priority of the state of affairs (*eventus rei*) to which the proposition then refers. Aristotle, we recall, believed in a coherence between a proposition and the prior state of affairs to which it refers. And Boethius had argued that things give rise to intellections so that understanding proceeds from the anteriority of things. Abelard reaffirms that being, and things existing in relationships, are prior to and the condition for all signification. This gave rise to problems concerning statements about chimeras. But he will differ from what he takes to be Aristotle's form of empiricism in arguing that the coherence between things signified and their signifiers – be they images or words or ideas, is not of the nature of repeated similitudes which are themselves things, where for instance, the image *is* the idea. Rather, images, words, ideas relate in their own way to the object world itself without being real entities in themselves.

Abelard confirms that the definition of the term 'true' as a predicate of a proposition requires that the state of affairs referred to by the proposition exists. Propositional truth is defined as 'dicens illud quod est in re'.[31] This has important consequences for his understanding of the truth capacities of language in signifying past historical reality or events. If the state of affairs referred to by a proposition exists, then he says the proposition, if pronounced, is true.[32] But especially in the *Dialectica*, this does not mean for him that unless words are actually being spoken, we cannot truly say that there are universals such as genera, common names etc. The logic of language already exists, having been established from human choice, whether or not that to which some proposition refers actually exists. Thus there are some predicates that can be true (albeit vacuously) even when no thing exists to which it refers, such as a chimera. This is because there already exist the conventions of a linguistic theory which make speech sounds meaningful without our supposing either the existence of meaningful speech sounds now or the existence of the things they signify. An example would be the fact that the law makes certain acts illegal without supposing the existence of such illegal acts. For there to be universals like genera, common names, articles, etc. is simply for there to be certain established language conventions. And Abelard extends this to

31 De Rijk, ed., *Dialectica*, introduction, p. lviii and *Dialectica*, II, p. 205.
32 In the *Tractatus de Intellectibus* where Abelard states that all knowledge depends on the prior sensation of existents, he then says that as a result of the necessity of sensation for knowledge, there is derived a *necessitas consuetudinis*: 'sensus consuetudo adnectitur nobis, ut vix aut numquam aliquid intelligere valeamus quod non tanquam corporeum et corporeis proprietatibus subiectum imaginemur' (p. 107).

all cases where we posit in discourse items which *can* be concretely exemplified but whose existence is independent of the existence of those concrete exemplifications. Thus, even when no one is speaking, there are still genus and species.[33]

Abelard goes on to say that the truth of affirmative categorical statements is not *necessarily* true.[34] Their truth requires that the subject term denotes something that exists. But what is meant by 'exists'? Here Abelard explains that all things other than God have contingent existences.[35] Therefore, the natural sciences have to operate with these contingencies; they do so on the basis of a hypothetical necessity whereby a categorical proposition must be true so long as there do exist the things it is talking about. Abelard says this qualified necessity always rests on something hypothetical, that is, a law of nature, and the natural sciences always seek necessary entailments that hold between the natures of things that actually exist. The inference drawn by the natural sciences, that is, the conclusive force of an argument, rests on the sense of the antecedent. Take, for instance, 'a man is an animal'. He says this must be true as long as there are men (antecedent) and this conditional necessity depends on the 'law of nature' that the nature of man cannot exist without the nature of animal being in it. It is this kind of reasoning, based on hypothetical necessity, that we shall see again in the distinctive thought of William of Ockham in the fourteenth century.[36]

---

[33] *LNPS*, p. 524: 'His ita determinatis sciendum est genera et species nullo loquente non minus esse. Cum enim dico "genus vel species est" ipsis nihil attribuo sed institutionem iam factam.'

[34] *Dialectica*, pp. 208 ff. *Tractatus*, III *Topica*, I, *de locis*.

[35] Compare John of Salisbury, *Metalogicon*, II, 13, and see discussion below.

[36] Martin M. Tweedale, 'Abelard and the culmination of the old logic' in *The Cambridge History of Later Medieval Philosophy*, ed. Kretzmann, Kenny and Pinborg (Cambridge, 1982), pp. 143–58; p. 151. *Dialectica*, pp. 283–4:
Unde non alias categoricas ad hypotheticas antecedere concedimus, nisi quod rerum naturam ostendant, quae consecutionis necessitatem in perpetuum custodiat ut istam: 'animal est genus hominis' ad huiusmodi consequentiam: 'si est homo, est animal', et quaecumque rerum tales assignant habitudines, quae hypotheticarum sequentium vim consecutionis conservant. Videtur autem duae consecutionis necessitates: una quidem largior, cum videlicet id quod dicit antecedens non potest esse absque eo quod dicit consequens; altera vero strictior, cum scilicet non solum antecedens absque consequenti non potest esse verum, sed etiam ex se ipsum exigit; quae quidem necessitas in propria consecutionis sententia consistit et veritatem tenet incommutabilem ut, cum dicitur: 'si est homo, est animal', 'homo' proprie ad 'animal' antecedit, cum ex se ipso 'animal' exigit. Cum enim in substantia hominis animal contineatur, cum 'homine' semper 'animal' attribui contingit.
And he says (*Dialectia*, pp. 280–1):
Unde inhaerentiam, quam sola rei destructio aufert, lex naturae exigit, cum nullatenus hominem natura pateretur esse, nisi ei animal inhaeret. Unde et in natura sibi semper adhaerentia videntur, ex quo naturalem consecutionem semper custodiunt, vel ullam ad invicem oppositione recipere, sicut nec ipse homo sibi ipsi opponi potest, licet tamen a se ipso vere removeatur, cum omnino non sit: quod enim omnino non est, nec homo est.

What effect, we would ask, does this have on the truth of an affirmative statement whose existents are no longer? Perhaps more importantly, can there be a true affirmative statement about a hypothetical existent that was never experienced or even known? These questions are at the heart of the issue for us in so far as we are interested in the historical memory. In general, the way round the contingency of experience is for Abelard to posit, as do the natural sciences, a hypothetical necessity, a law of nature, that expresses the necessity of entailment based on the presumption that a statement's referents do, or can, exist, even if they do not do so at the moment. While a thing's existence is transitory, understanding is permanent, because, as Abelard says, the idea remains in the mind independently of the existent to which the idea refers. And the manner in which the idea is had in the mind is central to the problem.

Abelard's theory provides a logical and linguistic development of Augustine's belief that words which describe the experience of others can only have meaning if one has experienced something similar oneself at some time. But for Abelard, one may presume that a statement's referents do or can exist without our having an analogous experience ourself because the conventions of language have been established and these presume the world is constant and capable of being experienced as language describes and signifies it. But, as we shall see, Abelard believes that man only knows by means of sensation, although what man knows in this way is individual things, that is, by their accidents and not their natures. Therefore, what is not sensed can only be known as opinion and not as an intellection, because intellection requires similitudes of things based on sensibles that have been sensed.[37]

Furthermore, Abelard's theory implies the impossibility of cross-cultural or even trans-historical comprehension *unless* one assumes a hypothetical stability in existents to be experienced which can then be signified by propositions whose truth value depends on their possible present existence. There is, then, no distinctive and unique past that can have any meaning for men unless they make the assumption, as he believes they must, that what exists now and which may be experienced and signified, existed in like manner at some earlier time. So long as linguistic

Cum autem (ab) homine nullo modo existente nullus homo sit homo, non tamen ideo oppositus sibi ipse est homo nec ista vera consequentia: 'si est homo, non est homo', quam nec etiam oppositionis proprietas veram faceret, si etiam ipsum hominem sibi oppositum esse contingeret, ut in tractatu de vi inferentiae oppositorum apparebit ... Et fortasse si singularum enuntiationum sensus dictionumque impositionem attendamus, falsa erit consequentiae sententia. Sed si secundum rei naturam inferentiae necessitatem pensemus, quae nulla enuntiatione mutari potest, nulla variabitur significationis mutatione.

[37] *Sup. Porphyr.* III, p. 524.

conventions signify, logic cannot *prove* the prior existence of language referents.[38] This also means that the uniqueness or unrepeatable sensual element of the past as experienced by someone else, cannot be expressed in a statement; language cannot convey unrepeatable uniqueness; and were such a statement attempted it could not be called 'true'. Language can only signify the nature or properties of some past experience, whose nature or properties are had in common with other such experiences and this is what enables us to use words to describe them. Language can only convey common natures, presumed to be shared by discrete individual things of the same kind.

When we turn to Abelard's psychology of signification, elaborated in the *Dialectica*, the *Tractatus de Intellectibus* and the various treatises of the *Logica Ingredientibus*, we see that he considers the basic role of language to be an overt expression of *certain* of the activities of the speaker's *mind*. Boethius, likewise, argued that what is in vocal sound represents the signs of the *soul's affections*, since sound signifies both things and, principally, intellections, and things through them. These activities are seen as prior to and independent of language itself. For Abelard, as for contemporary Cistercians, for Anselm and of course, for Augustine, the soul may grasp an idea better than language can ever express.[39] Language may externalise thoughts but it is not a mere describer of thoughts. Anselm believed this as well. Words are used to talk about the same things that thoughts are *about*. Words, however, do not link ideas. When we say 'a man runs' the words put the very things 'the man' and 'running' into the mind of the hearer, and rational mind links them. Words deal with things.[40] Language therefore is a methodology employed by mind that is 'lower' than intellection. We shall see how for the later scholastics, words are taken to be signs of intellections or ideas which then refer to extramental entities, sensibly experienced. The study of language, for Abelard, addresses the question of how words, either on their own or in grammatical constructions, relate to things on the one hand and to intellections on the other. Language seems to bear analogy with imagination so that words are somehow

---

[38] This is a true understanding of Aristotle. See above, chapter 2.
[39] *Dialectica*, p. 118.
[40] *Dialectica*, p. 154. Also *Tractatus de Intellectibus*, p. 109:
Simplices quidem dicimus intellectus, sicut et simplices quasdam actiones aut tempora quae scilicet nullius succedentibus sibi partibus coniunguntur, compositos vero e contrario. Sicut enim sermonum qui intellectus excitant, ita est et intellectum natura, ut videlicet sicut sermonum alii simplices sunt, singulae scilicet dictiones, alii compositi, velut orationes, quas ex diversis necesse est confici dictionibus propriam in ipsis significationem tenentibus: ita et intellectus ex sermonibus habiti, vel iuxta ipsorum instructionem habendi, modo simplices sunt qui videlicet ex simplicibus habendi sunt sermonibus, modo compositi, qui ex compositi

signifying similitudes or representations of things just as images in the imagination are signifying similitudes in a different (lower) mode.

In the *Tractatus de Intellectibus*, Abelard lists five passions or affections of the soul: *sensus, imaginatio, existimatio, scientia, ratio*, ordered from inferior to superior. *Sensus* and *imaginatio* are possessed in common by men and animals. The others are only in man. Abelard has an Aristotelian/ Boethian notion, distinct from the Augustinian *anima/corpus* division, where instead of using the term *passio* and *affectio* with regard to the body, he prefers *vis* which refers to *anima*, the soul.[41] There is then the possibility of a passage from inferior to superior degrees of the *vires, sensus* to *intelligentia*, by means of the *anime vires: sensus, imaginatio, ratio, intelligentia*. As in Boethius, *perceptio* implies a general power of the soul of which representation is a particular specification. Imagination is the record of sensation where the sensed thing is absent. Imagination does not involve rational judgement: 'nihil ex ratione deliberat'.[42] Imagination is a *confusa animae perceptio*; it is not of a sensible object but is an *animae passio* according with the object *sine sensu*. And in order for one to have intellections one must have imagination's images. Now words signify ideas that images produce in the minds of hearers. This does not mean that for each word there is some *thing* it signifies. Words are common names so that no universal word, eg. man, signifies any specific *thing* since there is no thing the idea of which it introduces. Words, common names, however, are not as universal as intellections which, as we shall see, are creations of the intellect through its own activity.

Abelard asks, what is the reason for our applying or using universal words? This is the major question the answer to which puts Abelard in the vanguard of early scholastic thinking with its dependence on dialectic solutions to arguments. Abelard is treating three interrelated problems here. Firstly, what is the common cause (*communis causa*) according to which the universal is imposed; secondly, what is the mental conception or the intellection of the common similitude (*conceptio intellectus communis similitudinis*); and lastly, is the term (*vocabulum*) called 'common' because of the common cause in which things agree (*propter communem causam in qua res conveniat*) or because of the common conception (*propter communem conceptionem*) or because of both at once?[43]

In the *Logica Ingredientibus*, Abelard shows that intellections that are associated with these universal words do not indicate a something that is

---

[41] See Boethius, *Phil. Consolatio* and *In Isagogen Porphyrii Commenta*, ed. S. Brandt, (Leipzig, 1906) p. 16.
[42] *De Intellectibus*, p. 105.
[43] *Sup. Porphyr.*, in *LI*, pp. 19–24: Also see Stock, *Implications of Literacy*, pp. 395–6.

conceived by these intellections; furthermore, universal utterances do not deal with things either. Universals have no subject thing. All things in the world subsist distinctly in themselves; they do not agree in a shared *thing* which could serve as that in virtue of which universal names are applied. In other words, universals do not point to a thing-like essence or separable form in, for instance, individual men, which they share in being men. Therefore, we are still left with the question, what is the idea that is generated by the universal word an idea of? what is being signified? Abelard wants to show that a common name like 'man' is not correctly said to signify a specific individual like Socrates or anyone else, since no one individual is selected out by the force of the name although it is true that the word 'man' names or denominates individuals. Here, he draws upon a psychology that links sensible things with understanding: the *genera* and *species*, he says, have been given 'in' sensibles only in the sense that they name sensibles but they signify outside sensibles.[44] A common name like 'man' denotes things that are observable by the senses (individual men) but it does so in virtue of individual men having a property that is not observable by the senses, namely rationality. And rationality is not a thing. Rationality is what is signified by the common name without naming or denoting it. Signification does not therefore express a genuine relation between a sign and something else. Realists would say that the sign did express a real relation between itself and something else, that is, that rationality was a something. Thus, common names like 'man' signify but we cannot pick out the items or the things they denote and say 'these are what are signified'. Furthermore, a name can denote, as opposed to signify, even when what is named does not actually exist, for example, a chimera. But this would make the denotation of a nonexistent vacuously true.[45]

[44] *Sup. Porphyr*, in *LI*, p. 29:
Unde et nomina ipsa universalia et corporea dicuntur quantum ad naturam rerum (et si ea quae discreta sunt) et incorporea quantum ad modum significationis, quia etsi ea quae discreta sunt, nominent, non tamen discrete et determinate ... Et dicuntur universalia subsistere in sensibilibus id est significare intrinsecam substantiam existentem in re sensibili ex exterioribus formis et cum eam substantiam significent, quae actualiter subsistit in re sensibili, eandem tamen naturaliter separatam a re sensibili demonstrant.

[45] See Tweedale's discussion in the *Cambridge History of Later Medieval Philosophy*, pp. 143–58. Also *De Intellectibus*, 'Qui sani intellectus vel cassi', pp. 114–15:
Cassi vero quidem e contrario sunt, ut si videlicet intelligam chimaeram quae omnino non est, vel chimaeram esse aliquid, cum omnino nihil sunt. Quia enim hic intellectus chimaerae in rerum eventu rem subiectam non habet quae videlicet res secundum huiusmodi intellectum sane deliberari valeat, ut scilicet eam rem veraciter attendi chimaeram liceat, cassus est omnino intellectus.
Also *De Intellectibus*, pp. 126–7: 'Ad quod respondeo quod cum dicitur "intelligo chimaeram" vel "chimaera intelligitur" figurativa est locutio'.

In the *Logica Ingredientibus*, Abelard describes the psychological stages by which we can say we come to understand. He follows Boethius's interpretation of Aristotle's *De Interpretatione*. According to Boethius, the relationship between language, sense, imagination and intellectual understanding, based on Aristotle's *De Anima*, III, 8, is interpreted in the following way. When we use a name like Socrates we are signifying both a mental image as well as an intellectual understanding of the real man. Mental intellections are founded on sense and imagination. When a thing is perceived by sense or imagination, the mind creates a mental image and then later, the confused images of the imagination are sifted and coordinated for a fuller understanding. Boethius insists that Aristotle believes nouns and verbs to be signifying mental intellections rather than reflecting sense impressions or images directly.[46] Nouns and verbs enunciated in a sentence are vocal declarations of the *mind's affectations* and this is also true of writing which represents what is spoken. But it is important to realise that Boethius believes that every reception in the soul reflects the nature of reality *accurately* and the *passiones animae* are born through *adequate* likenesses or similitudes of things.[47] Abelard agrees with this.

Abelard says the first beginning stage in understanding occurs when the soul applies itself through a kind of inchoate cogitation and it does this before it *distinguishes* the *nature* of a thing or its properties. This first stage of inchoate cogitation is called imagination.[48] When the soul thereafter actively attends to or notes a nature of some thing in as much as the thing is the being (*ens*), or substance, or body, or white or Socrates, this activity is called intellection, since from confusion which belongs to the imagination, the soul has been led by reason to intellection.[49]

Understanding hinges on this active, intellective attention which is focused on the confused images of the imagination. Abelard distinguishes the act of intellection (*intellectus*) from acts of sense perception (*sensus*). Both sensing and intellection are the soul's activities in relation to external reality. In order to have an intellection one must first have sensed

[46] Boethius, *Commentaria*, Book I, p. 29.
[47] *Ibid.*, p. 34. See Stock, *Implications of Literacy*, p. 371.
[48] *De Intellectibus*, p. 105:
Differentia imaginationis ad intellectum. ... sed in his rebus quas sensimus nihil aliud imaginatio sit quam quaedam sensus recordatio, cum videlicet re quam sentiebamus absente, eo adhuc modo sese animus ... Est itaque imaginatio confusa animae perceptio, sine sensu eius scilicet rei quam imaginariam confusam dicimus, cum nihil ipsa ex ratione deliberet, sicut nec sensus. Saepe quippe sentimus ea quae nequaquam intelligentes attendimus, et cum ad exteriora quae occurrunt circumferatur sensus, animus tamen per intellectum ad alia dirigitur.
[49] 'Ubi vero attendit naturam aliquam rei vel in eo quod res est vel ens vel substantia vel corpus vel alba vel Socrates, intellectus dicitur, cum quidem de confusione quae imaginationis erat, ad intellectum per rationem dicitur' (*LI*, p. 317).

something in terms of the object's accidents. In the *Gloss on Porphyry*,[50] he
argues that the most perfect knowledge we can ever attain is the intellection of an individual, but this is achieved by first sensually experiencing the
thing's accidents rather than its nature. There are then, two kinds of
knowledge we may attain: superficial sensation on the one hand, and
intellection of a universal on the other, where intellection is dependent on
the image of an absent thing in the imagination. When we have an
intellection of a universal without having first perceived, sensed or experienced the individual which is signified by a universal, or where the
universal is imperceptible, such as *paternitas, rationalitas, mortalitas*, then
we have an opinion rather than an intellection. That power of the soul
existimatio, which is synonymous but not identical with *credulitas, fides* and
opinio, presupposes the *intellectus* but not vice versa.[51] Hence, there is a
difference between the object of faith and that of cognition. In the case of
opinion or faith, the object is not sensible whereas for *cognitio*, the *res* is, on
the contrary, capable of being experienced.[52] We may recall that Anselm
also used *intelligere* to refer to the confrontation between mind and
external reality where *ratio* is only exercised through reference to external
reality. *Ratio* remains unaffected by the truth of faith or divine revelation.
For both Anselm and Abelard, faith can lead on to understanding but
understanding does not lead to faith.

In effect, Abelard describes the *vis sensualis* and the *vis intellectus* as
powers of the soul to perceive and understand respectively. Both sensing
and understanding belong to the soul but with a difference, as Aristotle
had also said. Sense is exercised, says Abelard, only through corporeal
instruments which perceive bodies or what is in bodies. He provides the
example of seeing a tower or its visible qualities. The senses do not
perceive the substances themselves in their nature but only their accidents. Sensation allows us only to touch the object lightly; and while
opening up the world of body to us, sensation does not permit us to attain
the incorporeal or the absent. In order to grasp the incorporeal or the
absent we require the activities of imagination and intellection.

On the other hand, *intellectus* does not require a corporeal instrument,
nor is it necessary for intellection to have a subject body.[53] As for

---

50 *LI*, pp. 21–3.
51 'Omnis itaque qui aliquid existimat, id quod existimat necessario intelligit: non autem e
converso' (*De Intellectibus*, p. 108).
52 See Abelard's definition of faith in his *Introductio ad Theologiam, PL* 178, 1051. Ulivi, the
editor of the *De Intellectibus*, says there is no value judgement intended here in Abelard's
distinction between *estimatio/existimatio* and *cognitio*, only a reference to the diversity of
objects (p. 34).
53 *De Intellectibus*, pp. 103–4: 'Differentia sensus ad intellectum'.

247

Augustine, so too for Abelard, although intellection requires similitudes it does not require images of corporeal things as subjects on which it gazes. Rather, intellection is content with a similitude or likeness of the thing which the soul itself constructs for itself and it is this similitude towards which it directs its action of understanding.[54] Therefore, if the tower were destroyed or somehow removed from the senses, the sensing which dealt with the tower perishes also while the idea remains through a likeness of the thing that is retained by the soul.[55] If intellection is this active capacity to regard the soul's constructed likeness, then we are left with the question – just what is this likeness a likeness of? Abelard says the intellection relies on the similitudes that are created by the soul through its activity of imagining, so that the images in the imagination are that towards which intellection turns in order that the soul may thereafter construct its own likenesses. The soul's constructed likenesses are therefore likenesses of the images in the imagination. Abelard seems to be describing the activity of an active intellect here but is still within the Augustinian tradition of the interior vision of the soul turning its gaze actively on imagination. The imaginative similitude, however, is not the intellection which is yet another kind of similitude. The intellective similitude he describes as an activity, a noting, an active attention, which, with the aid of reason, leads to under-standing. Understanding is, then, the result of a noting of the constructed likeness of some nature or property which is not a thing.

Now, sense perception requires body or perceptible qualities, but it is argued that sensing is not of the thing as substance towards which the sensing is directed; rather one senses accidents of things. When the object that is sensed in this way is present to the senses, then thinking in the presence of the sensed object does not require an image. Imagination remains dormant when we think of what we are at the same time sensually experiencing.[56] The only time we need an image is when the sensible object no longer is present to the senses. This means that when we deal with the past or future, we must invoke images from imagination in order that the soul may construct voluntarily its own likenesses to be understood by higher mind.[57] Ideas rely on the similitudes that remain of bodies and further similitudes are created by the soul from the activity of sorting out images in the imagination. Ideas then are not likenesses or images which belong to the imagination. Rather reason, inspired by the will, takes these imaginative images and presents them to the attention of intellect. The

---

54 'Intellectus autem sicut nec corporeo indigens instrumento est, ita nec necesse est eum subiectum corpus habere in quod mittatur, sed rei similitudine contentus est, quam sibi ipse animus conficit, in quam suae intelligentiae actionem dirigit.'
55 *LI*, p. 20.   56 Compare *De Intellectibus*, p. 106.
57 'Ut tunc intellectus imagine non egeat cum praesto est ei substantiae veritas' (*LI*, p. 21).

idea is not the form of the thing which it grasps. Rather intellection is an action of the soul and the form or image towards which it is directed is a certain imaginary created thing (*res imaginaria*) which the soul voluntarily creates for itself. Its likeness is not substance or accident.[58] Abelard provides the example of those imaginary cities seen in sleep or the form for constructing a building which the architect conceives as a model of the thing to be constructed which, he says, we cannot call substance or accident. Now, these images or similitudes in imagination, or, thereafter, those similitudes formed by the soul in an act of intellection, are not real entities. Abelard uses the familiar notion of the mirror which has reflections, the reflections not being the things reflected but their similitudes.[59] We have already met this in Anselm and Aelred but it is more emphatic and explicit with Abelard. We have on the one hand a rejection of Aristotle's physical imprints as well as an attack on the Platonists. Abelard says:

If someone asks whether these imaginary forms by which we have imagination and thereafter intellections, are any things, we deny it. They are neither substances nor forms sustained by substances. When after having seen some tower I recall it, although it is absent or completely destroyed, the immense and long four-sided image which the soul constructs as though it is constructed before the mind's eye, is neither substance nor form.

We are left with the problem of just what this construction, this activity of mind is. It is certainly not a thing. We are also left asking just how we can say anything true about these similitudes or mirror images; and how we can affirm that they accurately resemble physical things. Abelard says that the image is not the mind formed into some similitude of singular things since the mind is completely indivisible.[60] And he rejects Aristotle when he takes Aristotle to say the image *is* the idea or intellection itself, quoting

---

[58] *LI*, p. 20:
Sicut autem sensus non est res sentita in quam dirigitur, sic nec intellectus forma est rei quam concipit, sed intellectus actio quaedam est animae, unde intelligens dicitur, forma vero in quam dirigitur, res imaginaria quaedam est et ficta, quam sibi, quando vult et qualem vult, animus conficit, quales sunt illae imaginariae civitates quae in somno videntur . . .
Compare Aristotle, *De Anima*, III, 8, 432a 3–14:
unless one perceived things one would not learn or understand anything and when one contemplates one must simultaneously contemplate an image; for images are like sense perceptions except that they are without matter. But imagination is different from assertion and denial, for truth and falsity involve a combination of thoughts. But what distinguishes first thoughts from images? Surely neither these nor any other thoughts will be images but they will not exist without images.

[59] *LI*, p. 21.

[60] 'Sed cum anima omnino indivisibilis sit'. See Aelred, as discussed above, ch. 12.

De Interpretatione that 'these and their similitudes are the same things'. This is unacceptable to Abelard. The idea which is a form of the indivisible mind cannot exceed its own subject,[61] so that it cannot fit itself to the quantity of all things nor transfigure itself into all forms. We have already met this in more inconclusive form in Aelred's *De Anima* where he also drew the analogy of the memory with a mirror. Thus, says Abelard, we concede that no thing whatever is an image or simulacrum of things which the soul makes for itself in order to contemplate in it a thing which is absent.[62]

He reminds us that so long as the thing is present and sensed we do not require an image of it;[63] the image is conceived only as a substitute for the thing when it is not present.[64] We have also been told that universal names give rise to intellections and they also signify intellections. Furthermore, Abelard has said that there is a close association between intellection and those mental images or similitudes in the imagination, but he does not identify the act of thinking of something with its associated image in the imagination. He is willing to call the intellection a mental thing itself although what it is an intellection of is not a thing.[65] He has rejected what he takes to be Aristotle's solution that the idea is an idea of the image where idea and image are the same thing, because this would imply that there were isolated entities, discrete similitudes in the mind which is indivisible. Instead, Abelard says that in intellection we *conceive*[66] an image, but ideas of different things might be *associated* with a single image.[67] Although the image is the same, there are many ways of conceiving it, and these many ways are mind's own activity, an activity which does not alter its indivisible nature.[68] Ideas are modes of signifying just as images are, but animals signify through images alone, whereas the human mind's *vis intellectus* has a mode of signifying *in discretione attendendi*, through

---

[61] '... subjectum suum non potest excedere.'

[62] Compare Aristotle, *De Anima*, III, 6, 430b 26: 'Every assertion says something of something, as too does denial and is true or false. But not every thought is such; that of what a thing is in respect of "what it is for it to be what it was" is true, and does not say something of something.'

[63] Compare Aristotle, *De Anima*, III, 7, 431a: 'Actual knowledge is identical with its object. But potential knowledge is prior in time in the individual, but not prior even in time in general; for all things that come to be are derived from that which is so actually.'

[64] 'Unde nil penitus esse concedimus huiusmodi imagines vel simulacra rerum, quas sibi animus fingit ut in eis res absentes contemplari queat ... Quippe similitudo non nisi pro re concepta erat. Ubi vero res tenetur, non est opus similitudine' (*LI*, pp. 314–15).

[65] *LI*, p. 314.   [66] 'concipit'.

[67] Aristotle, *De Anima*, III, 11, 434a: 'Hence we have the power of constructing a single image out of a number of images, that is, we have the ability to make one image out of many.'

[68] Compare *De Intellectibus*, p. 121.

discretionary attention, which pertains to reason.[69] Thus, the same image can give rise to diverse attentions which vary the idea about the nature of something.

We may well compare this with William of St Thierry's belief that words are only instruments by which one attains God who is above language. However, Abelard is going further in providing a psychology which regards the created world through the signifying capacity of established language and the given powers of the soul. An Augustinian and Plotinian influence seems in evidence when Abelard speaks of the mind's activities of voluntary attention. The *vis intellectus* can voluntarily use images in order to think of the characteristics which images exhibit, but it has a special ability to vary what the mind is attending to without altering the contents of the imagination. He says that 'when another person and I think about rationality and notice that it is what makes the soul able to discern, both our attentions are true and the same *although we establish for that same thing diverse images just as whoever uses some sign ought to establish it at his own willing*' (emphasis added). Abelard's dialectical focus is therefore on meaning rather than on transcendence. He is addressing the question of how we can ever say anything true about mental images if they are not things; how we can predicate truth of mirror images. How can we say that similitudes, be they images, words or ideas, resemble the objective world which we are signifying by these universals which are not themselves things? He is attempting to deny the current Platonic realism of ideas by meeting head on the question of whether there are ideas in our minds of things in our mind. This is analogous to the Platonic and Augustinian problem of ideas being *in* God's mind with the attendant problems of such ideas militating against the divine mind's simplicity and lack of division and multiplicity.

Augustine had baptised Plato's forms as divine ideas in God's mind, whereas Plato's ideas were not to be identified with or located within the Creator's mind. Rather, the world of ideas was generated by the Good which is not *in* the divine mind. Furthermore, for Plato, contemplation is the highest act of mind but where thinking is described as a motionless *reception* rather than a productive act. Augustine altered this on the basis of his reading of Plotinus. For Plotinus, the ideas are located ontologically in

---

[69] *LI*, p. 329. In *De Intellectibus*, p. 104, he distinguishes between *ratio* as a *habitus* and *rationalitas* as the faculty, the former being identified with *animus*: 'Rationem autem dicimus vim ipsam sue facultatem discreti animi qua rerum naturas perspicere ac diiudicare veraciter sufficit.' It is this capacity which distinguishes intellection from sensing and imagination. Intellection as an activity of *ratio* derives from *ratio* as its perpetual effect: 'Intellectum ... necessario ex ratione descendere tamquam perpetuum rationis effectum' (p. 105).

the divine Nous, the Intellectual Principle that emanates from the unknowable One, as we have seen. They are eternally thought by the eternal mind as its co-natural object, mind thinking itself. The question that emerged however, was over the relative priority of mind (Nous) and its ideas. Neo-Platonism after Plotinus came down on the side of the absolute priority of mind as the ultimate spiritual agent over all ideas, so that all existential acts must precede the idea. Abelard's emphasis on the activity of mind constructing its own images towards which the intellect turns its gaze and by which it produces ideas which give rise to the mind's understanding, is a correlate of this neo-Platonist tradition.

It was through Plotinus's speaking of the Intellectual Principle, Nous, as a dynamic and active generator of ideas, taken up by Augustine, that the tradition was presented to the Latin west. The modified realism of the fifth- and sixth-century neo-Platonists of the Alexandrian School who commented on Aristotle's logical works, also emphasised the priority of mind as activity over its ideas.[70] This tradition would continue into the thirteenth century, especially in the new metaphysics of Aquinas for whom the divine ideas are the signifying signs of things, the meaning of things (*intentiones rerum*) and not the things themselves.

We shall have more to say about Aquinas later, but here it is important to draw out the implicit legacy that Abelard's dialectical analysis left for the next century. The being of things in the world is distinct from their meaning for Aquinas so that the subjective being of ideas which are identified with the act of mind that thinks them is distinguished from their objective content; their intentional meaning and reference can be multiple and distinct. Aquinas's anti-Platonist stance here seems to have taken Abelard's psychology of signification one step further, and we shall

[70] See Linos Benakis, 'The problem of general concepts in neo-Platonism and Byzantine thought', in *Neoplatonism and Christian Thought*, ed. Dominic J. O'Meara, (Albany, N.Y., 1982), pp. 75–86. For an interesting argument that the Greek medieval tradition, derived from the Alexandrian neo-Platonists commenting on Aristotle's logic, provided a variation of Platonic and Aristotelian realism (and not nominalism) which influenced Avicenna and thereafter Anselm and Abelard (p. 77). Byzantine philosophy of the ninth through fourteenth centuries dealing with the problem of general concepts does not resemble the dispute in the west because in the east there was an almost universal acceptance of solutions of the Alexandrian neo-Platonists who were moderate conceptual realists (p. 85). In the west, the Alexandrian solution appears as a compromise between realist and nominalist extremes, and was adopted by Abelard, Albertus, Aquinas, through Avicenna (p. 86). For a different but complementary approach to this influence, see Tullio Gregory, 'The Platonic Inheritance', in *A History of Twelfth-Century Western Philosophy*, ed. P. Dronke (Cambridge, 1988), pp. 54–80. Gregory argues that the Timaen physics enriched with Stoic elements already provided an interpretative scheme of becoming in which room was thereafter found for the suggestions of Arabic cosmology and philosophy. It is therefore not surprising that new translations from the Arabic of scientific texts originate from twelfth-century Platonic circles (p. 66).

observe this more closely later. But there is already in Abelard a distinction between an intrinsic act of existence of things in their own right as individuals, and their intelligibility. There is a dimension of being outside the mind to which is added an enrichment of the universe through the operations of the *vis intellectus* which uses images in such a way as to vary what the mind of a thinker is attending to without altering the contents of imagination or the world of experience to which images relate. What is being toned down in Abelard as it will be for some of the thirteenth-century scholastics, is the notion that all creatures exist in a higher more perfect state in the exemplary idea of each of them in God's mind than in their own created being. A thing's own being is not to be found in its idea taken as a separable immaterial entity. Rather, a thing's own being is to be found in its meaning, its intelligibility, for Abelard. Meaning, the force of an idea, consists in the mind's distinction of attention to the natures of things, an activity pertaining to reason and which beasts lack. Thus there are many ways of conceiving the same image so that there are many ways of interpreting the world and endowing it with true meaning, a meaning which goes well beyond the imagination's images.[71] In his *Gloss on the Perihermenias*, Abelard says that the plurality of *dicta* that may be possible in a proposition, that is, that a word or phrase may have multiple meanings, is not because of the word itself (*ex vi vocis*) but stems from the plurality of interpretations which might be made of a proposition. Interpreting mind is given the freedom instead of the emphasis being placed on ambiguity as an inherent quality of language.[72] The force of an idea does not consist in its mode of signifying but consists in the distinction of attention which pertains only to human reason.

Abelard is explaining the vast capacities of mind's active interpretation where the rational mind's activity is somehow independent, using images and words to construct meaning. Although Abelard does not allude to the ideas of justice, truth etc. as being somehow placed in the human mind from the beginning, he would affirm that universals, like justice, signified just properties.

His logic also implies that the mind has conventions of activity unique to itself which run parallel with those linguistic conventions which men establish to speak about and think about the world. It is of some importance that he makes no mention of the intellect's capacity to judge true or false against immutable truths already in the mind. In fact, he does not

---

[71] His itaque intellectus non in modo significandi consistit, quod et bestiae faciunt per imaginem, sed in discretione attendendi, quod ad rationem solum pertinet, cuius omnino bestiae expertes sunt' (*LI, Sup. periermenias*, p. 329).

[72] As pointed out by Constant Mews, 'On dating the works of Peter Abelard', *AHDLMA*, 52 (1985), pp. 73–134; p. 88. See above, n. 71.

seem to believe in immutable truths in the mind. What is in the mind depends on a sensed experience of the world in order that one may have intellections of the natures of such things. When one has universals in the mind like mortality, rationality, paternity, which are either never sensually experienced or simply imperceptible, we have, he says, opinions rather than intellections.[73] Thus intellectual judgement or meaning relates to the existential world. His concern in his logical writings is to show how meaning is generated by mind's activities through the use of universals: images, words, ideas. The *vis intellectus* for Abelard is equivalent to the understanding of universals, common names. The force of an idea, its meaning, belongs to reason rather than to images or modes of signifying and it is not in a one to one correspondence with images. Since the mode of understanding is different from the mode of subsisting, something can be understood in a way that is different from the way it exists.[74] Understanding is based on a process of abstraction so that one thing can be understood separate from another whereas in reality there is no separation at all. Through reason's application, mind can think of the matter or form of a thing which exists both in matter and form inseparably. What we call the isolation or the distinction occurs in the mind.[75] It is precisely this mode of understanding through a voluntary attention of the *vis intellectus* that is responsible for our being able to consider the future through images picturing items as though they were present. It is also the attention of the *vis intellectus* through which we come to understanding, which enables us to consider the past through images as though they were present. Our lengthy introduction has prepared us for Abelard's analysis of what it is to remember, how we understand the past, and how the past is given meaning.[76]

He says

perhaps it would be better to say that intellection is not judged true or false according to the conception or disposition of images, but rather according to the attention of the mind, that is, that mind attends to an image as being or not being as things are or are not, or as having been or having not been as things were or were not, or as going to be or going not to be as things will be or will not be. For I do not gather images in my mind only in order that I may attend presently to what is, but also that I may presently attend to what happened before or what is going to happen. The *vis intellectus* which is through reason, pertains more to discretionary distinction[77] than

---

[73] *Sup. Porphyr.*, p. 23.
[74] 'Et aliter tamen quodam modo quam sit, dicitur intelligi, non alio quidem statu quam sit ut supra dictum est, sed in eo aliter, quod alius modus est intelligendi quam subsistendi' (*LI*, p. 25).
[75] *Sup. Porphyr.*, pp. 25–6.   [76] *Sup. periermenias*, p. 328.
[77] Note that 'distinction' according to Aristotle's *Categories*, is an act of distinguishing between the various meanings of things said in several different senses. Distinction is therefore an investigation of the different senses in which each word may be predicated. It

to the conception of images, which latter belong to imagining. Therefore, whatever images we use or however we dispose them, they do not refer to the truth of the intellection as long as there is distinctive attention. Otherwise memory of the past and foresight of the future would never be associated with valid or correct conceptions.[78] While therefore we conceive presently the future or the past, that is, presently we attend to what is not, the power of conception is sane or valid which pertains to the intellection because whoever considers presently does not attend to what is present but rather to what was or what will be. Therefore the truth or falseness of intellection pertains not to the conception of images but to the attention paid to things through images since we make images as signs of things rather than images being that which is signified.[79]

Thus a valid conception is entirely dependent on the rational *vis intellectus'* distinctive attention paid to the past which remains in the mind as a similitude, an image, as yet unjudged and in the present. And the judgement of intellection's truth is always in the present. The truth of intellection is constant no matter how we dispose of images.

But then what is it that makes the true meaning which results from mind's attentive judgement of images of the past in the present, objective

appears clear that Abelard uses this notion of mental distinction derived from logical operation. There is here a probable origin, in dialectic, of the development of *distinctiones* as used by sermon writers. On sermon *distinctiones* see Richard and Mary Rouse, '*Statim invenire*: schools, preachers and new attitudes to the page', in *Renaissance and Renewal in the Twelfth Century*, pp. 201–28. Also on *distinctiones* see Abelard's Prologue, *Sic et Non*.

[78] Compare John of Salisbury, *Metalogicon*, III, 4 and the discussion below.

[79] Illud etiam fortasse convenientius dicetur intellectum neque verum neque falsum iudicari, secundum conceptionem vel dispositionem imaginum, sed secundum attentionem animi quod videlicet ita attendit esse vel non esse, uti est vel non est vel fuisse vel non, uti fuit vel non, vel fore vel non, uti erit vel non. Non enim ad hoc imagines in animo colligo praesentialiter ut praesentialiter sic esse attendam, sed sic antea contigisse vel contingendum esse. Magis enim vis intellectus qui rationis est, ad discretionem pertinet quam ad conceptionem imaginum quae est imaginationis. Quibuscumque ergo imaginibus utamur vel quomodo eas disponamus, nil refert ad veritatem intellectus, dummodo attentio discretionis sit. Alioquin numquam memoria de praeteritis vel providentia de futuris sanae conceptionis essent. Cum ergo futurum vel praeteritum praesentialiter concipimus, sed praesentialiter esse non attendimus, sana est vis conceptionis quae ad intellectum pertinet, quia qui considerat praesentialiter, non attendit praesens esse, sed sic vel fuisse iam vel adhuc futurum esse. Ideo autem non ad conceptionem imaginum sed ad attentionem rerum, per imagines veritas intellectus vel falsitas pertinent, quia imagines tantum pro signis constituimus non eas quidem significantes, sed in eis res attendentes ... Unde si sana est attentio rationis, qualiscumque sit dispositio imaginum vel forma, sanus est intellectus. Cum enim vim et naturam rerum insensibilium attendimus sicut spirituum vel qualitatum quas non sentimus, alius aliam fingit imaginem et alius aliam, cum tamen utraque vim naturae recte attendat ... Et saepe in eadem imagine diversae attentiones variant intellectus ... Vis itaque intellectus non in modo significandi modo consistit, quod et bestiae faciunt per imaginem, sed in discretione attendi quod ad rationem solum pertinet ... Est enim discretio vis deliberandi et attendendi rerum naturas vel proprietates. (*LI*, pp. 328–9)

about the past? How do we know we are dealing with the past at all? Abelard is not implicitly operating with the Augustinian notion that images and experiences in the mind as images are always judged according to a-temporal immutable truths already in the mind. Rather, he is saying that there is an objective reality as well as a reality of the activity of intellection and that language and imagination's images are merely instruments which enable us to speak and think about the natures of things, language however, being conventionally established, but thought presumably being divinely established through our endowed rationality. Indeed, following Boethius, he says that *intellectus* rather than *voces* are the same among different peoples, so that human understanding, based on a distinctively human and permanent mode of mental conceptualisation, is a fixed aspect of what 'being a man' means.[80] What is diverse among men of different linguistic cultures is their mode of signifying. Language has tenses but mental operations and the natures of things do not. If the *vis intellectus* has a tense at all, it is the continuous present.[81] Aquinas as we shall see, would reaffirm these epistemological conditions to come to the same conclusions about how we know the past.

In his *Gloss on the Perihermenias*, Abelard says:

Plato calls images incorporeal and therefore they are not capable of being sensed by corporeal senses. Some hold that (incorporeal images) are what words designate [i.e. realists]. Aristotle [and Abelard] oppose this. It is not on account of the similitude of things nor on account of a similitude of ideas that words are established, but more on account of things and their ideas, in order that there might be a doctrine about the nature of things and not a doctrine about this sort of image or figment. Words are also images or figments. Images or figments are signs of things which then set up ideas. It is rather merely through such images or figments when we substitute them for absent things as though they were signs of them, that we are able to have an account of things and their ideas. Thus by these figments used as signs, words set up ideas of things and not ideas of images or figments. The words (*voces*) lead the mind of the *listener* to a similitude of a thing so that mind will attend via that similitude to the individual thing for which it substitutes, and not to the similitude itself.[82]

As we have already seen, the images are not what we think of and words do not cause us to think of images but on things. For Abelard, then, images and words serve as intermediaries by which we think of things that are not images, but that are part of the objective world. At either extreme, the

---

[80] *Sup. periermenias*, p. 323.
[81] 'Ideo autem non ad conceptionem imaginem sed ad attentionem rerum per imagines veritas intellectus vel falsitas pertinent ...' (*LI*, p. 328). See above, no. 80.
[82] *LI*, p. 315. This is evidence of Abelard's classroom context where he addresses listeners rather than the contemplative reader.

active attention of mind and the *res* are constants. But different languages employ different modes of signifying. Images and words are *intersigna*, intermediary signs. The mind has the independence to use images and words as it will. Words and images do not initiate meaning; the *vis intellectus* endows with meaning. Images and words are only established means to meaning. Signifying common names are made diverse by intellection.

We have already said that Abelard faces directly the Platonic issue of whether universal names signify forms that are in the divine mind. He acknowledges that this view, found in the grammarian Priscian, is one held by the great authorities. But he does not appear to be able to accept this doctrine because it would contradict his own belief that words signify the real world we think and talk about, rather than mental entities (similitudes) we use to think of things. Thus he continually denies that the natures and properties which universal words signify are themselves things. Justice and truth are not things. And this has great importance for his analysis of the trinity. Here we see the school dialectician entering a theological debate with the tools of logic to clarify meaning.

In his *Theologia Christiana*,[83] he defends the simplicity of God by saying that if forms are in the divine mind they are not there as things and not really *in* God who is simple. The diversity of the three divine persons depends on *our* being able to think of a diversity in a unity and we must therefore be able to develop some mode of differentiation which still maintains the divine simplicity.[84] He says that something can be called the

---

[83] E. M. Buytaert, ed., *Petri Abaelardi Opera Theologica*, CCCM, XI, XII (Turnhout, 1969), vol. 2, *Theologia Christiana*. Also *PL* 178, 1237–41.

[84] William of St Thierry argued against the notion of compositeness in God, against Abelard, quoting Augustine, *Epistola*, 169, ii, 7 (*PL* 33,745) that the Word endured immutably in His own nature, in which nothing composite with which He might subsist should be suspected: 'Permanente tamen verbo in sua natura incommutabiliter, in qua nihil compositi cum quo subsistat ulla phantasia humani animi suspicandum est.' William found it abhorrent to speak of a division of Christ's person and a commixture of his human and divine substance. He read Abelard as having said a creature cannot be part of his Creator and if not part of God, the human creature which Christ assumed, could not be a person of the Trinity. *Adversus Abaelardum*, III, PL 178, 278C–280B. At least in Abelard's logical writings there seems implicit a discussion of human motivation and understanding without reference to man's divinity and the consequent necessity of alluding to theological rather than natural arguments. Logic as an *ars sermocinalis* makes this possible. But in the *Theologia Christiana* (Buytaert, vol. 2), 'De deo trino et uno', Book II, Abelard defends appealing to pagan letters in Christian theology, especially the disciplines of grammar, dialectic and rhetoric, in order to better understand the sources of Christian doctrine *if* it is done inside the limits assigned by the Church to such practice (II, pp. 116–29). In Books III and IV he considers the trinity from the viewpoint of natural reason (III, 1–2) and dialectically considered (III, 3–187). Dialectic is good *per se* but must be applied to theology with the same prescribed prudence (pp. 3–52). And he says he will stay with this rule of Christian prudence (pp. 53–8).

same or diverse in definition or property, and here he explains what he means by property, nature or *status*.

He says we commonly speak of the same *status* or nature or diverse natures when we speak of items which are the same or diverse by definition, and he gives as an example of the same *status* that of a blade and a sword.[85] Likewise, the divine persons are distinct in definition but not in essence. The different properties are not forms in God. Rather they are *quasi propria*, just as Aristotle says it is common to every substance (1) not to be *in* a subject, (2) not to sustain more or less, and (3) to have nothing contrary to it. By these 'common natures' which Aristotle assigns, he does not mean forms. The common natures are not different from the substances they are in.

Abelard is attempting to deal with Aristotle's composite first category–substance. Thus, he says we can speak of something distinctive to the Father, Son and Holy Spirit without speaking of separate forms in God. The divine properties are relations (*proprietates vel relationes*) which are similar to expressions or mental images, none of which are things.

This would mean that mind itself, at the human level, is simple so that the traditional Augustinian distinction between *memoria*, *ratio* and *voluntas* are only relations, properties, displaying a common nature or *status* so that these properties are not essentially distinct from one another or from mind itself.[86] Thus whenever we refer to what Abelard calls a man's nature or *status*, his 'being a man', his *modus essendi*, through the use of the common noun 'man', we are not referring to a thing, since 'being a man' is not a thing. The verbal noun-phrase 'being a man' is equivalent to a nature and we call the nature of man his 'being a man' which is not a thing. It is this nature or *status* which is the common cause of the application of universal nouns to singulars in as much as they agree with each other.[87] Natures or *status* are the causes of common nouns; they are not themselves universal but that which universals signify.

Most important for us is that Abelard believes that past actions can also be called causes of universals even though they are not now things. Abelard's concern here is to deny that talking about 'being a man' or 'past actions' (both of which cause universals) or, indeed, any such nature or *status* that may be signified, forces us to accept that there is some universal to which we are referring over and above the concrete individuals that share such a nature.[88] The realist theory of universals which says that a

[85] In his *Theologia 'summi boni'*, III, ed. H. Ostlender, BGPTMA, 35, vols. 2–3 (1939), Abelard emphasised that identity of essence is distinct from identity of property or definition.
[86] Compare Alcuin's *dignitates* and Aquinas, below, ch. 20.   [87] *LI*, p. 20.
[88] See Tweedale, *Abailard on Universals*, p. 207.

common noun is actually referring to a universal and separable thing is impossible for Abelard. The natures of past actions are not separable things. Past actions are discrete events, the *natures* of which cause common nouns or universals to signify them.

That a nature or *status* may be signified by a common noun ties in with Abelard's assertion that there is no *necessity* either in ordinary discourse or in logic to employ names for what verbs and sentences signify. So too in talking about objects of thought (what ideas are ideas of), we need not treat psychological discourse as containing names of things which are these separable objects. If we did so we would be affirming that there were things to which we referred and 'man' as a universal is not a thing.

This theory is doing something extraordinary. It is working against the tendency we examined that continued to develop further among twelfth-century Cistercians, to classify sense impressions through to intellectual conceptions as things of greater or lesser corporeity, by showing that such schemas do not understand the nature of universals. In effect, Abelard seems to be attempting to revive the Aristotelian understanding of first substance as composite by arguing that the discipline of logical dialectic shows us that signs, be they images, words or ideas, enable the natures of things to have meaning without extracting this nature or *status* from things as though it were a separable something. Meaning for Abelard is not naming. Both the rational mind on the one hand and a world in which *status* can be found on the other are required for us to establish universal words, but in his logical works it appears to be the world comprising individual things that is the more important cause of our being able to speak with meaning. Thus, universals are found in the world of things but they are not themselves in that world. Words are universals but they signify an objective *status* and this *status* depends for its existence on the hypothetical existence of concrete individuals which share *status* to which words refer. When sentences say something, they do not signify merely by naming what they signify. Thus, rational mind's activity, on the one hand, and a world in which *status* are found, on the other, are required for there to be language, that is, universal words, and meaning.

Abelard is precisely aware of the consequences of his opponents' tendency to treat what he refers to as *status*, as well as *dicta* or statements of propositions, as though they were things, or separated essences. He notes that if 'being a man' were treated as a thing then we would be dealing with Plato's eternal realities. He acknowledges that because we are not God we do not have correct or complete conceptions of natures

259

that our ideas are of; indeed, intellection is limited.[89] Noting that the grammarian Priscian viewed the world as constructed on the basis of forms in God's mind and that our words signify these extramental forms in a confused manner, Abelard does not, in his logical works at least, commit himself. He is perhaps too deeply familiar with Aristotle's texts to do so. Or else he is too deeply influenced by Porphyry's attempt to separate logic from ontology in his commentaries on Aristotle. For Porphyry, Aristotle's categories deal with the simple expressions which signify the structure of reality that our *language* presupposes, and this could well be different from the structure metaphysicians would posit. We mentioned in the previous chapter that earlier monastic authors had great difficulty in dealing with Aristotle's first category of substance as the composite individual. Porphyry argued that Aristotle was correct in considering individuals prior to universals in discussing *language*, even if metaphysicians would seek, as early medieval authors did, to reverse the order and consider Aristotle's second substance (universals) as ontologically prior to individuals. Abelard appears to have been almost unique in his time in following Porphyry by attempting to argue that logic was not concerned with discussing whether there were metaphysical realities which correspond to the universals of logic and logical universals were not to be considered things. Universals are a function of predication; they are 'found' in the world of things but they are not themselves things in the world.

Indeed, the neo-Platonist school of fifth- and sixth-century Alexandria led by Ammonius and his disciplines and successors (including Philoponus), in commenting on the logical writings of Aristotle, interpreted the universal as a concept of the knowing subject. Rejecting Plato's understanding of the idea as prior to sensible things, nor was it in things, these Alexandrians said the concept derived from individual sensible things through mind's conceptual apprehension of their common characteristics. It was this tradition that made its appearance in the Latin west perhaps even before the translations of Avicenna's works and both Anselm and more especially Abelard are thought to have been affected.[90]

What is perhaps most important for our purposes is Abelard's understanding of language as established by convention but caused by the world being as it is and experienced as such: so too, 'being imagined' or 'being

---

[89] Compare Gilbert of Poitiers, discussed in N. Häring, 'Commentry and hermeneutics', in *Renaissance and Renewal in the Twelfth Century*, pp. 173–200; pp. 195–6.

[90] Benakis, 'Problem of general concepts'. Avicenna's works, however, are thought to have been translated after the years in which Anselm and Abelard wrote. The dating of the translations is fraught with difficulties. See J. Jolivet, 'The Arabic Inheritance', in *A History of Twelfth-Century Western Philosophy*, ed. P. Dronke, pp. 113–48, esp. pp. 123–4, 129–34.

thought' do not require an actually existent subject, but in order to be sane our ideas must presume a hypothetical 'law of nature' which asserts the possibility of such existents. What we have in the mind when we have mental images and ideas are not entities but an act of imagining and thinking whose content or object is a similitude of something sensed but which is in the mind as a reflection in a mode peculiar to mind's own agency. That we understand the world as it was is dependent on the world as it is, expressed through language and given meaning through linguistic conventions that are based on language's capacity to signify common natures in the world of individuals without this commonness being a thing itself. Abelard takes this further when he classifies intellections according to their truth and thereby invokes logic in order to distinguish between sane and empty intellections. In his late *Glosses on Porphyry*, he says that

sane intellection [sanus intellectus] is only had of an individual thing and is, in effect, a kind of remembrance of a sensation experienced. The senses are the guides of intellection and they perceive things as discrete with their exterior accidents. Intellections, which imitate sensation conceive in a mode peculiar to this act of mind's attention the very same discrete things.[91] True knowledge is only of the previously sensed individual thing, but even here intellection cannot grasp the true nature of such a thing as God conceives it.

Abelard therefore presumes that sane intellection is an active consideration of the natures of individual things as they are, in so far as we can attain this.[92]

An empty intellection, more properly an empty opinion, refers to chimeras and the like where there is no application to a real nature.[93] Both when expressed through propositions can be judged true or false, but an empty opinion which refers to

---

[91] *Sup. Porphyr.* III, p. 524.   [92] *Sup. periermenias*, p. 326.
[93] *Sup. periermenias*, p. 321:
'Per identitatem rerum ostendit a simili vel a causa identitatem intellectus. Nam quia res apud diversas gentes eadem permanent nec propter commutationem linguae suam substantiam commutant, intellectus qui ad naturam rei percipendam applicantur, necesse est eosdem esse. Hoc enim loco passiones animae pro sanis intellectus tantum ponit, qui videlicet cum statu rei concordant, non pro cassis opinionibus. Quippe causae opiniones quae ad nullam rei naturam applicantur, nullam identitatem ex substantia rei habent, quia id quod non est, quoquo modo fingant, nil impedit. Praeterea intellectus similitudo rei dici non potest ipsa re non existente, quod enim non est, similitudinem non habet. Unde qui audit 'hircocervus' hoc nomen, et cetera nomina non existentium, conceptionem quidem aliquam in animo sumit, sed cum nulla res huiusmodi existat, in rerum natura nullius rei similitudo est quae concipitur … Unde cassam oportebit opinionem esse quam hic nullo modo nomine intellectus includit, sed sanas tantum, ut dictum est, animi conceptiones.' Boethius uses this wide notion of *intellectus* to include *conceptiones* of the soul; but finally shows that an empty intellection should not be called an intellection. (p. 322).
Also see *De Intellectibus*, pp. 114 ff.

things not in the world and therefore incapable of being sensed, is only vacuously true or false.

Thus, the problem of uniting the sensible with the intellectual world as conceived by Cistercians who posited two memories linked somehow by a *vis sensualis* that is almost spiritual and a *vis phantasticum* that is almost corporeal, is, for Abelard, replaced by the logic of language. As in then current psychology, images are the instruments by which we think of things, just as logic or semantics is a study of the universals which serve as instruments by which we think of and speak of things. Everything hinges on the *vis intellectus* 'which is through reason' and which enables us to distinguish and judge intellections and words about reality. The truth of our ideas depends not on images or similitudes but on mind's discretionary attention to these whereby intellection interprets in various ways a single image or sign. Language effectively serves as a bridge between *intellectus* and *res* for Abelard: 'Intellectus sunt idem apud omnes et res eadem sunt'.[94]

Abelard therefore believed that the heart of Aristotle's discussion of meaning depended on mental conceptions rather than on the naming of things because the meaningful words in a sentence do not make things exist. Rather, words stimulate the *vis intellectus* to contemplate what already exists through their signifying function. Meaning in the mind, the *vis intellectus'* active judgement of existents through words, images and intellections, is for Abelard *interpretatio*.[95]

That interpretation, the disclosure of meaning, is of crucial importance to Abelard shows up clearly in his project in the *Sic et Non* where apparently conflicting patristic statements may be brought to resolution through the active engagement of the *vis intellectus'* willing judgement focused on expressions, propositions, texts.[96] Even where his theological discussions were judged to be erroneous, Abelard's use of logic in construing texts would be enormously important in the development of an interest in understanding the literal sense of the past, the past as expressed

---

[94] *Sup. periermenias*, p. 322. Also see *LI*, p. 324.

[95] *Sup. periermenias*, p. 309:
Cum autem hic secundum significationem intellectus tantum de vocibus intendat, recte eas interpretationes nominant, quia interpretari vocem non est rem assignare, sed intellectum aperire ... Rerum quippe significatio transitoria est, intellectus vero permanens ... Nil quippe voces in substantia rerum faciunt, sed tantum de eis intellectum excitant.

[96] The first draft of the *Sic et Non* is dated 1122–27. *Petrus Abelardus, Sic et Non, prologus*, ed. B. B. Boyer and R. McKeon (Chicago and London, 1976–7) See E. Bertola, 'I precedenti storici del metodo del "Sic et Non" di Abelardo', *Rivista di filosofia neoscolastica*, 53 (1961).

through language. For according to Abelard, patristic, biblical and conciliar authorities are to be understood as synonymous with their texts. This is extremely important. Texts like words and images are intermediary means to meaning situated between the world as it is and the mind as it is. He says in his prologue to the *Sic et Non* that we ought not to be afraid to judge the various statements of the saints when they demonstrate diverse or even contrary truths. His purpose is not to condemn errors and falsehoods so much as to show that they were made out of ignorance rather than from duplicity or sin. Surely the saints spoke with God's spirit in them. Our problem in understanding their meaning is, however, that we may not be familiar with their mode of speaking and with the diverse significations of their words. We cannot assume that one mode of signifying is the same as another. The diversity of things requires a diverse use of words, often employing less used or even unknown words in order to signify more subtly. Furthermore, Augustine, in his *De Doctrina Christiana*, IV, had warned those responsible for teaching others that they had best use an unornamented style, for it is not rhetorical eloquence but the *proprietates sermonis*, which counts.[97]

In his prologue to his commentary on Paul's *Epistle to the Romans*, Abelard shows that in order to teach or move the reader, divine Scripture employs the persuasive methods of oratory.[98] But in the *Sic et Non* he appears to wish to emphasise that when one is in a milieu of young students, one must speak plainly of the *proprietates sermonis*. Hence, he cites Augustine, asking, what is the point of speaking if those who listen do not understand? It is not easy to determine if Abelard is consciously arguing against the highly ornamented, allegorical manner of textual exegesis brought to such a high point by Bernard. But he clearly seems to be defending his own profession in the non-monastic schools where a master of logic and dialectic acted as *arbitror*, responding to students' queries on the logical consistency of set texts.[99]

Thus, he continues, without negative judgement but rather in loving attention we should observe the sayings of the saints which are sometimes

[97] Quod etiam diligentissimus ecclesiae doctor beatus attendens Augustinus, cum in quarto De Doctrina Christiana ecclesiasticum intrueret doctorem, omnia illum quae intelligentiam praepediunt eorum quibus loquitur, praeterire admonet et tam ornatum quam proprietatem sermonis contemnere, si absque istis ad intelligentiam facilius poterit pervenire, 'non curante' inquit, 'illo qui docet, quanto eloquentia doceat sed quanta evidentia. Diligens appetitus aliquando negligit verba cultiora'. (*Prologus Petri Abaelardi*, p. 90)

[98] . '... docet quippe dum quae fieri vel vitari oportet insinuat, movet autem dum sacris admonitionibus suis voluntatem nostram vel dissuadendo retrahit a malis vel persuadendo applicat bonis' (*Opera Theologica*, ed. Buytaert, vol. I).

[99] See the *De Intellectibus* where he fields questions *ad quod respondendum arbitror*, pp. 123 ff.

opposed or alien to the truth because false titles or corrupt writings purveyed errors. There are, for instance, many apocrypha attributed to the saints which none the less have been taken as authoritative. Jerome warned us to beware. But these errors were made through ignorance rather than malice. Furthermore, some of the writings of the saints were retracted or corrected. And we also know, from Gregory the Great, that numerous conflicting interpretations of Scripture, for example, Ecclesiastes, abounded. And sometimes heretical opinions were inserted into a tract which then acquired authority and praise, as Jerome, writing to Augustine, admitted when he said that he had followed Origen's writings wrongly.

It is also important to realise that some authors spend a great deal of time presenting the opinions of others in their works, opinions with which they do not necessarily agree. Abelard gives Cicero as an example (*De Officiis*, II) where there is a discussion of the virtues: can justice be separated from prudence? Some, of course, say that he who has one has all the virtues and others separate them. Cicero notes that the various meanings of 'virtues' depend on to whom one is speaking. And when we speak commonly (*ut vulgus*) we might call some men good, others strong, and others prudent. Words in popular discourse follow action and use as we speak.

Abelard is not only defending the principle of contextual interpretation here: he is also mounting a self-defence and a defence of the teaching methods in the urban schools where explanations, oversimplifications, current issues raised from the floor of the debating chamber had to take into consideration the audience and the context of propositions. Statements can be true or false depending on their context as well as on their logical consistency, something with which Bernard, responding to the demands of monastic milieux, could not feel sympathy.

But this gives rise to a potential problem area. Abelard says that in our daily use of words we judge according to our corporeal senses. For instance, although there is nowhere in the whole world which is an empty place, that is, not filled with one or another body, we none the less find it useful to say that some place is empty in which we perceive nothing.[100] Because of our senses we assume something to be permanently the case even when such things are not apparent to us at the time, so that we refer to the sky as 'starry' and the sun as 'hot'; thus it is not surprising if the truths uttered by saints or the Fathers are extended in meaning. On the one hand the same thing may be referred to in diverse ways, or we can

---

[100] John of Salisbury, *Metalogicon* IV, uses a similar example and also has interesting comments on how Abelard was forced to oversimplify for his students. See discussion below, ch. 14.

collect together diversities under a single principle or rule. For instance, the same thing can be intended as a remission of sins that can also be taken as an exhortation to perfection. According to the different intentions of speakers or writers we can come to a solution as to their meaning. In effect, when we read we are seeking the author's intention.[101] If a precept is true, be it general or particular in application, it may be directed to all in common or to some specifically.

Furthermore, if we are to penetrate a writer's meaning we must distinguish the time at which he wrote and the immediate causes of his writing, because often what in one time may be allowed, in another is prohibited.[102] It is particularly important to distinguish such things in the decrees of church institutions or in the canons of law. So that we can have an easier time grasping the meaning of authorities if we are aware that the same word is used in diverse authors to signify in diverse ways.

In general, then, these rational considerations on the ways to solve the controversies that appear in the writings of the saints should be diligently adhered to. If, however, a controversy cannot be solved by reason, then one consults the authorities and he whose testimony is stronger and the more confirmed must be retained. Abelard gives the example of Isidore writing to Bishop Massionem, where the decision of the more ancient authority holds.

Abelard notes that the prophets prophesied with the spirit of grace but some also prophesied from the habit of prophesying, believing themselves to have the prophetic spirit, and through their own spirit unknowingly proffered falsehoods. One must distinguish what they knew (*cognoscerent*) truly through the Holy Spirit of God and what they knew through their own existence (*et quales per suum existerent*) when they were not aware that they falsified from not having the gift of grace. God does not confer all gifts on one; neither are all minds filled or illuminated in the same way. Rather one in one manner, or another in another. To some a revelation is open and to others it is closed and secret.

---

[101] It was believed that Hilary of Poitiers (d. 367) had brought to prominence the exegetical principle of examining authors' intentions. Heresy, he said, flows not from the words used but from the user's intentions or his interpretation of words. *De Trinitate*, II, 3, in *PL* 10, 51B: 'De intelligentia enim heresis non de scriptura est: et sensus, non sermo fit crimen.' See N. Häring. 'Commentary and Hermeneutics' in *Renaissance and Renewal*, p. 196. The distinction between grammatical meaning and a writer's intention is also emphasised somewhat later by Gilbert of Poitiers, Simon of Tours and John of Salisbury.

[102] Distinguenda quoque tempora sunt et dispensationum causae, quia saepe quod uno tempore est concessum alio reperitur prohibitum; et quod ad rigorem saepius praecipitur ex dispensatione nonnumquam temperatur. Haec autem in institutionibus ecclesiasticorum decretorum vel canonum maxime distingui necesse est. Facilis autem plerumque

Now in his preface to his translation of the Pentateuch,[103] Jerome had also noted that God's inspiration worked on the minds of the human authors of Scripture in such a way as to supply the content of what they were to say, but the choice of words and imagery was left to them. Their various skills and educational attainments therefore, created the varying texture of Scripture. When he speaks of those who translated Scripture, Jerome says that errors were made. There is a distinction to be made between a prophet (*vates*) and a translator or commentator (*interpretes*). Without this distinction we would have to say that Cicero, who translated books of oratory from Greek to Latin, was inspired by the 'spirit' of rhetoric (*rhetorico afflatus spiritu*). If we insist that all translators of the Pentateuch were inspired by the Holy Spirit, we would have to explain anomalies (*inconveniens*); but if we assume they were not thus inspired, there is no difficulty in understanding the source of their errors.

Likewise, Abelard says that it is not surprising that the multiplicity of the writings of the holy Fathers often succumbed to errors because of the causes he has outlined, many of which were linguistic or scribal, errors made out of ignorance, grammatical or logical, of one kind or another. Abelard reaffirms that he is not imputing sin to anything that is said out of charity and for edification, since with respect to God, every statement depends on one's intention, on one's meaning. It is one thing to lie and quite another to err in speech and to recede from the truth through error in words, rather than through evil.[104]

Written texts may therefore be faulty, due to the ignorant errors of copyists, or to an author's own inclusion of heretical statements which he later retracted. Furthermore, meaning depends not only on the diverse ways one might use language but also on the author's intention. Especially when one speaks colloquially, one tends to rely on the evidence of the corporeal senses and thereafter extend from one experience to a general statement covering all such instances, some of which were and never will

controversiarum solutio reperietur si eadem verba in diversis significationibus a diversis auctoribus posita defendere poterimus. (*Prologus, Sic et Non*, p. 96)

103 *PL* 28, 181A–182A.

104 'Aliud itaque est mentiri, aliud est errare, loquentem et a veritate in verbis per errorem non per malitiam recedere' (*Prologus, Sic et Non*, p. 99). Abelard does, however, acknowledge that a reading of ancient poets and philosophers, whose mythic and fabulous language was a vehicle of hidden meanings and truths, could be unveiled by a hermeneutics geared to revealing true teachings under the veil of the letter. *Theologia Christiana*, I , 102, ed. E. M. Buytaert, *Opera Theologica*, II (Turnhout, 1965), p. 114. See Tullio Gregory, 'Abélard et Platon', in *Peter Abelard* (Leuven-The Hague, 1974), pp. 38–64. And this methodology was applied not only to ancient poets and philosophers, but also to the books of the Bible. See Tullio Gregory, 'The Platonic inheritance', pp. 58–9: 'The further the "surface of the letter" seems from the truth the more it requires a non-literal translation.' The aim is harmony not discord.

be experienced. Abelard is also insistent to point out that meaning depends on the context of the utterance, its time and the conditions in which the author lived. But he is NOT thereby attributing a relativistic dimension to meaning; he is instead affirming that a dialectical analysis of a text is a rational means of distinguishing an author's intention if we are aware of, or can discover, the situation which gave rise to his utterance. The nature of this situation must be repeatable in present circumstances. Such a situation cannot be completely different from our own or it would be meaningless. Universal words, as we saw, are only possible because we must assume that the things such words apply to may exist somehow; the prior existence of that of which universal nouns are predicated is a necessary condition for language. The state of affairs referred to by a proposition must have hypothetical existence and because of this the proposition when pronounced is true. But because language's logic has already been established, propositions can be 'true', albeit sometimes vacuously so, even when that to which they refer does not exist. The existence of language conventions means that there are always instruments which enable sensed experiences, which remain in the imagination as images or similitudes, to be endowed with meaning by the *vis intellectus*, because language conveys meaning through its common nouns. And it is because intellection operates in its own mode, attending to words or images in order to construct, through reason, the soul's own kinds of similitudes on which the willing mind gazes and reflects, similitudes that somehow relate to imaginary and verbal similitudes and thence to the world, that the conditions in which past utterances were made can be investigated via language conventions. These conventions are the static rules of grammar, already established; only the modes of signifying are various and depend on the author's intentions in his context.

Since mind interprets words as well as images through its discretionary attention pertaining to reason, the past is available to us in the present because we now judge something as having been or having not been as things were or were not. The careful use of language and its logic is the established and conventional means by which meaning is conveyed. The mind's act of intellection has an independence to use its images and words as it will. Mind *must* use these images and words which place before it similitudes of the world of experience. The commonnesses or status 'in' the real world which universal words signify have always been and shall always be, according to this theory, based on the hypothetical necessity we discussed earlier. Abelard believes then, that a careful use of language and an analysis of saintly writings can bring us to the truth of past utterances in the sense that mind may endow these with correct meaning, that is, mind can grasp the author's original intention. But the original intention, in order to be understood, must be an intention which a person now could have. It cannot be unique or it would be meaningless and indeed, inexpressible through language. It is the literal analysis of a text in conjunction with what we know Abelard believes of the mind's capacity to read meaning into signs, that permits us to see that in his logical writings he is technically doing something very different from the monastic tradition of reading texts and uncovering their meaning. Here, Abelard is not interested in the metaphorical significance of words which enable them to refer to a higher truth.

We recall that the *disciplina claustralis* was an imitation of the apostolic life in the cloister achieved through an interiorised assimilation of the text of the Gospels, so that the claustral imitation of Christ's life was an imitation based on verbal concordance where textual parallels evoked historical parallels, rather than the reverse. One does not have to do the same thing as Christ and the apostles, that is, one need not imitate people in the past. Rather, one does something else which has essential or conceptual affinities to a past act rather than accidental ones. Thus, the monk lived and thought and read in an allegorical mode.[105]

Abelard, whose training and teaching in the logical interpretation of a text's statements occurred in the arts course of urban cathedral schools, was interested in how language conventions allow us to understand the way things are or were in themselves and in their contexts. The conventions of language and those of mind ensure that we know and understand things as they are or were, *if* we accept the hypothetical laws of nature that presume constancy in mind's operations and in the world, over great tracts of time. Universals, that is, common names, can have no historicity in themselves because the world which gave rise to these conventions is presumed to be as it is, and presumably mind is as it is. Although words are used to talk about the same things that thoughts are about, that is, the world as it is, a unique, concrete event would be transformed by language into something that was already known and describable through the conventions of signification. However, since we are told that the soul can grasp an idea that signifies the nature of something better than language can ever express it, there may still be room for a mental intuition about the past's nature or the nature of the future. But when expressed in language the nature of the past would lose something of its specificity[106] through

---

[105] See Pierre de Celle, *De disciplina claustrali*, c.1 and I. E. Lozano, 'De vita apostolica apud Patres et scriptores monasticos' and 'De Vita apostolica apud canones regulares', in *Commentarium pro religiosis et missionariis*, 52 (1971), pp. 97–120 and 193–210.
[106] As well as of its intellectual universality.

conventional expression. We are also told that only the *vis intellectus* has the special active ability to vary what it is attending to without altering the contents of the imagination or, presumably, of texts. But reason's guiding of the *vis intellectus* is not random and wildly creative because both *intellectus* and *res* are fixed for Abelard. This means that mind's application to a text can elicit a meaning which goes beyond that expressed through the text's words. The static conventions of language may be transcended by the active wilful operations of the *vis intellectus* but not in a random, subjective way. Words put what they signify into the mind but meaning derives from mind's activity where mind's activity is a constant for the human, rational species, so that meaningful interpretation cannot be at random. Rather, it operates according to what the discipline of logic enables us to call the fixed rules of how men think when they have 'sane' intellections of reality experienced and this is what 'being a man' means.

The more open technique of monastic concordance, verbal reminiscence, conscious metaphor, all in the service of the allegorical and moral sense of Scripture, contrasts with this literal, dialectical school activity of discretionary, rational attention to words and propositions. Such attending is not a conscious device of grammar and rhetoric but an act of mind grasping the individual natures of events and things and open to explanation through the rules of logical dialectic. If Abelard was interested in distinguishing between the disciplines of grammar and rhetoric and thereby promoting the logic of dialectic, linking the latter more directly with philosophy and psychology in order to study the literal sense of texts, he also extended the functions of attentive reason, that activity of mind which endows the world, past, present and future with its meaning in a fixed and regulated way. He did not imply that such meaning is arbitrary or even subjectively and individually creative. Abelard wished to affirm that meaning is disclosed in a fixed manner peculiar to that property we call rationality, which is signified when we speak of 'being a man'. The past *is* knowable according to this theory, but we must assume hypothetically that things as well as men's minds have always been as they are now. We remember the past as it was because of how the present is for us, that is, enshrined in language.

The *Sic et Non*'s selection of texts to be analysed according to the rational methodology outlined in the prologue influenced the development of the *disputatio* and *distinctio* in the late twelfth- and thirteenth-century legal and theological schools.[107] But as a repertory of texts, it had offered little that was new. Carolingian controversies had also produced works made up of extracts, just as canonical collections attempted to reconcile

---

[107] J. de Ghellinck, *Le mouvement théologique du XIIᵉ siècle* (Bruges, 1948), p. 164.

269

authorities from at least the time of Isidore of Seville. But Abelard's original methodological ordering of the texts was influential: the *Sic et Non* served as an arsenal of patristic texts arranged *pro* and *contra*. And the prologue in particular, dealt with a way to resolve the problem of harmonising troublesome texts, a problem that had already loomed large on the theological and canon law horizon.

Stephen Kuttner has shown how the new Roman jurisprudence of the twelfth century adhered to the motto 'diversa sunt non adversa', and this became a powerful tool in lawyers' modes of argumentation. 'One could indeed reduce many of the literary forms employed by the glossators (of both laws) to *solutio contrariorum* as a common denominator.'[108] In the earliest glosses on Gratian (post-1140) one already finds *solutio contrariorum*. 'Thus we have collections of *distinctiones*, especially among canonists, where a quoted text, followed by an adversative *auctoritas*, is the subject matter of the distinction.'[109] And if a general argument was countered by a contrary opinion in the same source, a dialectic solution would be found so that the *regula juris* suffered only an *exceptio* rather than a *contrarium*. Indeed, early legal glosses of the generation just after Abelard show simple antinomies in their sources as well as hypothetical cases, difficulties in interpreting a legal term and the didactic device of formulating statements as questions. For all these problems, the *quaestio decretalis/legitima* offered a broad area of dialectic *solutiones contrariorum*. For Abelard, as too for lawyers, the *quaestio* and the *quaestio disputata* emerged from the technique of lecturing in the urban schools. The intellectual bond between lawyers and dialecticians, indeed between all scholastic fields of learning, has often been noted. But Abelard's extraordinary powers of dialectical analysis of texts raised him, in the eyes of younger contemporaries like John of Salisbury, well above the standard teachers of logic in Paris. His method not only indirectly influenced Peter the Lombard and Gratian and their respective glossators. Within the school of Hugh of St Victor, a sophisticated study of Abelard's thought provided the springboard for many doctrinal developments of the future.

The Victorines increasingly placed a stress on the literal sense of a text, although they claimed that the literal sense of the Pentateuch was taught them by Jewish exegetes.[110] And as we shall see, John of Salisbury in his *Metalogicon* (1159) would provide a parallel defence of the use of logic to

---

108 S. Kuttner, 'The revival of jurisprudence', in *Renaissance and Renewal*, pp. 299–323; p. 311. Also see Häring, 'Commentary and hermeneutics', pp. 183–5.
109 Kuttner, 'Revival of jurisprudence', pp. 313–14. See R. W. Hunt, 'Hugutio and Petrus Helias', in *Medieval and Renaissance Studies*, 2 (1950), pp. 174–8.
110 Beryl Smalley, *The Study of the Bible in the Middle Ages* (Notre Dame, Indiana, 1964), p. 102 on Andrew of St Victor's comments on his master Hugh.

determine an author's (especially authors of canonical Scripture, the Fathers and the Evangelists) true, noncontradictory meanings.[111] John noted that Abelard's disciples still existed (*c.* 1159) and were his friends.[112] Indeed, the *Metalogicon* is quite astonishingly Abelardian in its analysis of the various logical books of the trivium, despite John's quibbles with a very few of Abelard's teachings, eg. on universals (where he excuses Abelard as having been forced to oversimplify for his students) and on hypothetical propositions.

The outline of a method that would allow a complete synthesis of theological truths, as found in Abelard's Prologue to the *Sic et Non* inspired the subsequent era of 'summists' when, by the 1230s, theology was taken to be a science according to the deductive principles of Aristotelian *demonstratio*, applied to revealed givens. Abelard, as a school dialectician, along with men of similar training, no longer circumscribed by the demands of the cloister, irreversibly affected the rational element of future theological method and scriptural exegesis.

For Bernard, as we have seen, one's memory of the past was not to be seen as a constituent of the reformed monastic self so much as something to be denied, purged and blanched. In order to live the present reformed monastic life, the uniqueness of one's own past had to be replaced rather than retained and built upon. The dichotomy of body and soul was set against the continuous essential present evoked through monastic scriptural reminiscence. But Abelard's analysis of signification and interpretation led to very different conclusions.

Abelard affirmed the constant nature of intellection and things. We recall that he argued that we only have sane intellections or ideas of individual things where the intellection is a kind of remembrance of a sensation experienced. What kind of remembrance? Since the senses guide intellection, they perceive things as discrete by means of their accidents. Intellections then 'imitate' sensation, but in a mode peculiar to mind's conception. True knowledge can only be had of a previously sensed thing but what is grasped of the individual is the thing's nature in so far as it is graspable, incompletely by the human mind, completely by God's. The most perfect knowledge we can ever attain is the intellection of an individual but this requires that we first sensually experience the thing's accidents rather than its nature. Superficial sensation as one kind of knowledge is followed by intellection, which uses images or words that

---

[111] *Metalogicon*, I, 19.
[112] *Metalogicon*, II, 17. It is particularly interesting that John heard Abelard teaching dialectic *c.* 1136 on Mont Ste. Geneviève, *after* Abelard had become a monk following his disastrous affair with Heloise.

signify the *status* of the thing first sensed and now absent. If we have not first had a sensual experience of the individual's accidents, or where a 'thing' as signified by universals is imperceptible such as is the case for *paternitas, rationalitas* or *mortalitas*, then we have an opinion rather than an intellection of the 'thing'.

We also recall that concrete and specific events of the past could be revealed in texts only through the more universal signification of common names which signify the natures of such past events. But whatever images from the past we use or however we dispose them, he said, we are not referring to the truth of the intellection because intellection's truth does not depend on images or similitudes but on the present distinctive attention of mind engaged in distinguishing the meaning of images or words which signify the world. The present attention of mind therefore de-temporalises past and future, in effect, harmonises them rather than showing them to be incommensurable, in order that mind's understanding comes to valid or correct conceptions about the past. The truth is not culturally or temporally relative although language is. The memory of the individual nature of things has meaning only in a mode of intellectual judgement in the ever-present. Although mind is dependent on images and words which signify past or present reality, mind interprets signs endowing them with meaning in the present.

Here Abelard is doing something different from the monastic tradition of textual exegesis when he affirms that dialectic is a rational means of distinguishing any author's meaning if we are aware of or can discover the prior situation which gave rise to his utterance. But we must note that he assumes prior circumstances can be understood if we simply construe the grammar and logic of the sentence aright. The evidence of the text is sufficient. Words are universals signifying an enduring *status* which depends for its existence on the hypothetical existence of concrete individuals which share *status* to which words refer.[113] We can grasp the meaning of the past through texts in the same way as the present may be understood, without however, turning the past into the present. But for Abelard, one need not investigate the past beyond the evidence of the text

---

[113] Compare St Anselm in the *De Veritate*. After discussing the nature of utterance he says there are two senses in which a statement may be true: (1) because as a proposition it satisfied logical requirements, (2) but also because it signifies what really occurs. Normally we do not call a statement true when it refers to a condition which in reality does not exist. When it does refer to an existing state it signifies both what it is taken to signify as well as what it is really signifying. Meaning is achieved both through words alone as well as through the correlation between words and things. *De Veritate*, II, in Anselm, *Opera Omnia*, ed., F. S. Schmitt, 6 vols., vol. I (Seckau, 1938, reprinted Edinburgh, 1946), p. 179.

itself. Indeed, Abelard substituted texts for events: texts are primarily significations of events.[114] Thereafter, the variety of modes of signifying combined with the independent constancy of the *vis intellectus* to use its images and words as it will, imply a human capacity to grasp the ways things are or were in themselves and in their discrete contexts, by means of signifying instruments, words and images. The world can *be* many things and experienced in many ways. The way it is or was to a speaker or writer of texts at any moment, determines what he says about it. But its subsequent interest, its meaning and truth for a twelfth – (or any other) century reader of past texts is not the 'otherness' of its pastness; rather its interest rests on the belief that since language has been conventionally established, men can speak truly of their experiences and convey the nature of these through language to our present, their future. Abelard believes that language reflects the stability of the nature of things over time. Language enables us to establish continuities between the past and present without destroying the distinction between the past and the present. Language's logic is a-temporal. Abelard's concern for literal textual exegesis along dialectical or logical lines, therefore, affirmed that it was possible to come to some understanding of a past author's intention in the present. The truth of the conception of a past intention, expressed through its logical coherence, may be discovered by a present activity of mind analysing fixed grammatical and logical conventions. These conventions were used by Latin readers and writers in the past in the same way as contemporary readers and writers used them. John of Salisbury, one of Abelard's pupils, would be influenced by the significance of what he was saying regarding our capacity to grasp the nature of the past through an analysis of different modes of signifying, and the ability of *language* to create a bridge from past to present. But a concern for the past as so unique and different as to be impossible of true verbal communication was alien to him and to all his contemporaries. This has become our problem: it was not Abelard's.

[114] In his prologue to the commentary on Paul's Epistle to the Romans, Abelard says that 'exempla quoque ex historiis necessarium erat adiungi in quibus tam remuneratio obedientium quam poena transgressorum ante oculos ponerentur'.

Chapter 14

MEMORY AND ITS USES: THE RELATIONSHIP BETWEEN A THEORY OF MEMORY AND TWELFTH-CENTURY HISTORIOGRAPHY

... the following are the main types of transformation [of an original story] likely to occur:

1. There will be much general simplification, due to the omission of material that appears irrelevant, to the construction gradually of a more coherent whole, and to the changing of the unfamiliar into some more familiar counterpart.

2. There will be persistent rationalisation, both of a whole story and of its details, until a form is reached which can be readily dealt with by all the subjects belonging to the special social group concerned. This may result in considerable elaboration.

3. There will be a tendency for certain incidents to become dominant, so that all the others are grouped about them.

It also seems probable that a cumulative form of story favours the retention of the general series of incidents with little change, and that whatever causes amusement is likely to be remembered and preserved. It may be to this last factor that the preservation of the novel in a commonplace setting is largely due.

F. C. Bartlett, *Remembering, A Study in Experimental and Social Psychology*
(Cambridge, 1932), p. 138.

Whenever a sign appeared at first glance to be relatively meaningless, or when it was seen to be unusually elaborate, or when, for any reason whatever, it was disliked, it was generally faced by a determined effort to remember. Such an effort gives rise to an interesting and complex attitude, the first component of which is dissatisfaction, depression, unpleasure ... Now it is precisely this sign, or the detail of it, which is most likely of all to be omitted. So far as I can see, the mechanism of omission is somewhat as follows. Whenever occasion arises for the reproduction of material of this difficult type, the first thing to be reinstated is the attitude with which the material was faced. The first and dominant component of this attitude is the 'I shall never be able to reproduce this sign' state of mind. And this obtrudes a barrier to the process of reproduction ... there is no doubt whatever that in these experiments a special determination to remember was promptly followed by omission. Similar cases are common in everyday experience. [Conclusions]: Signs not obviously or readily related to other material already used by a subject [are omitted].

274

Signs not accorded any distinctive name [are omitted].

Signs arousing a definite determination to remember [are omitted].

Any detail in a representative sign detached from the central structure was liable to disappear.

If any conventional representation was already established possessing the same assigned meaning as that of a given sign, the sign was certain to be transformed so as to become more like the already existing conventional character.

Subjects could be classed broadly into a) visualisers, and b) vocalisers, though no person used one method only:

a) The typical visualiser relied more upon direct memorisation, treated the different signs of a series more definitely as individuals; sometimes used analogy and secondary association, but not specifically as aids to reproduction; was in general rapid and confident in his method of work;

b) The typical vocaliser used description, names, secondary associations and analogies definitely as aids to recall; was on the whole more hesitating and less confident in his method of work.

Both types made much the same errors in reproduction with a slight preponderance of blending in the case of the vocaliser ... Determination to remember was constantly correlated with actual forgetting.

F. C. Bartlett, *Remembering, A Study in Experimental and Social Psychology*, pp. 115–17.

INTRODUCTION

The writing of history, perhaps even more than the reading and interpreting of past historical texts, depends on an attitude to memory: what it is, how it operates, and how human rememberers determine what is worthy of being remembered. During the twelfth century the writing of history developed further and beyond the monastic enclosure into a professional endeavour. Much has been written about twelfth- and thirteenth-century historians but largely without any attempt to relate how their theories of knowing and remembering affected how they went about their historiographic task. Frequently, these medieval historians are derided for having no interest in the pastness of the past, and it has even more frequently been said that they 'simply' lacked 'a sense of the past'. The silliness of the latter is akin to arguing that cultures that admire artists who paint iconically in two-dimensions have no capacities to see and live in a three-dimensional world. It is true that twelfth-century historians had little interest in verifying past, authoritative, written accounts or in establishing as important how *different* men were in the past. But there were serious reasons for this. We shall also find this to have been the case for fifteenth- and sixteenth-century Renaissance historians as well. But the *reasons* for their (to us) unhistorical stance have a great deal to do with what on the one hand they understood memory to be capable of, and even more importantly on the other, how they thought memory should be used. It is abundantly clear that even in modern psychological theories of remembering, based on numerous experiments like those of Bartlett, remembering is not an unproblematic recollection of all things past but is determined by social and cultural factors which help to determine what is worthy of remembrance. Where for modern rememberers such social and cultural factors remain implicit, indeed unknown, for the medieval historians we shall examine, they were explicit and examined: remembering was an exercise in constructing harmonies between the past as recorded in texts and the present for use in the present. And they came to understand precisely the distinction Aristotle had drawn between the historian – our eyewitness journalist – and the rhetorician *cum* poet who interpreted the literally reported experiences as set down in a text. What *we* refer to as the history written by medieval 'historians' was for them largely an exercise in oratory just as Cicero and other Roman models taught them it was, but now set within the overarching, exemplary theme of God's design for man's salvation, the *meaning* of which had no historical dimension other than that of the ever present. Any modern Christian sitting in Church and hearing the Gospels is likely to know exactly what this means.

HISTORIA AS PRIMARY SIGNIFICATION: BEDE, ISIDORE

Abelard takes us to the brink of something new. Indeed the twelfth century is often taken to be the turning point in medieval intellectual history. To pursue our interest in attitudes towards memory and its uses we must now ask questions which go beyond an analysis of individual writers' discourse on language and its uses. We must ask a more general question: is there any relationship between theories of memory and the activity of writing history? Indeed, is history writing as practised during the monastic middle ages and then in the cathedral schools a remembrance of things past? Is there some relation between theories about memory and the practical attempts that were made by historical writers to learn about and to interpret the past? Can we trace the links, if there are any, between philosophies of mind and language and practising historians' attempts to interpret the past? What is required for someone to study the past as past? And is there a kind of history writing that does not study the past as past but rather interprets everything in the light of present applicability? Should we call this history? Was anyone who had been trained in a monastic setting or who had undergone an education in the liberal arts, 'doing' history at all in its modern sense of studying the past for its own sake?

To come to some decision on the matter let us begin, once again, with Aristotle. In the *Poetics*, Aristotle noted as we saw, that history lacks both form and universality which are the ingredients of serious art. History lacks form because events in the world have no dramatic unity, and since it is the historian's task to record events faithfully and in the order of happening, the dramatic form of beginning, middle and end, has no place in the finished historical record. Furthermore, the historian's record has to be as chaotic as life itself and its universal truth must therefore be missing from its written account (*Poetics*, 1459a–b). The statements of an historian, describing things that have been, are therefore valid for one time and place only. The universal, exemplary lesson to be drawn from the recording of successive and discontinuous facts is the task not of the historian but of the poet, the rhetorician or the interpreter.

Now, effectively this means that the historian merely records in words what he physically sees and experiences. He does not interpret and does not seek to find lessons for other actors who might find themselves in similar situations. He is merely a recorder, a literal representer of experience that is prior to its linguistic description. Is there any evidence that medieval writers understood this meaning of the historian? My answer will be 'yes'. We have already examined how Abelard was interested in literal textual analysis and we shall see that this would be shared to some extent by Hugh of St Victor, an Augustinian canon, and by the Chartrains.[1] What this means is that the having of an experience can be recorded by letters so

---

[1] For the development of the method elaborated by Abelard see Richard H. and Mary A. Rouse, '*Statim invenire*, schools, preachers and new attitudes to the page' in R. L. Benson, G. Constable and C. Lanham, eds., *Renaissance and Renewal in the Twelfth Century* (Cambridge, Mass., 1982), pp. 201–25; pp. 201–5. The distinction between preaching and the classroom is largely artificial (p. 218). It should be noted that preaching is referred to as *in artem sermocinandi* and therefore is similar to the grammatical and logical emphasis on the *sermo*. The Rouses illustrate the increasing emphasis on the authority of a whole text rather than extracts and the necessity of reading statements in context during the second half of the twelfth century, leading to a significant change in terminology: *codices integri* become *originalia scripta*, where the whole work of an author is best grasped through reading his words in context and as a whole text rather than extracts (p. 223). Note that this context is verbal, that is, grammatical and logical. Also see Nikolaus M. Häring, 'Commentary and hermeneutics' in *Renaissance and Renewal*, pp. 173–200, on the difference, according to William of Conches, between *glosa* which takes into account the *continuatio* or the *expositio* of the *littera* – the authoritative text, and the *commentum* which deals with the *sententia*. The *glos(s)a* explains individual words and pays attention to the (linguistic) context; the *commentum* is a résumé of the author's doctrine (*sententia*) (p. 179). We note that *continuatio* is the extension of meaning, the interpretation of the literal text, an extension of the primary signification of the text or *littera*. Thierry of Chartres's Commentary on Genesis (*c.* 1142), ed. N. Häring (Pontifical Institute of Medieval Studies, Toronto, 1971) is a *glosa continua* interpreting the text *secundum phisicam* and deliberately disregarding allegorical and moral meanings as expounded by earlier (monastic) commentators. *Tractatus*, I. Abelard's *Expositio in Romanos*, PL 178, 785 B is a *glosa continua*.

that the experience can be set before a reader's eyes by means of its representation in a text. And, indeed, the literal reading of a text became assimilated to 'history' most clearly and self-consciously during the twelfth century. But to say that letters are stable representations of experiences is to say nothing of whether the experiences were in the past or were contemporary with the writer. And some medieval authors would be careful to use the word *historia* when they were writing of events in their own life times which they themselves had experienced, and at no other time. We shall give evidence of this shortly. But was this use of *historia* as the literal representation of experience limited to the twelfth century?

Before we can judge whether something new and distinctive was developing during the twelfth century regarding what we might refer to as historical interests, we ought to return to an earlier age, that of Bede, to provide ourselves with comparisons and contrast. It is often said that prior to the mid-twelfth century, the European historical tradition was a particularly elaborate rhetorical and exegetical art, inspired by Roman models but set within the overarching theme of God's design for man's salvation) Hence, it was not in line with Aristotle's definition of the practice of recording history, the describing of things that have been which were valid for one time and place. If before the twelfth century, history writing was in Aristotle's terms 'unhistorical' it was in part because history was an activity that was not fully appropriated by man.[2] Instead, as we have seen when we discussed the monastic milieu, men were engaged in an exercise in providing commentaries on lengthy patristic extracts to describe the working out of an already established divine plan for humanity. Monks were not remembering the past. The object of their memories was the text, scriptural and patristic, which clothed timeless, eternal, universal truths. But that extraordinary monk, the Venerable Bede wrote in addition to scriptural commentaries, an ecclesiastical history of England. What, if anything, did Bede think *historia* meant and what, more specifically, did he take to be the literal sense of a text?

Bede's preface to his *Historia Ecclesiastica* closes with a plea that his readers not blame him if, what he has merely written down from the collections of *fama vulgante*, is not true! He asserts that the *vera lex historiae* is simply that which can be collected from oral report and general belief for

---

[2] R. W. Southern, 'Aspects of the European tradition of historical writing: 1. The classical tradition from Einhard to Geoffrey of Monmouth', *TRHS*, fifth ser. 20 (1970), pp. 173–96; G. Bourdé and H. Martin, *Les Écoles Historiques* (Paris, 1983), pp. 12–18. Also R. W. Southern, 'Aspects of the European tradition of historical writing: 2. Hugh of St Victor and the idea of historical development' *TRHS*, fifth ser. 21 (1971), pp. 159–79, and '3. History as prophecy', *TRHS*, fifth ser. 22 (1972), pp. 159–80.

the instruction of posterity.[3] In theory, *historia* for Bede is the recording of first hand accounts of witnesses. Similarly, in his commentary on Luke i, 1–4,[4] Bede emphasises that the Evangelists spoke 'veritas historiae' because they had eyewitness experiences. This use of *historia* employs the long standing *topoi* to be found in the prefaces of Roman histories[5] and it is akin to Aristotle's understanding of the historian's task as Aristotle described it in the *Poetics*. But there is a problem here in that to record events faithfully and in the order of happening, as Aristotle would have it, is not quite the same as recording the first hand accounts of witnesses. Bede was doing the latter as had Gregory the Great in his *Dialogues*, as we have seen. The question of the nature of reliable evidence is at issue here, intimately tied up with the nature of language and men's confidence in its capacities to report this evidence accurately. But Bede was even more concerned than Gregory to give specific information about his sources, using the Gregorian terms of 'traditio seniorum' or 'traditio priorum', or mentioning others by name. Especially in his *Ecclesiastical History*, he relied on innumerable faithful witnesses 'who either knew from actual experiences or somehow remembered the facts'[6] of events Bede recorded. But as would be the case for all those recording the experiences of *others*, Bede's *historia* is the writing down of testimony he *believes* to be reliable but whose factual quality, not having experienced the situations he records himself, he was not in a position to judge.[7] Bede's *historia*, then, is not *his* memory of experiences.

But it is clear that Bede believed that moral edification can only be based on the experiences of men, and such experiences, when recorded, comprised the 'literal' deeds in words, the events reported *secundum litteram*. There was no question of verifying purportedly eyewitness testimony or beliefs.

In his *De tabernaculo*, 1.11. 784–5, Bede defined *historia* in the following way: 'historia namque est cum res aliqua quomodo secundum litteram facta sive dicta sit plano sermone refertur'.[8] It is the literal recording of things without moral or rhetorical embellishment or interpretation. In this

---

[3] 'Lectoremque suppliciter obsecro ut, signa in his quae scripsimus aliter quam se veritas habet posita reppererit, non hoc nobis imputet qui, quod vera lex historiae est, simpliciter ea quae fama vulgante collegimus ad instructionem posteritatis litteris mandare studuimus.' See Roger Ray, 'Bede's *vera lex historiae*', *Speculum* 55 (1980), pp. 1–21. Edition used: Bede, *Historia Ecclesiastica*, eds. Bertram Colgrave and R. A. B. Mynors (Oxford, 1969), p. 6.
[4] *In Evangelium Lucam Expositio*, I, CCSL, 120, ll.12–56.
[5] Elmar Herkommer, *Die Topoi in den Prooemien der römischen Geschichtswerke*, (Tübingen, 1968).
[6] Ray, 'Bede's *vera lex historiae*' p. 12.   [7] *Ibid.*, p. 13.
[8] *De Tabernaculo*, I CCSL, 119A, ll.784–5.

way one accepts the gospel testimony as the unembellished accounts of the eyewitness experiences of the evangelists.

It has been pointed out, however, that actual eyewitness testimonies comprise only a small part of Bede's materials, and that the closer he came to his own times when first hand witnesses could have been found, the less he wrote.[9] Most of Bede's narrative in the *Ecclesiastical History* drew on a small supply of written sources and on *fama vulgante*, much of the latter more than a century old and therefore, seldom if at all verifiable. Gregory of Tours and Gregory the Great had already provided an authorised genre of history writing based on believed but unprovable oral tradition,[10] although in Gregory the Great's case, much of the oral testimony drawn upon came from near contemporaries. Now Bede is often called the 'Father of English History'. But we must ask, 'what kind of history did he write and what relation was there between his memory and that of others to the events as they actually happened'? Bede must have reflected on this not least because there was already, in his times, a rigorous definition of the historian's task. Isidore of Seville (d. 636) had demanded that historians do much more than record unprovable oral tradition. Isidore said that *historia* narrates real events, true events that really happened (*Etymologies*, I, 41.1–2). And he noted (I, 44.5) that the word 'history' came from the Greek *historein* meaning to see and comprehend. History must therefore be a record of events within the sight of the narrator himself. Isidore pointed out that no one in antiquity wrote history unless he took part in and saw what he recorded. He said 'it is better therefore to discover by seeing than to collect by hearing; things seen are published without lying'. And he added that this historical discipline pertains to *grammatica* because whatever is worthy of being remembered is committed to letters or writing. Letters, he said, are for the memory of things because things absent from experience are bound in letters lest they fly into oblivion.[11]

---

[9] Ray, 'Bede's *vera lex historiae*', p. 13.

[10] See Margaret Deanesly, *The Preconquest Church in England* (London, 1963) p. 166, where she discusses Adomnan of Iona's writing a book on Palestine's holy places from a word of mouth account given him by Arnulf, Bishop of a city in Gaul. Adomnan says that whatever *he* deemed worthy of remembrance from Arnulf's account he wrote down.

[11] 'Apud veteres enim nemo conscribebat historiam, nisi is qui interfuisset, et ea quae conscribenda essent vidisset. Melius enim oculis quae fiunt deprehendimus quam quae auditione collegimus. Quae enim videtur, sine mendacio proferuntur. Haec disciplina pertinet ad grammaticam quia quidquid memoria dignum est litteris mandatur.' *Etymologiae*, I, 41, 1–2, ed. W. M. Lindsay, 2 vols. (Oxford, 1911). Furthermore, Isidore said: letters are for the memory of things; things absent from experience are bound in letters lest they fly into oblivion. *Etymologiae*, I, 3, 2: 'Litteràe autem sunt indices rerum, signa verborum, quibus tanta vis est, ut nobis dicta absentium sine voce loquantur. Usus litterarum repertus propter memoriam rerum. Nam ne oblivione fugiant, litteris alligan-

On Isidore's definitions, then, virtually none of Bede's works could be called *historia*! Bede was aware of Isidore's definitions and Roger Ray has argued that Bede's concern to give his sources was his response to this author with whom Bede appears to have been at odds many times in his life.

Bede collected and wrote down these opinions and experiences of others which he believed were worthy of being recorded for posterity and he called this *historia*. According to the strict definitions of both Aristotle and Isidore, Bede's enterprise was not historical at all. But Bede would influence many to write in a similar vein for centuries to come. *In practice*, the kind of enterprise Bede was engaged in continued into the twelfth century and well beyond. But in *theory*, by the twelfth century, much finer distinctions were being drawn between *historia* and hearsay, *historia* and interpretation.

When we examine what *historia* means to twelfth-century writers, we can observe not only the influence of Isidore, who saw *historia* as the *narrator's* eyewitness testimony, which, when written down was a part of *grammatica*. We can also observe how the grammatical and logical disciplines of the contemporary arts course of the cathedral schools reinforced this understanding of *historia* as the literal freezing of events experienced through representative texts. What is important for us to realise, is that the testing of the accuracy of verbal descriptions of experiences was never in question. Because of the nature of grammatical and logical education in the schools, both monastic and cathedral, history as *littera* could not be transformed into a study of *res*, the things which gave rise to *littera*. The introductory texts of Porphyry and other late antique authors insisted that the only way to things, past or present, was through words. And words were adequate signs of things.[12] The art of grammar was the study not of

tur. In tanta enim rerum varietate nec disci audiendo poterant omnia, nec memoria contineri.'

12 This does not mean that the *sermo* expresses the *res* in its entirety *ut est*. Gilbert of Poitiers as well as Abelard realised that human understanding is limited and cannot grasp the *res* in its entirety the way God can. So too, the linguistic expression lags even further behind reality, since mind can grasp reality better than words can express it, but not in the way things subsist eternally. See Häring in *Renaissance and Renewal*, p. 196. Indeed a thing's existence is not considered one of its characteristics, essential or accidental, since 'is' is or has been already imposed on all things in accordance with their *essentia*; 'is' names everything. Predication through common names presupposes substantial existence and does not express it fully. And we can only 'transfer' this language to God when we speak of Him. Abelard says:

Quod vero onmis hominum locutio ad creaturarum status maxime accommodata sit, ex ea praecipua parte orationis apparet sine qua, teste Prisciano, nulla constat orationis perfectio ex ea scilicet quae dicitur 'verbum'. Haec quippe dictio temporis designativa est, quod incepit a mundo. Unde si huius partis significationem attendamus, oportet per eum cuiusque constructionis sensum infra ambitum temporis coerceri, hoc est ad eas res

the past but of texts which represented in letters the experiences experienced by narrators. History was part of grammar. And grammar has no historical dimensions, no historical depth as we understand these terms today. Grammar is the construing of a text whose veracity is unquestioned. The truth or falsity of propositions is a logical truth or falsity. Grammar's truth or falsity does not refer to the accuracy or otherwise of a matching of words to non-textual experiences which give rise to words.

Hence, according to Hugh of St Victor, 'historia est rerum gestarum narratio quae in prima significatione litterae continetur'.[13] He says, the word *littera* is synonymous with *historia* understood in the large sense. In its large sense, history is not the things narrated so much as their first signification which the properties of the narrative words express. This is what is meant by our reading the biblical texts literally or historically.[14]

And it is important to realise that this literal sense, the history related by the primary signification of the words of the narrative, is not a reference to the pastness of the past. *Historia* can be of contemporary experiences. The literal sense is an assimilation of *historia* to the exterior and sensible aspects of things signified by words. What is involved here is a specific understanding of the way language relates to knowing and remembering, clearly pointing to the current understanding of the soul's powers to relate the external world with interior understanding *through* signs. As Abelard noted, we cannot have true intellections without first having experienced the world through the sensing of individual things, but it is words and thought which are used to refer to such things. In his prologue to the commentary of Paul's *Epistle to the Romans* (1135–39) Abelard had noted that scriptural *exempla* 'quoque ex historiis necessarium erat adiungi in quibus tam remuneratio obedientium quam poena transgressorum *ante oculos ponerentur*' (Through literal reports, placed before one's eyes, one sees the necessary connections between obedient repayment and punishment for sins).

This understanding of the literal sense and of primary signification was

---

tantum inclinari quae temporaliter contingere, non aeternaliter subsistere volumus demonstrare. (*Theologia Christiana*, III, 125, *Opera Theologica*, XII, CCCM, ed. Buytaert, vol. 2, p. 242).

13 *De Sacramentis*, prologue, c. LV, *PL* 176, 185A.

14 *Didascalicon*, VI, c. iii, *PL* 176, 801A:
Si tamen hujus vocabuli significatione largius utimur, nullum est inconveniens ut sc. "historiam" esse dicamus "non tantum rerum gestarum narrationem, sed illam primam significationem cujuslibet narrationis, quae secundum proprietatem verborum exprimitur" secundum quam acceptionem omnes utriusque Testamenti libros ... ad hanc lectionem secundum litteralem sensum pertinere puto.
Hugh of St. Victor said that 'our imitation of the saints is the imprinting of their lives in us as a seal moulds wax on which it is pressed' (*De Institutione*, c. 7, *PL* 176, 932D–33C).

treated in arts course texts like Aristotle's *Topics*, book VII and in Boethius's commentaries on the *Topics*. John of Salisbury discusses it in *Metalogicon*, III, 9 where he says: 'The primary and literal sense occurs when the identity is designated by an alternative name or definition, as when a "tunic" is referred to as a "garment" or "a man" as a "two-footed animal able to walk".' *Historia* as primary signification is the designation by an identical but alternative substitutive common name signifying a sense experience and through the text placing this now absent experience before one's eyes. The experience, signified by words which substitute for it, is now before us, unjudged as yet and to be taken literally. Experiences themselves cannot be verified. Truth and falsity pertain to propositions. Every student who was the product of an education system based on the late Roman grammarians knew this. Language, conventional though it was, could refer adequately to things, past, present and future. This is a very specific, indeed technical notion of *historia* as primary signification. It is not what we mean by history nor does it refer to the past as past.

Therefore, it is common to find Isidore's definition that history is related to seeing things and is contrasted with the fictions of poets, fables and *argumenta*. For Otto of Freising,[15] the chronicler, history, taken in its etymological sense, is first what one knows from having seen it. For the chronicler William of Tyre,[16] history is what is brought forward to the mind by means of eyewitness testimonies so that it is less subject to being forgotten than that which one learns from hearsay. For John of Salisbury, 'letters, that is shapes, are primarily signs of sounds. Thereafter, they set before the mind things [seen] through the windows of the eyes and frequently the expressions of the absent are spoken voicelessly'. (*Littere autem, id est figure, primo vocum indices sunt; deinde rerum, quas anime per oculorum fenestras opponunt, et frequenter absentium dicta sine voce loquuntur*).[17] History for the twelfth century, is then, the recording in words or letters, which directly substitute for events experienced by actors and observers.

Isidore had distinguished between history as the signification of events as sensually experienced by the narrator, and annals, which are narratives written down *in other times* (i.e. by men who had not themselves witnessed events?], dealing with events which our age did not see. Was Bede then an Isidorean annalist? William of Malmesbury understood this distinction because he used the title 'chronicle' for the three first books of his work

---

[15] *Gesta Frederici primi*, II, c. 41, in *Monumenta Germaniæ Historica [MGH]*, vol. 46 *Scriptores rerum germanicorum*, ed. G. Waitz and B. von Simson (Hanover, 1912), p. 150.
[16] *Historia rerum in partibus transmarinis gestarum*, XVI, prologue, *PL* 201, 639.
[17] *Metalogicon*, I, c. 13, ed. C. C. J. Webb (Oxford, 1929), p. 32.

but was careful to reserve *historia* for the narration of contemporary experience. He says that the letter as well as the *gesta* may be said to teach through the facts being retold as seen, the historical text denoting (not signifying) the *gesta* or event. What William is referring to is the manner in which the text's words denote sensual experience before they are seen to signify experience through propositions which then are interpreted and endowed with higher, more general meaning.

Hugh of St Victor also has a cognition theory in mind when he says that the 'fundamentum et principium doctrine sacrae, historia est'.[18] He says he is undertaking to give an account as a memento of the principal events of sacred history for his students' use. It is the sensual aspect of events to which words literally refer, that is best retained in the memory, enabling the soul thereafter to comprehend and the memory to retain.[19] History as the recording of sensual experience is for Stephen Langton as well the foundation of allegory and this is the meaning found in the language of scholastics.[20]

History, then, as the literal sense, was meant to be transcended by being

---

[18] *Didascalicon*, VI, iii.

[19] On the Augustinian canons' concern to teach by word and example see Caroline Bynum, *Jesus as Mother* (Berkeley, 1982). Hugh makes a direct reference to corporeal memory places of the Ciceronian, rhetorical tradition. See Hugh of St Victor's *De Tribus maximis circumstantiis gestorum*, as discussed by William M. Green, *Speculum*, 18 (1943), pp. 484–93 and the discussion of mnemonic devices including historical tables to be memorised: 'Historiam nunc in manibus habemus, quasi fundamentum omnis doctrinae primum in memoria collocandum. Sed quia ... memoria brevitate gaudet gesta autem temporum infinita pene sunt, oportet nos ex omnibus brevem quamdam summam colligere, quasi fundamentum fundamenti, id est, primum fundamentum quam facile possit animus comprehendere et memoria retinere' (*De Tribus maximis*, p. 491). It is clear, however, that for Hugh the sensual experiences recorded in sacred writing are not the experiences of his students. But they must be similar to sensual experiences they might have or else they would not be understood. Others would be more specific that *historia* is the recording in writing of one's own sensual experiences. Everything else is classified as annals or chronicles. The chronicle of Romuald, archbishop of Salerno (1153–81) ends with a statement implying that what he had not witnessed he could not claim to speak about with authority. However: 'Haec autem omnia quae praediximus ita gesta fuisse nulli dubitationis vel incredulitatis scrupulum moveant quia Romualdus secundus Salernitanus archiepiscopus qui videt et interfuit scripsit haec et sciatis quia verum est testimonium ejus', and this must refer to his account of the Venice negotiations at which he was present. (*Romualdi Salernitani Chronicon*, ed. C. A. Garufi, *Rerum Italicarum Scriptores*, VII, i [1909–35], pp. 293–4). See D. J. A. Matthew, 'The chronicle of Romuald of Salerno' in *The Writing of History in the Middle Ages, Essays Presented to R. W. Southern*, pp. 239–74. In general, see Michael McCormick, *Les Annales du Haut-Moyen Âge* Typologie des sources du moyen âge occidental, 14 (Turnhout-Belgium, 1975); Bernard Guenée, 'Histoires, annales, chroniques, essai sur les genres historiques du moyen âge', *Annales E.S.C.* 28 (1973) pp. 997–1016.

[20] Henri de Lubac, *Exégèse Médiévale, les quatres sens de l'Ecriture*, 2 vols. (Paris, 1959), II, p. 438.

interpreted and understood, the sense experience of something represented as a primary signification, thereafter must be conceived by intellection in its universal, a-temporal nature. This is how they interpreted St Paul's second letter to the Corinthians, where he said: 'written not with ink but with the spirit of the living God: for the letter killeth but the spirit giveth life'.

An understanding of what is meant by *historia* in this period, therefore depends on an understanding of the faculties of the soul and how it comes to know and understand the meaning of individual sensual experiences in a more universal mode, through words, which directly substitute for the absent sensual experience. History, thus understood, is a direct consequence of grammatical studies in the arts course, premised on a theory of cognition through signs. If this is the case, then it raises some very serious problems for modern medievalists who use medieval chronicles as evidence of a past that purportedly happened. What these chronicles tell us is what their compilers valued and thought worthy of remembrance, whether or not what they re-recorded from previous recorders like Bede – who did not, for the most part, record what he experienced – ever happened or not!

THE 'NEW' HISTORY IN THE TWELFTH CENTURY: A RECOGNITION OF THE PASTNESS OF THE PAST? JOHN OF SALISBURY

With this understanding of 'history' as the literal record of sensual experience of the narrator, as yet unjudged and without moral interpretation, we are now able to examine aspects of the 'new' history during that period which has, with justice, come to be known as the twelfth-century Renaissance.

Brian Stock has rightly argued that the eleventh and twelfth centuries witnessed a modification in the interdependence between an oral and written tradition, where texts increasingly served as a reference system for everyday activities outside the monastic community (as well as within it), giving shape to many larger vehicles of explanation.[21] Codes generated from written discourse were employed not only to produce new behavioural patterns but to restructure existing ones. We have already seen this to have been the case amongst the Cistercians in the monastic setting. *Extra muros*, the writing down of events, the conversion of sensual

---

[21] Brian Stock, *The Implications of Literacy: Written Language and Models of Interpretation in the Eleventh and Twelfth Centuries* (Princeton, New Jersey, 1983).

experience into signs on the page, gave rise to parallels between literature and life, readers being able to live texts.[22] An interest in discovering what a text says literally, instead of immediately transforming its meaning by allegory and metaphor had already been demonstrated during the eleventh century. By the twelfth century this was taken further, leading away from the methods and purposes of the allegorical, monastic history-writing to produce a literal but exemplary historiography practised by new groups that sought to achieve something closer to a literal *imitatio christi* than they believed monks had achieved. History as a succession of discrete, exemplary anecdotes to be understood literally as the primary significations of experience, would emerge to stand side by side with history as allegory. And along with this literal 'new' history would come a new conception of time that was no longer the continuous essence of the monastic experience but a conceptual form serving the needs of both mind and body by dividing and measuring the present and past into discrete discontinuities.[23]

It has often been argued that an oral tradition unnoticeably transforms the past, editing out irrelevant aspects of the past which would be incomprehensible to the present hearers, whereas written texts inspire comparative reflection through the static appearance of the described past as unlike the present.[24] Writing tends to elicit the discontinuities between past and present so that men actively seek change, either to restore what they take to be the past or to modify the present. During the twelfth century there was an increasing awareness of discontinuities.

During the twelfth century there was an observable break with the older monastic tradition of static intellectual truths clothed in metaphor. The writings of the renegade Cistercian Joachim of Flora at the end of the century emphasised the importance of the past of the self and of human

---

22 *Ibid.* p. 4. Also see, Franz Bäuml, 'Varieties and consequences of medieval literacy and illiteracy', *Speculum*, 55 (1980), pp. 237–65. John F. Benton also points to the increasing naturalness of verbal portrayals in the twelfth century. We note that presentness is emphasised for readers now and in the future, but there is no concern with the pastness of the past. See 'Consciousness of self and perceptions of individuality' in *Renaissance and Renewal*, pp. 263–95.

23 Jacques Le Goff, *Pour un Autre Moyen Âge, temps, travail et culture en occident* (Paris, 1977), part I, p. 75.

24 Jack Goody, *The Domestication of the Savage Mind* (Cambridge, 1977); Goody, 'The consequences of literacy' in Jack Goody and Ian Watt, eds., *Literacy in Traditional Societies* (Cambridge, 1968); Michael Clanchy, *From Memory to Written Record, England 1066–1307* (London, 1979); Harvey J. Graff, ed., *Literacy and Social Development in the West: a Reader* (Cambridge, 1981); Michael Stubbs, *Language and Literacy: The Sociolinguistics of Reading and Writing* (London, 1980); Harvey J. Graff, *Literacy in History: An Interdisciplinary Research Bibliography* (New York, 1981); Janet Coleman, *English Literature in History c. 1350–1400: Medieval Readers and Writers* (London, 1981), chapter 4.

history as part of his schema of an unrepeatable and progressive pattern of human development. But this was based not on recorded evidence of man's lived life but rather on Joachim's distinctive exegesis of the Gospel text.[25] Another break with the older tradition can be seen in the increasing literacy of western culture whereby the past came to be observed as fixed in a text whose interpretation in the present brought to light discontinuities between how it is now and how it was then. Furthermore, the increasing availability of Aristotle's natural science writings, especially the *Physics* posed the problem of successive motion made up of discrete, individual moments which led to a discussion of the nature of time as unrepeatable and progressive, a continuity of discontinuities. And the blossoming of anecdotal history seemed to indicate a readiness, but only in the first instance, to observe the discontinuities of life in the world. But discontinuities were not left as such.

The earlier monastic, universal and comprehensive view of human progress, strangely indifferent to time other than that of the fixed liturgical rhythm of the year, and read against the one truly historical text, the Bible, gave way to observations of discrete events and anecdotes. But this in turn gave rise to systematic prophecy as the framework of certainty for the course of contingent discrete events, past, present and future.[26] Prophecy was not merely taken to be prediction of the future, but the divinely revealed pattern of knowledge of all matters past, present and future, lying beyond the scope of human observation. Therefore, on the one hand, an increasing scientific observation of things as they are in their discreteness combined, on the other, with an overarching prophetic attention to all else that was indeterminate and contingent, serving to explain in two modes the direction and shape of history as it had been, as it was in the present and as it was to be. The continuous or the harmonious was created out of the discontinuous.

An instance of the discrete observation and recording of things is the typical scholastic book in the form of *glossa* or *summa*, which took shape in the twelfth century. Interlinear glosses proliferated to elucidate the text or *littera*. The *glossa* or *summa* aimed to cope with the increasing number of documents that were being produced. The scholar bishop Robert of Melun, Bishop of Hereford, 1163–7, defined the *summa* as a concise

---

[25] Marjorie Reeves, *The Influence of Prophecy in the later Middle Ages: a study in Joachimism* (Oxford, 1969); and Reeves, *Joachim of Fiore and the Prophetic Future* (London, 1976); Ann Williams, ed., *Prophecy and Millenarianism, Essays in Honour of Marjorie Reeves* (Essex, 1980).
[26] See the discussion below of John of Salisbury's distinction between the ancient and modern meaning of 'contingent' in the *Metalogicon*.

encyclopedia of instances, a compendious collection of instances.[27] One collected together discrete instances in a *summa* or *florilegium*. *But* thereafter one arranged these in such a way as to enable commentators to illustrate the *harmony* of instances. Abelard's methodological prologue followed by contrasting instances in his *Sic et Non* had attempted to do just this.

In what is often called the oral society of the earlier middle ages, nonliterate jurors who swore on the Gospels, were asked to reveal what was recorded in people's living memories. What passed for truths without documents was the current collective attitude depending on the word of one's fellows, and this was the flexible, updated, remembered truth of the oldest living member. But by the twelfth century, the written record increasingly froze past archaisms for all those who could read to see.[28] While there is no clear point of transition from a nonliterate to a literate society, in areas like property law and the canon law of marriage,[29] oral customary traditions were increasingly superseded by administrative, institutional and legal texts during the later twelfth and thirteenth centuries. The right to hold land on the basis of a customary memory 'from time out of mind' would no longer be honoured without a document that enshrined such rights.[30] From the middle of the twelfth century there was an increase in records of all sorts, produced by a growing number of specialists in administration whose technical skills were based on the written word, on reckoning, on setting down for posterity a fixed memorial of the present, who thereby measured and divided up the present and the past into discrete discontinuities.

But thereafter, continuities were constructed. The administration of European governments increasingly was founded on precedent. Such administration of men and things expanded with the growth of a technical, artificial memory, the written document. The written word therefore, came to transform men's conceptions of themselves and their societies,[31] not least, by extending the reader's membership beyond a localised customary community to a wider, normalised community outside the sphere of influence of the memory of family and community. An instrumental rationality came to structure the contours of men's lives. And in

27 'Singulorum brevis comprehensio, singulorum compendiosa collectio'. (M.-D. Chenu, *Nature, Man and Society in the Twelfth Century*, trans. J. Taylor and L. Little (Chicago, 1968) p. 292).
28 Clanchy, *From Memory to Written Record*, pp. 229–33.
29 Janet Coleman, 'The *Owl and the Nightingale* and papal theories of marriage', *Journal of Ecclesiastical History*, 38 (1987), pp. 517–68.
30 Janet Coleman, 'Property and poverty', in *The Cambridge History of Medieval Political Thought, c. 350– c. 1450*, ed. J. H. Burns (Cambridge, 1988), pp. 607–48.
31 Stock, *Implications of Literacy*, p. 18.

church and nascent state it was insisted that law as opposed to custom, was the equivalent of truth, 'the search for which would lead to the restoration or renewing of the authentic practices of the apostles and the primitive church'.[32] Facts were not only recorded in texts but were embodied in texts, the text as the literal, primary signification, substituting for the event it literally described.

Thus far we can say that history as text at first transformed the perception of tradition into a series of discontinuities. But as we have also seen, new methodologies emerged to evaluate and reconcile opposing texts. And here is the heart of the issue: the new scholastic logical techniques, so well exemplified by Abelard's dialectical analysis of propositions, were bent on reconciliation and harmonisation of perceived discontinuities. There was no attempt to evaluate the past in its own terms and thereby preserve discontinuities. After the literal reading of a text came exegesis and interpretation and these were not exercised in order to set forth the uniqueness of the objective contents of a text. No one was interested in stopping at the discrete, literal level of the text's ability to denote experience. What mattered was a text's meaning and meaning was the consequence of an activity of rational mind engaged in intellection and interpretation.[33] As Anselm had remarked in his *De Grammatico*, what matters is meaning and not words which hold a syllogism together.[34] If *historia* is the literal word, the primary signification of events, then it is

---

[32] *Ibid.*, p. 37. Their concern with a *renovatio* reveals their intention to take from antiquity what they could deposit in the twelfth century without any interest in the continuity of change. They sought a reproduction of the past and present, based on a belief in the possibility of a renewal of sameness. There was little concern for Rome's uniqueness, distinctiveness, distance and otherness. What they believed was possible was an *essential* repeat performance.

[33] The Rouses point out that the needs of teaching from the page motivated the development of techniques of layout; hence the artificiality of the distinction between preaching and the classroom (p. 218). Preaching as *in artem sermocinandi*. Peter of Capua (d. 1242) compiled a collection of distinctions entitled *Alphabetum in artem sermocinandi* (*c.* 1220–5): when one wishes to make a sermon one should lay as his foundation some authority, i.e. a scriptural passage ... since one builds more suitably on a stable foundation. Then one should consider *diligenter* how many *dictiones* are contained in this authoritative passage and *a quibus litteris ipse dictiones incipiunt, quibus etiam rebus conveniant proprie dictiones ipse; quo diligenter prenotato, secundum premissam duplicem ordinem de facili poterit in hoc opere* [Peter's collection] *de singulis dictionibus tractatus singulos invenire, quibus inventis, facile erit lectori ipsos coniungere et ex ipsis sermonem texere iuxta suam discretionem'*;
One constructs sermons on the basis of focusing on individual words in the authority, looking them up in Peter's collection, and then linking them; from the consequent expressions formed one then weaves a meaning according to one's discretion. Compare this with Abelard's discretionary attention. There is no analysis by the Rouses of the dialectical or cognitive terms used in this passage. The text is cited from the MSS in Rouse and Rouse, in *Renaissance and Renewal*, p. 219 n. 56. Also see p. 218 n. 51.

[34] *De Grammatico*, ed. D. P. Henry (Oxford, 1964), p. 149.

only propaedeutic to meaning. For most religious thinkers, the discrete individuality of the past or present as represented by words of a text, was of little importance. The historian must be superseded by the orator, the poet, the interpreter.

Consequently, Stock's argument that the twelfth century came to recognise the pastness of the past so that 'archaic modes of thought were no longer able to envelop the present and to dissolve it as an independent realm of experience'[35] should be stated the other way round. What most men understood as the presentness of mind's operations and the stability of language conventions as taught by the *ars grammatica*, eliminated the pastness of the past. Present modes of thought enveloped those of the past and dissolved the past as a discontinuous and independent realm of experience. Once one goes beyond the text as *littera*, the text as *historia*, one engages rationality to interpret the text, giving it meaning at the more universal level so that this meaning is applicable in the present. If the present was the vantage point from which the past could be discussed and debated it was largely in order that the past, the *littera*, would be interpreted by mind's present activity of construing the unchanging rules of grammar and logic, thereby transcending the literal text. What appears to have been 'new' in the attitudes of the *moderni* of the twelfth century was their delight in a consciousness of their presentness, their attention to human acts and intentions, whereby ancient authorities would serve the present through an exegetical analysis of their present relevance.[36] What changed during the twelfth century was not the evidence of the past but exegetical modes, the mechanics of textual interpretation, based mainly on Aristotle's logic as a key to the meaning of texts whenever they happened to have been written.

Once again, *historia* is not necessarily about the past. *Historia* is the enshrining, in words, of those experiences which would otherwise 'fly into oblivion'. Such primary significations of sensual experience stand in for experiences and when scratched into vellum are signs of fleeting experience. The literal sense, *historia*, is not about time but about the transformation, through signifying representations, of experiences. At the level

---

[35] Stock, *Implications of Literacy*, p. 517.
[36] Where antiquity was referred to, it provided the form while the twelfth century (the contemporary period) and its needs and perceptions provided the substance. See Robert L. Benson, 'Political *renovatio*: two models from Roman antiquity' in *Renaissance and Renewal*, pp. 339–86; p. 359, on the use of 'revivals' of republican and imperial Roman models in the Roman commune of the twelfth century. Benson's two themes: historical continuity (that is, *no* distance and distinctiveness of old Rome) and Romanness of the contemporary Empire, left their imprint on the language of twelfth-century political consciousness and self-perception (pp. 373 ff). Hence, German princes were *optimates* or *senatus*; German knights were called *milites Romani*.

of meaning, exegesis and interpretation, there can be no recognition of 'archaic modes of thought'. Thoughts and propositions are either true or false. They have no historical depth. For twelfth-century thinkers the ancients were pretty clever but many moderns were even cleverer. See what John of Salisbury says in the prologue to his *Metalogicon*, I:

I have not been ashamed to cite moderns whose opinions in many instances I unhesitatingly prefer over those of the ancients. I trust that posterity will honour our contemporaries, for I have profound admiration for the extraordinary talents, diligent studies, marvelous memories, fertile minds, remarkable eloquence and linguistic proficiency of many of those of our own day.[37]

John has no interest in showing that the ancients saw things differently. He is only interested in deriving truths from texts, whenever they may have been written, that may be applicable for the present. He is convinced that all things read or written are useless unless they have a good influence on one's present manner of living. If the ancients are ever wrong it is only because they are grammatically or logically inaccurate or implausible judged by present standards. In the prologue to Book III of the *Metalogicon*, John says:

These opinions of the ancients are admitted (today) simply because of their antiquity, while the far more probable and correct opinions of our contemporaries are, on the other hand, rejected merely because they have been proposed by men of our own time . . . I also desire that credit be given those to whom I owe what little I know or think. For I am an Academician and am not ashamed to acknowledge the authors of my own progress.[38]

Most specifically, John's respect for the moderns is emphasised in *Metalogicon*, III, 4 where he discusses the arts course text, Aristotle's *Perihermenias* (*De Interpretatione*):

While the sense of the words that were used by the ancients and those that are used by moderns may be the same, their greater age has made the former more venerable. I recollect that the Peripatetic of Pallet (Abelard) made the observation, which I believe was correct, that it would be easy for one of our own contemporaries to compose a book about this art (of interpretation or logic) which would be at least the equal of any of those written (on the subject) by the ancients in both its apprehension of the truth and the aptness of its wording, but (at the same time) it would be impossible or extremely difficult for such a book to gain acceptance as an authority . . .

Neither the truth nor the rules of logical or rhetorical composition have any historicity for John. Scholars can refine their logic and improve their

---

[37] John of Salisbury, *Metalogicon*, trans. McGarry (Berkeley, 1955), p. 6.
[38] *Ibid.*, p. 145.

rhetorical skills, but each is based on the stability of language conventions be they ill or well used:

> Our own generation enjoys the legacy bequeathed to it by that which preceded it. We frequently know more, not because we have moved ahead by our own natural ability but because we are supported by the [mental] strength of others and possess riches that we have inherited from our forefathers.

These riches are truths for the present.

> Bernard of Chartres used to compare us to dwarfs perched on the shoulders of giants. He pointed out that we see more than our predecessors not because we have keener vision or greater height but because we are lifted up and borne aloft on their gigantic stature. I readily agree with the foregoing. Teachers of the arts, even in their Introductions, explain the basic elements of the art and many truths of the science equally as well and perhaps, even better than do the ancients. Who is content even with what Aristotle gives in his *De Interpretatione?* Who does not add points obtained from other sources? . . . They, so to speak, dress the message of the authors in modern style, which becomes in a way even more splendescent when it is more brilliantly adorned with the jewels of antiquity.[39]

And in *Metalogicon*, III, 6 John reiterates that 'scholars of our own day, drawing inspiration and strength from Aristotle [on the *Topics*] are adding to the latter's findings many new reasons and rules equally as certain as those he himself enunciated'. Hence, 'we are indebted not only to Themistius, Cicero, Apuleius and Boethius for their contributions but also to the Peripatetic of Pallet [Abelard] and to others of our teachers who have striven to promote our progress by developing new doctrines as well as by elucidating old ones'.[40] The old doctrines are not archaic and to be replaced by the new. Both old and new contribute to the truth of the science of logical interpretation of texts.

Bernard of Chartres's reputed reference to contemporary students as dwarfs standing on the shoulders of past giants and seeing further because raised inadvertently, should not be interpreted as a veneration for the ancients as opposed to the moderns. He undoubtedly believed in his generation's ability to see further than its predecessors as did John of Salisbury.[41] And this was because of additional and more subtle exegetical

---

[39] *Ibid.*, p. 168.   [40] *Ibid.*, p. 177.

[41] We shall have occasion to indicate later how some of our current historians of the Renaissance refrain from reading medieval history and literature while at the same time are concerned to show how Renaissance thinkers, during the fifteenth and sixteenth centuries, held attitudes that we can recognise as modern, having consciously left the middle ages behind. Here, it may only be noted that there is some cause for concern when the distinguished Renaissance historian Donald R. Kelley in his otherwise interesting and important review article on the various historical and literary schools of contemporary scholarship, can use the following quote from John of Salisbury's *Metalogicon*, 'nos esse

doctrines, a more sophisticated mechanics of interpretation of texts as the key to meaning, as the key to timeless truths, applicable to any text be it past or present. What changed during the twelfth century was an approach to texts and not the development of a method to investigate nontextual evidence.

If the twelfth-century Renaissance may indeed be seen in part as an awareness of progress through difference, it was the achievement of this Renaissance to perceive the difference and then dissolve it by reinterpreting it, conceptualising it, in accordance with the present, based upon their understanding of language conventions and the operation of intellectual understanding and interpretation of texts. In so far as they perceived the past as distinct from the present, and developed an interest in seeking out causal relations between events, they then transformed these through the mind's interpretative exegesis into that which had meaning for the present. They had little if any interest in allowing either the past or present, as *littera*, to remain uninterpreted as to its more universal truth.

Contrary to what is often believed, the *moderni/antiqui* dualism of the twelfth century had little historical depth as we understand these terms. There was no sympathy with the past as other because they did not appear to have thought that Latin texts written at other times disclosed the kind of difference that revealed values that were incommensurable with their own. What became apparent to twelfth-century thinkers was that language was a means of signifying experiences through fixed conventions. Such grammatical and logical conventions signified a fixed world that was to be understood by fixed conventions of mind. Although men could and did signify variously, if they did not abuse grammatical and logical conventions then they meant the truth which was not historically specific. When one text said one thing, another said something else, it was assumed each could be harmonised with the other. The twelfth-century concern to harmonise rather than to show unrepeatable disharmonies of the past in relation to the present is indicative of what we today would call a lack of historical depth. John of Salisbury would gladly have shared a straw pallet with Cicero without the slightest worry that the Roman would have any difficulty understanding what John meant. The truth was not relative. John, like all of his contemporaries, was engaged in constructing harmonies between the past as recorded in texts and the present for use in the present. What we must realise is that once the past is recorded in a text,

quasi nanos gigantium humeris insidentes, ut possimus plura eis et remotiora videre' and attribute it to Bernard of Clairvaux rather than Bernard of Chartres! See 'Horizons of intellectual history: retrospect, circumspect, prospect', *Journal of the History of Ideas*, 48 (1987), pp. 143–69; p. 152.

once past experiences are enshrined in language, they become universal and timeless like the common names that represent them. The written document was an artificial memory whose meaning was taken to be as relevant to the present as it was to the past.

One last example of the heightened concern for the present is the practice of forgery. Michael Clanchy has argued that forged documents were often based on earlier authentic documents or on good oral traditions. The purpose of forgery, however, was to produce a record in a form that was acceptable in the *present*, particularly in courts of law. 'Forgery was necessary because contemporaries had no historical sense'. But this does not mean that they did not distinguish past from present; rather, it was that the present relevance of aspects of the past was all that meant anything: 'A good oral tradition or an authentic charter of an early Anglo-Saxon king might be rejected by a court of law because it seemed strange, whereas a forged charter would be acceptable because it suited contemporary notions of what an ancient charter should look like'.[42] Forgeries looked like what they *thought* an old document looked like, forgers recreating the past in an acceptable literate form in the present. Indeed, 'those monastic writers who are most insistent in the prologues to their works on the importance of telling the truth are often those who were involved in fabricating charters'.[43] William of Malmesbury and Eadmer of Canterbury knowingly included forged material despite their reputed concern for evaluating evidence.[44] The 'new' history of the twelfth century was *not* concerned with the recognition of the pastness of the past, any more than the pastness of the past was a concern of history-writing as practised during the monastic middle ages.

CHANGES IN HISTORIOGRAPHIC TECHNIQUES DURING
THE TWELFTH CENTURY

Let us examine more closely historical writing at Bec in the time of Anselm and his followers and thereafter, treat the historical efforts of other authors who were not only monks but also Augustinian canons, secular clergy and mendicants into the thirteenth century. We shall better be able to observe the nature of the changes in historiographic technique and purpose during this period and get closer to what importance they gave to remembering the past and, indeed, what they meant by this.

The monk Anselm, as logician and theologian, stretched the term

---

[42] Clanchy, p. 249.   [43] *Ibid.*, p. 250.
[44] Antonia Gransden, *Historical Writing in England, c. 550–c. 1307*, (London, 1974), pp. 177–8.

'history' to mean theology and as a sacred historian he was largely interested in the logical necessity of historical events as set out in the Bible. In his *Cur Deus Homo*, for instance, Anselm proposed to demonstrate that even if Christ had not become man and we were ignorant of the events which followed his incarnation, it would still be possible to reconstruct the sequence of those events by considering the circumstances in human history which *logically necessitated* the incarnation, and this necessity he said, could be demonstrated *by reason alone*. What he proposes is a closed logical system based on sacred history where the end of the story is already known. Nothing is unpredictable and there is neither uniqueness nor unintelligibility of events because, following Augustine, understanding is of what is universal and not of the particular. As Evans has pointed out, 'Anselm enjoys an unquestioning confidence in the inevitability of what happened. He is able to discover a necessary sequence in the events with which he has to deal'.[45] Thus, he sees his task as a historian to be an explicit discussion of logical necessity in human history. He 'generalises from the observations he has made about historical cause and effect in which God is directly involved (in his work of atonement) in order to postulate the existence of much the same laws in the working out of ordinary events ... he makes no allowance for alteration or modification of the rules under changing circumstances, because he has no sense of period'. Indeed, Evans rightly points out that 'there can be no room in a philosophy of history based upon the events of sacred history for any sensitivity to differences in the particular flavour of one age for another'.[46]

We have already seen the degree to which Anselm was influenced by Augustine for whom sacred historical truth was classed as uninvestigable *credibilia*. The events of biblical history, not being abstract or universal, can never be understood; they can only be believed.[47] Therefore, authoritative biblical history, the only history that matters, lies in the uninvestigable realm of the assent of faith which is, thereafter, open to analysis only in terms of the logical necessity of its truth.[48] Because belief is a lower kind of thinking for Augustine when contrasted with understanding as a result of reasoning, he arranges a hierarchy in the objects of thought from historical, temporal things (*scientia*) to a knowledge of eternal objects of thought (contemplation). And because the soul is immortal and immaterial for Augustine, rational knowledge cannot enter the mind from outside. It must, in some way, already be present to mind, logically and necessarily.

45 Gillian Evans, 'St Anselm and sacred history', in *The Writing of History in the Middle Ages*, ed. Davis and Wallace-Hadrill, pp. 187–210; p. 206.
46 *Ibid.*, p. 195.
47 See above, ch. 13, Abelard on 'opinion' for a further elaboration on this.
48 Augustine, *De Div. Qu. LXXXIII*, 48, and *Epistle*, 147, 6–8.

In so far as the human soul is subject to mutability in that it suffers repentance and sin, the soul has an empirical history that cannot be completely divorced from the vicissitudes of life, but the *meaning* of its history is disclosed by the operations of reason for which there is no unintelligibility and only an inevitability of what happened. As for Augustine, so too for Anselm, how we interpret the events of past sacred history is by the same method employed to interpret the present's truth, a truth which is necessary and a-temporal, so that what one derives from particular historical events is a meaning that is not historical but ever-present and relevant in and to the now.

So too in his *De Veritate*, Anselm describes 'a world that is comprehensible and interesting because it is concerned not with the quirks of individuals but with reason and truth: not with the miscellaneous causes of the passing moment but with the mind of God'.[49] And as Gibson points out, Anselm as well as his contemporaries at Bec were indifferent to what we mean by history, keeping no records of events beyond the most practical: monastic professions, land-grants, and notes of legal and fiscal privilege. 'They showed no interest in the Norman past nor in world history as a whole ... they were not even concerned with the historical books of the Old Testament, nor with the historical circumstances in which Christianity was anchored: if the infidels were to doubt the historicity of the Incarnation, they would be sufficiently answered by a proof of its necessity'.[50]

When the climate at Bec began to change during the twelfth century and Milo Crispin compiled his *Vitae Abbatum*, he saw his task to be the composition of a hymn to Bec's founders, writing down their achievements 'for the edification of posterity; theirs was the pattern of life to be emulated'.[51] He simply added his own lives of Boso and William to the hagiographical accounts of Anselm and Herluin by Eadmer and Gilbert Crispin,[52] the whole work of 'history' being little more than a 'local necrology and a local store of unwritten anecdote'.[53] Later historians of Bec, like Robert of Torigny, seemed primarily interested in genealogies and chronology rather than in the moral value of history or the intention of its actors. This is indeed, literal *historia* without rhetorical embellishment and plausible interpretation. It is evidence of an old-fashioned kind of history writing that did not draw on school dialectic and rhetoric.

It has been argued that monastic history writing during Henry I's days

[49] Margaret Gibson, 'History at Bec in the Twelfth Century', in *The Writing of History in the Middle Ages*, ed. Davis and Wallace-Hadrill, pp. 167–86; p. 168.
[50] *Ibid.*　[51] *Vitae Abbatum, praef., PL* 150, 695 C.
[52] Gilbert Crispin also wrote a *De Anima:* BL Ms Add. 8166 fos. 37–39v.
[53] Gibson, 'History at Bec', p. 171.

began to change because it was inspired by a more hostile scrutiny of the monastic vocation by new monastic foundations, and by canons and secular clergy who challenged monks' authority to exercise jurisdictions beyond the cloister. With a growth in the activity of bishops and their diocesan agents, monks were experiencing a regulation of their conduct of external affairs as never before. So they set to writing justifications of their interpretation of the past through a presentation of saints' lives, customs, rights and estates established by precedent, seeking to assert a continuity of experience from before the Norman conquest, defending ancient titles to lands and rights threatened by 'ignorant newcomers'.[54] Eadmer of Canterbury not only revised and rewrote the lives of saints on whose relics, miracles and traditions his church depended, but he also was a shrewd observer of current events. He wrote his *Historia Novorum* as a narrative of *contemporary* events providing documentary illustration some of which he knew to be forgeries, despite his protestations that he only presented the truth.[55] We note that his use of *historia* for contemporary events is in line with the understanding of *historia* as the literal sense. But we also note that when he cites documents earlier than his lifetime his purpose is to establish precedents for how Canterbury understood its situation in the present. He is not simply displaying the past but converting it into the present, thereby going beyond the mere recording of uninterpreted, literal *historia*.

Eadmer's contemporary William of Malmesbury also harnessed interpretative hagiography to literal *historia*, arguing in his *Miracles of the Virgin Mary* that it is not deception to alter your stories if you make them more dramatic and edifying for the present reader: 'If indeed any grandeur of language has outrun the true facts, the man who is fair-minded will not therefore judge it any less true'.[56] As Carter says, 'the problems of truth are not for William what they are to us: those that exercise him are not mundane matters of time and place but rather questions of faith about the other world . . . how else can spiritual truths be understood unless they are couched in material terms?'[57] And for William, the truth of the interpreter who uses the literal words or *historia*, is to be found in authoritative books, interpreted to suit his own present purposes, books which he says he took

---

54 Martin Brett, 'John of Worcester and his contemporaries', in *The Writing of History in the Middle Ages*, pp. 101–26; p. 125.
55 R. W. Southern, 'The Canterbury forgeries', *EHR*, 73 (1958).
56 Prologue, Book II, ed. J. M. Canal, 'El libro de laudibus et miraculis sanctae mariae de Guillermo de Malmesbury O.S.B.', *Claretianum VIII* (Rome, 1968), p. 127. Peter Carter, 'The historical content of William of Malmesbury's Miracles of the Virgin', in *The Writing of History in the Middle Ages*, ed. Davis and Wallace-Hadrill, pp. 127–66; p. 163.
57 Carter, 'The historical content', p. 164.

great trouble to find in order to compose his other works – his five books on the deeds of English kings, five more on the deeds of bishops, a revised *liber pontificalis* to illustrate the relations between England and Rome, a history of Glastonbury's antiquities, a revised life of Wulfstan of Worcester, and other saints' lives. In none of these works is it clear that William worried over the conflicting evidence he found in his numerous sources.[58] Instead, he took books or texts to be trustworthy and these texts were unexamined evidence implying a stability of *res*, as authoritatively narrated, on the basis of which one then created a narrative whose plausibility for present understanding was all that mattered. For William, a chronicle was composed by means of what we would call a curious combination of historical 'fact' and a romancer's liberty of invention, made-up conversations, events, dates, names: it was a rhetorical genre which united hagiography with history in an uneasy alliance. He was doing what Aristotle had said poets and interpreters do to the chaos of the historical record. But he knew the difference between this kind of narrative composition and what he calls *historia*: only the latter is based on contemporary sensual experience and denotes *gesta* which are then interpreted.

This kind of 'historical' author is not retrieving the pastness of the past. He is rigorously selecting events and deeds which he believes ought to be transmitted to the future because of their exemplary value for the present. The perceived purpose of annals and chronicles in general, their distinction having been lost during the twelfth century, illustrates this well.[59] Chronicles originated in the literary tradition which took as its model Jerome's translations of Eusebius's *Ecclesiastical History* while annals originated in the marginal comments on a text with a liturgical purpose, only incidentally including disparate historical notes. Chronicles were interested in history from creation, that is, universal history, while primitive

---

58 *Pace* Rodney M. Thompson, 'William of Malmesbury as historian and man of letters', *Journal of Ecclesiastical History*, 29 (1978), especially pp. 393–8, and R. M. Thompson, 'John of Salisbury and William of Malmesbury: currents in twelfth-century humanism', in Michael Wilks, ed., *The World of John of Salisbury*, (Oxford, 1984), pp. 117–25; especially pp. 119–20. As C. N. L. Brooke says in the introduction to the edition and translation of Walter Map's *De Nugis Curialium*, ed. M. R. James, C. N. L. Brooke, R. A. B. Mynors (Oxford, 1983), pp. xli–xlii:

Educated men in the twelfth century seem commonly to have drawn a distinction between history and fiction; but there were many intermediate stages and no twelfth-century writer wrote history solely or mainly out of regard for the love of truth. There were men like William of Malmesbury who had a strong interest in discovering what had happened in the past and strong weapons to help them in their study; but even William was also much concerned with history as entertainment, as story-telling ... [T]his notion of history as literature, edifying and true but also intended to amuse ... [allows twelfth-century historians to be read] more like historical novels than sober history.

59 Michael McCormick, *Les Annales du Haut-Moyen Âge* (Typologie des sources du moyen-âge occidental, 14) (Turnhout-Belgium, 1975).

annals consigned themselves to annotations on noteworthy events. Chronicle history recorded selected events in the history of man's salvation in chronological order, working against the larger, fixed backdrop of the meaning of such events in relation to salvific history. Primitive annals were larged divorced from what we would call a well-defined historical curiosity. *But neither of these two traditions saw any interest in the past for itself.* Either the past was an example of moral behaviour seen in the light of the universally present, or the present was merely recorded as the present. As Gervase of Canterbury said: 'The historian proceeds diffusely and elegantly, whereas the chronicler proceeds simply, gradually and briefly'. He distinguishes them in terms of rhetorical genre and not in terms of the subject matter they treat:

Cronicus autem annos incarnationis Domini annorumque menses computat et Kalendas, actus etiam regum et principum qui in ipsis eveniunt breviter edocet, eventus etiam, portenta vel miracula commemorat. Sunt autem plurimi qui cronicas vel annales scribentes, limites suos excedunt, nam philacteria sua dilatare et fimbrias magnificare delectant.[60]

Gervase merges chronicles and annals and says they teach men by means of telling the stories of exemplary personages like kings and princes or by recording and preserving miracles. But he complains that current authors were exceeding the limits of the genre by elaborating on their exemplary material to amuse readers.[61] They thereby extended their briefs as chroniclers. Gervase saw himself as writing for his own monastic family rather than presenting the past to the public at large.[62] Other chroniclers, like Matthew Paris, exceeded these limits. But no one was telling anyone about the past for its own sake. The historical consciousness that did emerge more distinctly in the twelfth century saw no purpose in elaborating on the pastness of the past unless some moral, exemplary and universal aspect of that past could be interpreted for use in the present. As Gervase of Canterbury said, there is a distinction to be drawn between memorable events (*memorabilia*) and those worth remembering (*memoranda*). Only the latter were worthy of retention and should be recorded.[63] His aim, like other historians, was to convey to posterity a deliberately created and

---

[60] Gervase of Canterbury, Chronicle, Prologue, ed., W. Stubbs, *Opera Historica*, vol. I (London, 1879), pp. 87–8.
[61] McCormick, p. 19. A.-D. von den Brincken, *Studien zur lateinischen Weltchronistik bis in das Zeitalter Ottos von Freising* (Dusseldorf, 1957); A.-D. von den Brincken, 'Die lateinische Weltchronistik' in *Mensch und Weltgeschichte: zur Geschichte der Universalgeschichtsschreibung*, ed. A. Randa (Salzburg and Munich, 1969), pp. 43–58 and especially pp. 59–60.
[62] Michael Clanchy, *From Memory to Written Record* (London, 1979), p. 78.
[63] Gervase, Chronicle, *Opera Historica*, I, p. 89.

rigorously selected version of events for the use of the present and future reader.[64] The *gesta temporum*, the deeds of the past, were to be recorded because they were acts performed by a morally responsible 'someone' who could be imitated. Only events judged worthy of being remembered and imitated are *notabilia facta*.

MONKS AND JOHN OF SALISBURY'S RHETORICAL HISTORY

There is an argument here that historiography even after the mid twelfth-century's recognition of the distinction between the past and the present, had much in common with the purposes of hagiography. Authors of *Miracula* presented testimonies of their time, writing about the remarkable events they had seen or transmitting true testimonies of others of what they had seen in order that such events would not be lost to oblivion. The specific purpose of such recorded testimonies was to edify and not only to inform and to interest. When an author of miracles was not in attendance on the facts, he often made an appeal to oral tradition where others had witnessed the event in question. The conception of history which dominates hagiography as well as much history writing is that of the immediacy of the testimony of sensual experience. And like authors of miracles, historians aimed to write for posterity so that the events witnessed in their own time would not disappear from the collective memory.[65] Much the same intention was therefore shared by historians and hagiographers: the expression of 'les événements à chaud'.[66] From 'warm memories' would be drawn a universal lesson, by the author, reader or preacher.

The peculiarity of the medieval *exemplum*[67] in hagiographical and historical writings shows up in stark contrast with the ancient *exemplum* as a rhetorical instrument. The ancient *exemplum* proposed an historical

64 Clanchy, *From Memory to Written Record*, p. 119. Also see, Bernard Guenée, *Histoire et Cultures historiques dans l'Occident Médiéval*, (Paris, 1980). Also see B. Guenée, ed., *Le Métier d'Historien au Moyen Âge, études sur l'historiographie médiévale* (Paris, 1977). Guenée, *Histoire et cultures historiques*, p. 29; 'Il arriva que les historiens, lorsqu'ils étaient clercs, furent plus soucieux d'efficacité pastorale que de verité'.

65 P.-A. Sigal, 'Histoire et hagiographie: les miracula aux XIᵉ et XIIᵉs.', *Annales de Bretagne et des Pays de l'Ouest*, 87 (1980), pp. 237–57 = *L'Historiographie en occident du Vᵉ au XVᵉ siècle, Actes du congrès ... à Tours (1977)*; 235.

66 *Ibid.*, p. 245 n. 43. On the necessity of writing 'adhuc calente memoria', see Richard de la Trinité, *Itinerarium peregrinorum et gesta Ricardis regis*, prologue, ed., *Britannicarum Medii Aevi Scriptores* (Rolls series) (London, 1858–96), vol. 8, pt. 1, p. 4. Also see Bernard Lacroix, *L'Historien au Moyen Âge* (Montreal and Paris, 1971), pp. 152–55.

67 Claude Bremond, Jacques Le Goff and Jean-Claude Schmitt, *L'Exemplum*, (Typologie des sources du moyen âge occidental, 40) (Turnhout- Belgium, 1982), p. 82. Jacques Berlioz, *Le Tractatus de diversis materiis praedicabilibus d'Etienne Bourbon*, Troisième partie: *De dono scientie*, Etude et édition. See *Positions des thèses de l'Ecole Nationale des Chartes* (Paris, 1977), pp. 25–33.

personage whose historic virtue was erected at the level of a model and whose fame authenticated the account. The heroes of medieval *exempla* in contrast, sink into a kind of anonymity of a simple *quidam*;[68] the authenticity of the account rests with the worthiness of the informer, the preacher, the narrator. From this essential difference between the ancient and medieval use of exemplary historical personages, several important consequences have been seen to follow.[69]

Roman history mentioned illustrious persons in texts. The material extension of this memorial in the collective memory was realised in the form of ancestral images, statues and inscriptions which filled a city's public space. Their rhetorical interest in mnemonic memory was simply another aspect of the Roman tendency to create concrete realisations of abstractions. But during the middle ages men of the church in particular, never sustained a cult of ancestors in the manner in which they celebrated the cult of saints. Exemplary types were honoured rather than individuals of excellence. And yet it has been pointed out that these exemplary saints were rarely the heroes of *exempla*. The even more anonymous *quidam*, the ordinary individuals, most frequently played this role. What was perhaps most distinctive about medieval *exempla* is demonstrated in the thirteenth-century alphabetical collections which insist that the same story can be used for *different* moral ends. The historical example was not meant to be unique in its excellence but universal in its significance, brief, plausible, amusing and memorisable.[70]

It is of some importance, and no surprise, that a monastic author of the mid twelfth century, Peter the Venerable, would set out the requirements and purposes of history writing in a work devoted to miracles.[71] He said:

I am often angered by the laziness of a great number of men who, though distinguished for their knowledge, love of learning and eloquence are yet so sluggish that they do not hand down in writing to those who are to come after them the marvelous works the Almighty repeatedly accomplishes in different parts of the world to strengthen his church. It was an ancient custom, not only with the first

---

68 See the interesting discussion by Alexander Murray, 'Confession as a historical source in the thirteenth century', in *The Writing of History in the Middle Ages*, ed. Davis and Wallace-Hadrill, pp. 275–322, where confessors' manuals, especially those composed by friars, reveal private confessions of parishioners from all social strata and are used in *exempla* for both pious behaviour to be imitated as well as cautionary tales of irreligion and disbelief.

69 Jean-Claude Schmitt, compte rendu: rhétorique et histoire. 'L'exemplum et le modèle de comportement dans le discours antique et médiévale': Table Ronde. L'Ecole française de Rome, 1979, in *Bibliothèque de L'Ecole des Chartes*, 140 (1982) = Extrait de *Mélanges de L'Ecole française de Rome. Moyen âges. Temps modernes*, 92 (1980), pp. 7–179.

70 *Ibid.*, p. 105 for a discussion of the work of J.-M. David and J. Berlioz.

71 *De Miraculis*, II, prologue, *PL* 189, 907–9.

fathers of the Christian faith but even with the gentiles, to consign to writing every undertaking, good or evil: but our contemporaries . . . nonchalantly allow to die out the memory of everything that is happening in their own times and which could be so useful to those who might come after them (*universa suis temporibus accidentia, quae succedentibus non parum possent esse utilia, languentes animo perire permittunt*) . . . How will [the works of God] be known to those who have not seen them if they are not related to them? How are they to persist in the memory of ages far distant from ours which will replace us, if they are not written down? . . . This apathy which encloses itself in a sterile silence has reached the point where everything that has happened for four or five hundred years, whether in the Church of God or in the kingdoms of Christendom, is practically unknown to us as to everyone else. In fact, our times are so different from former times that, while we are perfectly informed about everything that happened five hundred or a thousand years ago, we know nothing about later events or even what has taken place in our own lifetime. Thus we have a great number of ancient histories, ecclesiastical acts and great doctrinal books containing the Father's precepts and examples; but as for the events which have occurred in periods close to our own, I am not at all certain that we possess even one book which treats them . . . In our times those who know Latin act very differently [from Egyptians who learned Greek, the Greeks Latin, the Latins Greek etc]; not only do they take no interest in anything outside their own native land but they will not condescend to find out what is happening only two steps away or inform the public about it either in the spoken or the written word.[72]

Peter's aim is to inspire historical writing of the immediate experience of God's works for posterity. While he is aware that his times are not like former times, the purpose of writing history just as the purpose of writing miracles, is edifying in intention. It has never been, according to Peter, simply a curiosity about the past for itself. History is written to display examples to be imitated, and as Oderic Vitalis noted, it should be sung like a hymn in honour of the creator God.[73] Thus, in all medieval accounts of the past, even when during the twelfth century it became clear that the past was somehow unlike the present, the writer had to be able to distinguish between what pertained to historical 'accuracy', to a recording of primary significations, and what was relevant to the desire to exhort.

The thesis that hagiography had much in common with history writing of the interpretative variety does not intend to obscure the difference

---

[72] The translation is in Jean Leclercq, *The Love of Learning and the Desire for God*, p. 194. Compare this with what Walter Map says is his *De Nugis Curialium*, ed. M. R. James, C. N. L. Brooke and R. A. B. Mynors (Oxford, 1983):
The industriousness of the ancients is in our hands; they even make their past present in our times and we are struck dumb; their memory lives in us and we are without memorials of our own. What a miracle! The dead are alive and the living are buried by them.
[73] Orderic Vitalis, *Historia Ecclesiastica*, prologue, ed. Marjorie Chibnall (Oxford, 1969–).

between the two genres. At the level of collecting facts alone, the two genres may be distinguished and this reflects the different audiences for each genre. Whereas the historian increasingly saw his mission as providing in as complete a manner as possible a narrative of all the discrete events which he considered worthy of being remembered, in order to pass these on to posterity, the author of *miracula* permitted himself a wider choice among events because he was primarily concerned to edify through a specific interpretation of these events. Historians sought to edify *and* inform. So concerned to relate miraculous events, the hagiographical author often gives the impression of having 'enmagasiné dans sa memoire un certain nombre de faits miraculeux qu'il ressort en fonction des associations d'idées successives surgies à l'évocation de ses souvenirs'.[74] This is a method we have already observed more generally among monastic authors and hagiography shows much closer ties with the circular time of the liturgy than with the chronicler's sense of time as extended duration marked chronologically. But from the mid twelfth century, especially when a hagiographer's intention is to launch a cult of a forgotten or insufficiently recognised saint, he does what an increasing number of historians do: he collects a dossier of texts as evidence of the saint's worthiness. It is of some importance that in the second half of the twelfth century the process of canonisation was elaborated by the papacy, a crucial element of which was the presentation of a dossier.[75] The dossier came to substitute for the events literally described therein, but what mattered was their interpreted, a-historical meaning.

Bredero has recently argued that 'when writing a biography nowadays, it is customary to place the life of the subject in his historical context. In this way the human qualities of such a person can be better understood and judged. Medieval hagiography had rather the opposite in mind. Someone's *Life* was told to express something which was not timebound, his holiness'.[76] The effect of such a *Life* was to rouse in a reader or listener a devotion to this 'saint' in order to bring him to imitate the virtues recommended as an expression of the Christian life. Therefore, the saint must appear in hagiography as an a-historical being and his earthly life must be seen as having purely accidental value.[77] That the written *Life*

---

[74] Sigal, 'Histoire et hagiographie', p. 250.
[75] *Ibid.*, p. 257. Stephan Kuttner, 'La réservation papale du droit de canonisation', *Revue historique du droit français et étranger*, 4e serie, 17 (1938), pp. 172–228. E. Kemp, *Canonization and Authority in the Western Church* (Oxford, 1948).
[76] Adriaan H. Bredero, 'The canonization of St. Bernard and the Rewriting of his life', in John R. Sommerfeldt, ed., *Cistercian Ideals and Reality* (Kalamazoo, 1978), pp. 80–105; p. 80.
[77] *Ibid.*, p. 81.

came to occupy an important place in the process of canonisation by the mid twelfth century can best be illustrated by the relationship between the *Vitae* of St Bernard and his canonisation in 1174. St Bernard died in 1154 but in the years immediately thereafter he still existed 'within living memory'.

Bredero has argued that the revision of the *Vita Prima* of St Bernard was previously explained by the need felt by Geoffrey of Auxerre, its author, who was still alive, to endow the manuscript with a greater historical reliability. 'Apart from the fact that such an explanation attributes to Geoffrey a desire which was alien to his time, the absurdity of this hypothesis is shown by an accurate comparison of both versions of this *Life*. The image of the practice of heroic virtue by St Bernard and the narrative of his miracles were slightly touched up in the second version simply to accentuate even more strongly the special favors bestowed on him'.[78] Therefore, in Geoffrey's revision (1163–5) the narrative dealing with the practice of virtue and with the miracle stories had to be a standard text and not one that was open to historical verification. This meant that the text could no longer contain any clues that could lead to verification. Bredero suggests that the motive behind the revision was to omit any miracle stories in which well-known persons were mentioned as witnesses. Where witnesses were still alive, the miracles associated with their witnessing were edited out. 'The authenticity of the narrative was no longer allowed to be open to historical research.'[79]

At first, the revised text was held in little esteem, but it was accepted once again at Clairvaux *c*. 1171. Bredero says that 'the *Life* described St Bernard as a 'time-less' saint. His earthly life played only an accidental role in it. In this respect there was no substantial difference between the first and second version. However, the resistance against the second version which led to the postponement of the canonization, had arisen because at that moment the concrete historical memory of St Bernard had not yet disappeared.'[80] 'As long as the revision of his *Life* still provoked repercussions because St Bernard himself still appeared as a historically known person, the time was not ripe for his canonization.'[81]

When the text of his life could come to substitute for the lived events themselves, then canonisation of, in effect, a dossier, rather than an historic individual, took place.[82]

---

[78] *Ibid.*, p. 84. Also see A. Bredero, *Etudes sur la Vita Prima de St. Bernard* (Rome, 1960).
[79] Bredero, 'The Canonization' p. 88.   [80] *Ibid.*, 98.   [81] *Ibid.*, 99.
[82] Similarly on the 'Gegenwart der Toten', the presentness of the dead in memorial pictures and grave pictures (Grabbilder und Epitaphien), see Otto G. Oexle, 'Memoria und Memoriabild' in *Memoria, der geschichtliche Zeugniswert des liturgischen Gedenkens im Mittelalter*, ed. K. Schmid and J. Wollasch (Munich, 1984), pp. 384–440, especially c. II,

If much of what has so far been described seems largely applicable to historical writing in twelfth-century monastic milieux, we ought to extend our investigation to other historians outside the monastic enclosure. John of Salisbury provides abundant evidence of contemporary attitudes to the past and discusses the methods by which the historian remembers the past and for what purpose.

John probably wrote his *Historia Pontificalis* entirely in 1164 when he was a clerk and advisor to Theobald's successor as archbishop of Canterbury, Thomas Becket.[83] About 40 per cent of the *Historia* reflects the period 1148–52, immediately following his twelve years of logical and theological studies in France. John was, from 1148–52, secretary and confidant to archbishop Theobald and the *Historia Pontificalis* originates in his own recollections of his experiences of the papal world's inner workings as a result of Theobald's business having taken him to the papal court several times. It is dedicated to the abbot of St Remi at Reims, Peter of Celle, with whom John resided when he preceded Becket into exile on the continent. But only the dedicatory prologue mirrors the monastic tradition of history writing.

Although the *Historia Pontificalis* appears in a late thirteenth-century manuscript as a continuation of the chronicle of Sigebert of Gembloux, John made no attempts whatever to supplement the pre-1148 record. In fact, his references to Sigebert's and Hugh of St Victor's chronicles are perfunctory and Marjorie Chibnall has recently argued that it is even doubtful whether he read them at all.[84] There is, however, much overlapping material from his contemporary letters which reflected his own experiences and therefore served as *historia* as we now understand them to

pp. 391 ff and pp. 437–9. Oexle argues that a present relationship rather than an historical one was established between the dead and the living so that the dead maintained a status in the present. It was only in the eighteenth century (and he cites references to Goethe's *Elective Affinities*, ch. 2) that the memory of the dead was 'merely' reduced to an evocation of the dead past:

Freilich darf bei der Beurteilung diesen Bilder Individualität in der Darstellung Lebender und Toter nicht von vornherein gleichgesetzt werden mit Porträtähnlichkeit im neuzeitlichen und modernen Sinn. Diese Gleichsetzung von Porträtähnlichkeit und Individualität und die Annahme von deren gemeinsamem Gegensatz zu einer aufblosse 'Typen' bezogenen Personendarstellung scheint ein modernes Missverstandnis zu sein. Aus der Sicht der Sozialgeschichte möchte man vielmehr der Aufmerksamkeit lenken auf die Frage nach den Mitteln und Ausdrucksformen von Individualität in der Personendarstellung gerade auch dort, wo der moderne Betrachter zunächst weder Individualität noch gar Porträtähnlichkeit feststellen kann oder feststellen zu können glaubt. (p. 438)

[83] Roger Ray, 'Rhetorical scepticism and verisimilar narrative in John of Salisbury's *Historia Pontificalis*', in E. Breisach, ed., *Classical Rhetoric and Medieval Historiography* (Kalamazoo, Michigan, 1985), pp. 61–102.

[84] Marjorie Chibnall, 'John of Salisbury as historian' in M. Wilks, ed., *The World of John of Salisbury* (Oxford, 1984), pp. 169–77; p. 170.

have used this term. Mrs Chibnall has suggested that his letters became material for his future history in the *Historia Pontificalis* but that in the *History* he looked at events from rather different angles when he wrote them up as rhetorical interpretations. What precisely does this mean? It means that he telescoped events, dressed up legal arguments in plausible rhetorical speeches and made up likely speeches which he put in the mouth of, for instance, Ulger of Anger in reply to Arnulf of Lisieux whose views were pro-Stephen and anti-Matilda, the empress. This was a reply that Ulger might have argued had he thought of it at the time, which he seems not to have done until much later! Mrs Chibnall notes rightly that such speeches were normal devices of historians when they wished to explain the motives of their characters even when they never so expressed themselves in reality. This is precisely what Aristotle taught in his *Rhetoric* when he distinguished between the historian and the orator/poet and which Cicero passed on with even greater enthusiasm for the orator's task, indeed duty to his own generation and posterity. Did John of Salisbury have a theory behind this kind of enterprise?

We can find it at length in his *Metalogicon* (1159)[85] and in his *Policraticus*. John had been educated in Paris under Abelard and probably at Chartres. He was well-versed in the dialectical logic of those who supplemented Priscian, Boethius and Porphyry's texts with Aristotle's and their own commentaries. In the *Metalogicon*, he complains against the Cornificians, in particular against that Cornificius who now teaches what he learned formerly at a time when there was no 'letter', no literal sense, in liberal studies. 'Previously, everyone sought "the spirit" which, so they tell us, lies hidden in the letter, and poets [NB] who related history [that is, the primary signification of experience] were considered reprobate; if anyone applied himself to studying the ancients he became a marked man and the laughing stock of all.'[86] Such teaching still abounded in the cloisters of his own day and John condemns it for not making use of the new dialectic in analysing the literal sense of speech and texts. He says, the Cornificians only read Boethius and no Aristotle so they know no logic. John asserts that logic in its broadest sense is the science of verbal expression and argumentative reasoning (*loquendi vel disserendi ratio*).[87] Logic includes grammar as the starting point for speaking and writing correctly in all liberal studies.[88] His belief in the stability of things in the world matched by a stability in the modes of mind's operation is like Abelard's as well as

---

[85] C. C. J. Webb, ed., *Joannis Saresberiensis episcopi Carnotensis, Metalogicon libri III* (Oxford, 1929).
[86] *Metalogicon*, I, 3; McGarry translation, p. 15.   [87] *Metalogicon*, I, 10.
[88] *Ibid.*, I, 13; McGarry, p. 37.

others treating how words enter our ears and arouse understanding. The instability is in modes of signification and not in the world or in the mind. 'Letters,' he says, 'are written symbols and in the first place represent sounds. Secondly, they stand for or substitute for things which they conduct into the mind through the windows of the eyes. They can communicate without emitting a sound, the utterances of those who are absent.'[89] Although natural things are everywhere the same, grammar varies from people to people, having developed as an invention of man. But this invention is not arbitrary; it imitates nature from which it partly derives its origin.[90] As with Abelard, John believes that the accidents of substances are more familiar and more readily perceptible by our sense than are words. Words are more universal substitutes for things in the world when we are not sensing them directly.[91]

Furthermore, like Abelard, John believes signification must only be of that which can be experienced. Although the rules of grammar permit one to say absurd things, that is, joining terms which could never in reality be linked, he says it is dialectic which determines what is or seems true or likely.[92] 'That "man is rational" is, in view of present reality, in a way necessary. That "man is able to laugh" is probable. That "man is white" is possible but also doubtful for its chances of being false are about equivalent to its chances of being true. That "man is able to bray" is impossible for this positively cannot be true.' He measures all these statements against existential reality experienced. The grammarian however, will repudiate none of these statements, for in each of them he finds his own rules observed. 'The logician, however, challenges and disproves the last, for it is his function to determine truth and falsity',[93] and by this John mean's language's congruity with the world of things signified by it. John believes the logician determines truth or falseness on the basis of what he takes to be a stable reality so that what is stated in a proposition must signify what exists or can exist in nonverbal reality. Like Abelard, he argues that our reason endeavours to make words cognate to things discussed,[94] and we are ruled in our speech by custom or convention. Those who speak correctly according to established grammatical rules give us the best idea of language's conventions.[95] The rules of grammar help us to learn to discriminate between what is said literally, what is said figuratively and what is said incorrectly if one is ever easily and accurately to comprehend what one reads.[96]

[89] *Metalogicon*, I, 13; McGarry, p. 38.
[90] *Metalogicon*, I, 14; McGarry, p. 39, and also see p. 41.
[91] McGarry, p. 42.   [92] *Ibid.*, p. 45.   [93] *Ibid.*, p. 46.   [94] *Metalogicon*, I, 16.
[95] *Ibid.*, I, 17; McGarry, p. 50.   [96] *Metalogicon*, I, 18; McGarry, p. 55.

Speech, we are told, was not only invented to signify things, but also as a means of communicating mental concepts. And, like Abelard, John asserts that if we are aware of how authors signify, that is, if we know the rules of language which permit us to get at the intention, the purpose behind what they say literally, then we can determine meaning.

Otherwise even in the canonical scripture the Fathers would be at odds and the evangelists themselves would be contradicting each other, if we are foolishly to judge only from the surface of their words without considering their underlying purposes ... The meaning of words should be carefully analysed and one should diligently ascertain the precise force of each and every term both in itself and in the given context so that one may dispel the haze of sophisms that would otherwise obscure the truth.

For John, the truth is a-temporal and can be got at by an analysis of words spoken or written according to grammatical rules. He is as clear as Abelard when he asserts that no matter when the text was written 'the considerations prompting the speaker may be accurately surmised from the occasion, the kind of person he is and the sort of listeners he has, as well as from the place, time and various other pertinent circumstances that must be taken into account by one who seriously seeks the truth'.[97] Like Abelard and any other contemporary student of grammar, logic and rhetoric, John sees the study of language as a means to establish the harmony of meanings across time. If people in any age speak the truth it has no temporal or cultural dimensions as we saw Cicero to have said as well. The theory is that so long as you have like experiences which can then be signified by more universal words in propositions, then any text at its level of true meaning can be understood now as it was in the past, and in the same way. Numerous passages in the *Metalogicon*, can be cited to support this view but we shall refer here only to the Prologue to Book III where John says:

The truth of things endures, impervious to corruption. Something that is true in itself does not melt into thin air simply because it is stated by a new author ... who, except a foolish or perverse person, will reject a (true) proposition simply because it has been advanced by Gilbert, Abelard or our own Adam ... While it is true that words are used differently by different authors in different contexts, it is possible through grammar and logic to understand the truth behind such a varying use of words; we use the word 'contingent' today in a way that is different from the way Aristotle used it, and custom prevails over Aristotle. But the actual truth itself cannot be changed by man's will since [unlike language] it was not established by man.

---

[97] *Metalogicon*, I, 14; McGarry, p. 58.

John concludes that 'both the original words and their meaning should be preserved if possible, but if both cannot be preserved, the words should be dropped without losing the meaning. Knowing the arts does not consist in merely repeating parrot-like the words of authors; rather it involves comprehending their meaning and understanding the thoughts they present.'[98]

To confirm that what is stated in a proposition must signify what exists or can exist, and be experienced in nonverbal reality, he says: 'As we have already remarked, if we are unable to find examples of our mental concepts among actually existing things, then our ideas are empty'.[99] He then uses the word *historia* to mean an accurate, literal account, the primary significations of experience, when he says: '*Historia* of nature includes all particular things but excludes anything that is actually never found existing. Since they are known from their subjects, things that are predicated are, as Boethius observes, such as their subjects' permit ... Furthermore, when we investigate the truth it is necessary that the reality in question [in a proposition] be not entirely beyond our comprehension.'[100]

Because 'grammar prepares the mind to understand everything that can be taught in words', John says the proper subject of the grammarian 'is language and if he goes further, history, and if he proceeds still further, poetry'.[101] And John is enthusiastic about ancient authors who elaborated on 'the crude materials of history, arguments and fables as well as other topics by diacrisis'. This diacritical technique is defined as separation or discernment or interpretation, which, he says, we may translate as vivid illustration or graphic imagery copiously embellishing what would otherwise be the crude, literal historical text. Interpretation of this kind does not distort but rather ornaments primary significations, 'the crude materials of history'. And running through the interpreted text is logic which, he says, contributes plausibility by its credible proofs.[102]

Logic in its narrow sense is the science of argumentative reasoning (*ratio disserendi*) which provides a solid base for the whole activity of prudence. Logic is exercised in every inquiry into the truth, but as John will later point out, a knowledge of the absolute truth is not possible for the human mind. What is sought is the probable truth, the likely and plausible truth behind what authors say. John is drawing upon the rhetorical doctrine of probability as found in Cicero's *De Inventione*, I.[103] While the various poets

---

[98] *Metalogicon*, III, 4; McGarry, p. 170. [99] *Metalogicon*, III, 3.
[100] *Ibid.*, III, 5; McGarry, pp. 162 and 175.
[101] *Metalogicon*, I, 21; McGarry, pp. 60 and 63.
[102] *Metalogicon*, I, 23; McGarry, pp. 66–7.
[103] He also draws on Marius Victorinus's *Explanationes in Ciceronis rhetoricam*. See Cicero, *De Inventione*, I, 21, 29. John will note that it must be the opinion of wise and important men and not the *vulgi morem* which is to be taken into account.

whom John cites express themselves differently, he says, their meaning is the same.[104] In so far as men can ascertain the truth by reasoning they do so by means of the discriminating science of logic. And Aristotle is the master in this field.[105]

John then divides logic into demonstration, probable proof and sophistry. For our purposes and his, it is probable proof which is of the greatest interest because this kind of logic is concerned 'with propositions which, to all or to many men, or at least to the wise, seem to be valid.' This kind of probable logic includes dialectic and rhetoric. The dialectician and the orator, he says, trying to persuade an adversary and a judge respectively, are not too much concerned with the truth or falsity of their arguments provided only that they express a likelihood. Dialectic in particular, simply makes inquiries into truth using the ready instrument of moderate probability.[106]

John has a more explicitly sceptical attitude towards the degree to which the human mind can ever ascertain truth than did Abelard, for where the latter posited a hypothetical *necessity* which must be assumed as the basis of the further presumption of the congruence between signifiers and signified, John will argue for man's imperfect mind having to come to terms with how things really are or were through *probability*.[107] Abelard believed that language could tell us, if we did not abuse it, something more about how things are and were because it serves as an accurate mirror image of the nature of experiences no longer being sensed. Like Abelard, however, John affirms that dialectic investigates the meanings expressed by words and the truth of such meanings. He will later describe how meaning arises.[108]

As a whole logic is concerned with divisions, definitions and inferences. The natural scientist (*physicus*) as well as the moral philosopher can only construct their principles on the basis of the proofs supplied by *logicians*. As with Abelard, the natural sciences must work with a hypothetical necessity, a logical plausibility or a demonstrative necessity based on experience.[109] Whether we are dealing with invention and judgement and

---

[104] McGarry, p. 75.   [105] *Metalogicon*, II, 2; McGarry, pp. 76–7.

[106] *Metalogicon*, II, 3; McGarry, p. 79. See the discussion above, ch. 2, on Aristotle's enthymeme.

[107] But see above on Abelard's view that mind's intellections of *status* are incomplete when compared with God's knowledge. Abelard's invective against false dialecticians in the *Theologia 'summi boni'* and the *Theologia Christiana* is meant to emphasize that human language is limited by its very nature in its capacity to describe eternal truths. See Constant Mews, 'Man's knowledge of God according to Peter Abelard', in *L'Homme et son Univers en Moyen Âge*, 2 vols., ed. C. Wenin (Louvain-la-Neuve, 1986), pp. 419–26. Speaking about God is only through analogy and example.

[108] *Metalogicon*, II, 4.   [109] *Ibid.*, II, 5; McGarry, pp. 81–2.

whether they divide, define or draw inferences, the same *rational* systems are always used. John is not offended by situations in which a rational argument is advanced only in order to win acceptance of an opinion; although opinion may err it need not be false. He is only offended, as was Aristotle, by the kind of sophistry which misuses words in order to bring about the acceptance of an opinion which is neither true nor probable but only seems to be so. It will be clear from this that his concern in the *Historia Pontificalis* was not to dissemble but to construct plausible opinions which approximated to the truth of situations as he experienced them. If we wish to win assent to a given proposition, he says that we must first posit something from which it may be inferred as probable or necessary.[110] And as we shall see, John believes it is usually presumptuous to posit necessity concerning worldly matters.

He concludes that the dialectic methods he has discussed are always the servant of eloquence. When dialectical logic is applied to other studies it can destroy falsehood and at least enable one to speak with probability. This probability is what really interests him and we note that probability or plausibility have no derogatory sense for him.

John tells us that after he studied dialectic with Abelard for two years and then with Alberic for another two in Paris, he transferred to the grammarians. Only later did he study rhetoric under Peter Helias. Throughout his studies he seems to have been attracted far less to the Platonists than to the peripatetic Aristotelians. He even taught the first principles of logic to keep soul and body alive. And he ended his studies with Gilbert of Poitiers, Robert Pullen and Simon of Poissy in theology. He tells us that he never wanted to use dialectic on its own and when he returned to visit old friends in Paris, he found they were still enmeshed in introductory studies of dialectic for its own and sterile sake.[111]

Dialectic must come into play in all studies. The dialectician must leave what is known as the hypothesis, namely, that which is involved in particular circumstances, to the orator. The circumstances of who, what, where, by what means, why, how and when are enumerated in Boethius's fourth book of the *Topics*. Where dialectic focuses on the more general nature of reasoning, oratory descends to particulars. Eloquence or oratory for John is, then, a part of logic and one has to be trained in logic before one can apply it to rhetoric.[112] But when one talks about particular human affairs to a wide audience of learned and unlearned, one is in the domain of the rhetorician whose concern, like that of the dialectician, is with probable logic; the orator however, leaps across by inference from one

[110] *Metalogicon*, II, 6; McGarry, p. 86.   [111] *Metalogicon*, II, 10; McGarry, pp. 99–100.
[112] *Metalogicon*, III, 10; McGarry, p. 199.

thing introduced by way of example, to another. We recall Aristotle's enthymeme. The orator's method serves more to persuade than to convince.[113] Probable logic and rhetoric, then, deal with verisimilitude rather than with necessary truth. But verisimilitude is not akin to false fables. It evokes a true likeness of experienced particulars by using familiar examples, for these have greater cogency whereas strange ones lend no conviction concerning what is doubtful.[114] This, then, is what the writing of a work like the *Historia Pontificalis* is for John. As he learned it, Greek and Roman historiography was rhetorical and what is meant by history was the business of the orator because it spoke in plausibilities to a large range of people rather than to learned disputants. The degree to which John is a Ciceronian in his 'historical' activities is overwhelmingly evident.

Speech is an instrument used in common both by dialecticians and rhetoricians. Rhetoric, however, aims to sway judgement of persons other than the contestants in a dispute and usually employs prolonged oration and induction owing to the fact that it is addressed to and solicits assent from a crowd. But dialectic expresses itself succinctly and generally in the form of syllogisms for its judge is only the opponent in dispute. In both cases, reasoning is the instrument to determine the force of the speech, its meaning. The real force of speech derives from the thoughts or judgements it expresses, without which it would be dead, powerless and meaningless.[115] What distinguishes dialectic from rhetoric is simply their respective methods of proof and their audiences, rather than the meaning they wish to convey.

John's scepticism emerges most fully when he asserts that although demonstrative logic is concerned with necessary proofs, no one, or hardly anyone ever fully comprehends the laws of nature in their necessity. And since God alone knows the limits of possibility it is frequently both dubious and presumptuous to assert that a thing is necessary.

For who has ever been absolutely sure about where to draw the line between possibility and impossibility? Since probable or contingent things are subject to change they are not necessary. If it is a difficult matter to perceive the truth, which (as our Academicians say) is as indefinite in outline as though it lay at the bottom of a well, how much energy is not required to discern, in addition to the truth, the hidden secrets of what is possible?[116]

John says that the logical method of argumentation is usually feeble with regard to the facts of nature for these are corporeal and changeable things.

---

[113] *Metalogicon*, III, 10; McGarry, p. 192.   [114] *Ibid.*
[115] *Metalogicon*, II, 12; McGarry, p. 102.
[116] *Metalogicon*, II, 13; McGarry, pp. 104–5.

Therefore, what one needs when one deals with the particular events of the world is a good grasp of probabilities.

But what is probability based on for John? There is no doubt that it is experiences in his own world and time. And John is happy to cite Cicero's *Tusculan Disputations* where Cicero says: 'we who take probability as our guide cannot do more than assent or affirm that a thing seems true and are prepared both to argue against the views of others without becoming angry and to be ourselves corrected without obstinacy.'[117] Furthermore, he says: 'according to our Academy we have a right to defend any proposition that seems probable'.[118] And a proposition is probable

if it seems obvious to a person of good judgement and if it occurs thus in all instances and at all times, or is otherwise only in exceptional cases and on rare occasions ... There are some things whose probability is so lucidly apparent that they come to be considered necessary whereas there are others which are so unfamiliar to us that we would be reluctant to include them in a list of probabilities.[119]

This means that the otherness of the past would indeed seem improbable and would therefore be rejected. Of course, as Aristotle says, we perceive only by our senses and things can be otherwise than we sense them. None the less, we must base plausibility on the shaky probability of repeated sensual experiences in the present.

We have here a scepticism that would become famous in Hume's *Essay Concerning Human Understanding*, even to the extent of the same example being given: the sun sets and we do not know with certainty its continued course over the earth since our sensory perception of it has ceased. But we assume its course and its return to our hemisphere and believe, without adequate proof, that the sun will rise again the next morning. Such connections are made in our minds.[120] Thus, anyone who is in possession of his senses, faulty as they may be, says John, will not posit something which either seems plausible to no one or is apparent to everyone or at least to those whose judgement is sought.[121]

In so far as John's rhetoric is a logic that he classifies as part of philosophy, he notes in his *Policraticus* (II, 26)[122] that he is familiar with epistemological theories of how men know. He says that what men see are appearances and God made his deeds (*historia*) look as though they were the deeds of men. Since the divine will is an uncaused cause it is unintelligible to us and this means we can form no meaningful statements

---

[117] Cited in *Metalogicon*, II, 2; McGarry, p. 5.   [118] Citing Cicero, *De Officiis*.
[119] *Metalogicon*, II, 14; McGarry, pp. 106–7.
[120] *Metalogicon*, II, 14; McGarry, p. 107.   [121] *Metalogicon*, II, 15; McGarry, p. 109.
[122] *Policraticus*, ed. C. C. J. Webb, 2 vols. (Oxford, 1927).

about it. We have no means of comprehending the works of God in specific events of the past or the present. But the role of the historian-orator, as he speaks of it in the *Policraticus*, is to provide provisional, hypothetical statements about matters that do not permit of certitude.[123] Nothing definite can be stated about *God's* purpose in historical events.[124] What man is provided with is a power of reasoning: he possesses this naturally and its role is to explain in contingent language the strictly *human nature* of experiences rather than the underlying purposes of God. Both dialectic and rhetoric are concerned with sensible reality about which one can be deceived. But it is all we have. Therefore, probable opinion is the only consequence of the application of logic to words that refer to events of the past.

Abelard, we recall, had argued that we can only make sense of statements about the past by assuming a hypothetical law of nature that expresses the necessity of entailment based on no more than the presumption that a statement's referents do or can exist. John, however, was disappointed with Abelard as well as Aristotle on hypothetical propositions. For Abelard and John, logic or dialectic is an art which aims to distinguish between valid and invalid arguments using contingent speech to elucidate meaning. But where Abelard sought to contrast the domains of logic with that of grammar and rhetoric, John's concern is to show that it is rhetoric as an extension of logic that deals with the likely meaning of particular events. John is more the sceptic in his affirmation that the sensible world is, as neo-Platonic philosophy taught, a problematic object of thought, and we may well postulate that the Platonism of John's rhetorical mentor Peter Helias,[125] was precisely the kind of thinking Abelard opposed. Where Helias argued that apparently necessary truths about observable reality took their force from probable truth or *opinio*, and this is the realm of rhetorical method, Abelard sought a more direct and stable means of relating words to things in the world on the one hand, and to thoughts on the other. Abelard affirmed that *res* and *intellectus* were constants and what varied was the contingency of language. John on the other hand, asserted that it was presumptuous to assert that a thing is necessary in the sensible world so that 'no one with any wisdom will waste his time on the futile pursuit of certain truths among changeable phenomena. Instead, he will arm himself with a knowledge of probabilities.'[126] John's understanding of

---

[123] *Ibid.*, 2.26 and 2.22.
[124] Compare the prologue to the *Metalogicon*: 'Being an Academician (sceptic) in matters that are doubtful to a wise man, I cannot swear to the truth of what I say. Whether such propositions may be true or false, I am satisfied with probable certitude' (McGarry, p. 6).
[125] Karen Fredborg, 'Petrus Helias on Rhetoric', *Cahiers de l'Institut du Moyen Age Grec et Latin de Copenhague*, 13 (1974), pp. 31–41.
[126] *Metalogicon*, II, 13 and 14.

the probable truth of rhetoric and therefore of history is based on a neo-Platonic distrust of the instability of our perception of sense data and not on a distrust of the stability of things themselves, so that 'neither eyes nor ears nor even the testimony and writings of credible men could ever give us access to the pure truth of history as God knows it.' The historian-orator is only positing a probable truth of the past and this is what John sees his task to be in the *Historia Pontificalis*. Gone is the theory that verbal signs necessarily and truly relate to things as we sense them; in its place is the standard of rhetorical verisimilitude to govern his narrative of the events he saw and remembered.

The power of the rhetorical narrative to achieve the desired results through plausible likenesses rather than through an accurate portrayal of objective truth, governs the rhetorical art of writing about events as John's Roman mentors understood it. If a narrative were skilfully conceived but at variance with an audience's views or customs, then it would be cast aside as implausible.[127] This lesson of Roman rhetoric must have inspired a licence for medieval forgeries. It was a message that could be so evidently unconcerned with what had once happened, because it held historical truth to be unattainable beyond plausibility, that we can see why Abelard would have wanted to distinguish in a more explicit way between logic and either grammar or rhetoric. Instead, Abelard argued, following Boethius, that similitudes held in the memory, either as images or words, really did bear some true relationship with that with which they were similar. For John, rhetorical verisimilitude only produces the likely, the probable, the plausible; words are not the true keys that they are for Abelard. When we substitute words for absent things as though they were signs of them, Abelard believed we then have a true and necessary account of things. Words do signify the real world we think and talk about for Abelard; for John the rhetorician, words are of the less certain category of the merely plausible verisimilitude. But words are all we have.

In his preface to the *Historia Pontificalis*, John does not describe his own work as history nor does he think of himself as an historian.[128] Indeed, the *Historia Pontificalis* is not history as the word was technically understood, but interpretation according to rhetorical principles. When John uses the word *historia* he does so in the same way as Hugh of St Victor, to refer to the first signification of his own experiences which the author conveys and surveys. History is the primary signification of events seen or experienced

127 See the important discussion in Ray, 'Rhetorical scepticism', p. 84 for the source of this in Marius Victorinus's *Explanationes*.

128 See John O. Ward, 'Some principles of rhetorical historiography in the twelfth century' in Ernest Breisach, ed., *Classical Rhetoric and Medieval Historiography* (Kalamazoo, Michigan, 1985), pp. 103–65; p. 107.

which may then be interpreted as edifying. John provides the interpretation and singles out the memorable events, *the materia papatiae*, to present them in narrative form, the numerous anecdotes of occurrences which come into the mind from the letters of the parchment, the voiceless utterances of the absent. To read his *Historia Pontificalis* requires that one brings to it an assessment of its factual content by means of grasping his rhetorical purpose and technique, centred on plausibility, as well as grasping how any twelfth-century writer of narratives understood what mind does to the first significations of the *gesta* set down. The writing down of *gesta* like the writing down of any text employs a conventional means of revealing – for John, the probable truth – for Abelard a more fixed truth based on hypothetical necessity and on already established linguistic conventions, a presumed fixity of things in the world and a fixed rational interpretation of signs. For both men, language tells us about the world, but with greater or lesser certainty of how it was, based entirely on how it is.

The 'crude materials of history' – John's own letters based on his experiences, were used as the foundation of his rhetorical enterprise in the *Historia Pontificalis*. But Abelard's description of his own experiences, written as a letter (to Heloise) and conserved in medieval manuscripts as *Abelardi ad amicum suum consolatoria* (*not* as a 'history', the *Historia Calamitatum*, but correctly called *historia* by contemporaries) must have been intended as the unembellished crude materials of his history, the literal account of his experiences. For he says experiences, literally described, in other words, *exempla*, often serve to arouse or mitigate human passions better than do words. 'So that from these my experienced misfortunes described in writing to someone absent, you may compare your own experienced misfortunes [that is, the events themselves] and recognise yours as of little or no account and thereby more easily suffer them' (*Sepe humanos affectus aut provocant aut mittigant amplius exempla quam verba. Unde post nonnullam sermonis ad presentem habiti consolationem, de ipsis calamitatum mearum experimentis consolatoriam ad absentem scribere decrevi, ut in comparatione mearum tuas aut nullas aut modicas temptationes recognoscas et tolerabilius feras*).[129]

And indeed Abelard believed that had he not written down these events in words, the things or facts themselves would cry out and indicate the outcome: 'Quod si ego taceam, res ipsa clamat et ipsius rei finis indicat'.[130] Others, like Otto of Freising in his *Deeds of Frederick Barbarossa*, would

---

[129] Abelard, *Historia Calamitatum, texte critique avec une introduction*, ed. J. Monfrin (Paris, 1967), p. 67. For a list of the nine MSS and their contents, see pp. 9–61.

[130] *Ibid.*, p. 67. That is, Abelard provides the primary significations of his experiences and the reader interprets these, comparing the represented events with her own experiences.

distinguish further between *plana historia dictio* (the first signification of events) and *oratio* which is elevated 'ad altiora velut phylosophica acumina', that is, oratory provides meaning and interpretation of the first signification of things which the properties of the narrative's words express. Otto also recognised the different levels of mind's understanding by expanding the purpose of historical writing to encompass a philosophical understanding of the more universal import of a text's mere primary significations. As Ward has argued, Otto's is

the confidence of the rhetorical historian, contrasted with the temerity of the annalist or the caution of the exegete, who like to keep the historical sense to the simple linear narrative, the first meaning of a piece of writing, and reserve interpretation to other senses and levels. The exegete's distinction between the historical or literal level (text/event) and the allegorical level or interpretation ... forms an analogy for the distinction Otto draws between narrative (facts) and digression (interpretation).

He aggregates the whole process and calls it history, not stopping at the literal sense but advances to mind's more universal understanding.[131]

It has recently been argued that twelfth-century history writing in general, attempts to close out doubt and encourage or create certainty by its spare use of antinomy and its paratactic style,[132] what Galbraith once referred to as the narration of 'one damn thing after another'. At the level of interpretation of the narration of actions there is little exploration of the views of two or more sides but rather the presentation of a harmony in the guise of a single interpretation. This rhetorical method shared with scholastic method an understanding of the a-temporality of interpreted truth and both were practised by the technical leaders of society with grammatical, logical, rhetorical and sometimes philosophical and theological educations, as abbots, bishops, the upper clergy *cum* administrators. Their interest in writing history was to persuade a present and future readership of the universal lessons to be drawn from exemplary historical moments, narrated in the most plausible and appealing way. The reality of their history was in the re-telling of events which had to be endowed with meaning, a process that was enhanced by the finest verbal skills that rhetoricians could employ to evoke images in the minds of those absent from the events, through verbal resonances, figures, colours. These devices clothed the *historia*, the *nuda verba* of the annalist, presenting more memorable figures to the attention of the mind's vision. One told in the first instance what was memorable, not all that had happened but all

---

[131] Ward in *Classical Rhetoric and Medieval Historiography*, pp. 117–18.
[132] *Ibid.*, p. 148; and Nancy Partner, *Serious Entertainments: The Writing of History in Twelfth-Century England* (Chicago, 1977).

that was judged to be worthy of being recalled. History was a serious entertainment; it was story-telling as present edification.[133] A study of grammar, logic and rhetoric supplied not merely a method of composition and oration. It also taught an epistemology and brought with it a range of perceptions, values, in effect, all that was seen to make up the life of the mind. Rhetorical history's concern with verisimilitude was analogous to logic and psychology's concern for mental similitudes. Each was ultimately concerned with the degrees of accuracy attainable by the mind's representative thoughts of sensual experiences, externalised through the medium of language. Words, as well as images in the imagination and memory, served as the conventionally established means of triumphing over the chaos of a world filled with individual things and events and acts, providing the tools for reason's comprehension of universals and meaningful wholes. It is not surprising therefore to find that when twelfth-century historians discussed more theoretically what they believed themselves to be doing, especially in the prefaces to their writings, that they were talking not about facts or evidence, but about language and its relation to reality. History was discourse rather than a revelation of the pastness of the past, and its interpretation was an activity of mind rather than a passive observation of the past's incomprehensible debris. They had no interest in reconstructing the past and its experiences for its own sake: they retold that past only in the light of the present.

When an historian did not re-tell what he had seen but took on the larger task of writing an *Historia Anglorum* like the archdeacon, Henry of Huntingdon, he was told by the bishop of Lincoln, to whom the work was dedicated, to follow a well-tried procedure: start with Bede's *Ecclesiastical History* and then use chronicles preserved in old libraries up to the point at which you, the author, have first-hand material. The editions of Henry's *Historia* run from 1129 to several revisions up to 1154. In his prologue he defended the writing of history as a kind of literature that traced the tracks left by men who had lived outstanding lives (with reference to Horace's *Ode*, I, 32, 14).[134] Henry is not attempting to prove by means of examining

---

[133] Nancy Partner, 'The new Cornificians: medieval history and the artifice of words' in Breisach, ed., *Classical Rhetoric and Medieval Historiography*, pp. 5–59 especially p. 38: 'What the historian creates is the significant, intelligible structure of history from language which both refers and creates. The historical construct is not a reconstruction – the past as experience is irrecoverable – and that is nothing to be mourned or regretted: the past was merely experience; in the present we make history.'

[134] Cum in omni fere literarum studio dulce laboris lenimen et summum doloris solamen, dum vivitur, insitum considerem, tum delectabilius et majoris praerogativa claritatis historiarum splendorem amplectendum crediderim. Nihil namque magis in vita egregium, quam vitae calles egregie indagare et frequentare. Ubi autem floridius nitescit

evidence, *res*, that great men lived as old texts say they did. Rather he is re-telling from these authoritative accounts that they did so. History is believed, God is the judge of the acts of men and nations, and we learn from these *gesta* because they are didactic *credibilia* as Augustine said: 'sic etiam in rebus gestis omnium gentium et nationum, quae utique Dei judicia sunt, benignitas, munificentia, probitas, cautela, et his similia, et contraria, non solum spirituales ad bonum accendunt et a malo repellunt, sed et saeculares ad bona sollicitant et in malis muniunt'.[135] How then are exemplary lives in their contexts to be presented by narrative history? Henry gives the by now familiar answer. He says that history *represents* the past *as though* present to sight; it determines the future through the past by (present) imagination (*Historia igitur praeterita quasi praesentia visui repraesentat; futura ex praeteritis imaginando dijudicat*).[136] History, therefore, as a first signification of acts, events, things, is a conventional verbal means of representing, creating similitudes for the sight of the reader who was not present to observe what happened. And this past as represented in the present imagination is now to be judged and determined. Henry is alluding to a cognition theory in which language plays its role in representing the past for mind's understanding. Furthermore, he says that a knowledge of the past distinguishes rational men from beasts; those men who wilfully remain ignorant of their nation's history and past events are no more than beasts: 'Habet quidem et praeter haec illustres transactorum notita dotes, quod ipsa maxime distinguat a brutis rationabiles: bruti namque homines et animalia unde sint nesciunt, genus suum nesciunt, patriae suae casus et gesta nesciunt, immo nec scire volunt.' To know the past and its meaning is an act of willing, rational men, their distinguishing characteristic being their reason turned to (textual) representations or similitudes of the past, their wills focusing their reason on these similitudes in order to understand the meaning of *historia*, their pasts. He then lists his sources and says that when he comes to his own times he will not depend on authoritative texts but represent the past as heard and seen, 'usque nostrum ad auditum et visum praeterita repraesentavi'.[137] Then he invokes God's aid in order to begin.

We should not be surprised to find Henry disinclined to engage in extensive investigations of matters of fact or novelties, nor should we be astonished that his chronology is unreliable. He does, however, reliably reproduce Bede his authority. We should also not be surprised to find

---

virorum fortium magnificentia, prudentium sapientia, justorum judicia, temperatorum modestia, quam in rerum contextu gestarum? (*Historia Anglorum*, ed. T. Arnold, RS 74 (London, 1879), p. 1).

[135] *Historia Anglorum*, ed. Arnold, p. 1.   [136] *Ibid.*, p. 2.   [137] *Ibid.*, p. 3.

copious moralising, nor that he plans his work around five plagues that God inflicted on Britain in the form of belligerent nations: Romans, Picts, Scots, Angles, Danes and Normans.[138] His theme is divine vengeance, but the five plagues are a formal, rhetorical device for controlling his material, and his overwhelming interest seems to be to moralise on what becomes of the powerful and how the world's glory comes to naught. The themes of the inevitability of death, the lack of endurance of worldly values, have caused Nancy Partner to refer to the whole work as a *memento mori* addressed to royalty, where kings who set aside their crowns to become monks are worthy exemplars. The *contemptus mundi* theme is everywhere.[139] Henry has no interest in the pastness of the past, and even his present is a transitory moment to remind us of the vanity of sin and the necessity of the world's pleasures passing away.

Can we look elsewhere and find a contemporary historian who *is* interested in recovering evidence to grasp the uniqueness and unrepeatable nature of the past?

William of Newburgh is often seen to be such an historian: he has been called 'the father of historical criticism'.[140] But even his greatest admirers have noted that his *Historia Rerum Anglicarum* does not provide us with exact facts and his dates are nearly always wrong! William was an Augustinian canon, educated at Newburgh priory in Yorkshire. This education seems to have centred round the Bible, the Fathers and the classical poets. 'The difference in William is a matter of conscious refinement and caution' because he pays 'scrupulous attention to secular events before venturing an interpretation'.[141] 'The tradition of historical writing in which William worked demanded also that an historian attempt to be a higher critic and judge who 'reads' morally as he records ... His respect for the profundity and obliquity of the divine mind made him unwilling to blot out the complexity of human experience for the sake of an edifying (and simplifying) lesson'.[142] He talks about testimony, plausibility, interpretation and explanation in terms of veracity, completeness and reliability; these, as we have seen, are logical and rhetorical criteria. He measures himself against Bede and Bede against other *authorities*. And as an Augustinian canon, writing for a Cistercian abbot of Rievaulx, we should expect to find evidence of an Augustinian understanding of history, not only concerning how one writes it but also how one knows the

---

138 Nancy Partner, *Serious Entertainments*, p. 24.
139 *Ibid.*, p. 30. For an exhaustive treatment of this theme in an earlier period see Robert Bultot, *Christianisme et valeurs humaines: la doctrine du mépris du monde en occident, de S. Ambroise à Innocent II*, 2 vols (Louvain, 1963).
140 Partner, *Serious Entertainments*, referring to others, p. 51.   141 *Ibid.*, p. 52.
142 *Ibid.*

past and its meaning mixed with an assertion of why and how one records the present for posterity.[143]

The *Historia* was written late in life, begun in 1198 and composed quickly. Most of his prologue is concerned to show how Geoffrey of Monmouth's 'history' conflicts with the authoritative text – that of Bede, in order that the wild Britons might be raised falsely to historical note.

Geoffrey of Monmouth had written his *Historia Regum Britanniae* to show his readers the cyclical nature of historical events: a hero who conquers a land and founds a kingdom is followed by a period of peace and good law, succeeded by the next generation in which everything falls apart until a new ruler arises and begins again.[144] Providing on the one hand, a chronology and a genealogy and on the other, endlessly repeated dramas of campaigns, destruction of kingdoms, noble and just kings, renewed conflict, he created a narrative to glorify a British past. He raised the folklore of Britons to the status of national history. Like other 'historians' Geoffrey was a *fabulator*. But William of Newburgh reserved this as a term of opprobrium for Geoffrey alone. William attacked Geoffrey because he believed he wrote false *historia* to William's true *historia*. Geoffrey had resurrected a king Arthur who was, to William, not only implausible but unlikely.[145] William saw Geoffrey as having written a partisan, minority and fabricated British ideological history, not founded on the literal *historia*: 'How could the old historians whose careful attention let nothing important escape being written down, who are known to have committed even commonplace things to memory, have passed over in silence ... this incomparable man [Arthur] and his outstanding deeds?'[146] William refers to 'our Bede's true genealogy of Saxon kings in contrast to 'quantum mera historiae veritas hoc loco compositae praejudicet falsitati, vel lippienti mentis acie clare videri potest'.[147] Geoffrey had replaced Ethelbert with Arthur who was then shown to outshine all men in his exploits. William comments: 'Inde fabulator ille, ut suum Arturum ad summum evehat, facit eum Romanis bellum indicere; ante hoc bellum singulari certamine mirae multitudinis gigantem prosternere'. But note that the implausibility of this is because: 'cum post Davidica tempora de

---

143 See Caroline Bynum on Augustinians seeing themselves as both learners and teachers in *Jesus as Mother* (Berkeley, 1982), p. 37 n. 45 and p. 40: 'Teach by example and word'.
144 Gibson in *The Writing of History in the Middle Ages*, ed. Davis and Wallace-Hadrill, p. 185.
145 For the influential rhetorical doctrine of probability as expounded by Cicero, see *De Inventione*, I, 19.27–21.30: 'Probabilis erit narratio ... si res et ad eorum qui agent naturam et ad vulgi morem et ad eorum qui audient opinionem accommodabitur'.
146 William of Newburgh, *Historia rerum Anglicarum*, ed. R. Howlett, RS 82 (London, 1884), p. 17.
147 *Historia rerum Anglicarum*, ed. Howlett, p. 15.

nullo gigante *legatur*'. This story-teller has his Arthur declare war against the Romans before which he kills a giant, but after the times of David we *read* of no giants. 'Profusiori mentiendi licentia', Geoffrey has Arthur defeat the combined forces of all the nations of the earth, in fact, he names more kingdoms than could fit on our globe. But most importantly, all these 'glorious' exploits have found no place in the works of authoritative, old historians, *historiographi veteres*. Geoffrey must be making it all up because what he describes cannot be corroborated *by a reading of accepted authoritative texts*. Instead, Geoffrey must have drawn upon *fabulae Britannicae*. William will have nothing to do with these kinds of sources and instead sings the praises of Bede, 'de cujus sapientia et sinceritate dubitare fas non est, fides in omnibus habeatur'. Why we should trust Bede and his sources, and not Geoffrey and his, is never debated. Bede is an accepted authority and therefore we know him to have been sincere. It is not that William unearths new facts in his own *History* but rather that he contrasts what he believes to be one authoritative text with another that is not. In his prologue, William cites Gildas and Bede (and models his antipathy to the Britons on that already found in Bede) in opposition to Geoffrey of Monmouth's 'sources'. Gildas and Bede have nothing about a falsely glorified British past and therefore Geoffrey is a *fabulator* because he has not given readers the literal *historia* that is authoritative. This is clearly a dispute in the present between present partisan readings of lesser or greater authoritative texts. It is not a dispute over true and false history based on an examination of evidence beyond the literal text.[148] It is an assertion about an unexamined authoritative source text in which a conservative writer has faith and another text without such authority.

William goes on to say that after relying on acceptable authorities like Bede and Gildas, he will proceed by treating the neglected current times, as though in response to Peter the Venerable's complaint that no one today seems to think it important to write in order to record worthy events around him: 'nostris autem temporibus tanta et tam memorabilia contigerunt, ut modernorum negligentia culpana merito censeatur, si literatum monumentis ad memoriam sempiternam mandata non fuerint'.[149] This kind of literature, recording current experiences, William believes to be a monument to sempiternal memory and he sees the task set him by Erwold, abbot of Rievaulx, to be the preservation for posterity of the events of English history during his own lifetime, that is, the recording of

[148] In general, see the important work of Partner, *Serious Entertainments*; and 'The new Cornificians: medieval history and the artifice of words', in Ernst Breisach, ed., *Classical Rhetoric and Medieval Historiography*, Studies in Medieval Culture (Kalamazoo, 1985), pp. 5–59.

[149] On Peter the Venerable, see above, pp. 301–2.

memorable current events to which the author was either witness, or at least, of which he heard from those whom he believes to be reliable witnesses.

William's *Historia* has been described as a very 'bookish' book relying heavily on recent previous historical work supplemented by various documents, oral testimony of reliable men and a very little first hand experience. William wrote his own prose instead of copying directly from his uncited sources, distinguishing witnesses from those who only spoke with them.[150] It has also been pointed out that although his prologue praises Gildas and Bede and damns, by contrast, Geoffrey of Monmouth, William never consulted his favourite authorities because he was writing contemporary history beginning with the Conquest. And in providing the first signification of events, individually recorded, he often seems prepared to leave the ultimate 'reading' to someone else.[151] This is because he believed that interpretation is not the historian's task. Rather he should narrate experience or reliable testimony: 'Interpretatur quisque ut voluerit signum mirabile cujus utique didici simplex esse narrator, non etiam praesagus interpres; quid enim Divinitas eo significare voluerit nescio'.[152] Indeed, William says it is because of the weakness of our *senses* that we are unable to trace the explanation of apparent miracles and prodigies, the signification of which only God knows.[153] This, of course, agrees with the views of John of Salisbury. He knows several of Augustine's works, citing him usually on demons and miracles, but it is of some importance that the texts used come from the *De Genesi ad Litteram* and the *De Trinitate*, both of which deal extensively with the problems concerning the appropriate manner in which the primary signification of texts may be *used* in order to enable the discovery of *principles* that make occurrences described therein intelligible in the present.

All of the writers discussed were educated clergy whose familiarity with the intricacies of Augustine's relation of psychology to language would not have been unusual. Certainly they also knew the logical and grammatical sources on which Augustine himself worked as well as Boethian, Porphyrian and grammatical commentaries along with Cicero, Quintilian, Valerius Maximus etc. An understanding of what language was and what purposes it served was, in effect, a key to understanding the exegetical interpreting mind. The study of classical grammar and later commentaries along with the rules and functions of oratory allowed them to create an

---

[150] *Historia rerum Anglicarum*, ed. Howlett, p. 498.
[151] Partner, *Serious Entertainments*, p. 59.
[152] *Historia rerum Anglicarum*, ed. Howlett, p. 308.
[153] *Historia rerum Anglicarum*, ed. Howlett, p. 87.

aesthetic of historical narrative where the universality of episodes, arranged serially and often without development, was meant to open up to interpretation, by means of the primary mode of signifying – through words, the events beyond language which required interpretation. This rhetorical aesthetic, working with oratory's colours and plausible fictions, served a present concern for timeless edification with a direct reference, albeit often implicit, to the role of *ratio* in the interpretation of *historia*, the present similitudes of the past for present purposes.

This may not be what we mean by history but it is what twelfth and thirteenth-century authors meant by it because *historia* was what they took to be the preconditions for the activities of remembering and interpreting. What men remembered was a universal truth and not the sensual particularity of the disordered and meaningless past. The remembrance of things past, through their primary significations in historical narratives, had as its purpose a timeless edification rather than a curiosity about the past in its own right. From the written text that represented a lived life, exemplary truths would be construed grammatically, logically and rationally from the twelfth century onwards.

PART IV

ARISTOTLE NEO-PLATONISED: THE REVIVAL OF ARISTOTLE AND THE DEVELOPMENT OF SCHOLASTIC THEORIES OF MEMORY

INTRODUCTION

Part IV presents the scholastic evolution of theories of knowing and remembering, culminating in the magisterial teaching of Thomas Aquinas. Most of the texts analysed are not easily accessible and they have rarely been expounded in English, especially with the purpose of tracing the changes in theories of knowing and remembering and their consequences for scholastic attitudes to the past: how men recall it and why they do so. The Arabic and Jewish analyses of the soul, only meagrely presented here, are part of an immensely impressive intellectual endeavour, far more so than many Christian Latin attempts simply to understand them and produce a synthesis acceptable to Christian orthodoxy. Until Aquinas.

It is frequently asserted that St Thomas Aquinas is an extraordinary medieval mind and indeed later centuries, notably the nineteenth, determined his as the voice of Catholic orthodoxy. But after confronting the writings of his numerous learned thirteenth-century forebears and contemporaries, a reader faced with his *Summa* cannot help being overwhelmed by his clarity, his comprehensive knowledge of all contemporary debates, and for the most part by his inspired, largely optimistic sympathy for men and their capacities. It is probably not enough simply to say this. One has to read the other scholastics first, not only to understand why Aquinas chooses to argue the ways he does, but also to see the difference. So much has been written on Aquinas that the sections in this book can only attempt a poor beginning.

Chapter 15

ARABIC AND JEWISH TRANSLATIONS OF SOURCES FROM ANTIQUITY: THEIR USE BY LATIN CHRISTIANS

The 'Prose Salernitan Questions', Isaac Israeli, Avicenna (Nemesius of Emesa, John of Damascus)

Whether beautiful or ugly or just conveniently at hand, the world of experience is produced by the man who experiences it ... There certainly is a real world of trees and people and cars and even books, and it has a great deal to do with our experiences of these objects. However, we have no direct, immediate access to the world, nor to any of its properties ... Whatever we know about reality has been mediated, not only by the organs of sense but by complex systems which interpret and reinterpret sensory information. The activity of the cognitive systems results in – and is integrated with – the activity of muscles and glands that we call 'behavior'. It is also partially – very partially – reflected in those private experiences of seeing, hearing, imagining, and thinking to which verbal descriptions never do full justice.

Ulric Neisser, *Cognitive Psychology* (New York, 1967), p. 3.

The Syriac-speaking peoples of the Near East cultivated the art of translation from as early as the fourth century and provided Syriac versions of ancient Greek writings on science and philosophy later used by the Arab world. In the eastern Mediterranean, the ancient syllabus continued to be taught in Syriac translations.[1] As we have seen, from the twelfth century, western scholars began to benefit from the Arabic medium of transmission: ninth-century Baghdad had been one centre where Syriac versions were rendered into Arabic and from here the works of Aristotle, Ptolemy, Euclid and Galen were disseminated throughout the Islamic world. In Arab-occupied Spain and in southern Italy, multilingual scholars then set to translating these works into Latin. This translation effort is the beginning of what has been called the twelfth-century Renaissance of ancient Greek thought in the west.[2]

---

[1] R. Duval, *La littérature syriaque*, third edn (Paris, 1907), pp. 251ff; G. Furlani, 'L'introduzione di'Atanasio di Bâlâdh alla logica e sillogistica aristotelica tradutta dal syriaco', *Atti del reale Istituto di Scienze, Lettere ed Arti*, 85 (1926), pp. 319–44.

[2] Sebastian Brock, 'Aspects of translation technique in antiquity', *Greek, Roman and Byzantine Studies*, 20 (1979), pp. 69–87; Richard Walzer, 'Arabic transmission of Greek thought to medieval Europe', *Bulletin of the John Rylands Library*, 29 (1945), pp. 3–26; Marie-

As we have seen, some of the Arabic texts, when translated into Latin, were known and used by Cistercian authors and their contemporaries when they wrote treatises on the soul. The Cistercian theological anthropologies we have examined comprised one contribution to the wider twelfth-century interest in constructing a human psychology that classified the soul's powers. With the increasing availability of translations of Aristotle and his Arabic commentators, a more subtle and diverse tradition concerning the soul's cognitive powers than that found in Boethius, began to be incorporated into theories of the soul. As a result, that extraordinary technique of harmonising diversities and apparently conflicting authorites would be tested to its limits during the thirteenth century.

Aristotle's *De Memoria et Reminiscentia* appeared during the twelfth century in most of the Aristotle manuscripts of the predominantly Greek-Latin type.[3] At first there appears to have been no Arabic-Latin version of this work. The two twelfth-century versions of the *De Memoria* that survive are substantially the same 'Boethian' version of which a revision formed the standard text after the middle of the thirteenth century. The *De Memoria* was known under the more encompassing title, the *Parva Naturalia*, which included three short tracts, *De Iuventute*, *De Longitudine Vitae*, *De Respiratione*. Although there was no Arabic-Latin translation available, Averroes's paraphrase (*Epitome*, c. 1170) of the work was translated into Latin, probably by Michael Scot at the beginning of the thirteenth century. The source for Averroes's *Epitome* was the Hebrew translation of Hunain Ibn Ishak's Arabic version of the ninth century.[4] In the Greek, Arabic and Latin texts of the Aristotelian corpus, the *Parva Naturalia* follow almost invariably on the *De Anima* text, and thus, the *De Memoria* appears to have been seen as an appendix of that work. It is thought that the first Greek-Latin version of the *De Anima* was accompanied by the *Parva Naturalia* from at least the latter part of the twelfth century.[5]

The thirteenth-century list of Richard de Fournival attributes all the treatises of the *Parva Naturalia* to Boethius. But the 'Boethian' Latin

Thérèse d'Alverny, 'Translations and translators', in *Renaissance and Renewal*, pp. 421–62. Texts edited in L. Minio-Paluello, *Aristoteles Latinus*, III (Bruges, 1962).
3 S. D. Wingate, *The Medieval Latin Versions of the Aristotelian Scientific Corpus with Special Reference to the Biological Works* (London, 1931), pp. 46–50.
4 Harry Blumberg, *Averroes, Epitome of Parva Naturlia, Translated from the Original Arabic and Hebrew and Latin Versions* (Cambridge, Mass.: Medieval Academy of America, 1961); Emily Shields, ed., *Averrois Cordubensis Compendia Librorum Aristotelis qui parva naturalia vocantur; Libri Aristotelis de memoria et reminiscentia (versio Vulgata and versio Parisina)* (Cambridge, Mass.: Medieval Academy of America, 1949), pp. 47–72.
5 L. Minio-Paluello, 'Le texte du 'De Anima' d'Aristote: la tradition latine avant 1500', *Autour d'Aristote, recueil d'études de philosophie ancienne et médiévale offert à Monseigneur A. Mansion* (Louvain, 1955), pp. 217–43.

translation of the *De Anima* from the Greek was actually the work of James of Venice in the middle of the twelfth century (to some scholars he was known as the translator of the *libri naturales* – the *Physics*, *De Anima* and parts of the *Parva Naturalia*). During the thirteenth century, William of Moerbeke, the Dominican translator, revised James's work for chapters 4–8 and the beginning of chapter 9 of Book III. James's work was known as the *translatio vetus* and was still attributed to Boethius by Aquinas well into the thirteenth century. James of Venice was also credited with the Greek-Latin translations of Aristotle's 'new logic' (*Prior Analytics* and fragments of Alexander of Aphrodisias's commentary, as well as a partial version of the *Sophistici Elenchi*).[6]

James, however, was not alone. A number of anonymous twelfth-century translators, probably in Italy, was also at work in a milieu where a knowledge of Greek and an interest in Aristotle converged.

In Spain, another group of translators, also interested in ancient scientific and medical tracts, was at work, flourishing in Toledo during the second half of the twelfth century. The Latin translation from the Arabic of Aristotle's *De Anima* was probably the work of Michael Scot. In addition, the archdeacon of Toledo, Dominic Gundisalvi (Gundissalinus) collaborating with Jewish scholars, translated Avicenna's commentaries on Aristotle. Gundisalvi also wrote his own *De Anima*.

The agents of the transmission of all these translations from the Greek and from the Arabic were most frequently physicians who studied at Salerno or Montpellier and went on to Bologna, Paris and England. Any interest in memory according to the ancient tradition would, therefore, at first begin with what the medical literature had to say. It is these medical commentators on the ancient corpus to whom the twelfth-century Cistercians and their contemporaries referred as the *physici*. We must turn now to look more closely at the medical understanding of memory in order to understand how this tradition would play a role in the gradual eclipse of the eclectic use made of it during the twelfth century when thinkers still preserved the *corpus-anima* division.[7] We can begin to see changes in the *Prose Salernitan Questions*.[8]

---

[6] M. Th. d'Alverny in *Renaisssance and Renewal*, pp. 421–62; L. Minio-Paluello, 'Iacobus Veneticus Grecus, canonist and translator of Aristotle', *Traditio*, 8 (1952), pp. 265–304; L. Minio-Paluello, *Opuscula. The Latin Aristotle*, (Amsterdam, 1972); S. D. Wingate, *The Medieval Latin Versions*, p. 49.

[7] For an overview, see P. Michaud-Quantin, 'La classification des puissances de l'âme au XIIᵉ s.', *Revue de Moyen Âge Latin*, 5 (1949), pp. 15–34. For a detailed analysis of problems concerning Arabic texts in Latin translations, see J. Jolivet, 'The Arabic Inheritance', in *A History of Twelfth-Century Western Philosophy*, ed. P. Dronke (Cambridge, 1988), pp. 113–48.

[8] Brian Lawn, ed., *The Prose Salernitan Questions edited from a Bodleian MS (Auct. F. 3. 10), An Anonymous Collection Dealing with Science and Medicine Written by an Englishman c. 1200*

At the end of the twelfth century, an anonymous English master teaching natural philosophy or *physica* in an unidentified arts faculty, probably to medical students, compiled a collection of questions and answers dealing with current science and medicine. He seems unusually preoccupied with sexual matters and gynaecology. Thus, he asks the following question: 'do women stop wanting to mate after they conceive following sexual union, as other animals do?' The correct and standard answer is then given: 'men differ from other animals in that animals only have a knowledge of the present; but men have a knowledge of the present, memory of the past and the capacity to conjecture about the future. Therefore, when a woman remembers past delights she desires the same again'! Hence, the human capacity to remember even affects our sexual behaviour and marks us off from the animal world.[9]

It is likely that this English master trained either at Salerno, Montpellier or Paris before the year 1200, and the bulk of his questions and answers are Salernitan, heavily influenced by the doctrines of two great medical authorities there, Urso of Lodi and Maurus. This compiler also used material from William of Conches's *Dragmaticon*, Book VI, and there is some link between the compiler and a circle of scholars at Hereford whom Gerald of Wales also seems to have known.[10]

The Salernitan masters used translations from the Greek rather than the Arabic of Galen's *Tegni* and Constantinus Africanus's *Pantegni theorica*, as well as translations of the works of the Egyptian Jewish doctor and philosopher Isaac Israeli.[11] Furthermore, they drew on the standard early encyclopedists and philosophers Pliny, Seneca, Solinus, Macrobius and Isidore for their medical knowledge. As regards the genuine works of Aristotle, these compilations of Salernitan questions and answers have virtually no direct quotations from any of the newly translated *libri naturales* and, indeed, Aristotle is only quoted twice by our English master, and this comes from William of Conches. What they know of Aristotle comes through the Greek to Latin translations in the Salernitan medical literature and it is attributed to the *physici*.[12] Their discussions of the memory is of some significance to us.

(Oxford, 1979)., Also see Brian Lawn, *Quaestiones phisicales, the Salernitan Questions, An Introduction to the History of Medieval and Renaissance Problem Literature* (Oxford, 1963).

[9] Queritur cum cetera animalia post conceptionem a coitu cessant mulieres tunc libentius coeunt? ... In hoc differt homo a cetermis animalibus quia illa habent solum scientiam presentium; homo vero habet scientiam presentium, memoriam preteritorum, coniecturam futurorum. Unde fit quod mulier reminiscens preterite delectationis similem desireat precedenti. (Bodleian Auct. F.3. 10 = b. 23); Lawn, *The Prose Salernitan Questions*, pp. 13–14.

[10] Lawn, *The Prose Salernitan Questions*, p. xvii.   [11] See below.

[12] Lawn, *The Prose Salernitan Questions*, p. xxiii.

What happens, they ask, if some *literatus* falls ill with a mania and afterwards is cured; does he lose his knowledge of letters? We are told that when this occurs, its cause is a melancholic infection in the rational cell of the brain and this infection affects the memory which is a conserving and continuous faculty. Many melancholics, therefore, hate the present. When the infection affects the memory cell of the brain the memory can no longer conserve memories which, by necessity are collected together, and the knowledge of letters slips away. The reason and the memory are thereby weakened so that information is not preserved. A knowledge of letters therefore, requires two things: rational discretion and memory. Wherefore without this weakness in reason and memory, a knowledge of letters cannot be lost.[13] This question and answer tells us that anyone with a knowledge of texts cannot simply be using his conserving memory faculty but rather, must employ the reasoning as well as the memorial faculties of the brain if he is to know, that is, understand, the literature.

Later on we are told that wisdom only is to be found in the soul but the soul cannot exercise its wisdom unless it is attached to a subject body. The soul is, as it were, engraved into this corporeal mass. It may forget its wisdom as well as natural, sensual knowledge but through discipline these can be recalled (*reminiscitur*). Therefore, memory is nothing other than a record of the past (*recordatio preteritorum*).[14] The sensual affections that are had first in the brain are perfected here just as are imaginations. Some affections begin in the brain and are perfected in the heart; for instance, cogitations, cares and cunning. It is therefore necessary to have recourse both to heart and brain. The discipline of reminiscence brings back the already recorded past and the memory perfects sensual affections and imagination's images. This solution indicates that the memory is more than a simple conserving faculty: it perfects images. We note that there is no discussion of how the exterior world comes inward but, rather, that we are dealing with sensual affects and images already in the mind as insubstantial forms, although soul must be attached to a subject body.

13 Queritur quare quidam literatus arreptus a mania et postea liberatus, scientiam literarum amisit? Solutio. Huius rei causa est infectio melancholie in rationali cellula, cuius infectione inficitur memorialis que est conservativa et continua, que etiam multam melancholicam abhorret presentiam. Quoniam ergo ex presentia melancholici humoris cerebrum in memoriali cellula impediatur ne possit ei commendata memoriter conservare, necessitate cogente, ab ea literarum elabitur scientia. Nam ex huiusmodi oppressione sequitur rationis et memorie debilitatio, quibus debilitatis literarum nequit conservari notitia. Ad scientiam namque literarum duo concurrunt: discretio et memoria. Unde notandum est quod sine debilitatione tam rationis quam memorie literarum scientiam non potuit amittere. (B 241; Lawn, *The Prose Salernitan Questions*, p. 120. The sources: Constantinus, *Pantegni*, VI, 11; Isaac Israeli, *Lib. de Oblivio*, f. 209 (Lyons, 1515 = *Opera Omnia*)

14 See below, pp. 354–6 on Avicenna's use of *recordatio*.

There is also an implied distinction between the activities of memory and reminiscence (*recordatio*) but in a terminology that does not elaborate on the differences. Mind appears to be a function of the soul, enabling it to exercise its wisdom in a particular way.[15]

Furthermore, it is asked, why is one man more forgetful than another and one more capable of remembering? There are, we are told, three cells of the brain: the first is the *fantastica* (imagination); the second is *rationalis*; and the third is the *memorialis*. The *fantastica* is warm and dry, the better to represent appetitive knowledge; the rational cell is warm and humid, thereby discerning good from evil, pure from impure; and the third, the memory cell, is cold and dry in order to retain memories entrusted to it. In the *fantastica* there is much spirit and very little core or pith (*medulla*), the small amount of core not impeding perception. In the rational cell there is much spirit and core so that the temporate spirit may (move around and) discern good from evil, pure from impure. In the third memorial cell there is little spirit and core. If there were much spirit, motion would hardly be retained. If there were much core then its humidity and flexibility would prevent retention and therefore those who have too much core forget more than others.[16] As with Aristotle, those whose memories are more fluid have a more difficult time retaining images in such a medium.

The posterior cell of the brain is the instrument of the soul which perfects memory since it is both cold and dry in complexion; having little core and spirit means that there will not be much motion there; and the impressed forms will not slip away, the forms themselves being cold and dry and thereby firmly retained. Someone with this dryness and coldness has a perfect memory. If it happens that the core of this memory cell is made liquid and fluid, then the memory forms slip away and this is like liquefied wax when brought near a flame. Hence, figures and letters become confused, merged, and they disappear. If the substance of the brain is hardened so that the accidents of the forms to be impressed are not received, then no memories are retained and someone of this sort is judged to be useless at the study of literature. But if the brain's substance is somehow both moderately soft and moderately hard as well as pure, this

---

[15] Sapientia solius est anime, quam tamen anima exercere non potest nisi corpus subiectum inveniat. Anima igitur ipsius mole corporis gravata, scientiam quam naturaliter habet obliviscitur, cuius tamen postea per disciplinam reminiscitur, unde nihil aliud est memoria quam preteritorum recordatio. Attende autem quia affectionum quedam habent principium in cerebro ibique perficiuntur, sicut quedam imaginationes; quedam in cerebro incipiunt et in corde perficiuntur, ut cogitationes, sollicitudines, [et] astutie. Huiusmodi ergo ut fiant, necesse est fieri recursum a corde ad cerebrum, et e converso ... (B. 280; Lawn, *The Prose Salernitan Questions*, p. 134).

[16] Source: Maurus, *Super Isagogen Ioannitii*, 19 rb; Lawn, *The Prose Salernitan Questions*, pp. 224–5.

kind of person has a perfect memory. If, however, the substance is more soft than hard, the forms are more easily imprinted but the impression quickly disappears. Such are judged to have a nonenduring memory. If the substance of the brain is mainly hard such a person takes a long time to conceive and a long time to lose what he conceives, and this kind of person is said to have a tenacious memory. Those whose brain substance is equally distant from either extreme are capable of conceiving and then conserving forms in a middling way (*mediocriter*).

Those people who forget the present but not the past do so as a result of diverse cerebral substances, hard or soft, wet or dry, in the different parts of the brain. Those who can firmly retain forms (in the posterior memory cell) but whose middle, rational cell is also hard, cannot have conceptions, so that they can reminisce about the past but the present is forgotten. Take the example of wax which softens near a flame: if the edges of the wax are compressed towards the centre, the form impressed on the wax in a pure and subtle manner is thereby made large, and the more subtle impressions disappear. The initial subtle impressions of forms remain separate one from another but under compression they are brought closer together; but such moderate compression does not permit these larger forms to be deleted. This is what happens when someone has a knowledge of letters and other things. The accidents of the letters are forgotten through a moderate cerebral compression towards the central (rational) cell. This kind of knowledge is more subtle since the impressed forms are subtle and they disappear. But true knowledge which is less subtle and larger has larger forms which are impressed and they remain. Therefore, depending on the hardness or softness of the different cerebral cells' substances, a man has different capacities to remember well or ill.[17]

---

[17] Questio: unde contingat quod quidam in egritudine obliviscuntur tam presentium quam preteritorum tantum, et quare quidam litterarum tantum et non aliorum obliviscuntur? Ad quod dicimus quod posterior cellula conveniens existit instrumentum anime ad perficiendum memoriam, nec immerito quoniam frigida et sicca est de complexione, parum de medulla habens et spiritu quia non multus in eis debet fieri motus, parum de medulla ut forme impresse non elaberentur. Frigida fuit et sicca, ut frigiditate et siccitate formarum impressarum firma fiat retentio. Et si omnia ista habuit, perfecta fit memoria; si vero non, contrarium. Unde si contingat quod ex aliqua causa medulla dicte cellule nimis fiat liquida et fluida, forme impresse cito elabuntur, ut contingit in litargicis in quibus, propter mollitem posterioris substanti cerebri, forme impresse delabuntur, ut est videri in cera liquefacta ad ignem, in qua si figure et littere protrahuntur, illico evanescunt et confuse fiunt. Si vero substantia cerebri nimis sit indurata, ex quod accidenti formarum impressioni nullo modo cedit, unde nichil memorie commendat, quare tam isti quam predicti ad litterarum studia iudicantur inepti. Sed si contingat cerebri substantiam esse medietatem inter mollitiem et duritiem, et puram, in talibus potest memoria perfici. Si vero plus ad mollitiem quam ad duritiem, forme faciliter imprimuntur, et impresse cito elabuntur. Tales iudicantur labilis memorie. Et si magis ad duritiem vergat tale cerebrum, tarde concipit et concepta tarde dimitti, et tales dicuntur tenacis memorie. Quandoque

The analogies with wax and the reference to the cold and dry characteristics of the memory cell recall Aristotle's physiological explanation of
remembering. It also reflects Galen's interpretation of Aristotle.[18] Galen
argued that the substance of the soul is also a mixture of four qualities,
wetness, dryness, warmness and coldness. We noted earlier that the
ancient *physici* and their medieval medical followers, maintained an interest in the brain and in the heart as organs, leaving the more spiritual
activities of the soul to the philosophers for discussion. And yet in Galen
they saw an enduring concern to define the nature of the links between
soul and body. In his later works, Galen had become more convinced that
psychism submits to the influence of the body's composition of mixed
elements and he ended up by seeing the body and its parts as the very
cause of the soul. This, of course, is in direct contrast with Augustine's
view. For Galen, the substance of the soul was identical with the pneuma
of the brain's cavities and this pneuma was then taken to be the first of the
soul's organs. Galen interpreted Aristotle's dictum, that the soul was the
form of the body, in a distinctive way whereby the four elements enter into
the matter of natural bodies to produce a corporeal mixture equivalent to
the form. Hence, the substance of the soul was also a mixture of the four
qualities of wetness, dryness, warmness and coldness. This is what we see
adopted in the Salernitan questions.[19]

It is also clear that medical discussions of memory in the Salernitan

vero equaliter distant ab utroque extremorum et tunc formas mediocriter concipiunt et
conservant. Sed quidam presentium obliviscuntur et non preteritorum; diversitas substantie cerebri est in causa, quia contingit quandoque cerebrum indurari per partium
extremarum ad medium reductionem, et est videre in latere quod induratur ab igne per
subtilium partium consumptionem, unde formas et figuras quas prius habebant, retinet
firmius. Sic igitur potest in cerebro videri quod induratur propter subtilium partium
consumptionem. Formas sibi impressas firmiter retinet, unde propter duritiem aliam
concipere nequit, unde tale habens cerebrum preteritorum reminiscitur et presentium
obliviscitur. Si autem cerebrum induratur per partium accumulationem, ut est videri in
cera cuius partes extreme quandoque per compressionem ad medium reducuntur unde
forme prius ei impresse pure et subtiles, grosse vero remanent. Subtiles pereunt quia
partes in multum distant ab invicem, unde ex modica compressione pereunt. Grosse
remanent quia [non] multum distant ab invicem, unde non ex tam modica compressione
possunt deleri. A simili contingit quod quidam habeant scientiam litterarum et aliarum
rerum. Ex quod accidenti litterarum obliviscuntur per mediocrem cerebri compressionem, quia illa scientia, utpote subtilior, [per] subtiles formas erat impressa et ideo prius
evanescit; alie vero scientie, utpote grossiores, per grossiores formas, et ideo remanent;
item quidam bene imaginantur, ratiocinantur, et bene memorie non [sic] commendat.
Hoc habet fieri ex mollitie et duritie nimia interioris cellule et mediocritate medie et posterioris. Similiter dicendum est de alienatione et memoria perfecta et imperfecta. (Lawn,
The Prose Salernitan Questions, pp. 304–5: Source, Maurus, *Super Isagogen Ioannitii*).

[18] Paul Moraux, 'Galien et Aristote' in *Images of Man in Ancient and Medieval Thought: Studia
Gerardo Verbeke ... dicata*, (Louvain, 1976), pp. 127–46; pp. 138–9.
[19] This is a medieval example of what Richard Wollheim refers to as the archaic conception
of mind. R. Wollheim, *The Thread of Life* (Cambridge, 1984), pp. 142–3.

335

milieu tied in the capacity to conserve images in the posterior ventricle with the rational, middle ventricle of the brain where distinction between images in the present takes place. We shall see an increasing concern to distinguish sense memory from a memory linked with reason in the Arabic commentaries on the ancient medical literature as well as an increasing concern to determine the nature of the continuity between the sensed objective world and the internal workings of reason and memory. Aristotle's memory 'faculty', located by him in the lowest perceptual part of the soul and, therefore, classified as a faculty of the sensitive soul by medievals, would be paralleled by the reminiscent, intellectual memory in the realm of the philosophical, interpreting, rational soul under the influence of neo-Platonist interpretations of recollection.[20]

The tenth-century Jewish physician and philosopher, Isaac Israeli, provides us with a sophisticated entrée into the world of medical and philosophical understanding of the soul's capacity to think and remember in the neo-Platonic mode which was attractive to Arabic, Jewish and Latin thinkers well into the thirteenth century. Latin scholastics were acquainted with his *Book of Definitions*[21] and his *Book on the Elements*,[22] both of which were translated from the Arabic (but written in Hebrew characters) by Gerard of Cremona in Toledo. Isaac's more specifically medical writings were translated by Constantinus Africanus.[23]

Isaac was a native of Egypt and began his career as an oculist. But he later became the court physician to the shi'ite Ubayd Allah in al-Qayrawan (Tunisia). The main influence on his writings was al-Kindi as well as an unidentified neo-Platonist, the author of a now lost pseudo-Aristotelian tract, who is known as Ibn Hasday's neo-Platonist.[24]

In his *The Book on Spirit and Soul*[25] Isaac asserted that the soul is not a body, that it is simple, not composed, and has no qualities such as warmth, coldness, humidity or dryness. And it is invisible. But the spirit is humid and resides in the heart. He distinguishes three parts of the soul: the

---

[20] Generally, see P. Michaud-Quantin, 'Une division 'augustinienne' des puissances de l'âme au moyen âge', *Revue des Etudes Augustiniennes*, 3 (1957), pp. 235–48.
[21] Isaac Israeli, *Liber de definicionibus*, ed., J. T. Muckle, *AHDLMA*, XI (1937–38), pp. 299–340.
[22] S. Fried, ed., *Das Buch über die Elemente* (Isaac Israeli) (Frankfurt-am-Main/Drohobycz, 1900).
[23] Isaac Israeli, *Omnia opera Ysaac* (Lyon, 1515); *Thesaurus sanitatis de victus salubris ratione … libri II*, (Antwerp, 1607); Isaac ben Salomon, *De diaetis universalis et particularibus libri II* (Basel, 1570).
[24] A. Altmann and S. M. Stern, *Isaac Israeli, A Neo-Platonic Philosopher of the Early Tenth Century, Selected Texts Translated with Commentary* (Oxford, 1958).
[25] In Altmann and Stern, *Isaac Israeli*, pp. 109ff.

rational, the animal or sensitive, and the vegetative. The soul is in its own world 'above the sphere' but its faculty is attached to us: the soul is a part of the Intellect. The Intellect derives its wisdom from its Creator and the Creator emanates thereby to the rational soul which in turn emanates to the animal soul.[26] Man alone has an intellectual soul, his rational soul having come into being as a radiance of Intellect so that a certain degree of Intellect intervenes between the light of the Creator and the human rational soul. Likewise, a radiance went forth when the human rational soul was created to create the animal soul where one finds the estimative and imaginative faculties. There are two kinds of action appropriate to the soul: perfect and imperfect. Perfect actions are in accordance with the demands of the higher Intellect and imperfect actions are in accordance with the demands of the animal soul.[27]

In the *Book on the Elements*, we have a further elaboration of the animal and rational souls and how they operate in relation to the world.[28] In the anterior ventricle of the brain reside the common sense and the *fantasiya*. Only the latter is an interior sense,[29] a subdivision(?) of which is the imagination. Here are received from the corporeal senses, e.g., sight, the corporeal aspects of things which are then transmitted to the first spiritual sense, the imaginative faculty. The form of something corporeal and communicated by the external senses impresses itself more readily upon the anterior ventricle of the brain because of the latter's proximity to the corporeal sense. The form has to settle and impress itself thereafter on thought. Once in the anterior ventricle, it will then be possible to divest the form of its corporeality in order that it might be interpreted in a spiritual sense by means of allegory and analogy.[30]

How is this done? Isaac explains that when the intellect wishes to reveal to the soul what its Creator has caused to emanate upon the Intellect, namely an *understanding* of the spiritual forms which it finds in itself, the Intellect shows the soul these spiritual forms and the things which it finds in itself. The Intellect therefore imparts to the soul forms that are intermediate between corporeality and spirituality so that they may be more readily impressed upon the *sensus communis*. The Creator therefore uses the Intellect as an intermediary between Himself and the soul, in order to impart His intentions regarding the world. It is only the corporeal and imaginative form which will be impressed upon the common sense because of the proximity of the common sense in the anterior ventricle to

---

[26] *Ibid.*, p. 109.   [27] *Ibid.*, p. 111.   [28] Fried, ed., *Das Buch über die Elemente*, II.
[29] H. A. Wolfson, 'Isaac Israeli on the internal senses', *Jewish Studies in Memory of George A. Kohut* (New York, 1945), pp. 583–98.
[30] Altmann and Stern, *Isaac Israeli*, p. 135.

the corporeal senses. The *sensus communis* is intermediate between the corporeal sense of sight and the imaginative faculty which also is lodged in the anterior of ventricle and known as (an aspect of the ?) *fantasiya*. Thus there appear to be a succession of more or less corporeal/spiritual forms engaged in the process of understanding. The forms with which the Intellect clarifies the (purely) spiritual forms are intermediate between corporeality and spirituality because they result from the imaginative representations of the corporeal forms and are more subtle, spiritual and luminous than the latter. The corporeal forms are found in our waking state and are full of darkness and shells. Isaac says the ancients compared the intellectual forms to the forms in the higher world, and we possess such forms when we are asleep for it is then that their images are more spiritual, subtle and transcend the natural order. It is these more spiritual forms which teach us certain truths once they are interpreted by a truly wise person.

During sleep, says Isaac, the *sensus communis* sees the forms that are intermediate between spirituality and corporeality, that is, we see the forms in which the Intellect has clarified the spiritual forms, but the sleeping mind knows these only in their corporeal aspects, because the *sensus communis*, even when asleep, does not have the power to know more of these forms than their image because of the proximity of the common sense to the corporeal sense (e.g. sight). Once it knows their corporeal aspects it transmits them to the imaginative faculty which also resides in the anterior part of the brain.[31] The imagination receives these forms in a more sublte way since it is itself more subtle than the *sensus communis* and more remote from the corporeal senses. Then the imaginative faculty transmits the forms to the memory and deposits them there. When the person awakes from his sleep, he claims these forms from the memory, and memory returns to him the remembrance of all their traces, impressions and characteristics as these were received from the imagination. But once one remembers these images, one does not stop here. One seeks to understand their spiritual meaning through the engagement of the cogitative faculty in the middle ventricle. This faculty possesses a power to scrutinise, discern, combine and distinguish between the shells of all things and their kernels. Having discerned and purified them, the cogitative faculty then returns the forms to the memory faculty and memory receives them and stores them away until such times as they are required.[32] When a person has a cogitative faculty that is spiritual, pure,

[31] *Ibid.*, p. 136.
[32] *Ibid.*, p. 137. Compare the *De Spiritu et Anima* on judged images in the memory, above, ch. 12.

luminous and barely obscured by shells and darkness, then the Intellect will cause its light and brilliance to emanate upon it and make known to cogitation its own properties, forms and spiritual messages. The Intellect will also enlighten the cogitation as to the properties and forms of the soul and its faculties and as to the difference between its spiritual forms and its corporeal ones. Then these forms will be completely purified of all their shells and cogitation will interpret those dreams without error. But if one's cogitation is obscured by shells and darkness, then the Intellect will be unable to descend to its depth with its own light and cogitation will fail to know its own faculties and those of the soul. It will remain unenlightened as to the spiritual forms and those of the Intellect and soul. It will be unable to effect a complete and proper separation of the shells from the inner content of those forms in which some allegorical meaning is conveyed during sleep. It will not have understood their spiritual meaning and thereby will be unable to distinguish them from their corporeal expression. Such an obscured cogitative faculty will therefore only know the corporeal expression of forms and its interpretation of dreams wil be faulty.[33]

Isaac has a very distinctive analysis of the operation of Intellect conjoined with the Creator's textual messages, an analysis which would be closely paralleled by Hugh of St Victor's later description of how texts convey spiritual meaning. Isaac says that Intellect follows in the footsteps of the Creator and seeks to imitate His activity. The will of the Creator is only known to man through messengers which He sent to make known His will. Hence the Creator put His message in *spiritual*, unambiguous *words* to serve as guides and as a true teacher to those endowed with Intellect and understanding. They alone can attain an understanding of the meaning of those messages partly in corporeal and ambiguous terms.[34] The Creator put his messages partly in such corporeal and ambiguous terms for the benefit of those who are dull and deficient in Intellect so that at least they could come to some understanding by having their imaginative faculties impressed by the coarseness and corporeality of sensible forms. But such people, deficient in Intellect and morals, are in need of a moral teacher who will speak so that they may gain a deeper understanding of the spiritual meaning of God's messages. Isaac says it is impossible to gain an insight into the spiritual meaning of the corporeal expressions from books, seeing that books speak in a particular way and express their subject in a particular form; if the understanding of the book eludes the reader, then he will remain in ignorance until he goes to a scholar who interprets the book's allegorical meaning in a great variety of ways, offering him many explanations of the mere corporeal images. Such a

[33] Altmann and Stern, *Isaac Israeli*, p. 137.   [34] *Ibid.*, p. 139.

scholar will teach him first the corporeal aspect of the thing which is close to the senses, and if he notices that his pupil finds it easy and understands it well, he will proceed further; otherwise he will further elucidate the corporeal aspects of the matter and raise his pupil's level of understanding until he arrives at a point where he understands, and the form of the thing is impressed upon his sense. Then he will again explain the matter to him little by little until he reduces the words to their complete spirituality.[35] The journey from the literal, primary, sensual signification of a text, as Hugh of St Victor described it, is paralleled here in Isaac's explanation of intellectually reading spiritual meaning into corporeal forms.

We have noticed that Isaac describes the anterior ventricle of the brain as housing both the common sense and the imaginative fantasy, while at the same time delimiting the operations of the two faculties, the former being closer to sense experience than the latter which alone seems to be an interior sense. Aristotle did not make such a distinction. We shall see that Avicenna *identifies* the fantasy and common sense, and places the common sense in the category of an interior sense and hence further away from sense experience. It is also worthy of note that Isaac understands the memory as a store house not only of spiritualised corporeal forms recognised when asleep, but he also has excogitated memories returned to the memory store once they have been interpreted through the illuminating activities of Intellect. He allows a greater role to higher reason in the production of images: imaginative forms originate not in the normal process of imagination working on sense data but in a rational activity producing images and presenting them to the imagination via the common sense. The precise role of the Intellect in the actual production of images, other than its illuminative descent to cogitation, remains obscure. But it is clear that for him fantasy is not only operating on sense perception as a faculty of the animal soul but it also is at the service of the rational soul and works on rational, interpreted data. Hence the fantasy provides reason with the material delivered from sense perception and works from below upwards; and it also operates downwards by translating the material derived from reason into sensible images. The rational activity of the soul is most in evidence when man is asleep and his images are divorced from matter. But upon waking Isaac believes man's cogitative power is linked to the intellectual faculty rather than being, as Avicenna would have it, a special kind of imagination.

In his *Book of Definitions*, he makes this even clearer. He defines cognition as an intellectual faculty roving among things. Memory is defined as an understanding or comprehension of things which are in the soul, through investigation; whereas recollection (*recordatio*) is the coming back

[35] *Ibid.*, p. 140.

of a thing which had been forgotten, a kind of renewal of lost memory, by means of the intellectually influenced faculty of cogitation: 'Recordatio est inquisicio adventus rei iam oblitae a virtute cogitativa; memoria est comprehensio rerum existencium in anima cum [in] quisicione'.[36] There is no reference, in these definitions, to memory relating to any thing outside the soul. In other words, there is throughout his philosophico-medical writings an attempt to limit the role of the external world and its corporeal images on the soul, and a concern to emphasise early on the active role of Intellect and rational interpretation in the most basic of imaginative experiences of the soul.

In his purely medical writings, for instance, that work which came to be called his *Thesaurus Sanitatis* or the *De Diaetis Universalibus*, Isaac notes in his chapter *de cerebro*,[37] that the brain, following Aristotle, is the basis of sense and motion. Sensation and motion result from natural warmth and therefore it is impossible for the brain to be cold since coldness would constrain the natural humidity of the brain and restrict motion. If the brain were cold then man's memory, fantasy and reason would be destroyed. For those whose brains are dominated by phlegma or coldness have hardened or dull memories, confused power of discretion and disordered reason. As Aristotle well indicated, the brain is warm and moderately moist although it is supplied with sufficient accidental coldness so that cerebral motion does not overheat it.[38] Even in his medical analyses Isaac is concerned to link the memory faculty with the rational, cogitative middle brain cell. In his *De Oblivio*, used by the compiler of the *Prose Salernitan Questions*, an infection in the memory cell also affects the rational cell so that someone who once had a knowledge of letters no longer preserves the information. A knowledge of letters requires not only memory but also rational discretion so that a knowledge of texts requires the engagement of higher understanding, intellectual interpretation, the result of which will be stored in the memory.

Avicenna's *De Anima* was more than a commentary on Aristotle's work.[39] It was a systematic exposition and a new synthesis, very much focused on a new anthropology and placing great emphasis on man's psychology, incorporating much information from ancient Greek medical studies. Aristotle's psychology was reinterpreted in a neo-Platonic mode whereby the human soul has an immaterial character, is immortal, and is transcended

---

[36] *Liber de definicionibus*, ed. Muckle, p. 338.   [37] (Basel, 1570), Lib. I, c. xliiii, p. 209.
[38] As cited by Isaac, p. 210.
[39] *Avicenna Latinus, Liber de Anima seu sextus de naturalium* I, Lib. I–III, and II, Lib. IV–V, ed. Simone van Riet (Louvain/Leiden, 1972); vol. I: Introduction by G. Verbeke.

by an agent intellect. We have already seen the degree to which twelfth-century Christian thinkers in the Latin west were prepared to accept this analysis. Where Aristotle did not clearly distinguish the soul's five senses from post-sensationary powers, Avicenna, like other Arabic, Jewish and then Latin authors developed a doctrine of the internal senses and gave much greater emphasis to the mechanisms of visual perception. The internal senses were located in the brain and were said to operate without bodily organs. This reflects a neo-Platonic psychological dualism not found in Aristotle.[40]

For Aristotle, when one speaks of the soul, one is adopting a specific vantage point. Therefore, perception and the object of perception can be spoken of in a unified way: perception is potentially what the perceived object actually is.[41] Since both the activity of the object of perception and the activity of that which can perceive are 'in' that which can perceive, i.e. the soul, the activity of the object of perception and of that which can perceive, is one and the same activity. Furthermore, when one defines the soul, one does so in terms of its distinguishing characteristics, which include thinking, understanding and perceiving. Perceiving and understanding, however, are not the same; nor are perceiving and thinking the same. As we have seen, during the middle ages a sensitive soul and a rational soul were discussed separately, the sensitive soul often being seen as the preserve of physicians and the rational soul that of the philosophers. Avicenna reflects this in his own writings.

But how the two aspects of soul were linked became the subject of much debate as we have already observed it amongst twelfth-century Cistercian authors. A psychological dualism consonant with a radical distinction between body and soul in the Latin West was also to be found in Avicenna's *De Anima*. It is not to be found in Aristotle. Avicenna argued that the soul is the form of the body as did Aristotle, but went on to say that it is better to see the soul as the body's perfection, capable of acting as the form of a living thing but is itself a separable substance. He provides the famous allegory of a man, newly created and fully formed, dwelling in a vacuum, and incapable of receiving any sense impressions from his senses. If one can then assert one exists, as one must, then one asserts the existence not of a body of which one has no knowledge, but of one's soul.[42]

---

[40] H. A. Wolfson, 'The internal senses in Latin, Arabic and Hebrew philosophic texts', *Harvard Theological Review*, 28, (1935), pp. 69–133. See the *De Spiritu et Anima*, *c.* 1170, above, ch. 12.

[41] Aristotle, *De Anima*, III, 2, 426a 15 f.

[42] 'Anima humana ... non est impressa in materia sua, sed est providens ei' (*Avicenna Latinus*, p. 65, ll. 42–3; IV, 4). Compare Descartes's famous *cogito ergo sum*, although Avicenna does not refer to subjectivity since the intellect does not elaborate itself by the

The individual's identity is seized as existing outside of all sense perception. One's identity *is* the soul and it does not coincide with the corporeal organs nor with any organ because it is of another nature from the body; it is an incorporeal substance with diverse powers. To know the soul (in its self-knowledge) is to know what it is not, i.e. the body, and the soul's self-knowledge is an immediate intuition. The soul is not an accident of the body.[43]

Book I of Avicenna's *De Anima* lists an inventory of all the different psychological faculties which are then fully discussed in the subsequent four books. Books II and III deal with the inferior faculties of vegetative life: the nutritive, the growth, and the generative powers. Like Aristotle, he studies sensation in general: perception, sensible qualities, the necessity of having bodily organs and the function of the intermediary milieu between the object sensed and the cognitive power. He defines the sensitive soul which is the first perfection of the natural body, possessing organs by which it apprehends particulars and moves at will. Aristotle had said that the soul is discussed in terms of its two distinguishing characteristics: motion in respect of place, and thinking, understanding and perceiving. Avicenna therefore divides the sensitive soul into *motiva* and *apprehendens*. The motive power of the sensitive soul is ruled by the concupiscible and the irascible appetites, and the power effecting motion is infused in the nerves and muscles. When he turns to the apprehending power of the sensitive soul he enumerates the five external senses: touch, taste, smell, hearing and sight (in reverse order to Aristotle) and then passes, in Book IV, to the internal senses.

In Arabic and Hebrew philosophical literature, the term 'internal senses' was, from the beginning, a generic term which included a variety of post-sensationary faculties not developed by Aristotle. In general, they include three faculties: imagination, cogitation and memory. They correspond to Aristotle's discussion in the *De Anima* and the *De Memoria* of the powers beyond sensation. Some have argued that this three-fold classification is from Galen but Galen got it from Aristotle and neither used the term 'internal senses'.[44] What Galen did do, and what Arabic and Hebrew texts also do, is specifically to locate these faculties in the anterior, middle and posterior ventricles of the brain.

intelligibles which it knows, but rather, receives these from the transcendent agent intellect.

[43] See F. Rahman, *Avicenna's Psychology, An English Translation of the Kitab al-Najāt, Book II c. vi, with Historico-Philosophical Notes and Textual Improvements on the Cairo Edition*, (Oxford, 1952). The Najāt is a summary of the important passages of the Shifā' = *De Anima*.

[44] Wolfson, 'The internal senses', p. 71.

Arabic and Hebrew writings on the three-fold classification of the internal senses do not seem to use the same type of classification nor the same terminology, especially regarding the third, memory faculty. Some replace 'memory' by understanding, comprehension and wisdom; others replace imagination by a natural disposition or a creative power, largely in an attempt to come to terms with Galen's classification. But in general the third internal sense, 'memory', is discussed in two ways because there are two kinds of memory. One kind belongs to sense perception or imagination, and the other to thought. We have already seen that according to Aristotle, memory *directly* belongs to sense perception or imagination, the lowest perceptual part of the soul; but it *indirectly* belongs to thought.[45] Aristotle also says that in an accidental way, some of the things which are properly the objects of scientific knowledge may also be objects of memory, so that a person is said to remember that he has learned something where the something is an intellectual object of memory, or he has contemplated it at some time previous, and he can recall it through the discipline of reminiscence.[46]

Plotinus, as we have seen, also spoke of two kinds of memory; one of sensible objects, which belongs to imagination[47] and the other of intellectual conceptions, which belongs to reason.[48]

The neo-Platonic interpretation of memory as found in Nemesius of Emesa's *De Natura Hominis* (translated into Latin by Burgundio of Pisa)[49] also distinguished between the two kinds of memory whereby one retained sense images, the other intelligibles.[50] According to Nemesius, the sensible soul through its sense organs was thereby able to comprehend and have opinions of *sensibilia*; whereas intelligibles were remembered *per intellectum et fit intelligentia*. Whereas *sensibilia* are remembered in themselves, the *intelligibilia* are remembered *secundum accidens*. Excogitated memories are based on *phantasia* whereby we do not have the substance of those things we remember having said or heard; and intellectual conceptions are had either through the discipline of learning or through unlear-

---

[45] Aristotle, *De Memoria et Reminiscentia*, I, 450a, 12–14.
[46] *Ibid.*, II, 451a 28–9, and I, 450a 12–14; Wolfson, 'The Internal Senses', p. 75.
[47] Plotinus, *Ennead*, IV, iii, 29.   [48] *ibid.*, IV, iii, 30.
[49] G. Verbeke and J. R. Moncho, eds., *Nemesius d'Emèse, De natura hominis, traduction de Burgundio de Pise*, Corpus Latinum commentariorum in Aristotelem Graecorum (Leiden, 1975), c. XII, '*De memorativo*', pp. 86–9; *Gregorii Nysseni (Nemesii Emesini) Periphyseos Anthropou, liber a Burgundio in Latinam translatus*, ed., C. Burkhard (Vienna, 1891). On the confusion of Nemesius with Gregory of Nyssa, see P. Michaud-Quantin, 'Les puissances de l'âme au XIIᵉ s.', *Revue de Moyen Âge Latin*, 5 (1949), p. 18.
[50] '*Est autem memoria, ut Origenes [the neo-Platonist, not the Christian] quidem ait, phantasia relicta ab aliquo sensu secundum actum apparente; ut Plato autem, conservatio sensus et intelligentiae*' (*Nemesius d'Emèse* ed. G. Verbeke and J. R. Moncho, p. 87).

ned natural intentions.[51] If we say that we remember what we first knew or heard or otherwise cogitated upon, where what we mean by 'first' is in relation to past time, then it is clear that memories are made and destroyed and exist in time.[52] Something is absent from memory, not absent in itself, so that, when we speak of recollection we mean that which is brought back from forgetfulness which blocks out memory; *rememoratio* is the restoration of *corruptae factae*. Forgetfulness destroys memories and therefore oblivion is abandoned memories. There is a continuum of memories but a discontinuity of recollected memories.[53]

Nemesius also says that there is a certain kind of recollection which is not in relation to the forgetting of sensibles or intelligibles, but is rather related to forgetting natural intentions. He defines natural intentions as those which are had intuitively, without any teaching, for instance God's existence, and he says that Plato refers to this kind of recollection as a remembering of the idea or form.[54] This means that in general, intentions are kinds of ideas but not proper to *intelligentia* but rather to *excogitatio* in the sensible soul where one understands sensibles through the sense organs and has opinions of these.[55] Intuitive intentions however, are possessed naturally and correspond to Plato's preexisting and eternal ideas.

Nemesius then goes on to locate the memory in the posterior ventricle of the brain, referring to Galen, and he discusses the various incapacities which result from wounds in one or more of the three ventricles.

---

51 Nam sensibilia quidem secundum se ipsa memorantur, intelligibilia vero secundum accidens quia et excogitabilium memoria ex praesumpta phantasia fit; ea vero quae principaliter intelligibilia, si quid quidem didicimus vel audivimus, memoramur; substantiae vero eorum memoriam non habemus; non enim ex praecedenti phantasi intelligibilium resumptio, sed ex disciplina vel ex naturali intentione. (*Ibid.*, p. 87).

52 '...quae in tempore consistunt'.

53 Si vero memorari dicimur quae prius scivimus vel audivimus aut aliter qualitercumque cognovimus ('prius' autem relationem, habet ad praeteritum tempus) manifestum est quod memorabilia sunt quae fiunt et corrumpuntur; quae in tempore consistunt. Et est quidem absentium memoria, non tamen ab absentibus fit; rememoratio vero dicitur, cum oblivio mediaverit memoriam. Est enim rememoratio: memoriae corruptae factae restauratio; fit autem corrupta ab oblivione; oblivio autem est memoriae abiectio; sed haec quidem est continua, alia vero usque ad quantum, cuius est rememoratio. (*Ibid.*, p. 87).

54 Alia autem rememoratio est, quae non est oblivio eorum quae sunt ex sensu et ex intelligentia, sed naturalium intentionum oblivio; naturales autem dicimus intentiones quae sine doctrina omnibus adsunt, ut esse Deum; hanc autem Plato rememorationem esse dicit idearum; quid autem est idea, in sequentibus dicemus. Igitur phantasticum quidem tradit excogitativo ea quae apparent; excogitativum vero vel discretivum assumens et diiudicans transmittit memorativo. (*Ibid.*, pp. 87–8)

55 Anima enim sensibilia quidem per membra sensuum comprehendit et fit opinio ... cum igitur typos et eorum quae opinata est ... Videtur autem intelligentiam in his dicere Plato non eam quae propria est intelligentiam sed excogitationem ... quia et excogitabilium memoria ex praeassumpta phantasia fit. (*ibid.*, p. 87)

345

John of Damascus in the *De Fide Orthodoxa*, II, 20, followed Nemesius and further emphasised the third term, memory, when he meant a memory of intellectual conceptions, focusing therefore on the rational soul.[56] The posterior ventricle would be filled both with intellectual forms as well as sense memories, as yet unjudged and uninterpreted. This was also the case according to the neo-Platonist physician Isaac Israeli as we have seen.

This neo-Platonist tradition was in line with the Augustinian doctrine that opposed any real distinction between the substance of the soul and its faculties; the soul is manifested by its activities of memory, intelligence and will, each of which is of the same substance as the soul. But the Arabic and Jewish philosophers went even further than Augustine and Aristotle in elaborating on the internal senses and their functions.

Avicenna offers various views in his different writings on the combination of the different faculties of the internal senses. In the *De Anima* he provides a five-fold classification: (1) common sense (which he *identifies* with *phantasia*); (2) the retentive imagination; (3) a compositive imagination which in humans is called the *cogitativa*; (4) the estimative faculty, and finally (5) memory (which includes recollection). In the *Canon* (translated by Gerard of Cremona – twelfth century) he says that according to the philosophers the common sense which receives the images of things is distinct from the imagination which retains images. But according to the physicians, common sense and imagination comprise a single faculty although there is a distinction between reception and retention. However, in the *Risalah fi al-Nafs*, he says the common sense and the imagination are identical as a single faculty but then he makes no distinction between receptive and retentive powers. As Wolfson has argued, Avicenna appears to wish to contrast the two ways in which the internal senses may be viewed: the medical and the philosophical ways. The physicians who are concerned only with those faculties of the soul where there may be some hindrance in their functioning through injury, focus on the anterior ventricle of the brain and here are located both common sense and retentive imagination. Likewise, when he speaks of the posterior ventricle with its memorial faculty, he notes that philosophers are in doubt as to whether memory and recollection are two distinct faculties since they do not know whether these two have distinct functions. In the *Canon* he refers to different philosophical opinions as to whether memory and recollection

---

[56] On John of Damascus, see O. Lottin, *Psychologie et Morale aux XIIe et XIIIe siècles* (Louvian-Gembloux, 1949–60) especially volume I, pp. 393–424. On John's classification of the virtues, volume III, pp. 99–194. On the use of John of Damascus by Jean de la Rochelle, see below, ch. 17.

constitute one faculty or two; but in the *De Anima*, he makes no distinction between these two terms, although he does distinguish between sense memory and *recordatio*, as we shall see, in an important and influential way.[57]

From the beginning of the *De Anima*, Avicenna makes clear that the external senses are oriented towards the seizure of an exterior object. The internal senses are those which let us know interior objects.[58] The exterior senses seize the forms which come to them through a medium, for example, air. Thereafter, the internal senses are involved in making further distinctions: between the perception of the form and the perception of an intention. To know the form is the function of the external senses simultaneously with the internal senses. For instance, the form of length is seized first by the external senses and then transmitted to the internal senses. But in addition, some of the internal senses alone seize the intention of an object, that is, they have a certain knowledge of the object which is not perceived by the external senses: the intention is a kind of non-sensible excogitated idea rather than an intellectual idea. An example of this is given where a sheep knows the wolf as an animal to flee and fear over and above the sheep's external senses' perception of the shape of the wolf.[59]

Furthermore, the powers of the soul are divided into the power of acting and the power of knowing, active knowledge and passive knowledge. In certain cases the form or intention is simply reproduced in the cogitative faculty without any further action, but in other cases the internal sense known as the *cogitativa* or *imaginativa* (in animals) will combine the forms and the intentions or separate these. Lastly, the internal senses distinguish between an object seized in the first place from those known indirectly and in a secondary way, that is, by (intellect) reason and deliberation.[60]

More precisely, how does this series of further distinctions by the internal senses operate? Firstly, the common sense (*phantasia*) receives all forms perceived by the five external senses. Then the imagination (*imaginatio*) conserves the forms even when the objects perceived are no longer being perceived. Thereafter, the *imaginativa* (in animals) and the *cogitativa* (in men) combines certain forms and dissociates others. This is followed by the estimative faculty which has as its object the intentions or intuitions of value concerning each sensible object. Lastly the memory and the power of reminiscence *conserves the intentions of the estimative faculty.*[61]

---

[57] Wolfson, 'The internal senses', p. 99.
[58] *Avicenna Latinus, De Anima*, I, 5, pp. 82–3.
[59] *Ibid.*, I, 5, p. 86.   [60] *Ibid.*, I, 5, p. 87.   [61] *Ibid.*, I, 5, p. 87.

Avicenna has, therefore, given the imagination the role of retaining sensible forms and the memory the role of conserving intentions which have already been 'worked on', that is, evaluated by estimation.

Now in Aristotle there is no mention of a power or faculty known as the *estimatio* or *vis aestimativa*. But Aristotle does attribute to the human cogitative soul the motion of pursuit and avoidance based on an evaluation of potential harm or value. This capacity, he says, is also in animals and is determined by a combined action of the appetitive faculty and the imagination both of which are possessed by man and animals. In man, however, the imagination is rational and deliberative whereas in animals it is only sensitive. Avicenna, therefore, was led to distinguish between *imaginatio*, and *imaginativa/cogitativa*. The motion caused by the sensitive imagination according to Aristotle is a pursuit and avoidance of something that directly causes pleasure or pain, that is, good and evil. As he says: 'all imagination is either concerned with reasoning or perception, and in the latter animals share also'. But in the *Historia Animalium*, VIII–IX, Aristotle argues further that even animals plan for the attainment of remote or indirect pleasure. Whereas in man the rational or deliberative 'faculty' performs this task, working on man's imagination, in animals there must be some additional faculty which does this beyond sensitive imagination. Aristotle does not specifically name such a faculty, but in the *De Partibus Animalium* he does speak of animals having sagacity, prudence and forethought in a peculiarly animal way. This capacity for sagacity, prudence and forethought in animals is paralleled with the intellect in man. The Arabic philosophical texts names this capacity *wahm* (*æstimatio*).[62]

According to Avicenna, above the sensitive soul with its various activities engaging the external and internal senses, is the rational soul. This may either be focused on things above it, in contemplation, or it can be focused on things below it, that is, the body, and therefore it is active. When the rational soul acts with regard to things below it, it moves the human body towards a determined activity as a result of thoughts in so far as thought (cogitation) adopts certain intentions or *judgements of value that are established* (*ad placitum*), in effect by social conventions.[63] The rational soul can then exercise its action in union with the appetitive powers and produce conventionally induced shame, blushing, laughter. The rational soul's active faculty can also work in combination with the imaginative and

---

[62] Wolfson, pp. 9off.

[63] *Avicenna Latinus, De Anima*, I, 5, p. 90, ll. 64–6: 'Vis autem activa est vis quae est principium movens corpus hominis ad actiones singulas quae sunt propriae cogitationis, secundum quod intentionibus convenit ad placitum quae approprientur ei.' Verbeke notes also *De Anima*, I, 5, p. 80, ll. 12–16, where Avicenna makes a rare allusion to a kind of free will: 'agere actiones electione deliberationis' (n. 125, p. 44*, vol. I and no. 108).

estimative faculties, as when one discovers laws of contingent things or when one invents certain arts. Lastly, the active capacity of the rational soul can operate on its own, giving itself over to philosophy and finding rules of moral action that are universally in existence without being demonstrated by reasoning based on experience.[64]

When the rational soul focuses on things above it, it contemplates and has for its objects the universals that are abstracted from matter. If the objects of contemplation are forms that are by themselves immaterial, there is no difficulty in knowing them; but if these forms exist in matter, it is necessary first to abstract them and divest them of all that is material.

In order to determine just what is the intellect's receptivity to intelligible forms when the *virtus contemplativa* knows universals, Avicenna distinguishes different levels of potentiality in the intellect. First, we have the material intellect which is in absolute potentiality when it is not in possession of its intelligible objects.[65]

Secondly, we have a level of potentiality when the intellect is already in possession of first intelligibles, that is, self-evident first principles, for instance, that the whole is greater than any of its parts. This is called the *intellectus in habitu*. The third and final level of potentiality is the intellect in act, that is, in possession of secondary intelligibles, when it is capable of bringing its attention to these and to think actively when it wishes. This is the *intellectus accommodatus* or *acquisitus*. The intellect will only thereafter pass into perfect intellection in act when it is under the influence of an intellect that is always in act and separate from it, and this occurs when the *intellectus accommodatus* is joined to the separate and transcendent agent intellect and then it receives forms which the agent intellect imprints on it. This activity of the separated agent intellect on the third level of potential intellect provides the intelligible form now, in the present.[66] The *intellectus accommodatus* is therefore turned to the active intellect which in turn takes its place as the lowest neo-Platonic rung in the hierarchy of celestial intelligences, and it is man alone who is thereby capable of participating in the intelligible universe above him.

For Avicenna, then, all apprehension is the receiving of forms in different degrees of abstraction. The process of abstraction is a process of successive dematerialisation. Avicenna has taken up Aristotle's understanding of sensation and perception as the actualisation of a power in the soul but where the passage from potentiality to actuality occurs under the

---

[64] *De Anima*, I, 5, p. 94; also I, 5, pp. 90–2.
[65] 'et haec potentia vocatur intellectus materialis ad similitudinem aptitudinis materiae primae, quae ex se non habet aliquam formarum sed est subiectum omnium formarum' (I, 5, p. 96).
[66] 'forma intellecta nunc in praesenti est in eo' (I, 5, pp. 98–9).

influence of an exterior agent intellect. There is no true alteration in the potential intellect, no change from being one thing to being another. Rather, all sensation consists in receiving the abstracted form of the perceived object, and assimilating it, so that the knower becomes like what he knows. The form which is assimilated by the knowing subject is an abstract form divested of matter. Sight, for instance, is an abstraction of a kind whereby the object of vision does not enter the eye but rather a copy of it is made, and the copy reproduces all the accidents of matter in order for one to have a copy of, for example, a particular man. The *primum sensatum* is not an exterior object, the thing existing outside the knower, but the impression that is received in the sensitive organ.[67] Avicenna himself asks, what then does it mean to *perceive* that which is exterior?[68] The knower does not go outside himself to encounter the object; rather, the *form* of the exterior object is 'assimilated' by the sensitive faculty.[69]

The power of imagination then gives a greater abstraction; copies of material things existing in the *vis imaginatio* are not simply without matter, but exist even if their originals are no longer present or in existence. Imagination may contain an image of someone even if he is away somewhere else or has been dead for years. Imagination therefore still perceives the accidents of matter since its images are copies of individual things. That which is imagined does not exhibit the characteristics of all such individuals; what is reproduced are the particular characteristics of a specific object.

Thereafter, the estimative power abstracts even further, apprehending the non-material intentions of material things. Hence a wolf's *malicitas* is perceived by a sheep when the sheep scrutinises the mental image of a wolf and by *estimatio* it understands the intention, the *malicitas*, and runs away. This intention, this *malicitas*, is not apprehended by any sensitive power but rather the *intentio* of *malicitas* is conveyed by the sensible image and abstracted by the estimative faculty.[70]

The process of gradual dematerialisation in the soul is a two-fold one: the form must first be divested of matter, and then there must also be an

---

[67] 'Primum enim sensatum certissime est id quod describitur in instrumento sensus' (II, 2, p. 121).

[68] '... sentire quod est extrinsecus?'

[69] Videtur autem quod cum dicitur 'sentiri' quod est extrinsecus, intellectus eius est praeter intellectum sentiendi in anima. Intellectus enim huius quod dicitur 'sentiri extrinsecus' est quod eius forma assimilata est in meo sensu; sed intellectus 'sentiendi in anima' non est quod ipsa forma eius effigiata sit in meo sensu, et propter hoc difficile est constituere esse qualitatum sensibilium in corporibus. (De Anima, II, 2, p. 121).

[70] For a clear discussion of this process, see E. Ruth Harvey, *The Inward Wits, Psychological Theory in the Middle Ages and the Renaissance* (London, 1975).

abstraction from the material accidents.[71] The fact of the diversity of matter is realised at the level of sensible perception. But thereafter the rational soul abstracts the form by stripping it further of all material accidents. That we can speak of the 'form of man' as being multiplied in several individuals, is because this multiplicity is a material accident of the form; it is the same for quantity, quality, place and position. None of these determinations belongs to the essence of the form, however. Therefore, these categories can be disengaged or separated without any effect on the essential structure of the perceived object. And if one strips the form not only of its matter but also of its material accidents then one achieves something of a spiritualisation of the form, which is none other than its universality. The intellectual power of the soul achieves this complete abstraction regarding the pure forms stripped of all material specificities and limitations. Where abstraction by means of the act of vision is not a total dematerialisation, the form assimilated by the visual faculty being stripped of matter but not separated from its material accidents (since sight needs these accidents to perceive the form), abstraction via the imagination is a further dematerialisation. It is not necessary for the object to be present for it to be known in the imagination. And yet imagination does not strip the form of material accidents either since forms that are conserved in the imagination are not deprived of quantity, quality and position. Consequently, the human form in the imagination is never universal; it is not applicable to all individuals. It is always the image of, for example, a determined man.[72]

Thereafter, the estimative faculty, located in the central ventricle, attains a degree of abstraction slightly superior to that in imagination since it knows intentions which are not material, even though such intentions are realised in matter. The estimative faculty seizes these intentions which are not sensible, and yet even here the material accidents are not stripped off the form, since the very purpose of the estimative seizure is particularised in relation to a determined sensible form.[73]

Finally, however, intellectual abstraction occurs at such a level that the form *is* stripped of its matter *and* of its material accidents. The apprehended form is thereby a separated entity, distinct from quantity, quality, position and place. Hence, it is universal and can apply to all individuals of the same species.[74]

How can we ever be certain that there is any truth in sensation? Why may it not be the case that what one seizes is none other than a subjective

---

[71] *De Anima*,. II, 2, pp. 114–15.   [72] *Ibid.*, II, 2, pp. 117–18.
[73] *Ibid.*, II, 2, pp. 118–19.
[74] *Ibid.*, II, 2, p. 120.

impression of an exterior object, an impression that is somehow unique to each individual perceiver? Avicenna addresses this question as to whether sensible qualities exist in the reality of things thereby belonging to the real structure of objects. He gives the example of some people finding the taste of bile bitter, others tasting it as acid. Are sensible qualities purely subjective? He answers no. For Avicenna, qualities not only have a corresponding reality but this reality presents the same diversity as the perceived qualities. Hence, there is a parallel between the form received in the sensitive faculty and the real properties of known things. Like Aristotle, Avicenna maintains that sense impressions are usually reliable and that sense organs are taking impressions of the properties of exterior things. Images are faithful to their objects in reality.[75] And the sense organs are necessary for the soul's apprehension of the forms of matter. The abstract form of the object with its material accidents of quantity, quality, position, place, comprise the *primum sensatum* of perception and this *primum sensatum* provides a parallel of the exterior thing through being an adequate copy.

Perception, which occurs once the sensible impression is transmitted to the anterior ventricle of the brain where common sense resides, is like sensation in that both are types of passivity. The first term of perception is the assimilated form of the object so that the knowing subject in effect perceives itself, that is, itself as it has become like its object.

The object of sight, when illuminated, throws off a likeness of itself (*simulacrum*) to be received by the proper organ, the eye. The *simulacrum* enters the eye and thereafter comes under the scrutiny of the brain, the *simulacrum* being imprinted on the crystalline, humour of the eye. The images in both eyes are then carried by the *spiritus visibilis* along each optic nerve to a point where the two nerves cross and are superimposed on one another to create a conjoined image, which is transmitted to the front ventricle of the brain. The spirit which operates the *sensus communis* receives the conjoined image and the act of visual perception is completed. This image, given by sight to the *sensus communis*, is preserved by the imagination. We have reached that area where the external and internal senses meet, the borderline between the rational and the irrational, the material and the immaterial. The internal senses serve as the bridge between the exterior world that is experienced by body, and the interior interpretive understanding of mind. But we note that animals also interpret their world but in a manner that is intuitive and instinctive whereas men consciously reason about their corporeal experiences. The mind/body dichotomy has become much more complicated in Avicenna.

[75] *Ibid.*, II, 2, pp. 120–1.

Whereas each sense only can distinguish its own *sensibilia*, the general power which grasps all sensibles in order to compare and relate them, the *sensus communis*, serves as a place where all impressions are held momentarily (hence, the continuity of vision) before they are relegated to the next higher power, the conserving imagination, which is also located in the anterior ventricle. Hence, imagination is a kind of memory, because it is a treasury or storehouse of sensible forms, ready for the active operation of higher internal senses which will discern and judge them. As we have noted, Avicenna is the first to include the common sense in the category of the internal senses. The animal imaginative or the human cogitative imagination occupies the central ventricle. Here occur the operations of combining and separating the images from the *phantastica* or common sense. In man, the cogitative imagination is controlled by the rational soul; the estimative power then has those forms which are preserved in the *cogitativa* or *imaginativa* brought to it for evaluation. In animals, the *estimativa* is the *excellentior iudex*, the highest power, since it perceives intentions in sensations that are brought to it by anterior powers. It is set in the top of the middle ventricle, serving as a kind of natural instinct which judges on the basis of sensory experiences. In man it operates when, for instance, one refuses to believe in the existence of something which falls outside one's experience. Hence, one says that the *estimatio* in man cannot find a likeness in his imagination.

Lastly we come to the *memorialis*, the site of the memory of estimation's intentions. As we have seen, Avicenna distinguishes between the treasury of *phantasmata* and images from sense impressions, which is the imagination, and the treasury of more abstract intentions which is the memory. The awkwardness of the relationship between conserving imagination and conserving memory would be taken up later in the thirteenth century by Bacon amongst others.[76] Furthermore, in the *De Anima*, Avicenna appears not to distinguish between the terms memorial and reminiscent, referring to them both as capacities of the soul, saying only that 'there is the *vis memorialis* and *reminiscibilis* which is a power set in the hindmost ventricle of the brain. It retains what *estimativa* has apprehended, that is, the intentions of individual *sensibilia*, intentions which were not themselves perceived by the senses.'[77] Animals too have this kind of *vis memorialis et reminiscibilis*. While memory and imagination belong principally to the soul, it is only in a soul that has a body that imagination and memory can be manifested.

But in Book IV, 3,[78] we have a new departure: here Avicenna discusses animal intentions, that is, their capacity to estimate usefulness or harmful-

---

[76] Opus Maius, V, pars I, dist. I.   [77] *De Anima*, I, 5.   [78] Pp. 40–1.

ness of sense objects, and he says, as we would expect, that these estimative intentions are stored with their forms – that is, images, in the memory. While memory of this sort is in animals as well as in man, he then distinguishes a capacity for *recordatio*, which is the ability to call back from forgetfulness, and this only occurs in man.[79] Therefore, to know that something was once here which thereafter was effaced is none other than a power of reason.[80] If this capacity were anything except rational it would be estimative and embellished by rationality.[81] Therefore, *recordatio* is peculiar to man. Animals seem to remember, if they remember at all, in an all or nothing manner according to Avicenna. When they do not remember, he says they do not desire to remember nor think about it thereafter. It is this desire to recall which alone is in man.[82]

Recordatio is a relationship to something which once existed in the soul, that is, in the past; Avicenna says that some (wrongly) think it is similar to a capacity for (*discere*)–learning more/learning what one does not already know.[83] *Recordatio* is movement from an apprehended exterior thing or from an interior thing to others. Similarly, *discere* (*addiscere*) is a movement from the known to the unknown so that the unknown may be known.[84] *Recordatio* is, in effect, an inquiry so that one has in the future what one had in the past. But *discere* is only had/achieved in the future. Hence, *recordatio* does not occur as a result of the acquisitions of necessary intentions (the acquisition and preservation of which is the job of the estimative and memorial faculties of the sensitive soul), but rather *recordatio* proceeds *ad modum signorum*.[85] The soul is moved from an intention or idea which it has that is close to the intention which it no longer has, to that once-possessed intention or idea.[86] If one's mental disposition is different now

---

[79] 'Sed recordatio, quae est ingenium revocandi quod oblitum est, non invenitur, et puto, nisi in solo homine.' (Notes 79–86 all from pp. 40–1.)

[80] 'Cognoscere etenim aliquid ibi fuisse quod postea delectum est, non est nisi virtutis rationalis.'

[81] '... si autem fuerit alterius praeter rationalem, poterit esse aestimationis, sed quae decoratur rationalitate.'

[82] 'Reliqua enim animalia si memorant, memorant tantum; si vero non memorant, memorare non desiderant nec cogitant inde; immo hoc desiderium et hic appetitus solius hominis est.'

[83] 'Recordatio vero est relatio ad aliquid quod habuit esse in anima in praeterito, et imitatur discere secundum aliquid et non imitatur secundum aliud.'

[84] 'Recordatio etenim est motus a rebus apprehensis exterioribus vel interioribus ad alias; similiter discere est motus a cognitis ad incognita ad hoc ut sciantur [sic].'

[85] 'Recordatio vero est inquisitio ut habeatur in futuro quale habebatur in praeterito; discere vero non est nisi ut habeatur aliquid in futuro. Item in recordatione non itur ad id quod intenditur per aliqua quae sequatur acquisitio intentionis necessario, sed ad modum signorum.'

[86] 'Cum enim iam habetur id quod est propinquius intentioni, movetur anima ad intentionem tali dispositione qualis ipsa erat.'

from what it was in the past, even though the form in one's mind is close to the earlier intention, one will not be able to move from the present known to the once known. This is similar to the case where one's mind suggests some book through which is recalled a teacher who taught the book to one; but it is not necessarily the case that in recalling the book and its ideas or intentions, all men will also recall the teacher.[87] However, whatever leads us to know more or something new does necessarily lead us there by definition. Thus, there is a difference between *recordatio* and *discere*.

Avicenna has, therefore, used the traditional language of memory and reminiscence when he has spoken of the sensible soul. When he speaks of the rational soul however, he develops another terminology (already used in part by Isaac Israeli) and distinguishes between *recordatio* and *discere*, a disciplined and conscious recollective search on the one hand, and a power of knowing/learning new things on the other.

He goes on to say that many men find it easier to learn new things than to recollect (*recordari*).[88] Furthermore, the sort of person who is capable of retaining memories but weak in recollecting (*recordatio*) has a mental complexion that is dry and it therefore retains what is apprehended; however, such a person's cerebral matter is not obedient or sufficiently flexible regarding the action of the imagination and its representations when the soul is moved. This must mean that the restless inquiry of recollection (*recordatio*) cannot be undertaken if one cannot creatively respond to images in the imagination, whose substance must be moist rather than dry. Other men are the reverse of this. A person who recollects quickly has a greater *will* to grasp or hold on to mental objects, being more in command of sensible motion and intentions.

Other people are stronger in learning new things in the future but weaker in remembering, since learning new things and remembering old

---

[87] Si autem dispositio fuerit diversa, quamvis subeat mentem forma propinqua aut eius intentio, non tamen oportebit propter hoc moveri; sicut ille cuius mentem subit liber aliquis per quem recordatur magistri qui se docuit eum, non tamen est necesse ut cum recordatur libri et intentionis eius, recordetur etiam magistri sui omnis homo. Via autem quae ducit ad discere, necessario ducit nos, et haec est syllogismus et definitio. (p. 41, ll. 85ff)

[88] Sunt autem plerique homines quibus facilius est discere quam recordari; iste enim naturaliter habet cognoscere necessaria motus; quibusdam vero fit e contrario. Quidam enim ex illis est fortis in memoriter retinendo sed debilis in recordando, eo quod est siccae complexionis quae retinet quod apprehendit, sed materia cum movetur anima non est obediens actionibus imaginationis et eius repraesentationibus; alius vero est contrarius isti; qui enim citius recordantur sunt hi qui magis percipiunt nutus; nutus etenim operantur motum sensibilium ad alias intentiones et qui fuerit perceptibilior nutuum erit citius recordans. Alius vero fortis est discendo sed debilis in memorando, quasi enim inter discere et memorare contrarietas est: ad discendum etenim necesse est ut materia formae interioris sit multum facilis ad imprimendum ei, ad quod non iuvat nisi humor (IV, 3, p. 42, ll. 86–98).

ones are contraries. If one is good at learning new things one necessarily possesses an interior matter that is very easily imprintable with/by forms, and what is of use here is none other than the (moist?) humour; however, a good memory necessarily requires a cerebral matter from which it is difficult to delete impressions in it, and this is the work of a dry cerebral matter. It is difficult to have these two capacities, the capacity to learn more and the capacity to remember, simultaneously. [However, it does appear that the mental complexion required for recollecting and learning more is similar.] Those with good memories do not have much movement in their souls nor are their thoughts (cogitations) widely dispersed: hence those who have much movement and many thoughts do not remember well. Memory with its dry matter requires that the soul is quick to take up forms and that its matter is diligent regarding these forms, and that having them it is not possessed of anything else. Hence, children have humid cerebral material but retain forms in a firm manner. Their souls however are not possessed of those things which adults are possessed of; young people whose cerebral matter is warm and agile regarding motion, also possess a dry cerebral complexion and yet their memories are not like those of infants and children. Young people are in the most favourable position for remembering and learning new things. Old people only possess [moist] cerebral humours which prevent them from remembering [retaining].[89]

Avicenna then goes on to speak about emotions and how we recall them. Someone who feels sadness or anger does so because the memory adopts a similar disposition to the thing which caused these emotions, and therefore the real cause of sadness, anger or pain is none other than forms which were impressed in the interior senses in the past and a similar response now is had (to these forms) to that experienced in the past.[90]

---

[89] Memoriae vero necessaria est materia a qua difficulter deleatur quod impressum est in illa, et ad hoc opus est sicca materia, et ideo difficile est habere illa duo simul. Illi vero sunt memoriores quorum animae non habent multos motus nec disperguntur cogitationes eorum; ille etenim cuius anima habet multos motus et multiplices cogitatus, non bene memorat; ergo memoria, etiam cum sicca materia, eget ut anima sit velox ad formam et ad materiam studio, et ut habens illam non occupetur circa aliam. Unde pueri quamvis sint humidi, tamen firmiter retinent; animae enim eorum non occupantur circa quae occupantur animae magnorum, nec moventur ab eo in quo stant ad aliud; iuvenum autem propter calorem suum et propter motus suos agiles, quamvis complexio sit sicca, tamen memoria eorum non est sicut memoria infantium et puerorum; senibus vero accidit propter humorem qui prevalet in eis non memorare ea quae vident. (IV, 3, p. 42, l. 99–p. 43, l. 12)

[90] Sed aliquando ex dolore aut ira aut ceteris huiusmodi accidit cum memoria aliquid simile dispositioni rei qualiter acciderit: causa vero doloris et irae et tristitiae non est nisi quia eorum quae praeterierunt forma impressa est sensibus interioribus; quae cum redit, facit illud aut simile illius. (p. 43, ll. 12–16)

Furthermore, [being future-orientated], hope and desire are distinct from one another. Hope is an imagining of some thing to which is added an affirmation or opinion that this thing will be again; desire [being past-orientated] however, is an imagination of some thing and a longing for it and a judgement that an absent thing is desirable or pleasant. Fear is the opposite of hope, as its contrary, while diffidence or despair is the privation of hope. *All of these are judgements of the estimative faculty*, and hence are judgements of *intentions* rather than of images.[91]

In effect, to have any of these emotions is to engage the sensible soul. Here one has images of things and by this is meant that one possesses, as images in the soul, the dispositions of things, that is, sadness, pain, memories, which are joined to the body. One must have a body to experience such emotions in the soul, the soul possessing these emotions in imitative forms; this is not the same as saying that these emotions come directly from the body. For instance, one feels pain from a beating and the accident of pain is in the body, while the pain is had in the (internal) senses according to what it means (intention) to sense something whilst the cause of the pain is in the body. There is therefore a distinction between what the body submits to and what is its effect on the sensitive soul, the *passio animae*, the soul's experience.[92] Imagination comes from what is apprehended rather than from what is experienced by the body. It is the apprehended form that one has in the imagination and in the estimation rather than the object which is the natural cause of the interior senses' responses. Therefore, the perceptual act is not achieved in the sense organ. Rather, there must be a transmission of the sensible impression to the anterior ventricle of the brain where the first of the interior senses, the

---

[91] Desiderium quoque et spes faciunt etiam hoc; spes autem aliud est quam desiderium; spes enim est imaginatio alicuius rei cum affirmatione aut opinione quia erit; desiderium vero est imaginatio rei et concupiscentia eius, et iudicare quod delectabitur in illa si affuerit. Timor autem est oppositus spei ad modum contrarietatis, sed diffidentia vel desperatio est eius privatio. Et haec omnia iudicia sunt aestimationis. (IV, 3, pp. 43–4).

[92] Imaginatio vero et concupiscentia et ira et huiusmodi sunt animae sed ex hoc quod est habens corpus, et sunt corporis ex hoc quod principaliter sunt animae ipsius corporis, quamvis sint animae ex hoc quod est habens corpus, non dico ex corpore; similiter sollicitudo, dolor, et tristitia et memoria, horum nullum est accidens corpori ex hoc quod est corpus, sed sunt dispositiones rei coniunctae cum corpore, nec sunt nisi cum est coniunctio cum corpore; habet ergo ea corpus sed propter animam: anima enim habet ea principaliter, quamvis habeat illa ex hoc quod est habens corpus, non dico autem quod habeat illa ex corpore. Sed dolorem habet propter verbera et propter permutationem complexionis, et hoc accidens habet esse in corpore: solutio enim continuitatis et complexio sunt dispositiones corporis ex hoc quod est corpus, et etiam hic dolor habet esse in sensu sentientis secundum quod est sentiens, sed causa corporis.(IV, 4., p. 60, l.64– p. 61, l.79)
'Sed ex imaginatione et timor et dolore et ira principaliter accidit passio animae ...' (IV, 4, p. 61, ll.80–1).

357

common sense, resides and apprehends the sensible form, passing it on to the imagination and the other interior senses, through a process of abstraction and dematerialisation.[93]

By the time Avicenna reaches Book V he is prepared to speak about the very special nature of the human soul distinguishing those characteristics of man which set him off from the rest of living beings. Most characteristic of man is his ability to form universals. Universal intelligible intentions are entirely abstracted from matter as we have already seen. And man can proceed from known intelligibles to a knowledge of unknown intelligibles by means of a process of affirming belief and 'forming'.[94] The highest power of the human soul, man's potential intellect, deals with universals, with truth and falsehood, with the necessary and the possible. But precisely because we are at the level of extreme abstraction, Avicenna says that this capacity to deal with truth and universals does *not* rule over the individual actions of human life! Only when the rational soul focuses downwards towards bodily things does it concern itself with the right and wrong, the lawful and unlawful with regards to particular incidents in human life. Therefore, it is the downward focus of the rational soul which produces morality. But the *truth* of any morality is divorced from the particulars of life's incidents and hence from the specifics of history.

The highest capacity of the human soul is achieved when it trains itself to a proficiency of receiving the light of the separated agent intellect at will and habitually so that man's mind can turn to contemplate the intelligible forms that are separate from all material and temporal limitations. Starting with the exterior senses and proceeding to the interior senses, forms which are successively dematerialised are offered to the intellect. The intellect, by means of the impressions of individual things in the imagination, uses the light of the separated agent intellect to extract universals. The intellect requires the help of the sensitive soul and its interior senses only in the preliminary stages of thought. When the soul has become strong in thinking, it can, says Avicenna, operate alone. Hence, the soul is associated with a body but it does not depend on the body. When the soul gradually acquires an aptitude for turning to the agent intellect

[93] ... imaginatio enim etiam, ex hoc quod est apprehensio, non est de passionibus quas habet corpus principaliter; quamvis ex imaginatione accidat ut tendatur aliquod membrum; hoc enim non habet ex causa naturali, propter quam debeat complexio permutari vel calor augeri vel vapor generari qui diffundatur in membrum ita ut extendatur; sed quia forma habetur in aestimatione, secuta est permutatio in complexione et calor et humiditas et spiritus; et nisi esset illa forma, non haberet natura quid moveret eam. (IV, 4, p. 62, ll.88–95)

[94] ... que autem est magis propria ex proprietatibus hominis est hec: scilicet formare intentiones universales intelligibiles, omnino abstractas a materia ... et procedere ad sciendum incognitu excognitis intelligibilibus: credendo et formando. (V, I.).

in order to contemplate universals, it reaches that supreme stage when it can dispense altogether with the sensitive powers.

Indebted to Aristotle as Avicenna certainly is, his ultimate purpose is a Platonist one: the strict separation of sensory experience from the ultimate act of intellect.[95]

What is important for us is Avicenna's understanding of how the historical individual lives in his world and remembers it. On the one hand, his sensual experiences, sensed through the five external senses, are apprehended as abstract forms of individual experiences by the perceiving faculties of the interior senses. These also act on the dematerialised forms, conserving them, distinguishing amongst them, and evaluating them. The interior sense of memory, lodged in the posterior ventricle of the sensitive soul, conserves those immaterial intentions judged by the estimative faculty as it evaluates the distinct forms in the cogitative imagination which itself can only be filled by copies of things already sensed by the external senses. Although the *cogitativa* is somehow ruled over by reason, the rational soul focusing downward on the body and the sensitive soul, its objects depend entirely on the sensed world beyond the soul. But it also seems clear that any man living an historically specific life stores memories of sense experiences in a mediated and interpreted manner in the memory faculty, that is, what is stored by memory is the already evaluated intentions (or ideas) of the images of things. And as Avicenna makes clear in Book I as well as in the final book of the *De Anima*, estimation is dependent on historically specific social experiences and it is only in such a context that one exercises whatever free will we may have. Whilst the highest power of the human soul deals with a-historical universals, this capacity to deal with truth and universals does not rule over the individual actions of human life. Moral evaluations result from the rational soul's downward focus on the particularities of the experienced world as apprehended by the external and interior senses. And when the estimative faculty is active in a man it ensures that he will refuse to believe in the existence of anything that falls outside his own experience. Technically he will not be able to find a copy of an implausible experience in his imagination for his estimation to work on. And his memory will not, therefore, house anything other than the intentions his estimative faculty has abstracted (and judged according to social norms), intentions or ideas that are abstracted from the immaterial forms of the imagination; these forms are there in the first place because they have been experienced in the world in which the bodily organs operate.

[95] See Aquinas's recognition of Avicenna's Platonism in *ST* Ia Q. 84 a. 4. See the discussion below, ch. 20.

In discussing *recordatio* as a capacity to proceed systematically from what one remembers to what one has forgotten, a process that is peculiarly human and distinguished by man's desire to recall what he once knew, it is still clear that even this kind of intellectual memory search is tied to the sensitive power, the *vis memorialis*, which in turn is tied to the bodily organs. If one has not experienced something at some time in one's own lifetime, and furthermore, evaluated that experience in terms of one's cultural, social milieu, one will not remember it. Man's character is distinctively social, according to Avicenna, and his moral sense is developed from living in a particular culture. The process of abstraction, instrumentally described throughout the *De Anima*, is, even at the level of operation of the internal senses (*cogitativa* and especially *estimativa*) necessarily hedged round by cultural and historical specificities. Man cannot live, cannot even remain alive without society.[96] It is not only that the sensitive soul has a particular way of apprehending what the body experiences, passing on this apprehension to higher interpreting mind. It is also that even at the level of the sensitive soul, estimation is culturally specific, interpretive, and serves to edit out the implausible. Furthermore, Avicenna believes that man alone has the power to teach his associates what is in his own soul through conventional (not natural) signs.[97] And because men, unlike animals, have infinite appetites and infinite capacities, when considered as individual men, they have a natural, infinite means of self-expression. But he implies that language, with its conventional signs, necessarily limits this infinity of experienced expression.[98] So too, men agree on the creation of (social) arts, not through their instincts but through thought and hence there is variation in their creations, unlike the invariable arts of animals who, for instance, build nests, in the same way, instinctively.[99]

There is here an extremely interesting, albeit implicit, distinction being made throughout the entire discussion of the soul's operations: a distinction between a functional description of mind's operations in all men, constant for the species, and a contextualisation of the operations of reasoning. In other words, the medical approach that is so influential in Avicenna's discussion of the sensitive soul, gives way to a philosophical discussion of rational soul where judgements of perceptions are historic-

---

[96] 'Quarum prima est quod esse hominis, in quo creatus est non posset permanere in sua vita sine societate' (v, 1, p. 69).
[97] '... necessarium fuit homini habere naturaliter potentiam docendi alium sibi socium quod est in anima eius signo aut opere.'
[98] '... quod autem habet homo de hoc est ad placitum, eo quod humani appetitus quasi infiniti sunt; unde non potuit homo naturaliter habere sonos sine fine.'
[99] *De Anima*, v, 1. p. 73.

ally and culturally specific. Estimative intuitions of value concerning sensible objects are, for him, to some degree culturally and temporally tuned. If for Aristotle animals too could be described as having a capacity for sagacity, prudence and forethought regarding potential pain and pleasure, good and evil, it is man's intellectual estimation rather than an instinctual estimation that is brought into play. That man alone, *desires* to recall what he once knew but thereafter forgot, is indicative of a capacity for rational estimation – it is 'none other than a power of reason'. *Recordatio* is Aristotle's reminiscence. But Avicenna is clear that if one's mental disposition in the present is not similar to what it was in the past then one will not be able to move from what is presently known to what was once known. What he leaves undiscussed here is just how one's present mental disposition got to be what it now is, how it changed from what it once was other than through the inevitable ageing process which changes the constituency of the different ventricles. From what he says elsewhere he seems to be implying that what one is now is contextually and culturally determined through accumulated experiences that are socially mediated, and if this is the case, then the past, if it was experienced in a different context, is irretrievable as it once was. Hence, not everyone will recall the teacher who taught one a certain book even when one does recall the more general intention of the book itself.

Avicenna does, of course, also refer to the medical theory that a good memory but a lack of skill in *recordatio* (or reminiscence in Aristotle's terms) depend on the complexion of the cerebral matter. Hence, there is a physiological as well as a cultural and psychic dimension to memory. The latter is a further confirmation of Avicenna's ultimate rejection of human, individual subjectivity. His more familiar argument against man's total individualism is, of course, his proposal of the trancendent agent intellect in which all men share when they contemplate universals and truths.[100]

---

[100] 'Cum autem anima liberabitur a corpore et ab accidentibus corporis, tunc poterit coniungi intelligentiae agenti, et tunc inveniet in ea pulchritudinem intelligibilem et delectationem perennem, sicut dicemus suo loco' (*De Anima*, V, 6, p. 150). The reference is to the Metaphysics of the Shifā', IX, 7. The real distinction amongst men seems to be the aptitude to acquire this *intellectus sanctus*.
Debes autem scire quod sapientia sive habeatur ex doctrina sive non, non aequaliter habetur. Sunt etenim quidam discentium qui sunt aptiores ad intelligendum, quorum apititudo, quae est prior ea aptitudine quam praediximus, est fortior. Cum vero homo habet hoc in seipso non aliunde, vocatur haec aptitudo subtilitas; quae aptitudo aliquando in aliquibus hominibus ita prevalet quod ad coniungendum se intelligentiae non indiget multis, nec exercitio, nec disciplina, quia est in eo aptitudo secunda; immo, quia quicquid est, per se scit: qui gradus est altior omnibus gradibus aptitudinis. Haec autem dispositio intellectus materialis debet vocari intellectus sanctus qui est illius generis cuius est intellectus in habitu, sed hic est supremus in quo non omnes homines conveniunt. (V, 6. p. 151)

But his is not an argument which denies historical individuality; rather the reverse. And for our purposes, his diffused discussion of memory is a water shed in the medieval history of the subject, precisely because it was understood in the Latin west as part of the increasingly sophisticated discussion of the nature of the soul's ties with the body.

> Possibile est ergo ut alicuius hominis anima eo quod est clara et cohaerens principiis intellectibilibus, ita sit inspirata ut accendatur ingenio ad recipiendum omnes quaestiones ab intelligentia agente, aut subito, aut paene subito, firmiter impressas, non probabiliter, sed cum ordine qui comprehendit medius terminos (probata quae sciuntur ex suis causis non sunt intelligibilia). Et hic est unus modus prophetiae ... unde congrue vocatur virtus sancta ... (v, 6, p. 153)

The middle term of the syllogism is acquired either *proprio ingenio*, where *ingenium est actus rationis* or *ex doctrina* by which is meant that 'res terminantur sine dubio apud ingenia quas adinvenerunt homines ingeniosi, deinde tradiderunt eas discipulis' (v, 6, p. 152).

Chapter 16

JOHN BLUND, DAVID OF DINANT, THE *DE POTENTIIS ANIMAE ET OBIECTIS*

Once the *De Anima* and the *De Memoria et Reminiscentia* were available in Latin translations, Aristotle's theory of intellect had to be assimilated by a Christian neo-Platonic philosophical and theological tradition. Aided by Avicenna's neo-Platonic interpretation of Aristotle, Latin Christian scholars were then prepared to attempt a synthesis.[1] Gundisalvi was able to describe the human soul as a spiritual substance, the mover of the body and its perfection or form. To this Platonist residue was added the Avicennan notion of the intellect: the human soul was said to contain only a potential intellect whereas the agent intellect was described as an angel (*dator formarum*). The function of the potential intellect was to attend to phantasms or images and this attention prepared it to receive enlightenment from the (separate?) agent intellect whose role was to illuminate the phantasms and create abstract concepts within the potential intellect. In line with Avicenna then, Gundisalvi endowed man with the potential intellect as the highest part of the soul which was joined to the body as its form.[2] The soul then looks upwards to contemplate God above her. Without the Agent Intellect we have no understanding of the truth of a thing. Reason in men's minds (= God, the Agent Intellect) was a treasury of concepts whose function was to transmit intelligible forms into the receptive individual's potential intellect.

No sequal to this Spanish, Christian, Latin reception of the Avicennan Aristotle is known until the early thirteenth century, when one John Blund, an Englishman who was both student and professor at the Univer-

[1] E. Gilson, 'Les sources greco-arabes de l'augustinisme avicennisant', *AHDLMA*, 4 (1929–30), pp. 5–149; Z. Kuksewicz, 'The potential and agent intellect', in *The Cambridge History of Later Medieval Philosophy*, ed. N. Kretzmann, A. Kenny, J. Pinborg (Cambridge, 1982), pp. 595–601.

[2] D. A. Callus, 'Gundissalinus' *De Anima* and the problem of substantial form', *The New Scholasticism*, 13 (1939), pp. 338–55; Gundissalinus' *De Anima* is edited by J. T. Muckle in *Mediaeval Studies*, 2 (1940), pp. 23–103. Gilson, n. 1 above, has argued there is no separate Agent Intellect in the *De Anima* (pp. 23–7). But see R. de Vaux, *Notes et textes sur l'avicennisme latin aux confines des XII–XIII*s. (Paris, 1934).

363

sity of Paris arts faculty, wrote his commentary on the *De Anima* and incorporated, in encyclopedic fashion, much of this neo-Platonised Aristotle. We have already referred to the influence of the Greco-Arabic medical tradition on the physiological sections of the twelfth-century Cistercian tracts on the soul. These indicated the degree to which thinkers were prepared to absorb further physiological reflection combined with a philosophical analysis of the soul. Blund combined Augustine, Boethius and Avicenna in a manner which would be further clarified by mid thirteenth-century writers.[3]

In 1232, Master Henry of Avranches addressed a poem to Pope Gregory IX in support of the candidature of John Blund to the archbishopric of Canterbury.[4] Blund was indeed elected but never consecrated; he became chancellor of York Cathedral and remained there until his death in 1248. We know little else about him. From Henry we know that he studied and lectured at Oxford and Paris on Aristotle's texts newly translated from the Arabic. His regency in arts must have fallen within the first decade of the thirteenth century. He also studied theology in Paris.

At the beginning of the thirteenth century, Aristotle's newly translated *libri naturales* constituted a major intellectual excitement, especially in Paris. Numerous *Commenta* were produced by arts faculty lecturers, drawing on the medical and naturalist traditions made available during the twelfth century. It is thought that Blund wrote his *Tractatus de Anima c.* 1200–04 for arts faculty students either at Oxford or Paris, assimilating Avicenna's *De Anima*, the texts of Aristotle and the *physici*, and grafting this new learning onto the older stocks, especially Augustine's writings.[5]

[3] D. A. Callus, 'The introduction of Aristotelian learning at Oxford', *Proceedings of the British Academy*, 29 (1943), pp. 229–81; D. A. Callus and R. W. Hunt, eds., *Johannes Blund, Tractatus de Anima* (Oxford: British Academy, 1970); D. A. Callus, 'The treatise of John Blund On the Soul', in *Autour d'Aristote, receuil d'études de philosophie ancienne et médiévale offert à Monseigneur A. Mansion* (Louvain, 1955).

[4] J. C. Russell and J. P. Heironimus, eds., *The Shorter Latin Poems of Master Henry of Avranches relating to England* (Cambridge, Mass., 1935) p. 131, ll. 77–86:
Adde quod a puero studiis electus inhesit
primus Aristotilis satagens perquirere libros,
Quando recenter eos Arabes misere Latinis,
quod numquam fertur legisse celebrius alter
aut prius, ut perhibent Oxonia Parisiusque.
Non tamen est contentus eo quasi fine, nec artis
illi mundane suffecit adeptio, donec
humanos regeret divina sciencia sensus,
ad quam translatus lustris duobus et annis
in sudans totidem rexit dominanter in ipsa.

[5] But the following issues treated by Blund – whether imagination and memory are corporeal powers or powers of the soul, and that one knows God through images of creatures – sound similar to the treatment of David of Dinant, c. 1210, who discusses whether the soul is separated from the body and says that Aristotle deals with the idea that

His discussion of memory is an encyclopedic assimilation of conflicting traditions as these confronted scholars at the beginning of the thirteenth century. The work is a school production – series of questions and solutions, overtly citing specific works of Aristotle and Avicenna amongst others.

In speaking *de anima sensibili*, he notes that there are external senses (*deforis*) and internal senses (*deintus*); the body's diverse sensible instruments receive *inmutationes* specific to each sense organ, diverse *impressiones* being received by touching coldness, hotness, and by the eye and the ear receiving impressions appropriate to their own capacities as receptors of sense data.[6] The *vis apprehensiva deintus*, the internal apprehending sense comprises the *sensus communis*, the *vis ymaginativa*, the *vis estimativa* and the *vis memorialis et reminiscibilis*.[7] The soul apprehends through these various facultative powers.[8] Now the sense is a perceptual power (*sensus est vis apprehensiva*) grasping present things to the extent that what is present is so through *inmutationes* received in the corporeal instrument from outside. And everyone agrees that perception is of singulars. And yet some wish to show that the sense may apprehend universals as well.[9] Avicenna for instance, says that a sword is seized by the senses but it is also in the intellect; it is first an impression in the senses but the intellect grasps 'sword' as an aggregate universal of all swords according to its universal intention and hence this falls within the domain of intellect, first having been included in the sense (in an imperceptible way). For instance, light *per se* is seen. But light in terms of what light is, is a universal. In effect, singulars are felt or sensed whereas universals are known, so that we must concede that what is universal *is* sensed but not *as* a universal.[10] As we have already seen it in Avicenna, Blund will go on to argue that the intentions in those individual things that are perceived, can only be abstracted by certain activities of the internal senses of the sensitive soul.

After an elaborate discussion of the five external senses, Blund turns to the lowest interior sense of the sensible soul, the *sensus communis*, citing Augustine as having said that common sense is an interior sense served by the exterior senses.[11] And then following Aristotle's *De Anima*, he says

nothing is known (*intelligere*) without *passiones que fit in instrumento sensus a re sensata* etc. See below, pp. 377–81 on David of Dinant. Blund appears to be familiar with David's arguments.
6 Callus and Hunt, eds., *Johannes Blund, Tractatus de Anima*, 60 p. 18.
7 *Ibid.*, 62, p. 18.
8 *Ibid.*, 74, p. 21.   9 *Ibid.*, 84, p. 23.
10 *Ibid.*, 87, p. 23: 'potest concedi quod id quod est universale sentitur, non tamen universale'.
11 *Ibid.*, 237, p. 63: 'de viribus anime sensibilis apprehensivis'.

that the *sensus communis* receives the impressions of the five external senses; it is through the *sensus communis* that one perceives forms generated in the exterior senses. He also follows Avicenna's distinction between a power of receiving impressions and of retaining these. Some say that *Ymaginatio* has a double *corporeal* power, one which receives the similitudes of exterior bodies and another which retains these similitudes. If this double power of reception and retention is appropriate to the imagination, then we should also be able to speak of memory in this way.[12] But this would only be true if we spoke of imagination and memory as corporeal powers – that is, if we only discussed memory as the posterior cell of the brain, rather than as a power of the soul, and as imagination and memory are powers of the sensible soul, using similitudes of bodily things, such distinctions are inappropriate. The implication is that the *physici* would speak of memory as a corporeal power whereas a philosopher would speak of it as a power of the soul.[13]

What then is the imagination and how is it to be distinguished from other powers of the soul? Blund defines *ymaginatio* as a *vis ordinata* in the highest part of the anterior cerebral cavity, retaining received impressions committed to it by the (exterior) senses. As a retentive power it passively receives similitudes from the *sensus communis*, that is, similitudes of singular things, and through the imagination absent things can also be apprehended. The common sense does not have the capacity to retain singular images received from the five exterior senses, nor can it apprehend absent things, but is aware only of those present.[14] But he says that this means one could show that imagination is the same thing as memory, since imagination apprehends things first existing *in sensu*, and memory is a remembrance of the past, memory apprehending things as they first existed to the senses. What then is the difference between the imagination and the memory?

Avicenna, he says, notes that the *vis estimativa* and the *vis memorialis* both perceive and act at the same time, apprehending things and also composing or dividing these. Through the memory is had both the apprehension/perception of things and the remembrance (*recordatio*) that

---

[12] *Ibid.*, 247, p. 66, and 249, p. 67:
Similiter potest ostendi quod duplex est vis ipsius memorie, et ita plures essent virtutes quam distinguantur, et non esset ymaginatio una sola vis sed plures. Similiter et memoria.
[13] *Ibid.*, 249, p. 67:
Dicendum est quod, ut ostensum est, diverse sunt vires, vis receptiva et vis retentiva, et utraque illarum virium subservit ymaginationi. Et sunt ille due virtutes corporales; nec ponendum est illas duas virtutes esse de ymaginatione, nisi dicatur quod ymaginatio sit vis corporis et non vis anime.
[14] *Ibid.*, 250, p. 67.

things were previously perceived.[15] This recollection that one previously perceived something is known as *compositio*. But the imaginative power only apprehends things described as an image without composing or dividing. Imagination is merely a perceiving capacity and not one which then acts on the image of a subject. Hence by distinguishing two aspects of remembering, a passive perception of imaginative images as well as a simultaneous recognition that such images were previously perceived, the memory is more than a storehouse of images of past experiences but also possesses a self-reflective capacity that is aware of its own past perceptions. Blund will continue along these Aristotelian (rather than Avicennan) lines.[16]

Although one could say that the imagination intuits a thing according to what was first sensed (and therefore can intuit absent things on the basis of having first sensed these things), it is still the case that the imagination does not have its own perception that the thing was previously sensed, that is, the imagination is not reflective on its own activities or on whence its image came, dependent though it is on a previous sense datum. This consciousness of having perceived previously is a capacity of memory.[17] The capacity to distinguish priority in its actions is Blund's way of dealing with Aristotle's reference to the memory having the capacity not only to conserve images but also to know that such an image was previously experienced, so that one 'says in one's soul one has previously experienced something'.

Blund takes up the issue of the presence of universal intentions[18] in singulars when he discusses the next higher internal sense, the estimation. The estimative faculty is located in the middle cerebral cavity and apprehends *intentiones non sensatas* which are in singular and sensible things. By means of apprehending intentions one judges whether something is useful or harmful, and following Avicenna, Blund provides the example of the sheep who discerns the intention of a wolf, harmfulness itself being a

[15] 'Per memoriam enim fit apprehensio rerum et recordatio quod prius eidem res fuerunt apprehense'. Note the use of *recordatio* which implies that rational deliberation and judgement have already been applied.

[16] *Ibid.*, 252, p. 68.
... unde in ipsa recordatione est compositio; per vim autem ymaginativam apprehenditur solummodo res cuius ymago describitur in subiecto illius virtutis, sed non componendo vel dividendo aliquam passionem in aliquo subiecto fit per eam apprehensio. Unde vis ymaginativa apprehendit simpliciter rem non simul operando.

[17] *Ibid.*, 253, p. 68.
Dicendum est ad hoc quod licet ymaginatio intueatur rem secundum quod ipsa fuit prius sensata, non tamen est per ipsam perceptio quod res illa prius fuerit in sensu. Illud enim prius in ymaginationem non cadit, sed in memoriam.

[18] *Intentiones* are akin to Aristotle's 'supposal'. Aristotle *De Anima*, III, 3, 427b 1b f: 'That imagination is not the same kind of thinking as supposal is clear.'

non-sensed property of wolves with regard to sheep, recognisable by the sheep and inspiring it to run away.[19] Intentions are not grasped by the senses nor are they images either in the senses or in the imagination. Intentions are had in the estimative faculty alone by means of apprehension; since this is difficult to understand he says, we can say that a similitude of an intention *is* in the senses and the imagination but the soul cannot perceive it by means of sense and imaginative faculties, these powers not being of a concording nature with intentions. However, the estimation's faculty *is* of a like nature with that which is *per se et proprie* the subject of an intention and hence the estimative power can perceive intentions. And it is through the power of estimation that one apprehends universals.

But then are we saying that a sheep's estimative faculty enables it to grasp universals? Blund says that universals are not apprehended by animals. First we know that estimation does not apprehend anything other than singular things. Therefore, the animal estimative faculty does not apprehend that it must flee wolves, but rather, that it must flee this particular wolf. Likewise, if estimation is concerned with composition and division as well as with truth and falseness, animals are able to apprehend what is a particular case of the true or false but not according to a principle of truth and falseness, since it is not through the estimative capacity that one distinguishes (principles of) truth and falseness but through intellect and reason which animals do not possess.[20]

Blund has somewhat simplified Avicenna's argument, not distinguishing a cogitative imagination from an animal imagination, nor has he spoken of the rational soul's activity, when combined in man with the imaginative and estimative powers, to lead to a discovery of laws of contingent things or the invention of arts. Blund seems to reduce the estimative capacity here to one which works alone on sense images as they are retrieved from the imagination. Where Avicenna considered that the

---

[19] *Ibid.*, 254, p. 69: 'Nocitiva, ut illa proprietas que est in lupo propter quam ovis fugit lupum'.

[20] *Ibid.*, 260, p. 70:
Dicendum est quod universalia non possunt apprehendi a brutis animalibus. Estimatio autem non apprehendit nisi singularia: unde secundum vim estimativam non apprehenditur quod a lupo sit fugiendum, sed apprehenditur quod ab hoc lupo sit fugiendum, qui est in sensu, vel prius fuit in sensu ...
261, p. 71:
Dicendum quod licet in vi estimativa sit compositio vel divisio et circa illam sit veritas vel falsitas, non tamen per vim estimativam percipitur ibi esse veritas vel falsits, sed per intellectum tantum et per rationem. Unde a brutis, etsi percipitur id in quo est veritas vel falsitas, non tamen percipitur ab his verum secundum quod verum, vel falsum secundum falsum. Non enim apprehendunt veritatem vel falsitatem, cum intellectu careant et ratione.

animal *estimativa* was a kind of natural instinct which judges on the basis of sensory experiences, he also said that in man it operates in cases where one refuses to believe in the existence of something beyond ones own experience. Furthermore, Avicenna noted that the human estimative faculty, when embellished by reason (*decoratur rationalitate*) enables men to know that something was once present which thereafter was effaced. Blund has none of this here. He seems to regard estimation as an animal capacity which has no distinguishing characteristics even when in man. Since the *estimativa* is tied so closely to bodily images it can be assumed that universals are in things but are not sensed as universals. Therefore, the only example Blund gives of estimation in operation is that where a sheep apprehends a particular wolf's intention and rightly flees.

However, when Blund turns to the next higher internal sense, the memory, he does anything but oversimplify: rather he provides an elaborate discussion of various, sometimes conflicting, memory theories, harmonising them in a most interesting way.

Memory he defines as a *vis ordinata* located in the posterior cerebral cavity receiving impressions from the estimation and retaining these. And because images rest in the memory, the will turns the *aciem animi*, that highest part of the soul, towards the memory to examine those images through which it contemplates things previously apprehended.[21] Blund then presents an interesting, apparently current objection. Since the memory revisits, through images resting in its faculty, those things which were first contemplated and thereby revisits itself, examining itself, then in the memory there must be an image of priority. The noun 'priority' cannot be apprehended unless the thing which this noun signifies is recognised. But it cannot be recognised unless the memory retains it. The image of 'priority' therefore is in the memory since it remembers itself as being previously perceived. But nothing imprints images in the memory unless at a time when this thing was present to the memory. So that if there is an image of 'priority' in the memory there must have been a 'priority' in its present, imposing its image on the memory, and this would mean that 'priority' or the past 'is' which surely must be false.[22]

---

[21] *Ibid.*, 262 , p. 71:
Memoria est vis ordinata in posteriori parte concavitatis cerebri recipiens impressiones ab estimatione et eas retinens. Et quia in memoria reponuntur ymagines, voluntas convertens aciem animi ad memoriam invenit ibi ymagines per quas intuetur res prius apprehensas: unde memoria est ad memorandum prius apprehensa.

[22] *Ibid.*, 263, p. 71.
Sed obicitur. Memoria recolit per ymaginem repositam in suo instrumento res quas prius intuebatur et recolit se prius eas inspexisse. Sed huiusmodi memorari non potest nisi ita sit quod ipsa apprehendat hoc ipsum prius: sed quicquid apprehendit per ymaginem apprehendit. Ergo memoria est ymago prioritatis.

Furthermore, it is argued that since the memory takes up species or images from the estimation as the nearest and previous faculty, are we to say that the image of *prioritas* was first in the estimation? What then is the difference between the estimation or even the imagination and the memory?[23] And since *cognitio* of a thing precedes the memory of it, there can be no memory of anything unless it was first in the soul as images. But if the images are already in the soul, the soul knows the thing through its received images and therefore someone who remembers a thing first had to know it.[24] To recognise a thing, you remember it, and if you remember then you first knew it and therefore there can be no *cognitio prima*. How then does *cognitio* of something occur? He tells us that there is a similar ambiguity in Plato's *Meno* where it says that nothing is ever added to our knowledge unless we already know it; that is, that we simply remember what we already know.[25]

Blund tries to provide an acceptable solution to this long enduring logical and epistemological problem by answering that *prioritas* can be accepted by the memory since through the memory we revisit the things we previously saw. But the image of 'priority' is relinquished in the memory to presentness when the present thing imprints its image in the memory, and this image which then is a similitude in the present will be, ever after this time of impression, an image of 'priority' and of the past.[26] It is, indeed, the same in the case where 'now' is present and after this it will be past, and it is said it will be past at some time in the future.[27]

Now we know that the memory contemplates through memories deposited in the memory faculty, but there is a distinction to be made between the image, the subject of the image and the memory itself as an active capacity. The image represents the subject and is caused by the thing of

264, p. 71:
Preterea. Audito nomine prioritatis non apprehenderetur prioritas nisi agnosceretur res que illo nomine significatur; sed non agnosceretur nisi memoria eam retineret. Reliquitur ergo ymago prioritatis est in memoria, cum ipsa meminit se illud prius percepisse. Sed nihil imprimit ymaginem in memoria nisi quando ipsa res presens adest. Si ergo in memoria est ymago prioritatis aliquando affuit prioritas in presentia sui ei imponens ymaginem. Ergo tunc potuit vere dici prioritas est, quod est falsum.'

[23] *Ibid.*, 265, pp. 71–2.   [24] *Ibid.*, 266, p. 72.
[25] *Ibid.*, 268, p. 72.
Secundum hoc occurret Menonis ambiguitas, qui dicebat neminem aliquid addiscere nisi id quod ipse prius novit; quoniam si discit, novit in cognitionem eius quod discit; et si cognoscit, meminit illud, et ita si discit, meminit. Et ita a primo non discit aliquid nisi id quod prius novit.'
[26] *Ibid.*, 269, p. 72: 'cum res presens imprimit memorie suam ymaginem, et illa ymago que tunc fuit presentie similitudo semper post illud tempus impressionis erit ymago prioritatis et preteritionis.'
[27] *Ibid.*, 269, pp. 72–3: 'Illud idem enim quod nunc est presens post hoc erit preteritum, et dicetur fuisse prius in quolibet tempore quod modo est futurum.'

which it is the image, the thing being the subject. But is the subject to be regarded as the being or essence of its represented image? It is also said that memory remembers when it remembers itself so that memory remembers memory remembering. The memory, therefore, contemplates itself and there must, it is said, be two images through which it apprehends both its image and itself in the remembered image. How, it is asked, are these two images formed if the estimation did not first apprehend both of them? The problem is obviously complicated by an attempt to come to terms with what Augustine says of memory remembering itself in the *Confessions*, X, 12.

According to Blund the memory is its own subject and it remembers itself remembering through an imagination of that thing which, when remembered, was recalled (*recordatio*); through the act of remembering, something is in effect recalled, the image being firmly placed in the memory through this activity. Hence the memory contemplates itself not through having a representing image of itself but through the effect proceeding to its cause. Blund seems to be trying to deal with the active and passive aspects of remembering simultaneously, rather than distinguishing two images, the memory itself and the memory image.[28]

If it is asked why memory remembers itself remembering but sight is not able to see itself seeing, this is because in memory is deposited images which lead to absent things. Memory is of those things previously contemplated by the soul whereas sight does not retain the images of things seen. Absent visible things cannot be images to sight because sight only deals

---

[28] *Ibid.*, 271, p. 73:

Item. Quicquid intuetur memoria, intuetur per ymaginem repositam in subiecto memorie; sed contingit aliquem recolere quod illa ymago est in aliquo subiecto; sic ergo intuetur memoria suum subiectum. Sed aliud est ymago et aliud subiectum ymaginis. Ergo in ipso subiecto memorie, quanto illud memoria intuetur, est ymago representans illud subiectum. Queritur ergo a quo causetur illa ymago in esse; non nisi a re cuius est illa ymago, et illa res est subiectum in quo ipsa est ymago. Ergo ipsum subiectum constituit in esse suam ymaginem que in ipso est; ergo idem in seipsum agit, quod esse non potest.

272, p. 73:
Memoria meminit quandoque se meminisse, et ita memoria meminit memoriam meminisse. Intuetur ergo memoria seipsam; intuetur etiam hoc ipsum meminisse. Invenit ergo duas ymagines per quas apprehendit illa duo .... Queritur ergo qualiter ille due ymagines formentur in subiecto memorie, cum estimatio eas prius non apprehenderit.

273, pp. 73–4:
Dicendum est quod memoria apprehendit subiectum illud in quo reponuntur ymagines sine ymagine representante illud subiectum. Quoniam illud subiectum semper presto est ipsi memorie; se meminisse autem meminit per ymaginationem illius rei cuius rei per illud meminisse fuit recordatio; quoniam per illud meminisse fuit recordatio in effectum; quoniam per illud meminisse fuit firmius insita illa ymago in memoria; et cum illud meminisse fuerit a memoria per apprehensionem eius quod est meminisse, intuetur memoria seipsam per effectum procedens ad suam causam; causata enim sunt suarum causarum vestigia.

371

with present things that are imageable. Memory, however, can remember itself remembering whereas sight cannot see itself seeing.[29]

Blund then turns to deal with the difference between remembering and recalling, and says it is known that Aristotle distinguishes at the end of the books *De Anima* between remembering and recalling saying: the difference is not only with regard to time, but also in that both men and animals can remember whereas only men can recall. The cause of this is that recalling is like a syllogism (where we reason) that something was seen or heard or happened before. Therefore, reminiscence is only of universals, but remembering is both of universals (intentions) and singulars; and Aristotle says that meditation helps the memory in recalling. Blund is very terse here, appearing to assume that his students know the discussion in Aristotle's *De Memoria et Reminiscentia* rather than in the *De Anima*. This may be a further indication that *De Memoria* was seen as an appendix to the *De Anima*.

Blund then proceeds to discuss what happens when we forget. He believes that this process of recalling what is effaced in the memory is an act of a rational mind's reminiscence and he is attempting to come to terms with Augustine's *Confessions* and the *De Trinitate* by means of Aristotle and Avicenna. He says that one can say that forgetfulness is the deletion in the memory of the resting image so that oblivion is the privation of images through which the *recordatio* had been made. If there is no such image, then the memory cannot contemplate what it has forgotten. Now if one has totally forgotten something it is not possible for the memory to consider it, because it forgets itself to be this thing. But if part of the memory of the thing is held on to, and yet not perfectly held, then one can reflect that something has been forgotten, memory remembering itself previously having known it. This is like someone knowing a proposition through some medium which was the reason for retaining the images of this proposition, and yet the medium by which the proposition is appropriated is deleted. The image will none the less be retained as a universal while the image of the special medium, in particular, will be deleted. (This is similar to Avicenna's discussion of recalling a book's intentions but not the medium, the teacher, who taught you the book.) Through the medium's image as a universal, the memory can reflect that

---

[29] *Ibid.*, 274, p. 74:
Si autem queritur quare ita sit quod memoria meminit se meminisse et visus non videre possit se vidisse, dicendum est quod hoc contingit quia in memoria reponuntur ymagines, et manent rebus absentibus. Ideo memoria est eorum que prius intuebatur anima, visus autem est non retinens ymagines rerum visarum. Immo absentibus rebus visibilibus absunt earum ymagines a visu; et ideo visus est presentium tantum, et non potest visus videre se vidisse, sicut memoria se meminise.

the soul, through *some* medium, had knowledge of this proposition but there will be a defect in this similitude of the particular medium and hence memory will reflect on its having forgotten through which particular medium the knowledge of the proposition came.[30]

The soul can turn itself to the resting image in the memory by reflecting on the image being here; it is only through present images which are similitudes of things that one can think about absent things and those at a distance. The soul thinks of things of which it has images as signs or vestiges, just as the image in a mirror is a sign of a thing. Just as the soul perceives present images representing to it an absent thing, so the memory revisits the image here, memory revisiting the soul's knowledge of this image. Hence, images existing in the memory will be of some image already in the memory, and by reason of this second image there will be a third and so on to infinity. But Blund asks: If one image has another image, does it have it *per se* or *per accidens*? Blund believes it impossible for there to be an infinite unending number of memory images. And yet if the second image is had *per accidens* rather than *per se* he asks by what accident is it had? He says one can assign no accident to the image of the image in the memory, leaving the subject here.[31]

Next, it is asked how God, who is the first cause of all, can be accepted by the soul in its intellect and memory, since this cannot be through images. Since an image is finite, and the first cause is infinite, then the first cause has no image which can represent it and the first cause is not contemplated through images either in intellect or memory. Should we say that the first cause of all is incomprehensible and above all reason and

[30] *Ibid.*, 279, p. 75:
Solutio. Dicendum est quod si aliqua res sit totaliter oblita, non potest memoria recolere se oblitam esse illius rei. Sed si memoria partem illius rei teneat, et eam non perfecte teneat, propter illum defectum recolit se oblitam fuisse illius rei, et per illam partem que retinetur a memoria, meminit memoria se prius scivisse illam. Ut si aliquis sciverit aliquam propositionem per aliquod medium quod fuerit ratio illius scientie potest retinere memoria ymagines illius propositionis, deleta ymagine representante medium illi propositioni appropriatum; retinebit tamen ymaginem medii in universali, et erit deletio ymaginis ipsius specialis medii in particulari. Unde per ymaginem medii in universali recolet memoria quod animus per aliquod medium habuit scientiam ipsius propositionis; sed propter defectum illius similitudinis medii particularis appropriati illi propositioni recolit memoria se oblitam fuisse per quod medium animus venit in scientiam propositionis.

[31] *Ibid.*, 281, p. 76:
Si ymago habeat ymaginem, aut prima constituet secundam per se aut per accidens. Si per se, pari ratione et secunda tertiam, et tertia quartam per se, et sic in infinitum. Sed si aliquis per se et proprie est causa alicuius secundum quod ipsum est, ipso existente existit eius effectus. Cum eo ergo erunt simul constitute in effectum infinite ymagines in memoria; quod esse non potest, quoniam ubi est infinitas ibi non terminus. Si per accidens, queritur per quod accidens, et per quid aliud ab ipsa ymagine constituetur ymago ymaginis in memoria non est assignare.

intellect, since the first cause has neither matter nor form and what is intelligible is such only through matter or form? What then are we signifying when we name 'God'? Blund's solution is that we say that an existing image in the memory is not just any image of something else, for the image is first the memory itself, this memory contemplating itself. However, the memory also examines exterior things through images.[32] Therefore, it is said that the first cause is not contemplated by the sight of the soul (*anime acies*) through internal habitual images, but through things apprehended from outside which are the effects of the first cause. Therefore, creatures are signs or vestiges of the creator. And the soul, in understanding creatures, comes to a knowledge of the creator, just as through a knowledge of the good the soul comes to know the highest good.[33]

In the memory rest the images to which the will turns the sight of the soul in order to contemplate the things of which these are images. Thus, memory is like a stomach of the mind and a hiding place. Through memory is had a contemplation of things previously apprehended, but just as it is appropriate for someone to reflect on himself having previously apprehended sensible things, so too someone can reflect on himself apprehending universals like genera and species which are not sensible but only intelligible. Therefore, we must say that memory reflects on its universals as well as on sensibles.

Both Augustine and Aristotle note that animals have memories of their nests but does this mean they understand and remember 'nestness' as a universal? Since intellect and reason alone deal with universals, animals cannot be said to contemplate universals (for example, nestness) through memory. Since memory in man is stronger and more subtle than in beasts, because man's intellect is able to accept universal forms, memory in man is unique in that only his *vis apprehensiva* is a *vis* of a soul that is rational.[34]

---

[32] *Ibid.*, 285, pp. 76–7:
Dicimus quod ymaginis existentis in memoria non est alia ymago. Cum enim illa ymago sit presto illi memorie, ipsa memoria seipsa eam intuetur; sed res extra per ymagines inspicit.

[33] *Ibid.*, 286, p. 77:
Dicendum est quod primam causam non intuetur anime acies tantum per ymagines intus habitas, sed per res apprehensas extra que sunt effectus cause prime: creature enim sunt signa et vestigia creatoris. Sic ergo anima intelligendo creaturam venit in intelligentiam creatoris, et per cognitionem boni quod hic est venimus in cognitionem summi boni'.
Compare this with the pantheism of David of Dinant, pp. 377–80 below, who says Plato agreed 'mundum esse [deum] sensibilem'.

[34] *Ibid.*, 295, p. 79.
Dicendum est quod fortior et subtilior est memoria in homine quam in brutis animalibus propter intellectum, qui est in homine, qui accipit formas universales; et memoria potest postea easdem accipere, cum quelibet vis apprehensiva in homine sit vis illius anime que est rationalis.

Blund wishes us to understand that man's rational soul is not affected by sensible forms and the soul is not the body. The soul is an incorporeal substance.[35] Therefore, when the soul measures exterior space through its images to which it turns then these images are deposited in the memory cell which is corporeal and is not to be considered the soul. Only the intelligible images rest in the soul.[36] This means that when we speak of perceiving or apprehending we say that the power of perceiving is in the soul just as it is in the subject, and the soul can contemplate the *passiones corporis* without these *passiones* being present in it with respect to their essences. As a superior reason is assigned to man as a perfection, it is this reason which turns its intentions to the inmutations formed in the body, having these only as similitudes rather than as essences. The soul, existing in the body, can contemplate images formed in its body but not as these are present with regard to their essences but only as their images. Blund understands and follows Avicenna in this.[37]

Thereafter, Blund takes up the current positions on the various aspects of the intellect, speaking of the soul turning itself to the body over which it reigns as well as turning itself to the similitudes and images stored in the memory where what he calls the formal intellect in man mediates between these images and the Giver of Forms. He says some authors wish us to understand that the intellect turns to a form impressed by the intelligence as its minister,[38] the Giver of Forms as its authority, so that some call the agent intellect an angel which is the minister of man's soul.[39] He speaks, however, of some believing that the *intellectus agens* is a *vis anime apprehensiva* apparently in the soul rather than above it, abstracting universals from things and their accidents.[40] And the intellect *in habitu* is an intellect resting in the soul to which the will turns the *aciem animi*, in order for it to become the *anima intelligens actu*.

[35] *Ibid.*, 303, p. 82: 'quod anima est substantia incorporea'.
[36] *Ibid.*, 303, p. 82:
Dicendum est quod quando anima metitur spatia terrarum vel spatia firmamenti per ymagines eorum ad quas ipsa se convertit, tunc sunt ipse ymagines reposite in cellula memoriali, que corporea est, et non in ipsa anima. Sole enim ymagines intelligibiles reponuntur in anima.'
[37] *Ibid.*, 308, p. 83:
Solutio. Dicimus quod potentia percipiendi est in anima ut in subiecto, et potest intueri passiones corporis, licet ipsa ibidem non sit cum ipsis passionibus presens secundum sui essentiam; quia, ut assignata est ratio superius, ipsa semper, ut suam habeat perfectionem, habet convertere suas intentiones ad inmutationes formatas in corpore, et omnes illas potest intueri inclusa in corpore habens se ad similitudinem centri ... Similiter anima existens in corpore potest intueri ymagines formatas in ipso corpore, non tamen erit presens secundum sui essentiam cum ipsis ymaginibus.
[38] See Isaac Israeli, ch. 15 above.   [39] *Ibid.*, 344, p. 94.
[40] *Ibid.*, 341, p. 93: 'Intellectus agens est vis anime apprehensiva rerum universalium abstrahendo eas ab accidentibus.'

In concluding with the question whether there is a world soul, he says that he does not believe the world to have a soul other than the holy spirit.[41]

John Blund's *Tractatus de Anima*, and in particular his treatment of memory, has provided us with an important series of arguments in question and answer format. Here, we can observe the issues that were at the heart of university arts faculty debates concerning an anthropology that would absorb the medical *and* philosophical traditions available at the beginning of the thirteenth century.

As we have seen, the problem that was central to the biological as well as philosophical writings of Aristotle, as well as to the earlier neo-Platonic writings of the school of Chartres, was none other than the relation between the body and the soul as thinking mind. By the turn into the thirteenth century, scholars had a mass of material to harmonise in order to answer the fundamental question: *Utrum aliquid de anima separabile sit a corpore?* The growing tendency to represent the human *body* as an image of the world followed on from that earlier tradition in which man's *soul* was taken to be an obscure image of God. Now that the biological and medical worlds offered their information, the question of the relation of soul to body was 'physicalised'. One could link the senses, the imagination and the reason to bodily organs, especially if the *sensus*, the *imaginatio* and the *ratio* were lodged in the *cellulae capitis*. Aristotle had said that there could be no intellectual understanding without images based on sense experience.

According to the neo-Platonic tradition we have already examined (and as seen in the works of Thierry of Chartres and his disciple Clarembald of Arras), the soul perceives *either* with the aid of corporeal organs (through the *sensus, imaginatio* and the *ratio*) *or* without their aid and by itself (*intelligentia, intellectibilitas*). The soul thereby acquires either a knowledge that is mixed and uncertain (*opinio*) when dependent on the senses, or else it acquires an infallible knowledge (*intelligentia*) and the latter is only proper to God and a few god-like humans. But with the increasing availability of the medical writings of the ancient *physici* and their Arabic commentators, as well as the *libri naturales* of Aristotle, the question was once again raised: *Utrum aliquid de anima separabile sit a corpore?* It was answered in perhaps its most radical form, by Innocent III's former

---

[41] *Ibid.*, 360, p. 98. Compare David of Dinant, *Quaternuli*, fragmentum P¹ and P², *tractatus naturalis*, fol. 214 ra f, ed. Marian Kurdziałek, p. 71: 'Manifestum est igitur unam solam substanciam esse, non tantum omnium corporum, sed etiam animarum omnium et eam nichil aliud esse, quam ipsum Deum.' See below, on David of Dinant.

chaplain, David of Dinant.[42] His *Quaternuli,* or collection of extracts, paraphrases and citations from Aristotle in particular, and his knowledge of the Greek originals, provided arts faculty students and lecturers with a rational anthropology that would be seen as far too radical and physiological by church authorities.[43] In 1210, his works were condemned, burnt, and the *libri Aristotelis de naturali philosophia et commenta* were forbidden to be read either publicly or in private in Paris. A serious analysis of the relationship between soul and body, and the consequences for memory as Aristotle understood this, would not be publicly attempted again until mid century. What did David of Dinant and like-minded natural philosophers say that was so radical?

According to David, there are three things in the soul: the sense, imagination and desire. *Sensus* is the soul's perception of that which is an experience in the body.[44] The sense undergoes an experience from something outside and brought to it either through a medium or without a medium. The medium undergoes a sensed thing and then activates the sense instrument of the body. David equates experience (*passiones*) with what other authors call *inmutationes* or *impressiones*. For instance, when we speak of vision, we mean that something is perceived which the eye first experienced, for example, colour, which comes to the eye via the medium of air. Now, the eye is the mirror of the soul and David goes on to speak of its physical qualities, its surfaces, its moisture and its susceptibility to light.[45] He gives Plato's interpretation of sight and then shows Aristotle to have proved him wrong. The particulars of the argument are not important here except to indicate how keen he is to show Aristotle to be the master in physiological explanation throughout the *tractatus naturalis.*

Speaking of imagination, David says that imagination depends on preexisting sensation, so that if one has not previously seen something one cannot imagine it. When we speak of chimeras or anything else which cannot be seen and experienced, it is necessary that someone imagines parts of things by means of similitudes of those things which he *has* seen and the *imagination* somehow joins these similitudes together. The *sensus* and the imagination occur in the same part of the body, (anterior ventricle – but not said), differing only in that the *sensus* of some perceiver is an experience (*passionis*) had in the sense instrument from sensed things,

---

[42] Marian Kurdziałek 'L'idée de l'homme chez David de Dinant', in *Images of Man in Ancient and Medieval Thought . . . for G. Verbeke* (Louvain, 1976), pp. 311–22.

[43] Marianus Kurdziałek, ed., *Davidis de Dinanto, Quaternulorum fragmenta,* (Studia Mediewistyczne, 3, Warsaw, 1963).

[44] 'Sensus est perceptio anime earum que in corpore fiunt passionem.' Fragmentum P¹ and P², ed., Kurdziałek, pp. 65ff.

[45] *Ibid.,* p. 66.

whereas the imagination is an experience which remains in the sense instrument; both perceptions, and not the whole external thing brought inwards, are *passiones* which are signs or vestiges of preexisting experiences, as Aristotle says, for we are told that Aristotle emphasises: *non est intelligere sine fantasmate*. Hence, the experiences in the *sensus* and in the imagination are phantasms dependent on sense data. Plato said that the imagination could also perceive ideas so that ideas are imaged forms of a body. But Aristotle rejected this proving that there could not be ideas for everything.[46]

Furthermore, Aristotle said memory was the same kind of thing as imagination since memory works on the remains of phantasms located in the imagination. When we remember, we are investigating phantasms, now housed in the memory.[47] David then goes on to describe the workings of imagination when we are asleep.

We may recall that Abelard rejected Aristotle where he believed him to be saying that the images in the imagination were the same as the memory images; here, we see David arguing that the images which are *fantasmata*, *are* the same in imagination and memory, the difference only being that memory as a separate faculty works on them when they are located in itself, drawing them first from imagination.

Later in the same tract David turns to discussing another threesome in the soul: *scientia et intellectus et voluntas*.[48] Each one of these can be considered *passibilis*, that is, subject to impressions or experience: for instance when *scientia* is *passibilis* it is sensed, and when the intellect is *passibilis* it is imagination [sic]. When the will is *passibilis* it is desire. He has previously discussed how, according to Aristotle, the first and universal instrument of all sensation is the heart rather than the brain (against Galen and his followers) and now says that the *sensus* is nothing other than a perception of an experience which is had in the sense instrument from the things sensed. Similarly, imagination is impossible without having experienced something in the senses, imagination perceiving this experience as a sign or vestige of the sense experience. Furthermore, emotion or desire

[46] *Ibid.*, p. 67:
... ymaginacio autem perceptiva est passionis, que remanet in instrumento sensus a re sensata, ymaginacio autem perceptiva est passionis, etsi non tota, saltem tamen eius aliqua pars, quam Aristoteles signum vel vestigium preexistentis passionis appellat. Id ipsum autem fantasiam vocat, ubi ait: non est intelligere sine fantasmate ... Visum autem est Platoni ymaginationem perceptivam esse idearum et ideas esse ymaginarias corporum formas; cui Aristoteles repugnat, dicens et probans ydeas omnino non esse.

[47] *Ibid.*, p. 67: 'Dicit enim Aristoteles memoriam etiam idem esse, quod ymaginacionem, nam memoriam efficit remanencia fantasmatum in loco ymaginacionis. Rememoracio vero est investigacio fantasmatum in loco memorie.'

[48] *Ibid.*, pp. 69ff.

(*affectus*) cannot be had in the soul unless first it was experienced in the heart through systolic and diastolic experiences or through the heating or cooling of the blood in the heart. Since David sees prior sense experiences as the origin of knowledge, intellection and will, and thereby closely ties together the soul to the body, he is aware that Aristotle himself had to ask the crucial question of whether the soul is separable from the body. Thus far, the radical nature of David's physiological continuum between soul and body is a significant departure from earlier writings, but not unlike Galen's attempt to see the body, its parts and experiences as the very cause of the soul.[49]

David goes on to argue that none of the three aspects of the soul called *scientia, intellectus,* and *voluntas* can be had *except through body* and this means that nothing is experienced except through a *passio corporis,* a bodily experience.[50]

As we shall see, David went even further and argued that man's soul reflects better than the souls of other creatures, the visible world, and that human souls *like human bodies* are only individualised manifestations of the divine. His pantheism, expressed in a belief that man, body and soul, is an image of the world, was rightly seen as a radical anthropology. But it was a major aspect of this pantheistic anthropology to argue for a continuity of soul and body, reducing some of the highest aspects of soul to the soul's responses to the physiological experiences of sense data, and this constituted a major danger to the prevalent doctrine that man's soul was, ultimately, capable of acting in its most perfect manner, alone and untouched by the world of experience.

David did, however, try to come to terms with the idea of something being essentially separable and called it mind. Mind alone is *impassibilis* and only here are remembered (*memorata*) the threesome *scientia, intellectus* and *voluntas*. He explains this by saying that in whatever way a body is had *ad ylen,* then it is had *ad mentem*. What does this mean? He says there is only one mind but many souls, just as there is only one *yle* and

---

[49] *Ibid.*, pp. 69–70:
Dico igitur tria esse in anima: scienciam et intellectum et voluntatem; horum autem unumquodque est passibile. Dico passibilem scienciam esse sensum, passibilem vero intellectum ymaginacionem, passibilem vero voluntatem desiderium seu affectum. Nam sensus nichil aliud percipit quam passionem que fit in instrumento sensus a re sensata. Quoniam vero ymaginacionem impossibile est fieri nisi ex preexistente sensu, manifestum est, quod ymaginacio nichil aliud percipit quam signum vel vestigium passionis sense. Sed nec effectus potest fieri in anima nisi per inmutacionem (sistoles) vel diastoles, sive secundum calefactionem vel frigefactionem sanguinis, sive spiritus qui est in corde. Querit autem Aristoteles utrum aliquid in anima separabile sit a corpore.

[50] *Ibid.*, p. 69: 'Igitur nullum trium predictorum posse fieri nisi a corpore, quando nullum horum fit nisi cum passione corporis.'

many bodies. *Yle* is therefore a primary essential substance. Mind and *yle* are not subject to experience; it is only the body and the soul which are subject to experience. And both mind and *yle* do not differ one from the other. So that when the potential or passive intellect which is in the soul, understands something bodily, the mind comprehends only the *yle*. But the passive intellect, which he calls *ymaginacio* (!) does not comprehend anything unless it is assimilated to things sensed, and this passive intellect cannot therefore understand *yle* unless it has a similitude of it. Where could it possibly find such a similitude of *yle* especially since similitudes are experienes and subject to *passiones*? It is the separable mind and *yle* which work to collect together singular similitudes and David momentarily leaves behind his physiological Aristotelianism to accept support from Plato. Plato, he says, called the world the sensible aspect of God. And mind, which is not subject to change and experience, is nothing other than God. If the world, then, is the same as God and the world is perceivable by the senses as Plato, Zeno, Socrates and others said, then *yle* or the world is God and the form which enters *yle* is none other than God making Himself sensible. This must mean that there is only one essential substance, but it is not corporeal but rather 'the soul of all' which is God himself. This substance from which all bodies come, is called *yle*. And the substance from which all souls come is called mind. Hence, David concludes that God himself is the reason or mind of all souls and *yle* is the basis of all bodies. Both *yle* and mind appear to be, in origin, above nature, but somehow expressed in the world and sensed by us, as particular experiences. It appears that the only way an individual can know anything about separable, unchanging and impassive mind/*yle* is *through* experiencing the corporeity of the world. The essential separation of mind and *yle* from soul and body is not grasped by an individual's passive intellect but only by a divine mind. Man in all his aspects, corporeal and spiritual, is only a sensible image of the world.[51]

[51] *Ibid.*, p. 71:
... aut de anima nichil esse separabile, aut non. Aliquid est separabile in anima a corpore in esse, quod nos mentem dicimus. Unde manifestum est, mentem esse quod impassibile in quo sunt memorata tria eo, quod impassibilia sunt. Dico autem, quod quemadmodum se habet corpus ad ylen, ita se anima ad mentem: si autem sint corpus et yle passiva, ita anima et mens passiva. Dico autem, quod una sola est mens, multe vero anime; et una sola yle et multa vero corpora ... manifestum est, quod una sola est mens et una sola yle. Querendum autem, utrum mens et yle unum sint aut diversa. Cum igitur sola passiva different ad se invicem, videtur mentem et ylen nullo modo differe, cum neutrum eorum sit subiectum passioni. Rursus autem, quemadmodum passivus intellectus, qui est in anima, comprehendet solum corpus, ita et impassibilis intellectus, qui est in mente, comprehendet solam ylen. Manifestum est etiam, quod passivus intellectus, (hoc est ymaginacio) non comprehendet esse, nisi assimiletur rei sense, nam hoc supra naturam; per simile vero videtur quod nec passibilis intellectus possit comprehendere ylen, nisi

It is possible to see some of these views already surfacing in Blund's *Tractatus de Anima* and this may cause the proposed date of the work to be altered to the years during which David of Dinant was making his presence felt in Paris. The authorities, however, realised by 1210 that enough had been said for Aristotle's *libri naturales* to be seen as a real danger to a neo-Platonised Christianity. A condemnation was issued; and from Christmas of that year, no one was to read in public David's works or Aristotle's *libri naturales*.[52]

If arts faculty members were not to read Aristotle's *libri naturales*, theologians appear to have remained immune from the prohibition. Surely the nature of the soul was a theological issue and an anthropology was rightly the preserve of those professionally concerned to classify the powers of the soul.[53] While the Franciscan John of la Rochelle was the first to give a systematic account of these powers, *c.* 1233+ he was heavily indebted to an anonymous tract known as the *De potentiis animae et obiectis* which contrasted Avicenna's interpretations with those of unknown others. Most important was this tract's assertion that the active or agent intellect was *not* to be considered a substance *separata a substantia anime* but rather an immanent faculty of the soul. The agent intellect is distinct from the

habeat similitudinem cum ea aut ei sit idem. Non autem potest esse ei similis cum similitudo non sit nisi eorum, que passiva sunt et sunt subiecta eidem passioni, cuiusmodi sunt duo alba aut duo nigra. Ex hiis ergo colligi potest mentem et ylen idem esse. Huic autem assentire videtur Plato, ubi dicit mundum esse (Deum) sensibilem. Mens enim, de qua loquimur et quam unam dicimus esse eamque impassibilem, nichil aliud est quam Deus. Si ergo mundus est ipse Deus, preter se ipsum perceptibile sensui, ut Plato et Zeno et Socrates et multi alii dixerunt, yle igitur mundi est ipse Deus, forma vero adveniens yle nil aliud quam id, quod facit Deus sensibile se ipsum ... Manifestum est igitur unam solam substanciam esse [following Aristotle] non tantum omnium corporum, sed etiam animarum omnium et eam nichil aliud esse, quam ipsum Deum. Substancio vero, ex qua sunt omnia (corpora) dicitur yle; substancia vero, ex qua omnes anime, dicitur racio sive mens. Manifestum est ergo Deum esse racionem omnium animarum et yle omnium corporum.

Compare Gundisalvi, p. 363 above.

52 H. Denifle and A. Chatelain, eds., *Chartularium Universitatis Parisiensis*, 4 vols. (Paris, 1889–97), I, p. 70:
Quaternuli magistri David de Dinant infra natale episcopo Parisiensi afferantur et comburantur, nec libri Aristotelis de naturali philosophia nec commenta legantur Parisius publice vel secreto, et hoc sub pena excommunicationis inhibimus. Apud quem inveniuntur quaternuli magistri David a natali Domini in ante pro heretico habebitur.

53 Masters of theology (*in sacra pagina*) at the University of Paris wrote sermons, treatises on the *ars praedicandi*, and works devoted to the following subjects: *de vitiis, de anima, de articulis fidei, de praeceptis, de donis, de sacramentis* and numerous disputed questions. See Mgr. P. Glorieux, *Répertoire des maîtres en théologie de Paris au XIIIᵉ s.*, (Paris, 1934), II, notice 302, pp. 27 f; Also V. Doucet, 'Maîtres franciscains de Paris', *AFH*, 27 (1934), pp. 539–41; P. Michaud-Quantin, ed., and introduction, *Tractatus de divisione multiplici potentiarum animi* (John of la Rochelle) (Paris, 1964), p. 9.

passive or possible intellect but neither intellect is separate from the soul itself. Hence, no special illumination of the intellect is required from outside, except for that kind of rare knowledge of those truths that are above the capacity of the normal intellect, that is, known *divino modo*. For corporeal knowledge and intellectual understanding of the world, there is no need for any special illumination from a separated intellect or mind.

During the first decades of the thirteenth century theological circles show evidence of a wide knowledge of Aristotle and the new learning, particularly amongst such thinkers as William of Auvergne, Philip the Chancellor, and John of la Rochelle (chair of theology, Paris; 1238–45), who were intent on writing *summae de anima*. The anonymous *De potentiis animae et obiectis* is thought to have been written possibly by an English theologian, without the influence of the Latin translations of Averroes, which entered circles at the University of Paris *c.* 1230.[54]

The author speaks of the divisions between the powers of the animal, vegetative, sensible and rational souls. The objects of these diverse powers are different; in particular, the *anima sensibilis* in man, who has a rational soul, is a *substantia cognoscitiva* of corporeal forms moving the whole body from place to place. This means that the sensible soul in man knows corporeal forms – that is, that they are corporeal in material subjects – but it knows these as separated by means of cognition of the rational soul. The *anima rationalis* knows spiritual forms either *simpliciter* or as conjoined with bodies whereby it understands species in phantasms.[55] The sensible soul is an incorporeal, unseparated, but corruptible substance whereby sensibles are known by it according to the separable species in such sensibles, separated according to the operations of rationality (or *cognoscitiva*). One can speak of an understanding which is had through the body and another which is had through the rational soul.[56] One of the characteristics of the rational soul is its power to perceive as well as its power of *compositio* which enables it to abstract from phantasms, thereby understanding the forms. A sensible form is in matter and it must be abstracted from this matter as a sensible species or similitude. This perception of the similitude of the sensible species is had externally and the remnant which is had from the received form in the senses is had internally (*ab intus*).[57] The author

54 Text cited in D. A. Callus, 'The powers of the soul, an early unpublished text', *RTAM*, 19 (1952), pp. 131–70.
55 *Ibid.*, p. 148:
    Et intelligitur sic, quod est cognoscitiva formarum corporealium ut quod cognoscit et quo cognoscitur sit corporale sed hoc in subiecta materia, illud vero non, et per hoc fit separatio a cognitione anime rationalis, quo cognoscit aut per formas spirituales simpliciter, aut spirituales coniunctas corporibus, prout dicitur quod intelligit species in phantasmatibus.
56 *Ibid.*, p. 149.   57 *Ibid.*, p. 150.

believes that the properties of sensible things are accepted by the senses and only thereafter are we led to an understanding of the principles in sensible things.

Magnitude, number, movement, rest, form and shape are accepted by the common sense. Thereafter, these perceptions are converted by an internal sense known as imagination; the fantasy then moves from one image to another, composing and dividing.[58] Memory conserves the sensible phantasms so that memory deals only with what was first sensed. But within the memory are the intentions or forms which are in matter and yet not material themselves because intentions are not sensible *per se*. Intentions are, for instance, good, bad, harmful, useful (*bonitas, malitia, nocumentum, iuvamentum*). These depend on bodies but are more noble powers.[59]

Now these intentions which are in material things but are not themselves sensible are perceived by the power called estimation (*estimativa*) – judging things sensed or judging what is imagined to be good or bad. Just as estimation moves the appetite, so does the fantasy (or imagination) but the fantasy moves the appetite by means of forms received from that which is simply sensed, whereas the *estimativa* moves the appetite according to those intentions which are innate in sensed things. There are, therefore, some forms which the sensible soul cannot touch or experience, for example, justice and prudence, and these forms are understood not as universals but rather as individual qualities like colour and magnitude. One requires the powers of the rational soul to understand spiritual forms and the *estimatio* cannot do this.[60]

Although Aristotle does not speak of a material intellect as such, the author cites the *De Anima* where the rational soul is described as passive and corruptible and calls this the material intellect. Here are received the

[58] *Ibid.*, p. 154.
[59] *Ibid.*, p. 154:
Dicitur etiam memoria secundum conservationem phantasmatum sensibilium sine qua conservatione non procedunt actus predictarum virium. Dicitur autem memorativa inquantum memoratur aliquid prius sensatum. Quia vero intentiones sive forme que possunt esse in materia, et non materia que sunt non sensibiles per se, vel communiter, ut sunt bonitas et malitia nocumentum, iuvamentum, hec autem forme predictis sunt nobiliores. Nam prime non ꞏpossunt proprie esse sine corpore, hec vero possunt esse in corporibus et non corporibus, ideo nobilioris potentie et posterioris in hac via erunt.
[60] *Ibid.*, pp. 154–5:
... hec vis dicitur estimativa: estimat enim de re quam sentit, vel quam aliquis esse imaginatur esse bonum et malum ... sicut autem tam estimatio quam phantasia moventes appetitum, sed phantasi movet ex formis receptis simpliciter ex sensu, estimativa vero ex illis et ex aliis que sunt innate. Quia vero sunt quedam forme quas non potest attingere anima sensibilis, sicut iustitia, prudentia et huiusmodi, et sunt alie forme quas, licet possit comprehendere, non tamen comprehendit eas inquantum sunt universales, sicut sunt color et magnitudo ...

separable intelligible species that are in phantasms. This material intellect abstracts intelligibles from phantasms, and as such is a power acting in communication with the sensible soul.[61] The phantasms in the material intellect have their intelligible species thereafter abstracted from them by the active or agent intellect. The material intellect's power comprises the rational soul which is, of necessity, conjoined with a body, and as such the activity of abstracting intelligible species from images goes on in the *cellula logistica sive rationalis*. It is called a rational power because it accepts universals that are in particulars, but it does not know or experience these universals as universals. As such, this rational power is inseparable from the body, receiving as a passive intellect the species abstracted from bodies.[62]

Thereafter, there is an intellect which *is* separable from the body and is considered two-fold: an *intellectus agens* and an *intellectus possibilis*. But the active intellect is not separate from the soul's substance.[63] And the author goes on to reject a theory of illumination from a separable agent intellect in order that the soul may know intelligibles. Instead, the agent intellect is itself an interior light along with the possible intellect.[64] All of these increasingly immaterial powers of the soul respond to intelligible species which are received in the fantasy or imagination and which are, in turn, served by the senses. The difference between the different powers is only with respect to the increasing degree of abstraction in the superior powers.

There are also forms acquired by the soul which, however, are not there through a process of abstracting from images of particular sensible things. These are the virtues and moral knowledge.[65] The soul acquires virtues

[61] *Ibid.*, p. 155: 'Et hec vis est tamquam anime actus intellectualis communicans cum actibus anime sensibilis.'

[62] *Ibid.*, p. 155:
Loquamur ergo prima de prima vi in ordine isto anime rationalis, scilicet intellectus materialis qui ponitur in libro De Anima, passivus et corruptibilis. Et ipse recipit species intelligibiles in phantasmatibus ... Et hec vis est tamquam anime actus intellectualis communicans cum actibus anime sensibilis. Nam hec ad phantasma terminatur, illo vero ex phantasmatibus materialiter tribuit species intelligibiles abstrahendas ab intellectu agente. Hec autem virtus numquam est anime rationalis nisi dum coniungitur ad corpus; provenit enim in coniunctione anime rationalis ad corpus, et nominatur alio nomine rationalitas, a qua dicitur cellula logistica sive rationalis ... quia potens est accipere universalia in particularibus, non tamen universale per modum universalis, aut particulare per modum particularis. Hec autem est virtus inseparabilis a corpore, scilicet intellectus passibilis, qui recipit species abstractas a corpore.

[63] *Ibid.*, p. 156: 'intellectus autem agens non est separatus a substantia anime'.

[64] *Ibid.*, p. 156: 'ideo ad hec comprehendenda non est necessarium illuminatione substantie separate, sed sufficit intellectus agens, qui est lumen interius, cum intellectu possibili'.

[65] *Ibid.*, p. 157:
Sed sunt alie forme que non indigent hac abstractione, sed sunt tamen non sine ipsa, et sunt adquisite in anima, quemadmodum sunt virtutes et scientie morales, et non oportet quod species istarum rerum abstrahantur a phantasmatibus rerum sensibilium.

and moral knowledge as kinds of universals which are not sensed and yet which are already in particular instances. There is a kind of intellect which knows the quiddities of things, that is, the principles of things; it is able to know, for instance, what is the whole and what is part, what greater and what lesser. This intellect is known as the *intellectus in habitu*. It must be considered a stage (*gradus*) in the more general possible intellect which is, still, served by the senses.[66]

The only kind of rational knowing which is not dependent on sensible images is a kind of speculation regarding forms in the intellect, placed there *per illuminationem superiorem*, that is, through grace; these forms can issue in the power of prophecy or inspired visions in sleep, or in a kind of inspired comprehension of philosophical and moral truths. Here, however, we are dealing with souls that have received something beyond their normal capacities (*a gratis data non gratum faciens, aut gratem faciens*). This is from God.[67]

What is striking about the *De potentiis animae et obiectis* is the author's concern to explain the many capacities of the individual human soul to respond to sense experience and come to the most abstract and universal knowledge through its own natural activities. Furthermore, the most abstracting activity of the possible and agent intellects is always, in origin, dependent on the perceptions of the sensible soul and its experience of the exterior world. Since there are intelligible species in all things as perceived by the sensible soul, a continuum is established between those aspects of abstracting intellect most closely connected with particular images and a higher abstracting intellect concerned with universals. The memory is one of those aspects of the sensible soul which houses not only images of past sense experiences but also intentions, universals in particulars, which have been judged by the estimative faculty. The heart of this theory then, is its affirmation of species which are resemblances, more or less abstract, of something sensed. The species is an image of a sensible object or of an intellectual concept

---

[66] *Ibid.*, p. 157:
Particularia enim horum universalium non sunt sensibilia, sed cum sint aut esse possint in anima secundum rem, non indigent speciebus quibus cognoscantur que non sunt res ... Quarum prima est circa quidditates, secunda vero circa complexiones primas, que dicuntur principia scientiarum; et primus intellectus dicitur intellectus in actu cum cognoscit quidditates ... intellectus autem cognoscens huiusmodi principia (id est quid est totum et quid est pars ...) vocatur intellectus in habitu. Cum ex hiis principiis informatur intellectus in cognoscendo conclusiones vocatur intellectus adquisitus, quia alia ratione dicitur scientia. Et hii sunt gradus in intellectu possibili ad rerum quantum ad illam partem que fit ministerio sensus.

[67] *Ibid.*, p. 158.

and it is thanks to the species that we know, sensually and intellectually.[68]

Precisely how the species is born and thereafter fulfils its function of uniting the exterior sensible world with interior intellection poses a series of problems which our author declines to elucidate. In general, the sensible species is conceived as a sort of emanation from the object to be known. In the thirteenth century most authors admitted the existence of what the term 'species' designated and hence retained a realism which increasing Aristotelianism would force some to reject.[69] Some refused to give the species any ontological density when compared with the object, defining it as did Matthew of Aquasparta as having only an intentional function, intending the cognitive faculty of the rational soul towards the object which alone has an autonomous and proper reality.[70] The more platonising authors, especially Franciscans, however, continued to see the species as not entirely disengaged from all corporeity.[71] However viewed, it was the species which, having been seized by the sense organ, then becomes the object of the internal sense and receives the designation which indicates its role regarding various faculties of the soul: *imaginaria, in imaginatione, memorialis, species spiritualis.* Where the earlier medical tradition referred to the *spiritus* as a mysterious fluid, a pneuma, which was somehow affected by sense data and transmitted the data in a form receivable by interior senses (a congruence theory of elements), thirteenth-century authors referred to the species as somehow abstractable by mind. When the species was the object of the interior senses, especially imagination and memory, it was also called *phantasma.*[72] Hence, they were able to follow Aristotle's parallel description of a sensory and an intellectual activity, a lower and higher mind while preserving a continuity. Our anonymous author is content to speak of a progressive dematerialisation of the species. Others would argue, however, for a rupture which enabled the intervention of the agent intellect to confer on the species an immateriality and universality which it did not have initially. It would be Aquinas' solution to the problem to posit the acquisition of a species only after the possible intellect actively abstracted the *phantasma* from the imagination. Hence, the species was only in potency prior to being abstracted as intelligible.

---

68 P. Michaud-Quantin, 'Les champs sémantiques de *species*. Tradition latine et traditions du grec', in *Etudes sur le vocabulaire philosophique de Moyen Age* (Rome, 1979), pp. 113–50.
69 See below, ch. 22, on Ockham's rejection of the reality of species.
70 Matthew of Aquasparta, *Questiones de anima separata*, ed., G. Gál (Quaracchi, 1959), Q. IV, solutio 13, p. 74.
71 John Pecham, *Quodlibet Romanum*, 23, ed., J. M. Delorme (Spicilegium Pontificii Athenaei Antoniani, fasc. 1, Rome, 1938), pp. 58 ff.
72 Michaud-Quantin, 'Les champs sémantiques de *species*', p. 121.

All agreed, however, that the species of a thing is distinct from the thing of which it is the image and hence the species is not the object of knowledge but an image of that which is the object, the sensed object. The species is therefore that *by which* one knows the world rather than *what* one knows, and hence it is a diminished being, offering less of reality than the object which it represents.[73] Our author says nothing new about the memory, for it is clear that he treats it as the conserving power in the posterior ventricle which receives and preserves estimation's intentions as well as images from imagination, all in the form of the species appropriate to the level of abstraction of this part of the sensible soul.

To remind us that a divided tradition still was maintained during the 1230s by theologians, a tradition which recognised but never coordinated the discussions of memory *secundum physice vel philosophice* and the discussions of memory according to theologians, especially Augustine, we need only turn briefly to the fragment which survives of the *Summa Douacensis*, a work that influenced Philip the Chancellor.[74] It was written by an anonymous author, a contemporary of William of Auvergne, and is slightly earlier than the writings of Alexander of Hales and Albert the Great. It contains a *De Anima* which is heavily Augustinian (including reference to the pseudo-Augustinian *De Spiritu et Anima*) and expands on the traditional question of the distinction between image and similitude in the Genesis passage where God is said to have made man in his image and similitude.

When he comes to speak of memory the author says that Augustine in particular provides the best definitions (*De Trinitate*), memory being a dignity of the soul in conjunction with intellect and will. While some attribute memory to the Holy Spirit, others identify memory with the mind of God the Father (*mentem Patri*). Following Augustine, he says one can speak of memory as the conserving of similitudes of God in the soul through which similitudes the soul is led naturally to what it naturally knows and loves, that is truth and the *summe bonum*. These two acts of natural knowledge and love refer to a cognition of affective remnants (*reliquus ad affectum*). Memory, therefore, is none other than that which leads to a natural knowledge and love of God. Hence, memory must be accepted as coming *before* such knowledge and love and is, therefore, attributed to the Father. Others, however, believe that memory is had from the Holy Spirit which issues from the Father.

But a third way of speaking of memory is that of the *phisice vel philosophice*. They say that memory is a treasure house in which is received

---

[73] See below, ch. 21, on Duns Scotus for a further elaboration.
[74] P. Glorieux, ed., *La 'Summa Duacensis' (Douai 434)*, (Paris, 1955).

images of things or species, that are accepted through similitudes of external things.[75] But our author says that this kind of memory attains nothing of the above two natural capacities of knowing and loving. So that this kind of memory differs in innumerable ways from the memory that is identical with the Father. The higher memory, given to man and attributed to the Father, is naturally and indelibly in man. The medical and philosophical memory, however, is only in man accidentally and *delebiliter* (capable of destruction).[76]

[75] 'Per extrinsecas similitudines accepte'.
[76] Glorieux, ed., *La 'Summa Duacensis'*, p. 21:
Alio autem modo et diverso loquitur Augustinus attribuens memoriam vel mentem Patri. Unde secundum hanc viam loquentes, describere possumus memoriam sic dicendo: memoria est conservatio similitudinis Dei in ipsa anima per quam ipsa anima naturaliter ducitur in id quod naturaliter est intelligendum et naturaliter diligendum, hoc est in primum verum et primum et summe bonum. Et illorum duorum actuum primus referendus est ad cognitionem, reliquus ad affectum. Unde patere potest quod memoria nichil aliud est quam ipsa ductio in duo predicta ... Quare memoria per hunc modum accepta prior est, et ita merito Patri attribuenda ... secundum autem aliam Spiritui Sancto ... Tertio autem modum accipitur memoria secundum phisice vel philosophice loquentes hoc modo: memoria est thesaurus in quo recipiuntur ymagines rerum vel species per extrinsecas similitudines accepte. Hoc autem nichil attinet memorie supra dupliciter diffinite; imo differt multipliciter a memoria secundum quod Patris est. Et primum per hoc quod memoria secundum quod est in homine et Patri attributa, inest homini naturaliter et indelebiliter et in opere prior naturaliter. Sed modo tertio accepta est hominis accidentaliter et delebiliter et ultimo loco operativa.

Chapter 17

JOHN OF LA ROCHELLE

During the decade 1230–40 in Paris, theologians judged the various competing psychological doctrines to represent a very serious problem. In effect, they were faced with three conceptions of man: one that was theological where man was understood as a morally engaged agent in the economy of salvation; another, from the Greco-Arabic tradition, which considered man as an element amongst others comprising the universe; and increasingly, a third in which man was conceived as capable of developing the *habitus* of virtues, a conception drawn from the rhetorical and moral treatises of Cicero and other ancients on the virtues.[1] *De Anima* tracts written in this period were linked with treatises *De Bono et Virtutibus* whereby the classification of the virtues was closely linked with the soul and its powers. The treatise by the eighth-century monk, John of Damascus, his *De Fide Orthodoxa*, was also drawn upon to show the connection between virtues and the soul's powers.[2] These traditions would be combined, at first uneasily, to produce important consequences for an enlarged understanding of the memory.

On the one hand, Augustine and Peter the Lombard influenced theologians to focus on sensuality, reason and the free will, while on the other, Aristotle read through Avicennan eyes inspired them to concentrate on the external and internal senses, the appetite, the practical or potential

[1] R. Baron, 'A propos des ramifications des vertus au XIIe siècle', *RTAM*, 23 (1956), pp. 19–39.

[2] John of Damascus, a monk in the monastery of Mar-Sabas near Jerusalem, was the son of a local Christian notable who served in the financial administration of the Caliphate of Damascus. John had been educated in Greek philosophy and theology by his Sicilian tutor and became well known when he wrote three orations championing icons in the Byzantine world, for which he was anathematised at the iconoclast council of 754. He argued that the Godhead was uncircumscribable and therefore incapable of any form of representation. But depictions of the human Christ were justified as images of the Word incarnate and as a reminder of the salvation of men through God's redemptive powers. His views circulated widely at the end of the eighth century. See B. Kotter, ed., *Die Schriften des Johannes von Damaskos* (Berlin, 1975). John of Damascus, *De Fide Orthodoxa*, ed. E. M. Buytaert (Louvain and The Hague, 1955).

intellect and the will. The Franciscan theologian, John of la Rochelle, brought these traditions together when he compiled one of the most thorough treatises on the various classifications of the powers of the soul without explicitly taking sides.[3] Hence, he has been seen as a true *compilator* rather than as an *auctor*, allowing for an uneasy coexistence of the numerous classifications available. He provides students with the differing points of view from which one might argue, either theologically or philosophically and medically. His *Tractatus de Anima* is not, therefore, to be seen as a magisterial or even personal exposition, as is his *Summa de Anima*,[4] but rather as an auxiliary manual for a course in the theology faculty sometime between 1233 and 1239. Whereas the earlier treatises on the soul from monastic milieux or those written by canons regular did not separate the problems concerning the nature and activity of the soul from considerations of moral action in the economy of salvation, John of la Rochelle's *tractatus* shows some evolution in that it does separate the study of the soul in itself and in its activity from that of the moral and supernatural end it pursues.[5] Here, John of la Rochelle is influenced by a reading of Aristotle's *Ethica vetus* and *Ethica nova* (he does not seem to know a complete translation of the *Ethics*),[6] where there is a distinction drawn between moral philosophy and the criteria for human action on the one hand, and natural philosophy which studies the whole soul on the other. If he mildly criticises any tradition, it is the classification of the powers of the soul according to Arabic medicine, and he reports this largely according to Avicenna's *Canon*.[7]

In Part I of the *Tractatus de Anima* he provides the following sources for *twelve* different definitions of the soul: John of Damascus, the pseudo-Augustinian *De Spiritu et Anima*, Alfred of Sareschal, Plato, Aristotle, Nemesius and Seneca. In Part II he provides five tables of classification of the soul's powers grouped under three heads: Avicenna (*De Anima*) and

---

[3] Jean de la Rochelle, *Tractatus de divisione multiplici potentiarum animae*, ed. and intro. P. Michaud-Quantin (Paris, 1964). John of la Rochelle (at Paris 1238–45) was the disciple of the Franciscan Alexander of Hales who gave the Order their first university chair in theology. Alexander accepted the *De Spiritu et Anima* to be by Augustine and during the late 1230s and early 1240s this treatise was connected with the beginnings of Franciscan theology, as the current which provided the centre for a neo-Augustinianism in the thirteenth century. Philip the Chancellor recognised that the *De Spiritu* was not by Augustine. See P. Michaud-Quantin, 'Les puissances de l'âme chez Jean de la Rochelle', *Antonianum*, 24 (1949), pp. 489–505.

[4] *Summa de Anima*, ed. T. Domenichelli (Prato, 1882), dated *c.* 1233+ but probably written after the *Tractatus*.

[5] *Tractatus*, ed. Michaud-Quantin, p. 19.   [6] *Ibid.*, p. 23.

[7] *Ibid.*, pp. 102–3, secunda pars, c. xxvi, 'de ordine potentiarum anime secundum Avicennam'. But also see D. H. Salman, 'Jean de la Rochelle et l'Averroïsme Latin', *AHDLMA* 16 (1947–8), pp. 139–42.

the philosophers; the medical tradition citing Johannitius and Avicenna's *Canon*;[8] and, finally, John of Damascus and both the pseudo-Augustinian *De Spiritu et Anima* and Augustine himself. In Part II he is primarily concerned to examine the principal terms: *ratio, intellectus, voluntas, memoria*, etc. In Part III he discusses the theological perfection of the soul whereby grace and man's supernatural life are considered in the light of the virtues, culminating in a discussion on beatitude. What he has to say about memory provides us with the most comprehensive summa of competing authorities we have thus far encountered, particularly because he usually remains faithful to whatever source he is using. And because he uses a wide range of sources, his treatment of memory conflates the physiological and philosophical traditions with the reappearance of the rhetorical tradition of memory places, as Cicero, the authority on the virtues, had explained these.

In his discussion of the internal senses (*de vi sensibili apprehensiva deintus, scilicet sensu communi, ymaginatione, ymaginativa, estimativa et memoriali*),[9] he follows Avicenna's *De Anima* closely and clearly. The memorial power (*vis memorativa*) is, he says, a *vis ordinata* located in the posterior cavity of the brain, retaining what the estimative power has apprehended from the intentions of sensibles. We are told that Avicenna says that one can compare the *vis memorativa* and the *estimativa* in the same way that one compares the imagination with the common sense; just as the imagination retains and is the treasure house of sensible forms apprehended by the common sense, so the memorial power is a treasure house conserving the intentions of sensibles apprehended by the *vis estimativa*.

There is, however, a difference between *memoria* and *reminiscentia*, that is, there is a distinction between *recordatio* and irrational *reminiscentia*. John has accepted Avicenna's linking of *memoria* and *reminiscentia* as powers of the sensible soul. Avicenna, we are told (*De Anima*, IV, 3) says that memory is in all animals but only *recordatio* is in man. *Recordatio* is the ability to call back, by means of a search, what has been forgotten and only men are good at this. To know that something was, that is thereafter deleted from memory, can only be a power of reason. And yet John distinguishes between *reminiscentia* and *memoria*, both in the sensible soul, in a distinctive way. Memory is the retention of a species or an intention of a sensible or its representation. Reminiscence, however, is the search for those forms in the memory that have been destroyed through forgetfulness; it is a search that is pursued *per similia* just as when the identity of a person whom we have seen is forgotten and we return to the place, the time and the acts through

---

[8] *Ibid.*, pp. 103–4 ff. Secunda pars, de divisione potentiarum anime secundum medicos.
[9] *Ibid.*, secunda pars, c. V.

which we recorded the person, seeing him in such a place at such a time and doing something and thereby recognising him. Suddenly we have here the introduction of the Ciceronian rhetorical memory places of which Avicenna said nothing.[10] John then continues with the Avicennan distinction between *recordatio* and *addiscere*, remembering what one once learned and learning something new. The difference here, he says, is that *addiscere* is a movement from something not known to something known. *Recordatio* is, on the other hand, a search for the already known in order to know it in the future as it was known in the past. *Addiscentia* is the very discipline of learning whereby the soul is extended from what it knows to what it does not yet know and, therefore, it had no prior knowledge of what it can learn. We have here an acceptance of Aristotle in contrast with Plato.[11]

As soon as John speaks about the divisions of the intellectual powers of the soul he shifts into the language of an Augustinian analysis of memory. Hence in Part II c. xxiii (*de divisione virtutis intellective secundum differentiam ordinis*) he says that the *virtus intellectiva* may be subdivided into a superior and an inferior part. The superior part Augustine calls *intelligentia* which is the supreme power linking the apprehending capacities of the soul and its knowledge of uncreated truth. This is possible because images or species of the Trinity itself are impressed on creation and are determined or judged by the three powers of the soul: memory, intelligence and will. Here, the memory is that power in which is conserved or retained the

---

[10] Francis Yates, *The Art of Memory*, pp. 246–52, says that Albert the Great was the first to provide a synthesis of Aristotle's reminiscence and Cicero's places or memory aids in the *De Bono*, article 2. But the synthesis is already here in John of la Rochelle.

[11] *Tractatus*, Michaud-Quantin, X, '*de vi memorativa*', p. 77:
Vis memorativa est vis ordinata in posteriori concavitate cerebri, retinens quod apprehendit vis estimativa de intentionibus sensibilium. Comparatio enim vis memorative ad estimativam secundum Avicennam est qualis est comparatio ymaginationis ad sensum communem; quia sicut ymaginatio retinet et est thesaurus formarum sensibilium, quas apprehendit sensus communis, sic vis memorativa est thesaurus conservans intentiones sensibilium quas apprehendit vis estimativa. Ad quorum evidentiam videndum est, que sit differentia memorie et reminiscentie, et an sit recordatio sive reminiscentia irrationalium. Ad quod dicendum secundum Avicennam, quod memoria est in aliis animalibus, sed recordatio, in solo homine. Recordatio enim est revocatio ingenii, ad querendum, quod oblitum est, quod non convenit aliis ab homine; cognoscere enim sibi aliquid affuisse, quod postea deletum est, non est nisi virtutis rationalis. Differentia ergo memoria et reminiscentie est, quia memoria est retentio specierum sive sensibilium intentionum vel representatio earumdem; reminiscentia vero est requisitio formarum a memoria deletarum per oblivionem per similia, sicut obliti alicuius persone, quam vidimus, recurrimus ad locum, ad tempus, ad actus, per que recordamur persone, quam vidimus tali loco, tali tempore, tali facientem. Nota etiam differentiam inter recordari et addiscere, conveniunt enim in hoc, quod utrobique est motus ab incognitis ad cognita, ut sciatur. Sed in hoc differunt, quod recordatio est requisitio cognitorum, ut cognoscantur de futuro, que quidem fuerunt cognita de preterito. Addiscentia vero, sive disciplina, est extensio anime ad cognoscendum incognita, que non fuerunt cognita prius.

similitude of primary truth introduced into creation. *Intelligentia* is the contemplation of primary truth through a similitude of truth impressed in creation. The will is a love of the primary truth through a fixed desire for it in creation. Otherwise, says John, memory can also be considered that superior intellectual power (*ipsa vis intellectus superioris*) by which a rational creature may think about (*cogitare*) his efficient principle by means of that which was not always, but certainly was from that efficient principle. *Intelligentia* is an impressed superior intellectual power (*impressa vis intellectus superioris*) by means of which a rational animal can think of the present primary truth. The will is that intellectual power that inclines the soul towards its future, its primary truth as its end.[12]

These intellectual powers are for us impressed judgements of truths concerning the principles of knowledge, for instance, that the whole is greater than its parts, and we know these because they are naturally innate, learning them through the light of the primary similitude of truth impressed in us, just as the Psalm says: 'signatum est super nos' etc. This intellectual power is of the same substance as the agent intellect whose nature can be considered an apprehensive power otherwise called *intelligentia* or *mens*.

If we consider the inferior aspect of the intellect according to its nature, we call it the possible intellect and its acts, considered therefore as *apprehensiva* or speculative intellect or *ratio*.[13] The principal act of the intellectual virtues or powers is to understand by means of sensibles and therefore, one can speak of the intellectual powers in four ways: *inventiva*, *judicativam*, *memorativa* and *interpretativa*. The *via inventionis* is an inquisition concerning truth *per se*; the *via iudicii* in discussion of the truth accepts (information) from others. Hence, the *via inventionis* is a *via*

[12] *Ibid.*, XXIII, p. 95:
Sciendum ergo quod intellectiva virtus subdividitur per superiorem partem et inferiorem: superior vero intelligentia dicitur ab Augustino (*De Spiritu et Anime*, 4), est autem huiusmodi vis suprema inter apprehensivas ad cognoscendam veritatem increatam, secundum ymaginem vel speciem Trinitatis sibi a creatione impressam, que ymago Trinitatis secundum Augustinum (*De Trinitate*, I, 11–12, 17–19) determinatur secundum tria, memoriam, intelligentiam et voluntatem. Et memoria dicitur ipsa vis, inquantum est conservativa sive retentiva similitudinis prime veritatis a creatione indite; intelligentia autem est, inquantum est contemplativa prime veritatis per impressam similitudinem veritatis a creatione; voluntas vero, secundum quod est amativa prime veritatis per infixum appetitum ipsius a creatione. Vel aliter: memoria, ut hic dicitur, sit ipsa vis intellectus superioris, qua rationalis creatura potest cogitare suum principium efficiens per hoc quod non semper fuit, unde certa est quod fuit ab illo; intelligentia vero est impressa vis intellectus superioris qua potest cogitare anima rationalis presentem primam veritatem, ut presentem lucem sibi et exemplarem causam; voluntas est vis intellectus superioris, qua inclinatur anima in ipsam primam veritatem ut in finem. (*De Spiritu et Anima*, 35).
[13] *Ibid.*, p. 95.

experiendi, a process of understanding through experience, whereas the *via iudicii* is a *via addiscendi*, a process of learning something new. Experience is *per se* whereas learning is by means of something or someone else. The *via inventionis* had through experience proceeds by means of composition whereas the *via iudicii* proceeds by means of resolution. The *via inventionis* is a knowledge of cause through its effect, whereas the *via iudicii* is a knowledge of an effect through its cause. Experience is therefore inductive and judgement or learning is deductive.

Now *memorativa* and *interpretativa* as the other two intellectual powers may be distinguished in that the memorial power is a power to retain already known species whereas the interpretative power is *dativa cognitionis*, the habit of providing knowledge. Furthermore, whilst the investigative and memorial capacities are in man *respectu sui*, investigation (rational) and invention (experiential) seek the unknown whereas remembering retains what is already known. Experience (invention) therefore precedes understanding whereas remembering follows understanding. Judgement and interpretation occur as a result of others but whereas judgement depends on another's cognition, interpretation is a distillation and transference into another (*transfundendo in alium*). Judgement, therefore, is had before one understands whereas interpretation is a result of understanding. Hence, for John, judgement is closer to received opinion which is uninvestigated, whereas interpretation is exercised in the light of some intellectual understanding and verification.

When we speak of the investigative power we are speaking of acts of natural experience, apprehensions, conception and reasoning. *Ingenium* is, he says, the extension of the intellect from the unknown to the known whereas experience is the certitude of things had through the senses. Apprehension is the acceptance of a simple perception (*simplex*) by the intellect, a capacity of animals and man; and conception is the acceptance of a composite or complex perception by the intellect, for instance, that man is an animal or that man alone is capable of laughter (*homo est risibile* = *complexa*). Reasoning is the acceptance of syllogistic arguments by the intellect, for instance, since man is an animal, man is *sensible*. John goes on to define and distinguish further between judgement and other modes of knowing (*via cognoscendi*) through reasoning, defining, *discernere* (*hoc est diiudicare*) and doubting, opinion and the comprehension of truth.[14]

Then he says that the memorial power, *memorativa*, is rational and has three acts: firstly, it can retain intelligible species; secondly it can represent them; and thirdly it can restore forgotten or obscured species and the latter, third capacity of *memorativa* is reminiscence. And all these species

[14] *Ibid.*, pp. 96–7.

are had by *memorativa* from sensibles.[15] *Memorativa* is distinguished from *memoria*. It is noted that *memoria* is three-fold. Firstly, memory is a conserving power of sensible species; then, it is also a power conserving intelligible species; and finally, it is a power that conserves the divine similitudes introduced into creation.[16]

Interpretation, the *vis indicativa intellectus*, is two-fold: it is a power that acts either by means of *excogitatio* or by means of *significatio*. Excogitation is a configuration or an informing of thought which portrays the exterior (world); on the other hand, signification is thought formed through signs and words in order to demonstrate (logical truths). Because signs as manifested in the world, *in opere*, are confused or equivocal to the intellects of others, one uses words that are specific and proper in order to make clear one's meaning and by this means the intellectual meaning is had through locutions. Locative speech is an expression of interior mental conceptions or thoughts manifested outwardly through uttered words. This is not quite the same as merely uttering sounds (*vocativa*) because magpies can do this but are not expressing an interior meaning; they are simply emitting vocal noises! Magpies do not proffer ideas (*intentione proferre*) and if by accident they seem to utter a meaningful word they intend nothing by it.[17] John has obviously included here a discussion of that inferior aspect of intellect, that is, the possible intellect and its acts of apprehension, reasoning, remembering, interpreting and judging, from the stand-point of the logician as such issues would have been dealt with by lecturers in the arts faculty.

Passing on to John of Damascus' treatment of the soul's powers, John of la Rochelle notes that after the imaginative power comes the excogitative

---

[15] *Ibid.*, p. 97: 'Memorativa vero rationalis triplex est actus: primus intelligibiles species retinere, secundus representare, tertius amissas vel oblitas species reparare, et hoc est reminisci, et hoc habundat a sensibili'.

[16] *Ibid.*, p. 97: 'Notandum enim quod memoria triplex est: est enim memoria vis conservativa speciei sensibilis; est etiam vis conservativa speciei intelligibilis; est etiam vis conservativa divine similitudinis indite a creatione'.

[17] *Ibid.*, p. 97:
Interpretative vero, que est vis indicativa intellectus, duplex est actus: excogitatio et significatio. Excogitatio est configuratio vel informatio cogitationis ad exprimendum exterius; significatio vero est cogitationis formate per signa et verba demonstratio. Qui vero signa in opere confusa sunt et equivoca ad intellectum accomodandum alteri, ideo accomodata sunt verba ad manifestationem intellectus, ut signa discreta et propria, et ideo significatio intellectus facta est locutiva. Est autem locutiva verbi interioris mente concepti, id est cogitationis, per verbum exterius demonstratio. Hec autem virtus non est eadem cum vocativa, id est cum emissiva vocis: vocativa enim est sensibilium et irrationabilium, locutiva vero rationabilium tantum. Unde nec pica nec dormentes locuntur, loqui enim vel dicere est cum intentione proferre; quia ergo pica vel dormens, et si proferant vocem significativam, nichil intendunt, cum locuntur, solius ergo proferentis cum intentione est loqui et virtus locutiva; tale autem est rationale homo.

395

power which, he says, his source considers equivalent to opinion – the capacity to judge sensibles.[18] Thereafter, we have the *memorativa*. What, he asks, is the cause of remembering? Memory is a derelict, left-over fantasy from one of the senses following the present experience or act of sensing, *or else* it is the accumulation of understood sense data.[19] The sensible soul perceives and has opinions through the senses. Intelligibles are had through the intellect and it thereby has understanding. The memory is the custodian of both *typi*, that is, figures of those things of which it has opinions as well as of those things it understands. John of Damascus wishes to show that intelligibles are had not through the senses but only through learning (*disciplina*) or through a natural ability (*naturali ingenio*). *Sensibilia* are entrusted in themselves to the memory whereas intelligibles, if someone tells them to us, are memorised, where the substance of the memory is not had by us (i.e. we only have the intentions).[20]

We are told that John of Damascus uses the term *rememorativa* to mean the restitution of memories lost by forgetting, and indeed *oblivio*, forgetfulness, is nothing but mislaid memories. The fantasy or imagination which receives matter through the senses, hands over to excogitation or discretion what it receives, and excogitation then judges and in turn transmits judgements to the memorial capacity (*memorativa*). The memory organ is the posterior ventricle of the brain and the animal spirit is in it.[21]

Now according to John of Damascus, mind and intellectual knowledge pertain to reason and there are three ways we come to intellectual knowledge: through experience (*secundum viam inveniendi*), through having been taught (*viam docendi*) and through a kind of logical learning (*viam addiscendi*).[22] He understands the *via inveniendi* as a process of sensual

---

[18] John of Damascus uses *excogitativa* and not *opinio*. *De Fide Orthodoxa*, cc. 33–7.

[19] *Tractatus*, ed. Michaud-Quantin, p. 115: 'Est autem memorativum memorie et rememorationis promptuarium et causa. Memoria enim est fantasia derelicta ab aliquo sensus secundum actum apparentem, vel coacervatio sensus intelligentie.'

[20] *Ibid.*, pp. 115–16:
Anima enim sensibilia per sensus percipit et fit opinio; intelligibilia vero per intellectum et fit intelligentia. Cum igitur typos, id est figuras, eorum que opinatus est et eorum que intellexerat, custodit memorari dicitur. [John of Damascus, *De Fide Orthodoxa*, ch. 34]. Oportet autem scire, quod intelligibilium susceptio non fit nisi ex disciplina vel naturali ingenio, non enim ex sensu. Nam sensibilia quidem secundum seipsa memorie commendantur; intelligibilium vero, si quid quidem didicimus, memoramur, substantie vero eorum memoriam non habemus.

[21] *Ibid.*, p. 116:
Rememorativa vero dicitur memorie ab oblivione deperdite restitutio; oblivio autem est memorie ablatio. Fantasticum igitur, id est ymaginativum, per sensus suscipiens materias, tradit excogitativo et discretivo, idem enim sunt utraque, quod suscipiens et diiudicans transmittit memorativo. Organum memorativi est posterior ventriculus cerebri et spiritus animalis, qui est in illo.

[22] *Ibid.*, p. 116.

experience leading to the knowing of intelligibles (*ad intelligibilia cogno-scenda*). Thus, the irrational powers are ordered towards and with respect to the rational. The senses of the soul create an image (*passio que vocatur ymaginatio*) and imagination constructs opinions whereby the mind judges these opinions as to their truth or falsity and this determination is called understanding (*intellectus*). However, there is, according to John of Damascus, another way of describing mental motion. *Cognoscere*, the first movement of understanding, deals with intentions or ideas, whereby the idea remains in the soul as understood as a thought (*excogitatio*). The power to think and examine oneself is called prudence (*fronesis vocatur*). This can be shown syllogistically as when we give the example: every whole is greater than its parts, and every continuum is a whole, therefore every continuum is greater than its parts. The motion of mind is focused on a universal proposition which it understands and accepts in an indeterminate way. John continues to show how the mind's logical operations work to achieve a conclusion based entirely on the logical relation of ideas, a kind of thinking, *excogitatio*, which remains and can be reflected upon, and therefore is called prudence, an interior perfection of the motion required to attain the most perfect of new knowledge (*per viam addiscendi*).[23] The third kind of intellectual movement appropriate to mind or intellect, (the *via docendi*) is the transference of what is in one mind to another (*transfundere intellectum in alterum*).

In summary, then, John of la Rochelle says that according to John of Damascus cognitive powers can be considered both rational and irrational. The irrational powers of knowing are exterior, like the senses, or interior, like imaginative, excogitative and memorial powers. The rational powers of knowing, collectively known as mind or intellect, are subdivided according to the mode of search employed: 'in via inveniendi et diiudicativam, in via discipline et interpretativam, sive locutivam in via doctrine'.[24]

The last discussion of the soul's divisions comes from the pseudo-Augustinian *De Spiritu et Anima* and from Augustine's *De Trinitate* and the *De Genesi ad Litteram*.[25] From the *De Spiritu* he shows that in the first cerebral compartment where the *vis animalis* resides, one finds the *fantastica*, otherwise known as *ymaginativa* because here images of things and similitudes are imprinted (*imprimantur*). In the middle cavity one finds what is called *rationalis* because here the images are examined and judged that were represented through the imagination. In the ultimate part of the brain is the *memorialis* because here are entrusted the memories judged by

---

[23] *Ibid.*, p. 117.   [24] *Ibid.*, p. 118.   [25] *Ibid.*, pp. 122ff.

reason.[26] These powers may be considered as much of the body as of the soul because the soul is *in corpore*. And thereby we understand the quantity of something according to the particular power of the soul but not the substantial quantity. But the soul also may be considered as having its own powers which Augustine, we are told, divides into the rational, the irascible and the concupiscent. Only through the rational power is the soul illuminated to know what is above it, in it, next to it and within it. For instance, it knows that God is above it, that the soul is in itself, that angels are next to the soul and that whatever the heavens contain is within it.[27]

Augustine divides the powers of the soul in the *De Genesi ad Litteram* in the following way: the sense (*sensus, vis anime*) perceives the present corporeal forms of corporeal things. The *ymaginatio* is a power of the soul which receives the corporeal forms of corporeal things which are now absent. The senses perceive the forms in matter, the imagination perceives these without matter. John of la Rochelle adds that one refers to the forms of exterior things as perceived by the senses as being the same as the forms transferred to the imagination, where we understand 'sameness' in terms of sensitive cognition. Imagination's origin is, therefore, in the senses and varies according to the varieties of diverse things.[28] The reason is a power of the soul whereby the *natures* of corporeal things, the forms, differences, properties and accidents, are perceived as incorporeals but not, John adds, 'extra corpora nisi ratione subsistentia'. The process by which such forms are abstracted from bodies is a process of reflective contemplation rather than an activity in itself. Hence, reason's capacity is to know the abstracted universal from the singular; thus, reason knows the universal in the sensible form.[29] We ought not to be surprised to find him citing Boethius or Porphyry in confirmation. And because reason is thus linked with the senses, John sees it as corruptible. However, intellect, dealing with the intelligible, has no direct relation with the sensible and is, therefore, incorruptible. John proceeds with a discussion of the divisions of intellect.

According to John, the distinction, even made by Aristotle in the *Posterior Analytics*, shows that, on the one hand, *scientia* is the having of conclusions based on corruptible reason, but understanding, *intellectus*, is the acceptance of incorruptible principles. Once again we see the contrary motion of inductive and deductive reasoning which divides the soul, at first in relation to the sensible world, and thereafter alone and by means of

---

[26] *Ibid.*, p. 123. *De Spiritu et Anima*, 22.   [27] *De Spiritu et Anima*, 4.
[28] *Tractatus*, ed. Michaud-Quantin, p. 125.
[29] He cites Boethius on Porphyry in confirmation, and the *De Consolatione Philosophiae*, V, pr. 4 and 5.

its own logic.[30] John returns to the pseudo-Augustinian understanding of memory when he defines the memory as three-fold: memory is that power which conserves sensible species which are common to men and animals. But memory is also the conservation of intelligible species, a capacity which is to be found only in men. Angels, he says, do not know by means of a reception of species. And lastly, memory is the conservation of the divine similitude which we do have in common with the angels.[31] That memorial capacity which is also rational in us is three-fold in its activity: firstly, it retains the intelligible species; secondly, it represents this species; and thirdly, it is capable of retrieving forgotten species and we call this reminiscence, the retrieving of species which men have from sensibles.[32]

The substance of the rational soul is called spirit, animating the body. Therefore, the spirit may be considered an inferior part to reason because according to Augustine (*De Spiritu*) the spirit is some power in the soul inferior to mind whereby corporeal similitudes of things are imprinted. But the spirit can also be called the superior part of reason according to Augustine because this spirit is made in the image of God in which is the knowledge of truth and the love of virtue. The apostle Paul calls this spirit 'mind'.[33]

In the third part of the *Tractatus de Anima*, John of la Rochelle cites Cicero, by means of Augustine, to illuminate the division of the virtues as part of a larger discussion of the perfection of the soul. He tells us that at the end of the first book on *Rhetoric* 'Tully' speaks of the virtues as being possessed as habits by the rational soul, and as having four parts: prudence, justice, fortitude and temperance. Prudence is the knowledge of good and bad things and its parts are memory, providence and intelligence. Memory here is described as that virtue through which the soul revisits (*repetit*) those things which were. 'Memoria est virtus, per quam animus repetit illa que fuerunt.'[34] Intelligence or understanding is the virtue through which the soul perceives those things which are now; and *providentia* is the virtue by which the soul sees something in the future before it actually happens.[35] And John enumerates definitions for the other virtues as discussed in Cicero's *De Inventione* (II, 53) combining this with the phraseology of Augustine. He says that the term 'virtus' used in

---

30 *Tractatus*, ed. Michaud-Quantin, p. 131. In general on the theory of abstraction, see J. Rohmer, 'La théorie de l'abstraction dans l'école franciscaine', *AHDLMA*, 3 (1928), pp. 104–85.
31 *Tractatus*, ed. Michaud-Quantin, p. 132.   32 *Ibid.*   33 *Ibid.*, p. 133.
34 *Ibid.*, p. 155.
35 *Ibid.*, p. 155: 'Intelligentia est virtus per quam perspicit ea que sunt; providentia est virtus per quam futurum aliquid videtur; antequam factum sit.'

the above definitions is not explained by the author but is to be understood.[36] He continues by juxtaposing the classifications of Cicero with those of Plotinus, Aristotle, Augustine, and his contemporary Philip the Chancellor.

John of la Rochelle has provided a compilation of coexisting arguments which show that the soul is both a spiritual substance and a substantial form which assures the life of the body. It possesses a great number of powers that one can set out purely organically, as cognitive sensible powers or as cognitive rational powers, the latter responding to the image of God in man, rendering him capable of an intellectual and moral life. The soul is perfected ultimately through grace and in the exercise of virtues.

[36] *Ibid.*, p. 156.

Chapter 18

AVERROES

The 'Epitome' of the 'Parva Naturalia'; the 'De Memoria'

The mind of man, like that of an animal for that matter, is something that we cannot see or touch or stimulate. It is the faculty which is responsible for that portion of human behaviour which does not seem to be automatic ... Everyone knows that the mind of man is something that depends upon the action of the brain. Things are seen, heard, felt or smelt only when electrical currents are conducted along appropriate nerve tracts to the brain. Problems are worked out by using the brain. A voluntary act is dictated somehow at a high level of organization within the cranial cavity. Then executive messages are flashed down the spinal cord ... It is obvious that there must be a co-ordinating centre within the 'house', a sort of telephone exchange or switchboard to which messages come, and from which messages depart after appropriate decisions be reached, decisions that are based upon memories of previous experience and influenced by present desires. The brain is a large spherical organ that is divided into two partially separated halves, the right and the left hemisphere. A superficial layer of nerve cells covers the whole of the cerebral hemispheres in an outer mantle of grey matter. This is the cerebral bark, or cortex ... The cortex covers the surface of the two hemispheres with a mosaic of functional areas. One area is devoted to vision, another to hearing, another to the sense of touch ... and still others to skills of hand and skills of mouth, such as speaking ... Almost all inward flowing currents of sensation may be said to go to the cortex for elaboration and then on to the upper brain stem [= the grey matter of the old brain, called the thalamus, and the midbrain, in a central position deep within the hemispheres] ... The large sheet of cortex which covers the front part of the brain seems to be utilized by man when he is thinking of new plans and seeking greater insights into life's problems. [A leucotomy], which amputates both frontal lobes, does not produce loss of memory because other parts of the cortex are used for the recording of memory ... In occasional cases of focal epilepsy there is chronic irritation of the cortex on the side beneath the temple and the ear. This is the temporal lobe ... In such conditions, stimulation may awaken a memory or cause the patient to experience a dream that is made up of materials from the storehouse of his memory ... Other evidence has suggested that the similar cortex of the opposite hemisphere contains duplicate recordings of memory patterns. Now, if the individual were to recall voluntarily, the appearance of his mother's living-room, we may surmise that he would activate the same pattern of cortical nerve connections. But he would be activating it from within . . . Thus I am suggesting that the master motor area in the brain of man may be found at the level of the upper brain stem where sensory information of finger position [in playing the piano] is available . . . where the memory of the music is available, as well as the auditory effect, and where conscious control is exerted upon the mechanisms of movement. Such a headquarters switchboard as that is so delicate, so complicated, as to stagger the imagination, but the evidence is overwhelming that it does exist. And it is the seat of consciousness . . . In a sense, therefore, the higher brain stem, together with that portion of the cortex which is being employed at the moment is the seat of consciousness. It is the 'physical basis of the mind', this hypothetical mechanism of nerve cell connections . . . What is the real relationship of this mechanism to the mind? Can we visualize a spiritual element of different essence capable of controlling this mechanism? . . . [A patient] would agree that something else finds its dwelling-place between the sensory complex and the motor mechanism, that there is a switchboard operator as well as a switchboard.

Wilder Penfield, 'The cerebral cortex and the mind of man', in *The Physical Basis of Mind*, ed. P. Laslett (Oxford, 1950), pp. 56–64.

Averroes' *Epitome* of the *Parva Naturalia* was written in Seville around the year 1170.[1] Here the author dealt with memory and reminiscence. A Latin translation, probably by Michael Scot, reached Paris sometime around 1230. With its appearance, the University of Paris was *not* made familiar with a passage by passage, line by line commentary on Aristotle's *De Memoria et Reminiscentia*. Instead, scholars were provided with a summary of Aristotle's conclusions and with Averroes' original ordering and elaboration of these. Where Aristotle mentioned the common sense, the imagination and the memory, Averroes, like his contemporaries, increased these three 'internal senses' to five by drawing on Galen, Alexander of Aphrodisias, Alfarabi and Avicenna. But there is much else that shows not only a sensitive reading of Aristotle but also an extension of his meaning that would, to a considerable degree, help to redirect the course of later thirteenth-century analyses of the memory and its significance.

Averroes begins by distinguishing *rememoratio* from other consequences of perception. He says that we say of things that are perceived by us that they are either perceived at the present time (*in instanti et in tempore presenti*), and instantaneously as with objects of sense, or that they will

[1] Harry Blumberg, *Averroes, Epitome of the Parva Naturalia, Translated from the original Arabic and Hebrew and Latin versions, with Notes and Introduction*, (Cambridge, Mass.: Medieval Academy of America, 1961); Emily Shields, ed., *Averrois Cordubensis compendia librorum Aristotelis qui parva naturalia vocantur* (Cambridge, Mass.: Medieval Academy of America, 1949), the analysis of the *de memoria et reminscentia*, pp. 47–72. Page references below are to the Shields edition.

come into existence at a future time, as with things that are judged (*et iste sunt res existimabiles*), or else, that they were already perceived in a past time. *Rememoratio* is that kind of apprehension based on having perceived in time past, for man remembers in the present those intentions which he has grasped previously, at some time in the past. 'Rememoratio est in istis: non enim vocamus rememorationem nisi illius quod presciebatur in preterito. Rememoratio enim est reversio in presenti intentionis comrehense in preterito.'[2] He is careful to use the term *rememoratio* as applicable to man alone and he sees further that an investigation *per rememorationem* is an inquisition that is voluntary into those intentions or ideas had from images in the imagination, in order to make them present after the things of which they are intentions are no longer present to the senses. 'Investigatio autem per rememorationem est inquisitio istius intentionis per voluntatem et facere eam presentari post absentiam.'[3] *Rememoratio* is, therefore, a kind of recall that is appropriate to man alone, based on what he once experienced and knew in the past. This is distinguished from memory (*memoratio*) which is in all those animals that also have imaginations, Aristotle however, judging that there are some kinds of animals that are not able to imagine.

Recall (*rememoratio*) differs from retention (*conservatione*). Retention refers to that which always was in the soul after it was understood (*comprehensum*). But recall (*rememoratio*) refers to that which was forgotten so that recall is a discontinued retention (*est conservatio abscisa*)[4] while retention is a continuous recall (*conservatio autem est rememoratio continua*). Hence, the rememorative power or faculty is one subject but can be considered two according to its mode of operation. *Rememoratio* (recall) therefore, is firstly the cognition of something that was already known (*quod fuit cognitum*) after the knowledge of it has been discontinued (*postquam cognitio eius fuit abscisa*). Secondly, the investigation that is had through recall (*per rememorationem*) is an acquisition of knowledge through mental labour. The cognitive faculty is exercised in the representation of what it once knew. It is, therefore, the reinstatement of past knowledge voluntarily pursued through a cogitative search. It is this activity which is called the *rememorativa*'s power. Averroes clearly is discussing the reminiscent capacity of which Aristotle spoke. It is the power of recall, the *rememorativa*, that distinguishes man from other animals and engages cogitation.

The *rememorativa* is a faculty that perceives particular, individual things and hence *rememoratio* is none other than a faculty operating after the engagement of sense and imagination. First, there must be an object of

2 *Ibid.*, p. 48.   3 *Ibid.*   4 *Ibid.*, p. 49.

sense and then of imagination for there to be, thereafter, recall. However, the *rememorativa* cannot perceive universals, that is, it does not grasp the *nature* of quantity, which the intellect can apprehend. The *rememorativa* only grasps determined quantity which the senses have already, individually, perceived, and of which imagination has formed a particular image. In what way the universal can be recalled will be discussed below.

The *rememorativa* faculty is, therefore, particular and depends on two prior faculties, *sensus* and imagination. How does it differ from the imagination faculty? They are not the same although they communicate in their activities. All recall and all reminiscence – which is an investigation through recall – occur *propter ymaginationem*, but the intention in recall is different from the imaginative intention: 'tamen intentio rememorationis alia est ab intentione ymaginationis et quod actio istarum duarum virtutum est diversa'.[5] The *rememorativa* faculty's activity has the purpose of making present the intention of the imagined thing after it has disappeared and also to judge it as being the same intention which was previously sensed and imagined. 'Actio enim virtutis rememorative est facere presentare rei ymaginate intentionem quam ante sensit et ymaginabatur'.[6] We note that recall deals only with the making present of intentions and with the judgement that its intention is the same as that previously sensed and imagined. Averroes does not speak here of a corporeal similitude being abstracted by internal senses which, at the level of the estimative faculty just prior to memory, is abstracted further as an intention as well as a spiritualised corporeal similitude, each of which is distinguished and rendered present. He is, here, apparently simplifying the work of the internal senses to a grasping of intentions alone at differing levels of abstraction.

There are four things involved in this process: the image, the intention of the image, the making and presentation of this intention as present, and lastly, the judgement that the intention of the image is the same as that which was previously sensed.[7] The capacity to make an image and present it as present is different from the power to perceive an intention. The faculty that simply perceives intentions acts in one of two ways. If the perception were continuous then the faculty would be called retentive; but if the perception (of the intention) were discontinuous, then the faculty would be called *rememorativa*. 'Facere igitur ymaginem esse presentem necesse est ut sit alterius virtutis a virtute que comprehendit intentionem.

---

[5] *Ibid.*, p. 51.   [6] *Ibid.*

[7] *Ibid.*, pp. 51–2: 'Sunt igitur quatuor, ymago et intentio illius ymaginis et facere illam intentionem que prius sentiebatur et iudicare eam esse intentionem illius ymaginis que prius sentiebatur.'

Et ista virtus invenitur duobus modis. Si comprehensio eius fuerit continua, dicetur conservans; si divisa, dicetur rememorative.'[8] The power to
judge that this intention is from the preceding image is a power that is, in
man, in the intellect because it is intellect which is capable of judging
affirmatively or negatively. In animals, the rememorative faculty is one
which is only *similar* to the intellect. In man, the power to affirm or deny
whether an intention or idea is the same as the imaginations' intention is
performed *per cognitionem*, as when one investigates through recalling.
Animals have this capacity from nature rather than through cognition and
we therefore speak of a kind of animal recall, but they cannot investigate
(wilfully) through recall: 'Et in animalibus rememorativis est simile intel-
lectui; ista enim virtus est in homine per cognitionem et ideo investigat per
rememorationem. In aliis autem est natura, et idea rememorant animalia
sed non investigant per rememorationem.'[9] We do not have a name for
this animal capacity although Avicenna called it *existimatio* (*aestimatio/
vis aestimativa*). Animals are therefore capable of fleeing the harmful
naturally even without having sensually experienced it (*licet numquam
senserit ipsa*).

   Averroes then clarifies his distinction between an image of a thing and
the intention of the image of the thing. In the imagined form there is
something like a subject (*aliquid quasi subiectum*), such as the outline or
shape, and something else which is like a form and this is the intention or
meaning or idea of the shape (*et aliquid quasi forma, et est intentio illius
figure*).[10] Now the individual thing that is outside the soul is composite (in
the Aristotelian sense of being body and form simultaneously). Each of
these, body and form, is received in the soul by two different faculties and
they are combined (once again) by a third faculty.[11] Therefore, what we
have in the soul are three faculties: a faculty which makes and presents the
image of the thing (that is sensed); a faculty which makes and presents the
intention of the image, and a faculty which combines the intention with its
image: 'esse tres virtutes: virtutem scilicet que facit presentari ymaginem
rei, et virtutem que facit presentari intentionem illius ymaginis, et virtutem
que componit illam intentionem cum sua ymagine.'[12] Hence, the process
of investigating through recall (*investigatio per rememorationem*), depends
on these three faculties, in effect, on sense, imagination and cogitative
estimation, whereby each of these faculties makes what is peculiar to itself
and presents it. Aristotle declares that the *virtus rememorativa*, the recall

---

[8] *Ibid.*, p. 52.   [9] *Ibid.*, p. 53.   [10] *Ibid.*, p. 54.
[11] *Ibid.*, p. 54: 'Individuum enim extra animam, quia est compositum, accidit ei ut sit in
anima secundum hoc, et quod receptio duarum partium ex quibus componitur sit duarum
virtutum diversarum, et quod compositio earum sit tertie virtutis.'
[12] *Ibid.*, p. 54.

faculty, is different from the imaginative faculty: we are able to apprehend the intention of an imagined form without the imagined form; also, we are able to apprehend the form without its intention. We can retain many more intentions than we can imagine, that is, there are more ideas of things than there are images of them. Just as the imagination apprehends a subject and retains it in the image – this is similar to a painter who describes the subject on a wall and the image is therefore retained in two dimensions – so too the *rememorativa* apprehends the intention of the picture and not simply the image:

> Et iam diximus quod virtus conservationis et rememorationis est idem in subiecto et duo secundum modum. Quod igitur virtus ymaginativa comprehendit de subiecto est illud quod pictor describit in pariete. Et illud quod comprehendit virtus rememorative est intentio illius picture.[13]

This means that what exists in the *rememorativa* is more spiritual than that which is in the imagination (*quod existit in rememorativa magis est spirituale quam quod in virtute ymaginativa*).[14]

Averroes then provides a slight variation on the now standard description of the process of perception. He describes the diversity of sensible things which then are sensed; the imagination imagines or provides images of what was sensed; then there is a distinction or separation of the intention of this form from its described image; and then the intention alone is retained by the retentive faculty which has received this distinguished or separated intention from the distinguishing faculty. He does not refer to the latter as the *estimativa*, apparently because Avicenna used this term to describe the natural, animal power alone. Men, however, cogitatively distinguish intentions.[15] The human memory faculty therefore retains the intentions which have been distinguished or separated from the images with which they were associated in the imagination. If the sensible thing is no longer there to be sensed, then the memory faculty will restore the intention of the image of the once-sensed object by means of combination, *secundum compositionem*, that is, linking intentions with imagination's images. The activities described in this complex process take place in different parts of the head: the imagination being in the front of the brain, the *cogitans* in the middle and the *memorans et conservans* in the

---

[13] *Ibid.*, p. 55. [14] *Ibid.*, p. 56.
[15] *Ibid.*, pp. 56–7:
Divisio autem est in definitione rei sensibilis, dum fuerit sensibilis. Et hoc erit quando sentiens senserit primo rem extra animam deinde ymaginaverit ymaginans, deinde distinxerit distinguens intentionem illius forme a suo descriptio, cuius est intentio, deinde recipit conservans illud quod distinguens distinguit.

posterior part of the brain.[16] Injuries that may occur to any of these faculties can be regionally located in the brain.

As soon as one speaks in the language of physicians about the location of various faculties of the soul in the brain, then it appears appropriate for Averroes to backtrack and deal with a process of dematerialisation of bodies as the different capacities of the soul deal with them. Averroes describes five stages beginning with a corporeal stage of sensible forms outside the soul. As for Aristotle, it is the corporeal, sensible form rather than the corporeal object that is to be taken inwards even at the level of sense experience. The soul responds to forms in things and the form of a sense object outside the soul is a corporeal form. Secondly, this form comes to be in the *sensu communi* which is the first of the spiritual stages. Thirdly, the form has existence in the imaginative faculty and this is more spiritual than the previous stage. Fourthly, the form exists in the distinguishing faculty, in *virtute distinctiva* (not *aestimativa*).[17] Fifth and lastly it exists in the rememorative faculty, separated (*distinguunt*) from its rind (*cortice*).[18] It appears that the retention of this most spiritual aspect of the form, the intention, is had when the sensible intention is continuously apprehended and this retention is possible, naturally, in animals as well. Forgetting, however, is the cessation of the existence of the intention of a sensible object. By implication, animals can also forget. *Rememoratio* however, is the return of the intention of the sensible object after it has been forgotten and this seems, for Averroes, to occur only through a willed *investigatio rememorationis*, a conscious recollective search whereby the intention is restored and this is only a process proper to man.[19] As in previous discussions, especially that of Avicenna, we are told that animals naturally remember their nests but there is no reference to the possibility of them having forgotten and then recalled because this *rememoratio*, aside from the retentive capacity common to animals and man, requires in man a willed reference to conscious, logical, rational judgement.[20]

Averroes is primarily interested in man, so he says we must now consider how man remembers what he once experienced and forgot. 'Et ideo considerandum est quomodo homo rememorat illud quod sensit et oblitus est.'[21] This occurs when the intention of a thing once sensed is

---

[16] *Ibid.*, p. 57.   [17] Compare Aquinas's *ratio particularis*, ch. 20 below.

[18] Shields, ed., *Averrois Cordubensis*, p. 59.

[19] Aquinas adds that the intention *and* the image are restored but in a series of operations. See below, ch. 20.

[20] Shields, ed., *Averrois Cordubensis*, pp. 59–60: 'Et declaratum est quod conservatio est continuatio esse intentionis sensibilis in hac virtute sine abscisione et quod oblivio est amissio eius et quod rememoratio est reductio eius post oblivionem et quod investigatio rememorationis est acquisitio eius et quod est proprium homini.'

[21] *Ibid.*, p. 60.

made present again. It is as though the perception process runs in reverse. When the *virtus rememorativa* presents the intention, the imagination creates the form of the thing and the distinguishing faculty combines with this imaginative image the intention which it has distinguished and divided, that is, which it has abstracted and separated. The intention of the imaginative form is then re-presented to the *rememorativa*. The role of imagination is one of (symbolic) description and the *distinctiva* faculty combines the intention with its imaginative description. Therefore, through a meeting and joining of these three faculties the forgotten thing in its most spiritual aspect as an intention is presented by means of the recollective search, the *investigatio rememorationis*.[22] This is a natural process in man. When the active recollection of a forgotten object of thought, an intention, proves difficult, it is only because of some weakness or impairment in one of these faculties. And such impairment in a lower faculty will usually be transmitted to a higher faculty by the lower. Therefore, an impairment in *rememoratio* results from an impairment in the lower *distinctiva*. And hence the more spiritual suffers when the corporeal suffers, but the converse – that the corporeal will suffer when the spiritual is impaired – is not true.[23]

There is an interesting consequence of the conjunction of these faculties in representing a thing as an intention linked with its image which once was experienced (*sentiebatur*) but is now forgotten: in some people there will be presented the forms of sensible things which they never experienced themselves(!): 'sed etiam in quibusdam hominibus presentantur apud congregationem earum forme rerum sensibilium quas numquam sensit'. Only the dispositions or attributes of these things will be conveyed to them without their having perceived them.[24] Hence, we are told that Aristotle speaks of one of the ancients being able to form the image of things that were conveyed to him by hearing alone. But when these forms were examined, they were found to have the same attributes as appeared to a person who saw them. This is how one can imagine an elephant without ever having perceived one: 'Et secundum hunc modum potest ymaginari elephantem qui nunquam sensit ipsum'.[25] This occurs as a consequence of the joining of the three faculties, an active conjunction of faculties that occurs by means of the rational soul because the faculties described are obedient to reason and are not merely passive in responding to sensation.[26] Where the faculties are actively, in effect, consciously

---

[22] *Ibid.*, p. 61.   [23] *Ibid.*, p. 62. Compare Aquinas and Ockham below.
[24] Compare R. Wollheim's discussion of Q-memories and acentrally remembering in *The Thread of Life* (Cambridge, 1984), pp. 101–12.
[25] Shields, ed., *Averrois Cordubensis* p. 63.   [26] Compare Aquinas, *ST*, I, 84, 6 ad 2.

joined in man, they are separated in beasts. But Averroes believes that this conjunction of the faculties is difficult to achieve even in man, occurring only when one actively and freely cogitates alone and when one is removed from the distractions that affect the senses. It is then that the common sense, the first spiritual internal sense, helps the other faculties because thinking, even at the most abstract level, never is possible without sensible images.[27]

The uniting of these faculties, without the object of sense being present, occurs in sleep, when the faculties will see the wonders of the world. There are mental dispositions that are akin to sleep which also produce this unity of interior faculties.[28] Aristotle tells us that there are times when the faculties need not be conjoined for any one of them to present the image or intention appropriate to each. There are, therefore, instances when the *rememorativa* and the *imaginativa* present their own images or intentions, operating alone, so that one can imagine without remembering, and recall without imagining.[29] But these are relatively rare occurrences.

The motion in the soul, when one is engaged in recall (*rememoratio*) is an interrupted motion, a movement running over the parts of an object to be recalled as these are represented in the soul through similitudes. What happens is that one moves by passing from known things to the parts of the forgotten things to be recalled. However, the motion involved in simple retention is continuous. The process of recall is a movement from a similar object in the soul, a similitude, to the parts of the thing to be recalled, that is, we recall through similitudes.[30] The motion in *rememoratio* is a non-equal movement from a similar thing in the soul, a similitude, to the thing itself. But because retention is continuous, Averroes believes it to be more noble than the interrupted process required when one recalls.[31] The discipline of looking for a lost object by means of a mental similitude is not, therefore, as important or noble in man as the capacity to retain what one once knew. The conserving or retentive faculty generally will present

---

[27] This is where the Ciceronian memory places may be fitted in, and are so discussed by Albertus Magnus and Aquinas.

[28] Shields, ed., *Averrois Cordubensis*, p. 64: 'et etiam in dispositionibus similibus sompno'.

[29] Compare Wollheim's discussion of noniconic memory, *The Thread of Life*, pp. 98f.

[30] Shields, ed., *Averrois Cordubensis*, pp. 64–5:
Et differentia inter motum anime super partes rei et facere illam presentari secundum rememorationem et inter motum anime super partes rei et facere illam presentari secundum conservationem est quod motus eius super partes rerum conservan darum est motus continuus, et motus eius super partes rerum rememorandarum est abscisus, et secundum translationem de rebus extraneis ad partes rerum rememorandarum: quod enim rememoratur, rememoratur per suum simile.

[31] *Ibid.*, p. 65: 'Et ideo conservatio nobilior est rememoratione: motus enim equalis continuus nobilior est absciso diverso'.

the intentions of parts of objects retained in a continuous way. A good retentive memory will therefore house the intentions of past perceptions without their corporeal aspects. *Rememoratio* occurs with forms that are easy to recover whereas a recollective search, *investigatio rememorationis*, occurs when the forms are difficult to recover. Universal concepts can indeed be recalled but only by virtue of the imaginative images joined to them;[32] hence, there is no remembering without sensible phantasms, as Aristotle said. Forgetting can occur in the case of universals just as with regard to the intentions of particulars. The ease with which *rememoratio* proceeds depends on the forms in the imaginative and common sense faculties being more corporeal than spiritual. The forms that are difficult to recover are those that are mainly spiritual. The common sense deals with corporeal forms, taking longer to abstract their spirituality from their corporeality. Hence the form lasts longer in the common sense, especially when the common sense receives a more spiritual form. Averroes has placed great value on the sense memory and the necessity of retaining corporeal sense images for there to be any higher mode of thinking and recalling. And he thereby concludes his discussion of the means by which the processes of *rememoratio* and the *investigatio rememorationis* occur and how they differ from retention.[33] Thus far, he seems to have discussed the internal activities and interconnections between mind or soul, so that no emotion attends recall or the recollective search. But then he asks why the person who recalls (*rememorans*), sometimes experiences pleasure and pain even though the pleasurable or painful things themselves are not actually present. And why are some people good at recalling (*rememoratio*) and others good at retaining (*conservatio*)?

We say that a person good at recalling, experiences pleasure through recalling things which are not actually present because recall is induced by means of other things, similitudes, which *are* present and these necessarily are similar to the thing recalled: 'Dicamus igitur quod rememorans delectatur per rememorationem rerum que non sunt in actu, quia illa que induxerunt ipsum ad rememorandum presentia sunt in actu, et sunt necessario similia rebus rememorandis'.[34] This emotionally-linked recall is a special case of the nonemotional kind described above. Memories do not, in themselves, induce emotion. Only the presence of similitudes representing past remembered things inspires emotional responses which then get linked to the mental thing, or intention, being recalled. The thing that is similar to that which he wishes to recall is apprehended *actually* and

---

[32] Hence Cicero's advice to link abstract ideas with corporeal images that are the more easily recalled.

[33] Shields, ed., *Averrois Cordubensis*, p. 67.   [34] *Ibid.*, p. 68.

therefore, the person who recalls, experiences the pleasure or pain associated with the similitude perceived and he has a kind of hope that something, some mental intention, will actually occur to him in conformity with its similitude. Thus, the mental thing to be recalled, that is, the intention, has the possibility, the potential, of existence is so far as it is like that which is its similitude and which is already in existence and represented in the common sense and imagination. When the soul recalls something through a similitude of the mental thing to be recalled, it perceives that this sensible similitude is of the same kind (*est de genere illius*) as that which had being, only potentially, that is, the intention, and he perceives that it is possible to bring this intention into existence like the similitude that already exists and which excites or stimulates the soul. Hence, pain and pleasure can be recalled in the same way as these would occur were the 'thing' with which these emotions are linked existing in actuality.[35] The 'thing' that is similar to 'that which' one wishes to recall, is a similitude or phantasm, and the 'thing to be recalled' is an intention and not the exterior substantial thing. It is striking that Averroes refers to the 'thing to be recalled' which is an abstracted intention, as a 'thing' (*rem*), a mental species. This analysis in the *Epitome*, would be crucially influential on Albertus Magnus and Thomas Aquinas, as we shall see.

A capacity for good recall (*rememoratio*) in man depends on the complexion of the posterior part of the brain which should be dry to retain the forms which it receives with difficulty. Once the form is received, then innately (*innata*) it is grasped and retained for a long time. Those with humid posterior parts of the brain are not able to recall things since forms exist for a short period in moisture, but such people will be able to grasp things quickly because the humour easily receives the form although they do not endure. Those who have much dryness in the brain retain little but recall much. Those who have much humidity in the posterior part of the brain are quick at grasping but forget a great deal and recall with difficulty. The best thing is to have a medium complexion in order to retain and remember well.[36] A good memory is associated with youth; man recalls many things that he experienced in childhood because in childhood he

---

35 *Ibid.*, pp. 68–9.
Quia igitur simile rei est comprehensum in actu ab eo, accidit rememoranti delectatio et contristatio apud illum, quod accideret ei si illa res esset in actu; et quasi habet spem ut illa res exeat in actum, et quasi esset apud animam possibile, quoniam, quando simile rei fuerit tunc erit res quam possibilis ut sit. Quando anima fuerit rememorans aliquid per aliquod simile illi rei, statim percipiet quod illud sensibile est de genere illius quod erat ens in potentia et quod est possibile ut exeat in actum, sicut est possibile quod excitat in actum hoc simile, per quod fuit excitatus super illam rem; et tunc accidit rememoranti de tristitia aut de delectatione, quod accideret ei si esset in actu.

36 *Ibid.*, pp. 70–1.

loves the forms and is eager to receive them. Hence they will be fastened in him and removed only with difficulty.

There is a distinctive emphasis in Averroes's presentation of memory in his *Epitome* which we will find reaffirmed in Aquinas. He has definitely linked the experiences of the body with the rational powers of the soul. However, he says virtually nothing about Aristotle's imprinted similitudes and nowhere implies that the memory, as the lower perceptual aspect of the soul, may be likened to wax imprinted with a signet ring. Furthermore, he seems intent on focusing on *rememoratio* and the *investigatio per rememorationem*, the first being the faculty or power which apprehends intentions of ideas that are always based on one having perceived them in more corporeal manner in a past time through the senses and the imagination's images of the sensed form. Averroes insists that *rememoratio* requires a *knowledge* of something in the past and *rememoratio* is the cognition of something previously known after the knowledge of it has been discontinued. The investigative recollection had through the operation of the *memoratio* is a laborious activity rather than a passive capacity, whereby the cogitative faculty is exercised to re-present a mental 'thing', that is, what it once knew as a result of sensed experiences. The rememorative faculty in man is linked to intellect because before one can recall one has to have the judgement that the intention retained in the memory is the same as the intention associated with the sensible, more corporeal imaginative image and with the sensed form in the common sense. Aquinas will also place great emphasis on this. Averroes is unwilling to allow animals any serious capacity for affirmative or negative judgement because, he says, they evaluate not through cognition but naturally, as though unconsciously. Certainly, they cannot use their memories to initiate a wilful search for things forgotten. Averroes has emphasised, as Aquinas will after him and to a greater degree, the role of wilful cognition in the process of intellection and recall.

What is very distinctive is his discussion of the interrelated faculties of the soul, which enable imagination and recall to proceed simply on the basis of mind's interconnectedness based on sensible similitudes. It is only when we feel emotions attached to certain memories that he is willing to say that the reason for this is not because emotion can be retained in the soul, but emotion is attached to a disposition we manifest when we confront mental similitudes of things in the world and which, when actually experienced as sensible similitudes, engage the emotions; the mental dispositions, the intentions, are in potency and depend on the actuality of the images and intentions that are present in our imaginations and memories. Imagination and memory in themselves are devoid of feeling. And in particular, both recall at the continuous retentive level or at the discontinuous level of a search for what has been forgotten, are involved with the most spiritual entities or intentions which, in being dependent on more corporeal similitudes, are actualised from being merely potential. Aquinas will clarify this further.

What is also interesting is the presentness of images and intentions in the soul. *Rememoratio* is based on a knowledge of something known or experienced in the past, but the memory itself presents present intentions, based on present, imaged similitudes of past things, intentions which appear to have no temporal depth. The temporal dimension emerges only through an investigative search in mind for what has been forgotten and which can be retrieved through present similitudes so that the meaning or intention of the memory sought for and found, is present. There is no image or intention representing a time lapse. And as we shall see for Aquinas, time is not imaged or represented as an intention either; time is somehow known through one's consciousnes of mental activities. The more spiritual an intention, the less tied it is to change. Therefore, it is more noble according to Averroes, for the mind to be continuously retaining intentions of past experiences than to have to work at what it has forgotten. A continuous, ever-present memory, a recall of numerous ideas or meanings or intentions, comprises a near-perfect memory faculty. If a man has the capacity for largely continuous presentation of intentions based on past experiences which he knows through the present, actual, similitudes in imagination, we must ask whether he has any grasp of the past as past at all? Or is he living a resplendent present not unlike Funes the Memorious? Aquinas will make the definitive statement that at the level of understanding, the past as past is irretrievable because irrelevant to the universals with which understanding mind operates.

Like Aristotle, Averroes employs a potentiality–actuality mechanism whereby the activity of remembering what has been forgotten is akin to the memory being potentially, and thereafter actually, what the experienced or known thing is in thought. Although Aristotle did not explicitly apply this to the memory faculty, he argued that the activity of the object of perception and of the sense organ is one and the same, and Averroes extends the argument to the conserving, retaining memory and the active search to restore the intention to an actualised present. As with Aristotle, the perceptible form as well as the perceiving, imaging and judging capacities are all in the perceiver. And it is clear that Averroes's *rememoratio* is always linked to perception and hence, dependent in the first instance, on having experienced the world. But like Aristotle, he provides for the possibility of imagining and remembering not based on sensual

413

experiences of one's own but rather on the reports of others; hence the ability to think of an elephant accurately, based on an aural/oral rendering of its characteristics, without ever having seen one. This is because Averroes, like Aristotle and like Aquinas after him, emphasises the active role of reasoning and distinguishing along with the congruence between the world and man's conscious thoughts, based on adequate imaged similitudes which allow for the accuracy of syllogistic deduction.

Averroes has focused extensively on Aristotle's recollective or reminiscent process – which Aristotle described as a logical, reasoning process, a search starting from one's thinking of something rather than from one's perceiving it. It is a wilful, deliberate undertaking. As for Aristotle, recollecting is not learning for Averroes, but rather a deliberate, self-motivated, autonomous search process in mind. It can culminate in remembering but it does not require, as remembering in the sense that continuous retention requires, sense images themselves. *Rememoratio* rather, involves the voluntary and laborious association of and comparison and distinction of ideas or intentions, based on sense experience's mental similitudes. *Rememoratio* like Aristotle's recollection, assumes there has been a gap during which knowledge has been forgotten. The recovery of previously known intentions is not possible for animals just as Aristotle said recollection or reminiscence is not possible for animals. Recollection or *rememoratio* begins with a consciously chosen starting point and is based on mental things being recognised as related in some succession and order along with the ability to recognise necessary similarities between what one is looking for and other mental things that are present in the mind. It requires that one reason that one formerly saw or heard or knew something. *Rememoratio* is a mental syllogism in operation, based on the adequacy of mental symbols to the sensually experienced world.

This analysis will be found to be co-extensive with the more famous and influential elaboration by Thomas Aquinas. What is extraordinary is that in Averroes's other commentaries, on the *De Anima* and the *Metaphysics*, for instance, he presents aspects of a theory of mind that are not in harmony with what he says in the *Epitome*, and Aquinas would argue strenuously against these propositions when he returned to Paris in 1269. Averroes's monopsychism, his anti-creationist theory of the eternity of the world, the doctrine of an incompatible double-truth – one according to faith and one according to philosophy, the doctrine of union in the soul by means of intermediate images, the teaching on the pains sustained by the separated soul, the supposed doctrine that the soul contains innate intelligibles, as these were defended by heterodox Aristotelians like Siger of Brabant,[37] put Aquinas on guard during the early 1270s. But virtually none of these doctrines surfaces in the *Epitome*.

[37] See especially Siger of Brabant, *Quaestiones in Tertium de Anima*, ed. Bernard Bazán (Louvain and Paris, 1972), Qq. 9–12; pp. 25–43; Q. 14 on the eternity of the separated agent intellect, pp. 52–3, and Q. 15,2 on the single intellect (monopsychism) for all men, p. 55. But Siger says (Q. 11) that the doctrine of the soul containing innate intelligibles is not only one with which he does not agree, but one which does not represent Averroes' meaning. Furthermore, Siger says in Q. 9, p. 28: In *De Anima*, III, 5 Averroes says: 'intellectus speculativa iam ipse in omnibus est unus secundum recipiens, diversus autem secundum receptum ... unde intellectus speculativus in hoc homine est corruptibilis, est tamen secundum se et simpliciter aeternus (ut dicit Averroes).' On Averroes reading Themistius as holding that the intellect is one for all men, see E. P. Mahoney, 'Themistius and the Agent Intellect in James of Viterbo and other thirteenth-century philosophers (St Thomas, Siger of Brabant and Henry Bate)', *Augustiniana*, 23 (1973), pp. 422–67. For the doctrine of monopsychism – that the potential intellect is one for all men and that it contains the first principles of knowledge which are required by men in order to think – see *Averroes, Commentarium magnum in Aristotelis de anima libros*, ed. F. Stuart Crawford (Cambridge, Mass., 1953), III, comm. 5, pp. 406–7. In what is believed to be Siger's later work, the *Quaestiones de Anima Intellectiva*, he sets out the arguments against the multiplication of the intellect and then admits these are difficult to maintain. See *Quaestiones de Anima Intellectiva*, ed. P. Mandonnet, in *Siger de Brabant et l'averroisme latin au XIIIᵉ siècle*, part II (textes inédits) second edn (Louvain, 1908), pp. 143–71, pp. 164–7. Here, there is one agent intellect which illuminates the many agent intellects in men's souls, and these in turn illuminate the potential intellects of men's souls. For a more recent and comprehensive edition of the *De Anima Intellectiva* along with the *Quaestiones in Tertium de Anima* and the *De Aeternitate Mundi* see the edition by B. Bazán (Louvain and Paris, 1972), cited above.

Chapter 19

ALBERT THE GREAT

Coming from a generation of theologians who wrote treatises on the *De Anima* linked with tracts *De Bono et Virtutibus*, Albert the Great included in his *De Bono*[1] a discussion of memory, both from the standpoint of psychology and from that of Cicero's *Rhetoric* and the *De Inventione*. As was clear in earlier tracts like that of John of la Rochelle, memory and reminiscence were already linked with the virtue of prudence, following John of Damascus's classification of the virtues.[2] Whilst memory, according to Albert, is said to pertain to the sensible part of the soul, prudence pertains to the rational part since, we are told, according to Aristotle's definition, reminiscence pertains to the rational part and hence is the type of memory which constitutes a part of prudence. By this Albert means to distinguish the stored results of the human estimative cogitation which judges the intentions of sensible experience, from the subsequent activity which leads to an attempt by reason to recall the mental similitude engendered by imagination's similitude.[3] Prudence is for Albert a moral *habitus* and hence reminiscence is a psychological *habitus*, an active, discontinuous, syllogistic search amongst mental similitudes, whereas the recollection of impressions and events of the past is not a *habitus* in and of itself. As John of la Rochelle said, summarising John of Damascus, when the motion of mind is focused on a universal proposition which understands in an indeterminate way, the mind's logical operations achieve a conclusion based on *the relation of ideas* to be reflected upon. This is prudence and the means to its achievement is *per viam addiscendi*. Memory

---

[1] Albertus Magnus, *Opera Omnia*, ed. H. Kühle, C. Feckes, B. Geyer and W. Kübel (Münster in Westphalia, 1951), XXVIII.

[2] See O. Lottin, *Psychologie et Morale aux XIIe et XIIIe siècles* (Louvain and Gembloux, 1949–60), I, pp. 393–424, and III, pp. 99–194, on John of Damascus' influence. The Ciceronian divisions of the virtues came to the Latin west directly or via Augustine and Macrobius, prior to the penetration of the complete text of Aristotle's *Nicomachean Ethics*. Lottin, *Psychologie et morale*, III, pp. 99 ff. Also R. Baron, 'A propos des ramifications des vertus au XIIe siècle', *RTAM*, 23 (1956), pp. 19–39.

[3] Albertus Magnus, *Opera Omnia*, *De Bono*, a. 1, pp. 245–6.

can be considered a moral *habitus*, says Albert, only when one *uses* it to recall past things in view of prudent conduct in the present and regarding a prudential view for the future. Only when memory as reminiscence can be *used* to draw useful lessons from the past is it a part of prudence.[4]

In Article 2, where he analyses Cicero's mnemonic *ars memorandi*, taking into account the rules for places and images, Albert notes in a distinctive way that the artificial memory should be seen as a *habitus* pertaining to the rational part of the soul because the *ars memoria* is a *use* of recalled impressions and is not to be equated simply with the technical 'imprinting' process. An elaborate synthesis of Aristotle's discussion of reminiscence and Cicero's education of memory is thereafter attempted.

Albert advises that one use real places of the memory, memorised in real buildings without constructing imaginary systems. The places that are best imprinted on the memory are corporeal, *loca corporalia*. These are found in the imagination as a result of imagination's reception of corporeal forms of sensory impressions. Such places are not found in the intellectual part of the soul for here one does not speak of memory but of reminiscence and the latter uses not real but imaginary places for rational ends.[5] Like his predecessors, Albert asserts that the memory is not only a collection of forms or images, since this is rather the definition of the imagination. Memory is also the collection of intentions drawn from the imagination's images, received in the memory by way of the estimative faculty. Taking the well-worn Avicennan example of sheep and wolves, Albert reaffirms that the estimation not only contains the image recalling the form of the wolf but also the wolf's intention, the idea of wolfness, as evaluated by the sheep.

Francis Yates has discussed the important use of Cicero's advice on remembering images for words and remembering images for things to be found in Albert's *De Bono*, along with Albert's criticism of this technique.[6] It is his criticism that is of greater importance: would it not be better, he says, to recall events by their *propria* rather than through an imprecise metaphorical representation of things?[7] Indeed, is not the soul's epistemology more important than rhetoric? Albert acknowledges that *propria* give more exact information about the thing itself, even though *metaphorica* moves the soul and aids the memory; for this reason it is believed that the first philosophers expressed themselves poetically.[8] Like Averroes's discussion of emotion which sometimes attends recall, emotional response to

---

[4] *Ibid.*, a. 1 second response.   [5] *Ibid.*, *solutio* to the twelfth point, p. 251.
[6] Francis Yates, *The Art of Memory* (London, 1966), pp. 69 ff.
[7] Albertus Magnus, *Opera Omnia, De Bono*, 16, pp. 247–8.
[8] *Ibid.*, *solutio* to point seventeen, p. 251. Yates (*The Art of Memory*, p. 78) is wrong in saying that this appeal to the emotions is uncharacteristic of scholasticism's puritanism!

417

metaphor is *an addition to* the remembering process and not its essential nature. Memories do not, in themselves, induce emotion. Averroes had argued that only the presence of similitudes representing past remembered things inspires emotional responses which then are linked to the mental image, the mental thing being recalled in a recollective search.

Albert is not interested in memorial techniques but the rational and prudential purposes to which these might be put. Hence, he concludes his discussion of Cicero's twentieth point in what was called his *Secunda Rhetorica* by saying that Tully's *ars memorandi* is the best technique to aid the recall of those things which touch on life and judgement. And such artificial memory holds special interest for the moral man and for the orator since the activities of human life comprise particular things and are in the soul by means of corporeal images. They will not remain in the memory without such images and therefore, of all things comprising prudence, memory is the most necessary. Memory guards the intentions of past sensibles, but the *habitus* of prudence is the *use* of the memory for exemplary purposes and an *ars memoria* has as its purpose the *use* of images for moral ends. This is because past things direct us towards the present and future, the past may be used to learn something about the present and the future.[9] We note that for Albert the past in its particularity is of no interest in and of itself. In effect, it cannot be grasped by the higher, understanding mind which only deals with abstracted *species intelligibles*, that is, universals.

Albert also wrote a commentary on Aristotle's *De Memoria et Reminiscentia*.[10] He provides the standard Avicennan psychology whereby sensory impressions pass by different stages from the common sense to memory and are progressively dematerialised. He emphasises Aristotle's distinction between memory and reminiscence and shows that although reminiscence is more spiritual and characteristic of the intellectual part of the soul, this activity still has traces of corporeal forms. Therefore, the things to be recalled pass through different faculties from the sensitive part of the soul to attain, with reminiscence, the domain of the intellect which distinguishes them. Memory, as an *art*, pertains to reminiscence rather than to sensual memory, and the best mental temperaments are those of dryness and coldness in the posterior ventricle of the brain.

While it is, of course, interesting that Albert includes in his discussion of reminiscence the prudential art of memory, it should not be concluded that his primary focus is here. Rather, like so many of his contemporaries,

---

[9] Albertus Magnus, *Opera Omnia*, p. 249.
[10] Albertus's commentary on the *De Anima*, ed. A. Borgnet, in *Opera Omnia* (Paris, 1890), V, and on the *De Memoria et Reminiscentia*, ed. A. Borgnet, in *Opera Omnia*, IX, pp. 97ff.

he collected information from the most varied of sources in order to elaborate on those areas of epistemological concern that were so central to Aristotle in his *De Anima* and his *De Memoria*, especially as these had been analysed by Averroes. And a major interest, demonstrated clearly by Albert's own conclusions, was that sensitive memory and rational, prudential memory were not to be entirely separated but rather linked through the increasing dematerialisation of species or similitudes.

At the heart of the scholastic theory of logical signification was the assumption that when the mind and the senses are working correctly and the things to be signified are not in themselves confusing, the spoken sign or the mental similitude or image signify their objects with an automatic truth, a truth that is real because it denotes the *resemblance* between the word or concept and the existing thing it represents. In effect, for them a real thing has entered the mind of a subject by means of its dematerialised similitude. By this similitude a person is judged to have a correct knowledge of what the similitude represents and he is thereafter capable of conveying it to others and relating similitudes, by analogy, to other things which he knows. Scholastics increasingly employed the formal discipline of logic to the conceptual realm whereby the world is signified in the mind by ideas which are formed to signify the intentions or intelligible species of things; words are the tools required to signify ideas in so far as one wishes to communicate them to others, and these ideas have their origin in sensibles. Thus, in general, knowledge of the world begins with sensation and sense impressions automatically and naturally signify the objects they represent as similitudes The phantasm, as an accurate sensible sign that is formed out of sensory impressions, is then transformed into an intelligible sign by a faculty of mind. The significative content, the intention of the imaginative image of the sense experience, is distilled by the activity of progressive abstraction to reveal the intelligible species, that aspect of the phantasm or imaginative similitude which is capable of being conceptualised. As Aquinas, Albert's student, was to point out, in accordance with earlier theories that we have examined, the active intellect is responsible for this distillation of the significative content of the phantasm, and the intelligible species that results from this process is then impressed on the possible intellect in so far as mind can know all things. It is the possible intellect which creates a *verbum mentis* and this is directly analogous to the imaged phantasm that is produced automatically and naturally. Sensory data require processing to allow for the extraction of intelligible components.

By the mid thirteenth century, this processing was understood as an activity that brings the world inwards. The *verbum mentis* is not a sign of a purely intellectual object of knowledge known by intuition divorced from sense experience. Instead, as Averroes had argued, the validity of a mental sign, a mental similitude, must be actively judged as truly representative of its object, and the intentionality of this judgement makes it clear that similitudes require a conscious acknowledgement of their accuracy on the part of the knower and rememberer. As we saw in Blund and thereafter, the subject must be simultaneously aware of the object of his thought and memory as well as of the contents of his mind. The knowing and remembering subject actively measures the concept or the signifying word against the yardstick of its object.[11] As Colish has correctly argued, the beings signified are always the criteria of the correspondence[12] and therefore, the truth of ideas that men have of objects depends on sense experiences *that are imaged.*[13]

This also means that for scholastics there is a confidence in the ability of language's logic to describe or represent the proper structure of the world:[14] relations between things in nature can be explained by means of logical relationships. Abelard had already affirmed this. And yet for Abelard as for later scholastics, mental similitudes as well as verbal signs are different from their objects. As Aquinas would point out, men do not know objects perfectly. But at the other end of the process of knowing, those universal causes of things, those entities devoid of matter, while being the most actual and therefore the most intrinsically intelligible of things in the universe, are even less known, because separate substances cannot be known in their essences perfectly. Therefore, mind, with all its capacities to abstract intelligible species or intentions from material objects and hence to operate at the level of universals, must depend on the im-mattered world. Being and its modes is, as Aquinas would make clear, always prior to knowledge and its modes. Hence, intelligibility is a property of things in themselves. Things do not acquire intelligibility once they exist in the understanding mind. Men know whatever they know in terms of a limited, imperfect, sense-bound mode of knowing. Aquinas's careful elaboration of this thesis would show him to be the greatest synthesizer of an already developing thirteenth-century epistemology which sought to link matter and form, the world of sensual experiences and interpreting

---

11 But note, the object is not directly the extramental *res* but its similitude in sense and intellect.

12 Marcia Colish, *The Mirror of Language, A Study in the Medieval Theory of Knowledge* (New Haven, 1968), p. 174.

13 Aquinas, *ST* Ia Q. 85 a. 7 and 2. Truth in the intellect consists in the fact that things are known to be as they are (*Veritas enim intellectus in hoc consistit, quod intelligatur res esse sicuti est*).

14 But there is no concern to *prove* this correspondence because any study of signs, linguistic or psychological, cannot approach the things to which signs refer.

mind, body and soul, in opposition to the Franciscan Platonism champto by his contemporary Bonaventure. Platonism was in partial eclipse: mind, for Aquinas, can never get rid of existing things. Sensibly derived intelligible signs do not leave the knower or rememberer trapped in his own mind. As David of Dinant propounded it in radical terms and as Aquinas would propound it in more accommodating ones, any investigator of the world, any experiencer and rememberer, must have a prior knowledge of God in order to appreciate fully the importance of the world of creation and its resemblance to Him, a resemblance that was couched in terms of spirituality *and* materiality. Aquinas would point out that God had expressly constructed the world to be like Him and He has provided a set of *signa Dei* for man,[15] which aid in the restoration of a right relationship between man and God which is obstructed by sin. Aquinas, like others of his time, was philosophically certain that the world resembles God who is its first cause, and hence, he believed that the world can, indeed must, provide us with information about God through reasoning based on our sense experience of creation.[16] Aquinas would summarise eloquently a long-developing doctrine of the accuracy of similitudes which placed overall emphasis on the 'fact' that we derive analogical concepts about God from our experience of nature at large. Hence, the most important similitude we can ever know is the mind of man. Psychology, as expressed in Aristotelian terms, was ultimately of greater importance than cosmology for Aquinas, so that in the now familiar tradition, established during Abelard's generation and thereafter, legitimate comparisons *were* to be drawn between the interactions of man's mental faculties, the process of the formation of images and concepts, the relation of man's inner ideas and his external expressions of them on the one hand, and the relationship amongst the persons of the Trinity. Augustine could thereby be seriously reintegrated into an Aristotelian psychology, but with Augustine's Platonism quite remarkably suppressed.[17]

---

[15] Colish, *The Mirror of Language*, p. 182.

[16] The essence of God (as opposed to limited creatures with determined existences, *creatura habet esse finitum et determinatum*) is a perfect likeness of all things and of every aspect found in all things as the universal cause of all (*Sed essentia Dei est perfecta similitudo omnium quantum ad omnia quae in rebus inveniuntur, sicut universale principium omnium*). We note that for Aquinas, *ST* Ia Q. 84 a. 2 ad 2 God is the perfect similitude of creatures rather than David of Dinant's reversal of this.

[17] See the discussion below, ch. 20. In *ST* Ia Q. 77 a. 5 ad 3 Aquinas says Augustine is *not* affirming but merely giving an account of Plato on sensation! (*non asserendo sed recitando*).

Chapter 20

THOMAS AQUINAS

One of the crucial points of difference between Aquinas and many of his Christian predecessors and contemporaries was over the role of man's body both in perception and intellection.[1] Here, he was indebted to Averroes and to an extremely close reading of Aristotle.[2] Aquinas forthrightly argued against all dualist theories of man, especially those of Avicenna, his Franciscan contemporary Bonaventure, and all the other neo-Platonists including the pseudo-Augustinian author of the *De Spiritu et Anima*.[3] Man's nature is composite; he is a being made up of both body and soul, so that intellect always owes a debt to sensation. The whole world of sensory experience, the external world which leaves phantasms or impressions in the soul, is not only necessary for man's development and essential to his very nature, but also he achieves blessedness through it. The body is not merely the soul's garment or its prison. The soul does not merely *use corpora*. Sensation, rather, belongs to the soul and body conjoined and this makes man a kind of hybrid. Averroes had similarly emphasised this, but had not satisfactorily individuated men within the species. In the *Summa Theologiae* where Aquinas begins his so-called 'treatise on man', he wrote that man must be considered a compound whose substance is both spiritual and corporeal

---

[1] Bruno Nardi, 'Anima e corporo nel pensiero di San Tommaso (1942)', *Studi di Filosofia medievale*, Storia e Letteratura, 78 (Rome, 1960), pp. 163–91.

[2] On Aquinas's use of Averroes and his not quite accurate description of the details of Averroes's scheme, see H. A. Wolfson, 'The internal senses in Latin, Arabic and Hebrew philosophic texts', *Harvard Theological Review*, 28 (1935), pp. 69–133; pp. 121–2. According to Wolfson, in general, the thirteenth-century Latin authors (Aquinas, Albertus, Roger Bacon etc.) all fail to reproduce with accuracy the use of the term *cogitativa*, in both Avicenna and Averroes. The shift is evident from a Galenic and medical tradition to an Aristotelian one, in so far as they can get at it through the commentaries of Avicenna and Averroes.

[3] *ST* Ia Q. 77, a. 8 ad 1 speaking of the *De Spiritu et Anima*, Aquinas says 'this book has no authority'.

(Ia q. 75).[4] Writing this between 1266–8, roughly at the same time as his commentary on Aristotle's *De Anima*, Aquinas argued[5] that the soul has no activity without the body, not even the act of understanding.[6] Understanding never takes place without images and there are no images apart from the body[7] as Aristotle had said. The body, Aquinas argues, is necessary for the activity of the intellect, not as the organ through which it acts, but rather in order to supply it with its object; for images stand in relation to the intellect as colour in relation to sight.[8] When some argue that 'the soul is the man', Aquinas says that they sometimes mean that the form alone pertains only to the individual – say, Socrates – and not to the type or species. But, he says, this cannot be the case. For the nature of a specific type, a species, includes whatever its strict definition includes,[9] and in things of the physical world this means not only form but form and matter.[10] Thus, materiality is part of the specific type in physical natures, not *this* determinate matter *here*, which individuates a thing, but materiality in general (*unde materia est pars speciei in rebus naturalibus; non quidem materia signata, quae est principium individuationis, sed materia communis*).[11]

Therefore, when we speak about sensation we must not understand this to be an activity of the soul alone. Sensing, says Aquinas, is an activity of the whole man, even though it is not peculiar to man. Man is no mere soul (*Homo non est anima tantum sed est aliquid compositum ex anima et corpore*).[12] But this does not mean for Aquinas that the intellective soul, the *anima intellectiva* is composed of matter and form. If it were thus composed, the forms of things would be received into it in all their concrete individuality so that intellection would always and only be of the singular as he believes is the case for sense knowledge. But since the intellective soul knows forms in isolation from their concrete materiality, that is, since man's concepts are universal rather than individual, the intellectual soul cannot itself be composed of form and matter.[13] Hence, the receptive capacity of the intellectual soul is quite different from the receptive capacity of prime matter as is obvious from the different natures of what they receive; prime

---

[4] *ST* Ia Qq. 75–83, The Treatise on Man, Latin text and English translation by Timothy Suttor (Blackfriars, 1970), XI. The translations in this chapter are modifications of that in the Blackfriars edition. *ST* Ia Q. 75: 'qui ex spirituali et corporali substantia componitur'.
[5] *ST* Ia Q. 75 a. 2, 3.   [6] *Ibid.*: 'nec etiam intelligere'.
[7] *Ibid.*: 'quia non contingit intelligere sine phantasmate'.
[8] *Ibid.*: 'ad tertium ... corpus requiritur ad actionem intellectus, non sicut organum quo talis actio exerceatur, sed ratione objecti; phantasma enim comparatur ad intellectum sicut color ad visum'.
[9] *Ibid.*: 'ad naturam speciei pertinet id quod significat definitio'.
[10] *Ibid.*: 'sed formam et materiam'.
[11] *Ibid.*, ad 4.   [12] *Ibid.*, Q. 75 a. 4.   [13] *Ibid.*, Q. 75 a. 5 responsio.

matter, we are told, receives concrete individual forms (*materia prima recipit formas individualis, intellectus autem recipit formas absolutas*), but the intellect receives forms stripped of their concrete individuality, and hence receives them absolutely. The Platonists, like Bonaventure, were therefore confusing potentiality with materiality. The potentiality of mind is not like prime matter's potentiality. The way each undergoes change is different.[14] The intellect has a capacity to receive intelligible things into itself (*quod est in potentia ad species intelligibiles*). As Aristotle says, there is a distinction between the shift from potentiality to actuality in things compounded from matter and form, and the shift from potentiality to actuality in nonmaterial intellectual substances. In the latter, Aquinas argues, there is a composition of potentiality and actuality but not of matter and form.[15] Rather, what one has in intellectual substances is the form and its participated existence.[16] Instead of speaking of matter and form, one is, or ought to be, speaking of the really distinct categories of essence and existence in all creatures. When intellect undergoes the change peculiar to intellectual substances, it moves from ignorance to knowledge rather than from matter to form.

In general, Aquinas's Aristotelian principle is that all things desire to exist in the manner proper to them. Hence, in things that have awareness (*cognitionem*) the desire to exist in the appropriate manner depends on this awareness.[17] Sense, of course, knows being only as here and now; but the intellect knows being as such, and in a timeless manner, since no intellectual substance can pass away.[18] The consequences for remembering particular past events and thereafter knowing their universal meaning, will be discussed later with special reference to the exemplary nature of the past. But here, as elsewhere, Aquinas does not wish to give the impression that he is arguing for a disembodied aspect of mind that operates in incorporeal timelessness. Insofar as man's soul is united to body whilst he is alive, man only comes to understanding through imagery as the proper operation of the soul. Only when the soul will be separated from the body, after death, will there be another mode of understanding and that will be

---

[14] *Ibid.*, a. 5 responsio, ad 1.   [15] *Ibid.*, a. 5 ad 4.
[16] *Ibid.*: 'in substantiis intellectualibus est compositio ex actu et potentia, non quidem ex materia et forma, sed ex forma et esse participato'.
[17] *Ibid.*, a. 6 responsio.
[18] *Ibid.*:
Potest etiam hujus rei accipi signum ex hoc, quod unumquodque naturaliter suo modo esse desiderat. Desiderium autem in rebus cognoscentibus sequitur cognitionem. Sensus autem non cognoscit esse nisi sub hec et nunc, sed intellectus apprehendit esse absolute et secundum omne tempus. Unde omne habens intellectus naturaliter desiderat esse semper. Naturale autem desiderium non potest esse inane. Omnis igitur intellectualis substantia est incorruptibilis.

like the understanding possessed by disembodied natures. But man, in life, is not thus disembodied.[19] He closes *ST* Ia Q. 75, a. 7, ad 3, with the reminder that properly speaking it is not the soul that belongs to the human species but the composite of soul and body, for the soul requires the body in order to act: 'anima quoddammodo indiget corpore ad suam operationem'.

In *ST* Ia Q. 76 Aquinas shows a distinctive concern for each person's individuating intelligence, each person's unique understanding whilst still being considered part of the human species with universally shared characteristics. Here he was determined to move away from the psychology and anthropology of Averroes and even more so from Avicenna. Indeed, he was also rejecting the neo-Augustinian notion of matter as imperfect actuancy, of the soul as a complete and separated substance, and he thereby attempted to supersede Bonaventure's Platonising system. Aquinas would be condemned for this interpretation during the years 1277–86 but his conception of man's unity would eventually come to prevail over the Franciscan elaboration of the older doctrine of the multiplicity of forms.[20] In *ST* Ia Q. 76, he would argue that the mind at work was always aware of the sense origin of its intellectual life so that there was always a bond between sense particulars and the universals of understanding. As we shall see, his notion of the agent intellect as that power to use the image as an 'objective instrument' of understanding, depended on a radical Averroistic use of Aristotle in understanding the process of how intellect abstracts an intelligible nature from an image. He argued that what makes this abstraction possible is the fact that both understanding and the senses are concerned with, *and indeed are*, the same thing.[21]

Aquinas asks, how, when we speak of the act of understanding, do we make this an act of a particular person? Each person is aware that it is he himself who understands.[22] When we say that Socrates or Plato understands, it is obviously not attributed to him *per accidens*, for it is attributed to him in virtue of the fact that he is a man which is predicated of him essentially. So we must either say that Socrates understands through his whole self, holding as Plato did that man is an intellective soul, or else, we

---

[19] *ST* Ia 75 ad 3: 'intelligere cum phantasmate est propria operatio animae secundum quod corpori est unita. Separata autem a corpore *habebit* alium modum intelligendi, similem aliis substantiis a corpore separatis ...'.

[20] This included a *forma corporeitas*.

[21] As Suttor points out in his commentary to his translation in the Blackfriars edition, p. 264.

[22] *ST* Ia Q. 76 a. 1 responsio: 'oportet quod inveniat modum quo ista actio quae est intelligere sit hujus hominis actio. *Experitur* enim unusquisque seipsum esse qui intelligat.'

must say that the understanding is some part of Socrates. The first is untenable, since the same man perceives himself both to understand and to have sensations, and sensation involves the body which is part of man. Therefore, intellect, whereby Socrates understands, is also part of Socrates, so that intellect is in some way united to the body. Now Averroes says this union takes place through the automatic intelligibility of the mind's contents, that is, that the (intention or) intelligible species is had in two ways: one, through the possible intellect shared by the species and the other, as phantasms which are in corporeal organs. This intelligible species serves as a link, a continuation between the possible intellect and the body of this or that man. But this continuation or union does not, according to Aquinas, suffice to make the intellectual act under question Socrates's own intellectual act; it is not individualising enough. Having the images or phantasms in the possible intellect which, according to this theory, is not unique to the individual, does not mean that it is Socrates who understands them. Rather, we must return to what Aristotle said. Each man understands because *his* intellective principle is *his* formative principle and from the very act of understanding it is clear that the intellectual principle is united to the particular body as its form.

It is the activity of understanding[23] that is peculiar to man and which allows him to transcend all animals. Indeed, as Aristotle said, it is the understanding that constitutes man's final or ultimate felicity. Hence *intelligere* is the *forma* proper to man, and it allows the human soul to transcend the material world. The intellect is dependent on images but it understands them independent of their materiality. The human soul then, is both nonmaterial (*est quidem separata*), and yet im-mattered (*sed tamen in materia*). Therefore, there must be as many souls as there are bodies. There cannot be only a single intellective principle for all men, *contra* Avicenna.[24]

Aquinas puts his case in *ST* Ia Q. 76 a. 2 in an extraordinarily clear way. He says that my intellectual activity might differ from yours thanks to our different sense images, that is, because the image of a stone in me was one thing and its image in you another. This could be the case, provided the mere sense image, in its individuality in me as distinct from you, were what informs the recipient understanding, the possible intellect, for the same agent produces different actions according to the different qualities it has, as for instance there are different objects of sight. *But the sense image is not*

---

23 And not simply the having of similitudes be they phantasms or intelligible species. Understanding is an activity and not a passive response. In Averroes's commentary on *De Anima*, III, Averroes says: 'intellectus est de natura virtutum passivarum. Item intellectus est possibilis, ergo est passibilis.'

24 The target here is Avicenna more than Averroes.

what informs the recipient understanding – this phantasm is not the form in the possible intellect. Rather, what informs the possible intellect is the intelligible species which is abstracted from the phantasm.[25] What *is* intelligible to the receptive possible intellect is the idea, the intention latent in the images from which it is abstracted.[26] And the possible intellect, from the diverse images or phantasms of one kind of thing, *abstracts only one intelligible idea*! This is plain in any one man for whom there may be diverse phantasms or images of stone and yet from all of these there is abstracted only one intelligible idea of stone.[27] It is therefore the *nature* of stone that one understands.

Now if there were one intellect in all men, the various sense images in this man and that could not give rise to different acts of understanding attributable to this man and that respectively, the way Averroes imagines.[28] And yet for Aquinas, it is clear that the different acts of attributable, individual understanding of the nature of stone arrive at the same intelligible object: the *intellectum* of the nature of stone. This is no argument for a subjectivist interpretation of the nature of the experienced world. The very natures of the things we experience are constant, there to be abstracted by the activity of minds acting individually on the basis of their images derived from such experiences. Hence, in Ia Q. 76 a. 2 ad 3

---

[25] Ia Q. 76 a. 2: 'Sed ipsum phantasma non est forma intellectus possibilis; sed species intelligibilis quae a phantasmatibus abstrahitur'.

[26] See Averroes's *Epitome* above for the same argument.

[27] 'Sicut in uno homine apparet, in quo possunt esse diversa phantasmata lapidis et tamen ab omnibus eis abstrahitur una species intelligibilis lapidis per quam intellectus unius hominis operatione una intelligit naturam lapidis non obstante diversitate phantasmatum.

[28] In Averroes's commentary on the *De Anima*, III, 5, 5, he says, 'intellectus speculativa iam ipse in omnibus est unus secundum recipiens, diversus autem secundum receptum ... unde intellectus speculativus in hoc homine est corruptibilis est tamen secundum se et simpliciter aeternus'. Siger of Brabant in *De Anima*, III, Q. 11: 'Unde, cum intellectus in potentia se habeat ad intentiones imaginatas, determinate respicit intentiones imaginatas hominum, eo quod omnes intentiones imaginatae hominium unius rationis sunt. Ideo intellectus unicus in omnibus est secundum substantiam suam et secundum suam potestatem' (citing Averroes, *De Anima* III, 31). Also, Siger explains Averroes's point in *De Anima*, III, 5, in his *De Anima*, Q. 14 (Bazán edn, p. 52) as follows:
Intellectus copulatur humanae speciei, et intellectus copulatur huic individuo humanae speciei. Et intellectus copulatio humanae speciei essentialior est quam copulatio quae est huic individuo, propter hoc quod humana species aeterna est et quia intellectus qui ei copulatur aeternus est. Copulatio autem intellectus huic individuo humanae speciei minus essentialis est. Unde etiam individuum separatur, licet intellectus a specie humana numquam separetur ... Unde in natura intellectus non est quod ipse copuletur huic individuo, sed in natura eius est quod sit in potentia ad intentiones imaginatas cuiuscumque hominis.
With reference to Averroes, *De Anima*, III, 5 and III, 20: 'Et cum ipsi sunt omnes eiusdem rationis, propter hoc intellectus, unus ex se existens, essentialiter unitur sive copulatur humanae speciei sicut accidentaliter se habet ad intentiones imaginatas huius individui.'
With reference to Averroes *De Anima*, III, 37.

he asserts that although the knower is an individual and his knowledge is an individual piece of knowledge, this does not preclude it from being knowledge of something universal.[29] Aquinas believes that if the form is abstracted from the individual material conditions, it will be a reproduction of the *nature* without the things that individuate it when shared by many, and thus something universally valid will be known.[30] What is thereafter in the mind is not the particular stone but the intelligibility of the stone, the *species lapidis*. Nevertheless, the particular stone is what is understood.[31] If we understood the *species lapidis* rather than the stone itself, knowledge would always be of ideas rather than of things (*alioquin scientiae non essent de rebus sed de speciebus intelligibilibus*). As was the case with Abelard, Aquinas is certain that knowledge is of the world and not of ideas about the world. This is because knowledge, following Aristotle, involves the assimilation of knower to the known and hence the same thing can be known by different knowers.[32] The nature of a thing is not simply a product of mind; it is outside mind in things themselves but when it exists in the mind it does not exist in the same manner as it does outside mind. Plato was wrong in thinking that a thing understood has the same sort of existence both outside mind as well as in the understanding, because he posited natures of things separated from matter.[33]

In a. 7 he rejects fully the doctrine of Bonaventure and other neo-Platonists who argued that the intellectual soul is united with the body through a bodily spirit; nor does light unite the body with the soul. Instead, one should say that the soul informs the body; it has no existence apart from body; and being conjoined to the body it has an existence without any intermediary. Here he argues specifically that matter must be seen as *ens in potentia* and the soul is the form or actuality of the matter to which it is conjoined.[34] Furthermore, activity like existence, belongs to the compound whole because it is what exists that acts.[35] The soul has one being as a substance but one can speak of its many different powers which are distinguished in terms of their acts and objects.[36] Bonaventure had maintained that since the soul and its powers comprised a self-sufficient unity, there could be no direct impact of the external material world on the soul or its powers. Therefore, sense perception was a purely bodily

---

[29] *ST* Ia Q. 76 a. 2 ad 3: 'quod individuatio intelligentis aut species per quam intelligit non excludit intelligentiam universalium'.
[30] *Ibid*.: 'Si vero species sit abstracta a conditionibus materiae individualis, erit similitudo naturae absque iis quae ipsam distinguunt et multiplicant, et ita cognoscetur universale'.
[31] *Ibid*.: 'et tamen lapis est id quod intelligitur, non autem species lapidis'.
[32] *Ibid*.: 'Et quia cognitio fit secundum assimilationem cognoscentibus ad rem cognitam, sequitur quod idem a diversis cognoscentibus cognosci contingit, ut patet in sensu'.
[33] *ST* Ia Q. 76 a. 2 ad 4.   [34] *ST* Ia 76 a. 7 responsio.   [35] *ST* Ia Q. 77 a. 1 ad 3.
[36] *ST* Ia Q. 77 a. 3 and a. 2 ad 3. Compare Abelard above, ch. 13.

function to be transcended. Aquinas rejects this and cites Aristotle to the effect that sensation belongs neither to soul nor body separately, but to both in conjunction.[37] But it is clear that some of the soul's activities, namely understanding and willing, do not take place in bodily organs. The powers which are the source of these activities take place in the soul, while other activities of the soul take place in bodily organs, for example, sight ... but the powers which are the source of such activities have the body-soul as their subject of inhesion and not just the soul alone – 'et ideo quae sunt talium operationum principia sunt in conjuncto sicut in subjecto, et non in anima sola'. Plato's (misinformed) opinion was, however, that sensation is an activity belonging exclusively to the soul just like understanding. And, extraordinarily, Aquinas adds that in many matters of philosophy Augustine makes use of Plato's views, not affirming them but simply giving an account of them: 'quod opinio Platonis fuit quod sentire est operatio animae propria, sicut et intelligere. In multis autem quae ad philosophiam pertinent, Augustinus utitur opinionibus Platonis, non asserendo sed recitando.'[38]

Aquinas takes up the traditional discussion of the various external senses in Q. 78, a. 3 *responsio*. Here, he defines a sense as a passive power which is meant to be set in action by an object of sense that is external to it. This outside source of internal change is the *per se* object of sense perception. But one can speak of two sorts of change within things: natural and spiritual. When we discuss sense activity we are speaking of that *spiritual* change in which the *form* of the source of change is received in the subject of change supraphysically as when the form of a colour is in the eye which does not physically become the colour it sees. Rather, the intention [*sic*] of the sensible form is had in the sense organ.[39] In Article 4 he proceeds to the traditional internal senses. We are told that in the *De Memoria* Aristotle maintained that imagination and memory are receptiveness at the primitive level of sensation, and we are reminded that imagination and sense memory are not powers distinct from sense. When we speak of the activity of the *cogitativa*, which in man brings together and fuses or separates, as well as the act of reminiscing, which uses a kind of syllogism in its search to recall, we are as far away from sense memory and any instinctual estimation as such estimation is from imagination. One might say that cogitation and reminiscence require powers that are distinct from instinctive estimation and sense memory but only in the sense of

---

[37] *ST* Ia Q. 77 a. 5 responsio.   [38] *ST* Ia Q. 77 a. 5 ad 3.
[39] 'Ad operationem autem sensus requiritur immutatio spiritualis per quam intentio formae sensibilis fiat in organo sensus'. (Compare Averroes on intentions in the sense organs.)

being the same, but more perfect powers in man, along what will prove to be a continuum from sensation to conscious, willed intellection.

If we consider that the life of a higher animal requires that it apprehend a thing not only when present but also when absent, then an animal has not only to receive forms of sense objects when these actually affect it (*cum praesentialiter immutatur ab eis*), but also to retain and conserve them. Furthermore, animals are not only moved by things that are pleasurable and painful to the senses but also by the useful and the harmful. Aquinas provides the Avicennan example of sheep shunning the wolf as a natural enemy. When this is the case, an animal can perceive things which no external sense can perceive so that the source of this apprehension has to be other than an impact on the senses. Following Avicenna, Aquinas says that the reception of sensible forms is had in the common sense which transfers these forms to the fantasy or imagination. Here is the treasure house of forms received through the senses (*est enim phantasia sive imaginatio quasi thesaurus quidam formarum per sensum acceptarum*). Then the estimative instinct apprehends the intentions which are not objects of simple sensation.[40] Thereafter, memory conserves these intentions, *vis memorativa, quae est thesaurus quidem huiusmodi intentionum*. The intention is the reason why animals remember something harmful or useful, and, Aquinas adds, the very fact of pastness, which is what memory attends to, enables intentions to be reckoned and compared: 'cuius signum est, quod principium memorandi fit in animalibus ex aliqua hujusmodi intentione, puta quod est nocivum vel conveniens, et ipsa ratio praeteriti quam attendit memoria, inter hujusmodi intentiones computatur'.[41] At this level, sense memory is therefore dependent on the instinctive estimation or opinion and on cogitation. And while animals and men are affected in the same way by external sensibles, there is a difference regarding the reception of intentions. In animals the intentions are instinctively known whereas in men they are had *per quandam collationem*, by a process of comparison under the operations of cogitation. For this reason, cogitation in man is called *ratio particularis* and the *medici* assign this activity to the middle part of the head. Its role is to compare individual intentions in the same way as the reasoning intellect compares universal intentions, that is, by analogy.[42] Man not only has the kind of memory that animals have, in terms of a sudden recollection (*recordatione*) of the past, but man also has

---

[40] 'Ad apprehendendum autem intentiones quae per sensum non accipiuntur ordinatur vis aestimativa'.

[41] *ST* Ia Q. 78 a. 4 responsio.

[42] *Ibid.*: 'est enim collativa intentionum individualium, sicut ratio intellectiva intentionum universalium'. (Compare Averroes above.)

the capacity for reminiscence (*reminiscentiam*) which is a quasi-syllogistic search amongst past memories according to their individual intentions.[43] In effect, Aquinas has described four powers of the interior sense: the common sense, the imagination, the estimation and the memory. Whereas animals have an instinctive *æstimatio*, man has a cogitative power known as particular reason, *ratio particularis*. When one speaks of intellective activity, one must always recall that the origins of such activity is in the senses and yet *in re apprehensa per sensum* the intellect is able to know much more than what the senses merely perceive. Hence, intentions which are not discernible to the senses are known by the estimative power.[44] In man, cogitation and memory attain a special eminence through their affinity with and closeness to abstract reason, by a kind of overflow rather than through anything that belongs to the sensitive part of the soul as such.[45] Man's cogitation and sense memory are simply more perfect than animal estimation and memory; they should not be considered as other powers in man. As elsewhere, Aquinas is concerned to maintain something of a continuum with lower nature rather than a break between the higher animals and man.

In Q. 79 a. 2 he discusses how the human understanding is in a state of potentiality in relation to what it can understand; initially it is like a blank page on which nothing is written as Aristotle said. Initially we are only *able* to understand; afterwards we come actually to understand. The understanding is a natural power of the soul which is oriented in some particular direction; immediately it is focused on the understanding of the *being* of sense objects; mediately it is oriented towards understanding other things by analogy.[46]

The process by which we come to understand what we experience of the material world depends on the fact that nothing in the physical world is actually ready for understanding. Hence, one has to posit a power of the intellectual order which makes things actually able to be understood by abstracting the species from material conditions. Thus we come to speak of the agent or active intellect, the *intellectus agens*.[47] This agent belongs to each individual soul.[48] We know this from experience when we see our-

---

43 *Ibid.*: 'Ex parte autem memorativae, non solum habet memoriam sicut cetera animalia in subita recordatione praeteritorum, sed etiam reminiscentiam, quasi syllogistice inquirendo praeteritorum memoriam, secundum individuales intentiones.'
44 *ST* Ia Q. 78 a. 4 ad 4.
45 *ST* Ia Q. 78 a. 4 ad 5: '... illam eminentiam habet cogitativa et memorativa in homine, non per id quod est proprium sensitivae partis, sed per aliquam affinitatem et propinquitatem ad rationem universalem, secundum quandam refluentiam. Et idem non sunt aliae vires sed eadem, perfectiores quam sunt in aliis animalibus'.
46 *ST* Ia Q. 79 a. 2 ad 2.   47 *ST* Ia Q. 79 a. 3.
48 *ST* Ia Q. 79 a. 4. Aquinas well knew that some of his contemporaries, mainly Franciscans, argued that there is only one agent intellect, i.e. God.

selves abstract universal natures from particular conditions, and this makes them actually understood.[49]

In Q. 79 a. 6 Aquinas asks the crucial question of whether memory is in the intellectual part of the soul. Some have argued that since animals also remember, memory cannot belong to the intellectual part of the soul. Furthermore, it is said that since memory is of past things and the past means a fixed point in time, the memory knows something in terms of a fixed time, which is to say, here and now. Such here and now knowledge is the province of sense and not of intellect. Memory therefore must be in the sensitive part of the soul. We recall this issue from Blund's analysis. Furthermore, it is said that memory preserves *species rerum* that are not actually being thought about; but this cannot happen in the understanding because we know that the understanding passes into act when it is informed through the intelligible species, the object of thought. The actuality of the thing understood is the understanding itself in act, and therefore the understanding actually understands anything it has as an intelligible species. The memory cannot therefore be *in parte intellectiva*.

Aquinas responds by arguing that since we define memory as the conservation of the species of things that are not actually being attended to, we must find out whether such thought (*species rerum*) can be conserved *in intellectu*. Avicenna said this was impossible: the similitude in the understanding must be actually understood. According to Avicenna, this means that as soon as someone stops thinking about something, the thought, the species of the thing, ceases to exist in the intellect.[50] If one wishes to think about it again one must turn to the agent intellect – which he posits as a separated substance – (over and above the individual) in order that the *species intelligibiles* flow from it into the potential or receptive understanding. This means that at the intellectual level nothing is pre-served except when it is actually present to intellectual attention.[51] But Aristotle says otherwise. He says that when the possible, receptive intellect becomes what it knows, then it is in act, and this occurs when it can act through itself. It is still in potency though not as before. The possible intellect becomes things when it receives them as species of singular things. From the capacity to receive *species intelligibiles* the possible intel-lect can then think about them when it will, although it is not always doing

---

[49] *ST* Ia Q. 79 a. 4: 'Et hoc experimento cognoscimus dum percipimus nos abstrahere formas universales a conditionibus particularibus, quod est facere actu intelligibilia'.

[50] *ST* Ia Q. 79 a. 6 responsio: 'In intellectu autem (secundum Avicenna) qui caret organo corporali, nihil existit nisi intelligibiliter, unde oportet intelligi in actu illud cujus simili-tudo in intellectu existit'.

[51] *Ibid.*: 'Secundum igitur hanc positionem nihil conservatur in parte intellectiva quod non actu intelligatur'.

so.[52] The kind of potential it maintains is that which is appropriate to anyone having habitual knowledge to which one then can desire to turn one's attention.[53] Furthermore, things are received according to the manner of the receiver. In so far as memory is taken to mean a power to conserve species then we have to say that memory *is* in the intellectual part.[54]

But if we say that the very reason for memory being as it is, is because it has as its object the past as past, then indeed it is *not* part of the intellect.[55] Because the past as past means that something is determined within time, it pertains to the realm of the particular and, therefore, to sense memory alone.[56]

This is perhaps the clearest statement towards which the entire tradition we have been examining necessarily leads: that the past as past, as unique, as particular, is not capable of being understood. The past preserved as past in the mind is an irrational, sense memory with no meaning, because meaning requires abstract and universal ideas, a processed past which makes it, of necessity, present and generally meaningful in an exemplary way.

Aquinas says that when we speak of memory as the conservation of intelligible species, or thoughts, we are only speaking of mankind, because these species are not preserved in the sensitive part of the soul (which we share with animals), but rather in the conjunction of the body and soul, the embodied soul.[57] The memorial power *is* an organic act but the understanding, of itself, is capable of retaining species apart from the physical organ and this is distinctive of man.

Aquinas is even more clear about this: pastness (*praeteritio*) can be considered in two ways: either in relation to the object known or in relation to the act of knowledge. These two are combined in the case of sense knowledge which is an apprehension of something because it is affected by a present sensible. Hence an animal remembers, simultaneously, that it formerly sensed some *thing and* that it *sensed* a past sensible

---

[52] 'Ex hoc quod recipit species intelligibilium habet quod possit operari cum voluerit ... non autem quod semper operetur'.

[53] 'Quia et tunc est quodammodo in potentia, licet aliter quam ante intelligere; eo scilicet modo quo sciens in habitu est in potentia ad considerandum in actu'.

[54] 'Sic igitur, si memoria accipiatur solum pro vi conservativa specierum oportet dicere memoriam esse in intellectiva parte'.

[55] 'Si vero de ratione memoriae sit quod ejus objectum sit praeteritum ut praeteritum, memoria in parte intellectiva non erit, sed sensitiva tantum, quae est apprehensiva particularium'.

[56] 'Praeteritum enim ut praeteritum, cum significet esse sub determinato tempore, ad conditionem particularis pertinet'.

[57] Animals do not have embodied, uncorruptible souls; indeed they have no immortal souls.

433

thing.[58] *But to the intellectual part, pastness is irrelevant to a thing when that thing is taken precisely as an object of understanding:* 'Sed quantum ad partem intellectivam pertinet praeteritio accidit, et non per se convenit, ex parte objecti intellectus'. Mind understands man as man. And it is irrelevant in the consideration of man as man, whether man exists in the present, past or future: 'Intelligit enim intellectus hominem inquantum est homo. Homini autem, inquantum est homo, accidit vel in praesenti vel in praeterito vel in futuro esse'.[59]

Were Aquinas to leave his analysis here, we would be confronted with the clearest summation of previous views on how the particular past is understood as past, that is, not at all. But he recognises the difficulty in having effectively destroyed the relevance of the particular past as a consequence of his analysis of the operations of higher mind and, therefore, returns to the distinction he made between considering the past in relation to the thing known and the past in relation to the act of knowledge. When it comes to an act of knowledge, he says that pastness *can* be found even in the understanding just as it is in sensation. Because any of our intellectual acts is a particular act existing in this or that time, we say that man understands or thinks now or yesterday or tomorrow. And this is not incompatible with the nature of intellect because such acts of understanding, although particular, nonetheless are immaterial acts just as the intellect is immaterial.[60] Just as the understanding understands itself, even though it is some particular understanding, in the same way it understands its own act of understanding which is a singular or particular act, be it in the past, present or future. Therefore, the very meaning of memory as memory of what is past, is in the intellect with respect to understanding, knowing that it has previously understood something. But this is not a knowledge or understanding of the past in its here and now character: 'Sic igitur salvatur ratio memoriae, quantum ad hoc quod est praeteritorum, in intellectu secundum quod intelligit se prius intellexisse. Non autem secundum quod intelligit praeteritum prout est hic et nunc.'[61]

---

[58] *ST* Ia Q. 79 a. 6 responsio ad 2: 'praeteritio potest ad duo referri, scilicet ad objectum quod cognoscitur et ad cognitionis actum. Quae quidem duo simul conjunguntur in parte sensitiva, quae est apprehensiva alicujus per hoc quod immutatur a praesenti sensibili. Unde quodlibet animal memoratur se prius sensisse in praeterito et se sensisse quoddam praeteritum sensibile'.

[59] *ST* Ia Q. 79 a. 6 ad 2.

[60] *ST* Ia Q. 79 a. 6 ad 2: 'Ex parte vero actus, praeteritio per se accipi potest etiam in intellectu, sicut in sensa, quia intelligere animae nostrae est quidam particularis actus in hoc vel in illo tempore existens, secundum quod dicitur homo intelligere nunc vel heri vel cras. Et hoc non repugnat intellectualitati, quia hujusmodi intelligere, quamvis sit quoddam particulare, tamen est immaterialis actus, ut supra de intellectu dictum est'.

[61] *ST* Ia Q. 79 a. 6 ad 2.

Where Aristotle had said that we *sense* a time lapse in addition to possessing the impressions of past experiences in the lowest, sensitive part of the soul, Aquinas has moved this into the intellectual part of mind where one understands that one has known or understood something previously.[62] He is responding to Aristotle's statement that when we remember we are somehow aware of having known or experienced something previously for we say to ourselves, say in our minds, that this has occurred before. Aquinas appears to have grasped this self-awareness, this self-regarding activity of the human knower and rememberer and thereby emphasises something like a conscious, because rational, awareness of acts of understanding in time which animals share only instinctually and therefore irrationally. The intellect only knows itself not by its own essence but by means of its activity of self-awareness.[63] It is, however, merely an assertion rather than an explanation of what this self-conscious awareness actually is.

At the close of Q. 79 a. 6, he argues – like Averroes – that mind, when in a state of habitual knowledge, is somewhere between potentiality and actuality so that we can understand concepts or species potentially even when mind is not actually attending to such species, and in this way understanding does have a capacity to conserve species which are not actually being reflected upon.[64]

This leads on to Q. 79 a. 7 where he presents an important conclusion that intellectual memory cannot be seen as a power that is distinct from understanding because it is essential to memory that it be a treasure house or conserving place for species. In its most important sense, rational memory has no time dimensions in the same way that understanding is a-temporal, that is, with regard to the objects of thought and memory. Memory is not a power distinct from understanding.[65] Aquinas is able, here, to interpret Augustine's analysis of memory, understanding and will, not as three distinct powers but as three activities with regard to objects; we are told that Augustine takes memory to express the soul's ability actively to retain things habitually, and he uses the word 'understanding' to mean the *act* of understanding, and the will is to be taken as the *act* of

---

[62] *ST* Ia Q. 85 a. 5 ad 2. The intellect, while it does abstract from sense images, nevertheless cannot actually understand except by turning to sense images (*non intelligit actu nisi convertendo se ad phantasmata*). And it is by reason of that aspect in which it turns to images that time is attached to the intellect's combinations and separations. 'Et ex ea parte qua se ad phantasmata convertit, compositioni et divisioni intellectus adjungitur tempus'.

[63] *ST* Ia Q. 87 a. 1 responsio.

[64] *ST* Ia Q. 79 a. 6 responsio ad 3: 'et tunc dicitur esse intellectus in habitu, et secundum hunc modum intellectus conservat species etiam quando actu non intelligit'.

[65] 'Unde patet quod memoria non est alia potentia ab intellectu. Ad rationem enim potentiae passivae pertinet conservare, sicut et recipere'.

will. The soul's powers are only distinguished in terms of their different 'formal' objects; there are no real distinctions in mind.[66]

Aquinas continues his disagreement with ancient and contemporary Platonism in *ST* Ia Q. 84 where he is concerned to show that Plato was wrong in believing that things understood must exist in themselves in the same way as they do in the understanding mind.[67] Because things are received according to the nature of the recipient, Aquinas argues that intellect receives material and species of material things in an immaterial and unchanging way. The soul knows material things through the intellect with a knowledge that is immaterial, universal and necessary. This is why Augustine's words (that material things cannot be understood by the intellect nor a body seen except by the senses)[68] must be understood as referring to that *by which* the intellect knows and not *what* it knows.[69] Thereafter, we are given a series of moderate realist assertions: The intellect does know material things intellectually but not by means of material things or material and corporeal similitudes of things; rather by immaterial, intellectual species *which can really exist in the soul*.[70] What exists in the mind of the knower exists there immaterially. The act of knowing is extended to things outside the knower, for we do, he affirms, also know things which are outside ourselves.[71] But the form of a thing is limited by its matter to the one thing. And so it is evident that the essential meaning of knowledge is opposite to the nature of materiality, and that things that receive forms only in a material way are non-knowers, eg plants.[72] And the more immaterial a thing's way of having the form of things known, the more perfect is its knowledge. The intellect which abstracts the species not only from matter but even from individuating material conditions therefore, has more perfect knowledge than the senses.[73]

---

[66] Compare this with Abelard's assertion that there were no real distinctions in mind or in the Trinity although one could speak of similitudes.

[67] *ST* Ia Qq. 84–9, Human Intelligence, Latin text and English translation by Paul T. Durbin (Blackfriars, 1968), XII.

[68] Augustine, *Soliloquies*, x, 6.

[69] *ST* Ia Q. 84: 'est intelligendum quantum ad ea quibus intellectus cognoscit, non autem quantum ad ea quae cognoscit'.

[70] *ST* Ia Q. 84 a. 1 ad 1: 'Cognoscit enim corpora intelligendo, sed non per corpora neque per similitudines materiales et corporeas, sed per species immateriales et intelligibiles, quae per sui essentiam in anima esse possunt'.

[71] *ST* Ia Q. 84 a. 2: 'Et hujus ratio est quia actus cognitionis se extendit ad ea quae sunt extra cognoscentem; cognoscimus enim etiam ea quae extra nos sunt'.

[72] *Ibid.*: 'Et ideo quae non recipiunt formas nisi materialiter, nullo modo sunt cognoscitiva, sicut plantae'.

[73] *ST* Ia Q. 84 a. 2: 'Unde et intellectus qui abstrahit speciem non solum a materia etiam a materialibus conditionibus individuantibus, perfectius cognoscit quam sensus'.

Now Aristotle said that the soul is 'in a way' all things; he did not say that it was made up of all things. Rather the soul is in a state of potentiality with respect to all things; to sensible things by means of the senses and to intelligible objects by means of the intellect.[74] The essence of God, as opposed to our essence as limited creatures with determined existences, is a perfect likeness of all things and of every aspect found in all things because He is the universal cause of all. We, however, are only in potency as knowers of all creation and we must activate this potency through mind's creation of similitudes, mind making images out of itself, not however in the sense that the soul or anything belonging to it is changed into this or that image, but analogously in the sense that a body is said to become coloured when it is informed by a colour.[75] Man's soul, as a knower, is in a state of potentiality regarding both the similitudes that are the principles of sensation and the similitudes that are principles of understanding.[76] This is why Aristotle held that the intellect, by means of which the soul understands, has no naturally innate species; rather it is initially in a state of potentiality regarding these species. Plato's view, that the intellect contains all species and is impeded from coming to a state of actuality by being united with the body, does not seem to fit the facts. If the soul did have a natural knowledge of everything, it would seem impossible for it to be so forgetful of this natural knowledge that it would not know that it had such knowledge. No one forgets things that are naturally known, says Aquinas, and he gives the example of an axiom that the whole is greater than any of its parts, as unforgettable. Furthermore, it would be inappropriate for a natural operation of a thing to be totally impeded by something belonging to the thing naturally, and, it is natural for the soul to be united to the body. Why then, Aquinas asks, *is* the soul united to the body?[77]

If the soul were, by nature, such that it could receive species through the influence of certain separated immaterial principles alone, and not from the senses, it would not need the body to understand and there would be no purpose in the soul being united to the body. He argues that the species which our soul understands do not come from subsistent, separated, immaterial forms. The species our intellect has by participation, come ultimately from a first cause which is a principle that is essentially intelligible, namely God. *But* they proceed from that principle through the medium of sensible, material things from which we gather our

---

[74] *ST* Ia Q. 84 a. 2 ad 2.
[75] *ST* Ia Q. 84 a. 2 ad 1 and ad 2: 'Et sic de seipsa facit huiusmodi imagines: non quod anima vel aliquid animae convertatur, ut sic haec vel illa imago, sed sicut dicitur de corpore fieri aliquid coloratum, prout informatur colore'.
[76] *ST* Ia Q. 84 a. 3.   [77] *ST* Ia Q. 84 a. 4 responsio.

knowledge.[78] Now the intellectual light in the human soul is nothing more than a participatory likeness of the uncreated light in which the divine ideas are contained; but since besides this light in us, species taken from things are required for our knowledge of material things, we do not have these merely by participation in the divine ideas as the Platonists think.[79]

Aristotle argued that the activities of the sensible part of the soul are brought about by an impression made on the senses by sensible objects. He also held that the intellect has an activity in which the body does not communicate. To cause intellectual activity, a mere impression made by sensibles is not enough: something of a higher order is required, the active being superior to the passive. But this does not imply Plato's position that intellectual activity is caused merely by an impression from things of a higher order. Rather, that higher superior agent, which Aristotle calls the agent intellect, by a process of abstraction makes images received from the senses actually intelligible.[80] Thus, Aquinas says we must conclude that intellectual activity is caused by the sense, by way of these phantasms, where these phantasms must be made actually intelligible by the agent intellect in order to effect a change in the possible intellect. We should call sensible knowledge not the total and complete cause of intellectual knowledge but rather, it is somehow the material cause. Hence we must interpret Augustine[81] as meaning that the light of the agent intellect is required for us to know the truth found in changeable things in an unchanging way and to distinguish real things from similitudes of things.[82] Because sense knowledge is not the whole cause of intellectual knowledge it is clear that the operations of mind, *intellectualis cognitio*, go beyond sense knowledge, allowing us to understand the natures of things beyond their particular being.[83] But we never know natures of things without first having images of particulars we experience.[84] As Aristotle said, we never think without an image. Aquinas affirms that it is impossible for our intellect, in its present state of being joined to a body that is capable of receiving impressions, actually to understand anything without turning to sense images. It is obvious that for the intellect to understand actually – not only in acquiring new knowledge but also in using knowledge already

---

[78] *ST* Ia Q. 84 a. 4 ad 1: 'Quod species intelligibiles quas participat noster intellectus, reducuntur sicut in primam causam in aliquod principium per suam essentiam intelligibile, scilicet in Deum. Sed ab illo principio procedunt mediantibus formis rerum sensibilium et materialium, a quibus scientiam colligimus'.
[79] *ST* Ia Q. 84 a. 5.   [80] *ST* Ia Q. 84 a. 6 responsio.   [81] *Liber 83 Quaestiones*, 9.
[82] *ST* Ia Q. 84 a. 6 responsio ad 1: 'Requiritur enim lumen intellectus agentis, per quod immutabiliter veritatem in rebus mutabilibus cognoscamus, et discernamus ipsas res a similitudinibus rerum'.
[83] *ST* Ia Q. 84 a. 6 responsio ad 3.   [84] *ST* Ia Q. 84 a. 7.

acquired – acts of imagination and of other sense faculties including memory which use corporeal organs, are necessary.[85]

Since the human intellect is of necessity joined to a body, what is its proper object? Aquinas answers that it is a nature, a *quidditas*, a 'whatness' found in corporeal matter. This *quidditas* as the object of the intellect, is the only means by which the intellect rises to its limited knowledge of invisible things, that is, by way of the *natures* of visible things. But by definition a nature of this kind exists in an individual which has corporeal matter; for instance, it is of the nature of stone that it exist in this or that particular stone. Thus the nature of stone or of any other material reality cannot be known truly and completely, except insofar as it exists in a particular thing. We apprehend the particular through the senses and the imagination. If it is actually to be understood, then the intellect must turn to sense images in order to look at the universal natures existing in particular things (*ut speculetur naturam universalem in particulari exist-entem*).[86]

As Aquinas has already made clear, the species that are conserved in the possible intellect remain there habitually when the intellect is not actually understanding; we must use these habitually stored species, judging them in accord with the things of which they are species, which are natures existing in particulars.[87]

Because the imagination does not transcend the world of time and extension and since our intellect cannot actually understand a thing without turning to see the phantasms, some argue that it must follow that intellect could not understand anything incorporeal. Aquinas takes up this objection[88] by arguing that we do know incorporeal realities which have no sense images, but only by analogy or comparison with sensible bodies which do have images. In the same way we understand truth in the abstract by a consideration of concrete things in which we see truth.[89] In

---

[85] *Ibid.*: 'Unde manifestum est quod ad hoc quod intellectus actus intelligat, non solum accipiendo scientiam de nova, sed etiam utendo scientia iam acquisita requiritur actus imaginationis et ceterarum virtutum'.

[86] *Ibid.*: 'Intellectus autem humani, qui est conjunctus corpori, proprium objectum est quidditas sive natura in materia corporali existens; et per hujusmodi naturas visibilium rerum etiam in invisibilium rerum aliqualem cognitionem ascendit'.

[87] *ST* Ia Q. 84 a. 7 responsio ad 1: 'Species conservatae in intellectu possibili, in eo existunt habitualiter quando actu non intelligit ... unde ad hoc quod intelligamus in actu non sufficit ipsa conservatio specierum, sed oportet quod eis utamur secundum quod convenit rebus quarum sunt species, quae sunt naturae in particularibus existentes'. Abelard would have agreed with this and would simply affirm that such natures are not things. Aquinas's argument here is parallel with that of Averroes.

[88] *ST* Ia Q. 84 a. 7 ad 3.

[89] *Ibid.*: 'Ad tertium dicendum quod incorporea, quorum non sunt phantasmata, cogno-scuntur a nobis per comparationem ad corpora sensibilia, quorum sunt phantasmata'.

439

our present state we cannot know other incorporeal substances except negatively or by analogy with corporeal realities (*alias etiam incorporeus substantias, in statu praesentis vitae, cognoscere non possumus nisi per remotionem vel aliquam comparationem ad corporalia*). Thus, when we understand anything of these incorporeal beings, we necessarily have to turn to images of sensible bodies, even though incorporeal beings do not themselves have such phantasms.

It must be clear that everything we come to understand depends on the intellectual abstraction of images or phantasms of corporeal and material things. The object of every sense faculty is a form that exists in corporeal matter, but this form is not a separable subsistent entity; it is im-mattered. The intellect knows these forms which exist individually in corporeal matter; and yet the understanding does not know these precisely as existing in such or such individual matter. This is what is meant by the capacity to abstract forms ie, when we say that we know something which in fact exists in individuated matter but not *as* existing in such or such matter.[90] In effect, we know the generic but the specific eludes our understanding. Plato, paying attention only to the immateriality of the human intellect and not to the fact that it is somehow joined to a body, held that the object of the intellect is immaterial ideas and that we understand, not by abstraction but rather by participation in abstract entities. Aquinas rejects this time and again. And he proceeds to analyse how abstraction occurs.[91]

That we are capable of considering a species of material reality, for example, stone, man, horse, without their individuating conditions because such conditions are no part of their definition as species, is an example of abstracting the universal from the particular. And it is because sense images as similitudes of individuals that exist in corporeal organs do not have the same mode of existence as ideas and the human intellect, we require the agent intellect to turn to sense images which represent the realities of which they are images, whereby a similitude specific to mind is effected in the possible intellect; but this similitude represents only a specific nature. Only in this way are species said to be abstracted from sense images, and not as though a form, numerically the same as the one that existed before in the sense images, should now come to exist in the possible intellect in the same way in which a body is taken from one place and transferred to another. Abelard, we recall, had also argued that the sense images were not the same as similitudes in higher mind. David of

---

[90] *ST* Ia Q. 85 a. 1.   [91] *ST* Ia Q. 85 a. 1 responsio ad 1.

Dinant however interpreted Aristotle as saying that the images in the different faculties were the same.[92]

The agent intellect illuminates sense images and by its power intelligible species are abstracted from them. The agent intellect renders sense images apt to have intellectual intentions of species abstracted from them. By means of the agent intellect's abstraction of species from sense images, we can consider specific natures without their individuating conditions; it is by the likeness of these natures that the possible intellect is informed rather than by sense similitudes.[93] The intellect, therefore, both abstracts species from sense images, but also understands these species in sense images.[94] Lest we think that we are caught within autonomous mind, Aquinas stresses that the sensible images from which species are abstracted, are not what is sensed; sensible images are that *by which* sense takes place.[95] The things we understand are not, therefore, only the species or intentions existing in the soul, but through these species, things existing outside the soul. What is understood first is the reality of which a particular species is a likeness.[96]

More particularly, in the sense part of the soul of man there are two kinds of activity: one takes place by way of a change effected from the outside (*solam immutationem*), from sensible objects (*per hoc quod immutatur a sensibili*). But the other activity is a 'formation' (*alia operatio est formatio*) by which the faculty of imagination formulates for itself a model of something absent or even of something never seen: 'Secundum quod vis imaginativa format sibi aliquod idolum rei absentis vel etiam nunquam visae.' Both activities are joined in the intellect (*haec operatio conjungitur in intellectu*).[97] First, there is an effect produced in the possible intellect insofar as it is informed by a species, and secondly, when it is thus informed, it formulates either a definition or else an affirmative or negative statement which is then signified by words. First then, we have a *species impressa* and this leads on to a *species expressa*. The meaning which a name signifies is a definition. An enunciation or a proposition signifies the

[92] There is an ontological premiss here about the differing modes of being appropriate to similitudes at different levels of abstraction that ties in with the logic of language. For Abelard and for Aquinas, there is a deep gulf between statements about an identified individual and statements about a class. Naming is not explaining or understanding. Such statements are of a different logical type. In effect, logic is a relatively poor model of cause and effect, although we do use the same words to talk about logical sequences and about sequences of cause and effect. But there is a recognition that if-then syllogisms are different from the if-then of cause and effect. As Aquinas argues, we conflate the two by analogy.

[93] *ST* Ia Q. 85 a. 1 ad 4. [94] *ST* Ia Q. 85 a. 1 ad 5. [95] *ST* Ia Q. 85 a. 2.

[96] *ST* Ia Q. 85 a. 2 responsio.

[97] *ST* Ia Q. 85 a. 2 responsio ad 3. Compare Averroes's reference (to Aristotle) speaking of elephants imagined but not seen.

intellect's combining or separating.[98] Words do not signify the effects produced in the possible intellect. Rather, words signify those things which the intellect formulates for itself in order to understand things outside.[99] Aristotle too had said that words signify the intellect's conceptions: 'voces significant conceptiones intellectus ut dicit Philosophus'.[100]

Aquinas was previously at pains to individualise for each man the operations of mind as it responded to sensibles. He asks in a. 7 of Q. 85 whether the same reality can be understood better by one man than another. He has argued that from diverse images or phantasms of one kind of thing, the possible intellect of each person abstracts only one intelligible idea. From all the diverse phantasms of stone comes only one intelligible species, the nature of stone. Hence, he argues that *ex parte rei intellectae*, with respect to the thing understood, one man cannot understand the same reality better than another for either he understands the thing as it is or he understands it other than as it is and therefore is mistaken. But if we say that 'better' qualifies not the act of understanding with respect to the thing understood but rather the person who understands (*ex parte intelligentis*) then yes, one man may have a greater capacity for understanding than another. This is due to material, physical qualities like better vision. Forms and actualities are received in matter according to the capacity of the receiver; therefore, some men have bodies that are better disposed and consequently souls with greater capacities (*quanto corpus est melius dispositio tanto meliorem sortitur animam*).[101] Those in whom imagination, the cogitative faculty and sense memory are better disposed, (clearly in the medical sense), are also better disposed for understanding. Once again, we have an affirmation that the world is as it is and natures in the im-mattered world are abstracted by mind and are as they are. As Aquinas says, truth in the intellect consists in the fact that things are known to be as they are.[102] Implied here is that men with different cerebral dispositions, for example, the moist and the dry, receive what there is to receive in different ways, since these physical qualities render them capable of greater or lesser reception and retention of impressions. Once again we are returned to intellect's dependence on sense experiences; those with greater understanding are by nature more perceptive and impressionable regarding the world in which they live and there are physiological pre-

---

[98] *Ibid.*: 'Unde ratio quam significat nomen est definitio, et enunciatio significat compositionem et divisionem intellectus'.

[99] *Ibid.*: 'Non ergo voces significat ipsas species intelligibilis sed ea quae intellectus sibi format ad judicandum de rebus exterioribus'.

[100] *Perihermenias*, I, 1, 16 a. 3, noted by Aquinas, *ST* Ia Q. 85 a. 5.

[101] Compare Ockham, ch. 22 below, on the mechanics of perception and its failings.

[102] *ST* Ia Q. 85 a. 7 ad 1 and 2.

conditions for this receptivity. This is the medical, psychological equivalent to the dialecticians' affirmation that only *modi significandi* vary, not the truth.

Indeed in Q. 86, when he asks what it is that our intellect knows regarding material realities, Aquinas once again responds that directly and immediately our intellect cannot know the singular in material realities. Intellect understands by abstracting species from matter and species are universal. But it knows the singular indirectly, by a kind of reflection[103] because even after the intellect abstracts species, it cannot actually understand by means of these intelligible species except by actively returning the attention to sense images in which it understands the realities of which the species are similitudes.[104] But because the intellect is infinite in power in so far as it is not limited by corporeal matter, it knows the universal and therefore, it is not limited to any individual object but extends to an infinity of individuals.[105] One cannot keep an infinite number of individuals in the mind but one can have categories which encompass the infinite number of things in reality. Hence, the intellect has a knowledge of contingent things in a manner that is specific to itself. Since contingency depends on matter, (the contingent is what has potentiality to be or not to be), and necessity (its opposite) is a natural consequence of form, contingent things as contingent, like the past as past, are known by the senses directly. But they are known by the intellect indirectly. What the intellect knows in relation to the contingent is the universal and necessary aspects of contingency. Once again, *understanding* of contingency relates directly to the timeless and unchanging necessity of the universal nature which inheres in things, be they past, present or future.[106] What the intellectual aspect of mind knows as its object in our present state is the specific being and truth that is found in material things, known in its abstracted more universal mode as a mental similitude, an intelligible species.

And this knowledge or understanding can be linked to emotions, but the affections are not in the intellect as similitudes as are the species of contingent particular sensibles; he says that emotions are derivatives in origin (*sed sicut principatum in principio*) and exist in the understanding 'by way of certain notions' as Augustine said. Aquinas is less clear here than Averroes on the mechanism by which emotions get attached to memories or thoughts which are mental similitudes of experiences.[107]

---

103 *ST* Ia Q. 86 a. 1: 'indirecte autem et quasi per quandam reflexionem ...'.
104 *Ibid.*: 'etiam postquam species intelligibilis abstraxit, non potest secundum eas actu intelligere nisi convertenda se ad phantasmata in quibus species intelligibilis intelligit'.
105 *ST* Ia Q. 86 a. 1 responsio ad 4. Compare Averroes on man's infinitude, ch. 18.
106 Compare Abelard's hypothetical necessity.   107 *ST* Ia Q. 87 a. 3 ad 3.

When in Italy (*c.* 1268+) or perhaps before, Aquinas was busy commenting on Aristotle's *De Memoria et Reminiscentia*,[108] and he is thought to have perfected this work in Paris. The years 1266–72 saw the appearance of his commentaries on the *De Anima* and the *Liber de sensu et sensato*. As was usual, the *De Anima* was linked with other treatises to be commented upon in the *Parva Naturalia*. Not only does Aquinas demonstrate a masterly control over all the competing traditions including Cicero's, but he is the most perceptive and faithful commentator on Aristotle we can observe for the period. The most interesting aspect of his commentary is his examples and explanations, drawn from his own world of scholarship and experience. The major focus of his analysis of the difference between memory and reminiscence is, of course, Aristotle's text, but he begins by signalling its wider, practical importance by drawing on Cicero. We are told that in the *De Inventione Rhetorica*, II, 53, Cicero speaks of the parts of prudence. Prudence comprises providence – through which the future is set out; and understanding, through which the present is considered. And memory is also a part of prudence through which the past is apprehended. Therefore, he provides the Ciceronian threesome of providence, understanding and memory as parts of prudence. In animals who participate in a kind of prudence, it is necessary not only to have a sense of the present but also a memory of the past. But animals have an imperfect kind of prudence and in particular, their memory is not as perfect as that of men. Men not only remember (sense memory) but they also recollect. Therefore, we must be more precise in investigating just what memory is and what is the act of remembering; what is its act and its causes and to what part of the soul does the *passio memorandi* pertain? Furthermore, what is recollection? They are not the same and men good at remembering are not necessarily good at recalling. Good recollectors are quicker at inventing or finding and learning. And this is because habits of mind depend on bodily dispositions. Those bodies which receive impressions quickly do not retain them. Remembering is nothing other than conserving, whilst reminiscence is like *reinventio*, a finding again what was first accepted by mind but not preserved. Those who *learn* quickly are better at reminiscing.[109]

We are told that Aristotle says that memory is of the past. Aquinas says we can show this *ex communi usu loquendi*, according to the ordinary way of speaking. When, for instance, men see something white in the present, they call this activity 'sensing'. And when something is considered in act or

---

108 Thomas Aquinas, *In Aristotelis libros de sensu et sensato, de memoria et reminiscentia, commentarium*, ed. R. Spiazzi (Rome, 1949, 1973). Also see Aquinas, *Opera Omnia*, XCV, 2, *De Memoria et Reminiscentia*, ed. Leonine Commission (Rome, 1985). References below are to the Spiazzi edition.
109 *Ibid.*, Lectio I, § 298–302.

actually, we call this 'knowing' or understanding. So that when someone has habitual knowledge and the power or capacity to sense but without actually sensing, then we call this remembering a past act. We do not say we remember when we are actually thinking and understanding.[110] Something is remembered from the previous sensible apprehension of it. When the soul remembers it does so because it first sensed it. One can also say that one remembers something learned from someone else or thought about *per seipsum*. Aristotle does not mean to say that we remember only things which were in the past and thereby exclude from memory those things which still may exist in the present. Rather, he emphasises that memory is of something which *we* perceived in the past, and memory includes that we once sensed or knew, whether or not these things continued to endure. Hence memory is neither a sense experience of the present, nor is it *opinio* which can be of the future. Aristotle shows, instead, that memory pertains to time or to a habit or disposition. Memory only pertains to sense or opinion when there is an intervening time lapse between the sense perception or the intellectual opinion and the subsequent remembering. Memory is of past perceptions or past opinions. Only those animals which can sense time (*quae possunt* sentire *tempus*) can remember.[111] We note here that Aquinas, faithful to Aristotle's text, includes time as a perception rather than as an aspect of understanding as he does in the *Summa Theologiae*. There are important consequences and conclusions to be drawn if we say that time is sensed rather than rationally, consciously understood (as a mental construction) as we shall see.

In Lectio II Aquinas reiterates Aristotle's statement that man cannot know without phantasms or images since phantasms are similitudes of corporeal things. When we understand (*intelligere*) we abstract universals from particulars.[112] Man cannot, according to Aristotle, understand anything where there is no continuity and time (*sine continuo et tempore*). This is why to understand requires phantasms, which establish a continuity between the singular thing, here and now being sensed, and its similitude. From these phantasms or similitudes the understanding abstracts intelligible species.[113] In fact, we can show from experience that men with injuries sustained in the organ where images are produced cannot under-

---

[110] *Ibid.*, § 307: 'sicut nullus dicit se memorari illud quod per intellectum actu considerat et intelligit'.

[111] *Ibid.*, § 309.   [112] *Ibid.*, Lectio II, § 313.

[113] Phantasma autem oportet quod sit continuo et tempore, eo quod est similitudo rei singularis, quae est hic et nunc, quod non potest intelligi sine phantasmate. Quare homo autem non possit intelligere sine phantasmate, de facili potest assignari ratio quantum ad primam acceptionem specierum intelligibilium, quae a phantasmatibus abstrahuntur. (*Ibid.*, § 314)

stand anything new but rather, consider only what they previously knew. This shows that those who acquire understanding through species cannot understand what they know unless they go back to the corresponding phantasms.[114]

Some say [Avicenna] that the intelligible species do not remain in the possible intellect except when they are actually being thought about; after this activity they disappear.[115] But this is expressly contrary to what Aristotle says in *De Anima*, III. Here he says that the possible intellect becomes a singular intelligible thought through its species and remains potentially to be actualised by understanding. The possible intellect understands species in phantasms, the species being present according to the diverse degrees of being pertaining to intelligible forms (for example, intentions, intelligible species), which relate to the diversity of material experiences.[116]

Now magnitude, motion and time are known by the same part of the soul.[117] Magnitude (in general) is known by the common sense as is motion. But when we say something is perceived by sense we can speak in two ways. Firstly, when the sensible object affects the senses; but also through a secondary motion related to the first change in the senses through the sense object. This secondary motion remains after the sensible has disappeared and it pertains to imagination. The phantasm which appears by means of this *immutatio secundaria*, is a *passio sensus communis*. Aquinas affirms that magnitude, motion and time, by means of this second kind of alteration (*immutatio*) are *in* the imagination and therefore are understood and known through the common sense.[118]

Memory is not only of sensibles but also of intelligibles as when some one remembers himself understanding or knowing. But this too cannot occur without phantasms. Sensible objects, after they have already been, are no longer apprehended, unless through phantasms. So too with understanding or knowing something that is no longer present. Aristotle

---

[114] Sed experimento patet quod etiam ille qui iam acquisivit scientiam intelligibilem per species intellectas, non potest actu considerare illud cuius scientiam habet nisi occurrat ei aliquod phantasma. Et inde est quod laeso organo imaginationis impeditur homo non solum ab intelligendo aliqua de novo, sed etiam considerando ea, quae prius intellexit, ut patet in phreneticis. (*Ibid.*) See Averroes, ch. 18 above.

[115] *Ibid.*, Lectio II, § 315.

[116] '... propter diversum gradum essendi formarum intelligibilium ... sed etiam ut eas quodammodo in phantasmatibus inspiciat ... Species igitur in phantasmatibus intellectivum intelligit' (*Ibid.*, § 316).

[117] *Ibid.*, § 318.

[118] 'Unde manifestum est quod praedicta tria, scilicet magnitudo, motus et tempus, secundum quod sicut in phantasmate, comprehenduntur et cognoscuntur per sensum communem' (*Ibid.*, § 319).

therefore concludes that memory can be considered in the intellective part of the soul *per accidens*, but it is *per se* from the senses, phantasms appearing in the common sense. A knower supposes (*proponit*) that there is a determined quantity in phantasms and when he understands he considers the absent thing according to its phantasms. Furthermore, to memory pertains the perception (*apprehensio*) of time *according to some determination* such as distance from the present moment. In itself, *per se*, memory therefore pertains to the presence of phantasms but *per accidens* memory pertains to intellectual judgement.[119]

The imagination (*phantasia*) and the memory are, as Avicenna demonstrated, diverse powers of the soul. The reception of sensible forms pertains to the power of sense while the conservation of these forms pertains to the imagination. The *æstimativa* conserves what is received through the senses as well as intentions not apprehended by the senses.[120] The *vis memorativa* retains the remembered thing, not absolutely (*cuius est memorari rem non absolute*) but rather, as it was apprehended in the past by the sense or by the intellect (*sed prout est in praeterito apprehensa vel intellectu*.)[121] Because memory *per se* is *primi sensitivi*, it follows that memory is also in animals which lack intellect. It is not only in man and others having opinion which pertains to the speculative intellect and to prudence which pertains to the practical intellect. If memory could be an aspect of the potential intellect how could it be in animals which evidently have memories but no intellects?[122] It must, therefore, follow that memory pertains *per se* to the sensitive part because even if we suppose that only men amongst mortals have *intellectus*, memory is not in all animals but only in those having a memorial capacity to sense time (*solum illa habent memoriam quae sentiunt tempus*). Once again we have a reference to time as something sensed directly rather than understood indirectly by rational reflection. Some animals perceive nothing unless it is presently sensed; if they do not *know* first

---

[119] Memoria autem non solum est sensibilium, utputa cum aliquis memoratur se sensisse, sed etiam intelligibilium, ut cum aliquis memoratur se intellexisse. Non autem est sine phantasmate. Sensibilia enim postquam praetereunt a sensu non percipiuntur nisi sicut in phantasmate: intelligere etiam non est sine phantasmate, ut supra habitum est. Unde concludit quod memoria sit intellectivae partis animae, sed per accidens; per se, autem primi sensitivi, scilicet sensus communis. Dictum est enim supra, quod intelligens proponit in phantasmate quantum determinatum, licet intellectus secundum se consideret rem absentem; ad memoriam autem pertinet apprehensio temporis secundum determinationem quamdam, secundum scilicet distantiam in praesenti nunc. Unde per se memoria pertinet ad apparitionem phantasmatum, per accidens autem ad iudicium intellectus. (*Ibid.*, § 320)

[120] Note that both Avicenna and Averroes said intentions alone were in the *æstimativa*.

[121] *Ibid.*, § 321.   [122] *Ibid.*, § 323.

447

and after, they do not have a memory.[123] This kind of knowledge of first and after (*cognoscere*) depends on sense experience as opposed to rational reflection on and linking of ideas. As the soul always acts through its memory, therefore, it senses what it first saw or heard or learned.[124] Before and after pertain to time rather than to the understanding; and time is sensed.[125] Hence memory pertains to that sensitive part of the soul to which imagination also pertains and one remembers by means of *phantasia*, images, that is, ultimately through *sensibilia*.[126] But *per accidens* memories are intelligibles which cannot be apprehended by man without images.[127]

Those men who have subtle and spiritual powers of contemplation are less able to remember,[128] because those memories which are best remembered are gross and sensible. Indeed, Cicero shows that if we wish to remember rational intelligibles easily, we must link them with other (more sensible) images, because memories that are larger and sensible are best.[129] Aquinas knows that there are others who disagree and wish to place memory in the intellective part directly.[130]

In Lectio III he discusses the process by which memories are had in the soul as a kind of *habitus*, an enduring impression not unlike a picture.[131] The sensible imprints its similitude in the sense and this similitude remains in the imagination even when the sensible is no longer present. The movement sustained by the senses by means of the sensible, impresses in the imagination a kind of sensible figure which remains there not unlike the impression in wax caused by a signet ring after the ring is removed. Now the motion of impressing, the *passio* sustained, does not pertain only to the soul but to the soul and body conjunction.[132] Therefore, memory is called a habit when we are not actually apprehending but

---

123 ' . . . et propter hoc non possunt cognoscere prius et posterius'.
124 'Semper enim cum anima agit per memoriam, ut prius dictum est, simul sentit quod hoc prius vidit, aut audivit, aut didicit; prius autem et posterius pertinent ad tempus'.
125 *Ibid.*, § 325.
126 ' . . . ad quam partem animae pertinet memoria, quia ad eam, ad quam pertinet phantasia; et quod illa sunt per se memorabilia, quorum est phantasia, scilicet sensibilia' (*Ibid.*).
127 ' . . . per accidens autem memorabilia sunt intelligibilia, quae sine phantasia non apprehenditur ab homine' (*Ibid.* § 326).
128 ' . . . est quod ea quae habent subtilem et spiritualem considerationem, minus possumus memorari' (*Ibid.*).
129 'Si aliquas intelligibiles rationes volumus memorari facilius, quod eas alligemus quasi quibusdam alii phantasmatibus, ut docet Tullius in sua Rhetorica [*Ad Herennium*, III, 24] . . . Magis autem sunt memorabilia quae sunt grossa et sensibilia' (*Ibid.*).
130 'Memoria tamen ponitur a quibusdam in parte intellectiva' (*Ibid.*).
131 'Dicimus esse quemdam quasi habitum, quae quidem passio est quasi quaedam pictura' (*Ibid.*, Lectio III, § 328).
132 ' . . . non pertinet ad solam animam, sed ad conjunctum' (*Ibid.*, § 329).

conserving past experiences.[133] It is through *signa* that we remember by having a present movement or *passio*. Minds that are too moist or in flux do not retain these *signa* or impressions, and this is the case of either children or old people.[134] But if that which is present in the rememberer through this kind of movement or *passio* is there as a figure or picture representing what was first impressed in the sense by sensibles, is it not the case that this memory will be other than *of* the figure or picture, and instead be *of* the thing itself? Surely we can know this from experience.[135] Indeed, Aristotle distinguishes between two ways in which a picture or image can be understood: either as a depiction of something else or as a picture which is an image in itself.[136] When we speak of an image depicting something else which we first sensed or knew, then we consider it as an image leading to that other thing and this is the principle or cause of remembering. But when we consider the image as an image in itself, we are dealing with what pertains to the sensitive part of mind. Therefore, when the soul turns itself to the image which is preserved of some form in the *parte sensitiva*, we have an act of imagination or of intellect considering this universal form. When the soul turns to that which is the universal's image which was first heard or known, we have an act of remembering. And since the very being of the image signifies an intention of a form, Avicenna has said that memory deals with intentions and imagination with the form apprehended by means of the senses.[137]

Aristotle also says that frequent meditation on what we have sensed or known strengthens and conserves the memory and enables us to reminisce about what we have seen or known. Meditation is none other than frequent consideration of something, whose image has previously been apprehended, but not only as an image in itself but also as an image of or for something else. This meditation as a means of conserving memories

---

[133] *Ibid.*, § 329.
[134] 'Manifestat propositum per signa, scilicet quod in memorando sit praedicta passio praesens' (*Ibid.*, § 330).
[135] 'Et etiam hoc experimento patet'.
[136] ' ... vel prout est aliquod in se, vel prout est phantasma alterius' (*Ibid.*, § 340). Clearly this is Aristotle. 'In current neurophysiology and psychology, one speaks of two hemispheres of the brain, a symbolic, affective hemisphere (right hand side) which is probably unable to distinguish a name from the thing named; and a dominant left hemisphere with which we can regard such things as a flag as a sort of name of the country or organisation that it represents. But the right hemisphere does not draw this distinction and regards the flag as sacramentally identical with what it represents. So 'Old Glory' is the United States ...' As Bateson points out, there will always and necessarily be a large number of situations in which the response is not guided by the logical distinction between the name and the thing named. See Gregory Bateson, *Mind and Nature, A Necessary Unity* (London, 1979), p. 31.
[137] Aquinas, *In Aristotelis ... de memoria*, Lectio III, § 343.

449

pertains to the very purpose of memory.[138] This activity of knowing that some image is an image of something previously sensed pertains to the *primum sensitivum* part of the soul to the degree to which we know time through this part.[139]

In Lectio IV Aquinas turns to reminiscence which is neither remembering nor learning something new and for the first time. It is a motion, a movement towards remembering and hence memory follows reminiscence as the goal of its movement.[140] The cause of reminiscence is a certain order of movement which releases what we first apprehended, the movement being from first to next, according to some custom or developed habit of ordering things. If one frequently thinks of one thing ordinarily coming after another, then one can think quickly along these lines. This ordered way of thinking in series is not equally habitual in all men.[141] Reminiscence is nothing other than a search (*inquisitio*) for a forgotten memory according to such an ordered technique. It is a search for consequences of that which came before and which we hold in our memories,[142] as when we search by means of demonstration, we proceed from something prior and which we know to something posterior of which we are ignorant. This is the way we find what has escaped from our memories. Aquinas gives the following example: We begin with something we remember and proceed to something else in one of three ways. Either by remembering Socrates and through this, coming to Plato who is similar to Socrates in wisdom. Or we reason from contraries as when we contrast Hector with Achilles. Or else we reason from what we know to something close or neighbouring, as when we remember the father and thereby proceed to the son.[143] But we use the word reminiscence in its proper sense only when we mean that we proceed from something prior and search for that which is posterior and momentarily lost. If one wishes to retain what one studies it is therefore advised that one learn it in some order. Secondly, it is advised that one concentrate one's mind; also, that one frequently meditate in an ordered fashion. And fourthly that one

---

[138] Et dicit quod frequentes meditationes eorum quae sensimus aut intelleximus conservant memoriam ad hoc quod aliquis bene reminiscatur eorum quae vidit aut intellexit. Nihil autem est aliud meditari quam multotiens considerare aliqua, sicut imaginem priorum apprehensorum et non solum secundum se; qui quidem modus conservandi pertinet ad rationem memoriae. (*Ibid.*, § 348)

[139] '... sed inquantum phantasma est imago alicuius prius sensati ... ad quam partem animae earum ... pertineat [id est] ad primum sensitivum, inquantum per ipsum cognoscimus tempus' (*Ibid.*, § 349).

[140] *Ibid.*, Lectio IV, § 356.

[141] *Ibid.*, § 361.

[142] *Ibid.*, 'Et ideo reminiscendo venamur, id est inquirimus id quod consequenter est ab aliquo priori, quod in memoria tenemus' (*Ibid.*, § 362).

[143] *Ibid.*, § 364.

begin the process of reminiscing from the beginning of the material one has consciously ordered along the customary lines of before and after.[144] Reminiscence is, therefore, a willed recuperation *sub ratione memoriae* of the knowledge that is now lost, preferably in the order in which it was first learned.[145] Once again, we are reminded that learning something new is not the same as reminiscence.[146] There is no room here for Plato's epistemology. And Aquinas returns to the Ciceronian method of reinforcing reminiscence by describing how some men recall best in places in which they heard or learned or thought something previously, thereby using places as a kind of principal cause of reminiscence.[147]

In Lectio VII he takes up the crucial problem of the way time is known differently when we remember and when we reminisce. He says that Aristotle shows how someone who reminisces knows time, that is the past, which concerns memory in which one searches to find what has been lost. Time or the past is known to the man who reminisces when he consciously proposes a certain measure, as for instance, one knows that one has sensed something three days previously; or else, when one proposes a more indefinite means of measure, that is, one that is indeterminate, for instance when one recalls that one has sensed something at some time or other.[148] But how does the soul know temporal measure? Aristotle says that first there is something in the soul by which one judges greater and lesser temporal measure. This something is rational. This is similar to the way the soul judges of corporeal magnitude. Something is of a certain magnitude with regard to or in comparison with quantitative distance from the perceiver's body, or regarding the quantitative distance from a place; by *analogy* there is a proportional quantity of time which is judged according to its distance from the present and now.[149] Magnitude is therefore known by the soul but not by extending the intellect (quantitatively) but rather, in an intellectual manner, that is, by analogy, proportionally.[150] The movement from a sensible thing is released in the soul and is judged proportional to the exterior magnitude. Within the soul are forms and movements similar to things through which the soul knows

---

[144] *Ibid.*, § 371.
[145] *Ibid.*, Lectio VI, § 372.
[146] *Ibid.*, § 373.   [147] *Ibid.*, § 377.
[148] *Ibid.*, Lectio VII, § 386.
[149] Et primo ostendit quomodo anima cognoscat mensuram temporis ... Dicit ergo primo quod aliquid est in anima, quo iudicat maiorem et minorem mensuram temporis. Et hoc rationabile est esse circa tempus, sicut et circa magnitudines corporales; magnas quidem, quantum ad quantitatem corporum visorum, et procul, quantum ad quantitatem distantiae localis, cui proportionatur quantitas temporis, quae accipitur secundum distantiam a praesenti nunc. (*Ibid.*, § 387)
[150] Compare Averroes's commentary on *De Anima*, III for a similar argument.

451

things.[151] Aquinas like Aristotle, merely affirms that the interior forms and motions correspond proportionally to exterior magnitudes.[152] This assumption allows for analogous thinking. What is required in the act of remembering is the simultaneous occurrence of the movement of the things recalled in the soul and the past time (*quando in anima simul occurrit motus rei memorandae et temporis praeteriti, tunc est memoriae actus*). If the movement is had but without temporal movement, one does not reminisce: one needs both. 'Unde si motus rei fiat sine motu temporis, aut e converso, non reminiscitur.'[153] It is, however, possible to recall something from the past but without determining precisely when in the past, and this results from weak impressions, not unlike seeing something from a great distance away which produces an indeterminate recognition.[154]

Aside from the difference regarding the way time is dealt with in remembering and in reminiscing, that is, either sensed movement or an intellectual analogy consciously invoked, there are other differences between the two. Lectio VIII focuses on reminiscence which is a syllogistic relationship between similitudes. Deliberation is performed *per modum cuiusdam syllogismi* and only men can do this. Animals operate through a kind of unconscious natural instinct rather than through conscious deliberation. Thus, operations of the intellectual part of the soul take place without corporeal organs and are distinguished in man by his will to choose or not choose as he wishes. Hence one has a choice to reminisce or not. But where corporeal organs are involved one has no power to resist or induce sensation. While there is a kind of biological determinism implied here at the level of sensation and experience,[155]

---

[151] Huiusmodi autem magnitudines cognoscit anima non extendendo ibi intelligentiam ... non ergo cognoscit anima magnitudinem ei se coextendendo, sed per hoc, quod quidam motus a re sensibili resolutus in anima, est proportionalis magnitudini exteriori. Sunt enim in anima quaedam formae et motus similes rebus, per quas res cognoscit. (*Ibid.*, § 388)

[152] *Ibid.*, § 390.

[153] *Ibid.*, § 396. Note that time is sensed as a motion and not as an image. Time is sensed movement or activity. Understanding must return to the sensed time in order to create or draw its analogy by setting up judgemental measure.

[154] *Ibid.*, § 397.

[155] Put in a modern way, Gregory Bateson argues as follows:
The *processes* of perception are inaccessible; only the *products* are conscious and, of course, it is the products that are necessary. The two general facts, first, that I am unconscious of the process of making the images which I consciously see, and, second, that in these unconscious processes I use a whole range of presuppositions (habitual knowledge) which become built into the finished image, are, for me, the beginning of empirical epistemology ... we all know that the images which we 'see' are indeed manufactured by the brain or mind. But to know this in an intellectual sense is very different from realizing that it is truly so. (*Mind and Nature*, p. 32)

Aquinas has, at the same time, opened up a freedom of wilful intellectual response to stimuli at the level of interpretative understanding of universals.[156] As he made clear in the *ST* Ia Q. 81, a. 3, an animal's judgement is controlled by his natural instinct, whereas man is free because of the willed activity of his reason making comparisons and drawing analogies between alternatives. In man the appetitive power is controlled by his *ratio particularis* instead of by the *æstimativa*. This particular reason acts by deducing from the general conclusions of 'universal reason' the particular mode of behaviour appropriate to circumstances. Likewise, in syllogistic matters, particular conclusions are drawn from universal propositions and hence the human appetitive powers are controlled by man's will and this is in turn governed by man's intellect. When animals are confronted by danger they proceed instantaneously and instinctively to a judgement which leads to action. But man, at least theoretically, can weigh up the circumstances and arrive at a course of action from fixed general principles. Then he assents willingly to this course of action and acts.

Once again Aquinas seeks to emphasise man's independent activity and individual responsibility in the way he interprets his world. The only way man needs outside help is in the general sense that all creation depends on God as a *causa omnium*. But man's body and soul conjunction indicates how he was made to come to intelligible knowledge through his body. Since mind can arrive at true knowledge of universals by its own efforts, that is, by contemplating the data of the individual's own sensory experiences, the intelligible, once grasped, remains in the mind even when the mind is not thinking of it. Hence intelligibles are somehow remembered even though Aquinas has affirmed, along with Aristotle, that memory is a

---

[156] Circa primum considerandum est, quod operationes, quae sunt partis intellectivae absque organo corporali, sunt in sui arbitrio ut possit ab eis desistere cum voluerit. Sed non ita est de operationibus quae per organum corporale exercentur; quia non est in potestate hominis quod ex quo organum corporale est mere eius passio statim cesset. (*Ibid.*, § 402)

This notion of free will regarding the interpretation of images of perception is wishful thinking according to Bateson who describes some extraordinary experiments devised by Adalbert Ames Jr. to show how we endow our visual images with depth etc. He concludes after having run through these experiments on image formation:

In sum, there is no free will against the immediate commands of the images that perception presents to the 'mind's eye'. But through arduous practice and self-correction it is partly possible to alter these images. In spite of this beautiful experimentation, the fact of image formation remains almost totally mysterious. How it is done, we know not – nor indeed, for what purpose. It is all very well to say that it makes a sort of adaptive sense to present only the images to consciousness without wasting psychological process on consciousness of their making. But there is no clear primary reason for using images at all or, indeed, for being *aware* of any part of our mental processes. (quoted in Bateson, *Mind and Nature*, p. 37)

sensitive organ, possessed by animals which have no power to understand universals. Since the memory is an organ and what is represented in it must be similitudes of sensibles, these similitudes have the limitations of individual and particular natures. But since phantasms or images or similitudes always accompany thought as well as sensing, there must be a continuous relationship between a remembered intelligible and a remembered image. The mind must turn its attention towards sensible similitudes to judge the accuracy of its universals or species. Intelligibles are thereafter preserved in the mind by way of symbols or similitudes stored in the sense memory. The sensible image or similitude and its intention in the sense memory are used by mind to prompt a recollection of an intelligible idea. This is a theory closely compatible with that of Averroes. Thus we have Aquinas's explanation of how Aristotle relates memory *per se* and memory *per accidens*, sense memory and intellectual memory or reminiscing. By means of intentions *and* phantasms or images stored in the sense memory, man can retain intelligibles through symbols. Because he has no source of natural knowledge other than his experience of the material world he must learn about creation above him through nature below him. His mind is a unique instrument which allows him to represent the world in abstracting likenesses as well as to express his knowledge of universals in similitudes drawn from material things. Aquinas comes in the end to a conclusion that is not very dissimilar to that of Abelard: that an intermediary world of symbolism, similitudes, of language, serves the natural process of knowledge, joining the fixed world of things with that of mind.

This hypothesis of the necessity of thinking by analogy, where the mind naturally compares its own products with the similitudes of sense data in the lower sensible aspect of mind, is of tremendous importance. Time, like magnitude, is known analogously by the human understanding. That a consciously constructed measure of temporality is as objective as the sensing of temporal movement in conjunction with the movement experienced in the act of sensible impression, depends on a belief that both organs and immaterial mind are congruent with the world to be experienced, their congruence differing only in their own, distinctive means of receiving impressions and acting on these. It is as though for Aquinas, at the level of sensing, time is a fourth dimension accompanying motion and to be sensed; time is there to be experienced whether or not we consciously are aware of experiencing it or not. This is very different from the Augustinian affirmation that time is nothing other than a mental or rational construction independent of the senses and which has no being outside understanding, created minds. For Augustine, animals have no time; and therefore no history. For Aquinas the issue is more ambiguous. Animals do sense time as do men; what they lack is an understanding of time and because they have no intellects cannot think analogously. By implication the capacity to think analogously is the determinant of man's conscious historicity for himself and others. Following Aristotle on reminiscence, where one proposes a peculiarly rational, conscious and prudential setting up of before and after in the search for lost (but necessarily learned or experienced and preserved) memories, Aquinas implies that what we mean by history is not remembering but reminiscence, a technique of structuring past experiences not only for easy retrieval but for understanding. That history as a rational construction is, therefore, artificial, like the artificial memory devices of the rhetorical tradition, is not in line with Aristotle's understanding of the historical which for him had no sequence: it was just one damn fact after another. But history as reminiscence, for Aquinas, must be of the aesthetic, poetic, exemplary, prudential order where the particular past as past is not understandable but where the past as usable is all that matters. The only reason one should turn to the history of ancient Rome, then, is for its exemplary message in the present, because mind can understand nothing else. Prudence uses experience of the past in order to know about the future and hence memory is a part of prudence.[157]

It is significant that if history is reminiscence, and we know that reminiscers are quick learners, then they enhance their ability to learn and retain through artificial aids to reminiscence, technical means to recall past images in order to understand them. They require writing and images of corporeal places to help them recall. They require alphabetical indices for preaching. In an oral culture a good rememberer would be valued; but by the thirteenth-century writing and recording the present for use by future generations was required for historical reminiscence. A literate culture is aware of the constructed ordering of the past, the art of sequence, the importance of rules of logical communication. The development of the use of a sophisticated theory of logic in the scholastic methodology to interpret seminal texts of a religious tradition, worked hand in hand with their theories of mind. As Aquinas said, Aristotle

---

[157] *ST* IIa IIae Q. 49 a. 1. The scholastic artificial memory was not, as Yates believed (*The Art of Memory*, p. 89) transformed by moral and pious intentions of theological authors, but rather by their concern to construct an epistemology for man as a moral agent as well as a rational being in the world. The *imagines agentes* of classical antiquity had indeed been transformed into corporeal similitudes or symbols of more spiritual, abstract *intentiones* because of the dominant thirteenth-century concern to establish a theory of mind. The extraordinary flowering of images and an elaborated system of these images in thirteenth-century religious art was no anomaly but a corollary of the continuum between *intelligibilia* and *sensibilia*. See *ST* Ia Q. 1 a. 9.

should be interpreted as asserting correctly that understanding requires a continuum and time. The continuity asserted is between sensible images and more abstract intentions and species, the latter being analogous to a consciously constructed continuity between prior and posterior, sequence and order, which are deemed to be implicit in the natural and unconsciously sensed world. Hence, the technique of the *ars memoria* is based on an assumed, a hypothetical necessity of there being a natural continuity between things and mind and language. To understand time one does not simply understand the interior operations of mind but one returns to the sensible by means of similitudes by which one senses or experiences time. The implicit continuity between things and mind, corporealities and spiritualities is based on the 'fact' of man being a composite being, a body and soul conjunction. Therefore, when Aquinas says that magnitude and time are sensed by the common sense through a secondary motion (immutation) which is necessarily related to the primary motion of impression in the senses, he is describing the beginnings of that apprehended continuity which ends in the relation between species in the mind at different levels of abstraction. Central to this theory of continuity is the 'fact' that the secondary motion remains in the imagination and memory after the sensible, which effected the primary motion and led to the secondary motion, disappears. The *immutatio secundaria* is a necessary *passio* of the *sensus communis*. Thus, understanding abstracts from the imagination where the similitude or image appears by means of secondary motion, a motion that is not true alteration but is rather a development from potentiality to actuality.

For Aquinas, a judged distance from the present moment is based on a perception of time which pertains to the sensitive memory. Sense memory operates with present images or phantasms, present, timeless abstractions from the past sensible images caused by sense experience. The knowing of first and after is therefore possible for animals which have memories because Aquinas affirms that sequence actually belongs to time rather than to understanding. There is, then, an objective before and after, there to be understood and sensed if it is suitably processed, independent of whether or not it is actually understood or sensed. Mental similitudes of whatever degree of abstraction are simply the means by which we know time and things rather than the similitudes being what is known. That we know that *signa*, symbols, similitudes are *of* other things and not self images, means that we assume a continuity with the world and mind's capacity to represent it adequately. The act of representing is equated to the mind becoming actually what it represents so that the knower becomes the known. And Aquinas is less ambiguous than Aristotle in asserting that memory retains the remembered thing, not absolutely, but *as it was apprehended* in the past by sense or intellect. However, the world being as it is, is there to be remembered as it is, and someone who remembers a past apprehension inaccurately, does so not because the world is open to conflicting interpretations but because the corporeal aspects of mind mistakenly represented the world as a result of the brain's physical inadequacies. There is here an important distinction being maintained, that between brain and mind, a distinction that for Aquinas does not permit of real discontinuity between the two.

Having asserted the continuity of sense similitudes and intellectual species, because of the soul–body conjunction which experiences the motion of impressing as a *passio*, Aquinas has, to a degree, 'saved' the phenomena. When time is understood as opposed to being unconsciously sensed, it is understood as a proportional quantity, *judged* as a distance from the present now. It is a rational capacity which judges the proportional relations between an exterior magnitude and its internal similitude. The resulting concept is believed to be generally adequate to its sensible object: 'adequatio rei atque cogitationes'. For Aquinas, the empirical world as it is underlies all empirical knowledge and all concepts as the *a priori of* knowing. But Aquinas also says that sense data are only the material cause of knowledge and what we know is more than what we sense. The intellect is dependent on images of sensibles but it understands them independent of their materiality. A mere impression made by sensibles is not enough and something of a higher order is required to cause intellectual activity. Operations of mind go beyond sense knowledge, allowing us to understand the natures of things beyond their particular being. We never know such natures without first having images of particulars we experience but we never understand particulars as such. This problem would continue to be addressed well into the eighteenth century and beyond.

Indeed, Kant rejected the argument that phenomena could be saved by reference to empirical observation alone since these never supply the universality claimed by concepts. For Kant, appearances might be so arranged that they were wholly discordant with the forms of unity postulated by the understanding. But did he believe this to be the case? No. The problem, therefore, remained well beyond the eighteenth century of how synthetic representations could be related to an object. Kant argued that the relation was *a priori* because otherwise concepts might not apply to some objects. He said that all experience does indeed contain, in addition to the intuition of the senses, through which something is given, a concept of an object (not unlike the medieval intention) as being thereby given, as

457

appearing. Therefore for Kant, concepts of objects in general, natures, underlie all empirical understanding, rather than sensing, as their *a priori* conditions. How far, in these matters, had Kant moved from Aquinas's position? Like Aquinas, Kant argued that we could never know 'the thing in itself' in its particularity.

The fundamental question remained from the scholastic analyses to modern times: how is reality incorporated into the concept; what is the relation of ideas, of reason, to the material world? The eighteenth-century Enlightenment experienced a crisis of idealism which mirrored that in the thirteenth century when there was so heated a debate concerning the divergence of Plato from Aristotle on these issues. The crisis of idealism was the breakdown of the identity between concept and object. Where idealism attempted to build out from the putatively secure ground of certainty based on the products of reflective reason alone to the given sensuousness of the world and historical reality, Kant argued that concepts were insufficient and they necessarily depended on something else, that is, the material of perception given to them. He criticised the independence of concepts postulated by Platonising idealists. He argued instead that *a priori* synthetic judgements and the synthetic unity of apperception, where the 'I think' accompanies all representations, salvaged the form to which the contingent material world had to adapt in order that it could exist, for us. But this was done at the expense of leaving the form purely general. Furthermore, Kant postulated a *cogito*, or transcendental subject, which consists of an abstraction 'I' which is identical, at this level of abstraction, in all thinking subjects. The parallels with Averroes's arguments seem clear. The various categories and forms which we use in thinking are, again, also identical in all subjects for Kant. However, the relationship between this transcendental subject and empirical (historical) subjects was seen to be the central issues in idealism, indeed its most problematic part.

Aquinas also saw it as a fundamental problem and, therefore, rejected the Averroistic view that the potential intellect was transcendental, that is, was not individualised in individual men. But as Kant was to do, Aquinas also argued that where individuals experienced differently, what they came to understand was a single nature of the particular experience; all men grasped the *nature* of stone, the intelligibility of stone, through varied experiences of different and particular stones. Understanding as a conscious, rational activity relies on the continuity of the abstracting activities of the diverse powers of mind, for Aquinas, where the internal senses are governed by reason's response at the level of the universal, the generic, the categorical.[158] Perception or apprehension then, is paralleled with a performance of thought based on the abstracting capacity of the common sense, the imagination, the particular reason and the memory to grasp, to 'perceive', similitudes according to these faculties' own modes of receiving the forms or categories implicit in the world of particulars. Mind cannot dispense with sensation of the particular. But it cannot know the particular as such. In opposition to all idealists, Aquinas argued that it was not the nature of our thought which determines what the world can possibly contain, but rather the reverse, that the world determines what we can think about but in a mode of thought that is particular to the representational capacity of the different powers of the mind.[159]

Aquinas's account of man's intrinsic capacities carries with it an insistence that man is naturally endowed with an ability to form true judgements and evaluations. Although he is a finite being amongst other finite beings, man is capable of exploring formal, universal truths and values of all being and therefore, of becoming in an intentional and consequently willed, cognitive way, all things.[160] And this openness to the formal truth of being is not any immediate evidence of divine reality. Man's certitude about being is not a function of his certitude about God. Rather, it is because he attains a certitude about the world through the activities of mind that he comes to a knowledge of God. It is not necessary, he says, that God, considered in Himself, be naturally known to man but only a likeness of God. So it remains that man is to reach the knowledge of God through his naturally endowed capacity to reason by way of the likenesses or similitudes of God found in His effects.[161] It is from man experiencing himself as a cognitive and appetitive, embodied subject in a world with others that he comes to construct a metaphysics of being and of God. This itinerary from what is prior according to human experience to what is prior absolutely and divorced from contingent material circumstances, is a natural journey embarked upon by the human intellect when it apprehends the realities the particular man experiences, including himself. The consequence of this openness to the being of what he experiences is a rational process of reflective discourse which elaborates, in trans-experiential and conceptual terms, an account of the ontological conditions

---

[158] For a contemporary expression of this, according to the physician Russell Brain in 'Speech and thought', *The Physical Basis of Mind*, ed. Peter Laslett (Oxford, 1950) p. 49, 'no matter in what regional accent or pitch, no matter what different patterns that are presented to our nervous systems, the word 'dog' even when written, still produces the same meaning'.

[159] Neo-Augustinians into the fourteenth century and beyond would not agree. See below ch. 21 on Scotus.

[160] *De Veritate*, Q. 2 a. 2.   [161] In *Contra Gentiles*, c. 11.

of his lived experience.[162] It has been pointed out that this itinerary from a phenomenology to a metaphysics rests on two *a priori* assumptions: first, that a metaphysical overview of man to whom being is intentionally accessible, is possible; and secondly, that man is integrated within an intelligible order of being.[163] Aquinas could never argue the position that there is no structure in a mind-independent reality, first because there is an eternally existing Mind, God; and secondly, because man's mind is only another aspect of that reality, in a mode specific to itself; therefore, both understanding and the senses are concerned with, because they are, the same thing. And they relate in different ways to an implicitly formal structured reality, a universal or categorical aspect of which mind grasps analogously. Between the two worlds of consciously structured learning and reminiscing on the one hand, and biological determinism at the unconscious sense level on the other, is the domain of the cultural phenomenon of explanation. This is nothing more than a mapping onto the tautology of definitions whereby the unfamiliarity and uniqueness of individual past experiences are made familiar, present, formal and exemplary if the past is to be understood. The aggregation of past phenomena into a meaningful system is coextensive with mind, it is prudence in action. But Aquinas is not speaking of mind that is separable and self-subsistent and subjective, but rather of a human, embodied mind that acts and expresses itself in a mode which Aquinas believes must be analogous to the modes of expression and action of other beings, all of which, in their different ways, are likenesses or similitudes of the divine *causa omnium*.[164]

---

[162] Patrick Masterson, 'Man and God in the philosophy of St. Thomas Aquinas', in *Images of Man ... for Verbeke*, pp. 335–51.

[163] *Ibid.*, p. 346.

[164] John Wippel, 'Thomas Aquinas, Henry of Ghent and Godfrey of Fontaines on the reality of nonexisting possibles', in *Metaphysical Themes in Thomas Aquinas*, (Washington, D.C., 1984), pp. 163–89, especially pp. 164–73.

PART V

LATER MEDIEVAL THEORIES OF MEMORY: THE *VIA ANTIQUA* AND THE *VIA MODERNA*.

INTRODUCTION

We are now about to launch into an examination of two immensely sophisticated theories of human cognition, that of John Duns Scotus and William of Ockham. It has been one of the main contentions of past chapters that epistemological theories, and the role given to the memory faculty within such theories, affected the way men wrote about the past. A theory about how the memory faculty or the capacity to remember processes experiences leads to assertions about what, if anything, of a past experience can be recovered in the present for present understanding and use. Both Scotus and Ockham were fourteenth-century Franciscans. With their theories of human cognition we reach the two epistemologies which effectively set the boundaries for all substantive debate into and beyond the early modern period. In what follows, an attempt is made to indicate how these two theories affected historical writing and attitudes to the past amongst Renaissance historians, all of whom, it is argued, can be seen to follow either the Scotist position or the Ockhamist position as these were taken up and modified by respective followers who travelled along what later was called the (Scotist) *via antiqua* or the (Ockhamist) *via moderna*. Modern historians of the Renaissance have often argued that Renaissance historians understood the past in ways similar to the way we understand it, whereas men of the middle ages had no sense of the past. This is untrue, and it will be argued that the two epistemologies stand in opposition well into the eighteenth century and in some cases beyond. What did change during the Renaissance were the narrative genres in which historians wrote about the past and communicated their views to contemporaries who were literate and no longer of the clerical stamp.

As we shall see, at the heart of the medieval *and* Renaissance discussion of how we remember the past is the contention that conventional language, which refers to mental discourse about the world, is the means by which the mind can make sense of past and present utterances. What it means to remember is, therefore, linked inextricably with the mediating function of language's logic. There is for medieval and Renaissance thinkers a language of thought and a conventional language of speech and writing. Without language we cannot remember anything that is meaningful for us; and some would argue that we cannot understand the texts of the past as being of the past without understanding how language, mental and spoken, works. Hence, the Scotist and Ockhamist epistemologies deal not only with how mind receives sense data, but how mind acts to transform such data, once internalised, and thereby gives sense experience meaning. The argument, in medieval and modern terms, is one between realists and nominalists (or conceptualists). It is between those who believe that individual experiences of the world have an essential, extractable, formal meaning to mind, somehow despite their sensual and temporal individuating qualities, and those who believe that all there 'is' in the world are individuals, and names which signify or substitute for such individuals in propositions, where the individuals are im-mattered and substantial. According to this latter view, we know individuals not merely their essences or some formal aspect of them, through experiencing the world of individuals and referring to these individuals through language.

In the concluding chapter I discuss briefly some current neurophysiological, psychological and computer analogies of mind and remembering in an attempt to show that they are, usually unacknowledged, realist positions of which there are numerous medieval precursors of considerable subtlety. How memory operates, even at the biochemical level, is distinctly unclear to us and the analogies drawn today between machines and mind or the reduction of mind to biochemical processes are not necessarily more illuminating than some medieval analogies. But the medieval analogies are rather unfamiliar or less congenial to us and this seems less caused by their medieval Catholicism and our modern secularism than by our unfamiliarity with Aristotle's writings on language, cognition and remembering. It was Aristotle's discussion of how human beings come to know and remember, especially in his logical works and in the *De Anima* and the *De Memoria et Reminiscentia*, which set the tone of later medieval and Renaissance discussions of mind, reinterpreted as these ancient texts were by the numerous attempts to harmonise what Aristotle said on the subject with various beliefs of the Church Fathers, especially St Augustine, and others dominated by a neo-Platonist conception of thinking.

What one sees in the debate between Scotus and Ockham is a conflict not over the truth of the past but rather over the means by which men come to know it. As we shall see, the debate would centre on whether the human mind knows the past as present and universal or as past and particular.

Chapter 21

JOHN DUNS SCOTUS

... Thou hast a base and brickish skirt there, sours
That neighbour-nature thy grey beauty is grounded
Best in; graceless growth, thou hast confounded
Rural rural keeping-folk, flocks, and flowers.

Yet ah! this air I gather and I release
He lived on; these weeds and waters, these walls are what
He haunted who of all men most sways my spirits to peace;

Of reality the rarest-veinèd unraveller; a not
Rivalled insight, be rival Italy or Greece ...

Gerard Manley Hopkins, Duns Scotus's Oxford

What the brain does with the spoken word – and no one can say how it does it – is to extract from it an electrical pattern in time and space which is distinctive of the word 'dog' and common to all the ways in which it can be pronounced, so as to be recognized.

Russell Brain, 'Speech and thought', in The Physical Basis of Mind, ed. P. Laslett (Oxford, 1950), p. 49.

In 1255 the faculty of arts at the University of Paris placed all the known works of Aristotle on the lecture programme.[1] The study of the authentic Aristotle, as translated into Latin,[2] was thereafter increasingly pursued by philosophers without the theological concern to baptize him. Indeed, during the 1260s the writings of radical Aristotelians such as Siger of

---

[1] Fernand Van Steenberghen, *Thomas Aquinas and Radical Aristotelianism* (Washington D.C., 1980); Fernand Van Steenberghen, *Aristotle in the West: The Origins of Latin Aristotelianism*, trans. L. Johnston, second edn (Louvain, 1970).

[2] William of Moerbeke not only revised the translation of Aristotle's *De Anima* but also provided a translation of Themistius' paraphrases. There was an active general interest in the early Aristotelian commentators: Themistius, Alexander of Aphrodisias, John Philponus etc. Averroes had used Alexander and Themistius extensively in his 'long' commentary on the *De Anima*.

Brabant and Boethius of Dacia caused alarm, not least to Aquinas.[3] And in 1270 and again in 1277 the Bishop of Paris, Stephen Tempier, condemned a series of propositions that were being defended by followers of an 'Averroistic' interpretation of Aristotle: the eternity of the world and the single intellect or world soul shared by all men.[4] But with the Parisian ruling that no theology should be taught in the philosophy faculty, an increasingly 'pure' Aristotle was sought by philosophers and allowed to speak for himself.[5] This continued into the fourteenth century.

As we have seen, there were various interpretations given to Aristotle's account in the *De Anima* of how the soul is only potentially knowledge and sensation and how it becomes aware of an external thing by somehow taking its form or similitude into itself. At the level of the external senses of sight and hearing or of the internal senses of imagination and memory, sensible species were involved in a process of continuous abstraction. But there remained a problem as to how sensory information could be conveyed to the intellective and nonmaterial part of the soul, and this centred on the fact that conceptual notions were incorporeal and universal.[6] Aristotle had been vague as to how the mind as potential knowledge, in what scholastics called the potential or possible intellect, became fully actualised through understanding. Reading Aristotle's text closely, it was seen that at least two factors were necessary: first, that some active agency, analogous to light, had to bring out the potential, just as potential colours of a darkened object were illuminated, so that the phantasm or sensible species was transformed in the imagination by having its potential intelligibility made actually intelligible. Some interpreted Aristotle's light metaphor as a way of speaking of the agent intellect's function, and numerous

---

[3] Fernand Van Steenberghen, *La Philosophie au XIIIe siècle* (Louvain and Paris, 1966) who refers to heterodox Aristotelianism rather than Averroism; Bruni Nardi, *S. Tommaso d'Aquino: Trattato sull' unità dell' intelletto contro gli averroisti* (Florence, 1947); Pierre Mandonnet, *Siger de Brabant et l'averroisme latin au XIIIe siècle*, I, II (textes inédits), 2nd edn (Louvain, 1908). Aquinas' attack: *Tractatus de unitate intellectus contra averroistas*, ed. L. W. Keeler, 2nd edn (Rome, 1957) which probably was directed at Siger's earlier works and not the *Quaestiones de anima intellectiva.*

[4] Text of the condemnations in H. Denifle and A. Chatelain, eds., *Chartularium Universitatis Parisiensis*, I (Paris, 1889), no. 432.

[5] Siger says he wants to determine what Aristotle said on the nature of the soul and is not interested in arriving at the truth! *Quaestiones de anima intellectiva*, c. 6 (ed. Bazán, p. 99): 'quod nostra principalis non est inquirere qualiter se habeat veritas de anima, sed quae fuerit opinio philosophi de ea'.

[6] The debate has continued into the twentieth century. See Peter Laslett, ed., *The Physical Basis of Mind* (Oxford, 1950). In the introduction Sir Charles Sherrington notes that 'Aristotle, 2,000 years ago, was asking how is the mind attached to the body. We are asking that question still' (p. 4). See in particular c. 4 by S. Zuckerman, 'The mechanisms of thought: the mind and the calculating machine', which begs all the relevant questions in ignorance that he is so doing.

theories were propounded to explain the precise function of this aspect of mind. Secondly, it was acknowledged that the potential object had to be already present in the mind itself for one to draw upon knowledge once acquired and to actualise it voluntarily. As Aquinas had argued against Avicenna, the intellect or understanding was a storehouse of virtual or habitual information and the understanding was a place of forms which could be brought to actual understanding at will. We have seen that the term intelligible species was used to refer to those distinct, universal forms in the possible intellect, ready to be actualised.

But here the interpretation of Aristotle met the Christian Platonism of Augustine and scholastics tried to reconcile the two. Augustine had argued that knowledge was more an activity of the soul than a purely passive reception of externally impressed objects. And he also believed that the human soul was the image of the Trinity where its higher part was a mutually interrelated set of activities of intellection, memory and will. The memory was of special importance because it was not only the capacity to recall things and events experienced in the past but was more significantly involved in actively producing mental conceptions of objects that either were no longer actually present to the senses, or never had been sensually perceived. Such notions had no strict counterparts in the sensible world, and Augustine, therefore, explained them by drawing on a Platonic illuminationism, mind being illumined by the divine archetypal ideas, mind intuitively grasping these transcendent natures or ideas that were over and above itself and any sensual experiences it may ever have had.

As Dominicans and Franciscans increasingly distinguished themselves from one another at the end of the thirteenth century, not only in terms of their respective understanding of their social roles in relation to mendicant poverty, and consequently their relationship to the papacy,[7] but also in terms of their adherence to an Aristotelian or Platonic epistemology, Augustine came to be reassessed, renewed, reinterpreted by either side of the ever widening debate. This debate, largely epistemological in origin, would give rise to the split between what would later be called the neo-Augustinian *via antiqua* and the more empirically based neo-Aristotelian *via moderna* of the fourteenth century within the Franciscan order itself.

The more Augustinian epistemologies of the later thirteenth century

7 See Janet Coleman, 'The two jurisdictions: theological and legal justifications of church property in the thirteenth century', in *The Church and Its Wealth (Studies in Church History*, 23) (Oxford, 1987), eds., W. Shiels and D. Wood, for the gradual separation of aims of the two orders, especially regarding attitudes to property and poverty, and to the authority of the papacy.

kept some form of special illumination in their theories of mind which was then integrated into explanations of how the agent intellect illumined the phantasms.[8] The rhetorical tradition's artificial memory technique reinforced this illuminationism by reminding those who were interested that memory places need to be well lit. By the early fourteenth century most scholastics, however, denied that anything more than a general illumination of the agent intellect was required to account for a natural knowledge of the world about us. And although they retained the Augustinian notion of memory as the source of the 'word' or the mental concept of the thing in the mind, emphasising the value of an analogical explanation to account for the eternal generation of the Word by the Father, the memory, as we already saw it in Aquinas, became synonymous with the understanding in so far as it contained the latent image of the object as a proportional representation. For Duns Scotus, this would be an *ens diminutum*, a diminished being, in the form of an intelligible species.

Some argued that the intellect was purely passive in conceiving of an object, maintaining that the simple impression of the intelligible species as the form of the object, was sufficient to produce actual knowledge, that is, that an impressed species caused the expressed species or the word. But others stressed the activity of the intellect and even denied the need for an intelligible species distinct from the sensible species, in the phantasm. This was the position of Henry of Ghent and Godfrey of Fontaines.[9]

One theologian, about whom we have very little biographical information but whose influence was to rival Thomism well into the seventeenth century, would provide an epistemology that sought to marry an Augustinian neo-Platonism with the current Aristotelianism. He would provide the most sophisticated justification of what would later be called the *via antiqua* to compete with a *via moderna* that would be elaborated not by a Thomist, but by another member of his Franciscan order. The epistemology of this thinker, John Duns Scotus, in partial confrontation with that of William of Ockham of the next generation, helped to define the contours of late medieval thought well into the Reformation and Renaissance, fostering a debate that spread outwards from the relative parochialism of early fourteenth-century Oxford, and more specifically an

---

[8] See for example the Augustinian James of Viterbo (d. 1308), *Jacobi de Viterbo OESA, Disputatio prima de Quolibet*, ed. E. Ypma, *Cassiciacum*, Supplementband 1 (Würzburg, 1968), q. 12, p. 160.

[9] Godfrey of Fontaines also eliminated intelligible species as an element of intellective cognition. Henry of Ghent's position is in his *Summa quaestionum ordinarium theologiae* (Paris, 1520) reprinted by The Franciscan Institute, (St Bonaventure, New York, 1943), f. 14 v. Ockham, as we shall see, would deny all species and replace them with intellectual habits.

Oxford heavily influenced by Franciscans, to Paris and then Germany on the eve of the Reformation. Sixteenth-century thinkers would distinguish between the *reales* (Albert and Thomas) and the *formales* (Scotus and the *Nominales*),[10] thus linking the two Franciscans in an alliance which often displayed anything but a united front.

Where both Franciscans were united, as we shall see, was in the common concern to determine a means by which to sever the association of God and necessity in order to replace a radical Aristotelian interpretation of a determined universe with a realm of contingency. This would enable man to understand God as free-willing, especially in the realm of His *potentia absoluta* where His freedom was not limited by His commitments to the world as it now is, *de potentia ordinata*. Their emphasis on our world as contingent led to an affirmation that God had committed Himself to this world rather than to possible other worlds, so that man was to look upon his world as issuing from a contract, a *pactum Dei*. The contingency of the world does not make it unreliable, however. Its creation and man's salvation were simply not ontologically necessary.

The Franciscan John Duns Scotus flourished at Oxford, Cambridge and Paris. He died in 1308 in Cologne but his influence endured for centuries. The seventeenth-century Cisterican theologian John Caramuel y Lobkowicz said that the Scotist school was, in his own times, more numerous than all the others combined.[11] After his period in Oxford, Scotus was selected as the candidate for the Franciscan theological chair at the University of Paris and he began his commentary on the Lombard's *Sentences c.* 1302, precisely at the time when the feud between King Philip the Fair and Pope Boniface VIII came to a head. It is sufficient to note here that Scotus sided with the pope and was exiled from France. But he was back in Paris in 1304. There he continued work on the *Ordinatio* of his lectures on the Lombard begun in Oxford, (*Opus Oxoniense*) and this work, combined with his last mature thinking, his *Quaestiones Quodlibetales*, secured him his fame as a philosopher and theologian until the early modern period. The *Quodlibets* indicate the interests of the university theology faculty of Paris at the beginning of the fourteenth century. The questions came from the floor of the debating chamber and the audience comprised a mixture of scholars at different stages of their course work.

---

[10] Heiko Oberman, *Masters of the Reformation, The Emergence of a New Intellectual Climate in Europe*, trans. Dennis Martin (Cambridge 1981), speaking of Wessel Gansfort, p. 39 n. 76.

[11] F. Bąk, 'Scoti schola numerosior est omnibus aliis simul sumptis', *Franciscan Studies*, 16 (1956), pp. 144–65.

The *Quodlibets* are dated 1306–7.[12] Here, we find Scotus's most mature thought on the nature of memory.

Where Aquinas considered the active or agent intellect to be a faculty of the individual soul that was really distinct from the possible intellect, Scotus considered that while it was a property of the soul, it was only formally distinct from and rather, really identical with the possible intellect and the soul's substance.[13] For Scotus, the function of the agent intellect was to render the potentially intelligible in the sense image or phantasm, actually intelligible.[14]

More importantly, Scotus defined in a more precise manner than we have previously encountered, a simple, nonjudgemental awareness of something as existing here and now, as intuitive cognition. He said that the senses have intuitive knowledge as does the intellect. Indeed, he posited at the intellectual level such prejudgemental acts which can be either intuitive or abstractive, depending on whether or not they are aware of the existence or nonexistence of the objects they signify. Intuitive, nonjudgemental acts know the thing as present and as it exists.[15] But although we have a direct, individual act of cognition, Scotus did not believe the individual in its singularity was the first object known by us. The first object is confused or indistinct knowledge, a species immediately 'above' the individual; the first object known distinctly by the intellect is rather, the *concept* of the individual's being, which is the most absolutely simple of concepts. Against Aquinas, Scotus argued that if a man's simple intellection was limited only to abstract concepts, that is, abstracted from sense experiences, then the face to face vision of God that is promised to man in the afterlife would be impossible. And so Scotus elaborated on those aspects of the soul's capacity for knowledge within the wider context of blessed, angelic and divine knowing. Indeed, he thought that rational considerations of every kind require some measure of intuition. But this intuition has its limitations in our present fallen state: it simply enables us

12 F. Alluntis, ed. and trans., *Questiones Quodlibetales, obras del Doctor Sutil Juan Duns Escoto* (Madrid, 1968); John Duns Scotus, *God and Creatures, the Quodlibetal Questions*, trans. with intro., notes and glossary, by Felix Alluntis OFM and Alan B. Wolter OFM (Princeton, 1975). This is the text cited below.

13 See St Bonaventure, *II Sententiarum* and the *Breviloquium* on the potential and agent intellects not as different faculties or parts of the soul but as two kinds of activity of the same substance, the soul.

14 *Quodlibet*, XV (a.1), 63.

15 Scotus, *Opera Omnia*, ed. L. Wadding, 12 vols. (Lyons, 1639); reprinted by G. Olms, 1968); *Opus Oxoniense*, II d. 3 q.9 n. 6 and *Opus Oxoniense*, III, d. 14, q.3 n. 14; Where new editions of Scotus' works are available, citations below refer to *Opera Omnia*, ed. C. Balíc *et al.*, Vatican Scotistic Commission, (Rome, 1950–): *Ordinatio*, prologue – d. 48, vols. 1–6; *Lectura in librum primum Sententiarum*, prologue – d. 7, vol. 16; *Lectura in librum primum Sententiarum*, d. 8 f. vol. 17.

to doubt something or to be aware of thinking something. It does not give us a knowledge of the individual in its singularity. The simple awareness or consciousness of existential situations which verify a proposition, is for him, required. And this simple awareness of existential situations cannot be a purely sensory knowledge because existential awareness often involves purely conceptual or nonsensory meanings.[16] What is important here, is that although we can be intuitively aware of an individual thing, we cannot know this thing as absolutely unique and singular.

Scotus rejected the need for intelligible species when he spoke of intuitive cognition. Intelligible species were only required as image substitutes for the object experienced when one engaged in abstractive cognition in order to explain why one's conceptual knowledge, that results from the combined efforts of possible and agent intellects with the intelligible species, reflects the universal characteristics of an object. There was another kind of intuitive knowing which did not require this processing. But in man's present state, although his soul is hypothetically capable of an intuition of pure intelligibles, this capability is deformed so that Scotus never really envisages the possibility of knowledge without species. And since individuals are more than their representative species, we cannot know the individual *ut hoc*; in our present condition, although we can have an intuited awareness of the presence and existence of something, we never know this thing *ut hoc*. We know what is intelligible about something *ut natura* and when we are simply aware of something as present and existing, we do not cognitively grasp its individuating difference and its singularity as such. The intellectual capacity to see individuating difference is somehow still with us but, *pro statu isto*, we have temporarily lost the power to exercise it. Therefore, in our present state, we only have a certain knowledge of individuals in their singularity. Even our senses do not perceive individuating differences. The senses perceive an 'indifferent' nature of the being present to them and the senses therefore permit the intellect to know abstractively the nature of this individual and also, intuitively, its existence. The intellect as we possess it in this life does not have an *intuition* of the individuating principle, the *haecceitas*, over and above the common nature of an individual thing. The intellect comes to a universalisation of this individuating principle only through abstractive cognition. The individual thing *is* intelligible but not as a singular. We come to know what is intelligible about a singular first by being aware that it exists and then by abstractively grasping its more universal 'thisness'

[16] Sebastian Day, *Intuitive Cognition, A Key to the Significance of the Late Scholastics* (St Bonaventure, New York, 1947); Camille Berubé, *La connaissance de l'individuel au moyen âge* (Paris and Montreal, 1964).

through species. Hence, as we shall see, the intellect knows by intuition if a nature exists because it has a knowledge of the sensitive act which seizes intuitively the existent *nature*. But it is by species that the object is present *sub ratione cognoscibilis sive repraesentati* and therefore, intellectual cognition must have its own object, the intelligible species, a representation of the individual in a more universal mode.

The relationship between intuitive and abstractive cognition, in sense and intellect, is of great importance for Scotus's conception of the past and the memory's role in knowing the past. Therefore, it is important to grasp Scotus's meaning here, that when we have a sensible intuition of an existent, our intellect knows that the *concept* of the individual's being is that of a singular, but its knowledge of the individual depends on the imaged species which says nothing of the presence and existence of the individual and is rather, more universal and hence, known by abstraction. Scotus's conclusion comes from his reading of Aristotle. He says that it was not Aristotle's intention to say that the individual was not intelligible, and therefore, only what is universal is intelligible. The singular *is* intelligible but not as a singular *ut hoc*. Scotus expresses this as follows: 'intellectus noster non intelligit nisi per sensum et dictum est quod per sensum non cognoscitur hoc singulare ut hoc sed solum ut natura, et sic potest intellectus noster intelligere singulare' (*Reportatio Parisiense* II d. 12, q.8, n. 10) '... nec est idem cognescere singulare actualiter et intuitive, et cognoscere existentiam singularis, quia singulare non est idem quod existentia cum abstrahat ab existentia' (*Rep. Par.*, III d. 14, q. 3, n. 6). Hence, *de potentia ordinata*, in this life as it is now for us,

non potest dici singulare per se intelligibile a quocumque intellectu, non quia objectum non sit in potentia propinquae quantum ex parte sui, sed quia intellectus non movetur nisi a phantasmate, vel a natura quae gignit phantasma, quorum neutrum est hoc ut hoc; natura enim est prius natura quam sit haec ut haec ... singularitas non movet intellectum nostrum ... nihil movet intellectum nostrum nisi natura vel phantasma, et ideo intellectus, qui sic movetur a re, non capit hoc ut hoc. (III d. 14, q.3, n. 8)

Scotus is often taken to be primarily interested in the unfallen capacity of the human soul's knowledge and in relating this to angelic and divine knowledge. Then is his intuitionism a purely theological nicety of primary importance only for a discussion of the face to face vision of the blessed? Surely not. This intuitionism is tied in with Scotus's neo-Platonism. He accepts that there are exemplars, or preconceptions, in the mind of, say, an artisan, and the preconceptual exemplar is an intelligent efficient cause which is then impressed on matter; the efficient cause is identified with the formal Ideas or the ideal types that form the intelligible world. The sensible world imitates these exemplars. Prior to sensible imitations are the archetypal exemplars, the ideas of all possible creatures in the divine mind. Thus, he describes a first act of intellection which corresponds to a first *intention* or quiddity, and this quiddity is the intelligible part of a thing. First intentions or formal concepts in the mind have objective correlates in the formal aspects of things.

Scotus is interested in reality as formally coherent because he focuses on Aristotle's reference to the form representing the quiddity or what is essentially intelligible about a thing. Hence the correlation between a distinct, formal concept or intention and an extramental entity is the form or quiddity of a thing and not its im-mattered existence. One and the same thing as formally distinct, is virtually many things. The quiddity of a thing has the capacity to produce objective notions or natural signs of itself that are conceptually separable. Therefore, the mind's *distinctio rationis* is not merely something created by the mind; rather, it is a symbolic expression of the quiddity of the object. This quiddity of an object is knowable through a natural sign in the soul, a first intention and first intentions *refer to* things and express some intelligible aspect, some essential, formal characteristic of things found in them.

This means for Scotus, that there is, as with Aquinas, *some* knowledge of the existent as such (intuitive) as in sense perception involving the external senses. There is also knowledge of the object but not as existing as such (abstractive). Here the knowledge is not of the object as actually existing or as present but rather as its conceptual representation.[17] But he goes further to show that a similar distinction can be shown in intellectual knowledge. Not only does he insist that there can be some intellection, necessarily abstract, of the non-existent, as Aquinas also affirmed; Scotus also argues that the object needs to be present to be apprehended by intuitive cognition. More importantly he argues that there can be intellectual knowledge of the existent *qua* existent, for the blessed will have such knowledge of the beatific object, that is, God.[18] Hence, the intellect *can* have an act whereby the object is grasped in its real existence, but only where that object is more noble or on par with the intellect.[19] This is what he means by intuitive cognition in virtue of which we affirm or deny contingent propositions, are aware of mental acts, and the blessed apprehend God's being.[20]

---

[17] Scotus, *God and Creatures, Quodlibet*, XIII, 27.   [18] *Ibid.*, 13. 28.
[19] *Ibid.*, 13. 29.
[20] Scotus, *Opus Oxoniense*, IV d. 45 q.2 n. 12; q.3 n. 17; d. 49 q.8 n. 5. See Rega Wood, 'Intuitive cognition and divine omnipotence: Ockham in fourteenth-century perspective', in A. Hudson and M. Wilks, eds., *From Ockham to Wyclif* (*Studies in Church History*,

We can observe here a return to the Avicennan and Averroistic *intentio* which represents a formal characteristic of an extramental thing without representing the whole of its intelligible essence. Avicenna's intention is similar to Scotus's *formalitas*. A formal distinction *a parte rei* is asserted to be compatible with the thing's physical or real simplicity where the formality or intention is conceptually separable, although it may be inseparable so far as the concrete individual in the world is concerned.[21] For Scotus, an intention is both a formal structure in a thing itself and also a concept.[22]

At the heart of this explanation is a concern for the formal, unique, individuality of things, their *haecceitas*, their 'thisness' which cannot be communicated to anything else, but which is knowable. The thisness of something is not determined by its im-mattered existence: matter is not the principle of individuation for Scotus as it was for Thomas and Albert. Rather, *haecceitas* is the unique, formal, intentional principle of individuation that makes the *nature*, which all individuals of the same species have in common, precisely this or that individual and no other. *Both* the common nature and *haecceitas* exist in reality as constituents of particulars and are formally distinct from one another. But *haecceitas* is a distinct, positive *formality*, an intention over and above the universal common nature of the individual. It is exemplified when we say that Petrinity inheres as a representative *haecceitas* of Peter. *Haecceitas* is a radically particularised universal, existing in things that are composite but capable of being separated out by mind, where it is absolutely universal.[23]

Therefore, when we speak of the relation between mental concepts and extramental things, that is, when someone apprehends something intuitively, we are, for Scotus, referring to real relations because there is really some extramental reality as a formal characteristic of a composite thing to which mental concepts refer. The relationship between matter and form really exists, distinctly (i.e. they are not identical) and holds independently of any intellectual consideration.[24] Intellectual consideration is predicated on these real relations and in Quodlibet 13.13 Scotus cites Aristotle's *Physics*, V, and VII c. 3, pointing out that acquired states of (formal) excellence or defects are not alterations because they represent relations: 'relatives are neither themselves alterations nor the subject of alteration or

subsidia 5) (Oxford, 1987), pp. 51–61; John F. Boler, 'Intuitive and Abstractive cognition', in *The Cambridge History of Later Medieval Philosophy*, ed. Kretzmann, Kenny and Pinborg (Cambridge, 1982), pp. 460–78.
21 A. B. Wolter, 'The formal distinction', in J. K. Ryan and B. M. Bonansea, eds., *John Duns Scotus, 1265–1965* (Washington, D.C., 1965).
22 See the introduction, *God and Creatures*.
23 Marilyn McCord Adams, 'Universals in the early fourteenth century', in *The Cambridge History of Later Medieval Philosophy*, eds., Kretzmann, Kenny and Pinborg, pp. 411–39.
24 *Quodlibet*, VI, 82.

becoming or in fact of any change whatever'. There is a continuum of form running from the world to mind and it is susceptible to degree. This would contribute to the heightened debate in fourteenth-century theological circles over the intention and remission of forms, where one discussed not real change but an *immutatio formalis* or *vitalis*.[25] In his earlier accounts, Scotus postulated that formalities had a double mode of existence: in reality as constituents of things, and in the intellect in a non-real mode of existence as concepts or objects of thought. Therefore, in abstract cognition real relations were not required because the object apprehended need not exist. In abstract cognition conceptual relations obtained.

One final distinctively Scotist concern which took Aquinas's wilful cognition further, is his concentration on the will as a rational faculty. Reaffirming the distinction between nature and will, between an unconscious, biological determinism and conscious choice, Scotus argued that only those secondary, purely reflexive, conceptual acts of the intellect that fall under the command of the will are to be deemed rational in the strict sense of being the result of a rational or conscious deliberation. Secondary acts of intellection correspond to second intentions or concepts. Second intentions refer to first intentions or primary concepts in the mind and include such logical notions as genus or species which the mind discovers by reflecting on how the formal content of one first intention relates to another. Logic, therefore, deals with second intentions which are conceptual comparisons and judgements that refer to the first intentions or formal quiddities of known things. Logic has nothing to do with the ontological status of things. The first intentional or ontological aspects of things are the concern of metaphysics rather than logic. Therefore, secondary acts of intellection focus on second intentions, purely conceptual, reflexive, judgemental, logical acts of mind and these, when under the command of the will, are alone strictly rational or conscious.

Scotus then added that the free will is rational in a further way, because it has an inborn inclination to love an object according to right reason. Once again we see him return to intuitive, inborn causes which incline the rational will towards that which in itself has intrinsic value. This inclination is not a result of sense experience but rather, of an autonomous intellectual experience, an *affectio iustitiae*, which is a higher, inborn inclination that serves as an aspect of the will's freedom in contrast with its freedom to incline towards some merely apparent good in an unreasonable, inordinate way. So instead of a continuum of knowledge which always and necessarily begins with the sense datum, Scotus takes up the

---

[25] Janet Coleman, 'Jean de Ripa OFM and the Oxford Calculators', *Mediaeval Studies*, 37 (1975), pp. 130–89.

Augustinian (and Avicennan) neo-Platonism which, in effect, argues for two separate sources of knowing, only one of which is sensual, in contrast and sometimes in conflict in the individual soul, with that which is innate and intuitive, based on higher, transcendent, exemplars. Once again a wedge has been inserted between the material and the spiritual or intellectual.

Throughout the cognitive process, be it at the sensory or intellectual level, Scotus argued for a cocausality of mind and object, where the soul is really identical with (and only formally distinct from) its cognitive faculties, and this soul functions as an active but partial cause, the conceptual, mental object or species as the other partial cause.[26] There are, as we shall see in greater detail below, essentially ordered causes in the soul whereby the agent intellect and the similitude or phantasm collaborate to produce the intelligible species, and in turn, and here is what is truly important, the intelligible species, combined with the intellect, seen as functioning as active *and* possible, produce actual knowledge or the mental word. When the co-causality of the intellect, mutually interacting as agent and possible, unites with the intelligible species to produce actual knowledge, Scotus says we are speaking of the intellect as memory. If the understanding is actually informed by the intelligible species, the memory passes from the state of essential or remote potentiality regarding actual knowledge, to one of accidental or proximate potency or potential. This is the perfect memory state where the 'passage' is from the object of the original act, that is, *what* one saw, heard or thought (remote potentiality) to the rememberer's own seeing, hearing or thinking (proximate potentiality). This perfect memory state, when one's own intellect expresses knowledge that is based on one's own prior intuitive and abstractive cognitive acts, is an intensely personal and individual intellectual activity. In its fullest sense it is the expression of who one actually is. As we saw, Aquinas also sought to express man's individuality to counter what he took to be the 'Averroist' denial.

The difficulty in this terminology is considerable but at least in one sense it is more apparent than real because we have already encountered Aquinas's argument that the truly significant function of memory is identical with the act of understanding. The most important aspect of intellectual memory, reminiscence, is none other than present understanding. Scotus, the Doctor Subtilis, takes this further with a prose whose difficulty repelled (not least) some Renaissance humanists. It is perhaps audacious here to indicate, without demonstrating, that the Renaissance humanists' opinions on Scotus's prose mattered little, not

---

[26] *Ordinatio,* I d. 3 nn. 496–503.

only in terms of the enduring influence of what he meant, but more specifically because Scotus would be seen to have successfully achieved a reintegration of Augustine into his theory of knowledge. A coming to terms with the Augustinian legacy was precisely the impetus behind the earlier humanists like Petrarch who sought a means to unite wisdom and devotional piety and thereby find a *sancta philosophia*. More will be said about this later.

When he wrote his Oxford *Ordinatio* on the Lombard's *Sentences*, Scotus used the term *memoria* in what has often been described as the more customary sense to mean that by which we recall or remember the past.[27] But there is something distinctive in his discussion of how this *memoria* operates. Reflecting on Aristotle's *De Memoria et Reminiscentia*, as did Aquinas, Scotus says that in an act of memory the object of the original act of seeing, hearing or thinking, can only be present as a species which was imprinted by the act of perception. Nothing new here. There is for him as for Aristotle, memory in the sensitive and intellectual faculties of the soul; whatever is remembered by the sensible memory is also remembered by the intellective while the intellectual memory can remember more than what the lower sensitive memory remembers. When we have an intellectual memory, that is, recollection (*reminiscentia*), what we must have is a memory of our past acts of seeing, hearing, thinking and this is achieved through the effort of mental discourse or by something external which acts as a reminder of that which has a discontinuous presence in our minds (the phantasm) but which is really there continuously as an intelligible species caused by the original act of perception or thinking. As was the case with Averroes, it is the phantasm which must be recovered by a kind of reverse process of consciously moving from the intelligible species back to the image in the imagination. When the intellect intuitively knows that I am seeing something that is present and existent, Scotus says that it can thereafter remember my now past act of seeing it, even if it does not remember the sensible object which I saw. But both my past acts of perceiving and thinking and that which I perceived and thought, *can* be the objects of both sensible and intellectual memory, respectively. I remember past sensible and intellectual acts which effected the imprinted species which grasped the quiddity of the object, by which I know something. Quiddity (*quidditas rei materialis*) only exists in a singular but the intellect can know it in itself without knowing that it exists in something. What the intellect sees first in the singular is not the quiddity but the common nature, thanks to which, knowledge of the universal is

---

[27] *Ordinatio*, IV d. 45 1.2. His discussion of imperfect intuition of the past would be taken further by Ockham and is discussed below, ch. 22.

possible. What, then, is the relation between the sensible species and the intelligible? *Pro statu isto*, we cannot understand anything as a universal unless by means of imagining its singular: 'quod nihil intelligimus in universali nisi cujus singulare phantasiamur' (*Opus Oxoniense*, I d. 3, q.6, n. 19). Hence, Scotus describes the two faculties of the soul, sensitive and intellectual, as operating *simultaneously* regarding their respective acts. The singular object engenders in the sense a sensible species, a phantasm, representing the object as a singular quiddity. This singular sensible species or phantasm is a partial cause of the production of the intelligible species which represents the object in its universal aspect. The other partial cause of this intelligible species is the agent intellect which engenders a species *of the same nature as itself*: intelligible and capable of universality (I d. 3, q.6, n. 15). The intellect universalises the common nature; it does not find the universal 'already made' or actual in the real but sees it there potentially to be universalised. *Pro statu isto* the phantasm with the common nature as its vehicle are simultaneously present with the act of intellection and this produces abstractive knowledge. But this abstraction is not what Aquinas thought it was. The intellect does not need to strip the quiddity in the phantasm: it is already there 'stripped', 'denuded', formal, in the thing to be known. However, the intellect in this life does not have an *intuition* of this individuating principle, the quiddity or *haecceitas* which confines the common nature to the singularity of the existent. The intellect only knows abstractively the nature of this individual. All it can know intuitively is the existence of the singular and not its individuating difference.

The species, then, is imprinted by my sensible or intellectual act. When the intellect later remembers my past act of sensing or thinking, it cannot have present to it either these acts or the objects which are no longer there. Therefore, it only knows them abstractively so that remembering says nothing of the presence and existence of its objects. What *is* present in the act of memory is the species, effected by previous acts of perception or intellection in confrontation with their objects. It seems that an intuitive act of cognition at the sensitive level knows its object as present and existent and effects the sensible species in the common sense and imagination; an intuitive act of cognition at the intellectual level knows its object as present and existent and effects the intelligible species in the possible intellect. The agent intellect does not abstract or extract anything but rather causes and produces in the possible intellect which receives it, a form, the intelligible species, which is capable of representing, as universal, the object that the sensible species or phantasm represents as singular (quiddity). Memory is never an intuited and always an abstractive kind of knowing and, therefore, says nothing of the presence and existence of its objects, be they sensible or intelligible. From such a memory a proposition is then formed which syllogistically leads to cases of a similar kind. Memory involves then, what Scotus refers to as imperfect intuition whereby the species is present but its objects are neither present nor existent. As we shall see, because memory cannot make any statements about the existence or presence of its objects, since it is an abstractive kind of knowing, it is a deductive exercise which provides clues to the probable rather than the actual. This will be shown to have important consequences for the human capacity to know and understand the past.

In his later work, his magisterial *Quodlibets*, Scotus used the word *memoria* to reflect the growing influence of Augustine on his thinking and he gradually extended its meaning to include, as Augustine made it include, everything the individual mind is capable of knowing or thinking about whether previously experienced or not. Therefore, he argued that every concept we form is a child of memory and every thought we bring to mind and actualise when we understand it, reveals or declares what is hidden in the mind's potential depths, in its memory. He cited Augustine's *De Trinitate*, xv c. 10 where Augustine said that 'the thought formed from that thing which we know is the word which we speak in our heart and it is neither Greek, nor Latin nor any other language'. Augustine, we recall, had spoken of the desirability of knowing all languages, every one of which expressed the word in our hearts. Memory, therefore, speaks its word. When memory speaks the word, it utters what Scotus referred to as declarative knowledge, actual knowledge as a *species expressa* being the child of the mind where mind reveals what lay hidden in the memory.[28] The soul as an image of the Trinity contained, in its superior 'part', the memory, intelligence or understanding and the will, and Scotus adapted this Augustinian analogy to elaborate his own understanding of the process by which the intellect functions and produces actual knowledge as a concept or quality within the soul.

In the Oxford lectures[29] he explained that the trinitarian image in man's soul can be seen first as the kind of perfection in which the power to produce knowledge in itself is called *memoria*. Then there was also a passive ability to receive knowledge thus produced and this is called *intelligentia* or understanding. Lastly, the soul's final perfection was its capacity to will. Therefore, memory represents an active, productive aspect of man's mind when man forms a concept or a mental word.

A perfect memory, seen as the total cause of the expressed or declared concept, therefore, includes both the intellect (active and possible) as well as the intelligible species, as cocausalities. Together they function as a

---

[28] *Ordinatio*, I d 32 n. 32: *Ordinatio*, III d. 32.   [29] *Ordinatio*, I d 3 nn. 580 f.

single principle, otherwise seen as essentially ordered causes leading to the mental word, the expressed, perfect memory. When perfect memory is defined more generally, Scotus says it is a pure perfection so that it can apply to God as well, in whom there is no distinction between His nature, His intellective power, and His actual knowledge.

In *Quodlibet* I, 54 he says that the perfect memory occurs when an intellect has actually present an intelligible object proportionate to itself. It follows that if memory were or could be a principle of expression for the person perfectly possessing it, it would or could express the declarative knowledge which corresponds to that memory. Is the perfect memory state merely a limiting condition for what never can be mortally achieved by man? Is it akin to that experience of mind transcending itself and becoming perfect memory described in Augustine's vision at Ostia with his mother? Is it a mystic leap beyond embodied self-consciousness? Scotus does not appear to believe that it is other than the highest moment when knowledge is actualised and expressed, and he draws on the Augustinian analogy whereby perfect memory in us begets our thoughts or mental words, the *verbum mentis*, by a kind of eternal speech act. He leaves it as a mystery as to how the Son proceeds from the Father, but describes it as a speaking of the Word, as an eternal generation of the Son or as a communication of divine nature to the second person. Lastly, he says it is an act of declarative knowledge in that the Word as image of the Father is a kind of eternal expression of what the Father is in Himself.

In the Prologue to his *Quodlibetal Questions*, Scotus cites Ecclesiastes i, 8 – 'All things are difficult', says Solomon, and immediately adds the reason why he thinks they are difficult: 'because man's language is inadequate to explain them'. The inadequacy of language to explain the divine nature, however, is less of a problem when Scotus analyses human capacities. He cites Augustine where the latter discusses divine intellectuality and understanding: 'the life which God is, perceives and understands all things; that is a life which perceives things mentally rather than corporally, because God is spirit'. Scotus explains that Augustine is referring to that life which is the divine essence, and as such it is necessarily intellectual.[30] Hence, Scotus wants to show how intellectuality can be essentially identical with the being to which it belongs. He says this is clear from the case of creatures, for intellectuality is part of the essential definition of every intellectual substance, and in the case of man, whose definition includes 'rational', this intellectuality is essentially identical with him.[31] Once again, as for the later Augustine, Scotus emphasises how what is essentially important about man is his essential nature, his immaterial mind.

[30] Augustine, *De Trinitate*, VI ch. 10 n. 11; Scotus, *Quodlibet*, I, 35.   [31] *Quodlibet*, I, 36.

And he goes on to show how a nature that is truly living in reality has or can have a vital operation, an essential activity that is a real being. This means that man's life has as its perfection, not a concept, not a thing of the mind. The act of cognition is not identical with the intelligible species. Rather, the act is cojointly produced by the species and the potential intellect which is actuated by the agent intellect. Man's life then, is an intellectual operation which is properly perfected as an intellectual nature. Here Scotus can draw upon Aristotle's reference in the *Nicomachean Ethics*, x, to man's ultimate happiness consisting in the *activity* of contemplation. The proper perfection of a nature which is living in reality, says Scotus, cannot be a thing of the mind, an intelligible species which has only diminished being. This species, he says, is so attenuated in being that it cannot constitute the essential perfection of a real being. Instead, what constitutes man's essential perfection is thinking as thinking, the activity of contemplation, an operation that is proper to a nature alive with intellectual life.[32]

We recall that for Scotus reality consists in formality, that is, in that which is understood through the knowable being that extramental things possess for us. When the mind represents the quiddity of a thing, it is responding to objective notions or natural signs in things that can then be conceptually separated. Therefore, he argues that when there is a *distinctio rationis*, a distinction of reason, we are deducing the order of entities so distinguished from the order they would have were they really distinct. And he means by their intrinsic order, that which stems from the *per se* or intrinsic meaning of the terms used to represent or supposit for them in statements. But we note that the essential or quidditative meaning, the whatness of a thing is intrinsic to the thing itself, and when we conceptualise the whatness of something we are not yet determining or judging whether the referents exist in reality or in the mind. First intentions or primary concepts do not relate one formal content with another. In so far as referents do exist either in reality or in the mind, they both possess some intelligible essential meaning that is, he says, independent of the precise way in which they might exist. But where one *is* aware of a distinction between things that have distinct being in reality and in the mind, he insists there is a similar intrinsic reason for their order and this is their respective essential meaning. For it is not its being in the intellect, it is not the thought itself, that gives something its essential or quidditative meaning but rather the knowable being of the world.[33] There is then, a formal meaning in the world; it is not a construction of mind.

When in *Quodlibet*, I, 54 he discusses how perfect memory occurs, that is, when an intellect has actually present an intelligible object propor-

---

[32] *Ibid.*, 44.   [33] *Ibid.*, 53.

tionate to itself, he is not only using the divine mind as a model. Rather, he draws the analogy with the operation, the 'life' of the intellectual mind, where memory speaks its word, and goes on to say that in the specific case of a rational creature, memory precedes speaking because memory is the principle of speaking. But this, however, is not true of God *if* we are talking of memory as such, or as distinct from essence.[34] But when we talk of memory as a productive act rather than of memory *per se*, then the production of mental words by the intellect in creatures is similar to one of the divine productions, that is, to speaking (the Word) because it does not presuppose any other production. And when we talk about the production of the creaturely will, we can say that this too is similar to the breathing of the Holy Spirit, once the 'speaking' is presupposed. In so far as we can discuss the workings of divine intellect at all, we do so because we note their resemblance to acts of the created intellect and will.[35]

In the thirteenth *Quodlibet*, Scotus presents Aquinas's position (unacknowledged) by arguing that in knowing, our intellect abstracts from the here and now and by the same token from anything concerned with the existent *qua* existent. This means that knowledge of anything as existing does not pertain to the intellect *per se* but rather *per accidens*.[36] But Scotus wishes to interpret this in another way. One could say that the common distinction made between intellective and sensitive knowledge, namely that we understand the universal but we sense the singular, must not be understood as referring to disparate but equal powers such as obtain between sight in seeing colours and hearing in perceiving sounds. Rather, the distinction is one between a higher cognitive faculty and one subordinate to it. This is a formal distinction. The superior power can know some object or aspect thereof that the inferior cannot know, but not vice versa. Only then could one admit that the intellect does not know the object as here and now because it grasps only its absolute quidditative form, whereas the senses cannot know the object in this quidditative fashion, because the power of each sense is limited to knowing its object under the aspect of its existing. But this does not mean that the intellect is so determined that it has to know the object only in some different way than as existing, for it is not limited to knowing it only in this way.[37] The intellect can know intuitively something as present and existing just as it can know abstractly whereby nothing is implied regarding the object's existence or presence. Scotus posits, as did Augustine, that in the case of intuitive knowledge, it is the thing in its own existence that is the *per se* motive factor objectively. But in the case of abstractive knowledge, what moves the intellect *per se* is something in which the thing has *esse* cognosci-

[34] *Ibid.*, 58. [35] *Ibid.*, 61. [36] *Ibid.*, XIII, 30. [37] *Ibid.*, 32.

bile, knowable being, whether this be the cause that virtually contains the thing as knowable (a first intention), or whether it be an effect such as an intelligible species or mental similitude that contains the thing of which it is the likeness representationally.[38]

In the end, Scotus wishes us to say that the object must be thought of simultaneously with the act of knowing and, more importantly, that the attainment of the object must be seen as a conceptual rather than a real relation in an abstractive act of knowledge. It is not the actuality of something real that we refer to when we say we actually understand but rather, the actuality of a conceptual relation.[39] Because as Aristotle says, the intellectual part of the soul is not altered since intellectual knowledge is not received *im*mediately from an external object, it is clear that for Scotus the knower is related, reflexively, to something internal, an object inside and not related immediately to an external object or its sensible form.[40] This is especially the case, he says, when a term does not exist extramentally but has being only in the intellect, so that any relationship to it must be one of reason, that is, it is a conceptual relationship. When an object no longer exists or when an act of cognition does not actually occur, the mind can only know nonexistential objects as well as nonexistent acts of cognition through reflection.[41] This is a matter of the second act of intellection working with second intentions. When objects no longer exist, one is dealing in the realm of historical remembering of the now-nonexistent. Scotus does not think one can have intuitive cognition of the nonexistent and nonpresent. Consideration of a nonexisting object of thought or of now nonexistent acts of cognition is the province of abstractive cognition.[42]

Scotus tells us that abstractive knowledge can exist as a direct first act (the production of a phantasm or sensible species – that which I see, hear, think) without the following reflex act (the production of the intelligible species – my act of seeing, hearing, thinking). This he describes as when the object can be the term of such a direct act without having to have the conceptual relation to the act (perceiving something without knowing it more universally and understanding it). But when the conceptual relation does exist, it is a necessary concomitant of direct acts of abstraction and is caused contingently after the direct and first act of intellection (the creation of the phantasm). And in this second conceptual, reflexive act the object of the direct and first abstracting act of knowledge, the first intention or phantasm, does not have to be the term of the reflex act. Rather, the object of conceptual relations is another concept (the intelligi-

---

[38] *Ibid.*, 33. [39] *Ibid.*, 100. [40] *Ibid.*, 61. [41] *Ibid.*, 43.
[42] On Ockham's views, see below, ch. 22.

ble species). This argument seems to run parallel with Aristotle's two-fold distinction between similitudes being considered substitutes of or for something extramental, and being considered in and of themselves as conceptual entities.[43] Hence, Scotus says that intelligible species are absolute qualities and they are the formal reason for understanding, because they, rather than phantasms or sensible images, essentially initiate the act of understanding. But he notes that the intelligible species is commonly called a likeness of the object (as though it were a sensible species or phantasm) because by its very nature it is a certain imitative and representative form of the object. Therefore, the intelligible species can either be considered in itself or, as is more commonly the case, its relationship can be included as well.[44]

Scotus then distinguishes in *Quodlibet*, XIV, between imperfect and perfect intellectual knowledge. He defines perfect knowledge as that which captures the object as such, that is, it is proper and distinct knowledge of the object as it is in itself. Ideally, the intellect is described as having the capacity to achieve this immediate and proper knowledge intuitively. In terms of the soul's essence, to which pertains its perfection, whether the soul be original, fallen or restored, it *essentially* remains the same and therefore, has defined capacities.[45] But the natural perfection of the soul is what the necessity of its essential nature demands in any of the three conditions it may be in. Essentially, then, perfect knowledge is possible although the soul's capacity to actualise this potential depends on its condition and *pro statu isto* all we are capable of is an intuitive awareness of a thing's presence and existence and not of a proper and distinct knowledge of a thing *ut hoc*, as it is in itself.

But the soul by its natural perfection, considering its nature in *any* state, is *unable* to attain knowledge of God that is immediate and proper, that is, intuitively, even with the cooperation of all the causes that naturally move it to know. The reason is that any such intellection *per se*, proper and immediate, requires the presence of the object in all its proper intelligibility as an object. If the intellection is intuitive, this means that the object is present as an object in its own existence. But if the intellection is abstractive, it is present in something (the species) which represents it in all its proper and essential meaning as a knowable object. However, God's

---

[43] Also see Porphyry, *Isagoge et in Aristotelis Categorias Commentarium*, ed. A. Busse (Commentaria in Aristotelem Graeca, IV, 1) (Reimer, 1887), pp. 57–8; and Boethius, *In Categorias Aristotelis libri quattuor*, *PL*, 64, 159 B–C, where it is observed that whereas signs have been imposed in order to signify non-signs, others are signs of signs. Therefore, words of first imposition are (conventional) signs of extra-linguistic entities and words of second imposition are (conventional) signs of linguistic entities.

[44] *Quodlibet*, XIII, 97.   [45] *Ibid.*, XIV, 8 and XIV, 4.

immediate presence must be a result of His free act. Only if God wills it is He present to any created intellect in all the proper and essential meaning of divinity and thereby known intuitively.[46]

Apparently, Scotus believes that the finite world can be known perfectly in its knowable being through the mediation of form, that is, abstractively. Finite being is all that any created intellect can reach by virtue of causes which naturally move it,[47] and finite being can be grasped by abstractive cognition which effects a conceptual representation (the intelligible species) in all its proper and essential meaning. This commensurate object that is naturally within the reach of our intellect in its present state is not the individual *ut hoc* but the quiddity of material things, or more precisely, the quiddity of a sensible thing, meaning by this not just that of the sensible proper but also the quiddity of what is essentially or virtually included in the sensible.[48] And although no created intellect is moved in a natural fashion by the (unmediated) essence of something as essence, and hence, there is no intuitive cognition of individuals, because we need first and second intentions to know individuals, all knowledge of this essence that is not caused by anything created is caused immediately by the divine will as in intuitive knowledge.[49]

Now this argument reflects the fact that as far back as 1282 the doctrine of the direct intellectual cognition of material singulars had been adopted officially by Franciscan theologians. It contrasted with Aquinas's denial of direct intellectual cognition of singulars. As we have seen, Scotus systematically developed this positive, Franciscan principle of individuation, *haecceitas*, when he distinguished between intuitive and abstractive cognition. In *Quodlibet*, XII, 27–32, he argued that we lack an intuition of individuality in the human intellect's present condition, but such formal understanding as we have derives from the process of abstraction. What is important here is that although the individuality of an actual thing is implied in our experience of objects, our sensual experience itself does not involve a cognitive grasp of this individuality. This is yet another way of saying that the mind does not *understand* present or by implication past individual events or experiences as existentially unique or individual. Rather, intellectual understanding grasps the quiddities or particular universals of things that it knows intuitively exist and are present by means of first intentions, and universalises these by means of second intentions. When we actively understand something, we know it by means of abstractive cognition in terms of its universal characteristics, and we say nothing

---

[46] *Ibid.*, XIV, 36 and *Ordinatio*, II, d. 3 q.9; I, d. 3 n. 57.   [47] *Quodlibet*, XIV, 39.
[48] *Ibid.*, 43.
[49] *Ibid.*, 63.

of the presence or existence, nothing of the actuality of that to which our knowledge refers. The active principle of our knowing something is not the object which we know through its 'accidents', somehow taken into mind, but rather it is the active engagement of mind thinking and reflecting on that which is of the soul's own nature, that is, species.

Scotus says in *Quodlibet*, XV, 5 that he assumes that there is perfect intellection, for instance, definitional knowledge of a definable object. Knowledge had by way of definition is distinct knowledge and is contrasted with the 'confused' manner in which any universal notion is known. Scotus asserts that if a simple term, some *ens* (being) is known at all, even though it may be universally extended, it can only be known distinctly. We know something 'confusedly' when one concept stands for an object similar to the way in which a name stands for something. But we know it distinctly, that is essentially and as not identical with anything else, when we can define it. This is because there is in every definition an undefined element, the *ens*, which is an irreducibly simple *concept*, the quiddity, known distinctly when it is known at all. All definitional, distinct, knowledge of real things includes the *ens* of these things as part of their essential definition.[50] Now definitional knowledge of a definable object, which he equates with perfect intellection, evidently depends ultimately on the divine exemplars and cannot exist without 'the word' of this distinct object in the mind. Therefore, when we say that something is active regarding perfect understanding, then it is somehow active in the formation of the word. Hence, he says we can say that the cause of our intellection in the present life can be investigated in a threefold manner. First, we assert that in the intellective part of man there is an active principle of intellection. We then go on to investigate whether this active principle of intellection is something of the intellective soul itself or whether it is only the object which is said to be in the soul as an accident, representative of the object, but not as part of the soul's nature. And thirdly, given that we will have proved that the active principle is something of the soul itself and not an accident, we ask whether this is the agent or possible intellect. Here we can observe Scotus's method of integrating Aristotle into Augustine.

As Aristotle says in the *De Anima*, II, c. 5, 'the objects that excite the sensory powers to activity, the seen and the heard etc are outside', and he continues,

the ground of this difference is that what actual sensation apprehends is individuals while what knowledge apprehends is universals, and these are somehow within the soul. That is why man can exercise his intellection when he wishes, but

[50] *Ordinatio*, I d. 3 n. 72.

his sensation does not depend on himself. For sensation a sensible object must be there. Therefore we have this certain conclusion that the active principle that suffices for this new intellection *is intrinsic to the intelligent subject.*[51]

Scotus then cites Augustine who says that what excels in the soul is called mind, and that man is not called the image of God according to everything that pertains to his nature but according to the mind alone.[52] Therefore, Scotus concludes that every image is in the intellective part which transcends the sensitive. But as Augustine also says, the image includes both 'parent and offspring'.[53] Hence, the 'parent' who begets this knowledge which is the 'offspring' and, therefore, is the active principle of intellection, is to be found only in the intellectual part of man. Therefore, anyone (like Aquinas) who claims that the reason for immediate generation of actual knowledge is the phantasm or some similar form in the sensitive part would not preserve Augustine's analogy where mind is the 'parent' of its thought.[54] Besides, Augustine says in the *De Trinitate*: 'The memory of man and particularly that which beasts do not have, namely, that in which the intelligible things are so contained that they do not come into it through the senses of the body, has in his image of the Trinity a likeness, unequal of course, but a likeness of whatever kind it may be to the Father'.[55] And he explains this by saying that 'that word of ours ... is so born from our knowledge as that Word was also born from the knowledge of the Father.'[56] Elsewhere he writes: 'We attribute to the memory everything that we know'.[57] Therefore, the memory which animals lack, that is, that which is properly intellectual, has a likeness to the Father and not to things sensually experienced.[58]

Thereafter, Scotus expands on his own position showing Augustine to be in agreement, that both the soul and the intellectual object (species) concur as active principles of intellection. The object is not the complete active principle of intellection. Rather, it is the voluntary effort that causes somehow a more perfect understanding and this would hardly be the case if the object alone were the active cause of this.[59] The object is not a free agent essentially, nor free by participation, because it is not of the same nature as the will. The object only accounts for the specific character of a given intellection, not as an intrinsic formal constitutive principle but as a *per se* extrinsic principle.[60] Therefore, as Augustine says in the *De Trini-*

---

[51] *Quodlibet*, xv, 6.
[52] Augustine, *De Trinitate*, xv, c. 7 n. 11; and *De Trinitate* xiv, c. 8 n. 11.
[53] *Ibid.*, ix c. 12 n. 18.   [54] *Quodlibet*, xv, 16.   [55] *De Trinitate*, xv, c. 23 n. 43.
[56] *Ibid.*, xv, c. 14. n. 24.   [57] *Ibid; Quodlibet*, xv, 17.   [58] *Quodlibet*, xv, 18.
[59] *Ibid.*, 28.
[60] *Ibid.*, 30.

tate, XII, c. 15 n. 24, 'The nature of the intellectual mind is so formed as to see things which, according to the disposition of the Creator, are subjoined to intelligible things in the natural order, in a sort of incorporeal light of its own kind, just as the eye of the flesh sees the things that lie about it in this corporeal light'.[61]

Now, since the image of God in us consists of what is best in our nature, the agent intellect belongs to that image and it must be part of memory. Memory however, has two functions: one is to conserve the object or likeness (species) of the object; and the second is to express or generate its actual knowledge. The first function of conserving memory cannot pertain to the agent intellect since it is not a receptive or conserving power. Hence, the function of the agent intellect must be the second aspect of memory, namely, expressing knowledge.[62] Since a corporeal agent can never be the immediate cause of something spiritual and hence, it cannot be the proximate reason why anything is transferred from one order to another, from the sensible to the intelligible, we must affirm that when an object that is actually intelligible becomes actually known, there is no transfer from one order to another. Instead, we must speak of metaphorical transformations.

The function of both the potential and agent intellects depends on the conception of their object. Now, since a quiddity, the formal whatness that exists in particular things, is not itself particularised, there is no need for any act of mind to liberate it from its individualising, material conditions. The agent intellect does not need to abstract it from something corporeal. Rather, within the phantasm or image or first intention there already is the nature, the formal knowability of the thing, which, when joined to the potential intellect by the action of the agent intellect, effects the intelligible species. We are not moving from the sensible to the spiritual but remaining in the realm of degrees of formal essentiality so that the intellect as a whole is the sole cause of the act of cognition.[63] The active power of the act of understanding has a potentiality which is only limited by the indeterminacy of the content of its act. This follows a distinctly Augustinian interpretation of the soul's direct and unproblematic self-knowledge. Augustine had asserted that ideas are the primary forms or the permanent and immutable reasons of real things. The soul cannot look on them unless it be a rational soul, and this occurs only in that part of the soul which excels, that is, mind, where, as it were, there is the soul's interior

---

[61] *Ibid.*, 43.   [62] *Ibid.*, 44.
[63] On this see Z. Kuksewicz, 'Criticism of Aristotelian psychology and the Augustinian–Aristotelian synthesis', in *The Cambridge History of Later Medieval Philosophy*, pp. 623–28; pp. 626–8.

and intellectual eye.[64] Hence, Scotus's concern for knowledge of the physical world is manifested in asserting that the flux of sensory experience is and must be organised in the light of intelligible forms by means of the mind's acts of cognition. These intelligible forms are located in an exemplary way in the divine mind.

The text of his argument runs as follows.[65] If one held to the first view, one could say that the agent intellect has two sequentially related actions. The first is to make the potentially intelligible actually intelligible, or the potentially universal actually universal. The second is to make the potentially understood actually understood ... From the phantasm or sensible image in the imagination there would be produced in the intellect, by virtue of the agent intellect, an intelligible species of something in which a thing appears as actually intelligible and which can be called, for brevity's sake, an intelligible species. And this very real production of one representation from another is accompanied by a metaphorical 'transformation' of one object into another, namely, of something sensibly imaginable into something intelligible. Scotus believes this metaphorical description is a reasonable account of what goes on because the object has a similar sort of (formal) existence as object, *esse obiectivum*, in the one representation as it does in the other. Therefore, in the real change whereby a spiritual representation is produced with the help of a corporeal representation, namely, where a universal representation is produced with the help of a singular representation, one can speak of or think of a similar 'transformation' of a corporeal object into a spiritual one, or of a singular object into a universal one. The second function of the agent intellect would consist in transforming the potentially known into the actually known. Here there is also a metaphorical 'transformation' of objects corresponding to a real transformation on the part of those things whereby one tends towards the objects, for actual intellection really follows the intelligible species. And just as the first transformation from potency to act is ascribed to the agent intellect, so also is the second, both metaphorically as regards the objects and really as regards those things in which the objects are represented. To the extent that the intelligible species would be generated by the agent intellect from the phantasm, the actually intelligible would be generated, metaphorically speaking, from the potentially intelligible.

Therefore, one can speak of a twofold activity of the agent intellect.[66] First, there is the reception of intelligible species from the phantasm

---

[64] Augustine, *Eighty-Three Different Questions*, Q. 46, 1–2, trans. in V. J. Bourke, *The Essential Augustine* (New York, 1964) pp. 62–3.
[65] *Quodlibet*, XV, 51.   [66] *Ibid.*, 52.

through the first action of the agent intellect. Secondly, there is the reception of intellection itself from the intelligible species through the second act of the agent intellect. And according to this interpretation, both agent and possible intellect would pertain to the intellective memory. The agent intellect, however, would not belong to it (memory) in virtue of its first function which is to make the potentially intelligible actually intelligible. Indeed, the memory in act would be the term of such an action for it would be in virtue of such activity that the intellect would have the object present to it as actually intelligible. It would be in virtue of its second action that the agent intellect would be included in memory, since the function of memory would be to make express the actual knowledge of intellection and the agent intellect's second action would contribute to this action. The possible intellect, however, would be called memory insofar as its reception of the intelligible species is concerned whereas it would be called understanding so far as the second receptive role is concerned.

But if one held the other view,[67] that is, that the possible intellect is the active factor in intellection and that the action of the agent intellect is limited to abstracting the object, then one would have to say that the agent intellect does not pertain to the memory but that its action (as regards sensibles) ends at the memory, since it ends at that form through which the object as actually intelligible is shown to the intellect, and this is the form that constitutes perfect memory. As for pure intelligibles such as spiritual things, it would have no action whatsoever, which would be true whether such things were understood directly or by means of a species, since they could cause such by their own power. The possible intellect however, would belong to the memory not only insofar as it retains all the representations of objects actually intelligible but also insofar as it actively expresses actual knowledge.

Now, Aristotle says in the *De Anima*, III c. 5 that 'light makes potential colours into actual colours' since it makes them actually visible.[68] Even though the nature of colour as an absolute quality remains the same in the dark, it is not able to be seen if we are speaking of proximate potency, for whenever two causes must concur to have an action, the second is not in proximate potency unless the first concurs. For colour to act on sight, another cause, light, is required for action. Therefore, colour is only proximately visible when illuminated. Similarly, the phantasm cannot produce the intelligible species without the concurrent action of the agent intellect. The agent intellect therefore makes all things actually intelligible in the sense of putting them in proximate potency to being known. In the intelligible species, the agent intellect makes appear what was only in

[67] *Ibid.*, 54.   [68] *Ibid.*, 57.

remote potency before, when they appeared in a material representation which presented them in their singularity ... The agent intellect's action is, therefore, coextensive with the possible intellect's receptivity and is to be taken in the sense as referring to making and receiving something actually intelligible and not something actually understood.

Reviewing these plausible accounts and his own comments, Scotus concludes[69] by saying that it seems that we should retain Augustine's distinction in the *De Trinitate*, x, c. 11 nn. 17–18 between memory, intelligence/understanding and will. Comparing Aristotle's distinction of the agent and possible intellects with this we see that only the possible intellect corresponds to understanding because only this receives the act of understanding. And Aristotle generally speaks of intellect as that *by which* we understand or that *by which* we receive intellections. The possible intellect also correspods to memory insofar as it pertains to memory to store habitual knowledge, according to Augustine, who speaks in the *De Trinitate*, xv, c. 10 n. 19 of 'the science of knowledge we retain in the memory'. Thus, Aristotle refers at times to the possible intellect as that by which we know or that by which we have knowledge or science which transforms the intellect from essential to accidental potency.

And as for the other act of the memory which consists in generating actual knowledge, it is clear that this still pertains to the possible intellect *per accidens* for when an active form exists in some subject, the action resulting from such a form pertains to the subject *per accidens*, just as one can give the example of wood warming *per accidens*.[70] The intelligible species by which the object plays an active role in producing intellection is a form in the possible intellect. Therefore, the possible intellect is at least productive *per accidens*. But the act of generating knowledge pertains *per se* either to the agent intellect alone or to the possible intellect alone, and consequently, the one or the other would belong to memory.[71]

Or one could postulate a third alternative: the act of generating understanding pertains to the agent *and* possible intellects but to the agent intellect to a greater degree than to the possible intellect. At any rate, the possible intellect is at least included in the memory.[72]

The exploratory nature of this complex discussion of the roles of the agent and possible intellects and their relation to memory should not obscure for us the consequences of this scholastic Augustinian elaboration of what it means to remember. Let us pose a number of questions. What does this theory tell us about historical comprehension? How does the working of mind affect not only an understanding of the past but what

---

[69] *Ibid.*, 60.   [70] *Ibid.*, 61.   [71] *Ibid.*, 62.   [72] *Ibid.*, 87.

does it tell us about the veracity of past experiences and descriptions, present or past, of that experience?

Firstly, Scotus accepts that people commonly refer to true likenesses of past sensations of things received and held in the mind, but he says this can only be true insofar as what is grasped is their knowable being. Furthermore, the dialectical activity of the agent and possible intellects is internal to mind and the intelligible species is a similitude of past experiences only in a universal, present and nonexistential conceptual mode. In so far as the conceptualisation of a second act of intellect focuses on the relation of conceptual intelligible objects brought forth from the intellectual memory store, preserved there as present particular universals or intentions, mind is of necessity unaware of the corporeity of past experience. The corporeal is irrelevant to the formal acts of mind. Furthermore, we noted that Scotus denied to sensation any capacity to grasp the formal individuating *principles* of things, their *haecceitas*. Experience does not involve a cognitive grasp of individuality. All we have in our present state is a capacity for formally understanding things derived from the process of abstraction of intentions. We lack an intuitive grasp of individuality. In the *Opus Oxoniense*, IV, d. 10 q.5 n. 4 and in the *Reportatio Parisiense*, II, d. 3 q.2 n. 11, Scotus did nowever, refer to our memory of past experiences as well as our vision of the future as imperfect intuition and suggested that we call this alternatively, a special habit. William of Ockham will take this further. For Scotus, what is characteristic of intuitive cognition is the awareness of the being of objects without reference to the sensible and therefore, without reference to anything other than their presence and existence. Even were we to assert the pastness of the imperfectly intuited being of objects of cognition, we would not be referring to their sensible, immattered existence but only to their formal, knowable being, their *haecceitas*. This is because for Scotus neither matter by itself, existence, nor any combination of accidents can individuate things. The unique individuality of things is a positive formality with an actuality of its own in things, and insofar as it is a principle, it is the nature, which exists as an incomplete universal, that mind knows. And when mind knows it as existing in the intellect, it is completely universal.

In so far as intuitive cognition is aware of the existence or nonexistence of objects *qua* existents, it characterises our intellect regarding the promise that we shall be like the angels and thereby have an intuition of the beatific vision and know it as actual. Likewise, when intuitive cognition applies to general, rational, prejudgemental awareness in existential situations, it is divorced from the individuating principle in the sense experience of the individual; most importantly, it is impossible for there to be intuitive cognition of an object that is not present and existent – it is only knowable through abstract cognition. What then of the past? The past, as conceptualised, is a present and existent thought existing in a mode unique to mind, noncorporeal and habitually present.

Thus, when we turn to abstractive cognition we are told that this process abstracts the object from existence or nonexistence, from presence or absence and therefore, is a kind of cognition where we have an understanding of a *principle* that is present in the intellect, whether what the conclusion or principle is *about* is existing or not, or present or absent. In abstractive cognition Scotus says we often experience a grasp of universals and essences of things whether they exist extramentally in some subject or not or whether we have an instance of them actually present or not. But what we have is an understanding of an existing thing in some intelligible object that contains the thing in question in an eminent way, as a species, that is, in a higher, more perfect and universal way. Therefore, we do not, because mind cannot know the sensual, material uniqueness of the past. Hence, material history gets transformed by the operations of abstract intellect. The material conditions of experience, past or present, are irrelevant to the formal being of things that we can know conceptually and related concepts are not immediately referring to extramental things.

Now, if one held, as some scholastics did, that the mind was more passive as a mere receiver of perceptual and then intelligible objects, then at least one could argue to some extent that the understanding person was formed by experience, in Aristotelian terms becoming what he perceived and understood through a process of abstraction from impressions, and directly at the mercy of material conditions, albeit transformed by the mind. The analogy here would be Aristotle's of wax impressed by the signet ring. But if one followed Augustine more closely, as did Scotus, so that memory not only included the power of recalling the knowable being of things or events and words or signs, but memory also produced mental concepts in some active way internal to mind alone, then the correlation between the likeness of mental conceptions and past sensual experiences is formal and conceptual because rational mind only operates conceptually. As Aquinas feared, this would lead to a theory, despite disclaimers to the contrary, of ideas being related to ideas rather than to individual extramental realities of composite, im-mattered forms.

What kind of likeness is assumed by Scotus for the intelligible species internal to intellect? It is not a corporeal or material likeness, and of course it would have no emotional content, for as Augustine said, when we recall past sorrows we recall them from memory but without their attendant emotions, because emotions are sensitive, appetitive affections and have no counterpart in higher mind. Because intellect is conceived as capable of being separate from the material world perceived by the senses, not only in Scotus's intuitive cognition but in abstractive cognition, where concepts relate to concepts, the 'alteration' in mind from the sensible to the intelligible being spoken of metaphorically, then the essentially ordered causes of cognition always relate to intentions or ideas which maintain a status that is formal and universal. Hence, the importance of Aristotle's memory as pertaining *per se* to the primary perceptive part of the soul has been transformed, and Scotus has irrevocably transferred memory as understanding and declarative knowledge to the far more abstract, immaterial, indeed transcendental realm where the cooperation between the intelligible species – that by which something is known – and the intellect, occurs, and only there is perfect memory. This is about as far removed from the actual conditions in which the original objects of knowledge, were they sensible at some time, could be. In moving from the common sense notion of memory as recollection of the past, to his notion that memory includes everything the individual mind is capable of knowing or thinking about whether previously experienced or not, Scotus opened up further, and with the help of Augustine, the notion of remembering to the realm of plausible mental fiction, that is, to the realm of mental possibilities rather than empirical certainties.

Scotus, like most thinkers after Bishop Tempier's condemnation of certain necessitarian theses held by radical Aristotelians in 1270 and 1277, was concerned to argue against the eternity of the world as the effect of an eternal cause. Nor can the human intellect be eternal. Aquinas had already argued that one simply cannot prove by rational demonstration whether the world began to be or not. Faith in divine revelation alone teaches that the world had a temporal beginning. Furthermore, Aquinas argued in *ST* Ia that the principle of demonstration is the essence from which we deduce its properties and since essences abstract from space and time, one cannot demonstrate that they have not always existed.[73] So too for Scotus, since abstractive intellection deals in universals divorced from space and time, mind can say nothing of the existence or nonexistence of its objects. Only in intuitive cognition do we have an indemonstrable and evident knowledge of the existence and presence of contingent things and we posit the divine will as the cause of such contingencies. He says in *I Sent.* d. xxxix, q.v. that it seems that the proposition 'there is a being that is contingent' is primarily true and cannot be demonstrated from causes ... those who deny any contingent being should be exposed to torture until

---

[73] See F. Van Steenberghen, *Thomas Aquinas and Radical Aristotelianism*, pp. 11–12.

they admit that it is possible for them not to be tortured'![74] He goes on to say that we suppose as being evidently true (*supposito ergo isto tamquam manifesto vero*) that there is a being that is contingent, and it is the divine will which is the prime cause of contingency. And it is abstractive cognition that helps us to know what is possible rather than what is actual (intuitive). All that experience does is confirm for us the cognitive possibilities open to the human intellect concerning what God's will does creatively. For Scotus, the senses serve only as an occasion and not as a cause of the truth or knowledge of principles. Indeed, he says that the intellect by its own power and by the meaningful force of the terms in the proposition: 'Every whole is greater than its parts' assents without doubt to such a proposition.[75] There is, in effect, no unconditional necessity in the natural world so that demonstrative science is itself concerned not with what is or has been necessary, but with what is possible in a world of contingents. Even science is not concerned, because it cannot be, given the limits of quidditative knowledge, with phenomena as they actually are or were but rather, it deals with propositions about what *can* occur or *could have* possibly occurred, and it does this by dealing with relations amongst our concepts. These are grounded in the assumption that there are indemonstrable premisses found in experience and known intuitively and nonjudgementally. He assumes that nature functions in a regular manner, determined by a formal linking of causes up to God's will, and that all our sensual experience enables us to do is identify natural, unfree, unwilled

---

[74] 'Ideo videtur ista, aliquod ens est contingens, esse vera primo et non demonstrabile propter quid ... qui negant aliquod ens contingens exponendi sunt tormentis, quo usque concedant quod possibile est eos non torqueri...'

[75] *Ordinatio*, I, d. 3, q.4: 'omne totum est maius sua partes, intellectus virtute sui et istorum terminorum assentiet indubitanter isti complexioni.' E. Gilson, sums up Scotus's position well:

En somme, et pour en finir sur ce point, la connaissance empirique possède une certitude propre qui peut être transformée en certitude actuelle grâce à l'application d'un principe général posé par l'intellect. On obtiendrait donc de la hiérarchie suivante des divers ordres de connaissance, en allant de la moins parfaite à la plus parfaite: certitude sensible immédiate en cas d'accord des témoignages des sens; certitude de la science expérimentale lorsque l'intellect garantit le témoignage des sens par le principe général de la constance des actions causales naturalles [tout ce qui arrive la plupart du temps en vertu d'une cause autre que libre est l'effet naturel de cette cause, *Opus Oxoniense*, I d. 3 q.4, a. 3 nn. 7–9]; certitude scientifique parfaite, *a priori* et par la cause, lorsque l'intellect peut découvrir un moyen terme qui permette de dire pourquoi l'effet produit doit nécessairement se produire tel qu'il s'est produit. Duns Scot fait donc largement confiance au sensible, et ce n'est pas surprenant, car sans nier la mutabilité essentielle de ses objets, il maintient la stabilité de leurs 'natures'. En somme, Avicenne vient ici faire équilibre à Saint Augustin, car ce n'est pas la *mutabilitas* augustinienne de l'objet sensible, c'est sa *natura* avicennienne qui agit sur le sens, offrant à l'intellect une 'occasion' faite pour lui d'exercer son jugement sur cette donnée de la sensibilité.'
E. Gilson, *Jean Duns Scot, introduction à ses positions fondamentales* (Paris, 1952), p. 566.

causes. Our minds, then, come to associate habitually these causes with repeated effects, but in so doing, what we know is only what is possible in certain contingent situations or circumstances. We do not and cannot *understand* what is actual or nonactual or what has been actual or nonactual, by means of abstractive knowledge, and therefore, *we cannot make any claims about the existence, now or in the past, of possibles*!

Scotus argued that mind was to be seen, following Augustine, as the parent of its thought set apart from body. The truth we can know in our hearts must indeed be higher, more universal than any singular sensible experience or material instantiation of the truth. What is far more important than anyone's particular, material experience is his universal, formal, conceptual understanding of these experiences. Perfect memory is not the recollection of a sequential ordering of individual experiences as the rhetorical tradition's *ars memoria* would have it. This is a trivial, corporeal device which bypasses the need to explain how we *understand* what we remember. Rather, perfect memory is the voluntary interior generation of a set of ideas, ideas that are abstracted, essential, formal meanings pertaining to the quidditative likeness of an object's *haecceitas* which is itself the formal individualising principle of the thing. It is only insofar as the mind can get beyond this formal individuality, metaphorically transform it into an intelligible and then unite with it to understand it and then express it as present and universal, that one has perfect memory. If material experiences possessed aspects incapable of being mentally conceptualised, then they simply would have no meaning. Meaning only pertains to the formalities of the world. As Augustine said, such experiences or statements about them would simply not be understood and it would be wrong to say we had not heard someone who expressed them. There is nothing wrong with our sense organs. But it is the mind that must understand in its own active mode before we can be said to have knowledge of some experience or statement. Mind, according to this neo-Augustinian tradition, seems to be a formal collection of powers whose unified ability to receive form and then respond to concepts is limited to itself or to some higher formal activity of the divine mind. The only kind of history there is, then, is conceptual history based on first intentions or quidditative forms of things. Scotus does not seem to treat explicitly of the Augustinian dilemma that other people's pasts may not be understandable to us unless we can draw upon analogous experiences to make someone else's descriptions our own, at least at the universal, exemplary level. But when Scotus argues that the distinction between intellective and sensitive knowledge is primarily a formal distinction between a higher and lower cognitive faculty, he implies that what we must have had was an experience of analogous *quiddity* in order to understand that of another. For Scotus, understanding is at the level of quiddities, particular universals and when they are thought in the mind they are completely universal. What we can know through experience then, is only that which is knowable to us, that which has knowable being. Hence only an aspect of material history is knowable, that which is capable of formal representation in universal, intelligible species and it is not these species alone which act, but they coact with intellect to be understood and expressed. As Augustine said, we must be capable of measuring what we measure; the conceivable must somehow be related to that which receives the conception. History then, can only be a peculiarly human because intellectual endeavour, as it was for Aquinas. But Scotus's knower of history not only knows something conceptual, internal to mind and universal. Truly rational, reflexive and purely conceptual acts of the intellect that are willed, open up history as a story of *conscious* deliberation. History is only about *men* in a contingent world; in effect it is deductive.

When Scotus says that what we know perfectly and distinctly is definitional knowledge of a definable object, he is, in effect, arguing tautologously in that we perfectly know within a closed logic of what has knowable being for us and such perfect knowledge cannot exist without 'the word' of the definable object being already in the mind, commonly spoken of as a likeness to extramental things but more properly called a likeness to the divine exemplar, the Word, expressed from the Father as memory. We only know what we conceive as definable. Insofar as the memory is expressed it is the coactivity of the agent and possible intellects with the agent intellect actually expressing. Hence history, like visionary poetry, as elicited from the storehouse of the memory, comprises entirely conceptual relations, with the material past having been radically dematierialised, detemporalised, indeed trivialised because it is unknowable *ut hoc* existentially or in its sensual individuality by the present cognitive action of the knowing mind.

The study of man's history, for Scotus, cannot have as its subjects individual cultural phenomena and temporally specific events. When a man reminisces, he actively seeks to recall a mental image that corresponds with his continuously present universal understanding of something. He has this understanding in consequence of all the intuitive and abstractive acts of cognition he has had throughout his life. He does not remember past *things* in themselves; he remembers past acts of knowing the formal aspects of things through sensible and intelligible species which represent those things in modes peculiar to active mind. He remembers only that which had and still has intelligible being for him.

497

It is clear that from the first Question of his *Lectura* and from the *Ordinatio*, Scotus signalled the disagreement between philosophers and theologians over the possibility that man can know distinctly his purpose, his end, and the means to achieve it.[76] As a theologian, Scotus must affirm that man's end is salvation, an immediate union with God through an intuitive vision of God's essence. It is not enough to say that through contemplation of God by means of sensibles alone, man achieves his end. Even if men could achieve their end philosophically, man's reason would fall into error in believing that there were rational means of attaining salvation and the vision of God. This would give no place to the necessity of God's freely willed initiative in man's salvation. It is not enough for the intrinsic acts of men to be evaluated for there must be a divine initiative which is a radically contingent acceptance of man. That an intellectual nature of a creature, man, is capable of receiving grace, the vision of God, does not diminish for Scotus the freedom of God's initiative through which the divine essence becomes itself an object for this rational creature. And being rational, man turns consciously towards his final end, not by a simple, biological tendency but through an act of will enlightened by reason whereby rectitude, truth, the *summum bonum* is willed for itself in a disinterested way, independent of all other interests. This natural and rational love of God, to the extent that the first being is rationally accessible as the Sovereign Good in itself, is effectively a commandment, a duty to love God more than anything else. This natural charity or love of the reasonable creature for God is a commandment of *reason*, responding to the existence of the infinite in itself, an abstraction 'metaphorically' transposed to 'being' from our capacity to discuss an intensive infinitude in quantity. We possess this rational love of God naturally, from which issues the moral order. But then religion begins for Scotus, beyond the moral order by means of the divine initiative. Man's natural love of God does not necessitate any union with the infinite in an eternal life. So that man's true final end depends on the radically contingent character of divine action *ad extra* by which God judges man's actions worthy or not. But this does not mean that man, in his finitude, has no positive value. Indeed, man's natural charity or love of God, his capacity for a specifically moral life which is disinterested, his human liberty in a contingent world, serve to indicate that each and every man must be held and hold himself intellectually responsible for his life. And each man's history is overarched

---

[76] For further analyses of the various aspects of the thought of Duns Scotus, see the contributions to *Deus et Homo ad mentem I. Duns Scoti*, Acta Tertii Congressus Scotistici Internationalis Vindebonae, 1970, *Studia Scholastico-Scotistica 5* (Rome, 1972), especially Paul Vignaux, 'Infini, liberté et histoire du salut', pp. 495–507.

by the historical character of the Christian vision of the universe whereby creation, the incarnation, from God's point of view, are free acts. The first cause according to Scotus, does not act by a natural necessity but rather through liberty and contingency, an historical response to historical men. The meaning of history is formal, coherent, ever present and essentially revealed to thinking minds.

Chapter 22

WILLIAM OF OCKHAM

To suppose that one word, in whatever context it appears, ought to mean one thing and no more, argues not an exceptionally high standard of logical accuracy but an exceptional ignorance as to the nature of language.

> R. G. Collingwood, *Speculum Mentis or The Map of Knowledge* (Oxford, 1924), p. 11.

When I was a schoolboy in Saragossa, I knew the names of all the Visigothic kings of Spain by heart, as well as the areas and populations of each country in Europe. In fact, I was a goldmine of useless facts. These mechanical pyrotechnics were the object of countless jokes; students who were particularly good at it were called *memoriónes*. Virtuoso *memorión* that I was, I too had nothing but contempt for such pedestrian exercises. Now, of course, I'm not so scornful ... You have to begin to lose your memory, if only in bits and pieces to realise that memory is what makes our lives. Life without memory is no life at all, just as an intelligence without the possibility of expression is not really an intelligence. Our memory is our coherence, our reason, our feeling, even our action. Without it, we are nothing.

> Luis Buñuel, *My Last Breath*, trans. Abigail Israel (London, 1984), pp. 3–4.

... and Professor Adrian confesses to the same 'misgivings' when he says that 'the part of the picture of the brain which may always be missing is of course the part which deals with the mind, the part which ought to explain how a particular pattern of nerve impulses can produce an idea; or the other way round, how a thought can decide which nerve cells are to come into action'. If this is a genuine problem, it is hard to see why further information about the brain should be expected to solve it. For however much we amplify our picture of the brain, it remains still a picture of something physical, and it is just the question how anything physical can interact with something that is not that is supposed to constitute our difficulty. If what we are seeking is a bridge across a seemingly impassable river it will not help us merely to elevate one of the banks ... as if mind and brain could be conceived as meeting at a point in space or as somehow shading into one another: but to me this is not even an intelligible hypothesis ... Descartes had the same problem, and he met it by suggesting that mind and body came together in the pineal gland; but how this conjecture could conceivably be tested he did not explain. The reason he had the problem, – the reason why we have it still – is that matter and mind were conceived by him from the outset as distinct orders of being ... as if ... no event could belong to both. . . . So if there is a difficulty here, it is not because our factual information is scanty, but because our logic is defective . . . In short, our problem is not scientific but philosophical . . . If there seems to be a mystery in this case, it is because we are misled by our conceptual systems; not by the facts themselves but by the pictures which we use to interpret the facts . . . The picture we are given is that of messengers travelling through the brain, reaching a mysterious entity called the mind, receiving orders from it, and then travelling on. But since the mind has no position in space– . . . it does not literally make sense to talk of physical signals reaching it. My conclusions is, then, that mind and body are not to be conceived as two disparate entities between which we have to make or find, some sort of amphibious bridge, but that talking about minds and talking about bodies are different ways of classifying and interpreting our experiences.

'The physical basis of mind: a philosophers' symposium', II: A. J. Ayer, in *The Physical Basis of Mind*, ed. P. Laslett (Oxford, 1950), p. 704.

OCKHAM

With the writings of William of Ockham (d. *c.* 1349) something happened that was to set the characteristics of theories of knowledge until the time of Descartes. If the picture of his direct influence on other contemporary thinkers remains obscure,[1] it is clear that he helped to focus the agenda that had emerged in Oxford earlier in the fourteenth century, an agenda that would inspire vociferous debate lasting well beyond his death and reaching beyond his Franciscan order.[2]

Our concern here is to discuss, first, his theory of cognition in order to understand how Ockham believes our minds remember the past. Once his epistemology is set out, and within it his theory of memory, we can observe how he uses his theory to explain not only how the past has meaning for individual men but also how individuals are to interpret past texts, especially those of Scripture. From his cognition theory emerges a distinctive approach to individual experience, to texts and authorities, to political formations, that would both inspire and alarm contemporaries and subsequent thinkers.

[1] 'Whether or not Ockham was the most important or influential figure around 1320, he certainly was one of the most controversial'. William J. Courtenay, 'The reception of Ockham's thought in fourteenth-century England', in A. Hudson and M. Wilks, eds., *From Ockham to Wyclif*, Studies in Church History, subsidia 5 (Oxford, 1987), pp. 89–107, p. 94; Katherine Tachau, 'The response to Ockham's and Aureol's epistemology (1320–40)', in Alfonso Maierù, ed., *English Logic in Italy in the Fourteenth and Fifteenth Centuries*, Acts of the fifth European symposium on medieval logic and semantics, 1980 (Naples, 1982), pp. 185–217.

[2] Indeed in this century, Etienne Gilson ruefully judged Ockham as excessively preoccupied with psychology, trying to solve metaphysical problems by psychological analysis. Gilson, *The Unity of Philosophical Experience* (New York, 1937).

Ockham's career was divided in two: his years in Oxford as a logician, philosopher and theologian followed by his years in Avignon (1324) and then with the radical Franciscans under the tutelage of the antipapal Holy Roman Emperor Louis of Bavaria (1328). During the first period he wrote the traditional late scholastic commentaries that we have come to expect from university milieux; during the second period he penned numerous polemical and political works. It is usually thought that the views of Ockham the logician-theologian have little in common with Ockham the political thinker, and indeed that we cannot work back from his political writings to his cognition theory which set forth the relation between the world and mental language. We shall see that this is not an accurate evaluation of his political works and that they are, in fact, based on the method and conclusions found in his earlier writings. Let us begin with what concerned him at Oxford and thereafter, when he taught in the Franciscan *studium generale* in London before he was summoned to Avignon.

In taking up many of the issues raised by his fellow Franciscan Scotus, and rereading Aristotle, often in the light of Augustine, Ockham went further in his treatment of individuals and how we have cognition of singulars. Acknowledging his debt to Scotus but disagreeing with him in important ways, Ockham also posited a theory of intuitive cognition of existents when he tried to answer the question: what do our concepts signify? How do we apply concepts to individuals? Affirming that concepts are the basic components of our thoughts, he argued that they are somehow caused by prior existent things so that knowledge is either of concepts or of extramental individuals and the latter must be prior. On the one hand, he argued that we have both intellectual as well as sensual knowledge of singulars, and on the other, following Aristotle, he argued that the scientific ideal of demonstration from necessary premises had to be based on terms because scientific demonstration is of the universal. Hence, although all knowledge is the result of the cognition of individuals, the universal character of our knowledge requires universal concepts.[3]

As we have already seen, earlier scholastics, treating the problem that was inherited from the ancient Greek philosophical tradition whereby objects of thought are universal but everything that exists is individual and singular, posited doctrines of moderate realism to overcome the gap between the intelligible and the existent. They suggested there were

[3] Ockham, *Expositio physicorum*, prologus, ed. and trans. P. Boehner, *Ockham: Philosophical Writings* (Edinburgh, 1957), p. 11. A good discussion and comparison with Scotus is in John F. Boler, 'Intuitive and abstractive cognition', *The Cambridge History of Later Medieval Philosophy*, eds. Kretzmann, Kenny and Pinborg (Cambridge, 1982), pp. 460–78. Also see Eileen Serene on 'Demonstrative Science' in this volume, pp. 496–518.

common natures in individual existing things which were distinct from their individuating principles, a distinction made possible only in thought. Therefore, the intellect must abstract from a particular presentation of sense experience a likeness, similitude or intelligible species in order to apprehend the common nature apart from its individuating conditions. Scotus said that the common nature was really identical with but formally distinct from the individuating principle, the *haecceitas*. Aquinas held that the common nature was distinct only according to the mode of consideration, although there was always some foundation in the thing itself. Revising the trend we have examined thus far, Ockham asked not how the individual derives from an essence or universal common nature, but how the world of individuals, which he says is all that really exists, can ever be known in a nonindividual and general manner. In his explanation, he completely rejected the need for species[4] and developed a theory of habits in the intellect to replace them. Universality and commonality are properties only of signs, of linguistic expressions and of acts of thought expressed by language. The problem of individuation is effectively a logical one showing how general terms used in propositions refer to individuals signified by them.

According to Ockham, science deals with the universal and necessary but knowledge is of the particular and contingent. How then do we come to acceptable scientific premises and general theories and yet also have knowledge of the contingencies that concern individuals and existence? Precisely this issue of individuality focused Ockham's mind in both his logical and theological writings, and this led to his theory of intuitive knowledge where he would disagree with Scotus by insisting on eliminating unwarranted assumptions, such as formal distinctions and the need for species. He was able thereby to define in a different way what he meant by intuitive cognition, by evident knowledge and by knowledge in experience, each of which was related to the role of propositional logic. In going beyond Scotus, Ockham argued that *both* intuitive and abstractive knowledge were immediate kinds of knowing individuals and that neither had any need of intermediary intelligible species, universal essences and natures. Unlike Scotus, general concepts for Ockham were not independent but merely the mind's way of knowing individuals. Cognition begins with an intuitive, immediate apprehension of the singular and not with some abstraction from images derived from sensory experience. For Ockham there is no precognitive phase prior to intellectual conceptualisation so that Aristotle's primary perceptual part is, from the beginning of

---

[4] Katherine Tachau, 'The problem of the *species in medio* at Oxford in the generation after Ockham', *Mediaeval Studies*, 44 (1982), pp. 394–443.

any act of knowing, always invaded by cognitive acts of intellect. But perhaps most important, for Ockham, immediate intuitive cognition as the means by which we know individuals, does not bring *ipso facto* certainty. The existence of anything, sensible or intelligible, can be doubted. This is because Ockham argues that our knowledge in experience derives from terms. At first glance this does not seem incompatible with Scotus's view. When we have evident knowledge of something we have knowledge of some true proposition whose nature is caused immediately or mediately by a noncomplex cognition of terms. Intuitive cognition is an incomplex apprehension of terms which substitute for really existing things, by means of which contingent propositions are evidently cognised.[5] It is on the basis of intuitive cognition – which is presupposed because it cannot be logically demonstrated – that we know whether or not contingent facts are true. But then Ockham insists on a corollary of fundamental importance which distances him from Scotus: when we know something intuitively we are not directly matching a proposition to which we assent intuitively with some extramental state of affairs. This is because there is no extramental composition, no formal or any other kind of ordering of which we can be certain, that is, which we can prove demonstratively, on to which predication is imposed.[6] Intuitive cognition of terms is and must be the presupposed starting point for our knowledge of contingent facts, but nothing known intuitively is absolutely certain.

Ockham then, like Scotus, argued for a certain autonomy of mind or the intellective soul whereby the intellect has direct cognition of individuals that exist. But just how the mind knows individuals is very different from the way Scotus supposed. This is because Ockham rejected Scotus's account of formal distinctions as constituents of real things. He argued that any creature that was formally distinct from another must also be really distinct.[7] This real distinction applied not only to assertions about beings, where propositions supposited or represented distinct real things,

---

5 'Et universaliter omnis notitia incomplexa termini vel terminorum seu rei vel rerum virtute cuius potest evidenter cognosci aliqua veritas contingens, maxime de praesenti, est notitia intuitive' (*Ordinatio*, I, prologus q. I). Editions used: Ockham, *Opera plurima* (Lyons, 1494–6), 4 vols., *Super quattuor libros Sententiarum*, vols. III and IV; Modern editions used, where available: *Scriptum in librum primum Sententiarum, Ordinatio, Prologus et Distinctio prima*, eds. G. Gál and S. Brown (*Opera Theologica*, I) (St Bonaventure, New York, 1967); *Scriptum in librum primum Sententiarum, Ordinatio, Distinctiones II–III, (Opera Theologica*, II) (St Bonaventure, New York, 1971); *Scriptum in librum primum Sententiarum, Ordinatio, Distinctiones IV–XVII*, ed., G. I. Etzkorn (*Opera Theologica*, III) (St Bonaventure, New York, 1977): *Scriptum in librum primum Sententiarum, Ordinatio, Distinctiones XIX–XLVIII*, eds., G. I. Etzkorn and F. Kelley, (*Opera Theologica*, IV) (St Bonaventure, New York, 1979).
6 Ockham, *Summa Logicae*, eds. P. Boehner, G. Gál and S. Brown, (*Opera Philosophica*, I) 2 vols. (St Bonaventure, New York, 1974), II, cc. 2–20.
7 *Ordinatio*, I, d. 2 q. I.

but also applied to distinct concepts or mental beings. For Ockham, real things and concepts are the only beings there are and there are no real beings that are not also real things. For him everything that exists in reality is singular and individual. Universals, like concepts, are nothing other than names, that is, they are either natural signs or terms in the mind that are general concepts, or conventional, linguistic signs of terms that correspond to natural signs. Such signs or terms contribute to the formation of propositions. The object of knowledge is the mental, spoken or written *proposition* comprised of terms, and not the substance, be it universal or particular to which this proposition refers. While it is individual substances which we know, such substances can only be known through propositions, mental or linguistic, that contain terms that supposit or represent them. Ockham asserted that no external corporeal substance can be naturally apprehended by us in itself;[8] we are only intuitively aware of substance, by which he means the individual substratum of qualities, as the subject of sensible qualities. Particular and individual substances really exist but we can only *know* these through propositions which contain terms that supposit for individual substances. The category of substance is therefore reduced to the referential purpose which language expresses, substance as the supposited referent. When we are immediately and intuitively aware of a real particular, the object of this intuitive cognition is identical with a real particular that is independent of mind. Indeed, it is that which is referred to by the term we apprehend. This means that he rejected the Scotist theory that intellect's proper objects were intelligible ideas or species divorced from their sensory and individual manifestations. For Ockham, intelligible knowledge of the universal was not superior to knowledge of individuals achieved through the senses. It was simply another way of mind knowing individuals.

Scotus, as we have seen, had a doctrine of direct acts of individual cognition as well, but he did not believe it was the individual in its singularity that was the first object known. Rather, the first object for him was confused or indistinct knowledge, a species that came immediately above the individual. For Scotus, the first object known distinctly by intellect was the *concept* of being as the most universal and absolutely simple of all concepts. For Ockham, the first object known is the individual through its supposited term.

What kind of being do concepts have for Ockham? Early in his career he argued that whatever is conceptualised must have some kind of existence in itself even when we can think of objects that do not or cannot really exist, such as impossibles (chimeras) or abstract objects like universals, or

[8] *Ordinatio,* I, d. 3 q. 2; I d. 2 q. 4.

unactualised possibles. Like Scotus, then, early in his career Ockham posited some nonreal mode of existence of concepts.[9] He said that they have a cognised existence. But in response to the criticisms of a fellow Franciscan, Walter Chatton, Ockham came to modify his earlier theory which, in effect had made cognised existence dependent on mind alone. He abandoned his distinction between cognised and real existence and came to identify concepts with really existent *acts* of intellect.[10] Likewise, universals were identified with really existent abstract general concepts. He therefore ends up with a kind of conceptualism,[11] very much like that of Abelard, whereby there is no reification of the relations between extramental things and mental concepts. Concepts or intentions are to be located entirely within the mind. An intention in the mind is a natural sign which signifies something for which it can substitute or which can be part of a mental proposition. The signs proper to spoken language correspond in a special way to intentions which are, as first intentions, natural signs of something that is not itself a sign. Spoken language is *ad placitum*, a conventional means of referring to natural signs in the mind.[12]

The effect of this anti-realist theory proved to be tremendous. Because Ockham believed that we can have a primary cognition of a conclusion obtained from a proposition that is necessary and evidently known, indeed that is what he means by a demonstrative syllogism, he is asserting that what we know must by logically consistent and based on a presupposed intuition of the proposition's terms. But he is not claiming that the

---

[9] *Ordinatio*, d. 2 q. 8:
... universale non est aliquid reale habens esse subiectivum nec in anima nec extra animam, sed tantum habet esse obiectivum in anima, et est quoddam fictum habens esse tale in esse obiectivo, quale habet res extra in esse subiective. Et hoc per istum modum, quod intellectus videns aliquam rem extra animam fingit consimilem rem in mente, ita quod si haberet virtutem productivam, sicut habet virtutem fictivam, talem rem in esse subiectivo numero distinctam a priori produceret extra ... Illud fictum in mente ex visione alicuius rei extra esset unum exemplar ... est exemplar ipsi artifici, its illud fictum esset exemplar respectu sic fingentis.'

[10] Gualterus Chatton, *Lecturae in 1 Sent.*, prol. q. 2, ed. J. O'Callaghan, 'The second question of the prologue to Walter Chatton's commentary on the Sentences', in J. R. O'Donnell, ed. *Nine Medieval Thinkers* (Toronto, 1955), pp. 248–9; Marilyn McCord Adams, 'Ockham's nominalism and unreal entities', *The Philosophical Review*, 86 (1977), pp. 144–76; p. 145. In the *Summa Logicae*, I. ch. 12, Ockham defines *intentio*, similar to Chatton's *intellectio* theory, where the concept is the *act* of cognition.

[11] P. Boehner, 'The realistic conceptualism of William Ockham', *Traditio*, 4 (1946), pp. 307–35; G. Gál, 'Gualteri de Chatton et Guillelmi de Ockham, controversia de natura conceptus universalis', *Franciscan Studies*, 27 (1967), pp. 191–212.

[12] Marilyn McCord Adams, 'Ockham's theory of natural signification', *The Monist*, 62 (1978), pp. 444–59. *Ad placitum* does not necessarily mean 'arbitrary' (ie. not bound by rules) but it does mean conventional. 'Mind' or the intellective soul is not located in the head but through the body. See *Quod.*, I, q. 12.

resulting science necessarily mirrors the inner constitution of nature. For Ockham, we learn contingent truths about what is the case by experience, but what he means by experience is something very precise: experience is a fact of life; we *know* our experiences by means of our knowledge of terms that supposit for things and this then gives rise to evident knowledge that is based on propositions. We thereafter transform these evident truths syllogistically into what we believe must be possible in similar cases. Hence, even more than for Scotus, Ockham is arguing that any demonstrative science, which necessarily deals with universals, concerns ideas and propositions which share common mental contents, and we can only assume this science reflects the causes of these ideas in the physical, extramental world.[13] Therefore, natural science can only be about mental intentions that are thought to be common to contingent and corruptible things in the world, such mental intentions suppositing for such things in propositions.[14] Hence, we must believe that intuitive cognition of particulars which really exist, is the basis of our knowledge. Even more than in Scotus, then, we have here an increasing focus on the probability rather than the certainty of our *knowledge* of the world beyond our immediate experience of it. But the evident contingent propositions resulting from our experience do provide certitude without fear of deception. Hence, Ockham concludes that scientific knowledge, general knowledge about the way things are in relation to one another is not, in fact, cannot be decisive and infallible, because a demonstrative syllogism is in principle no more certain than one which rests on probable premises even when such probable premises are considered by everyone, or the wisest, to be true.[15] Infallibility, no, but a high degree of certitude, yes. Thus, for Ockham, the cognition that we can acquire through scientific demonstration and that acquired by experience do not differ in kind with respect to the conclusion reached through each. The world as we know it or knew it is firmly circumscribed by how we mentally and linguistically construct it, based, originally, on intuitively knowing terms and having experiences. This is not to deny that there are assumed regularities in nature; nor does Ockham deny that moral norms are constant. Ockham did not deny causality or relation in general. Rather, he conceived of them as derived

[13] *Summa Logicae* (*OP*, I), p. 359.
[14] 'Nam obiectum scientiae est tota propositio nota' (*Ockham: Philosophical Writings*, ed. and trans. P. Boehner, pp. 2–16; p. 9).
[15] Serene in *Cambridge History of Later Medieval Philosophy*, p. 514.
Et si quaeratur an notitia accepta per experientiam alicuius conclusionis et notitia eiusdem accepta per demonstrationem sint eiusdem speciei; et similiter notitia accepta per diversas praemissas sit eiusdem speciei, potest probabiliter sit notitia conclusionis et nihil aliud, non est inconveniens ponere quod talis notitia sit eiusdem speciei specialissimae. (*Summa Logicae* (*OP*, I), III, ii, ll, p. 524)

from observation and abstraction, observation and abstraction that were, however, founded on an intuition of the singular and its consequent necessary generalisation to all other cases or individuals of the same nature. It is in this light that his so-called 'razor' is to be understood: 'Nihil debet poni sine ratione assignata nisi sit per se notum vel per experientiam scitum vel per auctoritatem scripturae probatum'[16] (Nothing should be posited without reason unless it is self-evidently known in itself, known by experience or proved by scriptural authority).

What we have here is a gradual and, eventually, a complete break with the neo-Platonised Aristotle with whom we have become so familiar. And we also have a break with Aquinas's interpretation of Aristotle in Ockham's doctrine of intuitive individual cognition.[17] We also have a break with Scotus's distinction between intuitive and abstractive cognition because Scotus described two different modes of knowing without a link between the two kinds of knowledge. For Scotus, knowledge presupposed an essential, quidditative concept so that one knows first in a confused and indistinct mode and thereafter, one knows the distinct. For Ockham, the individual thing is known as a singular or it is not known at all. We know distinctly and intuitively *before* we have a definition. Ockham overcame the Scotist duality by asserting that a direct intuitive cognition of individual existence was the starting point for all other kinds of knowledge, be it abstractive, individual, universal, contingent, necessary or self-evident. The only reality for him is the knowledge of individuals on which all different kinds of knowing are based. The sensitive faculty of mind ends in a cognition of the singular; the intellective faculty begins with individual cognition. Ockham notes that this is a deductive argument whose persuasiveness is based on Aristotle's schema of demonstrative knowledge being universal and necessary. Ockham, therefore, dispensed with intelligible species because for him all cognition had to be direct whether intuitively of individuals or abstractively of their representations in the intellect. In effect, he describes the two modes of knowing, intuitive and abstractive, as successive, indeed as related phases of immediate knowledge. The difference between intuitive and abstractive knowledge was determined by whether evidential or inevidential knowledge was provided. Intuitive knowledge is distinguished from abstractive on the basis of the certainty of existence alone. If something known in the mind can be shown

---

16 *Ordinatio*, I, d. 30 q. 1 E. Also less explicit: 'Quia frustra fit per plura quod equaliter fieri per pauciona', in Boehner, ed., *Reportatio*, II, qq. 14–15 = 'The *notitia intuitiva* of nonexistents according to William Ockham', *Traditio*, 1 (1943), pp. 245–75; p. 254.

17 Marilyn McCord Adams, 'Intuitive cognition, certainty and scepticism in William of Ockham', *Traditio*, 26 (1970), pp. 389–98. Criticisms in Gordon Leff, *William of Ockham, The Metamorphosis of Scholastic Discourse* (Manchester, 1975), p. 21 n. 76.

to exist extramentally, then it is evident knowledge; but if something known in the mind cannot be shown to exist in reality then it is abstractive knowledge as some form of apprehension, belief or opinion. Intuitive knowledge can tell the difference between the evident and inevident because intuitive knowledge is knowledge of real existence so that the validity of any mode of knowing depends in the first instance on intuitive knowledge. What is remarkable here is that Ockham asserts that we can be certain of experience but we cannot be absolutely assured of the necessary congruence of our immediate experiences with the world!

In the prologue to his *Ordinatio*, Ockham defines as evident that knowledge of a true proposition caused directly or indirectly by the knowledge of the terms of the proposition.[18] Evident knowledge is knowledge of what is contingent, it is of whatever can be known to be true. But simply to know the terms of an evident proposition does not suffice for evident knowledge because we also have to know the existence of that to which terms refer in fact. Thus, what is actual, within the range of what is logically possible (and whatever is not self-contradictory is possible) cannot be established by reason alone; it is established first and primarily by experience. Now, we can only know the existence of the terms of a proposition through intuitive knowledge.[19] Intuitive knowledge is therefore an act of immediate awareness in virtue of which it can be known whether a thing is or is not, and if it is, the intellect judges it to be and knows its existence evidently. Apprehension is an act of intellect distinct from judgement and the latter depends on an apprehension of what is signified by the terms of a proposition expressing the judgement. Intuitive knowledge then gives the knowledge of the real relation between things, for instance, the inherence of whiteness in Socrates, or the distance between things.[20] But it does not do so in an indubitable way. Only what is self-evident, *per se nota*, that is, a proposition evident from the meaning of its terms, is indubitable. Intuitive knowledge simply ensures for us the interconnectedness of individuals. It also ensures the distinction between the real and the mental and the relation between them. Intuitive knowledge is, for Ockham, the very source of all experimental knowledge of what is both contingent and necessary. Something is evident by experience, *nota per experientiam*, when it is established by generalisation from singular, contingent propositions that are evident by intuitive cognition. This kind of induction from the supposition of a common course of nature

18 For a clear discussion of intuitive and abstractive knowledge, sensory experience and the primacy of individual cognition, see Leff, *William of Ockham*, part I, chapter I.
19 Compare with Ockham's discussion of intuitive cognition in Boehner, ed., *Reportatio*, II, qq. 14–15, in *Traditio*, I (1943), pp. 223–75.
20 *Ordinatio*, prol.q. I, 31.

is not indubitable; rather it is hypothetical, because otherwise it would eliminate the possibility of God producing something without its natural cause.

The difference between intuitive and abstractive knowledge is that intuitive knowledge knows the existence of things for which terms in a proposition stand. Abstractive knowledge only knows the terms of a proposition or the concepts of such terms. An abstractive act of cognition is one in which it cannot be evidently known whether the apprehended object exists or does not. In virtue of an abstractive act of cognition an evident contingent judgement cannot be made. Each kind of knowledge knows the *same objects*, concepts or terms like 'man', 'dispute', 'lion', 'white man' (*incomplexa*) in a different way. When *incomplexa* are known we have an immediate apprehension of the object known, but no judgement on its truth of falsity is yet made since acts of judgement are *complexa* (propositions) rather than terms. Judgements presuppose apprehensions. If the terms of a proposition are known abstractively, that is, without knowing the existence of what they signify which would be known intuitively, then a proposition will only be known abstractively and inevidently, that is, in a nonexistential mode. If I observe Socrates seated, Ockham explains, I can evidently judge that he is seated. But if I leave the room and then judge that he is seated, the judgement is not evident and it may be false.[21] Thus, contrary to Scotus, *the same thing* is known both by intuitive and abstractive knowledge but in differing ways, existentially or not. The distinction between the two modes of knowing then, is with regard to *how* rather than *what* is known, since the *same thing* is known.

We recall that Scotus had insisted that abstractive knowledge does not seize the object in itself but only in a diminished likeness, in its intelligible species. Ockham disagreed. Both intuitive and abstractive knowledge are wholly of the same object known under the same object for both, so that anything known intuitively can also be known abstractively. The two forms of knowing, then, were not formally distinct for Ockham as they were for Scotus, because this would mean that while the object was the direct cause of our knowledge, we none the less required an intelligible species as an intermediary by which the object could be known abstractively. There are not for Ockham two distinct causes of intuitive and abstractive knowledge. Since intuitive knowledge knows the existence of the objects which the terms of a proposition stand for, it must have as its efficient cause the

---

[21] See the discussion of this in Ernest A. Moody, 'William of Ockham (1967)', in *Studies in Medieval Philosophy, Science and Logic, Collected Papers 1933–69*, (Center for Medieval and Renaissance Studies, University of California, Los Angeles, 1975), pp. 409–40; pp. 416–18.

existing object as present. Evident knowledge depends on what is present. The affection of the senses by an external object is a necessary condition for intuitive cognition. Ockham concludes that it is not *logically* necessary that the object of intuitive cognition be present or actually existent. But he insists that if the object is not present or actually existent, its cognition cannot yield an evident judgement that the object exists when it does not. Abstractive knowledge, however, can be of something which is no longer in existence because abstraction gives no clue as to the existence of the objects to which terms of a proposition refer.[22] *Pro statu isto* intuitive knowledge is always of what exists here and now and this will have an important consequence for Ockham's discussion of how we know the past as past.

Unlike Scotus, then, Ockham's intuitive knowledge differs from abstractive knowledge only as the latter is the nonexistential mode of knowing what is known existentially when known intuitively. There are no intermediary species either for intuitive or abstractive knowledge. Hence when intuitive knowledge is caused by *ipsa res nota*, the thing known, the efficient cause of abstractive knowledge is intuitive knowledge or a habit that inclines to abstractive knowledge. Therefore, there is a causal relation between intuitive and abstractive knowledge; abstractive knowledge follows a prior intuitive knowledge and is habitually conjoined with intuition. Because Ockham posits a causal primacy of intuitive knowledge as an evident principle known from experience, it is indemonstrable. We shall say more about the role of habits in knowledge, but what is clear and distinctive about Ockham's exposition of intuitive knowledge is that because it knows the individual as existing, intuitive knowledge is the prerequisite for all other knowledge. This is simply a fact of experience for him.

The primacy of individual cognition, however, raises a major problem for epistemology. If intuitively we know contingent individuals, how do we square this with the fact that we also know that the intellect knows universals? Where the intellect abstracts from what exists here and now, intuitive knowledge is of what is here and now. How, then, can the *intellect* be said to know intuitively? Ockham asserts that the intellect no less than the senses knows intuitively the individual and singular first as its object of knowledge. Aristotle had said that in knowing the individual first, the intellect knows it only imprecisely or confusedly. Ockham notes that when the intellect abstracts from the here and now it has abstractive knowledge without an existential component in its knowing; but when the intellect has immediate intuitive knowledge it judges whether or not something does

[22] *Ordinatio*, prol. q. 1, 38.

511

exist and is present. The same things are objects of both sense and intellect and can be known intuitively as well as abstractively and the thing known abstractively by intellect is not more abstract than it is for the senses. But because the intellect is immaterial, it can follow the initial, immediate, direct cognition of a present individual by an act of abstraction whereby many things can be known from the individual such as universal concepts, that are then known separately from their conjunction in real beings. Hence, according to Ockham, Aquinas had misread Aristotle. The intellect does not only operate by abstracting universals from material conditions as Aquinas had supposed. Prior to that abstraction is an intellectual intuitive cognition of the individual itself and intellect therefore does, intuitively, know what exists outside the intellect. Ockham interprets both Aristotle and Averroes as saying that sensory knowledge of individuals is what is known first, and where Aristotle said that the intellect cannot know without an image, Ockham takes him to mean that all intellective cognition presupposes sensitive cognition; he does not take Aristotle to mean that the intellect knows individuals *only through* images and phantasms which represent individuals as Aquinas had done. These are unnecessary intermediaries for Ockham.

Intuitive knowledge is for Ockham both of sensibles existing extramentally and also of intelligibles in the mind as individuals. He has not reduced all knowledge to sense perceptions, but rather, has incorporated the Augustinian dualism of sense and intelligible data as two different and unconnected objects of mind. In fact, he maintains that an awareness of our own interior states gives us the most certain of all knowledge possible. But this does not mean, as it did for Scotus, that there is a distinction between perceptual and conceptual knowledge. Rather, Ockham's distinction is between evidential and inevidential knowledge of the same object so that he is able to treat of the logical possibility of having, albeit extraordinarily, intuitive knowledge of nonexistents which for Scotus was impossible. According to Ockham, God, for example, could preserve intuitive cognition in the absence of an object. But in this case of a nonexistent object, intuitive cognition only enables judgement that the object is absent. The nonexistent object cannot lead to a judgement of its existence, because such a judgement would be self-contradictory. Therefore, it is not even in God's power for cognition to lead to an evident judgement that an object exists if it does not. An intuitive cognition of a nonexistent object is logically possible although realisable only by God's power.[23]

[23] *Quodlibet*, v, q. 5 in *Quodlibeta septem*, ed. Joseph C. Wey, *Opera Theologica*, IX (St Bonaventure, New York, 1980), p. 498, and *Quodlibet*, VI, q. 6 conclusio 2: 'Utrum

When we apprehend something Ockham says we are immediately aware of it. However much this awareness may be caused by the presence of its object, we can say that there is no judgement of the existence of the thing for which its term, an *incomplexa*, stands in a proposition. And there is no judgement as to the truth of the thing as there would be were we to form a proposition or *complexa* which included the term. Intuitive cognition is not identical with its objects. Intuitive cognition is a direct act of apprehension of what is signified by terms which represent objects. While naturally we can apprehend something without assenting to or dissenting from or doubting its existence, whenever we do assent, we are, in effect, presupposing a prior non-judgemental apprehension. These are really distinct from one another but naturally, once we assent, this assent is inseparable from prior apprehension. Hence, naturally and without God's intervention, we can only know intuitively what exists and this can only arise if the object is present. We cannot have knowledge of a nonexistent. Intuitively we can only know that something, which we do not apprehend, is absent.[24]

Now if, in Augustinian fashion, Ockham has asserted that our awareness of our own interior states is more certain and more evident than any other kind of knowledge (but not absolutely certain), what is the status of intuitive knowledge of external things? We have seen that Ockham argues that mind knows intelligibles just as immediately as it knows sensibles. This immediate knowledge enables us to know intuitively our own interior states.[25] Therefore, when we have faith we know it intuitively and this interior state is not concerned with sensibles. Those contingent truths which we know certainly and evidently can be divided into prior and posterior; those which come first for Ockham as sustained by Augustine, are intelligible truths because one may doubt *sensibilia* but not intelligible truths such as 'I know that I live' (*scio me vivere*).[26] But the difference between the certainty of intelligible and sensory knowledge is a relative one. Now, some intelligibles have been sensed first but others have not. Intelligibles are the most certain and evident because they do not presuppose other truths *by which* they may be known and such intelligibles require their own intuitive knowing.[27] Here, Ockham is drawing on Scotus to show that the mind has an intuitive knowledge of its own acts which derives from its recollective or memorial powers. Ockham emphasises that the intellect has a capacity to record *acts* which are entirely

cognitio intuitiva possit esse de obiecto non existente ... Secunda conclusio est quod naturaliter cognitio intuitiva non potest causari nec conservari obiecto non existente' (p. 606).
[24] *Reportatio*, II, q. 15 E, and *Ordinatio*, prol. q. 1, 31.   [25] *Ordinatio*, prol. q. 1, 41–2.
[26] *Ibid.*, 43 and *Quodlibet*, 1.   [27] *Ordinatio*, prol. q. 1, 43–4.

separate from the senses or from what comes through the senses. It is with the intellect's memorial powers that we can know both immediate and remote objects and thereby reason discursively and syllogistically.[28] Furthermore, he says that where intelligibles can be known intuitively, things which have been known in the past can only be known abstractively when they are no longer present. But because Ockham's theory of intuitive knowledge necessarily links intuitive with abstractive knowledge, he will be able to say the most distinctive, unique and indeed revolutionary things about the mind's capacity to deal with the past precisely as past, and so overturn the Thomistic and Scotist reliance on the present understanding of what can never be known as it once was.

We have, on the one hand, the intellect knowing sensibles through the senses intuitively, as well as, on the other, the intellect knowing intuitively interior intelligibles, which is a knowledge of acts of intellection or feeling which have no precedent in sense knowledge. This interior knowledge is mind's own act independent of and distinct from sensory perception of external, sensible things.[29] The intellect not only knows by intuitive cognition, the individual things as existing outside mind. Ockham rejects Scotus's distinction between direct acts of knowing things outside it and reflexive acts whereby it knows its own acts and therefore knows that it knows something similar to its acts. There is no such distinction between direct and reflexive acts of knowing for Ockham. Direct knowledge of our interior acts of intellection does not, as it did for Scotus, enable us to know these acts perfectly and distinctly. We cannot in our present condition distinguish reflexive from direct acts of cognition. And Ockham calls upon Augustine to confirm that the mind can know itself and yet not differentiate itself from others.[30]

Since all existence, other than God's, is contingent, what is known intuitively can only be known contingently – as existing or not existing, present or absent – because intuitive knowledge is of the existence or nonexistence of those things to which terms in propositions refer. The existence of the object known is not uncertain since it is the condition of all naturally engendered intuitive knowledge. We are certain of our experiences. This reflects a concern to establish the *cognitive* primacy of

---

[28] *Ibid.*, 46.

[29] Notitia intuitiva intellectionis vel affectionis vel delectationis presupponit notitiam obiecti illius intellectionis vel affectionis vel delectationis, et sic de aliis ... per hoc quasi innuens quod mens potest sentire – hoc est intuitive cognoscere – aliqua que exterius sunt; et similiter potest intuitive cognoscere aliqua que interius sunt, cuiusmodi sint actus intellectus et voluntates et delectationes et huiusmodi. Sine sensu, hoc est sine notitia intuitiva sensitiva illorum, quamvis notitia aliquorum necessario presupponatur. (*Ordinatio*, I, q. 1, 67–8)

[30] *Ordinatio*, q. 1, 68–9.

individual existence; we can have intuitive knowledge of something's existence while doubting the *nature* of what exists.[31] Our mental cognitive acts are, for Ockham, more immediate and certain than the certainty of the existence of other things. In denying a discrepancy between intuitive cognition of intellect and the senses, his is an optimistic view of the capacity of the intellect so far as natural experience is concerned. Leff has pointed out, following Baudry's criticism of Ockham,[32] that logically Ockham accounts for the asymmetry between terms and propositions on the one hand, and things on the other, but psychologically he does not recognise a discrepancy between the knowledge of existence and the judgement of the nature of what exists. He assumes they correspond.[33] When they do not, he simply argues for some malfunctioning or limitations of the sensual machinery. He gives the Aristotelian example in the *Ordinatio*[34] of children initially calling all men 'father'. He explains this by saying that when we confuse the universal with the singular, the cause is not in the intellect only knowing universals, nor in the priority of the universal over the individual. Rather, the cause is the senses which distinguish only what is dissimilar. Although the individual father is always immediately perceived, it is not immediately known distinctly unless it can be in some way differentiated from similar individuals, by colour, position, shape etc. The so-called original confused knowledge is really only due to the limitations of our senses. Apprehensions can cause false *judgements*. Hence intuitive knowledge of the individual is just about as certain as any contingent truths can be, which is not to argue for its infallibility. This interpretation should not be seen as scepticism, a position that future followers would indeed adopt in Ockham's name. For Ockham, we naturally *can* know the existence of all we can experience. The incompleteness in this knowledge, *pro statu isto*, is that it does not extend, naturally, to the nonexistence of something nor to that which is not immediately known here and now. What is known is certain as here and now. And the foregoing limitations can only be overcome by supernatural intervention.

Then how are we to deal with those things which are no longer here and now but which once, in the past, were? We must return to Ockham's analysis of the relationship between intuitive and abstractive knowledge in order to learn what kind of knowledge we can have of past experience. In the *Reportatio*, II, qq. 14–15 he looks at Scotus's discussion of recollection as Scotus analysed it in his *Sentences* commentary.[35] Here, Scotus referred to

31 As Leff has argued in *William of Ockham*, pp. 28–9.
32 L. Baudry, *Lexique Philosophique de Guillaume d'Ockham* (Paris, 1957), pp. 177ff.
33 Leff, *William of Ockham*, p. 29.   34 *Ordinatio*, I, d. 27 (*OT*, IV), pp. 243–50.
35 Scotus, *Opus Oxoniense*, IV, d. 10, q. 5, n. 4, and *Reportatio Parisiense*, II, d. 3 q. 2 n. 11. Ockham's treatment of imperfect intuition is discussed in Baudry, *Lexique*, pp. 177–8.

recollective knowledge as imperfect intuitive knowledge which depends on the existence of an object known (the species) and therefore, of the immediate present. Imperfect intuitive knowledge is the kind of knowledge we have of what no longer exists. Ockham says that imperfect intuitive knowledge differs from abstractive knowledge in having a temporal element in the sense that it is knowledge of what *has* existed. Abstractive knowledge we recall is without reference to something's existence or nonexistence. How, Ockham asks, is such imperfect intuition caused? And at what point does knowledge of existence as here and now become knowledge of past existence where the object of knowledge is no longer here and now?

Ockham treats imperfect intuitive knowledge as part of the larger discussion of the intuitive knowledge of nonexistents.[36] And here he makes clear his understanding of mental habits.[37] Imperfect intuitive knowledge is the result of a habit in a sequence which begins with perfect intuitive knowledge. Ockham himself gives two variations on an explanation:

Cognitio autem intuitiva imperfecta est illa per quam iudicamus rem aliquando fuisse vel non fuisse; et hec dicitur cognitio recordativa. Ut quando video aliquam rem intuitive, generatur habitus inclinans ad cognitionem abstractivam, mediante qua iudico et assentio quod talis res aliquando fuit, quia aliquando vidi eam.[38]

Now, either intuitive knowledge is alone the partial cause of this habit, or abstractive knowledge is a partial cause. It seems likely that Ockham's considered opinion is that the habit is due to abstractive knowledge as a partial cause.[39] The way a habit is built up, according to Ockham, is only through repeated acts of intuitive knowledge of present existence and these repeated experiences lead to imperfect intuitive knowledge of past experience. Such imperfect intuition of what no longer exists is also abstractive, which, we recall, makes no distinction between existence and nonexistence here and now: 'Ut videtur, cum cognitione intuitiva perfecta non manet cognitio abstractiva eiusdem, sed ex cognitione intuitiva frequentata generatur habitus inclinans ad cognitionem abstractivam sive intuitivam imperfectam'.[40] Such habits make the whole proposed mechanism of species superfluous for Ockham. As we have already said,

---

[36] The text is edited by Boehner, 'The notitia intuitiva of nonexistants according to William Ockham', pp. 245–75 and is cited below. See Leff's discussion of this, *William of Ockham* pp. 30f.

[37] Oswald Fuchs, *The Psychology of Habit according to William of Ockham* (St Bonaventure, New York, 1952).

[38] Boehner, ed., p. 250.   [39] See Leff, *William of Ockham*, p. 31.

[40] Boehner, ed., p. 253.

for Ockham, intuitive acts of knowledge engender abstractive acts of knowledge. With imperfect intuition we are presented with a half-way house: an imperfect intuitive habit is partially caused by imperfect intuitive knowledge so that we can say that it is intuitive regarding the temporal by which it refers to past experience and yet at the same time it is abstractive because it is knowledge of what no longer exists here and now. Hence, for Ockham, in recalling the past, both intuitive and abstractive knowledge exist together, concurrently, and they exist together after intuitive knowledge has caused the abstractive. This, Ockham says, can be proved by reference to our experience, for if someone has perfect intuitive knowledge of an object here and now, he can immediately thereafter form a proposition to which he evidently assents, even though the object has vanished or no longer exists. The proposition he forms is: 'This thing existed'. The very fact that we employ the past tense indicates the readiness of the intellect to draw forth this *act* of past knowledge where before it had none, and this is evidence of a habit having been established which inclines the intellect to such imperfect intuitive knowledge.[41] The only way we can have such an inclination is from an act of abstractive knowledge that is concurrent with perfect intuitive knowledge of what is initially known.

The procedure Ockham has outlined, therefore, runs as follows: first we have a perfect intuitive knowledge of an object which serves as a partial cause which leads to the concurrent abstractive knowledge of the same object and this, in turn, acts as a partial cause to produce a habit of imperfect intuitive knowledge which inclines the intellect, immediately, once the object no longer exists here and now, to a knowledge of its past existence. Starting with the fact of intuitive knowledge as an evident principle known from experience *tout court*, there is no other reason that is needed than experience itself to demonstrate that all knowledge is intuitive of existence. But since we can have no experience of abstractive knowledge as the concurrent partial cause of the habit to be established, that is, we have no experience of the effect of intuitive knowledge, we can only appeal to the Aristotelian principle that a like act leads to a like habit. Our knowledge of the past as past is dependent on the establishment of habits which incline the intellect to imperfect intuitions. *Hence, we conclude from reason, that is, on rational, deductive grounds*, that only abstractive knowledge can produce a habit because habits are only of abstractive knowledge which does not determine existence or nonexistence of objects, and therefore, of which we can have no experience. Since a habit of imperfect intuitive knowledge immediately follows the 'corruption' or cessation of

[41] *Ibid.*, pp. 250–1.

perfect intuitive knowledge, then abstractive knowledge, we rationally conclude, must be concurrent with it. On this model of what happens concurrently once the object experienced is no longer present, Ockham builds his entire cognitive theory of the grasping of the long distance past as well.[42]

Therefore, we have a first act of abstractive knowledge which runs concurrently with perfect intuitive knowledge and which, together with the object and the intellect, are partial causes. Then we have a second act of abstractive knowledge which is produced as a result of a habit that has been engendered from the first abstractive knowledge, and this habit leads to imperfect intuitive knowledge of what has existed, making all past knowledge abstractive. Ockham reiterates that in intuitive knowledge absolutely nothing, certainly not an intermediary species, is required besides the intellect and the individual object known.[43] And this intuitive perfect knowledge includes all immediate experience of what exists, be it outside the mind or internal to mind. For Ockham, the knowledge of what cannot be seen since it is interior, and that which can be seen through the senses, is no different in kind from intuitive knowledge. However, abstractive knowledge does require something other than intellect and the object known. Ockham considers abstractive knowledge to be a result of something left by intuitive knowledge: 'ergo habita cognitione intuitiva aliquid relinquitur in intellectu, ratione cuius potest in cognitionem abstractivam, et prius non potuit'.[44] This something left by intuitive knowledge, he says, is what Aristotle meant when he distinguished between a thing's essential and its accidental powers where for the latter something is added. So too when the senses sense something, an image or phantasm of the thing is perceived intuitively and it can remain in the imagination which is a repository of sense images after the thing known is no longer there. Thus, for Ockham, both the intellect and the sense imagination have, essentially, the same power of abstractive knowledge which is realised accidentally as a result of intuitive knowledge. In the

---

[42] Loquendo vero de notitia abstractiva, tunc aut loquimur de illa que semper consequitur intuitivam, aut de illa que habetur post corruptionem intuitive. Si primo modo, sic ad illa requiritur obiectum et intellectus et cognitio intuitiva tamquam cause partiales. Quod probatur sicut prius, quia illud quod posito etc. Si secundo modo loquimur, sic ad illam requiritur intellectus et habitus generatus ex cognitione abstractiva elicita simul cum intuitiva; et non requiritur obiectum in ista secunda cognitione abstractiva tamquam causa partialis, quia illa potest haberi, etsi obiectum annihiletur. Et est utraque istarum notitiarum abstractivarum incomplexa. Et ista secunda est causa partialis notitie complexe qua iudico quod res aliquando fuit. (Boehner, ed., p. 258).
[43] 'Prima est quod ad cognitionem intuitivam habendam non oportet aliquid ponere preter intellectum et rem cognitam et nullam speciem penitus' (Boehner, ed., p. 254).
[44] Boehner, ed. p. 255.

intellect what remains is what is left after the completion of intuitive knowledge. What is this remaining something if it is not a species? Ockham says what is left is a habit.

Here, he interprets Aristotle's *De Anima*, III, 3 where Aristotle spoke of mind having different potentialities, before and after the acquisition of knowledge. Mind, therefore, has an accidental potentiality to perform a similar act that is elicited through the presence of a habit and such an accidental potentiality is experienced only after an act of knowledge has been completed. When there is this preceding act of intuitive knowledge, the intellect, says Ockham, immediately knows itself to have the capacity for a further act of knowledge and this can only be the result of a habit left behind by the previous act: 'Et hoc non potest nisi per habitum derelictum in intellectu ex primo actu'.[45] This interpretation of Aristotle therefore leads Ockham to say that it must be in virtue of the intellect's own nature as a substance rather than because of a species which inheres in the intellect, that one knows both present and past. Because there is an immediate act of intellection following the cessation of intuitive cognition, no object can be assimilated to mind, considered as a recipient of an act of intellection that is caused by the object. There is no possibility, for Ockham, either in intuitive or abstractive knowledge, of species assimilating an object known to the intellect. He has conclusively rejected the Thomistic Aristotelianism which justified intellect's abstraction from material things by species converted in the imagination. Unless one posits an infinity of species, says Ockham, which is unnecessary, there is no need for species at all to unite object and intellect, either in intuitive cognition or in first abstractive knowledge. Only when one speaks of second abstractive knowledge, which requires something other than the object known and intellect, is there room for a third something and this is not a species but a habit. Such a habit inclines to complex propositional knowledge and results in something being known to have existed.[46]

Aristotle's 'species' has become Ockham's 'habit', not unlike Averroes's use of 'form' to render 'species' by which he meant an act of intellection or habit. The soul or mind is no longer the place of species but rather the subject of acts and habits. Whereas Scotus had said that at least in all nonintuitive knowledge species were required, so that the intellect could grasp the nature or species of something before knowing it individually, Ockham goes well beyond this and denies the presence of species as a condition of intellectual knowledge. He has destroyed the formal unity elaborated by Scotus between the natures of things and the universal known in the mind. For Ockham, universals do not exist extramentally.

[45] Boehner, ed., pp. 255–6; Leff, *William of Ockham*, p. 36.   [46] Boehner, ed., p. 259.

There is no way of defending Scotus's assumption that the object present to the intellect is a species. If the object is purely mental as a representation or image (*fictum*) it will be caused by an act of cognition and not by a previous species. And if an object exists extramentally, it has no need of species to be known by higher mind: it is already present to the intellect immediately and intuitively, just as it is immediately and intuitively present to the senses.[47]

The corollary of this theory is played out in Ockham's understanding of the role of the active or agent intellect. Having eliminated species, he now argues that the active intellect does not cause species by abstracting something from phantasms or by engendering something in them. The active intellect is simply the intellect's capacity to know and what it knows are individuals outside mind or their images or general concepts in mind. Abstraction then is nothing more than the intellect knowing intelligibly and immaterially and this is paralleled with the material nature of sense knowledge. Hence, whether one speaks of intellectual or sensory cognition, there is no conversion of images, even metaphorically, and in the case of intelligibles, these can be known not only actually but also by a habit. He refers to both the perfect intuition as well as the habit as providing perfect similitudes or similarities with the object known: 'cognitio est ita perfecta similitudo obiecti et perfectior quam species ... unde habitus ita perfecte est similitudo rei sicut species vel actus'.[48]

There are, then, for Ockham, no preexisting forms informing the intellect. Rather, the intellect directly and immediately has knowledge of individuals in themselves, and it has this cognition of the individual through the intellect's own acts and habits. He has, in effect, no distinction between the roles of active and possible intellects. The active intellect is nothing other than intellect in an act of knowing and the potential intellect is the intellect described under its passive capacity to receive. Neither illumination, nor purification of images is required. When we have images in the mind they are not the *principles* of cognition as they were for Scotus but rather the products of abstractive knowing dependent initially on intuitive, immediate knowledge.

Ockham does not jettison the entire thirteenth-century epistemological tradition which sought to examine the nature of the relationship between the sensory and the intellectual; instead, he argues for a parallel order in intellectual and sensory cognition. When one has a sensory experience, the thing perceived leads to its image in the senses. The image is impressed in the exterior sense organ as well as in the interior imagination and remains in each after the perception of the object has ceased. The

47 Boehner, ed., p. 268.   48 Boehner, ed., p. 274.

principle of vision or any other kind of sensation is the impressed visible quality of the object so that while the exterior object is the cause of the quality impressed, the object is only a partial cause of the act of sensing. Once impressed, the visible or sensible quality becomes a partial cause of an intuitive act of sensing the object's appearance. The interior and the exterior senses have, then, the same object, but what is impressed in the imagination, as had often been said previously, is not the same as the original object of the senses because the original object is no longer the actual thing sensed. Furthermore, when we speak of having an idea or concept of something, we *signify* the created individual thing known as well as connoting the *act* of knowing it. And when we use the term 'image' we signify the created individual thing imaged as well as connote the *act* of imagining. Hence, for Ockham, there are as many images in the interior senses as there are individuals imagined, caused partly by the physical object being perceived and partly by the act of imagination after the object is no longer present. Thus, when we have an immediate perception of an object in the exterior sense, we have this intuitively and this causes imagination in the interior senses. Imagining, as opposed to intuitive knowledge, says nothing of the existence here and now of the object to which it refers and hence imagination is abstractive knowledge.

This sequence that has led to imagination is paralleled in the intellect. The intellect has an intuitive experience of an individual, just as the sensory organ intuitively experiences the individual. This leads to a concurrent act of abstractive knowledge of the same individual, so that it is always the individual which is the first object of both what is sensed and what is imagined interiorly. The intellect alone can form propositions immediately it has intuitive knowledge of the same thing intuitively perceived by the senses, but it is the intellect alone which, as a superior power as Scotus would have it, is an act of assent or dissent over a proposition. Ockham believes that the close connection between the exterior and interior faculties makes the difference between them virtually imperceptible.[49] The concurrent schema then, is that of a sequence of immediate intuitive experience, both sensory and intellectual, which leads to complex knowledge (propositions) which then enables the formation of individual and contingent propositions as well as universal and necessary propositions. At the heart of this parallel between sensory and intellectual intuitive cognition is Ockham's interpretation of Aristotle's notion of the similarity of the intellect with its object, that is, its near identity. This means that the intellect does not create what it knows, as in a species, nor does it seize something (formally) from the object. Rather, something

[49] *Reportatio*, q. 18 P.

intuitively appears to the intellect as an object simply because the intellect knows immediately that object as such.[50]

Since only what is individual is real, for Ockham, concepts no less than images derived from the sensory are reduced to their individual meaning. In the *Ordinatio*, d. 27 q. 2 B Ockham appeals to our experience when he says that everyone accepts that there is something in the mind and engendered by the mind which is a likeness or an image of things. Augustine had described this. But it is not a species which is this likeness; rather the likeness is an act of knowing, or it can be a proposition, or more strictly, can be considered as a true word or term. The mental concept, he would in the end decide, was not to be distinguished from the very act of cognition.

How, then, does the mind form mental words or concepts? Once again we return to the relation between the word and memory. The memory, whether it is an intellectual habit derived from intellectual acts, as previously described, or as the sufficient principle of the word, is in both cases, of the soul's own nature.[51] Memory, he says, is the knowledge by which the soul knows itself before it thinks, and the reason it has this knowledge is because it already possesses knowledge in the memory from its previous acts of intuitive and abstractive knowing. Analysing, as did Scotus, the passage where Augustine says that the memory is to be seen as the parent of the word, Ockham says the memory is the mind's power whereby it has a quality or a habit left over from a previous act which enables the mind to produce a similar act independently of the exterior object which was the first partial cause of intuitive knowledge.[52] We can, he says, also understand the memory as the soul's power which strictly allows mind to refer to the past as past. This, once again, occurs as a result of a habit. When we consider the memory to be the capacity to know the past as past, we are not dealing with the intuitive and concurrent first abstractive act, but rather with the next moment in the sequence where propositions are recalled. This second sense of remembering, Aristotle's *reminiscentia*, following the established habit, where the past is referred to as past, is probably exclusively a capacity of the human intellect. Unlike the incomplex images of things past which can belong (as terms) to both the sensitive faculty and the intellect, there can only be a remembrance (reminiscence) of propositions in the intellect. We recall that only the intellect has the capacity to perceive and reflect on its own acts and propositions are its objects. It is exclusively the act of intellectual memory, then, when it distinguishes what cannot be really perceived outside the

[50] Leff, *William of Ockham*, p. 153.   [51] *Ordinatio*, d. 27 q. 2 R.
[52] *Reportatio*, IV, q. 12.

mind, in things, and thus when it knows the difference between the past and the present. But the senses are the prerequisites of the unfolding sequence ending in an intellectual memory act because from the senses we have individual experience which leads to the formation of imperfect intuitive knowledge, and the result of this imperfect intuition is an act of recollection as stated in a proposition. Thus, in order to have this intellectual act of memory we must first have had a sense experience, we must have seen or heard something in the senses and known it intuitively.

Therefore, the recall of a past act has itself two interdependent acts: there is the initial act of memory. There is also the act of reminiscing (recalling) by which the initial act of memory is apprehended as a partial object, whether or not the initial act of memory remains in the mind or not. An act of memory, therefore, has as its first object an *act* of remembrance which comes before the *act* of recalling the object actually remembered. This is Aristotle's distinction between memory and reminiscence through the spectacles of Averroes.[53] But Ockham, on the basis of his linking of intuitive and abstractive cognition in both sense and intellect, argues for a concurrent activity of first and second acts and this conjunction is what enables the past to be known as past. There is no room here for the Thomistic assertion that the past as past is only known to the senses, because Ockham believes that no less than the senses, the intellect can also experience individual particulars: 'Preterea intellectus potest cognoscere preteritum sub ratione preteriti ... preterea ratio adducta non concludit, quia non tantum sensus cognoscit singulare sed intellectus, immo sicut prius dictum fuit, singulare primo intelligitur.'[54] He then interprets Scotus to have agreed that since the intellect is a superior power and a superior power can do all that an inferior can do and more, then if the past can be known as past by the senses, the superior intellect can also know the past as past, precisely because recollection as an intellectual endeavour is always recollection of individuals, first known intuitively, just as the senses know the past object intuitively. Ockham has, of course, eliminated Scotus's assertion that what we intuitively know intellectually is only a formal uniqueness, a contracted nature, an incomplete universal, an individuating principle or *haecceitas* of an individual. Scotus, we recall, had

---

[53] Dico quod actus iste recordandi est respectu alicuius actus precedentis et preteriti inquantum precedens est ... Sed quia actus qui est obiectum actus recordandi sit precedens actus recordandi tempore, sive continuetur sive non, ita quod ad recordationem requiruntur duo actus. Primus est actus recordantis precedens qui est obiectum partiale actus recordativi. Secundus est actus recordativus quod apprehenditur primus actus, sive primus actus maneat sive non. (*Reportatio*, IV, q. 12 F).

[54] *Reportatio*, IV, q. 12 F; Leff, *William of Ockham*, p. 57.

said that we lack an intuition of individuality *pro statu isto*; our experience does not involve a cognitive grasp of the thing's individuality.

The intellectual act of memory then, is a proposition about past experience and as a work of the intellect, this proposition comes about through the act of imperfect intuitive knowledge as previously described. Memory is an end product of intuitive, abstractive and habitual knowledge which combine to produce imperfect intuitive cognition, as a proposition about what has been. What causes this intellectual propositional act of memory is in the soul itself, not through residual species but through habits. What is peculiar to mental habits and is not shared by species, is the awareness of the temporal. And because an act of intellectual recollection is complex (propositional) it must be deductively, rationally concluded that it is a result of like, complex habits that the mind is inclined to the recollective act.

Knowledge of the past is complex, that is, it is propositional. Since logic as a *scientia sermocinalis* deals with a system of signs that is used to make true or false statements about things signified by these signs, it is logic which effectively examines memory. Spoken and written language are conventionally instituted to signify what is naturally signified by acts of thought. Logic is the means by which we can study the properties of linguistic expressions to the extent that they refer to the logically essential functions of the soul's interior discourse. Recollection is therefore complex, having for its object a proposition that contains distinct terms which stand for things united by a verb. And the verb is always in the past tense. It is always in the form of the first person as well. Ockham gives the example: 'I have seen or heard or known this.' On the one hand, the complex knowledge of the past consists of a partial object which is an act of incomplex remembrance, intuitive and abstractive, in the intellect, senses or appetite, of some past act experienced by the person remembering. On the other hand, the total object is the proposition in which the predicate is joined to the subject by a verb in the past tense and first person. For Ockham, true memory and recollection must always have as their subject a person who remembers his own past experiences: 'De talibus [speaking, disputing, writing] non recordor nisi quatenus me recordor audivisse vel vidisse eum talia facere'.[55]

This means, of course, that other people's remembering cannot be proved true for oneself. Not all past knowledge, therefore, belongs to memory. Ockham distinguishes between a proposition recalling an experience and one which is merely a statement about a past occurrence based upon the memory but not itself remembered, because the latter

[55] *Reportatio*, IV, q. 12 H.

proposition is not from the experience of the person making the statement. His memory cannot be a partial cause of the remembrance.[56] Because memory in its strict sense can only record as a partial cause what has been directly and evidentially experienced in the past by a subject who recounts the proposition which recalls the past, the status of historical knowledge not personally experienced in the past by a person is less certain.

But since propositions as complexes which parallel recalled knowledge as complexes, are abstractive, they originate in intuitive knowledge but are themselves not intuited and only abstractive. Hence, such statements do not make claims about the certain existence of their contents. It is only because individuals who make statements about their past experiences are able to do so by assenting to propositions known by imperfect intuitive knowledge, which themselves presuppose perfect and evident intuitive knowledge, that we can personally have evident certainty of the past existence of an experience, as once having been experienced by us in a former here and now:

Illud complexum est evidenter notum ... Causatur ex notitia intuitiva terminorum sed intuitiva duplex est ... imperfecta. Tunc dico quod notitia evidens predicti complexi causatur ex notitia intuitiva imperfecta terminorum et hec presupponit naturaliter loquendo intuitivam perfectam.[57]

Memory is understood by Ockham in the same way as he understands all processes leading to evident knowledge. It is made accessible to intellect by a habit which is conserved in the mind. Because Ockham has not linked the content of memory with preexistent ideas or formal essences, he has confined it to an intellectual awareness based on experience. It has none of the characteristics of the Augustinian and Scotist higher source of separate awareness. It is always related to individual experiences of the rememberer. We can be as certain of these as we can be of anything.

Now whether or not Ockham's mental and sensual mechanics are plausible – and much discussion has arisen in the literature from his own times until the present of the inadequacies of some of his formulations[58] – and whether he rightly interpreted Scotus, it is important not to lose sight of the consequences of his understanding of memory. In his determination to argue that individuals alone exist and all our knowledge is based on intuitive cognition of individuals, Ockham concluded that the intellect

---

[56] For a modern discussion of this, see (with related issues) Richard Wollheim, 'Memory, experimental memory and personal identity', in *Perception and Identity, Essays Presented to A. J. Ayer*, ed., G. F. Macdonald (London, 1981), pp. 186–234.

[57] *Reportatio*, IV, q. 12; Leff, *William of Ockham*, p. 59.

[58] See Marilyn McCord Adams in *The Cambridge History of Later Medieval Philosophy*, pp. 420–2.

can and does know the past as past. And because he says we know the past through propositions about it, he effectively not only has a theory of mind but also a theory of historical writing, a theory of language that refers to the past. He has reversed the Augustinian belief in the independence of a nonsensory origin of intelligible knowledge as coming entirely from the intellect and he has reversed the Thomistic Aristotelianism whereby universal (confused) knowledge alone is the proper object of the intellect. This is undoubtedly the turning point for the emergence of a putatively Renaissance confidence in the uniqueness of the past as past, and it is based on an analysis of the intellect's capacity to know the individual past just as do the senses. What it does not affirm is the certainty of the existents referred to in anyone else's recollection of the past, if that past was not experienced by the subject himself. But in affirming that individual personality was indeed a consequence of the knowledge of one's past in its particularity, Ockham altered the epistemological course of western thinking on the nature of the active, thinking and experiencing subject.

In his final abandonment of Augustinian theories of mind, when he ultimately decided in favour of an *intellectio* theory of concepts against a *fictum* theory, Ockham put a seal on the autonomy of mind's *activities* and *habits* based on an unprovable but evident intuitive knowledge of all the individuals one has experienced. What appears at first sight to be a picture of a psychologically alienated individual wrapped up in his own experience of past and present, is modified by Ockham's belief in natural signs in the mind and the capacity of conventional language to signify these natural signs. As we said previously, however, he is not claiming that the universal knowledge we have necessarily mirrors an inner constitution of nature. We only have confidence in what we can and have experienced and from here we can only assume, as we must, a hypothetical necessity that science, which deals in universals, actually reflects the causes of our ideas in the physical world of particulars. *Pro statu isto* we live in a probable world of contingency beyond our immediate intuitive knowledge of things and concepts. Experience of particulars on the one hand, and syllogistic scientific demonstration on the other, give us the same kinds of conclusions based on the primacy of the intuitions of singulars and our consequent generalisations to all other cases of the same kind. Our theories about the world can only be about mental intentions that are thought to be common to contingent and corruptible things in the world, where mental intentions supposit for such things in mental and spoken propositions. We only know the individual substances of things by means of propositions that contain terms that substitute for them. And since knowledge acquired by scientific syllogistic demonstration provides the same kind of knowledge, in terms of conclusions, as experiential knowledge, we are as certain about our present as we are about our past. We rely on probable premises and to some extent fallible evidence, to make our way in the world of contingencies. This is simply how it is and has always been for all men barring an intervention by God into the order of things. This is not a radical scepticism as it would become for some of his followers. It is, rather, a statement about the probability of our knowledge now and of the past in obtaining the truth of how things are and were. One can, after all, construct laws of probability which provide a high degree of certitude. Nor is it a denial of the virtues of exemplary history. For in so far as memory, strictly speaking, can only be truthfully recalled as a past experience by a subject who experienced the world in the past, written history by others is not strictly speaking one's memory of the past at all.[59] *But* it is *someone's* true memory.

It is here that we see the consequences of Ockham's cognition theory, and the central role played by memory in it, applied by him to matters historical and political during his later polemical career. In what follows, we shall be able to observe the force of his so-called razor which established: 'Nihil debet poni sine ratione assignata nisi sit *per se notum* vel *per experientiam scitum* vel *per auctoritatem scripturae probatum*' (emphasis added).

Ockham spent many of his post-theological, political years (1328 onwards) engaged in an interpretation of papal and secular powers as exercised in the past and known from textual descriptions: but insofar as these were not experienced by present individual subjects themselves, such interpretations occupied another place in his hierarchy of truths that were demonstrable. Like Abelard, Ockham would point out, appealing to the Lombard's *Sentences* that *both* Scripture and the Fathers were in complete agreement so far as their meaningful content was concerned. They only used different terminology. Since one cannot have intuitive knowledge oneself of how past kings and past popes interpreted Scripture, canons of church councils or positive law, one was engaged in a different, exegetical enterprise based on the probability of language's capacity to signify adequately natural mental signs in *their* minds. The degrees of hypothetical certainty about these truths was less intense than that which derived from one's own experiences. It could, of course, be held on faith which itself, Ockham argued, could be an intuited and individual, intellectual experience. However, the probable certainty of propositions that

---

[59] This kind of knowledge of the past is abstractive and therefore makes no claims as to the existence of its subject matter!

are logically coherent and consistent, and formed as a necessary consequence of evident knowledge based on an intuition of terms which supposit for real individual things, establishes the validity of linguistic conventions which signify natural signs in the mind. Something real and true must have happened to individual, historical men in the past, and a textual expression of those experiences, understood abstractively and therefore, independent of time, place and claims to existence of its referents, must be based initially on *someone's* past intuitive cognition of the reality and existence of his experience. The exegete's task, was, therefore, to determine the true meaning behind the different terminology of past authors, a true meaning of individual past experiences. It is precisely here, in Ockham's exploration of the role of supposition logic, that we can see the beginning of a long enduring nominalist tradition to elevate the *distinction* between subject matter and expression, between rhetorical formulation and its object, already adumbrated in Abelard's writings, into a principle of textual interpretation.[60] Human minds classify things in the world into species and genera; such universals are not in the world to be classified. Singular things in the world do not *cause*, through phantasms, species, etc. universal thoughts. Rather, in apprehending an individual thing, the intellect actively produces a cognition which supposits for the thing. Thoughts of things are real acts of thinking to which correspond words in spoken or written language. The thought signifies naturally as the spoken word signifies conventionally, the *same* thing. This distinction between the world and how we speak of it, when raised to a principle of textual exegesis, would vastly influence a major strand in humanist, exegetical methodology.

Ockham's theory of individual cognition based on experience also played a role in his understanding of current political organisations, be they church or state, as when he was prepared to argue that collective opinion could only be a summation of individuals consenting to present, contingent circumstances on the basis of their own experience and thoughts. As a consequence, he was prepared to argue for a *kind* of conciliar decision-making but only where the whole was *nothing more* than the decisions of its individual parts. Hence, his premises seem fundamentally incompatible with other contemporary theories of representation which focused on a legally created collective. For Ockham, a corporation is not a legally created fictitious *persona* but a unified collection of real, individual persons. Just as a *persona ficta* cannot perform real acts, so it

---

[60] '... in propter diversitatem locutiones, hoc est, propter diversum modem accipiendi vocabula vel vocabulum' (Ockham, *Tractatus contra Benedictum*, chapter 3 in *Opera Politica*, ed. H. S. Offler (Manchester, 1956), III, pp. 233–4).

cannot possess real rights under law. Only real and autonomous, rational individuals are capable of a joint renouncing or holding of legal rights when unified in a corporation or religious order: 'Nec ordo est persona imaginaria et repraesentata, sed est verae personae et reales, quia est corpus Christi misticum, quod est verae personae ... et per consequens fideles sunt una ecclesia et ita ecclesia est verae personae et non est persona imaginaria et repraesentata'.[61] Ockham's appeal, then, was not to a formal entity but to a universal church *in time*, made up of individual, experiencing men who comprised the historical and unbroken witness of the faithful-prelates, laymen and women, to certain doctrines. Such witness depended on the contingent, temporal and hence, historical continuity of experience, language, meaning, which was far superior to any momentary General Council's authority.

As a supporter of his Franciscan Order's interpretation of its relation to property and *dominium*, Ockham would want to understand the general proposition 'all Franciscans wear grey' as equivalent to 'this Franciscan wears grey and that Franciscan wears grey and the other Franciscan wears grey ... '.[62] Thus, the reality of the Order as a conceptual generality had not been done away with, but had been shown to be identified with the reality of its individual members. Ockham argued, as did an increasing number of other thinkers of his generation, for the communal and political life made up of interactions among concrete individuals. He was talking in terms of the ecclesiastical tradition that was clarified in the heated dispute between Boniface VIII and Philip the Fair and thereafter, which spoke of corporate wholes as the very individuals comprising them. In asserting that the individual is responsible for alienation of property, the exercise of rights, freedoms, resistance to breakers of trust, be they pope or king, Ockham would express this in the form of the general proposition: 'The Church must resist heresy' and this is equivalent to: 'this individual Christian must resist and that Christian must resist and the other Christian must resist ... '.[63] But the individualism expressed in his political

---

[61] *Ibid.*, p. 191. On Ockham *against* the infallibility of a general council, *Dialogus*, I, book 5, ch. xxv–xxvi, in Melchior Goldast, *Monarchia Sancti Romani Imperii* (Frankfurt, 1614), II, especially pp. 494–5, where he argues: 'Illae personae quae, in diversis locis existentes possunt contra fidem errare, etiam si ad eundem locum conveniunt, poterunt contra fidem errare. Quia concursus ad eundem locum non reddit aliquos inobliquabiles a fide: quia sicut locus non sanctificat homines, ita et locus nullos confirmat in fide. Sed omnes ad generale concilium convenientes, antequam convenirent, poterant contra fidem errare.'

[62] Arthur McGrade, 'Ockham and the birth of individual rights', in Brian Tierney and Peter Linehan, eds., *Authority and Power, Studies ... presented to Walter Ullmann* (Cambridge, 1980), pp. 149–166; p. 157.

[63] *Ibid.*, p. 159.

works was less concerned to *give* individuals powers than to demonstrate *that* individuals have powers of various kinds before anyone or any political structure gives such powers to them. Individuals come first.[64] Thereafter, Ockham's political theory is not very radical concerning the exercise of rights. What *was* radical was his theory of the cognition of individuals which influenced his analysis of church governance. In his *Opus nonaginta dierum*, cap. 123, he denied that the pope or an ecumenical council could legislate in matters of faith. While the pope had a spiritual *potestas* he had no jurisdiction and therefore had no public and universal right to resolve the pluralities of beliefs, concerning for instance, the eucharist or the Virgin Mary's assumption, beyond that of the individual common believer.[65] But how could this be the task of the individual common believer?[66]

For Ockham, we must recall, that our general concepts are not merely mental constructs but are acts of each individual's mind which are dependent on each individual having an intuitive cognition of singulars based on his own natural experience and the limits upon knowledge which such natural experience imposes. Thus, all our knowledge must be reducible to knowledge of existence and verification which is based on our experiences rather than on rational demonstration. This knowledge is had through the analysis of the logical and grammatical forms of terms and their roles in propositions, mental or linguistic. When we analyse a scriptural text, therefore, we are analysing the linguistic use of terms which supposit for extramental things or for the thoughts of their author, expressed through conventional signs.

Since it is only by intuitive cognition of our own acts that we are aware of ourselves as intelligent beings, it is therefore, only through intuitive cognition that we are aware of ourselves as voluntary agents, free to choose between alternatives. We possess as individuals a *libertas* and we know of it only by experience. Ockham defined this individual liberty as 'that power whereby I can do diverse things indifferently and contingently such that I can cause or not cause the same effect, when all conditions other than this power are the same.'[67] Just as we cannot prove that we experience

[64] Janet Coleman, '*Dominium* in thirteenth and fourteenth-century political thought and its seventeenth-century heirs: John of Paris and Locke', *Political Studies*, 33 (1985), pp. 73–100.
[65] Also see Ockham's *De Corpore Christi* (= *De Quantitate*), cap. 5, ed. T. B. Birch (Burlington, Indiana, 1930), pp. 182–4 and cap. 36, p. 444.
[66] The following is based on Janet Coleman, 'The relation between Ockham's intuitive knowledge and his political science', *Théologie et Droit dans la Science Politique de l'Etat Moderne*, Table Ronde du CNRS (Rome, 1987).
[67] *Quod.*, I, q. 16, p. 87:
Utrum possit probari sufficienter quod voluntas libere causet actus suos effective ... In

individuals intuitively by demonstrative reason – we can only experience this as a fact, so too we cannot prove the will is free by demonstrative reason 'because every reason proving this assumes something equally unknown as its conclusion, or less known'. A man simply experiences the fact that however much his reason dictates some action, his will can will or not will this act. Hence human liberty, which we know from our intuitive knowledge of existents, we know evidently as a true term in a proposition, generalised through an extension by induction to all other individuals of the same nature. Liberty is the basis of our human dignity and the font of moral goodness and personal responsibility, more than is the power of reasoning, which only occurs after the simple intuitive apprehension of the term and therefore, what it signifies, even though reasoning is involved in willing or not willing. Our liberty is the basis of our human dignity because man is a free agent and therefore, in being responsible for his acts he can be judged worthy or not.[68]

Ockham's definition of liberty occurs in his Quodlibet, I, q. 16. But when he came to analyse papal power, he invoked a law of liberty which merely extended the operations of man's liberty in the specific and contingent realm of the application of his natural rights given man by God. In short, he argued that in Christ's institution of the Church, Peter was not given a plenitude of power but rather a limited and defined sphere of authority and power so that the pope cannot deprive any individual of his liberty. God gave men liberty and we know this from our experience, even before the coming of Christ and the establishment of his Church, so that man's liberty is an inalienable individual right possessed also by those nonChristians before Christ's coming.[69]

ista quaestione primo, exponam quid voco libertatem. a.1: Circa primum sciendum quod voco libertatem potestatem qua possum indifferenter et contingenter diversa ponere, ita existente alibi extra illam potentiam ... Utrum possit probari sufficienter quod voluntas est libera ... Circa primum dico quod non potest probari per aliquam rationem, quia omnia ratio hoc probans accipiet aeque ignotum cum conclusione vel ignotius. Potest tamen evidenter cognosci per experientiam per hoc quod homo experitur quod quantum-cumque ratio dictet aliquid, potest tamen voluntas hoc velle vel non velle vel nolle. (p. 88).

[68] *Quod.*, III, q. 19, pp. 275–6: 'Utrum aliquis homo possit mereri vel demereri ... dico quod sic ... tum quia homo est agens liberum et omne tale potest mereri et demereri'.

[69] *De Imperatorum et pontificum potestate*, ed. C. K. Brampton (Oxford, 1927):
Rursum 'in temporalibus potestatis plenitudo' potestatem et dominationem regum gentium comprehendit. Potestam ... Christi beato Petro ceterisque apostolis interdixit ut patet Lucae 22, Marci 10 et Matthaei 20 [p. 5]. Sed quaeret aliquis quae sunt iura et libertates aliorum quae a potestate apostolici principatus regulariter eximuntur. Hic responditur, quod ad illa iura et libertatis spectant omnia iura et libertates infidelium quibus ante incarnationem Christi ... [pp. 20–1]. Ex quo concluditur quod ad iura et libertates specialiter laicorum pertinent omnia illa quae ad dispositionem temporalium et negotiorum saecularium requiruntur ... [pp. 21–2] ... Ut autem generaliter explicitur, quae spectant ad iura et libertates aliorum laicorum et clericorum religiosorum et

Now, an individual's liberty gives him the capacity to dispose of temporal things and to operate amongst contingencies. All that the pope may do is teach God's word, maintain divine worship and ritual and provide such things that are *necessary* for Christians in their quest for eternal life.[70] The pope has no power to command, coerce or requisition things that are not necessary to this end, otherwise the liberty of the Gospel law would be a law of slavery.

How do we know that Christ's institution of the Church did not give Peter a plenitude of power over the contingencies of the world? Simply by analysing the logic of scriptural language! Scripture is a set of propositions whose coherence depends on any reader at any time analysing the meaning of its propositions in the light of his individual experience based on his intuitive knowledge of terms. Thus, if it can be found in Scripture that the pope was to provide for those things necessary for the Christian quest for eternal salvation, the determination of what is necessary as opposed to what is contingent, must be judged neither by popes nor civil rulers, but through an interpretation of the Gospel text by clergy, laymen and women, whether poor, rich, subjects or rulers![71] The Christian community is made up of private experiencing individuals who constitute the true Church.

In the *Breviloquium de potestate papae*,[72] Ockham says that a master in theology had claimed that if the pope were to contradict the Gospel one was bound to believe him rather than the Gospel itself. Ockham disagreed. Were papal power thus unlimited, it would stand opposed to the liberty of the Gospel law: the *lex evangelica* is a *lex libertatis*. It is not possible for the pope or anyone else to deprive a person of his rights and liberties as a created, rational individual, where those rights and liberties flow from God, nature or another man. *This Ockham believes can be demonstrated by his objective method of interpreting texts which are made up of propositions, themselves dependent for their meaning on individual readers' intuitive cognition of terms which comprise propositions.* And such intuitive cognition of terms of a proposition depends on men having individual experiences of a world of contingency, comprised of individuals. Our

saecularium, puto quod huiusmodi sunt omnia illa quae nec bonis moribus, nec his quae in novo testamento docentur inveniuntur adversa. (p. 22).

[70] *Ibid.*, c.x, para. 3 and 4. p. 23.

[71] *Ibid.*, p. 27:
Et si aliud dubitetur quanta sit, ita ut interpretatio sit necessario, huismodi interpretatio non spectat ad papam; sed vel spectat ad illum qui talem potestatem dedit papae, et ad successorem eius; vel iuxta prudentiam et concilium sapientis, sincerum zelum habentis, seu fuerit subditis seu praelatus. [p. 25] ... iuxta discretionem et consilium sapientissime sine omni personarum acceptionem zelantium, si possunt haberi, seu pauperes sint seu divites, seu subiecti seu prelati.

[72] Ed., Baudry (Paris, 1937), p. 42.

knowledge of internal states and of the external world can only be acquired in the natural order of things by our intuitive grasp of the facts of existence and presence. The human certitude regarding the existence of objects is based on the indemonstrable fact of intuitive cognition in virtue of which we then affirm or deny contingent propositions and we become aware of our mental acts. Hence, the only way we can possibly have any certitude about the meaning of a scriptural text is through evident know-ledge based on intuitive cognition of individual terms which supposit for things or thoughts and this is what he means by 'una auctoritas scripturae sacra *sane intelligenda*.'[73] Where the papacy has gone wrong in interpreting Scripture is precisely in transposing the terms of the ancients and extend-ing them illicitly. The terms of the ancients, 'quod posuit Christus, quando constituit beatum Petrum principem apostolorum et cunctorum fidelium, ante omnia manifestare studebo,'[74] he says. That certain limits were placed on Peter's powers can be studied by examining authoritative scriptural propositions and proved by reason.[75] 'Hoc etiam necessarium est papae "ne transgrediatur *terminos* antiquos, quos posuerunt patres sui"' (emphasis added).[76]

It is therefore important that the power of the papacy be disputed publicly and that authentic Scripture be made public 'et rationes de ea invenerint'.[77]

Ockham goes further to show that what the Roman Church calls its legislated customs cannot be recognised unless they are reasonable, and they are not reasonable if they are against divine law, or good mores, if they are prejudicial to the common welfare or to any person's liberty.[78] It

---

[73] *Prologue, De imperatorum et pontificum potestate*: 'verumtamen hoc certum habeant universi, quod in his quae fidei sunt et scientiae plus me monebit una ratio evidens vel una auctoritas scripturae sacra sane intelligenda, quam assertio totius universitatis mortalium propter quos intellectum omnino debeo in eorum obsequium captivare' (pp. 3–4).

[74] *Ibid.*, p. 4.

[75] *Ibid.*:
Tenendum est igitur in primis, quod Christus beatum Petrum constituens caput et principem universorum fidelium non dedit ei talem, temporalibus et spiritualibus plenitu-dinem potestatis, ut omnia de iure posset regulariter, quae neque legi divinae neque legi naturae refragant; sed potestati quae certos fines, quos non deberet transgredi, assignavit. Quod enim ei temporalibus talem non dedit plenitudinem potestatis auctoritate et ratione probatur.

[76] Citing Proverbs xxii, 28; *Prologue, De imperatorum et pontificum potestate*, p. 30.

[77] *Ibid.*, p. 30: And this is possible because 'omni propositio componitur ex nomine et verbo secundum sanctos et philosophos; sed nomen et verbum non sunt res extra animam sed signa earum' (*Quod*, III, q. 12, 4 p. 248).

[78] *Ibid.*, p. 34 '... potest autem ostendi quod consuetudo non est rationabilis si esset contra ius divinum, vel contra bonos mores, si est periculosa, si est scandalosa, si est praeiudicia-lis bono communi vel etiam alicui personae, cui non possunt licite tolli iura et libertates suae, et aliis modis'.

533

is insufficient for the Roman church to try to legitimate its customs through prescription. The papacy cannot simply say that elected kings and emperors are its subjects because this is not according to divine law and divine law may be known: 'ut liquet omnibus intelligentibus scripturas sacras.' Nor is the papal claim to superiority over kings and emperors *ex iure gentium quod praecessit imperium*, nor *ex iure civili*.[79] 'Nec est ex iure canonico.' And this presumed papal power is not *ex consuetudine*, because custom does not have the force of law unless it is rational. And it is especially not rational if it destroys individual liberty against the will of individuals who have such liberty from God, nature or other men.[80] Therefore, this assertion of papal power must be opened up to the disputes of literate men who can sanely interpret the propositions of Scripture.[81] And as Ockham was to reaffirm in his *Epistola ad Fratres Minores*, the holy rules of Scripture describe men's customs which may be daily verified *per experientiam*!

'Nam sanctarum regulas scripturarum mores hominum describentes, dum quotidie per experientiam verificari conspicio, magis intelligo.'[82]

Ockham insists on the authority of scriptural propositions prior to any decisions or interpretations made by means of the papal magisterial power of action. And therefore, he treats various writings of Pope John XXII as exercises in propositional logic, to show that the pope's arguments are not consonant with Scripture. Scripture as divine writ must be the final court of appeal, open to interpretation as to its true meaning by anyone literate. And even illiterates' views of the faith are to be taken into account because as living individuals they have evident knowledge. Furthermore, they can have revealed to them by God those truths hidden from wiser and more educated men.[83] But this would be an intervention into the natural and ordained order of things by God. In the ordinary course of things one must judge against good custom, natural reasoning and the certainty of experience. In treating John XXII's pronouncements in *Ad conditorem*,

---

[79] *Ibid.*, p. 35.
[80] *Ibid.*, '... nec ex consuetudine est talis subiecto, quia consuetudo non habet vim legis nisi sit rationabilis praesertim quae iuri vel libertati, quae tolli non debet ab invito, praeiudicare dinoscitur'.
[81] *Ibid.*, c. xxvi, 3: '... quamobrem omnes literati circa ipsa indagandam his periculosis temporibus occupari deberent'.
[82] *Opera Politica*, III, p. 17.
[83] *Dialogus*, I, 5 c. xxv, in M. Goldast, *Monarchi Sancti Romani Imperii*, vol. 2: Deus saepe revelat parvulis quae a sapientibus et prudentibus absconditur. Licet ergo in generali concilio errarent, et solum parvuli et illiterati ad concilium minime convenirent, non esset adhuc deperandum quin Deus veritatem catholicam parvulis revelaret vel eisdem veritatem notam defendere inspiraret.
This, however, should be seen as divine intervention in the natural order and not something that could be generally supposed from the natural order of things.

Cum inter nonnullos and *Quia quorundam*, Ockham says he will study and read the texts diligently. The result is that he finds 'quamplura haeretica-lia, stulta, ridiculosa, fantastica, insana et diffamatoria, fidei orthodoxae, bonis moribus, rationi naturali, experientia certae et caritati fraternae contraria pariter et adversa patenter (inveni).'[84] It is especially important that he judges against *bonis moribus, rationi naturali* and *experientiae certae*. He concludes that questions of faith are to be decided 'non solum ad generale concilium aut prelatos vel etiam clericos, verum etiam ad laicos et ad omnes omnino pertinent christianos', citing the *Decretum*, where the following famous statement is glossed: 'quod omnes tangit ab omnibus tractari debet'.[85] And he says: 'Ex quibus colligitur evidenter quod questio fidei etiam ad mulieres spectat catholicae et fideles'.[86] Clearly, the reason that even women may judge of religious matters touching them is that they, like all individuals, experience their world and know it through intuitive cognition from which they then generalise to all similar cases.

This does not mean that we can demonstrate the articles of faith. We cannot naturally experience that 'God is three and one'.[87] But in so far as we can define morality in its large sense as 'human acts subject absolutely to the will',[88] then the *scientia moralis*, when considered as a nonpositive science, is that which directs human acts without any superior precepts. The precepts known by all men are *pe se nota vel nota per experientiam*, and this is how any man can determine what is honest. That moral science called positive or the *scientia iuristarum* is not a demonstrative science because juristic rules are founded on human positive laws which are not propositions that are evidently known. However, the *disciplina moralis non positiva* IS a *scientia demonstrativa* because we deduce conclusions syllogis-tically from principles that are either self-evident or evident through experience.[89] And it is precisely nonpositive morality which is known most certainly by any and every human experiencer of the world!

Scripture, Ockham said, merely described the way men live in the world of contingencies, and one's natural, intuitively known, because experi-

---

[84] *Epistola ad fratres minores, Opera Politica*, III, p. 6.   [85] *Decretum*, C. 4 d. 96 'Ubinam'.
[86] *Opera Politica*, III, p. 10.   [87] *Quod.*, II, pp. 117–18 and pp. 120–22.
[88] '... quod "morale" accipitur large pro actibus humanis qui subiacent voluntati absolute' (*Quod.*, II, q. 14, p. 176): 'Utrum de moralibus possit esse scientia demonstrativa'.
[89] *Ibid.*,
     ... scientia non positiva est illa quae sine omni praecepto superioris dirigit actus humanos; sicut principia per se nota vel nota per experientiam sic dirigunt, sicut quod omne honestum est faciendum ... disciplina moralis non positiva est scientia demonstra-tiva, (where conclusions are deduced syllogistically from principles that are either per se nota vel per experientiam scitis) [p. 178]. ... Et ultra dico quod ista scientia est certior multis aliis, pro quanto quilibet potest habere maiorem experientiam de actibus suis quam de aliis. Ex quo patet quod ista scientia est multum subtilis, utilis et evidens.

enced, liberty could only be confirmed by rational arguments open to anyone who was sane enough to draw conclusions from his experience of individuals in his or her daily life. In this way, they would come up with universal knowledge or science, general theories based on the intuitive cognition of terms which supposited for extramental things or thoughts. But they would not be able to come up with supernatural knowledge unless God intervened in the natural order, which of course, He could do. Otherwise, the logic of thought and of written and spoken language is the only certain tool of analysis we have to help us ascertain what is true, contingent and necessary. Since the proposition, mental, written or spoken, itself was the object of knowledge, every individual experiencer of the world could and should analyse it, judging it true or false by the rules of logical thinking, speaking and writing.

This is not an argument in favour of a plurality of subjective and private interpretations of orthodoxy and Scripture. Ockham believes there is a single orthodoxy and a single, true reading of the propositions of Scripture. But the pope, the clerical hierarchy and general councils, do not have a privileged entrée into its meaning. All experiencers of the world who are rational have this entrée as a capacity of interpreting mind. This is, of course, an explosive doctrine and the more conservative forces throughout the Church knew precisely *how* explosive Ockham's theological and philosophical doctrine could become. It is not surprising that they sought to censure his logical, philosophical and theological views when such views became prevalent in university milieux,[90] among less cautious followers. This would take some time. And it came too late.

---

[90] There is much evidence of John XXII's and especially Benedict XII's opposition to Ockham. Ockham's views were investigated at Avignon but are not known to have been condemned, and Benedict's opposition was largely to Ockham's views on apostolic poverty to support those of his Franciscan Order. In 1339 the Paris Arts Faculty reaffirmed its rights to determine the list of books to be lectured on and specifically forbade the use of Ockham's writings. And they prohibited anyone in the faculty from lecturing or listening to lectures on Ockham, either in public or private gatherings, and from holding disputations or even referring to his opinions. *Chartularium Universitatis Parisiensis*, II, p. 485, n. 1023. The *doctrina Guillermi dicti Okam* refers to his logic and natural philosophy and Ockham was not yet a recognised authority to be lectured on in the Arts faculty. It seems fairly clear that the censorship of the substance, the *doctrina*, when it came somewhat later, was aimed rather at Ockham's followers, the *secta Occanica*. The real criticism comes with the Augustinian Gregory of Rimini who maintained a firm opposition to Ockham's epistemology, especially on intuitive cognition and to Ockham's elimination of species, although Gregory accepted his natural philosophy. See W. J. Courtenay, 'The role of English thought in the transformation of university education in the late middle ages', in *Rebirth, Reform and Resilience: Universites in Transition 1300–1700*, ed., J. A. Kittleson (Columbus, Ohio, 1981). Compare Rimini, *Lectura super primum et secundum Sententiarum*, ed. Damasus Trapp, (Berlin, 1978–), II, *Sent.*, d. 7, q. 3 with Ockham *Reportatio*, II, qq. 14–15 as ed. Boehner, *Traditio*, I (1943), pp. 223–75. Courte-

Ockham had described the kinds of powers men have as individuals prior to government in the realm of power over discrete things, and only as a consequence of man's real, individual status did Ockham then analyse the role of government in preserving or augmenting such power. In discussions of property, *dominium* was taken to be a logical conclusion to which men came as a consequence of human experience. Only a few modifications to this approach would lead to the blossoming forth of the classic individual rights theories so prevalent in the seventeenth century. I have discussed this elsewhere.[91] What needs emphasis here is that his cognition theory was extended by Ockham himself to the more explosive themes of scriptural interpretation and thence to the ordering of polities, ecclesiastical and secular. More specifically, by arguing that we sense and know individuals, that experience is certain, that we do remember past experiences and that we can interpret past texts which express the sensible and intellectual experiences of past others, Ockham was asserting a confidence in the human capacity to comprehend more than the formal coherence of present and past. With a little effort exerted towards analysing mental and spoken propositions, we can understand the present no less than the past in all their individuality and uniqueness. This is what it means to be a responsible, moral individual, to have individual experiences, understand them and recall them through mental habits established by one's active intellectual response to experience. By knowing one's past, one understands one's present and one makes one's future. We know individuals in themselves through our intellect's own acts and habits. All men possess memory, that power of the soul which allows our minds to refer to the past as past. We remember propositions in our minds and the necessary precursors of these propositions are the sensings of individual experiences of which we are intellectually aware. We can be as certain of the individual experiences we remember as we can be of anything. We remember our own pasts. We do not remember the events of the past signified in Scripture. But the authors of the Gospel had their experiences and signified them in language. We can know their meaning by rationally examining their language because what they described also refers to experiences that men may daily have in the present. Without such experiences, not least of our moral liberty, we cannot understand to what the texts of the past refer.

nay argues that Rimini was the first Parisian theologian to know Ockham's *theology*. Ockham's *Summa logicae* was widely available by c. 1345.

[91] See above, note 64.

Chapter 23

THE LEGACY OF THE *VIA ANTIQUA* AND THE *VIA MODERNA* IN THE RENAISSANCE AND BEYOND

The consideration in detail of how the drawbacks of imagery are surmounted demands a special study which would take us beyond the limits of our present discussion. But if we keep within the indications of the experiments, it would seem as if there must be some kind of supplementary relation between word and image formation ... There is a very general agreement that thinking and the use of language are closely connected, though nobody is justified in reducing the one to the other. In one important respect, words and sensorial images are alike; both act as signs indicating something else which need not be perceptually present at the moment. Thus they are both instruments of the general function of dealing with situations or objects at a distance. Words have the obvious additional advantage of being social, and they constitute the most direct manner of communicating meaning. The image, to be communicated, has itself to be expressed in words, and we have seen that this can often be done only in a most halting and inadequate manner. Words differ from images in another even more important respect: they can indicate the qualitative and relational features of a situation in their general aspect just as directly as, and perhaps even more satisfactorily than, they can describe its peculiar individuality. This is, in fact, what gives language its intimate relation to thought processes. For thinking, in the proper psychological sense, is never the mere reinstatement of some suitable past situation produced by a crossing of interests, but is the utilisation of the past in the solution of difficulties set by the present. Consequently, it involves that amount of formulation which shows, at least in some degree, what is the nature of the relation between the instances used in the solution and the circumstances that set the problem ... nobody ever thinks who, being challenged, merely sets up an image from a specific and more or less relevant situation, and then finds for himself a solution, without in any way formulating the relational principle involved. For carrying out this formulation, for utilising the general qualitative and relational features of the situation to which reference is more or less openly made, words appear to be the only adequate instruments so far discovered or invented by man. Used in this way, they succeed just where we have seen that images tend most conspicuously to break down: they can name the general as well as describe the particular, and since they deal in formulated connexions they more openly bear their logic with them.

Thinking, if I am right, is biologically subsequent to the image-forming process.

538

It is possible only when a way has been found of breaking up the 'massed' influence of past stimuli and situations, only when a device has already been discovered for conquering the sequential tyranny of past reactions. But though it is a later and a higher development, it does not supersede the method of images. Contrasted with imagining it loses something of vivacity, of vividness, of variety. Its prevailing instruments are words, and, not only because these are social, but also because in use they are necessarily strung out in sequence, they drop into habit reactions even more readily than images do. Their conventions are social, the same for all, and far less a matter of idiosyncrasy. In proportion as we lose touch with the image method we run greater and greater risk of being caught up in generalities that may have little to do with actual concrete experiences. If we fail to maintain the methods of thinking, we run the risk of becoming tied to individual instances and of being made sport of by the accidental circumstances belonging to these ... The image method remains the method of brilliant discovery, whereby realms organised by interests usually kept apart are brought together; the thought-word method remains the way of rationalisation and inference, whereby this connection of the hitherto unconnected is made clear and possible for all, and the results which follow are not merely exhibited, but demonstrated.

> F. C. Bartlett, *Remembering, A Study in Experimental and Social Psychology* (Cambridge, 1932), pp. 224–6.

'It's hard to imagine today, but when the cinema was in its infancy, it was such a new and unusual narrative form that most spectators had difficulty understanding what was happening. Now we're so used to film language ... flashbacks, etc., that our comprehension is automatic; but in the early years, the public had a hard time deciphering this new pictorial grammar. They needed an *explicador* to guide them from scene to scene. I'll never forget, for example, everyone's terror when we saw our first zoom. There on the screen was a head coming closer and closer, growing larger and larger. We simply couldn't understand that the camera was moving nearer to the head ... All we saw was a head coming towards us, swelling hideously out of all proportion ... like St. Thomas the Apostle, we believed in the reality of what we saw'.

> Luis Buñuel, *My Last Breath*, trans. Abigail Israel (London, 1984), pp. 32–3.

During the fourteenth and fifteenth centuries the problem of human cognition came to interest philosophers and theologians much more than did questions on the nature of the soul and its faculties, from which, of course, issues of human cognition initially derived. And during the fourteenth century, Aristotle's *De Anima* was, in arts faculty programmes, a text commented on by all *magistri*. As we saw, in Scotus and Ockham, so too in those after them, there was less of an interest in the nature of the distinctions between possible and agent intellects than in their functional activities. Philosophers and theologians focused on intuitive and abstractive cognition.

During the second half of the fourteenth century, there was a return to an earlier set of interpretations of Aristotle mixed with a revival of neo-Platonism and a neo-Augustinianism, but with hindsight, it seems true to say that nothing of lasting philosophical importance was achieved here. It was, rather, Scotus and Ockham who effectively set the boundaries for all substantive debate on cognition theories and their consequences for man's capacity to remember and use the past, during the next centuries. This means that in their attitudes to the past, in their understanding of how humans come to know, remember and then use what they know and remember, there was a penetrating extension of the substance of medieval discussions well into what we have learned to call the Renaissance, and this despite certain Renaissance thinkers abjuring the 'barbarity' of scholastic modes of discourse, distinctions and divisions. Renaissance philosophers and scientists continued to follow the medieval tradition of treating the study of the soul as part of natural philosophy as it was discussed in Aristotle's *De Anima* and the *Parva Naturalia*. They issued new translations from the Greek originals and studied these along with ancient Greek commentaries and paraphrases, some of which tried to reconcile Aristotle with neo-Platonism or Christianity. The story has been retold recently by Katherine Park and Eckhard Kessler in the *Cambridge History of Renaissance Philosophy*.[1]

Although the Renaissance emphasis on the *studia humanitatis* did not include the study of logic or the quadrivium as in the earlier medieval liberal arts course, Kristeller[2] has reminded us that 'humanism' did not represent the sum total of Renaissance thought and learning. Philosophy, theology, jurisprudence, medicine and the philosophical disciplines other than ethics, like logic, natural philosophy and metaphysics continued to be studied at late medieval and Renaissance universities. And Renaissance humanists were not as powerful in universities as they were in secondary schools which they came to dominate. Furthermore, what is often defined as the humanist educational system based on oratorical techniques, grammatical and philological analysis of terms and propositions, grew out of the medieval arts course concern with literary exegesis and the human capacity to attain knowledge of the truth from texts. There are, then, much greater difficulties in determining both the beginnings and the newness of the Renaissance than our present division of historical periods in university curricula would lead us to expect.

In what follows, I have tried to sketch an outline of continuities rather than point to the discontinuities in an effort to indicate some of the ways in

---

[1] Ed. Charles B. Schmitt, Quentin Skinner, Eckhard Kessler and Jill Kraye, (hereafter cited as *CHRP*) (Cambridge, 1988), pp. 455–534.
[2] *CHRP*, pp. 113–15.

which medieval theories of cognition and remembering, in which theories of language and representation played so large a part, led to the continuation of long-enduring theories and practices of how the past was to be recalled, understood and used. Ancient and medieval memories set the agenda for modernity.[3]

THE LEGACY OF THE 'VIA ANTIQUA' AND THE 'VIA MODERNA'

The earlier fourteenth-century developments in epistemology and the emergence of a clearer distinction between the respective domains of the arts and natural sciences played vital roles on the continent not least in establishing the battle ground between the *via antiqua* and the *via moderna* in the new German universities of the fifteenth century.[4] Although

---

[3] See E. J. Ashworth on signification from the thirteenth to the seventeenth centuries in *CHRP*, especially pp. 158 ff. For an excellent study of logic and sign theory in the fourteenth century now, see Joël Biard, *Logique et théorie du signe au XIVe siècle* (Paris, 1989). This study appeared too late to be taken fully into account in this book.

[4] Adam Wodeham, writing *c.* 1330s classified Scotus as *antiquus* and Ockham as *modernus*. (*Sent.*, I, d. 1 q. 12 P, Paris Univ. Ms 193 fol. 67ra), At both Paris and Oxford from the 1330s onwards, the dividing line between *antiqui* and *moderni* remains fixed at about 1310. See William J. Courtenay, '*Antiqui* and *Moderni* in late medieval thought', in *Ancients and Moderns: A Symposium, Journal of the History of Ideas* 48 (1987), pp. 3–10; p. 5. For the use of 'modern' to mean something positive and up to date, see my earlier chapter on twelfth-century *moderni* to be compared here with the nonpejorative use of the term in the fourteenth century. The labels *via antiqua* and *via moderna* appear in university and scholastic documents for the first time in the early fifteenth century and do not, as was once imagined, go back to competing schools of thought created by the disciples and opponents of Ockham. Courtenay believes that nowhere in the fourteenth century did *moderni* refer to a specific group, nor is it particularly associated with nominalists. It is clear, however, that Bradwardine speaks of certain contemporaries whose methods and conclusions in theological discourse contrast starkly, and to his mind erroneously, with his own, and these he does call *moderni*. N. W. Gilbert in 'Ockham, Wyclif and the "via moderna"', in W. Zimmermann, ed., *Antiqui und Moderni*, Miscellanea Mediaevalia, 9 (Berlin, 1974), pp. 85–125, argues that the *Wegestreit* is a fifteenth-century phenomenon issuing from Wyclif's attack on terminist logic culminating in a split between Wyclifite realism and the terminism of Pierre d'Ailly and Jean Gerson. To my mind this ignores the evidence of the fourteenth century which recognised Ockham and his followers as the perpetrators of a new methodology of textual analysis which disturbed church and university authorities in the 1340s, before the appearance of Wyclif on the scene of the debate. Courtenay is correct to emphasise that what comes to be the scholastic division between *antiqui* and *moderni* is rooted in the events at Paris and Oxford at mid fourteenth century and thereafter and that the term *moderni* had already begun to change its (neutral) meaning (i.e. contemporary opponent on a particular issue) by the second quarter of the fourteenth century. See Courtenay, '*Antiqui* and *Moderni*', p. 4. Already by 1388 the University of Cologne was a stronghold of the *via antiqua* and Erfurt, founded in 1392, of the *via moderna*. Also see Heiko Oberman, '*Via antiqua* and *via moderna*: late medieval prolegomena to early reformation thought', in *Journal of the History of Ideas*, 48 (1987), pp. 23–40; p. 24.

Ockham cannot be identified with followers who came to be referred to as Ockhamists, nominalists or even the later *via moderna*, it has been shown that the division between the *via antiqua* and the *via moderna* was often taken by later fifteenth-century contemporaries to be one between realists and nominalists and that Ockham was seen as the source of the Ockhamist *via moderna*.[5] Beyond its epistemological theories, this *via moderna* encouraged the study of physical phenomena divorced from a meta-physical super-structure. The empirical orientation of Ockham's confidence in experience, intuitively known, fostered *experimentum* and *experientia*, observation and experience of the world of contingencies, so that the sciences could be secularised in the sense that one could recognise the autonomy of the laws under which they operated. The only limitation set to this legal autonomy was a loyalty to a faith in the Church and its traditions. And here Ockham's understanding of the reality of individuals and his theory of universals played a primary role. As we have said, he viewed the Church as a corporation comprised of individual, historically-situated believers, with normative capacities peculiar to the human species throughout time, and who knew the world as they experienced it. This was a rejection of the realist notion of an essentially a-historical Church, a Church understood as an indivisible body of vital, formal and essential forces. For Ockham, the Church was not as the neo-Augustinians and neo-Platonists supposed, independent of specific time, place and its component members. Its reality was not in its conceptual abstractness.[6]

The confrontation between the *via moderna* and the *via antiqua*[7] in its

5 On the difficulties of establishing Ockham's influence where a position is ascribed to him by near contemporaries which was not unique to him, and where an author attributes a position to Ockham without direct reference or quotation, see William Courtenay, 'The reception of Ockham's thought in fourteenth-century England', in Hudson and Wilks, eds., *From Ockham to Wyclif* (Oxford, 1987), pp. 89–107. Gerhard Ritter lists the representatives of the *via moderna*, where Ockham is one of many including Marsilius of Inghen, Walter Burley, Robert Holcot, Gregory of Rimini, Pierre d'Ailly, Jean Gerson, Gabriel Biel. *Studien zur Spätscholastik: neue Quellenstücke zur Theologie des Johann von Wesel* (Heidelberg, 1926/7), III, p. 49. Also see Ruprecht Paqué, *Das Pariser Nominalistenstatut. Zur Entstehung des Realitätsbegriffs der neuzeitlichen Naturwissenschaft* (Berlin, 1970), p. 22 n. 13.
6 Ockham, *Tractatus contra Benedictum XII, OP*, III, p. 191: 'et per consequens fideles sunt una ecclesia, et ita ecclesia est verae personae et non est persona imaginaria et repraesentata'.
7 Alister McGrath, *The Intellectual Origins of the European Reformation* (Oxford, 1987), rightly refers to the opposition between several different schools, the *via moderna*, the *schola Augustiniana moderna*, the *via antiqua* etc., p. 17. On a coherent but multivalent school of thought, the *schola Augustiniana moderna*, see pp. 86 ff. See the work of Damasus Trapp, 'Augustinian Theology of the fourteenth century: notes on editions, marginalia, opinions and book-lore', *Augustiniana*, 6 (1956), pp. 147–265, and A. Zumkeller, 'Die Augustinerschule des Mittelalters: Vertreter und philosophisch-theologisch Lehre', *Analecta Augustiniana*, 27 (1964), pp. 167–262. But within the Augustinian Order there were polarisations between those following the *via antiqua* and the *via moderna* respectively. McGrath argues

ecclesiological manifestation continued into the Reformation in university circles. So did the epistemological divide, as it continued in Renaissance humanist circles between the neo-Aristotelians and neo-Platonists. The story that can be told by means of the confrontation between the 'two ways', the *via moderna* and the *via antiqua*, is rather different from the received version of the total break with the 'barbarity' of the medieval past supposed by some humanists themselves and which modern scholarship has sought to preserve and, as a consequence, has misunderstood. As Oberman pointed out: 'Nothing has so blocked our access to the *Wegestreit* as the humanist assumption that the *via antiqua–via moderna* antithesis, sustained by the scholastic *viri obscuri*, would shrink to its real dimensions, that is, trifling, ludicrous, scurrilous – when faced with the new antique–modern polarity born of the humanist recovery of classical antiquity and the liberation from barbarity'.[8] By looking briefly at the methods and aims of selected Renaissance historians we will clarify just what this 'recovery' really meant. We shall see that there was little new about it.

Neither medieval nor humanist readers of past texts discovered *historical* anachronism; both, however, were sensitive to anachronistic discourse, to different modes of signifying the experiences that men had and have. This awareness of linguistic anachronism was already explicit in the *via moderna*'s project to free the language of ancient authors from the Christianising and neo-Platonising straitjacket of the *via antiqua*, thus permitting the ancient individual to speak as an unbaptised experiencer and rememberer of his own world of individual contingencies.[9] We have seen that prior to Ockham and the *via moderna*, the radical Aristotelian Siger of Brabant had already said in his *De Anima Intellectiva* that he was going to try to determine the thought of the philosophers more than to discover the truth since he is treating matters *cum philosophice procedamus: quod nostra principalis non est inquirere qualiter se habeat veritas de anima sed quae fuerit opinio philosophi de ea*.[10] In reading his texts literally he was taking the first

---

that viewed from the standpoint of the subject matter of the arts faculty, the methods and natural philosophy of the *via moderna* and the *schola Augustiniana moderna* were practically indistinguishable. The difference emerged in the theology faculties regarding doctrines of salvation, justification, predestination. But note that in the case of Gregory of Rimini, who in some ways followed the *via moderna*, Gregory rejected Ockham's epistemology, especially his theory of intuitive cognition, which was a philosophical rather than a theological divergence.

8 Heiko Oberman, *Masters of the Reformation* (Cambridge, 1981), p. 34. Also see Eugenio Garin, 'La cultura fiorentina nella seconda meta del 300 e i 'barbari' britanni', in *L'età nuova: Ricerche di Storia della Cultura dal XII al XVI secolo* (Naples, 1969), pp. 141–66.

9 McGrath's summary of the characteristic features of northern European humanism unfortunately repeats the 'newness' of the humanist concern for texts and *specific historical situations of* interpreters. *The Intellectual Origins of the European Reformation*, p. 40.

10 Ed. B. Bazán, Siger de Brabant, *De Anima Intellectiva* (Louvain and Paris, 1972), cap. VII,

steps in a return *ad fontes*, a term usually reserved by modern scholars for the Renaissance approach to texts. It reflected not only, as van Steenberghen rightly says,[11] a thirteenth-century arts faculty professor whose purpose was to read (*legere/lectio*) the classical authors on the syllabus, but also an exegetical method born in a milieu crowded with arts faculty students and professors concerned with literal readings of texts, and with elaborating sophisticated theories of language and logic divorced from theological considerations.[12] Aquinas went further than a mere recapitulation of past utterances, which was suitable only to a literal gloss, when he noted in his *Commentary* on Aristotle's *De Caelo et Mundo*, I, that in analysing Aristotle's exposition of differing opinions of the ancients concerning the origin of the cosmos, the variety of interpretations need not trouble us since philosophical inquiry does not have as its purpose to know what men have thought but what is the truth concerning reality.[13] That

p. 101: 'diligenter considerandum, quantum pertinet ad philosophum, et ut ratione humana et experientia comprehendi potest, quaerendo intentionem philosophorum in hoc magis quam veritatem, cum philosophice procedamus'.

11 F. Van Steenberghen, *Thomas Aquinas and Radical Aristotelianism* (Washington, D.C., 1980), p. 86.

12 Klaus Jacobi, *Die Modalbegriffe in den logischen Schriften des Wilhelm von Shyreswood und in anderen Kompendien des 12. und 13. Jahrhunderts. Funktionsbestimmung und Gebrauch in der logischen Analyse* (Leiden and Koln, 1980), especially part II, c. vii: necessario, contingenter. For earlier material, see L. M. De Rijk, *Logica Modernorum*, 2 vols. (Amsterdam, 1962–7); Alain de Libera, 'The Oxford and Paris Traditions in logic', in *The Cambridge History of Later Medieval Philosophy*, ed. Kretzmann, Kenny and Pinborg (Cambridge, 1982), pp. 174–87; see the various articles by Alain de Libera *et al.*, in *Histoire, Epistemologie, Langage*, 3 (1981) = *Sémantiques médiévales, cinq études sur la logique et la grammaire au moyen âge*; J. Pinborg, 'The English contribution to logic before Ockham', *Synthèse*, 40 (1979), pp. 19–42. Note that Ockham's *Summa logicae* was written for students who required logic to apply to theological problems when they proceeded to theological degrees.

13 Aquinas, *In Aristotelis libros de caelo et mundo expositio*, I, lectio 22. For an extraordinarily similar view to Aquinas's without an appeal to God's truth, see the Introduction to *Philosophy in History*, ed. Richard Rorty, J. B. Schneewind and Quentin Skinner (Cambridge, 1984), where, on the one hand, there is described a possible *Intellectual History of Europe* whose author 'does not care, for purposes of her work, whether Paracelsus was right about sulphur or Cicero about republics. She only cares about knowing what each would have said in reply to various different sorts of contemporaries ... Her thousand volumes never take up the question "What are these people talking about?" much less "which ones got it right".' (sic.) That is why, we are told, she must write a chronicle rather than a treatise (p. 2). On the other hand, we are told that the author of a *History of Western Philosophy* needs to ask apparently timeless and universal questions 'at the centre of philosophy' and to discuss these problems separated from the 'transient concerns' of (say) Spinoza's day. (p. 3). Unsubtly and unproblematically, the authors continue: 'to construct criteria for answering such questions as "should we include Spinoza ... among the philosophers?" "among the *great* philosophers?" – is to have a view about the relation of intellectual history *to the way things really are* ... The author of *The Intellectual History of Europe* has *to pretend not to know the way the world is*' (emphasis added.) This is none other than the a-historical medieval attitude to the past which I have been at such pains to

there was and is such a truth, and that it is not historically specific, was not denied by the methodology of radical Aristotelians. It was, however, their methodological concern to determine first what the authors of antiquity said before they evaluated whether they were correct. They simply trusted the recorded memorials of past men's experiences and glossed the literal sense provided by ancient texts. Only thereafter would they interpret what the texts meant and, if they were philosophers, determine their truth concerning reality. Ockham would take this further and his followers in the *via moderna* even further.[14]

The *via moderna*, following Ockham's concern to emphasise an episte-mology based on intuitive individual cognition in the sense and intellect, along with an analysis of the mechanics of supposition logic, stressed as fundamental the awareness of the varying language of Scripture and the Fathers in order to ensure that the revealed plans of salvation remained contingent history. Men's language points to the contingencies of their experiences. This was diametrically opposed to the insistence of Scotists and the later neo-Augustinianism of Bradwardine and the like, that the revealed plans of salvation were a necessary, essentially fixed, self-expression of a divine essence. The *via moderna*, following Ockham and in the tradition of Abelard, placed linguistic exegesis at the centre of their concerns to interpret varying *modi loquendi* correctly in order to get at the a-historical truth that was meant for all time and all thinking men. But where modistic logic of late thirteenth-century Paris assumed that linguis-tic structures were not dependent on human conventions and instead, were part of the nature of things, Ockham insisted that meaning was revealed through an analysis of the conventional and linguistically contextual ways in which terms were used in propositions. At the heart of the debate, then, was, as it had always been, the proper relation between language, logic and reality.[15] Where neo-Augustinians and certain modistic logicians insisted that a mode of expression was inseparably bound up with the substance or

explain. It is hardly credible that Skinner, whose numerous important writings show such a sensitivity to philosophical and political texts in context, linguistic and otherwise, can have put his name to this introduction.

14 Hence, in the *De imperatorum et pontificum potestate*, I, 2, Ockham is concerned to show how the Avignon papacy has transposed the terms of ancient scripture: 'Proinde qualiter ecclesia Avinionica terminos transgreditur antiquos, inquantum est mihi possibile, promere cupiens universis, qui sint termini antiqui, quos posuit christus quando consti-tuit beatum Petrum principem apostolorum et cunctorum fidelium, ante omnia manifes-tare studebo' (C. K. Brampton, ed., p. 4).

15 Jan Pinborg, *Die Entwicklung der Sprachtheorie im Mittelalter* (Beiträge zur Geschichte der Philosophie u. Theologie des Mittelalter, 42.2) (Münster i. W., 1967); L. Kaczmarek, *Modi significandi und ihre Destruktionen: Zwei Texte zur scholastischen Sprachtheorie im 14. Jahrhundert* (Materialien zur Geschichte der Sprachwissenschaft und der Semiotik, I) (Münster in Westfalia, 1980).

meaning of a proposition's assertion, Ockham and the later *via moderna* distinguished style and modes of signifying from meaning and thereby pointed to the anachronistic hermeneutic enterprise in which the *via antiqua* was engaged. Thus, the doctrinal diversity that is so characteristic of the later medieval period was a major consequence of the disagreement not only over the nature of the sources of theology but over the status and method of interpretation of the language of Scripture and patristic authorities, especially Augustine.[16] And in Ockham's assertion that we know our experiences as certainly as we ever know anything, he focused on the probability of individual men arriving at the truth – not through a logical deduction of formal essences – but from recalling their own individual experiences, even when they signified these experiences through various and different *modi loquendi*. In effect, he provided individuals with a wider scope for self-determination in the natural order than any adherent of the *via antiqua* could sustain. According to Ockham, we recall our pasts as experienced, through acts of imperfect intuition which are founded on perfect intuition of what there is to experience. The pasts of others we understand abstractively, making no claims to the existence or nonexistence of what they recall, but presuming as we must, that they recall a truth based on *their* intuitive cognition of their experiences. Man was already at the centre of this 'medieval' philosophical inquiry, an inquiry stripped of its a-historical character only in the sense that it now treated seriously the transience and mutability of human experiences as set out in the varieties of more fixed, conventional discourse, preserved in textual memorials. What this inquiry did NOT propose was that the truth was mutable and relativistic: individual experiences and *modi loquendi* varied but the truth did not, and accurate literary exegesis could expose this truth. Therefore, much of what was to become characteristic of Renaissance philosophy and historiography was supported rather than denied by Ockham and the *via moderna*. Indeed, one of the outcomes of such a linguistic approach to the contingency of human experience would be the self-conscious affirmation of Renaissance historians that history, the recorded primary significations of experience, was a human appropriation, concerned not with the acts of God but with the recorded experiences and acts of men within their self-created political institutions, from which could be elicited universal regularities, that is, a-historical truths applicable throughout history. As we shall see, this would lead to Machiavelli's 'science of politics'.

The journey we have taken from the thirteenth-century neo-

[16] See Hermann Schussler, *Der Primat der Heiligen Schrift als theologisches und kanonisches Problem im Spätmittelalter* (Wiesbaden, 1977).

Augustinians to Scotus's attempt to harmonise Aristotle with Augustine, was followed by a revived 'anti-pelagian' Augustinianism and a continuation of modistic logic, that confronted head on, *not* the Thomistic Aristotelianism but rather, the *via moderna*, that is, a development of Ockham's brand of Aristotelianism which was seen by opponents like Bradwardine to have illicitly enriched the quality of unaided human actions prior to any emancipating gracious act of God which might elevate human achievements. The *via moderna*, said its theological opponents, defied the distinction between human acts performed in a state of grace and those done naturally.[17]

The rift between the *via moderna* and *antiqua* was not limited to epistemological discussion of opposing scholastics, nor to ecclesiologues on the eve of the Reformation. It survived in the very heart of early humanism as well, and cannot be limited by the received model of a north–south divide between the so-called secular Italian humanists and their northern Christian counterparts.[18] Indeed, the origins of an early humanism in the personality and writings of Petrarch can be shown to have been riddled with the dilemmas inherent in the *via antiqua*'s rejection of the methodology and aims of the *via moderna* in university circles.[19]

PETRARCH'S 'HUMANISM' AND THE 'VIA ANTIQUA'

Petrarch is usually singled out as typical of early Renaissance attitudes to history, philosophy and language. He is, therefore, taken to be more modern, more like us, than his 'medieval' contemporaries or predecessors. To what extent, if at all, is this accurate?

Petrarch's experience of mid-fourteenth-century Avignon where the papal court was in residence, brought him into contact with the writings of fourteenth-century biblical scholars like Trevet who were also classicists commenting on Livy. Classical studies were coming into fashion in Avignon by the second decade of the fourteenth-century, not least

---

[17] Heiko Oberman, *Masters of the Reformation*, p. 67; Thomas Bradwardine, *De Causa Dei*, ed. H. Savile (London, 1618, reprint 1964), cap. 39.

[18] 'The historian's carefully constructed model of a north–south axis with an alpine continental divide between a profane and a Christian humanism has buckled beneath the weight of recent research on humanism [by Kristeller, Bouwsma, Trinkaus and others]' (Oberman, *Masters of the Reformation*, p. 46).

[19] CharlesTrinkaus, '*Antiquitas versus Modernitas*: an Italian humanist polemic and its resonance', in *Ancients and Moderns, A Symposium, Journal of the History of the Ideas*, 48 (1987), pp. 11–21; p. 12: 'The early humanists (Petrarch, Salutati) were unquestionably 'ancients' in their appeal to Cicero, and Plato (as they knew him by reputation only), to Augustine and other ancient Christian writers, whom they regarded as superior to contemporary schoolmen.'

because several popes were keen collectors of ancient Latin texts.[20] Dominicans like Ridevall and Trevet are known to have 'invented' classicising biblical commentaries. Ecclesiastical Englishmen who were highly educated and employed in various ambassadorial or proctorial capacities at the papal court, carried the torch for classical studies by writing in accord with the strict rules of rhetorical dictamen. They collected formularies of high Latin letters, collected ancient books, praised Sallust, Cicero, Boethius, Macrobius, Lactantius and Martianus Capella, wished they could read Greek and wrote biographies of ancient sages with excerpts from their writings.[21] Some have argued that this incipient English humanism, if that is what it was, thereafter died in England, insular conditions dominating and cutting Britain off from the early 'humanist' continental, philosophical, literary and political trends. As a consequence, the bishop of Durham Richard de Bury's *Philobiblon* (1344) has been called a rhetorical treatise on the love of books and ancient authors that was no more than a one-off exercise in dictamen.[22] But he, like Petrarch, argued that one could not understand the Church Fathers or the Bible without the classical poets. 'Semi-pelagian' theologians like the Dominican Robert Holcot not only referred to Boethius and Hermes Trismegistus, as did his neo-Augustinian opponent Bradwardine in the *De Causa Dei*, but Holcot went on to cite Agamemnon, Ulysses and Hercules as heroes who laboured for glory and virtue with God's help.[23] The question is whether or not these men, educated in the current philosophical, logical and epistemological disputes at their source, in the university of Oxford, and who bolstered theological arguments with classical references, were wholly dependent on a pseudo-classical library circulating largely by means of scriptural lecture commentaries. Were they then drawing on the classics in a medieval and moralising way that Petrarch's classicising would leave behind? In other words, to what extent and to what degree is Petrarch's classicising an early example of what

---

[20] Diana Wood, *Clement VI, The Pontificate and Ideas of an Avignon Pope* (Cambridge, 1989), esp. ch. 3. Clement VI had been anticipated by John XXII who encouraged Italians to settle in Avignon, summoning Petrarch from Bologna in 1326. John, like Clement, was an enthusiast for classical learning, to such an extent that when Trevet offered to comment on the Pentateuch for him, John instead asked him to comment on Livy! See F. Simone, *The French Renaissance, Medieval Tradition and Italian Influence in Shaping the Renaissance in France*, trans. H. G. Hall (London, 1969), pp. 285–6.

[21] For a more extended discussion of the English–Avignon connection, see Janet Coleman, 'English Culture in the Fourteenth Century', in Piero Boitani, ed., *Chaucer and the Italian Trecento* (Cambridge, 1983), pp. 33–63. Also see M. Laclotte and D. Thiébaut, *L'Ecole d'Avignon* (Paris, 1983).

[22] Beryl Smalley, *English Friars and Antiquity in the Early Fourteenth Century* (Oxford, 1960).

[23] Robert Holcot, *In Librum Sapientie Salomonis* (Hagenau, 1494 and Paris, 1511), *Lectio* 120.

would flower as 'true' Renaissance humanism but that the English version is a misconceived imitation that cannot escape the Middle Ages? To what extent *could* Petrarch as an early humanist escape the Middle Ages, living and writing as he did in the Avignon where Ockham and his followers were brought to book precisely for their logical and theological positions?[24]

Petrarch defended the 'humanities', that is, poetry, rhetorical eloquence and ethics against what he took to be the claims of scholastic philosophy and science. He insisted that moral philosophy was the only part of philosophy which was to be recognised as part of humanist studies. But if one enumerates the kinds of concerns central to both Scotist and Ockhamist ethics, following on from the psychological theories that both united and distinguished them, one finds that moral concerns were at the heart of their discussion as well. Their agenda was dominated by debates on the role of Fate, fortune, providence, the individual's free will in directing his life, the ability of man to cope with the utter contingency of the natural and supernatural worlds. The world's contingency was now posited, as we have seen, in defiance of the necessitarianism of radical Aristotelians condemned by Bishop Tempier in 1277 at Paris. Put succinctly, the concern in pastoral, theological, philosophical, and literary circles, 'north and south' was now with the extent of an individual's moral autonomy and ability to be virtuous from his own nature, to 'do what was in him' (*facere quod in se est*) in order to live well and earn salvation.[25] What, it was asked, were the limitations on natural human experiences and action?

We have already discussed how Ockham and his English followers were involved in defending not only a radically individualist epistemology but also a methodology that insisted on a strict logic of ordinary and spiritual language. Those who took some of Ockham's ideas further were labelled by a group of neo-Augustinian theologians as semi-Pelagians. It was thought by men like Bradwardine, that they placed too much emphasis on man's ability to will his own salvation and his own virtuousness. Indeed, Ockham's conclusions led to a model of man as both appointed representative and partner with God within the limits of God's covenant or

24 The Parisian statute of 25 September 1339 stated: 'quod doctrina Okanica non dogmatizetur'. The difficulties of interpreting this has been frequently pointed out, but R. Paqué, *Das Pariser Nominalistenstatut*, sees it as an unproblematic condemnation of Ockham, pp. 306 ff. See below, n. 35.
25 Heiko Oberman, 'Facientibus quod in se est Deus non denegat gratiam. Robert Holcot OP and the beginnings of Luther's theology', *Harvard Theological Review*, 55 (1962), pp. 317–42. Also H. Oberman, *The Harvest of Medieval Theology, Gabriel Biel and Late Medieval Nominalism* (Cambridge, Mass., 1963; 2nd rev. edn, Grand Rapids, Michigan, 1967).

pactum, His free-willed choice to deal with *this* world of contingents and man's nature as it now is, rather than with possible other worlds. Man was indeed now responsible for his own life and his own society within the limits of the *pactum*. In contrast, Bradwardine asserted 'sola fide *sine* operibus praecedentibus fit homo iustus'; it is only by faith alone and not by precedent works, that man is made just.[26] Both sides of the controversy had their works epitomised and summarised and circulated outside university circles. Both sides drew on classical authors as never before to justify their positions. Their debate was deemed important beyond theological circles precisely because of its practical consequences in the pastoral and political spheres of men's lives. If the world was not absolutely determined by God or Fate or providence, and was utterly contingent as supposed by some, then how was it possible to teach and establish a fixed ethical order to guide Christians' lives? As we have seen, by the fourteenth century, questions about our experience of the world were being framed in the language of possibility rather than certainty. And linked with the Ockhamist assertion that reality could only be posited of discrete individuals – this man, rather than 'mankind' as a general concept, was real – was the logically necessary political and ethical conclusion: society was nothing other than the sum of discrete, responsible, autonomous individuals and all one could do was to follow the rules or dictates of reason and thereafter, hope that if one did one's best, did what was in one, the appropriate reward in the next life would be forthcoming.

These problems of individual responsibility, Fortune and man's free will were recognised by many – early humanists like Petrarch and medievals alike, and not least by Chaucer – to be issues that had confronted men of antiquity *as well as* modern men. The Boethian dilemma, which Chaucer turned into Troilus's dilemma, was now also the ancient *and* Christian problem set in the context of a pious and increasingly lay culture. Ancients, medievals and Renaissance men were believed to be confronted by the *same* problems.

Petrarch is well known for having rejected scholastic methods and style. While he valued philosophy for its contribution to the strengthening of human virtue, he had no time for philosophical subtleties of the logical kind current in contemporary university arts courses. But it has been argued that Petrarch's 'humanist' suspicion regarding scholastic theological methods and theology was based, in fact, on a scanty knowledge of that theology and philosophy of the schools. Trinkaus has argued further that Petrarch's humanism is less a reaction to the contemporary scene

[26] *De Causa Dei*, I, 43.

than a bypass of it. Having investigated Petrarch's citations of pre-Scholastics, Sophists and others, Trinkaus has shown that Petrarch's knowledge was usually no greater than what was currently available to numerous erudites of the medieval and clerical stamp. He could not read Greek and despite his admiration for Plato and his possession of some of Plato's writings in Greek, his acquaintance with his doctrine came, as did the acquaintance of most others, from the medieval Latin partial translation by Chalcidius of the *Timaeus*, the Latin *Phaedo* and *Meno* and primarily from Augustine, Cicero and Macrobius. Furthermore, Petrarch displayed the same medieval taste for encyclopedic epitomes of the classics and the compilations of rhetorical *loci communes* that his contemporaries in England shared.[27] And like those whom some have dismissed as northern, insular medievals, Petrarch preferred 'our Latin writers Cicero, Seneca, Horace' because he was more concerned with rhetorical form in conformity with faith than with philosophical subtleties. Rhetoric in conformity with faith provides a clue to his purpose. In his criticism of contemporary scholasticism, he revealed himself to be using a discourse that was shared by others. Indeed, what really influenced him was one of the main strands of current theology and its attendant methodological precepts concerning a proper interpretation of texts: the Platonising *via antiqua*. What linked him decisively with the *via antiqua* was this interest in Plato, following Augustine's lead, in order to show Plato's compatibility with Christianity. Therefore, we cannot be surprised to find that in true neo-Platonist fashion, Petrarch *contrasted* sense data and the welter of phantasms with higher truths in the mind. And this means that his view of man's memory was not unlike that of St Bernard. He, too, wished for a 'blanched' memory where the images of the sensual world would either disappear or be transformed. Petrarch, like the proponents of the *via antiqua* did not believe men's knowledge of their moral responsibility derived from their experience of the world but rather, imputed this morality to a higher source. Effectively, Petrarch was not interested in man recalling the past, remembering it and learning from it to become a morally determined person because he did not believe that man's moral choices ultimately were within his control. The world of experience was a disorderly distraction for Petrarch and it was best to forget it, if only one could. This attitude, as we shall see, led him to what today we would regard as a most distorted 'sense of the past'. In contrast to the *via moderna*'s emphasis on knowledge through sensual experience, Petrarch writes:

[27] Charles Trinkaus, *The Poet as Philosopher, Petrarch and the Formation of Renaissance Consciousness* (New Haven, 1979), pp. 11–12.

Thus, in fact, innumerable species and images of visible things, which entered by the bodily senses after they have entered singularly, are pressed together into a mass and condensed in the penetralia of the soul; the latter, neither born for this nor capable of so many deformed things, is weighed down and confused. Hence this epidemic of phantasms, dispersing and shattering your thoughts with an array of deadly concerns, blocks the road to the clarifying meditations by which the soul ascends to the one, only and supreme light.[28]

Petrarch closes the first dialogue of the *Secretum* in tones reminiscent of St Bernard's anguish over the cesspool of his sensual memory, saying:

And there comes to pass that inward discord of which we have said so much and worrying torment of the mind angry with itself; when it loathes its own defilements, yet cleanses them not away; sees the crooked paths yet does not forsake them; dreads the impending danger yet stirs not a step to avoid it.[29]

He attributes this state to a false dependence on externalities and fortune's vicissitudes. In such a state 'there is no wound old enough for it to have been effaced and forgotten'.[30] Augustinus says to the troubled Franciscus of the *Secretum*: 'If the tumult of your mind within should once learn to calm itself, believe me this din and bustle around you, though it will strike upon the senses, will not touch your soul'.[31]

Here we have a return to an earlier neo-Platonist tradition which teaches the separation of the autonomous soul from the senses, a doctrine derived from a reading of Augustine and the Latin Stoics, and showing numerous affinities with the ideas of St Bernard.[32] And yet Petrarch leaves his dilemma unresolved, unable in the end to choose between renouncing worldly ambition and spiritual peace. It is this irresolution that makes him appear 'modern' to us, but it is an irresolution found in the 'medieval' Chaucer's *Troilus* as well. However, Petrarch presents the reader with the neo-Platonist answer which is there to be taken up:

---

[28] *Secretum = De secreto conflictu mearum curarum libri tres*, in *Francesco Petrarca Prose*, ed. G. Martellotti *et al.* (Milan and Naples, 1955), prose 64–6: 'Conglobantur siquidem species innumere et imagines rerum visibilium, que corporeis introgresse sensibus, postquam singulariter admisse sunt, catervatim in anime penetralibus densatur'. Draper's translation is not sufficiently accurate. It may be noted here that it is customary to translate Renaissance Latin into melifluous English while frequently what is chosen (unconsciously?) for medieval Latin is an archaic, olde English which does little justice to the latter.

[29] Prose, 68. Compare St Bernard's *Sermon on Conversion*, discussed above, ch. 11. Petrarch's man, engaged in public life but always *inquietus*, without time to consider either earth or heaven, is contrasted with the man who employs his leisure in unbroken contemplation, in undisturbed tranquility. See Seneca, *De Otio*, v, 6. Also see Cicero, *Tusculan Disputations*, I, xix–xx, as discussed above, chapter 3.

[30] Prose 106–8.   [31] Prose 120.   [32] See prose 126.

that of contemplative detachment from the world. He, like Scotus, conceives of human life as active, thinking mind. Augustinus suggests an acceptance of the contingencies of the world and an insulation of the soul's real, essential life from such external flux. This means that for Petrarch, man is, essentially, thinking mind. This is the route that the *via antiqua* would continue to follow but in a new rhetorical key, drawing on an increasingly civic setting for illustrations of the kinds of disturbances experienced by the soul.

That Petrarch in the end could not identify himself either with the ambitious man of the world or with the contemplative recluse, does not vitiate his model of man as an autonomous soul troubled by sensual contingencies that are essentially divorced from it. For him, only divine aid can allow the individual to achieve that purity of soul divorced from sensual experience and its species. Human moral 'independence', ultimately with God's unmerited help, must be superior to and other than the accidents of circumstances, according to Petrarch. This is the older, pre-Ockhamist paradigm which we have already examined at length.

Furthermore, Petrarch attempted to analyse the nature of man's moral autonomy and to show that it was not merely a pagan concern that should be opposed to Christianity. Ciceronian and Senecan human autonomy was rather a position that was seen to be analogous with the role of the individual in the Christian doctrine of grace and justification. Petrarch admired Cicero and the ancients for having come far in their reverence for virtue, but added that divine grace determined salvation whereas man's worldly situation was 'somewhat' more in his own control. He says, 'and so where Cicero's and his companions' swift mind was stuck, our slow mind gradually progresses thanks to Him by whom both the progress of the mind and the plainness of the road are given'.[33] Indeed, after his spiritual crisis in Avignon that made him a disciple of Augustine, Petrarch argued for a position of *sola gratia* whereby man's virtuousness is not in his own hands at all but under God's or Fortune's or providence's auspices. Petrarch used the following example to illustrate this position in his *Epistolae familiares*, XX, 4, 30:

King Saul spared the life of king Amalech, yet for his clemency he merited the inexorable wrath of God. However, Finees murdered with his sword an Israelite and his foreign wife, and this severity was acceptable to God, useful to his people and glorious and just for himself, earning him perpetual fame. Indeed, according

---

[33] Petrarch, *De otio religioso*, ed. G. Rotondi (Studi e testi, 197) (Vatican City, 1958), p. 100, cited in Trinkaus, *In Our Image and Likeness* (Chicago, 1970), pp. 45–6.

to God's judgement and not just anyone's judgement, the cruel crime of homicide was pleasing and yet homicide is a reprobate act according to humanity.[34]

The determination of a man's virtuousness is, then, in God's hands and His ways are often inscrutable to human logic. To bolster his own position, Petrarch would recommend the *Milleloquium Divi Augustini* produced by a collection of Augustinians directed by Bartholomew of Urbino (d. 1350) as a fundamental collection of over 1,500 quotations from Augustine, often out of context. In line with the increasing suspicions roused against Ockham's followers' methods and conclusions in Avignon,[35] Petrarch, one-time chaplain to Cardinal Giovanni Colonna,

[34] Ed. V. Rossi and U. Bosco (Florence, 1933–42), IV, p. 20: 'Saul rex servavit regem Amalech, qua clementia inexorabilem iram Dei meruit; Finees vero israeliticum virum et alienigenam mulierem gladio confixit, que severitas et Deo accepta et populo utilis et sibi exstiti ad perpetuam fama iustitie gloriosa. Ecce non cuiuscunque iudicio sed Dei immane facinus homicidium, placet, humanitas reprobatur.'
[35] As we have seen, Ockham's logic and natural philosophy works were prohibited in the Paris Arts Faculty in 1339, a prohibition which included public or private readings or discussion of his opinions, *possibly* because his texts had not yet been approved. But Parisian students and bachelors of theology, including Nicholas Autrecourt, were called to Avignon to answer charges of erroneous teaching, and a series of opinions and practices, presumably associated with Ockham's supporters, was condemned. Autrecourt was specifically condemned at Avignon in 1346. *Chartularium Universitatis Parisiensis*, ed. H. Denifle and E. Chatelain (Paris, 1891), II, n. 1,023, pp. 485–6; n. 1,041 p. 505; n. 1,042, pp. 505–7; n. 1,124, pp. 576–87; n. 1,125, pp. 587–90. The relationship between Ockham's views and those of Autrecourt is disputed. Reference to 'Ockhamists' may well refer not to Autrecourt but to masters and students in the Arts Faculty, mainly of the English–German Nation. The Statute of 29 December 1340 reads: no masters, bachelors or scholars in the Faculty of Arts lecturing in Paris shall say that any famous proposition of the author whose text they are lecturing on is false absolutely or false literally, if they believe the author has the right intention in propounding it. They shall either concede it or distinguish the true meaning from the false sense because statements of the Bible might with equal reason be denied if taken literally, which is perilous. And since an utterance has no virtue except by employment and common usage of authors and others [this is Ockham's view] the force of an utterance is such as authors employ it and as the matter demands. ... No proposition is false according to the personal supposition of its terms ... for authors often use other interpretations ... No one should say no proposition is allowed unless it is literally true ... since the Bible and authors do not always use words in their literal sense ... A disputation based on literal meaning ... is nothing but a sophistical disputation ... No one should say there is no knowledge of things which are not signs, that is, which are not terms or expressions ... We have knowledge of things albeit by means of terms or expressions [which is also Ockham's view]. *Chart. Univ. Paris.*, II, n. 1,042, pp. 505–7.
This statute *conforms* to Ockham's teaching and indeed, does not mention his name in the body of the document. But it does provide us with information on the nature of disputes in the arts faculties, disputes with which Petrarch apparently had little sympathy. See William J. Courtney and Catherine Tachau, 'Ockham, Ockhamists and the English–German Nation at Paris, 1339–1341', *History of Universities*, 2 (1982), pp. 53–96, and Courtney, 'The reception of Ockham's thought at the University of Paris', in *Preuve et Raisons à l'Université de Paris: logique, ontologie et théologie au XIV* *siècle*, ed. Zenon Kaluza

recipient of canonries, the poet who wanted to become a cardinal but was disappointed in what Avignon popes offered him,[36] turned his back on the *via moderna*. The consequences of the programme inspired by Ockham's epistemology and logic, whereby experience of the world could be analysed free from the tutelage of faith, proved irreconcilable with the Platonically-inspired branch of humanism and its propensity for a *sancta philosophia*, a pursuit of wisdom through piety and devotion. Rhetoric was compatible not with philosophical metaphysics but with a fideistic theology. For a moral man to 'do what was in him' was simply not enough because one could not count on the probable certainty of a link between the way things are now and God's will.

Nor should we misconstrue Petrarch's 'humanist' interest in rhetoric as simply a concern for the style of *belles lettres* divorced from meaning. Just as neo-Augustinians and modistic logicians argued that form and content could not be separated, so too Petrarch's interest in rhetoric was ultimately an interest in lay Christian sermonising. He thought of himself and wished to be thought of as a *poeta theologicus*.[37] The lay poetic vocation included the role of moral counsellor and he was offended by the increasing practice of middle-ranking men acquiring letters, not as the light of the mind to secure an a-historical *sancta philosophia*, but only as an instrument for acquiring riches. His values, in common with the philosophical and theological *via antiqua*, would help to increase the rift between one dominant strand of emerging humanism and another, influenced by the *via moderna*. It was the latter which increasingly sought to reject metahistorical philosophies because they confused and belittled a human, self-determining, historically evolved body of laws and political institutions with immutable and divine justice, inscrutable Fortuna and an essentially fixed providence. With all of Petrarch's concern for extending the limits of man's moral autonomy, he can be seen to have opted for the stance that was common to adherents of the *via antiqua* when he said; 'Whatever is

---

and Paul Vignaux (Paris, 1984), pp. 43–64. A rejection of literal interpretation can also be found in Archbishop FitzRalph's *proposicio* of 1350, preached to the papal court at Avignon. See Janet Coleman, 'FitzRalph's antimendicant 'proposicio' (1350) and the politics of the papal court at Avignon', *Journal of Ecclesiastical History*, 35 (1984), pp. 376–90. I would venture a guess that the papal and university antagonism to literal biblical readings had nothing to do with Ockham's logic, but rather with certain Franciscan literal interpretations of Christ's and the Apostles' poverty. Indeed, possibly in oversimplifying Ockham's hermeneutics, some may have been 'dogmatising' and misusing his instructions for reading the *littera*. But Ockham does not seem to have been blamed for this possible misuse.

[36] *Liber sine nomine*, 8. Also see E. H. Wilkins, *Studies in the Life and Works of Petrarch* (Cambridge, Mass., 1955), pp. 63–80.

[37] C. Trinkaus, *The Poet as Philosopher*, pp. 90 ff.

well done by man is a divine achievement'.[38] As we shall see, there would be those later humanists, not least Machiavelli, who would, on the contrary, be the direct heirs of the *via moderna*'s interest in 'accurate' textual exegesis, individual responsibility and most importantly, a confidence in those laws of nature that were only derived from evident knowledge of individual experience. Faith need not be brought into the equation that defined a responsible individual and collective life.

Petrarch, like his medieval predecessors who recorded their own experiences literally and called their efforts *historia*, was equally concerned to record his own observations and experiences. When he read Giovanni Colonna's *Mare Historiam* along with the contradictory statements found in Jerome's translation of Eusebius he wondered: how did one put together contradictory statements about Rome with what one saw as the remnants of ancient Rome before one's very eyes? A good school question this: how to resolve contraries. In the *Rerum Familiarum* VI, 2 he observed the archaeological remains of the ancient Roman fora and then prepared a tour for Carthaginian ambassadors in his poem *Africa*. His observations and explanations are judged by modern scholars to have been on the whole remarkably accurate. But earlier historians who wrote down the primary significations of their own experiences, uninterpreted, providing readers with the literal sense, were always supposed to be accurate. Petrarch was not doing anything different. By engaging in this well-established tradition of writing down *historia* Petrarch would inspire followers to report their travel experiences and observations which led to systematic exploration of Rome and elsewhere. But why write down one's eyewitness experiences? Because, as we have seen, they could then be interpreted in an exemplary manner to inspire imitation or to justify present understanding. We cannot presume that Petrarch's intention behind his literal memorialisation of noteworthy experiences was simply disinterested investigation anymore than we can presume disinterested inquiry on the part of medieval historians. We need only note that Pope Martin V commissioned one of these post-Petrarchan 'explorers' Nicolo Signorilli 'to put together a list of all ancient and modern churches and a collection of inscriptions and documents regarding ecclesiastical jurisdic-

---

[38] *Liber sine nomine*, 4, speaking of Cola di Rienzo's service to Rome. 'If he had brought to completion what he had begun, it would have seemed a divine rather than a human achievement. Indeed, whatever is well done by man is a divine achievement ... Fortune must be held responsible for what happened afterwards.' Paul Piur, *Petrarcas 'Buch ohne Namen' und die päpstliche Kurie* (Halle, 1925). I do not think that this can be interpreted in a Ciceronian sense, that *man* is divine, but rather that achievements of moral value are not his at all.

tional rights'.[39] Such investigations were undertaken to justify and glorify Roman attainments because for men like Petrarch and his followers, ancient Rome lived in the present.

Twelfth- through fifteenth-century thinkers believed that the past was imitable. Everyone saw the value of the past to be its exemplary quality. Men looked for exemplary models in the memorials of antiquity whenever they believed their own age to be in moral and political chaos. Hence, when Petrarch insisted that he would have preferred to live in Augustan Rome, that he rated the past over the present, he was not desiring to live in what was still an essentially pre-Christian world and relive the Roman past as it really had been. He was taking up Livy's invitation to use history not as a means of solving problems of the present but of escaping from them. Indeed, Petrarch's letter to Livy, where he says he wishes either that he had been born in Livy's age or Livy in Petrarch's, is a testimony to Petrarch's longing to be elsewhere and he uses the language that has many affinities with millenarian longing for a new city of God. This letter to Livy tells us nothing about the past as it was. It simply tells us of Petrarch's longing to meet a man who wrote books he admired in what looks to Petrarch like a happy age filled with the kind of virtuous behaviour that Petrarch does not see around him in fourteenth-century Avignon, or elsewhere.[40] That he could imagine another, more virtuous place and time, just as numerous Christian millenarians could imagine some happy other place and simultaneously express a *contemptus mundi* for the present, tells us nothing of his accurate sense of the past. In fact, Petrarch was not accurate about Augustan Rome. Although he uses the expression 'evidence of the past', we must be careful to understand what he meant by 'evidence'.

What precision is there in his appeal to 'the evidence of the past' when he says in the *Liber sine nomine*, 4:

When was there ever such peace, such tranquility and such justice; when was virtue so honoured, the good so rewarded and the evil punished; when was there ever such wise direction of affairs than when the world had only one head and that head was Rome? Better still, at what time did God, the lover of peace and justice, choose to be born of the virgin and visit the earth?

For an historical record of the political brutality of Augustus's reign, Petrarch need only have read Tacitus, and of course his beloved Augustine's *City of God* contains a blistering condemnation of the Augustan age.

---

[39] R. Valentini and G. Zuccetti, eds., Signorilli, *Descriptio urbis Romane*, vol. IV, in *Codice topografico della città di Roma* (Rome, 1953). See Eric Cochrane, *Historians and Historiography in the Italian Renaissance* (Chicago, 1981), p. 38.

[40] *Epistolae Familiares*, XXIV, 8.

In this letter to the Roman people of the day, supporting the efforts of Cola di Rienzo who had briefly reestablished the Roman Republic, proclaiming himself tribune with dictatorial powers (1344), Petrarch speaks of an undifferentiated and continuous Roman republican history whose empire was always situated at Rome and 'belonged to the Roman people'. Indeed, Petrarch's letter to Livy tells us that Petrarch used his reading of Roman authors in an exemplary fashion. That he believed in the happy possibility of being transferred to another moment in time or that Livy could be who he once was were he brought into the fourteenth century, tells us of Petrarch's very 'medieval' conception of the presentness of the past.

THE MEDIEVAL AND RENAISSANCE SENSE OF THE PAST

In general, information about the past was effectively useless to medieval and Renaissance men; there was no interest in the mere 'facts' of the historical record for their own sake. And, indeed, historians would go on to construct fantastic genealogies based on mythic etymologies, forged documents, authentic fragments taken out of context, well into the eighteenth century. Hence, there is little doubt that during both the Renaissance and the middle ages, the past was only significant with regards to its interpretation, its present intelligibility.

But it has sometimes been suggested that the early humanists distinguished themselves from medieval 'historians' by adopting new standards of critical scholarship in their own historical works. Fifteenth-century humanists like George of Trebizond (*Rhetoricorum libri quinque*, 1433/4)[41] certainly believed that they were breaking with the recent past in writing history and he asserted that no one since the days of Livy and Sallust had written proper history. Why has it not been suggested more emphatically that these kinds of statements are a kind of rhetorically programmed amnesia? Historical accuracy was certainly one of their stated priorities but as Robert Black has commented in his study of Benedetto Accolti, 'the extent to which the humanists aimed at accuracy is not immediately obvious'.[42] Indeed, Accolti (1415–64), chancellor of the republic of Florence, used William of Tyre's medieval chronicle of the crusades in order

[41] Note the title of this work. See J. Montasani, *George of Trebizond, A Biography and a Study of his Rhetoric and Logic* (Leiden, 1976).

[42] Robert Black, 'Benedetto Accolti and the beginnings of humanist historiography', *English Historical Review*, 96 (1981), pp. 36–58; p. 38. Also see R. Black's 'Ancients and Moderns in the Renaissance, rhetoric and history in Accolti's Dialogues on the preeminence of men of his own times', *Journal of the History of Ideas* 43 (1982), pp. 3–32. Robert Black, *Benedetto Accolti and the Florentine Renaissance* (Cambridge, 1985).

to clarify a *current* political issue: Florence's response to the fall of Constantinople in 1453 and Pius II's call for a crusade against the Turks. As Cochrane says, 'his elegant Latin reworking of the original texts as well as his consistent reference to all Muslims as "barbarians" served to heighten the rhetorical effect of the speeches he put into the mouth of Peter the Hermit and his moral reflections on the discord among Christian subjects of the kingdom of Jerusalem'.[43]

When such historians depended on written sources, particularly when writing histories of remote periods, they did exactly what their medieval predecessors did: they took over entire accounts from past historians. Barely is there evidence that they sought documentary and other materials from which to reassess and alter rather than justify their views of another age. Rather, as Machiavelli does in the first part of his *History of Florence*, they excerpt from older histories and select those passages that strike a chord in the contemporary breast: that is, they look for and, of course, find, themes of republican virtue, evidence of a citizen militia serving a nation in superior faithfulness to that displayed by mercenaries, the constant theme of the foundation and destruction of cities. This is exemplary history as much as was its medieval predecessor, exemplary, ideological and consciously so.

It may seem perverse to point to those aspects of much Renaissance history-writing that show little of a so-called 'modern sense of the past' when so much history-writing demonstrated many new insights unexplored by the medievals, and not least a kind of investigation of sources which led to what we today recognise as a more accurate critical reading of Roman history. But this critical investigation of sources should be seen as a continuation of the medieval arts faculty tradition of reading a given ancient text 'literally', especially as it was furthered by the *via moderna*'s interest in the history of discourse as demonstrated by the varying modes of signifying men's experiences.

The historian Leonardo Bruni (*c.* 1415) clearly believed – one wonders on what evidence – that such university logicians as Ockham had gone too far. Bruni refers to the British 'barbarity' of sophisms that had confused true dialectical dispute with absurdities and trivialities. His complaint concerns the abuse of a certain kind of discourse and says nothing about whether his own discourse got at a truth that was distinct from that sought by medieval dialecticians. Indeed, their attitudes to the status of ancient texts were remarkably similar. Bruni translated many Greek books – which he appears to have been the first to read – into clear Latin, intelligible to ordinary, non-professional Latin readers.[44] He did not,

---

[43] Cochrane, *Historians and Historiography*, p. 27.   [44] *Ibid.*, p. 18.

however, consider his translation activities equivalent to the writing of history because, in line with Cicero's rhetorical understanding of history, there was no explanation in such translations of the memories recorded; nor was Bruni recording his own witnessed experiences. But Bruni never questioned the veracity of the original accounts. Instead, he provided a succinct record of all that the ancients who were available to him had transmitted about the political affairs of little-known ages of antiquity, but he reformulated this information in his own language, order and structure. We note, then, that he communicated the same truth but in another discursive genre. And he was the first, aside from Tacitus *whom he read*, to portray the Roman empire negatively, showing the principate to have been the death of the republic rather than its high point. Did he give reasons for choosing Tacitus's authoritative account over any one else's that may have conflicted with it? Was Bruni doing anything different from what William of Newburgh did when he rejected Geoffrey of Monmouth's account of Anglo-Saxon history and preferred Gildas's and Bede's authority instead?

If we look at his division of history into distinct epochs, characterised by the achievement of internal tranquillity and individual citizen creativity and the subsequent destruction of these ideals, we see that he offers a selection of preferred sources because they served as a justification of what he regarded as significant in his own city, Florence, in the fifteenth century. The goal whereby citizens were protected under just and equitable laws, a goal achieved through Florence gradually having become a mixture of 'the city' which was a cross between medieval commune and Greek polis, where power was in the hands of a fairly large number of citizens and the law ruled law-makers and subjects, was taken as an achieved and justifiable optimum. Republican Rome, found by ransacking archives, was not Florence's model but its fortuitous historical justification.[45] Republican Rome was not primarily a blue-print on which to base Florence's future: it was a reaffirmation of Florence's present success. If history, as Bruni believed, does anything, it teaches prudence, by which he meant that it is useful for justifying one's own affairs, a utility that medievals well understood.

Bruni warned Florentine humanist historians that the history of anti-

---

[45] We have already noted how twelfth-century Italian communes similarly referred to early Christian history to justify their own present activities. A relief, now in the Castel Sforza, dating from about 1171 on the Porta Romana in Milan, depicts the re-entry of Milanese citizens into the city after its rebuilding in 1167 under the protection of the confederated communes. Beside it, appears a parallel representation of St Ambrose and his struggle against the Arians. See Peter Classen, '*Res gestae*, universal history, apocalypse, visions of past and future', in Benson, Constable and Lanham, eds., *Renaissance and Renewal in the Twelfth Century*, pp. 387–417; p. 398.

quity had already been written. Therefore modern historians could only make summaries or add explanatory footnotes to the works of distant predecessors. This is what medieval readers called a literal gloss. No attempt was to be made to discover whether ancient historians were correct. As with the *via moderna*, what a distant experiencer and rememberer recorded was taken to be true and a modern's goal was to construe their grammar correctly. One did not set out to look for ancient archival documents that would gainsay the accounts of ancient historians or indeed show them to be describing and evaluating events in an unharmonious way. The historian Benedetto Accolti may have pointed out the inadequacies and undependability of the ancient historians but he demonstrated their unreliability largely by distinguishing, as Abelard had distinguished, between rhetorical and logical veracity, and not on the basis of newly discovered evidence. Accolti, normally in favour of republics, thereafter chose to write a kind of hagiographical, rhetorical biography of Francesco Sforza who had destroyed the Milanese republic.[46] Not only did no one before the eighteenth century question the authoritative testimonies of a Thucydides or a Dionysius of Halicarnassis.[47] They uncritically accepted the recorded *historia* of ancient authorities, chose amongst them for those who could confirm present beliefs, and they actively asserted, along with Bruni, that classical morals were universally applicable. True virtue and the gravity of morals were the same in the times of Plato and Aristotle as they are now.[48]

Like Bruni, Poggio Bracciolini (1380–1459) also understood that history alone could make the past present and therefore, it was exemplary.[49] Like Abelard, as cited by John of Salisbury in the twelfth century, Poggio believed that modern times were equal to ancient times so that contemporary great generals deserved to be remembered as much as did Caesar.

[46] See Cochrane, *Historians and Historiography*, p. 32.

[47] *Ibid.*, p. 434. See Mario Mazza, *Storia e ideologia in Tito Livio* (Catania, 1966), on how Livy's own motives for writing have been recognised only in the mid twentieth century

[48] Leonardo Bruni, *De studiis et litteris*, in *L. Bruni Aretino, humanistisch-philosophische Schriften*, ed. Hans Baron (Leipzig/Berlin, 1928), pp. 17–18: 'Quasi vero honestas gravitasque morum non nunc eadem fuerit quae nunc est?' Hence, one could cite both ancient and modern precepts and examples, sacred or profane, for their a-historical validity in moral argument. In Bruni's *Dialogi ad Petrum paulum histrum*, we have the Ciceronian model (*De Oratore*, including Ciceronian passages reproduced almost verbatim) of presenting a debate with a range of alternative views only to reveal, in *Dialogus*, II, the real and true harmonious reconciliation of the opinions of all the participants. There are numerous medieval examples of debates between pagan philosophers, Jews and Christians, with a similar dénouement. Also see Diana Webb, 'Eloquence and education: a humanist approach to hagiography', *Journal of Ecclesiastical History*, 31 (1980), pp. 19–39.

[49] Cochrane, *Historians and Historiography*, p. 29.

When Biondo, 'the first of all moderns' according to sixteenth-century followers, took up his scholarly investigation of Roman antiquities (*c.* 1443–59), he rejected identifications found in medieval guidebooks, preferring the testimony of 'ancient and trustworthy witnesses', that is, those presumed present at the time of their experience who produced the literal reports, the primary signification of their experiences. But since he accepted Cicero's judgements on Roman politics from his letters to Quintus, rather than Tacitus's judgements, he placed the first great age of Italy not at the time of the Etruscans or of the early Republic, as Bruni had done by following Tacitus, but in the first and second centuries of the empire which Bruni had excoriated. How did Biondo choose which historian to follow? He gives us a clue by telling us what he valued. Biondo said that the world dominated by Rome did not pine for its independence but 'rejoiced and glorified at being obedient to Roman government'. He believed that Rome had brought civilisation and morality to the world. Hence Biondo glorified this conception of a universal polis, the Roman empire, whose accomplishments rendered it worthy of being 'placed before the eyes of learned men of *these* times as a mirror and image of good living and every kind of virtue.' And, like Petrarch, he said he found this opinion of the Roman empire's glory in Augustine![50] For Biondo, good living and virtue were not historically specific.

Is this what we mean when we speak of the craft of the modern historian? Is this what we mean by 'a remembrance of things past'?

CURRENT HISTORIANS' VIEWS ON A RENAISSANCE SENSE OF THE PAST

This is not the place to examine in depth Renaissance historiography, and much that is illuminating has been said in recent years to afford a reevaluation of what Renaissance rememberers were in fact doing, as well as what they believed themselves to be doing.[51] What must be clear at this stage of our study is that the medieval mind was not a monolith, not a single enduring hypostatised entity that was suddenly transformed in the Renaissance. If we believe this, then we are perpetuating a caricature forged by some Renaissance thinkers who were still shackled to a shifting

---

[50] *Ibid.*, p. 39.
[51] See Charles Trinkaus, '*Antiquitas versus modernitas*', *Journal of the History of Ideas*, 48 (1987); Nancy Struever, *The Language of History in the Renaissance* (Princeton, 1970); Ernest Breisach, ed., *Historiography, Ancient, Medieval and Modern* (Chicago, 1983); Ronald Levao, *Renaissance Minds and their Fictions* (Berkeley, 1985); R. Landfester, *Historia Magistra Vitae, Untersuchungen zur humanistischen Geschichtstheorie des 14. bis 16. Jahrhunderts* (Geneva, 1972), to mention only a few reassessments.

medieval legacy. While there is a difference, at times vast, between certain attitudes to the past expressed in the Renaissance and that of certain medieval authors – just as there was a difference between the monastic and scholastic attitudes to memory and the past as well as a difference between what Scotus and Ockham respectively meant by memory – this difference cannot be illuminated by a false representation of what went through men's minds during a millennium of western European history. We cannot cite an author writing in, say 1490, and extrapolate to the 1980s and say, 'this is the attitude to history of the modern period, an attitude that medieval man did not share'.[52] To cite the eighth-century Bede and the fourth-century Martin of Tours as examples of the medieval mind in contrast with the Renaissance/modern mind is a fruitless distortion. At the heart of this distortion is the lack of interest modern historians seem to have in investigating the various epistemologies elaborated during the monastic and scholastic periods of the middle ages on the one hand; but perhaps more seriously, a lack of sensitivity to those genres used by medieval authors to convey to posterity their attitudes to the past and their understanding of memory and its uses. Renaissance genres with their undoubtedly greater rhetorical eloquence have caught the imagination of modern scholars to such an extent that their medieval predecessors have been forgotten and hence, the *continuity* of the medieval and Renaissance message has been obscured. More will be said below about the shift in genres but we must first examine what some modern historians take to be distinctive about Renaissance historiography in order to determine whether meaning as well as genres shifted.

Donald Kelley's influential *Foundations of Modern Historical Scholarship* argues that what we know as historical thought 'was not simply anti-Cartesian but to a large extent pre-Cartesian, and had its roots in the rich soil of Renaissance scholarship'.[53] His thesis is that the Renaissance sense of the past was different from the medieval: '[A]t least in the context of European civilization the humanists of the Renaissance were the first men to make a conscious and concerted effort to revive a dead past with some appreciation of temporal perspective and willingness to examine antiquity in its own terms'.[54] Is this true? We have already seen that questions

---

[52] See the influential book by Peter Burke, *The Renaissance Sense of the Past*, (London, 1969), chapter 1, 'Medieval historical thought', pp. 1–20. The distinguished Renaissance historian Burke is used below, to indicate that his clearly expressed views are models of widely held and repeated views in the historical profession today. Burke's own views were somewhat modified in his *Culture and Society in Renaissance Italy* (London, 1972) reissued with revisions as *Tradition and Innovation in Renaissance Italy* (London, 1974); see, for instance, pp. 40 ff.

[53] (New York, 1970), p. 7. [54] *Ibid.*

concerning temporal perspective – how, on the one hand, it is physically, sensually achieved, and, on the other, what its meaning is, how it is understood – was a central concern of monastic and scholastic authors when they dealt with the nature and activities of the soul. Those who, in short, believed that the mind only dealt with universals did not deny that men lived differently in the past, but rather asserted that what was meant by their lives, what was exemplary and universalisable about their living and experiencing, was what was important for posterity. It is not that they could not see that men, even one hundred years previously, dressed differently: one need only refer to the interesting episode in Matthew of Paris's Chronicle where he found old shoes in his monastery. Rather, it was that aside from the curiosity of such facts, the mind could not discover a meaning in this otherness unless it somehow translated the particularity of the past into a present, more generalised image. And this is what some believed was the very role of rational cognition. This, of course, can be interpreted by us as a lack of interest in the pastness of the past and we have already analysed the various theories of remembering that effectively made all interpretation of pastness necessarily a present activity with obvious ideological implications. The purpose of history was precisely that it could be used in the present. Ideology is not used here as a pejorative term. Even when the *via moderna*, following the radical individualising epistemology of Ockham, sought to uncover how the past was remembered by those who had experienced it, there was no attempt to cut off the uses of this uncovered past from the present. Instead, they pointed to the different modes of expression by which past actors signified past experiences. Experience was true but it could not be retrieved unless one was careful to analyse the language which signified events and connoted acts of mind, making coherent sense of terms which represented or substituted for such immediate experiences. What one sees in the debate between Scotus and Ockham is a conflict *not* over the truth of the past but rather over the means by which men come to know it when they study texts. The debate was over whether or not mind remembers and knows the past as past and particular, or as present and universal. This is not a debate that ends with the emergence of the Renaissance. As we shall see in the final chapter, it is still current in psychological, neurophysiological and philosophical circles. It was not that temporal perspective was ignored or seen as an impossibility, but rather that the distance between past and present, the distinction between the ancient Greeks and Romans and various medieval authors was a space that had to be overcome through the construction of relations and coherences, linguistic and conceptual, if men's actions – in what were taken to be like circumstances – were to be understood in a contingent universe in which an eternally fixed ethics had either to be essentially revealed (*via antiqua*) or individually discovered (*via moderna*), through language and texts.

What can we say, then, about the Renaissance humanists as the first men to make a conscious and concerted effort to revive a dead past with some appreciation of antiquity in its own terms? How dead was the past for them, what precisely was 'revived' and did they appreciate antiquity in its own terms?

We have already argued that contextual (in the sense of linguistic rather than historical) exegesis was the very heart of Ockham's suppositional logic, foreshadowed in Abelard's works. Ockham carried his theory over into his analysis of canonical, historical and patristic texts, not least in his polemical works against popes who he believed inaccurately interpreted the traditions of the Church. One can argue that Ockham, polemicist for the more radical wing of his Franciscan Order, and in the pay of the Holy Roman Emperor, antagonistic to the papal absolutism of the fourteenth century, employed his exegetical methods with less than pure motives. But as Kelley has also pointed out,

The motives of humanists were not always entirely pure. In the attempts to establish a splendid and heroic classical ancestry they tended to devote themselves to a myth-making rather than a historical impulse. Yet the remoteness and alien character of antiquity gave an unusual quality even to their idealizations. They created a new kind of myth which, it may be argued, lies at the roots of historicism'.[55]

But for Renaissance Italians, ancient Rome, its values and achievements, was not remote nor alien. The values and achievements of ancient Romans were exemplary and comprised the very identity of Renaissance Italians differentiating them from other peoples but not from their ancestors. And we must ask ourselves why we take their kind of myth-making to be more acceptable and historically-minded than that of the medieval stamp; why Romulus is a preferable ancestor to Brutus? What is being revealed here is not an attitude that is specific to the Renaissance but rather one that is specific to a modern sensibility which responds to a genre of historical writing that looks like nineteenth-century antiquarianism which pretended to a neutral curiosity in the lost past. But are there Renaissance *historians* whose purpose was so disinterested? Rather, the historical writings of the fifteenth and sixteenth centuries are rightly seen to be partisan ideologies spurred on to a *kind* of historical investigation that was, like its various medieval counterparts, little more than an

[55] *Ibid.*, p. 8.

attempt to protect certain myths, destroy others, and create still others by the selective use of sources. The investigation of the past was inspired by a concern to reinforce actions, rights, obligations in the present. This is not very different from what we have seen Gerald of Wales or Geoffrey of Monmouth to have been doing, especially in the latter's elaboration of the myth of Arthur.

It has often been asserted that what we define as history is not, in general, like poetry, something recollected in tranquillity. Kelley argues that it is precisely 'in times of crisis, in times of self-doubt and self-searching, that men begin most intensely to question their antecedents and to seek the reasons for their plight'.[56] Others, especially Hans Baron,[57] have argued further that the Italian Renaissance developed a modern approach to the historical past as a result of then, and only then, ransacking ancient texts to support republicanism. Apart from the fact that Renaissance historians always began with an agenda determined by their present and then selectively read past documents in order to find supporting 'facts' to bolster their own prejudices, we must also ask whether historical writing should be so narrowly defined as crisis literature. Should all other genres, the romance, the hagiographical saint's life, the discursive chronicle, all of which draw upon the past to show its relevance to a present argument, a present justification of affairs, be simply eliminated from the modern category of the historical? The narrowing of history to crisis literature, concerned with nothing but political history, was indeed Bruni's aim because he was concerned solely with the present collective acts of his Florentine political community and he was writing to urge the rulers of Florence to complete the city's history and hence draw it closer to what had been achieved by her Roman ancestors *as Bruni* 'remembered' these achievements. Thereafter, he believed his historical vocation would be at an end.[58] Surely this is not all that we mean by history and its concerns, and few would openly admit to investigating the past simply in order to demonstrate its uses in programmatic, political prophecy. If instead, we take Huizinga's notion of historical-mindedness of a period to be defined as 'the intellectual form in which a civilization renders account to itself of its past', as Kelley and others seem content to do, then on what grounds do we deny 'historical-mindedness' to the fourteenth-century historian Froissart who gives us the prejudices and interpretations of

---

[56] *Ibid.*, p. 11.
[57] Hans Baron, 'The *Querelle* of Ancients and Moderns as a problem for Renaissance scholarship', *Journal of the History of Ideas*, 20 (1959), pp. 3–22, and Baron, *The Crisis of the Early Italian Renaissance*, 2 vols. (Princeton, 1955).
[58] See Cochrane on Bruni's goals, *Historians and Historiography*, p. 9.

events of the class that patronised him;[59] to William Langland whose poem *Piers Plowman* records nearly forty years of social, economic, religious and governmental turmoil prior to and during the reign of Richard II?[60]

Such statements as 'during the whole millennium 400–1400 there was no sense of history even among the educated'[61] cannot now be seen to be either accurate or meaningful, especially if applied uniquely to the medieval period. What this so-called 'no sense of history' is taken to mean is (1) a lack of awareness of anachronism, (2) a lack of awareness of evidence, and (3) a lack of interest in causation. There is a sense in which these assertions are true, of both the medieval and Renaissance periods, in that what we may mean in the twentieth century by these terms is not what earlier thinkers meant by them or saw as important when they analysed the past and man's mind in dealing with either past experiences or language about the past.

CAUSATION, EVIDENCE, ANACHRONISM

Those fourteenth-century commentators on Aristotle's *Physics* known as the Merton College Calculators were precisely interested in investigating the cause of what they called the intention and remission of forms; they also examined the cause of an increase and decrease in heat, whiteness, motion and acceleration.[62] This medieval interest in the causation of intention and remission of forms was taken over by Pomponazzi. New techniques of logical analysis were invoked. But as Murdoch as argued,[63] during the Renaissance there was little shift in the *substance* of the

---

[59] For a discussion of Froissart's methods and aims see Janet Coleman, 'Late scholastic *memoria et reminiscentia*, its uses and abuses', in Piero Boitani and Anna Torti, eds., *Intellectuals and Writers in Fourteenth-Century Europe* (The J. A. W. Bennett Memorial Lectures, Perugia, 1984) (Tübingen, 1986), pp. 22–44; pp. 41–4; J. J. N. Palmer, ed. and introduction to *Froissart: Historian* (Suffolk, 1981), and George Diller, 'Froissart: Patrons and Texts', *ibid.*, pp. 145–60.

[60] See Janet Coleman, *Piers Plowman and the Moderni* (Rome, 1981). Guicciardini made use of Froissart's chronicles referring to Il Frossardo.

[61] Peter Burke, *The Renaissance Sense of the Past*, p. 1.

[62] Janet Coleman, 'Jean de Ripe OFM and the Oxford Calculators', *Mediaeval Studies* 37 (1975), pp. 130–89.

[63] In a communication at a conference at the Warburg Institute, London, 1987, in honour of the late and lamented Charles B. Schmitt. See Charles Schmitt, 'Towards a reassessment of Renaissance Aristotelianism', *History of Science*, 11 (1973), pp. 159–93, on the many Aristotelianisms in the Renaissance and the degree to which they were tied to a scholastic and textbook tradition. Only gradually and in the later seventeenth century was Aristotelianism erased from the universities. It was the criticisms of school philosophy by Galileo, Bacon and Descartes that became prominent and that subsequently have coloured historiography in a radically one-sided way.

problems being treated as they arose in Aristotle's *Physics*. In Renaissance discussions of the composition of continua, there was nothing added to the medieval understanding of the issues other than an increasing concern to cite new authorities from newly available Greek texts which served the eclectic character of Renaissance Aristotelianism. An interest in Aristotle's four causes had been taken up as soon as his scientific works were translated for the Latin west at the end of the twelfth century.

There had always been a theological concern for the cause of sin and evil, the cause of the Fall and of historical calamities. Both those who posited a necessarily caused and determined universe and those who opted for contingency were seriously engaged in the question of causation when they dealt with the origins either of a created or an eternal universe. And they dealt with the causes of justification and salvation.[64] If, what is meant by a lack of interest in causation is really a statement about the possibility of the world and men's experience of it to be investigated without reference to divine intervention, then that too was made possible by Ockham's optimism regarding the capacity of minds to experience intuitively and know evidently the world they inhabit and to link conceptually and linguistically (propositionally) individual experiences together in truthful statements, because God had covenanted that the world was to be as we know it. He could have done otherwise, and presumably still could do otherwise, but *we* can only operate within the probable certainties that govern the operations of reason and language in a universe that has been willed freely by God and which we can but trust. This conclusion issued from the debate over the relationship between God's ordained and absolute powers whereby a dialectic was established between things as they might have been and things as they actually are. The present created order was freely willed by God and did not issue from His acting out of necessity. But having created this order, God has now committed Himself to it in all its contingency.

Furthermore, Ockham was concerned to effect a considerable modification in the traditional Aristotelian doctrine of causation. Matter and form, as intrinsic causes, were to be construed physically rather than metaphysically: matter as actual in its own right, that is, as body having spatially distinguishable parts, and form understood as shape and structure of these material parts. This led in particular to his thesis that any whole *is* its parts, but also in general to a more mechanistic understanding of natural substances and events. Most important for us, is his attempt to prove that causal relations can only be known by experience rather than

---

[64] For a recent summary of the transition from a concept of ontological to covenantal causality, see McGrath, *The Intellectual Origins of the European Reformation*, pp. 82ff.

from rational deductions. Ockham here was dealing with the same kind of epistemological problem that Hume would entertain in the eighteenth century, although he was not as sceptical as Hume would be about the objectivity of causation because he believed we simply must accept the hypothetical principle of nature's uniformity.[65]

There was also a medieval interest in the causes of legal change. During the thirteenth century when feudal customs were giving way in land tenure to alternative developments in customary law based on the alienation of private property of possessors who came to be seen as *de facto* owners, even legal polemicists tried to analyse the cause for this change. They justified changes by appealing to the 'original' Roman understanding of the role of government as *protector* of private *dominium* or ownership. They argued against those who maintained, what would be a losing position, that *dominium* was Christ's and therefore the papacy's, or even against those who argued that kings were owners of what their subjects merely used.[66] As Milsom has pointed out,[67] *we* are the ones with the problems when we try to understand legal documents of the thirteenth and fourteenth centuries, not because such documents indicate that individual issues and evidence for plaintiffs' cases were not discussed, but because the records, the formulae for recording proceedings in courts, manorial or regal, excluded the distinct peculiarities of cases. The *forma*, the genre of legal recording obscured individualisms, but we cannot thereby assume that no one was confronting individual issues and evidence and discussing the whys and wherefores, the causes of litigious relations between men. We must, however, be aware that an interest in cause and effect is not an interest in neutral facts but rather is evaluative, based on prejudgements that are ensconced in contemporary social meaning.

Nor is it strictly true to assert that anachronism was not a critical category on the medieval agenda:[68] linguistic anachronism was certainly entertained, as we have seen.

And if we look at the great debate during the thirteenth century, that between the hierarchical church's interpretation of Christ's and the Apostles' poverty, what else can those radical groups like the Humiliati and the Franciscans themselves have been engaged in but a serious

---

65 Ockham, *Summulae Physicorum*, II, c. 12. Also see his *Quodlibet*, IV, qq. 1 and 2, when he says that Aristotle's statement 'nature acts for an end' is to be interpreted only as a metaphor.

66 See Janet Coleman, 'Property and poverty', in *The Cambridge History of Medieval Political Thought*, ed. J. H. Burns (Cambridge, 1988), pp. 607–48.

67 S. F. C. Milsom, *The Legal Framework of English Feudalism* (The Maitland Lectures, 1972) (Cambridge, 1976).

68 Burke, *The Renaissance Sense of the Past*, p. 1.

attempt to understand the present church as a deviation from and thus, as different from the true primitive church? They knew about this difference through texts. Not only was Scripture reinvestigated to get at the nature of Christ's and the Apostles' lives, in order to extract an exemplary message for those who wished to imitate it; but St Francis's very Testaments were treated as historical documents, linguistically analysed by popes, later Franciscans and Dominicans in order to get at his original intentions for his followers. Dominicans by the end of the thirteenth century simply asserted that neither the pope nor Franciscans knew the mind of Francis and that all the extra exemptions from the strictness of the original Rule were merely papal additions, concessions and misinterpretations of the saint's mind as expressed in his texts.[69] They recognised an anachronism, based on textual evidence, when they wanted to see one. They also recognised that certain apparent anachronisms could be domesticated through interpretation in the interests of a higher, more universal truth.

If we turn from learned literature to popular and vernacular texts, we cannot invoke pageant plays to indicate the lack of historical perspective of medieval people either.[70] In the Wakefield Cycle, Herod swears, anachronistically, by 'Mahoun'. Pageant plays, no more than the deathless exploits of Robin Hood or Batman and Robin, were not meant to be accurate reproductions of historical events. They were meant to illustrate universal types of good and evil throughout history. It is more than likely that the collectivity of authors of these kinds of plays was unaware that Islam had not appeared on the historical scene before the seventh century AD. The pageant play is simple, often barely literate entertainment: Herod is wicked, the Arabs unChristian and wicked, and the Arabs and Turks were on the fifteenth-century horizon.

There is still a genre in our modern world that contrasts the forces of good and evil and its purpose is exemplary rather than historical accuracy. It does not mean that viewers of Superman or Omen films have no historical perspective. The universe was not moralised only during the middle ages, as some recent Renaissance historians have, astonishingly,

---

[69] A. G. Little, *Grey Friars in Oxford*, OHS, 20 (Oxford, 1892) prints the text of a debate *c.* 1260 between Oxford Dominicans and Franciscans, taken down by an eye-witness, pp. 320–35. Dominican response:
Voluntas testamentaria fuit beati Francisci, quod fratres nullo modo quererent litteras expositorias, a sede apostolica, sed hoc non obstante quesierunt et papa annunente optinuerunt. Non solum ergo fratres sed et papa contra intencionem ejus fecerunt, ex quo videtur quod intencionem ejus non noverunt. (p. 325)
See the discussion in Janet Coleman, 'The two jurisdictions: theological and legal justifications of Church property in the thirteenth century', *Studies in Church History*, 23 (1987), pp. 75–110.
[70] Burke, *The Renaissance Sense of the Past*, p. 2.

supposed.[71] Are we then to believe that Rubens's majestic 'Herod's Feast' in the National Gallery of Scotland is evidence of this painter's lack of historical perspective because all his Biblical persons are dressed in sumptuous seventeenth-century dress? An anachronistic fork is lifted to the severed head of John the Baptist. And what kind of 'lack of historical sense' can we imply when we consider that Gavin Douglas's translation in Scotland of Virgil's *Aeneid*, followed by Dryden's translation, were meant, in Dryden's own words 'to make Virgil speak such English as he would have spoken if he had been born in England, and in the present age'?[72]

We have seen that much medieval writing was a formal affair where the framework often predominated. The form could exclude explanation, telling us perhaps nothing about how authors thought of cause and effect or evidence rather than telling us that they had no sense of either. Even when education was pursued in the earlier middle ages by a tiny clerical and indeed monastic elite, this education was based on oral debate, oral recitation, the writing and copying of formal letters, doctrine and laws. Preaching was according to a *forma praedicandi*, there was a *forma* for writing a romance, a *forma* for legal court records. Men of talent could always extend these recognised genres in original ways. We should be more concerned to examine what the role of the written document is for a period that is not widely literate, than to assert that formal and formulaic writing indicates no ability to analyse and deviate from the form. The latter assertion would be analogous to arguing that periods in which painting is formulaic and two-dimensionally iconic, give us evidence that painters and viewers could not physically perceive distance and did not operate in a three-dimensional world of perspective. This would lead us to assert that the mental properties of man had evolved suddenly, in say one hundred years, issuing in perspectival paintings at about the time of Giotto! Indeed, what did emerge around the time of Giotto was a method which had and still has to be learned for representing the world of appearances. An increasing interest in geometry, a recognition that vision proceeds in straight lines, led to a consciously reasoned technique of representing on two-dimensional surfaces the three-dimensional world of space in which men had always dwelt and knew that they did. To learn how to draw the particularities of the world in scaled-down relational proportions on a two-dimensional surface is a problem solved through asking questions about the logic of epistemological experience. Perspecti-

---

[71] *Ibid.*, p. 20.
[72] Douglas Gray, 'Some pre-Elizabethan Examples of an Elizabethan art', in Edward Chaney and Peter Mack, eds., *England and the Continental Renaissance* (Woodbridge, 1990), p. 24.

val representation is a learned logical solution to the question of representation, a science of perception that issues from matching a supposed logical theory of perception with experimentation in methods of representing perception. Its contemporary analogue was the logic of language and its representational capacities, so central to the arts faculty curriculum.

Finally, it is no longer credible to insist that the medieval attitude to law was that it was fixed, revealed and not invented. The work of Post, Tierney and generally, of those historians of canon, civil and customary laws, has demonstrated how thirteenth-century lawyers were concerned with the development of law and its changing qualities. Even Aquinas saw natural law as, in a sense, altering with the perfection of natural knowledge. But what is distinctive about this concern for development in law and for development in scriptural interpretaion is its purpose: to justify the present in the light of a past that was rendered useable. Such prudential use of the past is still with us. It was certainly still with all those later seventeenth and eighteenth-century republicans who justified their civic humanism in radically different contexts by an appeal not only to *their* conception of the Renaissance but also to *their* conception of antiquity. Rousseau was not alone in accommodating Sparta to the possibilities for eighteenth-century France and Corsica.

If there was an early period in medieval society when we can say that the law was taken to be fixed, it is only in the sense that thinkers during the early monastic middle ages referred to fixed authorities and principles while, in effect, reinterpreting these to suit their own circumstances. It was not King Alfred's intention, as some have argued,[73] to abolish old laws while he was not prepared to make new ones. What Alfred said was that 'many of them [the laws] which I did not like, I rejected with the advice of my councillors and ordered them to be differently observed. For I dared not presume to set in writing at all many of my own because it was unknown to me what would please those who should come after us.' This is a very important statement concerning the role of writing in fixing or changing traditions for future generations, a very perceptive comment from Alfred which anthropologists such as Jack Goody would applaud for recognising the difference it makes to society to inscribe its laws fixed on the page on the one hand, and to make laws for a culture that learns them orally and alters them imperceptibly in the future. Alfred's is a statement not about a fear of making new laws but about the consequences of writing them down.

---

[73] Burke, *The Renaissance Sense of the Past*, p. 4.

SHIFTING GENRES, STYLES AND AUDIENCES

I suggest that we reinterpret the so-called 'leap' from the middle ages to the Renaissance as a genre shift. The genre, the form of the various writings, taking into account the audience meant to read such texts, could and did help to determine the content and its subsequent interpretation by contemporaries and later readers. A consideration of medieval genres, which provided the *forma* of what *we* might classify as political thought, historical analysis, polemic, fiction, also enables *us* to determine what we mean by the beginnings of the Renaissance, late in the north and early in the south. It is far less that meaning differed in this north/south divide than that differing discursive genres were employed to express this meaning. Renaissance writers detested the scholastic mode of signifying truths that men of both periods shared. As McGrath has rightly pointed out,[74] using Erasmus as an example

The remarkable success of Erasmus' *Enchiridion Militis Christiani* in the first decades of the sixteenth century unquestionably reflects the fact that it was addressed to ... an articulate lay piety, expressing that piety in an intelligent and intelligible form. Thus Erasmus' criticisms of scholastic theology were directed against the form in which it was expressed – particularly in inelegant Latin employed by the scholastic theologians – rather than against the religious ideas thus articulated'.

Melanchthon was also to criticise the unintelligibility of scholastic Latin. The shift in literary structure, the alteration of the formulae of expression, leads us directly to the fact that audiences were changing as a consequence of increasing literacy from the fourteenth century onwards, and authors adopted suitable rhetorical forms to present plausible truths to the literate but nonclerical, as John of Salisbury already noted had happened to a more limited extent in the twelfth century. The content of the debate over the memory and its uses, already defined by Scotus and Ockham and their *via antiqua/via moderna* followers, did not change; what shifted were the literary genres in which such positions were elaborated.

The humanist movement at its high point has been characterised as the increasing employment of certain aspects of the medieval arts faculty trivium – originally, grammar, rhetoric and logic – which came to be called the *studia humanitatis*, and separated itself off as an independent discipline of philology. Philology was to become the scholarly means by which texts of the past were criticised, corrected and examined. It did *not* simply evolve out of the distinctive medieval rhetorical training in *ars dictaminis*

[74] McGrath, *The Intellectual Origins of the European Reformation*, p. 12.

which, for the most part, was a purely practical study to train notaries to compose documents and letters and lacked an ideological impetus to constitute an intellectual movement. Some humanists did, however, locate such political posturing in Brunetto Latini's *Treasure* and thereby established an elder authority of the uses of dictamen to whom they could appeal. Neither the mechanics of medieval dictamen nor grammatical studies which analysed and imitated ancient texts directly gave rise to the achievements of fifteenth-century humanism. Rather, philological exegesis of past texts should be seen as an extension of what was at the very heart of the *via moderna*'s project. In so far as the *studium humanitatis* was seen to be formally tied to the 'historical method' of analysing the grammar of past texts, it proceeded to identify such a method with the literal mode by which was meant the study of the letter, the terms and propositions which rendered a text grammatically coherent or incoherent. Avoiding allegory, indeed avoiding the neo-Platonising essentialist theories asserting a fixed, necessary history, they none the less, like Hugh of St Victor and other medieval grammarians and historians, identified the *sensus historicus* with the *sensus grammaticus*. But the so-called 'revival' of the literal sense of an account does not mean that literal history, which represents the first intentions of sense data, gives you the meaning or accurate interpretation of these data any more for these philologists than it did for Hugh of St Victor. Fidelity to the letter was simply propaedeutic to higher interpretation. The humanist call for a *fides historiae* is not in itself a call to what we take to be the foundations in empirical experience of historical understanding. It is rather a call for grammatical, stylistic and logical consistency in the copying of an ancient text in preparation for the reader's interpretation. *Fides historiae* is a reference to grammar being precise and rule-bound and by extension, the tale or story or account must be linguistically and stylistically coherent and consistent. It is not a call to check the nontextual evidence against the account. Time and again we have seen that there was a long-held belief in the adequate representation of men's thoughts, which referred to events, by means of terms and thereafter propositions, a belief to be found in the traditional Latin grammars of Donatus and Priscian which were reproduced in ever greater numbers during the Renaissance. The call to *fides historiae* was a call for grammatical and logical plausibility. It was a call to get the Latin cases right! In the twelfth century as in the fourteenth and in the sixteenth centuries, veridical implications were taken to be the properties of *linguistic propositions*. One did not thereafter have to believe Ockham and his followers that we have both a sensual and intellectual intuitive grasp of particulars and individual reality which thereafter, is represented to us in

574

terms of first intention or propositions of second intention. Humanist philologists were the heirs of those logicians who, as Scotus *and* Ockham affirmed, dealt with language as a conventional mode to signify thoughts and extramental realities. To this extent their project was not ontological and they were not concerned with constructing arguments that proved the certainty of the past's 'being'. They were simply affirming the plausibility of stylistically consistent and correct grammatical statements from and about the past as provided by the historical sense of a given text, just as we saw Hugh of St Victor arguing for the literal sense of a text being equivalent to its historical sense which represented, in words, the first intentions of sense data, as yet, uninterpreted.

Professed humanists rejected the pedantic and pedagogic conventions of scholastic discourse and this rejection of scholastic *forma* provided them with a real sense of their own separate identity in a world that boasted literate and professional men who were no longer clergy.[75] Medieval scholastic genres were replaced or altered; the debate form was traded in for the one-off rhetorical presentation or oration; but the methodological focus on the word, the grammar, the logic of the proposition was precisely what modal logicians of the thirteenth century and Ockham and his followers passed on to them, whether Renaissance propagandists were ready to acknowledge the legacy or not. Skinner has noted how all the early Renaissance rhetoricians and polemicists were, in fact, trained in the medieval *ars dictaminis* and many were academic professors of this old-fashioned *forma* in the universities of Europe.[76] But it was not simply the *ars dictaminis* but the trivium of the arts course, the grammatical studies and the focus on Aristotle's writings on rhetoric and logic along with the weight of authoritative commentaries, which they knew. If fourteenth-century Oxford was the centre of logical studies, Oxford's large body of international students, especially Italians and peripatetic mendicants, returned home with their manuscripts and commentaries to help spread English ideas and methods abroad and specifically to Italy.[77] Although it may be argued that much of the work of leading humanists had little significance for philosophy beyond the domain of ethics, much of the philosophical literature of the Renaissance was due not to the humanists but to those trained in scholastic Aristotelianism or in neo-Platonist metaphysics, influenced by the ancient ideas transmitted by both scholasticism and humanism. But even leading humanists demonstrate a greater

[75] Paul O. Kristeller, 'Humanism', *CHRP*, p. 121.
[76] See his important study, *The Foundations of Modern Political Thought*, 2 vols. (Cambridge, 1978), especially vol. 1.
[77] Kristeller, 'Humanism', *CHRP*, p. 134; also *CHRP*, pp. 22–3; on Blasius of Parma, see Eckhard Kessler, 'The intellectual soul', *CHRP*, pp. 486 ff.

continuity with a scholastic legacy than this division between Renaissance ethical humanists and Renaissance metaphysical philosophers implies.

In this light let us look at the attitudes of Lorenzo Valla (1407–57) who died just as the printing press was to make its appearance. Valla's main interests, it is of some importance to note, were classical philology, moral philosophy and *theology*, rather than history *sensu stricto*. In his most widely read work, the *Elegantiarum Latinae libri sex*, Valla focused on the study of words on which philosophy was based. He believed that such a linguistic study could correct errors about the past as well as help to transform manners and institutions in the present. He put forward what was an already well-established twelfth-century canonical interpretation in his *Declamatio* on the Donation of Constantine, that Constantine had never granted temporal jurisdiction over the western empire to the pope. He reinforced this thesis by adding philological arguments to the legal and logical ones, proving the document to have been an eighth-century forgery.[78] This philological analysis was then marshalled with an appeal for political action against the illegal usurpation of the contemporary papacy in the kingdom of Naples.[79]

Ockham had also denied the historicity and therefore, the legality of the Donation of Constantine, calling the tradition apocryphal on the basis of his study not only of chronicles and church history but by studying the text itself to show its linguistic distortions.[80]

Now, from what we have said thus far, it seems useful to subject Kelley's

[78] Compare this attitude to texts with the famous early-ninth-century example of Lupus abbot of Ferrières, who was unsatisfied with the single manuscript of Cicero in his possession. He requested of a friend a second copy 'so that from a comparison of the two texts the truth might emerge'. At another time Lupus, having examined an old manuscript (*codex reverendae vetustatis*) was surprised to recognise it was less truthful (*mendosiorem*) than the more recent manuscript in his possession (*posteriores non deteriores*). Earlier, Theodulf of Orleans, an adviser of Charlemagne, applied similar insights to the text of the Bible. The interest in both cases seems to have been, as in the Renaissance, in grammatical and orthographical correctness rather than in the historicity of ideas. See C. H. Beeson, *Lupus of Ferrières as Scribe and Text Critic* (Cambridge, Mass., 1930), pp. 3–4. E. K. Rand said: 'There is nowhere in the middle ages or in the early renaissance a closer approach than this [Theodulf's Bible] to the modern method of constructing a critical text'. 'Dom Quentin's memoir on the text of the Vulgate', *Harvard Theological Review*, 17 (1924), p. 228. Whether or not these are similar to modern criteria is another issue. But it is clear that an interest in producing 'pure' texts without at least linguistic and grammatical errors was as much a desideratum in the early middle ages as it was during the Renaissance. For Bede's similar attitudes to grammatical purity, see Paul Meyvaert, 'Bede the Scholar', in G. Bonner, ed. *Famulus Christi* (London, 1976), pp. 40–69.

[79] Wolfram Setz, *Lorenzo Vallas Schriften gegen die Konstantinische Schenkung* (Tübingen, 1975). Also see Linda C. Junk, 'Valla on rhetoric and history', in *History and Theory*, 12 (1973).

[80] Ockham, *Breviloquium de potestate papae*, ed. L. Baudry (Paris, 1937), Lib. VI, cap. 4, pp. 163–5.

summary of Lorenzo Valla's typical humanist method and achievement to the following test. Let us replace Valla's name with that of Magister X in order to determine whether Valla's distinctiveness, as described by Kelley, is unique to this distinguished Renaissance scholar. Is the *substance* of Valla's message a new departure?

Kelley says:

X demanded a return to human 'reality' for he was convinced that knowledge could be attained only through the examination of particular things. Not of course that X abstained from all generalisation ... X called for a return to original sources: for style was an organic part of doctrine and antiquity had to be allowed to speak in its own ultimately inimitable accents ... *Lastly and inevitably, X adopted an attitude that was both pluralistic and relativistic. Every age had literally to be understood in its own terms and truth could no more be separated from its cultural environment or from its cultural style than form could be separated from matter* ... X's historical thought was founded, in short, upon the recognition of a principle of individuality ...[81]

The statements in italics require further consideration because there appears to be an implication that X showed signs of historicism before its time. Whether or not X wished to acknowledge the fact, he was an heir to late scholastic terminism insofar as it was applied to authoritative texts; he was a terminist analysing the words in the sentence in their linguistic (not historical) context in order to determine the author's meaning. We saw that in his polemical writings Ockham had stressed that individual experiencers in any age use various styles and *modi loquendi* to express the individual experiences they have. And Scripture can be read by any reader as expressing those experiences which may be verified by anyone today. One need only look *not* at Ockham's tracts on logic but at his polemical, effectively rhetorical analysis of John XXII's pronouncements against the Franciscans and their supposed logical and grammatical misinterpretation of Christ's words and Christ's and the Apostles' understanding of the terms of voluntary poverty. Ockham had selectively brought in the machinery of ordinary logical and grammatical analysis to counter the papacy's interpretation of ancient texts, most notably in his *Tractatus contra Benedictum*[82] and in his *Dialogus*. And here, Ockham did not suggest that the average sane and literate man who confronted scriptural texts need be a professional logician, skilled in *suppositio* theory.

Valla, the language specialist, took this approach further, evaluating the Vulgate Latin Bible against the Greek original to the detriment of the former. That the Catholic Church continued to insist that the Vulgate was a doctrinally normative text led, of course, to a tension between humanist,

[81] D. Kelley, *Foundations of Modern Historical Scholarship*, pp. 45–6.
[82] *Opera Politica*, III, ed. H. S. Offler (Manchester, 1956).

multi-lingual, philological biblical exegesis and Catholic orthodoxy. Humanists insisted that *modi loquendi* changed. But so did Ockham and most other medieval analysts of language. However, it is very much to be doubted whether either Ockham or Valla was relativistic in the way Kelley describes. To understand a past text by focusing on its linguistic expressions and style, that is, to be aware that discourse has a history, is not necessarily to affirm that the truth uttered at some past moment is different from a truth expressed through verbal and stylistic alternatives of another age. The problem as both these men saw it was that the truth could not be retrieved at all if one did not examine the style, the logic and the grammar of a text. Both men shared an exegetical methodology. There was no concern to examine the text within or against a nonlinguistic, historical context. And the truth was neither multiple nor culturally situated.

Indeed, Valla, a good Ciceronian, argued that history was inseparable from rhetoric in that rhetorical rules, learned from ancient historians, required the adoption not only of a style capable of appealing to *current* readers but also of a vocabulary that current men could understand. Valla believed that in recalling the past he was writing for men of the present and future rather than for men of the past, and therefore, it was legitimate to use modern terms and borrow appropriately from the vernacular. We recall John of Salisbury's identical attitude. *Modi loquendi* change; the exemplary message does not. When grammar, dialectic and rhetoric are ill used in any age, they give rise to false and implausible opinions. The truth of history could, therefore, be expressed in later ages by another style, language and rhetoric. The historical and exemplary truth of ages past could be got at only through an investigation of past language.[83] When Valla argued that the dogmas, the religions, the false opinions of the action of virtues through which man ascends to heaven must be criticised in the pagan ancients, he did not believe the truth to be relative.[84] He did believe, like many medieval authors we have examined, that the *modi loquendi* had changed, and that language could be abused, inspiring men to

---

[83] See Cochrane, *Historians and Historiography*, p. 149.
[84] See Valla's prologue to Book IV, *Elegantiae*. Also David Marsh, *The Quattrocento Dialogue, Classical Tradition and Humanist Innovation* (Cambridge, Mass., 1980), chapter 4, 'Lorenzo Valla and the rhetorical dialogue'. Marsh shows how Valla's *De vero falsoque bono* (1441) extensively modifies its Ciceronian models *De finibus bonorum et malorum* and the *De natura deorum* along Augustinian lines, specifically Augustine's *Contra Academicos* and the *Epistle* 118. Valla depicts a debate between two classical philosophers adjudicated by a Christian theologian. 'Augustine's epistle formulates the duality of celestial truth and terrestrial falsehood underlying the argument of Valla's *De vero falsoque bono*, in which the false good of ancient philosophy is refuted in order to expound the truth of the Christian faith' (p. 57).

draw false conclusions. Language is merely a means to meaning. The truth is and ever has been immutable.

'Non lingua gentilium, non grammatica, non rhetorica, non dialecta, caeteraeque artes damnandae sunt, siquidem Apostoli lingua graeca scripserunt, sed religiones, sed falsa opiniones de actione virtutum per quas in caelum scandimus. Ceterae autem scientiae atque artes in medio sunt positae, quibus et bene uti et male.'[85] It is not the language of the Gentiles, their grammar, rhetoric, dialectic or any other arts that are damned, for the Apostles wrote in Greek, but rather religion, false opinions on the action of virtue by which we attain heaven. The arts are means, which may be used well or ill.

We may well compare this with Ockham's statement in his school textbook on logic, the *Elementarium Logicae*:

The sayings [of the experts] should not be spurned or reproved or denied before it has been established that they are at odds with the truth; but let judgement be held in suspence, whether they are sayings of the ancients or moderns, so that they will not be vilified on account of their novelty nor held on account of their age, but the truth should be extolled in all things; since whether the assertors are ancients or moderns, friends or enemies, it is holy to prefer the truth.[86]

John of Salisbury, we recall, had already proposed a similar stance towards moderns and ancients. As for Ockham so too for Valla, there is a truth that some past experiencer experienced and if he put this experience in writing as a memorial, presented us with the first intentions, gave us the literal text, *we* can get at its truth if we look closely at the coherence of his propositions and judge these against scriptural truth. We judge such propositions against the immutable truth of scriptural statements regarding celestial ascension. These statements are themselves open to any literate person capable of sanely reading the logic of language. If someone draws the wrong, that is, illogical or implausible, conclusions from his experiences, he is to be corrected and corrected with eloquence, says Valla. Language as a means to meaning can be used well or ill. Illogical or implausible conclusions are false interpretations, false opinions held, of the historical record of experience and it is these interpretations or opinions which need correcting. Valla, the philosophical rhetorician would argue that rhetorical plausibility rather than strict

---

[85] Cited in Eugenio Garin, *Prosatori Latini del Quattrocento* (Milan and Naples, 1952), pp. 620–22.

[86] Ockham, *Elementarium logicae*, ed. Buytaert, in *Franciscan Studies* 25 (1965), p. 275. Valla is saying that when the ancients were wrong we must say it as well as when they are right, judged against a universal notion of truth that is timeless. See Trinkaus, 'Antiquitas versus modernitas', *Journal of the History of Ideas*, 48 (1987), pp. 15 ff for a summary and elucidation of the debate between Poggio and Valla.

logical demonstration through the syllogism would sufficiently dissuade men from interpretative error, a point we have seen made abundantly clear by the twelfth-century Ciceronian John of Salisbury when he discussed Abelard's more strict logical method. Ockham's polemical writings show him to be more logically rigorous than Valla, but both men were focusing on the 'ordinary' language of Scripture to show that it revealed a-historical truths to ordinary, literate men who read it. A belief in the nonrelative stability of truth is confirmed in any age through rhetorically plausible arguments that employ current *modi loquendi* to express an exemplary truth.[87]

If this logical and philological approach to texts that was generally subsumed under *grammatica* was the making of that so-called intellectual revolution which coincided with the printed book, then it is only the latter event which can be deemed 'new' at the end of the fifteenth century.

The invention of printing, so important an aspect of the success of Renaissance humanism, occurred in northern Europe – in Germany, to be precise, a Germany riddled by the antagonism between the *via antiqua* and the *via moderna*. When the presses were set up in Paris (1470) by emigré Germans – Michael Friburger of Colmar, Ulrich Gering of Beromunster (Constance) and Martin Crantz of Constance – they came from the University of Basle as bachelors of arts, invited by Jean Heynlin, a Parisian theologian of German origins with an interest in *belles lettres*. The first text to be printed in Paris was a collection of Latin letters by the Italian humanist Gasparino Barzizza. But Heynlin was an adherent of the *via antiqua* and the humanist press was meant to send scholars back to study the Fathers and the Bible, St Thomas and Scotus, as voices of an ever-contemporary, formal set of immutable, a-historical truths. The texts of classical antiquity appeared in both manuscript and print side by side with the traditional medieval theologians, especially the commentaries on Aristotle of Aquinas and Scotus along with the major tracts of Augustine. It has been suggested that the humanist press of the Sorbonne was only able to publish humanist works at all because of the much larger funding provided by their publications of theological material and, in particular, that of the *via antiqua*.[88]

But if few university towns became centres of commercial publishing, the emergence of the availability of printed books is the crux of the issue. The philological tradition, so evidently an inheritance of the arts course,

---

[87] On humanists' logic and their concern for 'good' arguments, see Lisa Jardine, *CHRP*, especially pp. 175 ff.
[88] J. Veyrin-Forrer, *1470–1970, Hommage aux premiers imprimeurs de France*, (Paris, 1970). In general, see the various discussions in *CHRP* on manuscripts and printing, pp. 11–53.

was spurred on as the medieval tradition had not been, by the need to provide accurate texts for the printed page. And the medieval genres which presented eclectically gathered memorials of the past, be it from ecclesiastical history, the Bible, legal texts or from the classical ancient 'greats' were selectively remembered to suit a new audience, an expanded readership, a widened range of the politically powerful and articulate.[89] In the days before printed books, this had already been attempted by four-teenth-century Augustinians who collected and purified Augustine's writings to reinvigorate the *via antiqua*'s project, but nowhere near as many men could have to hand such laboriously copied out texts as would be the case when printing became available. As more sources of ancient philosophy, science, history and style were copied, edited, printed and dispersed, conflicting traditions emerged. This led to a widespread eclec-tic use of the welter of past memorials available. Renaissance readers and thinkers would become as *parti pris* as their medieval forebears in remem-bering and interpreting the past. The past was a living legacy to be preserved for use in the present by an expanding, nonclerical readership. There can be no justification for the modern assumption that investigation into either ancient history or the history of the primitive church suddenly took a new and 'modern' turn in the hands of humanists, especially if what is meant is that the Renaissance developed a disinterested grasp of the past in order to show how truth itself was in flux. They were not interested in discontinuities but rather in 'accurate' continuities and their criterion for accuracy was overarched by an ideological concern to justify their present, be it in terms of civic republicanism or an absolute princedom. Roman history especially was found to mirror their needs exactly. A philological analysis of ancient Roman texts showed them how they could even sound like their ancient forebears. And they adopted and adapted ancient formulae of discourse to address a wider public. To this wider audience they presented, as did their medieval forebears, an exemplary past, for as Matteo Palmieri declared, 'History is nothing other than the celebration of illustrious men'.[90] A wider audience did not require the kinds of logical proofs offered in dialectical debate. Rhetorical proofs would be sufficient. Hence, for Benedetto Accolti as much as for John of Salisbury, rhetoric enabled an historian to rescue the deeds of great men from oblivion as well as providing him with the tools to interpret these deeds to a mixed audience.

[89] For a recent summary, see McGrath, *The Intellectual Origins of the European Reformation*, pp. 11 ff. largely drawing on the many studies of Heiko Oberman and Paul Kristeller.
[90] Matthaei Palmerii, *De captivitate Pisarum liber*, ed. G.Scaramella, *Rerum italicarum scrip-tores*², XIX, pt. 2, 3, cited in Black, *Accolti*, p. 288 n. 25.

Renaissance historians developed the rhetorical comparison of the ancient and moderns further as a commonplace of panegyric. The debate between the ancients and the moderns, between the past and the present, had been an important theme of historical thought in antiquity and during the middle ages, and continued still in the Renaissance. The purpose was to contrast the present with the past. But in all these periods the quarrel between ancients and moderns could be used to point up the shortcomings of the present in comparison with some previous golden age or, on the contrary, to show the moderns to be the equals of the ancients if not even more virtuous, often because the latter were Christians and benefited from God's grace. The Renaissance emphasis on epideictic rhetoric led to a greater proliferation of rhetorical evaluations of the difference between antiquity and modern times. As Black has observed, 'Humanists, participating as they did in the quarrel [between ancients and moderns] as practitioners of epideictic rhetoric, chose the side of the arguments which was appropriate to the particular panegyric which they were composing and so there was no unanimity of opinion on the question of ancients and moderns in humanist literature'.[91] If Renaissance humanists expanded the use of panegyric, it none the less was not an invention of Italian humanists, and its theme, the contrast between ancients and moderns, was not unique to them. Its long history both preceded and followed the Renaissance well into the eighteenth century. And part of the long-enduring commonplace which praised moderns in having surpassed ancient (or medieval) achievements was the idea of a revival of the arts. History as rhetoric is not about fact but about narrative compositional techniques that make an unproblematic past useful for the present. Rhetorical history explains in ways found plausible to present readers. It aims explicitly to convince a present audience and not past actors, experiencers, rememberers. Its underlying premise is that men have not changed over the centuries and that like circumstances produce like responses albeit referred to by changing modes of expression.

Rhetorical history engages a distinctive sense of the past as present. It is not equivalent to a modern sense of the past as over and done with. And Renaissance historians tell readers precisely why they are using past exemplars as models for present action. Medieval authors often did the same.

The shift from the middle ages to the Renaissance becomes most clear if we observe the shift in genres, in the formulae of discourse. If we turn from the scholarly literature of scholasticism to the literature of the humanists, we encounter only to some extent the same literary genres we

[91] Black, *Accolti*, pp. 195, and see pp. 196–9.

saw developed during the middle ages. Here, too, are textbooks and treatises on rhetoric, moral philosophy, and a mass of commentaries on ancient authors. Such commentaries were written by humanists whose teaching activities fit them into what was still a medieval educational curriculum in European universities. Where the difference lies between scholastic and later humanist commentaries, even when the text commented on is the same, is in the methodology of interpretation of the text employed by some but not all humanists. The genre of dialectical analysis and argument came to be replaced by a grammatical analysis and a greater concern for the linguistic context of grammatical utterances. Such a trend was already evident in medieval commentaries on legal texts, both canon and civil. And many of the increasingly sophisticated tools for a linguistic and logical analysis of a proposition grew out of the linguistic concerns of logicians in the arts faculties of Paris and Oxford, techniques of analysis that reached something of a climax in the modern logic of William of Ockham and his followers. Behind such analysis of texts lay ontological theories that related words, statements, concepts and the extramental world.

The competing epistemologies of Scotus and Ockham survived well into the sixteenth century. What altered was the form of the analysis in that the *quaestio* was almost completely disregarded by humanists and the disputation was replaced by the oration. This reflects the social function of such commentaries in the two contrasted periods. In the later middle ages, the commentary on a text was an academic exercise. In the humanist age, the oration was to be *orally* delivered to a wider audience, and was composed for special one-off occasions.

If we compare the epistolary literature of the two periods, say, from the fourteenth to the sixteenth centuries, we see that medieval state documents were copied usually without names and often without dates and were written according to a *forma*, the *ars dictaminis*. The private letter was only beginning to appear and when it became widespread as a medium of communication we know that we are in an age in which literacy is extensive. There is further evidence in the growth in vernacular literature and this means an expansion in the ways of writing to different audiences. Different literary genres were intended for different groups of readers and some genres appear to owe their origin to a concern to define a new and discrete public. But the consequences for historical interpretation of the differing embattled methodologies of *via antiqua* and *via moderna* survived the shift in genres: men continued to argue over whose method accurately remembered the past for the purposes of the present.

WHAT MACHIAVELLI AND HOBBES INHERITED FROM
THE 'VIA MODERNA'

Let us turn, finally, to Florence of the 1470s where we find a Dominican Savonarola, preaching republican virtues in the language of the medieval visionary. Those who searched for an explanation of the incomprehensible and chaotic events of 1494 and 1499 turned for answers to the astrologers and prophets and not to the historians. Salvation was sought not in liberty and cultural creativity but in a Savonarolan New Jerusalem, for it was said once again, that God alone can improve man's history.[92] Machiavelli would argue that this priest's noble republican dream could not be adequately realised because he employed the exemplary lessons of history wrongly. Machiavelli proceeded to write his vast commentary on Livy to demonstrate that the importance of the past was precisely its exemplary character. The *Discourses on Livy* were meant to be a manual on how to read history and derive advantages for the present. Historical events of the past served as examples from which the laws of politics could be induced. And Machiavelli did not hesitate to distort history whenever it did not fit the universal laws of human action he believed he saw.[93]

Machiavelli went further than the traditional pre-Ockhamist medieval view when he said in the *Discourses*, I, 39: 'whoever considers the past and the present will readily observe that all cities and all peoples are and ever have been animated by the same desires and the same passions'. There is no historicism here. Indeed, he was arguing, as had Ockham, that men learn from their individual experiences and necessarily understand the world according to logical laws, inscribed in propositions about the past, which provide certainty about men's actions in given circumstances. Machiavelli says that 'it is easy by diligent study of the past [i.e. texts] to foresee what is likely to happen in the future in any republic, and to apply those remedies that were used by the ancients or, not finding any that were employed by them, to desire new ones from the *similarity of events*' (emphasis added). The world to be experienced, on the one hand, and its truth on the other, do not change. And men's responses to the world of experience remain constant and hence predictable throughout history. This is why we may follow the examples of the lives of good and successful rulers. In *Discourses*, II, 43, he notes: 'Wise men say not without reason what whoever wishes to foresee the future must consult the past, for

---

92 See Cesare Vasoli, 'L'attesa della nuova eta in ambienti e gruppi fiorentini del Quattrocento', in *L'attesa dell'età nuova nella spiritualità della fine del Medioevo* (Todi, 1962). Also Donald Weinstein, *Savonarola and Florence* (Princeton, 1970).

93 Contemporaries noted his distortions. See Cochrane, *Historians and Historiography*, p. 266.

human events ever resemble those of preceding times. This arises from the fact they are produced by men who have been and ever will be animated by the same passions and thus they must necessarily have the same results.' The contingency of the past as well as that of the present is inscribed in laws of probability based on that intuitive grasp of their experience that men who live and remember naturally achieve. Events as individual experiences and the constancy of man's nature in deriving understanding from what he experiences, rather than from separate intelligible truths that are essentially stable, led to Machiavelli's use of the past as exemplary. This kind of history is the direct legacy of the *via moderna* and it was written at a time when, in contrast, Ficino's neo-Platonist metaphysical absolutes and a general a-historical spirit had come to dominate Florentine culture. The merely contingent, individual and particular had fallen from favour. Machiavelli's is a rejection of the *via antiqua*'s assertion that a man's virtuousness was not in his own hands but rather, under the inscrutable auspices of God or Fortune or providence. For Machiavelli, Fortune was as fickle as a woman and with suitable beatings could be made to bend to the will of the man of self-determining virtù.

But did Machiavelli find such men of virtù in the past? Contemporaries knew that he misconstrued his textual sources and committed numerous errors of 'fact'. His successor as official historian of the Florentine republic, Scipione Ammirato said that Machiavelli 'altered names, twisted facts, confounded cases, increased, added, substracted, diminished and did anything that suited his fancy without checking, without lawful restraint, and what is more, he seems to have done so occasionally on purpose'![94] Machiavelli constructed his 'historical' man of virtù, the princely hero, by picking out passages from Villani and Biondo. As Cochrane admits, he 'recast the personages according to formulas borrowed from Diogenes Laertius and Diodorus Siculus, and ended up with a largely fictitious portrait of what seemed to him an anticipation of Cesare Borgia',[95] all in the service of showing fortune bending to individual self-determination. This is a view to which Petrarch would not have assented, but Machiavelli would find company in the later adherents of a *via moderna* who would make of Ockham's God a truly *absconditus* deity, effectively unconcerned with the world and men's actions.

If Ockham's epistemology and his logical subtleties, especially when used by less careful followers, offended Church authorities, Machiavelli

---

[94] Ammirata's *Istorie fiorentine*, ed., F. Ranalli (Florence, 1846), cited in Cochrane, *Historians and Historiography*, pp. 269–70.
[95] Cochrane, *Historians and Historiography*, p. 266.

would offend the wider world. But man, understood as an individual experiencer and rememberer, was already set to determine the course of contingent history, not least by determining on the basis of his individual experiences the nature of the political world he inhabited.

The seventeenth-century Hobbes would understand this as well as anyone. There is nothing startling in finding the first several chapters of Hobbes's *Leviathan* to be a recapitulation of medieval nominalist theories of language as conventional, where the focus is on the radical, individual experience of the sensual man in a contingent universe. Nor is it surprising to see the result of this epistemology and theory of language to be a discussion of the nature of rational individuals contracting into a political world made up of the individual and discrete wills of its members. Hobbes expresses high scorn for the kind of university Aristotelianism being taught where species were proposed to explain sensation and understanding. We have seen that this was not the Aristotle of Ockham and the *via moderna*, for the former eliminated species and instead spoke of an intuitive cognition of sensual and intellectual experience, sense experience being the very foundation of all the more general conclusions drawn from it about how things are for men in the world. Indeed, it is only through a system of signs, conventionally established, that men can draw conclusions about their particular experiences of the world, language signifying experiences and enabling connections to be made between cause and effect. The probable certainty of language which begins with precise definitions and fans out to establish syllogisms, enables men to establish the truth of their propositions, their representative reasoning about the world, rather than a truth about the world unmediated by language. For Ockham as for Hobbes, truth and falsity pertain to language rather than to things.

We can only surmise that where the *via moderna* continued to influence scientific examinations of the world through a precise method of definition, as in the geometry which Hobbes so praises, the *via antiqua* was reimported into university curricula in Hobbes's own times to encourage a reliance on authoritative school pronouncements rather than on man's own experience. But as we have by now seen, there was another methodology abroad and it undoubtedly fed into the first chapters of the *Leviathan*. That Hobbes defines memory as decaying sense, signifying something fading and past, and that memory depends on sense experience alone is what we have come to expect from Ockham and his successors. That Hobbes defines remembering of the reminiscent variety as prudence which attains only probable certainty, based as it is on plausible, presumed connections between past experiences, is by now a familiar utterance.

That speech signifies the world of experience and serves to transfer mental discourse into verbal communication, referring to the world, conventionally, but not implying an ordering of the extra-linguistic and extra-conceptual world, is central to both the Ockhamist and the Hobbesian enterprise. For both men, there is nothing in the world that is universal other than names, for the things referred to by such names are themselves individual and singular. No species, just experiences and signs, and a defined method of interpreting conventionally established signs to produce understanding in men, understanding being, as Hobbes insists, nothing but conception caused by speech. For Ockham, in a contingent world men sensually experience their lives in individual ways, but in accepting a strict logic of language come to communicate not only in generalities but by establishing relations between experiences as expressed through propositions. No divine voice tells an Ockhamist that there are laws of nature and of morality; rather, man comes to these as the dictates of prudence based on propositions which connect experiences and give them meaning. Where the arbiter of individual reckoning in an Ockhamist world is the language specialist, the literate logician, Hobbes politicises him and makes him sovereign. He is the absolute and last definer of terms. Ockham believes we are born with the faculty of reason, unlike Hobbes, but for Ockham we know of it only through its activity and such activity only comes about after we have experience, after we sense and remember the world and then make assertions about it methodically and unambiguously. For both thinkers, 'the light of human minds is perspicuous words', sense and memory being the necessary precursors providing us with knowledge of fact. And to come to true knowledge, do we return to examine nontextual evidence? No. We examine the definitions of former authors, we examine the logical probity of texts, for the world has no meaning other than the one imposed on it by language. Perhaps the time has come to let Hobbes say it himself:

But the philosophy-schools, through all the universities of Christendom, grounded upon certain texts of Aristotle, teach another doctrine, and say, for the cause of vision, that the thing seen, sendeth forth on every side a visible species ... for the cause of understanding also, they say the thing understood, sendeth forth an intelligible species ... which coming into the understanding makes us understand. I say not this as disproving the use of universities, but because ... I must let you see ... what things would be amended in them amongst which the frequency of insignificant speech is one.[96]

---

[96] That is, insignificant speech is speech that does not signify individuals, and species are not individuals to be sensed but are, instead, unnecessarily multiplied universals. This is a technical statement, which means more than that academics talk twaddle.

And this is it the Latins call imagination, from the image made in seeing; and apply the same, though improperly, to all the other senses. But the Greeks call it fancy, which signifies appearance, and is as proper to one sense as to another. Imagination therefore is nothing but decaying sense and is found in men and many other living creatures, as well sleeping as waking ... This decaying sense, when we would express the thing itself, I mean fancy itself, we call imagination ... but when we would express the decay and signify that the sense is fading, old and past, it is called memory. So that imagination and memory are but one thing, which for divers considerations hath divers names. Much memory, or memory of many things, is called experience. Again, imagination being only of those things which have been formerly perceived by sense, either all at once, or by parts at several times; the former which is the imagining the whole object as it was presented to the sense, is simple imagination as when one imagineth a man, or horse, which he hath seen before. The other is compounded, as when from the sight of a man at one time, and of a horse at another, we conceive in our mind a Centaur. So when a man compoundeth the image of his own person with the image of the actions of another man ... it is compound imagination and properly but a fiction of the mind ... There is no doubt but God can make unnatural apparitions; but that he does it so often, as men need to fear such things, more than they fear the stay or change of the course of nature, which he also can stay and change, is no point of Christian faith ... it is the part of a wise man, to believe them no farther, that right reason makes that which they say, appear credible. If this superstitious fear of spirits were taken away and with it, prognostics from dreams, false prophecies and many other things depending thereon, by which crafty ambitious persons abuse the simple people, men would be much more fitted than they are for civil obedience. And this ought to be the work of the schools: but they rather nourish such doctrine. For, not knowing what imagination or the senses are, what they receive, they teach ... Some say the senses receive the species of things, and deliver them to the common sense, and the common sense delivers them over to the fancy and the fancy to the memory, and the memory to the judgement, like handing of things from one to another, with many words making nothing understood. The imagination that is raised in man or any other creature indued with the faculty of imagining, by words, or other voluntary signs, is that we generally call understanding and is common to man and beast ... That understanding which is peculiar to man is the understanding not only his will, but his conceptions and thoughts, by the sequel and contexture of the names of things into affirmations, negations and other forms of speech ... By consequence or train of thoughts, I understand that succession of one thought to another which is called, to distinguish it from discourse in words, mental discourse ... In sum, the discourse of the mind, when it is governed by design, is nothing but seeking or the faculty of invention ... a hunting out of the causes, of some effect, present or past ... Sometimes a man seeks what he hath lost; and from that place and time wherein he misses it, his mind runs back from place to place and time to time, to find where and when he had it; that is to say, to find some certain and limited time and place, in which to begin a method of seeking ... This we call remembrance or calling to mind: the Latins call it reminiscentia, as it were a re-conning of our former actions.

Sometimes a man knows a place determinate, within the compass whereof he is to seek; and then his thoughts run over all the parts thereof, in the same manner as one would sweep a room to find a jewel ... or as a man should run over the alphabet to start a rhyme. Sometimes a man desires to know the event of an action; and then he thinketh of some like action, and the events thereof one after another; supposing like events will follow like actions ... Which kind of thoughts is called foresight and prudence or providence ... But this is certain; by how much one man has more experiences of things past then another, by so much also he is more prudent and his expectations the seldomer fail him. The present only has a being in nature; things past have a being in memory only, but things to come have no being at all, the future being but a fiction of the mind, applying to sequels of actions past to the actions that are present, which with most certainty is done by him that has most experience, but not with certainty enough. And though it be called prudence, when the event answereth our expectation; yet in its own nature, it is but presumption.

As prudence is a presumption of the future, contracted from the experience of time past, so there is a presumption of things past taken from other things, not future but past also ... But this conjecture has the same uncertainty almost with the conjecture of the future, both being grounded only upon experience.

There is no other act of man's mind that I can remember, naturally planted in him, so as to need no other thing to the exercise of it, but to be born a man and live with the use of his five senses. Those other faculties of which I shall speak by and by, and which seem proper to man only, are acquired and increased by study and industry; and of most men learned by instruction and discipline; and proceed all from the invention of words and speech. For besides sense and thoughts, the mind of man has no other motion; though by the help of speech and method, the same faculties may be improved to such a height as to distinguish men from all other living creatures ... Also because, whatsoever, as I said before, we conceive, has been perceived first by sense, either all at once, or by parts, a man can have no thought representing anything, not subject to sense.

The invention of printing, though ingenious, compared with the invention of letters, is no great matter ... But the most noble and profitable invention of all other, was that of speech consisting of names and appellations and their connexions, whereby men register their thoughts, recall them when they are past, and also declare them to one another for mutual utility and conversation, without which there had been amongst men, neither commonwealth nor society, nor contract, nor peace, no more than amongst lions, bears and wolves. The first author of speech was God himself that instructed Adam how to name such creatures as he presented to his sight, for the Scripture goeth no further in this matter. But this was sufficient to direct him to add more names as the experience and use of the creatures should give him occasion, and to join them in such manner by degrees, as to make himself understood.

The general use of speech is to transfer our mental discourse into verbal, or the train of our thoughts into a train of words ... so that the first use of names is to serve for marks or notes of remembrance. Another is, when many use the same words, to signify, by their connexion and order one to another, what they conceive or think of each matter; and also what they desire, fear, or have any other passion for. And for this use they are called signs.

... To these uses [of speech] there are also four correspondent abuses. First, when men register their thoughts wrong, by the inconstancy of the signification of their words; by which they register for their conception that which they never conceived and so deceive themselves. Secondly, when they use words metaphorically, that is, in other sense than that they are ordained for and thereby deceive others. Thirdly, by words, when they declare that to be their will which is not. Fourthly, when they use them to grieve one another ... The manner how speech serveth to the remembrance of the consequences of causes and effects, consisteth in the imposing of names and the connexion of them.

Of names, some are proper and singular to one only thing ... and some are common to many things, man, horse, tree, every of which, though but one name, is nevertheless the name of divers particular things; in respect of all which together, it is called an universal, there being nothing in the world universal but names, for the things named are every one of them individual and singular.

One universal name is imposed on many things, for their similitude in some quality or other accident, and whereas a proper name bringeth to mind one thing only, universals recall any one of those many ... By this imposition of names, some of larger, some of stricter signification, we turn the reckoning of the consequences of things imagined in the mind, into a reckoning of the consequences of appellation ... [Through words] the consequence found in one particular, comes to be registered and remembered as a universal rule, and discharges our mental reckoning, of time and place, and delivers us from all labour of the mind, saving the first, and makes that which was found true here and now, to be true in all times and places ...

When two names are joined together into a consequence or affirmation, as thus, a man is a living creature, or thus, if he be a man, he is a living creature, if the latter name 'living creature' signify all that the former name 'man' signifieth, then the affirmation or consequence is true; otherwise false. For true and false are attributes of speech not of things. And where speech is not there, there is neither truth nor falsehood; error there may be as when we expect that which shall not be, or suspect what has not been; but in neither case can a man be charged with untruth. Seeing then that truth consisteth in the right ordering of names in our affirmations, a man that seeketh precise truth had need remember what every name he uses stands for, and to place it accordingly, or else he will find himself entangled in words ... And therefore in geometry, which is the only science that it hath pleased God hitherto to bestow on mankind, men begin at settling the signification of their words; which settling of significations they call definitions and place them in the beginning of their reckoning.

By this it appears how necessary it is for any man that aspires to true knowledge, to examine the definitions of former authors ... So that in the right definition of names lies the first use of speech which is the acquisition of science ... which make those men that take their instruction from the authority of books and not from their own meditation, to be as much below the condition of ignorant men as men endued with true science are above it ... Natural sense and imagination are not subject to absurdity. Nature itself cannot err; and as men abound in copiousness of language, so they become more wise or more mad than ordinary. Nor is it possible without letters for any man to become either excellently wise or, unless his memory be hurt by disease or ill constitution of organs, excellently foolish. For words are wise men's counters, they do but reckon by them; but they are the money of fools, that value them by the authority of an Aristotle, a Cicero, or a Thomas or any other doctor whatsoever, if but a man.

Subject to names is whatsoever can enter into or be considered in an account, and be added one to another to make a sum or subtracted one from another and leave a remainder ... The Greeks have but one word, logos, for both speech and reason, not that they thought there was no speech without reason, but no reasoning without speech: and the act of reasoning they called syllogism which signifieth summing up of the consequences of one saying to another. And because the same thing may enter into account for divers accidents, their names are, to show that diversity, diversely wrested and diversified. This diversity of names may be reduced to four general heads ... Thirdly we bring into account the properties of our own bodies, whereby we make such distinction as when anything is seen by us, we reckon not the thing itself, but the sight, the colour, the idea of it in the fancy, and when anything is heard, we reckon it not, but the hearing or sound only, which is our fancy or conception of it by the ear, and such are names of fancies. Fourthly, we bring into account, consider, and give names to names themselves, and to speeches: for general, universal, special, equivocal are names of names. And affirmation, interrogation, commandment, narration, syllogism, sermon, oration and many other such, are names of speeches. And this is all the variety of names positive, which are put to mark somewhat which is in nature, or may be feigned by the mind of man as bodies that are or may be conceived to be, or of bodies, the properties that are or may be feigned to be, or words and speech. There be also other names, called negative, which are notes to signify that a word is not the name of the thing in question, as these words: nothing, no man, infinite ... All other names are but insignificant sounds.

When a man, upon the hearing of any speech hath those thoughts which the words of that speech and their connexion were ordained and constituted to signify, then he is said to understand it, understanding being nothing else but conception caused by speech. And therefore if speech be peculiar to man, as for aught I know it is, then is understanding peculiar to him also.

The names of such things as affect us, that is, which please and displease us, because all men be not alike affected with the same thing, nor the same man at all times, are in the common discourses of men of inconstant signification ... For

591

though the nature of what we conceive be the same, yet the diversity of our reception of it, in respect of different constitutions of body, and prejudices of opinion, gives every thing a tincture of our different passions. And therefore in reasoning a man must take heed of words, which besides the signification of what we imagine of their nature, have a signification also of the nature, disposition and interest of the speaker; such as are the names of virtues and vices; for one man calleth wisdom what another calleth fear; and one cruelty what another justice ... And therefore such names can never be true grounds of any ratiocination ... Reason is nothing but reckoning, that is adding and subtracting of the consequences of general names agreed upon for the marking and signifying of our thoughts; I say marking them when we reckon by ourselves, and signifying when we demonstrate or approve our reckoning to other men ... And therefore, as when there is a controversy in an account, the parties must by their own accord, set up for right reason, the reason of some arbitrator or judge, to whose sentence they will both stand or their controversy must either come to blows or be undecided for want of a right reason constituted by nature.

By this it appears that reason is not, as sense and memory, born with us; nor gotten by experience only as prudence is; but attained by industry, first in apt imposing of names and secondly, by getting a good and orderly method in proceeding from the elements which are names, to assertions made by connexion of one of them to another, and so to syllogisms, which are the connexions of one assertion to another, till we come to a knowledge of all the consequences of names appertaining to the subject in hand; and that is it men call science. And whereas sense and memory are but knowledge of fact, which is a thing past and irrevocable, science is the knowledge of consequences and dependence of one fact upon another.

To conclude, the light of human minds is perspicuous words, but by exact definitions, first snuffed, and purged from ambiguity; reason is the pace, increase of science the way, and the benefit of mankind, the end.

Thomas Hobbes, *Leviathan*, chs 1–5.

To include an extended quote from the seventeenth-century Hobbes in a chapter devoted to medieval and Renaissance attitudes to past texts and their use is meant to underline the importance of historical continuities without denying discontinuities. Descartes would counter the Hobbesian reliance on sensuality and physical experience with an assertion that personality was limited to the autonomous thinking subject, to mind divorced from bodily experience. We enter the eighteenth century with the debate still raging but in a new key. Whether explicitly or implicitly, theories of mind and remembering continued to serve to indicate how the past was either relevant or irrelevant to men intent on making themselves at home in their world. What remained central to opposing attitudes to the past well into the eighteenth century was the question of whether the world was to be remembered, known and understood as essentially ordered and hence its truth could be logically and formally deduced – as proponents of the *via antiqua* maintained; or whether it was remembered, known and understood as a consequence of men's individual experiences and their subsequent representational discourse.

MODERN DISCOURSE CONCERNING SENSES OF THE PAST

Antiquarianism for its own sake, indeed, a nostalgia for a world believed to be forever lost, would only flower abundantly in the later eighteenth and nineteenth centuries when a romantic sense of the lost and irrecoverable past would come to dominate the literary and historical imagination. That Rousseau in the eighteenth century could still reinterpret Sparta as a model for a pre-revolutionary France in his *Discourse on the Arts and Sciences* shows him to have been engaged in the same kind of rhetorical, exemplary historiography that was common to medievals and humanists reflecting on distant times. The nineteenth-century kind of sentimental history of a lost otherness is what truly characterises much, but not all, modern history, and it is this to which we are heirs. This attitude would be exemplified in the works of nineteenth-century historical theologians like Schleiermacher and Dilthey, whose early 'romantic' hermeneutics were premised on a desire to gain access to the otherness of the minds of past thinkers but who at the same time acknowledged a temporal, even a psychological gap to be leapt over. None of the medieval or Renaissance thinkers we have examined saw a gap to be bridged.

This is because both medieval and Renaissance historiography, whether adhering to the *via antiqua* or the *via moderna*, postulated universal hypotheses or general laws among the premises of explanation in history and both assumed that these general propositions had transhistorical applications. We met this most explicitly in Abelard's discussion of conventional language and dialectical analysis in the twelfth century. This means that both schools of thought were logically committed to the notion of universal regularities. *Where they differed was in how such regularities might come to be known: either as emanations of a divine essence, or by mind's establishing probable relations between discrete experiences.* Nor did this positing of universal regularities disappear as we entered the modern era. Hume's general principle and Hempel's general law,[97] combined with an assertion of the unlimited scope of such hypotheses and the transhistorical application of these in explanation are evidence of its liveliness. There is

[97] Carl Hempel, 'The function of general laws in history', *Journal of Philosophy*, 39 (1942), pp. 35–48.

still a vigorous belief in universal recurrence and it lies at the basis of positivism. Its eloquent opponents include Oakeshott.

The modern alternative to the continuity between ancient, medieval and Renaissance attitudes to and uses of the past, emerged in the romantic hermeneutics of the nineteenth century and it influenced the Anglo-American historical profession through the writings of Collingwood.[98] Here, we see a plausible rejection of methodologies which seek to uncover universal regularities throughout history. We are asked to focus instead on another hypothesis, that of a transhistorical, cross-cultural *difference*. This may imply that the thoughts we attribute to past writers and thinkers are probably not their own. Instead of viewing this approach as incompatible with any theory of historical explanation or linking it to scepticism, Collingwood focused on the process of thoughts existing as a changing continuity so that the parts are meant to be mutually exclusive, but the process is a continuum where the parts overlap with others. Over time, however, there is no identity between past and present. Recurrences in human behaviour and thought are not universal; qualitatively similar actions and ideas cannot be found in all times and places. It is not simply that human phenomena are unique but rather, that the recurrence of like phenomena is limited in scope.[99] This would lead to a recognition that the distant past was profoundly different from the present and the past could not, therefore, be considered as exemplary. Such an attitude was current during neither the middle ages nor the Renaissance precisely because the historical enterprise was intended as an exercise in a present-orientated self-understanding and as a justification of present institutions, ideas and actions. Collingwood's position denies – as the position of neither medieval nor Renaissance thinkers denied – a fixed constitution of the human mind; for them, mind was a constant and common characteristic of men throughout history. A study of the logic of language and of mental propositions demonstrated this. Where the *via antiqua* differed from the *via moderna* was in the degree to which each made room for the role of contingency in the determination of a mind's constitution. Theirs was not

---

[98] It is in this period alone that we begin to see a true historicism emerging. R. G. Collingwood, *The Idea of History* (Oxford, 1946). For the various competing methods by which current historians 'get at' the past, see the selections and comments in Preston King, ed., *The History of Ideas* (London, 1983). To counter historicism, according to Hans-Georg Gadamer, *Wahrheit und Methode: Grundzuge einer philosophischen Hermeneutik* (Tübingen, 1960), and his *Philosophical Hermeneutics* (collected essays), trans. David Linge (Berkeley, 1977), the knower, the reader of past texts *cannot* overcome his own present as if it were an accidental factor. The knower's own present situation is already constitutively involved in any process of understanding.

[99] See Rex Martin, *Historical Explanation, Re-enactment and Practical Inference*, (Ithaca, NY, 1977).

an argument that social and economic experience created human minds so that ancient Romans and their virtues were irrecoverable, discrete and peculiar to their time alone. There would have been no point in reading them except as curiosities had they believed this to be the case. It has only relatively recently been considered a possibility that even abstract truths do not survive as constants in radically different social and economic environments, that people's minds and what it is possible for them to think, are products of a changing social and economic base.

Collingwood believed that the true objective of historical investigation was to understand the actions of past others by somehow recreating or reenacting their deeds in our own minds. The degree to which this is conceived of as possible, the degree of historical accuracy that might result from such an imaginative reconstruction, constitutes one of the major dilemmas in current historical debates. Collingwood proposed a radical difference between past minds and those of the present. Others assert that the modes of thought of remote cultures are comprehensible to us only to the degree to which we share some of their basic categories.[100] How we might be certain even of this is under current scrutiny. Such shared categories were not doubted during the middle ages and the Renaissance. People remembered the past in one of two ways: experientially or essentially.

The medieval and Renaissance understandings of the past and its uses therefore, had much in common with one another as well as with only some modern theories of historicity.[101] The so-called beginning of what we take to be distinctive about modern historicity in the Renaissance falsely reduces the many modern approaches as much as it distorts the attitude of Renaissance historians. If instead, we look at theories of remembering, on the one hand, and their use, on the other, we find that it is the operation of memory as it was understood by the two contrasting epistemologies which lies at the basis of the rift between the *via antiqua* and the *via moderna*. This rift would survive into the Enlightenment and beyond. Rightly or wrongly, neither 'way' has been taken unquestioningly as the basis of an acceptable mode of understanding nor as suggesting an adequate methodology in contemporary schools of history. This is because, by and large, most contemporary schools of history consider that the past is irrecoverable in the sense of being inimitable, although it can, to varying degrees, be known in its otherness.

---

[100] Isaiah Berlin, *Historical Inevitability* (Oxford, 1954), p. 61.

[101] For a review of numerous alternatives, see Donald R. Kelley, 'Horizons of intellectual history', *Journal of the History of Ideas*, 48 (1987), pp. 143–69. Amongst the numerous essays on this subject in the journal *History and Theory*, see Dominick Lacapra, 'Rethinking intellectual history and reading texts', *History and Theory*, 19 (1980), pp. 245–76.

Every medieval and Renaissance historian who *interpreted* past texts thought his task was to judge and explain the truth of propositions, past or present. The uninterpreted 'facts' of the historical record were fixed forever on the page as the verbal representations of eyewitness experience so that these memorials would not fly into oblivion. As such, they *meant* nothing. And no one attempted to verify the literal record. When, however, they assembled these past utterances they became aware that discourse itself had a history. So that when they interpreted past discourse, extracting its truth, or when they reiterated past utterances in their own texts, they were not imprisoned by past discourse but employed inherited discourse in ways that were relevant to their current situation. To *our* retrospective eyes, they shifted meaning. But they thought the shift was only in terms of idioms, vocabulary, modes of signifying, that is, in the means to meaning.

Not only do we believe that idioms and vocabulary along with modes of signifying alter over time.[102] They can be transformed to constitute a new language as they adapt to new genres, other discursive practices and, perhaps most fundamentally, to external, contingent circumstances that create problems at particular moments that require linguistic formulation in arguments so that problems may be solved or explained. But the linguistic formulation in argument that addresses a particular problem is not created *de novo* for that particular circumstance. Linguistic formulations have their own rate of evolution and they depend on previously established linguistic formulations employed in a previous generation, when the constellations of experiences signified by them were different. The formulations, however, survive into the next, successive, set of contingencies.

If we observe certain words maintaining a continuity of sense over time, then it may be asked: to what degree do intellectual and moral dispositions also survive intact over time, despite social change, *because of* the continuity of sense and linguistic conventions? Has the world not always changed more rapidly and in a more disordered way than language could ever describe it? Language normalises the world of disparate experiences. That is its function. Hence, any historian seeking to get at the discordant past through texts which described it, necessarily confronts not that past but a particular writer's modes of signifying it. And signifiers are, by definition, more general, more universal, conventional counters which have no temporal qualities themselves. History writing, historiography, then

---

[102] See J. G. A. Pocock, 'The concept of language and the métier d'historien: some considerations on practice', in Anthony Pagden, ed., *The Language of Political Theory in Early-Modern Thought* (Cambridge, 1987), pp. 19–40.

becomes a textual hermeneutics rather than a direct confrontation with past acts that are other than speech acts. Historical interpretation is, then, explanation according to the rules of rhetorical plausibility. But plausibility for whom? For readers in our age who give meaning to words in social contexts that are different from those of earlier readers, writers and experiencers? Or plausibility to the inhabitants of a culture, a social context in which the text was written? Are the maxims of plausible good sense the same throughout history? Hume thought so in the eighteenth century. John of Salisbury thought so in the twelfth. Cicero thought so in the first century BC. For thinkers who believe this, history is exemplary. It assumes nothing novel, unique, singular, unrepeatable. Once one uses language to give an account of discrete practices, one offers a theory which links causes and effects through propositions which cohere through their own conventional laws that make sense of particulars. But language is a structure, not a prison.

During the middle ages and the Renaissance, no less than today, the professional historian had a métier, a craft, a practice.[103] He employed a shared discourse to give accounts. The discourse he used was shared most immediately by his contemporaries. To some extent we, in other ages, also share past discourse, but to what extent is a problem of which twentieth-century historians are peculiarly aware and to which various answers have been offered. Discourse itself has a history. But what this meant to medieval and Renaissance historians was that the history of discourse was a history of different modes of signifying. It was neither a history which charted the changes and evolutions in the world of nonlinguistic events, nor a history of mental evolution. John Pocock reminds us that we today do not say that the language context is the only context which gives the speech act its meaning and history. But as we have seen, medieval and Renaissance analysts of past and present texts did assert this to be the case. Thereafter, the language in its verbal context was related to a fixed truth beyond the text, a truth about how the world always is and about how sane human minds universally construe that truth. Ways of talking about the world, about politics, about how human minds know and remember what is and what was, change. But medieval and Renaissance historians did not believe that the meaning expressed by ways of talking changed at all.

For professional rememberers during the middle ages and Renaissance, the creation and diffusion of languages was largely a matter of clerical authority.[104] But as Pocock has noted more generally, clerisies, be they

---

[103] *Ibid.*, p. 20.

[104] Hence, for such authorities, 'the present is another name for the political organization of existence' to quote Sheldon Wolin *The Presence of the Past* (Baltimore/London, 1989),

churchmen, lawyers or political historians 'do not address themselves solely to their own members but impose their esoteric languages upon a variety of laities and lay publics.'[105] This became increasingly the case with the growth of a more numerous literate laity. The story told by a modern historian of discourse is

of how literate professionals have become involved in directing the affairs of others and have obliged others to discourse in the languages which they have evolved; but at the same time [it is] the story of how the laities have appropriated professional idioms to unprofessional purposes, have employed idioms from other sources in such a way as to modify their effects'.[106]

But it must be pointed out that the extent to which subjects can expropriate the rulers' language so as to reverse its effects is limited by the durable constraints a learned language imposes on all users at a particular moment. As medieval and Renaissance analysts of conventional language insisted, language sets its own rules, determining the legitimate ways in which its rules might be changed. And for medieval and Renaissance readers of texts and writers of others, who were interested in this issue of language's capacities, determined by the conventional language-game's rules, a prior theory concerned with how humans know and remember – and for what purpose – determined their use of texts to elicit meaning. The meaning was universally applicable to all times and places. With Cicero increasingly on their reading lists, along with other ancient Roman rhetoricians and rhetorical historians, they confirmed that both the study of the past and current discourse about that past were rhetorical exercises in uncovering plausible (to them), exemplary human action whose a-historical truth was to be imitated in their present. The 'facts' of history, men's signifying of their experiences, were meaningless prior to a more universal interpretation of the propositions which literally represented experiences known but not understood.

Throughout the medieval and Renaissance periods, modes of signifying and common uses of language were acknowledged to have changed over time. What they believed had not changed, and this would be revealed by a proper interpretation of a text from any age, past or present, was all these

p. 1:
It is constituted by competing/cooperating structures of power that advance and secure the expectations and advantages of certain classes, individuals, groups and organizations whose combination of authority and material resources enables them to concert power and thereby to exert a major influence over which of the possible presents a society is going to have or, at the least, which ones it will not have.
This is no less true of authoritative constitutions of a collective past which then are connected to present arrangements of power.

105 Pocock, 'The concept of language', p. 23.   106 *Ibid.*, p. 24.

speakers' or writers' true meaning. That is why ancient Rome could tell them something true about their condition, whether they lived in Italian Renaissance republics or princedoms. They established their identity through a constructed narrative reminiscence about their past which assured them of continuities with that past. *Historia magistra vitae.*

CONCLUSION: AN ALL TOO BRIEF ACCOUNT OF MODERN THEORIES OF MIND AND REMEMBERING

Materialism is the official philosophy of academic biology and is perhaps best summarised in the recent *Oxford Companion to the Mind* (1987). Steven Rose, the author of the entry, 'memory–biological basis', argues that 'it is axiomatic that in some way there must be brain representations of memory'. From this materialist assumption every twentieth-century neuroscientist has known how memories are encoded in the brain: briefly, there is a changed connectivity in particular neuronal circuits as a result of synaptic remodelling. As Rose has pointed out in another context, however: 'Everyone knows this; the only trouble lies in proving it'. Indeed. As a modern variant on ancient and medieval philosophical realism, these hypothetical memory traces persist in eluding their pursuers despite the ritual sacrifice of thousands of rats, cats, chicks and monkeys on the dissecting tables of the neuroscientists. Materialism may be wrong, or, as some classical and medieval thinkers believed, it may be only a part of the story, only one partial and inadequate way we can explain to ourselves what happens when we remember. We must include other things in our account of what it means to us to remember.

In scientific circles the brain is now universally accepted as the organ of the mind and certain parts of it are known to specialise in particular mental functions. In fact, what was recently laughed at as a quaint medieval model of the soul with its differentiated faculties, has been re-presented, unencumbered by a naive nineteenth-century craniology or phrenology, as a faculty psychology of a modular mind.[1] One such theory

[1] Jerry Fodor, *The Modularity of Mind: An Essay on Faculty Psychology* (Cambridge, Mass., 1984). Also see J. Z. Young, *Programs of the Brain* (Oxford, 1978), who argues against this faculty theory.
'Certainly we can say that a brain is not a general-purpose computer into whose memory *any* information can be placed. It is more like one that already has a system of programs within it' (p. 78). But Young goes on to say: 'In the earlier edition of [*The Oxford English Dictionary*, Supplement, prior to 1976] memory is the "faculty of remembering". The use of the word faculty indeed shows a sort of pre-scientific attempt to describe an agent. A "faculty" seems to be a sort of immaterial machine, but it would distract us to follow this

calls memory and perception horizontal faculties with the mind described as a two-dimensional layout. The horizontal faculties like a common memory for immediate information are actually fictions, that is, bundles of aptitudes and propensities. The cognitive modules which are vertical faculties, are mental faculties that specialise in a particular content domain whereby the output of a sense organ, like the eye, is translated into a representation of some aspect of the world which then becomes accessible to conscious thought. Conscious thought is conceived of as a nonmodular system which thinks and judges various inputs from modules. Each separate cognitive module or mental faculty, specialising in a content domain, depends on an innately determined and distinct neuronal structure of the brain which is designed for the relevant task. Hence, mental phenomena are not defined in terms of the brain's physical constitution (neurons or electrochemical events) but rather are defined in terms of the structure of operations that the brain carries out. This is in line with current theories which speak of mind metaphorically as a computer where its physical makeup is of secondary importance to its computational activity. Mind's computations could then be constructed from more elementary building blocks and rules of assembly.

While this is a vast oversimplification of one such theory, like most other theories of memory and thinking, past and present, it is and perhaps must be, couched in terms of analogy where today the most ready analogies are with machines and computers as they could not have been during the middle ages. Like its medieval counterparts, however, this is a variant either on philosophical realism or conceptualism. What is required is not merely a theoretical account of the machinery of remembering and thinking, but some plausible account of the code, the symbolic form in which experiences and information are actively registered. It was precisely this issue that twelfth to fourteenth-century thinkers addressed. They also addressed the possibility that the soul or mind might contain within itself all the potential memories that it could ever form. What appears to be a fantastic notion that every memory or thought is *either* innately *or* potentially within us is not simply the view of Plato or Aristotle and medieval Platonists and Aristotelians. It is also the view of modern geneticists who try to explain through descriptions of DNA and RNA molecular synthesis the processes by which events 'judged worthy' of long-term memory are committed to molecular memory. What modern

piece of history' (p. 79). 'I propose that we use the word memory essentially as the computer scientist does for the physical agent or system that allows for the setting up of programs of action effective for survival, modified to suit the experience of the individual ... Memories are thus physical systems in brains'.
So much for Fodor.

601

geneticists do is the modern equivalent of what the medieval *physici* did; they leave the discussion of the higher operations of mind to the philosophers and reduce mind to brain. Hence, the contemporary hypothesis in scientific circles argues that the change in the pattern of nerve connections *is* the memory. Thereafter, it is supposed that the chromosomes of our genes must store 'instructions' which are needed to allow the neuronal 'circuits' to alter without determining in advance which 'circuit' will be involved. Specific chemicals are found to be present when the circuits are activated, implying that we are genetically programmed with a potential, an ability to learn.[2]

The ghost in the machine, the switchboard operator has been found, diminutively seated on a chromosome giving orders so that enabling chemicals can be produced at the appropriate site. No doubt this does happen. But it is one partial way of explaining to us what we believe actually happens when minds think and remember. And it indicates that we simply do not know enough to be able to offer a good account of how the body and the nervous system enable us to live our mental lives.

The limiting determinism in this explanation could only be allowed by thirteenth and fourteenth-century thinkers at the level of biological response. They could not accept it at the level of a voluntarily chosen way of responding to the world's contingencies. For them, lived life and our understanding of it, could not be reduced solely to our modern scientific Darwinism whereby how we live in the world is evidence of a predetermined natural selection mechanism so that only genetic memories that are useful in survival are retained in our chromosomes. Genetic determinism strains credibility because it does not account for the enormous variability of thought and action. Genetic determinism is the trivial aspect of living and if presented to medieval thinkers, couched in analogies they could understand, it would illegitimately prescribe a model of man that is irresponsible. They believed man to be responsible for his immoral acts if not also for his moral behaviour, responsible before God and also before other men. We have observed how certain fourteenth-century thinkers made clear how men naturally come to know about this responsibility, whatever the limitations placed upon them individually by their more or less faulty sensual experience of the world. And if confronted with the above modern theories of remembering and thinking, they would have probably insisted that such descriptions were errors of categorisation and of language just as they are currently thus repudiated by many modern philosophers of mind. The possibility of further refining our chemical and electrical model of the brain so that it eventually will coincide with mind is

2 See Colin Blakemore, *Mechanics of the Mind* (Cambridge, 1977)

not an intelligible hypothesis for many today, not least because such an hypothesis is logically erroneous. At the very least it supposes that talking about electrical impulses and neuronal connections is equivalent to talking about sensations, thought and feelings. It assumes there are translation rules that map psychoanalysis into neurobiology. It also assumes, as medieval thinkers and many modern ones do not, that intellect has a specific organ.

This hypothetical debate is not simply one between the middle ages and modernity. P. W. Atkins in his recent review of Jean-Pierre Changeux's *Neuronal Man: The Biology of Mind* says:[3]

I find it extraordinary that in the Eighties a publisher [Oxford University Press] should still think it necessary to tread cautiously and to cotton-wool a book with remarks that it presents a 'radical and controversial hypothesis; that there is no "mind", nothing psychic, but rather only neurons, synapses, electricity and chemistry'. Sadly there remain people who think differently. Had the book presumed otherwise, it would not have been worth the death of a tree.

Several trees for my book have been needlessly felled! Atkins's view indicates that the apparent growth of our knowledge about the body and the nervous system has been so great as to give rise to the widely accepted presumption that all our mental life can be explained as the manifestation of the structure and functioning of the biological material comprising the body and its nervous system.

Hughling Jackson guessed and Wilder Penfield 'proved' that reminiscence occurred in the temporal lobe of the brain. Medieval thinkers placed sense memory in the back lobe of the brain, but they put logical and rational judgement in the middle. Reminiscence, a willed and logical procedure, which was not the same as iconic sense memory, also occurred here. Wilder Penfield was able to stimulate artificially the temporal lobe to induce 'hallucinations' of past experiences, tunes, scenes, lived experiences. The electrode inserted into this part of the brain did not stimulate fantasies but precise memories accompanied by those emotions which originally were linked to the original experience which, he believed, was somehow stored, frozen in the lobe. So Penfield has 'proved' that the brain can retain an almost perfect record of one's experiences as one experienced them. How he knows these are the past as experienced in the past and not some transformation is not clear to me. But it seems to have convinced many that the past as past is still with us. Effectively, it remains stored and unconscious, and we *need* to recapture it. Either we do so through a cerebral mishap like those described eloquently by Oliver

---

[3] *London Review of Books*, 21 May 1987, p. 17.

Sacks,[4] or we consciously reconstruct it (and probably) get it wrong. But somehow we need memories to ground our present, even if they are not memories of our original experiences! What an extraordinary thing to say! But of course Freud said it and with a vengeance. Neurosis *is* pathogenic reminiscence. And he believed that psychoanalysis enabled a patient to replace false memories with true reminiscences of their past.

Recently Oliver Sacks has asked the more fundamental question: in the so-called replay of the stored, inner record of past experiences as described by the experiments of Penfield and others, what is it that can be replayed in such a way as to reconstitute an experience?

Is it something akin to a film or record, played on the brain's filmprojector or phonograph? Or something analogous, but logically anterior – such as a script or score? What is the final form, the natural form, of our life's repertoire? That repertoire which not only provides memory and reminiscence but our imagination at every level, from the simplest sensory and motor images, to the most complex imaginative worlds, landscapes, scenes? A repertoire, a memory, an imagination of a life which is essentially personal, dramatic, and 'iconic' ... Our current concepts of cerebral processing and representation are all essentially computational. And as such they are couched in terms of 'schemata', 'programmes', 'algorithms' etc. But could schemata, programmes, algorithms alone provide for us the richly visionary, dramatic and musical quality of experience – that vivid personal quality which *makes* it experience? The answer is clearly, even passionately 'No'.[5]

Sacks opts for the possibility that 'above the level of cerebral programmes we must conceive a level of cerebral scripts and scores'. And then he offers the modern version of one aspect of Aristotle, for whom all thinking, even the most abstract, required images.

'Experience', Sacks tells us, 'is not possible until it is organised iconically; action is not possible unless it is organised iconically. The brain's record of everything, everything alive, must be iconic. This is the final form of the brain's record, even though the preliminary form may be computational or programmatic'. We are also told that 'all of this was hinted at a hundred years ago – in Hughling Jackson's original account of "reminiscence" (1880); by Korsakoff on amnesia (1887); and by Freud and Anton in the 1890s on agnosias. Their remarkable insights have been half-forgotten, eclipsed by the rise of a systematic physiology. Now is the time to recall them, re-use them...'[6] But as I hope to have shown in the preceding pages, all this was said rather a long time before the late nineteenth century, and this supposed iconicity of mind was not all that

---

[4] Oliver Sacks, *The Man Who Mistook His Wife for a Hat* (London, 1985).
[5] *Ibid.*, pp. 139–40.
[6] *Ibid.*, p. 141.

was said, not least by medieval thinkers interested in the formal structures of thinking as an activity.

During the nineteenth century, many historians and theologians came to believe that the past was completed and irretrievably other but somehow knowable by means of an imaginary leap across psychological distance. This was believed true of other men's pasts which were over and done with, but not necessarily of one's own past. Indeed, Freud came to argue that mental illness was due to the excessive influence of past events of one's own life, events which when stored as memories were somehow incorruptible and instead of being flushed away or swept up into some new network of associations, or simply forgotten, were fixed for continuous and pathogenic reminiscence. Wollheim[7] has recently traced the evolution of Freud's thoughts on the tyranny of the past. The evolution of Freud's theories provides an uncanny recapitulation in a new, positivist, key of certain aspects of theories of memory from antiquity to the middle ages. Freud attempted to account for the apparent paradox that we believe memories are permanently stored in the brain but that they are rarely recalled in their original form. Recollection is inaccurate. Wollheim tells us that after Freud posited incorruptible memories, he thereafter modified this account and argued that it was *forgotten* events, which lay in the unconscious, repressed there as a defence, that underlay hysteria. Then he hypothesised that the past tyrannises over us through unconscious infantile sexual desires, substituting desire for memory in his later theory. Lastly, it was through phantasies rather than through memories that people came to be tyrannised by the past.

Wollheim has characterised this along with the beliefs of positivists who reduce mind to brain and its functions, as an archaic theory of mind. He says that it generates in the minds of those who subscribe to it a characteristic misunderstanding of their mental life. Effectively, it blames mental events or states like imaginings for subsequent events. Archaic mind conceives of itself in corporeal terms and its activities are variously parts, products and processes of the body. He says,

> one way of characterizing how the archaic mind conceived of itself is through an overarching image of the mind as a whole and then, derivatively, through various applications of this image to the different phenomena of the mind: to dispositions, and to occurrent states and to activities and their vehicles. Each such application of the image or each self-presentation of a mental phenomenon would be iconic … [there would be] not just a self-presentation but a self-representation or, since it involved error, a self-misrepresentation of the phenomenon.[8]

---

[7] Richard Wollheim, *The Thread of Life* (Cambridge, 1984).   [8] *Ibid.*, p. 143

In the archaic theory, the processes of the mind are modelled upon physical processes that have been idealised. The mental phenomena then become as they are imaged, and mind conforms to its own prejudices about itself.

This criticism, applicable to Freud, is also, of course, applicable to Sacks and to most psychologists and to neuroscientists. It is also applicable to some medieval theorists. The problem is, at basis, that mind is not corporeal, as many medieval theorists insisted, that intellect has no specific organ, nor is it as those labels represent it so that we are dealing not only with the problem of labelling mind's contents. We are dealing with the labelling of mind's activities or its capacities to act as well as with its contents. We have seen that this was a major consideration of epistemologies from Abelard to Ockham. And because issues came to be formulated during the middle ages in terms of actuated or potential capacities, it became possible to rephrase questions about the past in terms not of its tyranny over the present but of its constitutive role in the present. Wollheim, in analysing critically some of Freud's hypotheses, seems to take something very similar on board. He says:

> By the time that Freud had come to think that the domination under which the person could fall was not that of memory [as he had once thought] nor that of desire [as he next thought] but was that of phantasy, was he still talking about the tyranny of the past? ... [W]e need to distinguish between a tyranny that merely originated in the past and persisted, and the tyranny of the past. For the domination of phantasy to be, like the domination of memory, the tyranny of the past, it seems as thought the past should enter in a substantive fashion into the explanation of why phantasy proves so dominant. Pastness should prove explanatory ... occurrent event phantasies that dominate the present should be dependent mental phenomena, that is, as they exert their *influence* over the present they preserve and transmit the *influence* of an earlier event in which the disposition that they manifested originated.[9] (emphasis added)

Wollheim believes that when phantasy dominates the present, the past substantively enters into the explanation of the condition in which the person finds himself. But this past is *not a past of events* but a past of phases in psycho-sexual development. He proceeds to describe as affective rather than as cognitive earlier phases in psycho-sexual development so that living comprises a series of desires which, in phases, cease to have a kind of intelligibility. 'At heart, the unintelligibility of an archaic desire is affective so that the person can no longer see what it is about the object of desire that makes anyone, not just himself, but anyone with a similar psychology, want it. Around this affective core, concentric circles of

[9] *Ibid.*, pp. 159–60.

incomprehension establish themselves.' It is this affective unintelligibility that is, for Wollheim, the direct mark of pastness. The affective unintelligibility of past sensual experiences and corresponding emotional states was also, as we have seen, a major tenet of Augustine's theory of mind. And as we have seen for Aquinas, Scotus and for neo-Platonists like St Bernard, in the normal course of events it is precisely the affective unintelligibility of past desires and past sensual experiences that permits the past to have being for us in the present and only in a universal mode. On the one hand, living a life, and on the other, understanding the life that one leads are two different but related activities for the medieval thinkers we have considered. They treated living and understanding as different vantage points in a discussion of what being a man is, rather than as conflicting and irreconcilable human situations. And it was the problem of remembering and then understanding one's life that most preoccupied them.

Earlier it was said that Wilder Penfield's experiments on human brains 'proved' that the brain retains almost perfect records of past experiences, and that either through some cerebral accident or illness, or through conscious reconstruction, such memories can be retrieved. When there is no cerebral mishap we consciously reconstruct past experiences and experiments have shown that we usually get it wrong. Indeed, today's psychological experiments seem to demonstrate that conscious memory – or as medieval thinkers and Aristotle would call it, reminiscence – is not simply a storing up of sensory images, but is rather a logical, syllogistic reconstruction of what *must* have been there, starting with ideas and reasoning. Conscious retrospection is not the retrieval of images but the retrieval of what you have been aware of before and the reworking of or recategorising of these elements into rational or plausible patterns in the present. Things like time, that in the physical-behavioural world do not have a spatial quality are made to have such in consciousness. Time is given spatial properties by analogy. And history is impossible without the spatialisation of time that is characteristic of consciousness. These insights are not modern ones. We have seen them argued for in the ancient world and passed on as a legacy to the middle ages.

Julian Jaynes has argued in his extraordinary book[10] that this consciousness is a culturally learned event that is balanced over the suppressed vestiges of an earlier mentality. If subjective consciousness can be not only learned but also unlearned, at least in part and within certain conditions, then Jaynes believes we are left with an erosion of that mind space and

[10] Julian Jaynes, *The Origin of Consciousness in the Breakdown of the Bicameral Mind* (1971; Harmondsworth, 1982).

hence with an inability to narratise. The loss of the ability to categorise events in time can cause a near total loss of specific reference, arranged in succession. This means one does not think of or write history as a succession of events implying cause and effect. Whether or not one is convinced by Jaynes's thesis of the breakdown of the bicameral mind in the ancient Greek world of the Dorian invasions, there is here a remarkable similarity with what some monastic thinkers sought to achieve: the replacement of subjective, private, sensual histories, recalled in succession, by an external, universal, authoritative scriptural history, the text of which would be memorised so that certain 'hook' words would inspire a free association of other biblical words out of context and order. What success St Bernard had in attempting to limit or eliminate self-consciousness and memory can only be guessed at. In modern times, Jaynes describes the loss of the analog 'I', its mind space and the ability to narratise, as producing behaviour that either responds to hallucinated directions or continues on by habit. The remnant self feels, he says, like a commanded automaton as if someone else were moving the body about.[11] This apparently is often the situation with schizophrenics who are unable to narratise and seem to have a more immediate involvement with their physical environment. In those now conscious but who have undergone experiences to unlearn aspects of consciousness, the internal authority of the pre-conscious bicameral mind apparently can be replaced with external methods of authorisation.

There is *no* implication here that St Bernard or his monks can be analysed as schizophrenics! There is, however, an intended parallel between what modern psychologists have learnt about the experimental requirements for remembering and forgetting, and the theory and practice of remembering and forgetting during the middle ages, in order to indicate the extraordinary insights of certain medieval men into the workings of imagination, memory and thinking, which, when put into practice, transformed lives.

Many recent neurophysiological and psychological theories have largely been concerned with fairly basic mechanistic operations of the brain as mind's organ. But recent books on the higher cognitive processes have gone somewhat further and adopted one of two orientations. On the one hand, information is followed as it enters the cognitive system and is processed, transformed and then stored. Information acquisition is its concern rather than how humans use this information in, for instance, problem solving. On the other hand, attempts are made to outline how the kinds of knowledge acquired are used. The analogies are usually network

[11] *Ibid.*, p. 423.

models to represent the structure of human concepts, and computer programmes are then developed to apply networks to content domains. Such models begin with assumptions about what concepts *are* and much dissatisfaction over these assumptions has been expressed.

Weisberg[12] has recently put together the range of current views on the higher mental processes like memory, problem solving, language use, development of thought and the question of the medium of thought. The general position that directs his work is that cognitive functioning in many different situations is a special case of a more general process: the selective retrieval of information from memory. Put in this way, the modern problem is none other than the long-enduring one which we have discussed with respect to scholastic formulations. That Weisberg concludes that there is no medium of thought, although imagery and language play a role in thinking, is the modern equivalent of certain medieval thinkers' concern to show thinking to be an activity, indeed a way of living, and it is not equivalent to the medium used to display its activity.

In summarising recent conceptual models, Weisberg says:

The basic assumption underlying this research is that knowledge is made up of concepts related to each other in various ways. These concepts are assumed to be abstract, in the sense that they are not related to any sensory modality. Thus, according to these models, comprehending a sentence or perceiving an event entails carrying out a 'cognitive act' – constructing the representation of that event out of concepts.[13]

For some recent psychologists concepts are mental objects that are assumed to have some sort of existence, analogous in some way to the physical existence of real objects. They represent the meanings of words or classes of objects that can be thought about. Weisberg is remarkably well-attuned to early modern and modern philosophical theories of mind and provides the analogous philosophical positions of realists, conceptualists and nominalists, and then shows how modern psychologists can be shown to hold to each of these positions. Plato is classed as a realist; Locke as a conceptualist; Berkeley, Austin and Wittgenstein as nominalists. Most philosophers today, he argues, seem to accept some version of nominalism in explaining concepts, and this raises problems for conceptual network models of concepts because there are no concepts out of which to construct them, since concepts are not things.

However, Weisberg rightly notes that philosophers have not had a particularly strong effect on psychological theorising. And therefore, most

---

[12] Robert W. Weisberg, *Memory, Thought and Behavior* (Oxford, 1980).
[13] *Ibid.*, p. 184.

psychologists explicitly assume that thinking entails the manipulation of internal representations of environmental systems, as do the conceptual network theorists. Psychologists are either realists or conceptualists. Frequently, there is in their accounts a smuggled-in hope and presumption that mechanism is all and that consciousness will one day be reduced to the epiphenomenon it is now presumed to be.

But the series of studies by Rosch points in another direction as Weisberg shows. It appears in these studies that many human categories are based on family resemblances. Most of our categories have structures in that their members can be ordered in terms of how typical they are of a category as a whole. The more typical members may serve to represent or stand for the whole category during perception or conception, where conception is thinking about the category in question. The most typical member would be thought about and would substitute for the category as a whole.[14] We have empirical evidence that there is no closed class of features that defines any given concept; this means that theories arguing that concepts have some sort of existence, as bundles of features or as nodes, are questioned. This may well help to explain why the search for memory molecules and zones of specific information storage in the brain have so far been fruitless – they may not be there. Mental life cannot be reduced to molecules alone. And if this is the case, then do we need an abstract or concrete symbol to stand for a concept when it is thought about? Are there 'species', asked Ockham, even 'intelligible species', which need to be posited when we think? And he answered 'no'. So too does Weisberg in his conclusion drawn from the empirical research of Rosch. Hence, we have an argument that concepts do not entail specific mental objects that are used in thinking. General terms do not always refer to one single sort of situation. And human categories are based, it seems, on family resemblances, similitudes, so that no single mental object could stand for the category. This means that the search for mental objects when we analyse the term 'concept' is misdirected. To acquire a concept does not mean that one's mental possessions have increased. One has simply become able to do things. This seems to be the conclusion of the neuroscientist Edelman as well.[15] Human intelligence is not knowing more but recategorising and generalising information. We have encountered this theory in Ockham and aspects of it earlier.

What is the role of language in all this? Weisberg concludes that language serves to summarise past experiences but it does not serve to

[14] *Ibid.*, p. 191.
[15] See Israel Rosenfield, 'Neural Darwinism: a new approach to memory and perception', *The New York Review of Books*, 9 October, 1986, pp. 21–7.

produce organisations of experience that could not have come about without it. We do not learn anything new when we learn words and they are simply a short cut, enabling us to pick up things without having to go through the experience ourselves.[16] For Weisberg we must reject the idea that we must learn to organise the world in a new way when we learn how to speak.

The view of most medieval theorists we have examined was that the world is already what it is, as is mind's capacities, with language serving as an accepted, conventional way to summarise the things there are for us. No medieval logician thought that *language* taught men anything new. Rather, language either referred to the world or language transmitted to us summarised knowledge without our having to experience every experience for ourselves. Experience would confirm what language transmitted and summarised. That medieval logicians like Ockham were more careful to specify the *probable* certainty on which conventional reference systems operated, a probability on which we must and do rely, takes his language theory further. Ockham, too, believed that thought is not equivalent to symbolisation; rather, thought is the behavioural activities peculiar to intellection.

The following extended quote from the immensely influential (but often misunderstood) work of F. C. Bartlett seems a fitting conclusion to a brief discussion of contemporary theories of memory. It is not a recapitulation of ancient and medieval views on memory and its uses in modern dress. But it provides a description and explanation of what has been learnt about memory in our own times. It serves as a frame of reference and a model against which the reader may judge of the plausibility of earlier accounts. What has not been attempted here, of course, is to provide an account of the nature of memory that might define the parameters of a contemporary inquiry. But if we are to read the accounts of past rememberers of a world we believe we have lost, then surely it must be of some importance to attempt to give an account of what *they* took to be significant about memory and its purpose. Some of their attitudes to knowing and remembering are still with us, especially when we require of the past exemplary behaviour to be imitated in the present. Much of what history is for us is firmly ensconced in the rhetorical mode. And as Bartlett shows, even the most empirical research methods into human remembering require at some stage in the experiment that the subject record *in words* what it is he remembers. We are reminded of the assertion of ancient and medieval grammarians and logicians that words are the only means we have of 'touching' things once experienced and now recalled.

[16] Weisberg, *Memory, Thought and Behavior*, p. 222.

Remembering obviously involves determination by the past. The influence of 'schemata' [an active organisation of past reactions] is influenced by the past. But the differences are at first sight profound. In its schematic form the past operates en masse, or strictly, not quite en masse, because the latest incoming constituents which go to build up a 'schema' have a predominant influence. In remembering, we appear to be dominated by particular past events which are more or less dated, or placed, in relation to other associated particular events. Thus the active organised setting looks as if it has somehow undergone a change, making it possible for parts of it which are remote in time to have a leading role to play. If only the organism could hit upon a way of turning round upon its own 'schemata' and making them the objects of its reactions, something of the sort might perhaps become possible. An organism which had discovered how to do this might be able, not exactly to analyse the settings, for the individual details that have built them up have disappeared, but somehow to construct or to infer from what is present the probable constituents and their order which went to build them up. It would then be the case that the organism would say, if it were able to express itself: 'This and this and this must have occurred, in order that my present state should be what it is'. And, in fact, I believe this is precisely and accurately just what does happen in by far the greatest number of instances of remembering, and it is to the development of a theory along these lines that the evidence which I have marshalled in the preceding chapters seems to point...

There is the low-level mental life which, being cut off from all but a few often-repeated environmental stimuli, shows unusual rote memory. All of us, in reference to some of our 'schemata', have probably completed the model and now merely maintain it by repetition. All relatively low-level remembering tends, in fact, to be rote remembering, and rote memory is nothing but the repetition of a series of reactions in the order in which they originally occurred ... [but] in remembering we are being determined by events out of their precise order in a chronological series, and we are free from over-determination by the immediately preceding event ... In fact, if we consider evidence rather than presupposition, remembering appears to be far more decisively an affair of construction rather than one of mere reproduction.

... In attempting to develop a theory of the whole matter, so far as I can see it, we must begin with an organism which has only a few sense avenues of connexion with its environment, and only a few correlated series of movements, but is devoid of all the so-called higher mental functions ... Any reaction of such an organism which has more than a mere momentary significance is determined by the activity of a 'schema' in relation to some new incoming impulse set up by the immediately presented stimulus ... circularity of reaction, the repetition over and over again of a series of reactions, is very prominent. Habits, moreover, are relatively easily formed, as is witnessed by a great amount of research ... From the outside, all this may look like continual re-excitement of well-established traces; but it is not. It is simply the maintenance of a few 'schemata' each of which has its natural and essential time order. However, in the course of development the special sense avenues increase in number and range, and concurrently there is an increase in number and variety of reactions. With this, and a matter of vital importance, as my experiments repeatedly show, goes a great growth of social life, and the development of means of communication. Then the 'schema' determined reactions of one organism are repeatedly checked, as well as constantly facilitated, by those of others. A new incoming stimulus must become ... a stimulus which enables us to go direct to that portion of the organised setting of past responses which is most relevant to the needs of the moment ... There is one way in which an organism could learn how to do this. It may be the only way ... An organism has somehow to acquire the capacity to turn round upon its own 'schemata' and to construct them afresh ... It is where and why consciousness comes in; it is what gives consciousness its most prominent function. I wish I knew exactly how it was done ... I can make one suggestion although I do so with some hesitation.

Suppose an individual to be confronted by a complex situation ... the case in which an observer is perceiving and is saying immediately what it is that he has perceived. We saw that in this case an individual does not normally take such a situation detail by detail and meticulously build up the whole. In all ordinary instances he has an overmastering tendency simply to get a general impression of the whole; and, on the basis of this, he constructs the probable detail. Very little of his construction is literally observed and often, as was easily demonstrated experimentally, a lot of it is distorted or wrong so far as actual facts are concerned. But it is the sort of construction which serves to justify his general impression. Ask the observer to characterise this general impression psychologically and the word that is always cropping up is 'attitude'. I have shown how this 'attitude' factor came into nearly every series of experiments that was carried out. The construction that is effected is the sort of construction that would justify the observer's 'attitude'. Attitude names a complex psychological state or process which it is very hard to describe in more elementary psychological terms. It is, however, as I have often indicated, very largely a matter of feeling or affect ... Here is the significance of the fact ... that when a subject is being asked to remember, very often the first thing that emerges is something of the nature of attitude. The recall is then a construction, made largely on the basis of this attitude, and its general effect is that of a justification of the attitude ... The need to remember becomes active, an attitude is set up; in the form of sensory images or, just as often, of isolated words, some part of the event which has to be remembered recurs, and the event is then reconstructed on the basis of the relation of this specific bit of material to the general mass of relevant past experiences or reactions, the latter functioning, after the manner of the 'schema', as an active organised setting ... In many cases, when the material had to be dealt with at a distance, as in remembering, the dominant features were the first to appear, either in image form, or descriptively through the use of language. In fact, this is one of the great functions of images in mental life: to pick items out of 'schemata' and to rid the organism of over-determination by the last preceding member of a given series. I would like to hold that this, too, could not occur except through the medium of consciousness. Again I wish I knew precisely how it is brought about ... What is it that gives to certain of these events other than the last, a predominant function, and at the same time tends to individualise them in the mass? It is appetite, instinct, interests and ideals, the first two being much the more important in early stages of organic development, and the last two advancing to positions of great, and very likely to chief, importance at the human level ... It now becomes possible to see that, though we may still talk of traces, there is no reason in the world for regarding these as made complete at one moment, stored up somewhere, and then re-excited at some much later moment. The traces that our evidence allows us to speak of are interest-determined, interest-carried traces. They live with our interests and with them they change.

Remembering is the re-excitation of innumerable fixed, lifeless and fragment-ary traces. It is an imaginative reconstruction, or construction, built out of the relation of our attitude towards a whole active mass of organised past reactions or experience, and to a little outstanding detail which commonly appears in image or in language form. It is thus hardly every really exact, even in the most rudimentary cases of rote recapitulation, and it is not at all important that it should be so ... It may be said that this theory after all does very little. It merely jumbles together innumerable traces and calls them 'schemata', and then picks out a few and calls them images. But I think this would be hardly fair criticism. All conventional theories of memory as reduplicative try to treat traces as somehow stored up like so many definite impressions, fixed and having only the capacity of being re-excited. The active settings, which are involved in the way of looking at the matter developed in the present chapter, are living and developing, are a complex expression of the life of the moment, and help to determine our daily modes of conduct. The theory brings remembering into line with imagining, an expression of the same activities; it has very different implications in regard to forgetting from those of the ordinary trace view; it gives to consciousness a definite function other than the mere fact of being aware. This last point is not entirely unimportant. There is an active school in current psychological controversy which would banish all reference to consciousness. It is common to try to refute this school by asserting vigorously that of course we know that we are conscious. But this is futile, for what they are really saying is that consciousness cannot affect anything that could not equally well be done without it. That is a position less easy to demolish. If I am right, however, they are wrong.

F. C. Bartlett, *Remembering, A Study in Experimental and Social Psychology* (Cambridge, 1932), pp. 202–14.

BIBLIOGRAPHY

SOURCES

Abelard, Peter, *Logica Ingredientibus*, ed. B. Geyer, *Peter Abaelards Philosophische Schriften*, BGPTMA, 21, vols. 1–3 (Münster, 1919–27).

Logica 'Nostrorum Petitioni Sociorum', ed. B. Geyer, BGPTMA 21, vol. 4 (Münster, 1933).

Tractatus de Intellectibus, ed. and introd. Urban Ulivi, *La psichologia di Abelardo e il tractatus de intellectibus*, (Rome, 1976).

Sic et Non, prologus, eds. B. Boyer and R. McKeon, (Chicago, 1976–7).

Dialectica, ed. L. M. De Rijk, *Petrus Abaelardus, Dialectica* (Assen, 1956, 2nd revd. edn 1970).

Theologia 'Summi boni', ed. H. Ostlender, BGPTMA, 35, vols. 2–3 (Münster, 1939).

Tractatus de Unitate et Trinitate Divina, ed. R. Stölzle (Freiburg, 1891).

Opera Theologica, ed. E. M. Buytaert, CCCM, 11, 12 (Turnhout, 1969).

Dal Pra, M. ed., *Pietro Abelardo. Scritti filosofici* (Rome, 1954).

Historia Calamitatum, ed. with introd. J. Monfrin (Paris, 1967).

Minio-Paluello, L. ed., *Twelfth-Century Logic, texts and studies*, II, *Abaelardiana inedita* (Rome, 1959).

Aelred of Rievaulx, *Aelredi Rievallensis, Opera Omnia*, 1 (*De Anima*), ed. A. Hoste and C. H. Talbot, CCCM, 1 (Turnhout, 1971).

Dialogue on the Soul, trans. and introd. C. H. Talbot (Cistercian publications, Kalamazoo, 1981).

Albert the Great, *Albertus Magnus, Opera Omnia*, 38 vols. ed. A. Borgnet (Paris, 1890–99).

De Anima, in *Opera Omnia*, 5 (Paris, 1890).

De memoria et reminiscentia, commentarium, in *Opera Omnia*, 9, ed. A. Borgnet.

De Bono, in *Opera Omnia* vol. 28, eds. H. Kühle, C. Feckes, B. Geyer, and W. Kübel (Münster, 1951).

Alcuin (?) *Libri Carolini sive Caroli magni capitulare, De Imaginibus*, in *Concilia aevi Karolini*, MGH legum sectio 3, III, supplement II (Hannover/Leipzig, 1924) and *PL* 98: 999–1248.

Bibliography

Dicta albini, super illud Geneseos: faciamus hominem ad imaginem et similitudinem nostram (Gen. I, 26), *PL* 100: 565–8.

Amalarius of Metz, *Amalarii episcopi Opera Liturgica omnia*, ed. I. M. Hanssens, 3 vols. (Studi e testi, 138–40) (Rome, 1948–50).

Anselm of Aosta, of Canterbury, St, *S. Anselmi Cantuariensis Archiepiscopi Opera Omnia*, ed. F. S. Schmitt, 6 vols., (Stuttgart-Bad Canstatt, 1968).

Obras completas de San Anselmo, 2 vols., ed. P. Juan Alameda (Madrid, 1952–3).

Anselm of Canterbury, 4 vols, ed. and trans. J. Hopkins and H. Richardson, vol. I: *Monologion, Proslogion, Debate with Gaunilo, Meditation on Human Redemption* (New York, 1974–5).

The Prayers and Meditations of St Anselm, trans. B. Ward (London, 1973).

De Grammatico, ed. D. P. Henry (Oxford, 1964).

Aquinas, Thomas, St, *De memoria et reminiscentia*, in *Opera Omnia*, vol. 95, 2 (Leonine Commission, Rome, 1985).

In Aristoteles libros De Sensu et Sensato, De Memoria et Reminiscentia commentarium, ed. R. M. Spiazzi (Turin, 1949).

In De Anima, ed. A. M. Pirotta, (Turin, 1959).

Quaestiones de Anima, ed. J. H. Robb, (Pontifical Institute of Mediaeval Studies, Toronto, 1968).

Summa Theologiae, Ia Qq. 84–9, 'Human intelligence', text and trans. P. T. Durbin (Blackfriars edn, London, 1968).

Summa Theologiae, Ia Qq. 75–83, 'Treatise on man', text and trans. T. Suttor (Blackfriars edn, London, 197).

Tractatus de unitate intellectus contra averroistas, ed. L. W. Keeler, 2nd edn (Rome, 1957).

Aristotle, *De Memoria et Reminiscentia, Aristotle on Memory*, Eng. trans and commentary, Richard Sorabji (London, 1972).

De Anima, trans. and introd. Hugh Lawson-Tancred (Harmondsworth, 1986).

De Anima II, III, trans. with notes D. W. Hamlyn (Oxford, 1968).

Categories and De Interpretatione, trans. and ed. J. L. Ackrill (Oxford, 1963).

Posterior Analytics, trans. and ed. J. Barnes (Oxford, 1975).

Prior and Posterior Analytics, ed. W. D. Ross (Oxford, 1949).

Parva Naturalia, ed. W. D. Ross (Oxford, 1955).

Topica and Sophistici Elenchi, trans. W. A. Pickard-Cambridge, in W. D. Ross, ed. *The Works of Aristotle translated into English* (Oxford, 1928).

Rhetorica, ed. and trans. J. H. Freese (Loeb Classical Library) (London, 1926).

Poetica, ed. and trans. W. H. Fyfe (Loeb Classical Library) (London, 1927).

Aristotle's Rhetoric, A Digest by Thomas Hobbes, ed. T. A. Moxon (Everyman Library) (London, 1949).

Aristoteles Latinus, Codices I (Rome, 1939) and II (Cambridge, 1955) *Supplementa altera* (1961), *Opuscula, The Latin Aristotle* (Amsterdam, 1972), ed. G. Lacombe, L. Minio-Paluello, *et al.*

Augustine, St, *Confessiones*, ed. P. Knöll, CSEL 33 (Vienna, 1896).

The Confessions, trans. F. J. Sheed (London, 1944).

Bibliography

De Trinitate in *Oeuvres de Saint Augustin*, vols. 15, 16 (Bénédictine edn), text with French trans, P. Agaesse and notes J. Moingt (Bruges, 1955).

De Trinitate, ed. W. J. Mountain, CCSL 50 (Turnhout, 1967); also *PL* 42.

Soliloquia, PL 32: 869–904.

De Diversis Quaestionibus LXXXIII, ed. A. Murzenbecher, CCSL 44A (Turnhout, 1975).

Epistolae, ed. A. Goldbacher, CSEL, 34, 44, 57, 58 (Vienna, 1895–1911).

Pseudo-Augustine (Anon.), *De Spiritu et Anima, PL* 40.

Categoriae Decem, ed. L. Minio-Paluello, *Aristoteles Latinus* I 1–5 (Bruges, 1961).

Averroes, *Averrois Cordubensis, compendia librorum Aristotelis qui Parva Naturalia vocantur*, ed. E. Shields, (Cambridge, Mass., 1949).

Averrois Cordubensis, commentarium Magnum in Aristotelis De Anima libros, ed. R. Stuart Crawford (Cambridge, Mass., 1953).

Middle Commentary on Porphyry's Isagoge, translated from Hebrew and Latin versions; and on Aristotle's Categories, translated from original Arabic, Hebrew and Latin versions, trans. and introd. H. Davidson (Cambridge, Mass., 1969).

Epitome of the Parva Naturalia, translated from original Arabic, Hebrew and Latin versions, trans. and introd. H. Blumberg (Cambridge, Mass., 1961).

Avicenna, *Liber De Anima seu sextus De Naturalibus* I-III, ed. S. van Riet, introd. G. Verbeke (Louvain/Leiden, 1972).

Kitab al-Najat, II, vi. *Avicenna's Psychology, English trans. with historico-philosophical notes and textual improvements on the Cairo edition*, trans. F. Rahman (Oxford, 1952).

Bede, *Bedae Venerabilis, Opera*, pars I, *Didascalicon*, ed. C. W. Jones and C. B. Kendall, CCSL 123A (Turnhout, 1975).

Historia Ecclesiastica, ed. B. Colgrave and R. A. B. Mynors (Oxford, 1969).

Benedict of Nursia, St, *The Rule of St Benedict in Latin and English*, ed. and trans. J. McCann (London, 1969).

La Règle de Saint Benoît, ed. A. de Vogüé, trans. J. de Neufville, SC, 181–6 (Paris, 1971–2), vol. 7 (Paris, 1977).

Bernard of Clarivaux, St, *Sancti Bernardi, Opera Omnia*, eds. J. Leclercq, C. H. Talbot and H. M. Rochais, 8 vols. (Rome, 1857–78).

De Conversione, ed. and introd. J. Leclercq, in *Opera Omnia*, 4 (Rome, 1966), pp. 69–116.

Sermons on Conversion, trans. and introd. M. B. Said (Cistercian publications, Kalamazoo, 1981).

On the Song of Songs, II, trans. K. Walsh, introd. J. Leclercq (Cistercian Fathers ser. 7) (Kalamazoo, 1976).

Brevis commentatio in Cantica, PL 184: 407–36.

Blund, John, *Tractatus De Anima*, ed. D. A. Callus (London, 1970).

Boethius, *Theological Tractates and Consolation*, text and trans, ed., E. K. Rand, H. F. Stewart, and S. J. Tester (Loeb Classical Library) (London, 1978); also *PL* 63–4.

In Categorias Aristotelis libri quattuor, PL 64.

Bibliography

Isagoge of Porphyry, trans., in Aristoteles Latinus I, 6–7, ed. L. Minio-Paluello *et al.* (Bruges/Paris, 1966).

Bonaventure, St, *Obras de S. Buenaventura* (Bibl. de Autores Christianos) (Madrid, 1957).

Bradwardine, Thomas, *Ars Memorativa*, Fitzwilliam Museum, Cambridge, McClean MS 169, fols. 254–6.

De Causa Dei, ed. H. Savile (London, 1618, reprint 1964).

Bruni, Leonardo, *L. Bruni Aretino, humanistische-philosophische Schriften*, ed. Hans Baron (Leipzig/Berlin, 1928).

Cassiodorus, *Opera* vol. I, ed. Å. J. Fridh and J. W. Halporn, CCSL 96 (Turnhout, 1973) including *De Anima*, ed. J. W. Halporn.

Cicero, *De Oratore*, text and trans. E. W. Sutton and H. Rackham (Loeb Classical Library), 2 vols., vol. 1: *De Oratore*, I, II, vol. 2: *De Oratore*, III.

Libri de oratore tres, ed. A. S. Wilkins (Oxford, 1902–3).

On Oratory and Orators, trans. J. S. Watson (Bohn's Classical Library) (London, 1855).

De Inventione, text and trans. H. M. Hubbell (Loeb Classical Library) (London, 1949).

Tusculan Disputations, text and trans. J. E. King, revd edn (Loeb Classical Library) (London, 1945).

Cistercian texts, Bouton, J. and J. van Damme, eds., *Les plus anciens textes de Cîteaux: Sources, Textes et notes historiques* (ser: Cîteaux, commentarii Cistercienses, studia et documenta, II) (Achel, 1974).

David of Dinant, *Davidis de Dinanto, Quaternulorum fragmenta*, ed. M. Kurdziałek, *Studia Mediewistyczne* 3 (Warsaw), 1963.

Gervase of Canterbury, *The Historical Works of Gervase of Canterbury*, ed. W. Stubbs, Rolls ser. 73 (London, 1879–80).

Gilbert of Poitiers. *The Commentary on Boethius by Gilbert of Poitiers*, ed. N. M. Häring, (Toronto, 1966).

Gregory the Great, *Grégoire le Grand: Morales sur Job*, ed. R. Gillet, SC 32 (Paris, 1950); also *Moralia in Job*, *PL* 76.

Les Dialogues de Grégoire le Grand, 3 vols., ed. A. de Vogüé, trans. P. Antin, SC 251, 265, 266 (Paris, 1978–80).

Gregory of Rimini, *Lectura super primum et secundum Sententiarum*, ed. D. Trapp (Berlin, 1978-).

Guigo II, *The Ladder of Monks, a letter on the contemplative life and twelve meditations by Guigo II, ninth prior of La Grande Chartreuse*, trans. E. College and J. Walsh (London, 1978).

Gundissalinus, Dominic, *Dominique Gundissalvi, De Immortalitate Animae*, ed. G. Bülow, BGPTMA, 2, 3 (Münster, 1897).

De Anima, ed. J. T. Muckle, 'The treatise *De Anima* of Dominic Gundissalinus', *Mediaeval Studies* 2 (1940), 23–103.

Henry of Huntingdon, *Historia Anglorum*, ed. T. Arnold, Rolls ser. 74 (London, 1879).

Holcot, Robert O. P., *In librum Sapientie Salomonis* (Hagenau, 1494; Paris, 1511).

618

Hugh of St Victor, *Didascalicon* VI, iii, *De Historia*, ed. C. H. Buttimer (Washington, D.C., 1939), trans. J. Taylor (New York, 1961).

De unione corporis et spiritus, PL 177: 285–94.

De Institutione, PL 176.

Isaac of Stella, *Isaac de l'Etoile: sermons*, I, 69–81, ed. A. Hoste (Paris, 1967).

Sermons, I, ed. A. Hoste and G. Salet, SC 130 (Paris, 1967).

The Letter of Isaac of Stella on the Soul, trans B. McGinn in *Three Treatises on Man: A Cistercian Anthropology*, trans. and introd. B. McGinn (Cistercian Fathers ser. 24) (Kalamazoo, 1977).

Israeli, Isaac ben Solomon, *Das Buch über die Elemente*, ed. S. Fried (Frankfurt am Main/Drohobycz, 1900).

Liber de definicionibus, Book of Definitions, trans. Gerard of Cremona, ed. J. T. Muckle, *AHDLMA* 11 (1937–8), 299–340.

Isaac ben Solomon Israeli, A Neoplatonic Philosopher of the Early Tenth Century, texts, trans. and comments, A. Altmann and S. M. Stern (London, 1958).

De Oblivio in *Omnia Opera Ysaac* (Lyons, 1515).

Thesaurus sanitatis de victus salubris ratione ... libri II (Antwerp, 1607).

De Diaetis universalibus et particularibus libri II, (Basle, 1570).

John of Damascus, *De Fide Orthodoxa*, ed. E. M., Buytaert (Nauwelaerts, 1955).

Contra imaginum calumniatores orationes tres, Die Schriften des Johannes von Damaskos, vol. 3, ed. B. Kotter (Berlin, 1975).

John of la Rochelle, *Tractatus de divisione multiplici potentiarum animae*, ed. and introd. P. Michaud-Quantin (Paris, 1964).

Summa de Anima, ed. T. Domenichelli (Prato, 1882).

John of Salisbury, *Ioannis Saresberiensis Episcopi Carnotensis, Metalogicon libri III*, ed. C. C. J. Webb, (Oxford, 1929).

Policraticus, ed. C. C. J. Webb (Oxford, 1909).

Historia Pontificalis, ed. M. Chibnall (Edinburgh, 1956, revd. Oxford, 1986).

Kilwardby, Robert O.P., *Robert Kilwardby O.P. on time and imagination, De Tempore, De Spiritu Fantastico*, ed. O. Lewry (Oxford, 1987).

Mamertus, Claudianus, *De Statu Animae*, ed. G. Engelbrecht, CSEL 11 (Vienna, 1885).

Map, Walter, *De Nugis Curialium*, ed. and trans. M. R. James, C. N. L. Brooke and R. A. B. Mynors (Oxford, 1983).

Matthew of Aquasparta, *Quaestiones de anima separata*, ed. G. Gál (Quaracchi, 1959).

Nemesius of Emessa, *Nemesius d'Emèse, De Natura Hominis, traduction de Burgundio de Pise*, ed. G. Verbeke and J. R. Moncho (Leiden, 1975).

Ockham, William of, *Elementarium Logicae*, ed. E. M. Buytaert in *Franciscan Studies 25* (1965).

Guillelmi de Ockham Opera Philosophica et Theologica, eds. G. Gál, S. Brown *et al.*, 8 vols. (St Bonaventure, New York, 1967–).

Summa Logicae, ed. P. Boehner, G. Gál and S. Brown in *Opera Philosophica*, I, 2 vols. (St Bonaventure, New York, 1974).

Quodlibeta septem, ed. J. C. Wey in *Opera Theologica*, IX (St Bonaventure, New York, 1980).

De imperatorum et pontificum potestate, ed. C. K. Brampton (Oxford, 1927), also in R. Scholz.

Reportatio II, Qq. 14–15. 'The *notitio intuitiva* of nonexistents according to William of Ockham', ed. P. Boehner, *Traditio I* (1945) 245–75.

Breviloquium de potestate papae, ed. L. Baudry (Paris, 1937).

Unbekannte kirchenpolitische Streitschriften aus der Zeit Ludwigs des Bayern (1327–59), 2 vols., ed. R. Scholz (Rome, 1914).

Scriptum in librum primum Sententiarum: Ordinatio, in *Opera philosophica et theologica, Opera Theologica* I ed. G. Gál and S. Brown (St Bonaventure, New York, 1967).

Philosophical Writings, ed. and trans. P. Boehner (Edinburgh, 1957).

Opera Politica, ed. H. S. Offler (Manchester, 1974 (1940)): *Octo quaestiones de potestate papae*; *An princeps*; *Consultatio de causa matrimoniali*, *Opus Nonaginta Dierum*, 1–6.

Opera Politica II, eds. H. S. Offler and R. F. Bennett (Manchester, 1963): *Opus Nonaginta Dierum*, 7–124.

Opera Politica III, ed. H. S. Offler (Manchester, 1956): *Tractatus contra Ioannem XXII*; *Tractatus contra Benedictum XII*; *Epistola Ad Fratres Minores*.

Dialogus, ed. J. Trechsel (Lyons, 1494) and in Melchior Goldast, ed. *Monarchia Sancti Romani Imperii*, 2 vols, vol. 2 (Frankfurt, 1614).

Odo of Cluny, *Odonis abbatis Cluniacensis, Occupatio*, ed. A. Svoboda (Leipzig, 1900).

Otto of Freising, *Gesta Frederici primi*, MGH *Scriptores rerum germanicorum in usum scholarium*, 46, ed. G. Waitz (Hannover/Leipzig, 1912).

Peter of Celle, *Pierre de Celle, L'Ecole du Cloître, De Disciplina Claustrali*, ed. G. de Martel, SC (Paris, 1977).

Peter the Venerable, *De Miraculis* and the *Statuta* of Cluny, *PL* 189.

Petrarch, Francesco, *De Secreto conflictu mearum curarum libri tres* in *Francesco Petrarca, Prose*, ed. G. Martellotti *et al.* (Milan/Naples, 1955).

Liber Sine Nomine in P. Piur ed., *Petrarcas 'Buch ohne Namen' und die päpstliche Kurie* (Halle, 1925).

Epistolae Familiares, eds. V. Rossi and U. Bosco (Florence, 1933–42).

De Otio Religioso, ed. G. Rotondi, *Studi e Testi*, 197 (Vatican City, 1958).

Philip the Chancellor, *Ex Summa Philippi Cancellarii Quaestiones de Anima*, ed. L. W. Keeler (Munich, 1937).

Plato, *The Collected Dialogues of Plato including the letters*, eds. E. Hamilton and H. Cairns, various trans. (Bollingen ser. 71) (Princeton, 1973).

Plato's Meno, ed. R. S. Bluck, text and introd. (Cambridge, 1961).

Pliny, *Historia Naturalis*, 5 vols., eds. L. Jahn and C. Mayhoff (Leipzig, 1822–1909) and text and trans. H. Rackham (Loeb Classical Library).

Plotinus, *Enneads*, trans. S. Mackenna, revd. B. S. Page, introd. P. Henry, 4 revd. edn (London, 1969) based on *Plotini Opera* I-III, eds. P. Henry and J. Schwyzer (Paris/Brussels, 1959, 1973).

Ratramnus of Corbie, *Liber De Anima ad Odonem Belovacensem*, ed. D. C. Lambot (Analecta Mediaevalia Namurcensia, 2) (Namur/Lille, 1951).

Salernitan Questions. *The Prose Salernitan Questions edited from a Bodleian Ms* (Auct. F. 3.10), *an anonymous collection dealing with science and medicine written by an Englishman c. 1200* ed. B. Lawn (London, 1979).

Scotus, John Duns, *Opera Omnia*, 12 vols., ed. L. Wadding (Lyons, 1639).

Opera Omnia, ed. C. Balíc *et al.*, (Vatican Scotistic Commission) (Rome, 1950–   ).

God and Creatures, the Quodlibetal Questions, trans. and introd., F. Alluntis and A. B. Wolter (Princeton, 1975).

Cuestiones Cuodlibetales, Obras del Doctor Sutil Juan Duns Escoto, text and Spanish trans. with introd., F. Alluntis (Madrid, 1968).

Siger of Brabant, *Siger de Brabant De Anima Intellectiva*, ed. B. Bazán (Louvain/ Paris, 1972).

Questiones in tertium De Anima, ed. B. Bazán (Louvain/Paris, 1972).

Stephen of Salley, *Un speculum novitii inédit d'Etienne de Salley*, ed. E. Mikkers, *Collectanea Ord. Cist.*, *Ref.* 8 (1946).

Thierry of Chartres, *Commentaries on Boethius by Thierry of Chartres and his School*, ed. N. M. Häring, (Toronto, 1971).

William of Auvergne, *De Bono*, ed. J. R. O'Donnell in *Mediaeval Studies*, 7 (1946).

William of Conches, *Moralium dogma philosophorum*, Paris BN lat. 2512 fols. 64v–86v.

William of Malmesbury, *Gesta regum Anglorum*, ed. W. Stubbs, Rolls ser. 90, 2 vols. (London, 1889).

William of Newburgh, *Historia rerum Anglicarum*, ed. R. Howlett, Rolls ser. 82 (London, 1884–5).

William of Saint Thierry, *Guillaume de Saint Thierry, Commentaire sur le Cantique des Cantiques*, ed. M.-M. Davy (Paris, 1958).

De Natura et Dignitate Amoris, PL 184; *De Natura Corporis et Animae, PL* 180; *Physica Corporis et Animae, PL* 180; *Speculum Fidei, PL* 180; *Aenigma Fidei, PL* 180.

Guillaume de Saint Thierry: meditations et prières, ed. and trans. J. Déchanet = *Meditativae Orationes, PL* 180.

Epistola Ad Fratres de Monte Dei, PL 184.

Three Treatises on Man: a Cistercian Anthropology, William of St Thierry, The Nature of the Body and Soul, I, II, trans. B. Clark, ed. B. McGinn (Kalamazoo, 1977).

William of Tyre, *Historia rerum in partibus transmarinis gestarum, PL* 201.

SECONDARY WORKS

The following works proved particularly useful and stimulating for this series of studies. Collections in which there are several important contributions, some of which have been mentioned in the footnotes, are cited here only as collections. More specific references to works used can be found in the footnotes to each chapter.

ANTIQUITY AND EARLY CHRISTIANITY

Armstrong, A. H., *St Augustine and Christian Platonism* (Villanova, 1967).
Armstrong, A. H., ed., *The Cambridge History of Later Greek and Early Medieval Philosophy* (Cambridge, 1970).
Arnhart, Larry, *Aristotle on Political Reasoning, A Commentary on the 'Rhetoric'*, (Dekalb, Illinois, 1981).
Arnou, R., *Le désir de Dieu dans la philosophie de Plotin* (Paris, 1921).
Barnes, J., M. Schofield, R. Sorabji, eds., *Articles on Aristotle*, vol. 4 (London, 1979).
Berti, E., ed., *Aristotle on Science: the Posterior Analytics, proceedings of the eighth symposium Aristotelicum* (Padua, 1981).
Block, I., 'Truth and error in Aristotle's theory of sense perception', *Philosophical Quarterly*, 11 (1961), 1–9.
'The order of Aristotle's psychological writings', *American Journal of Philology*, 82 (1961), 50–77.
Blumenthal, Henry, 'Neoplatonic elements in the *De Anima* commentaries', *Phronesis*, 21 (1976), 65–83.
'Neoplatonic interpretations of Aristotle on *phantasia*', *Review of Metaphysics*, 31 (1977), 251–2.
Plotinus' Psychology (The Hague, 1971).
Blumenthal, H. and A. C. Lloyd, eds., *Soul and the Structure of Being in Late neoplatonism: Syrianus, Proclus and Simplicius* (Liverpool, 1982).
Blumenthal, H. and R. A. Markus, eds., *Neoplatonism and Early Christian Thought, Essays in Honour of A. H. Armstrong* (London, 1981).
Bossier, F. and C. Laga, eds., *Images of Man in Ancient and Medieval Thought, Studia Gérard Verbeke* (Louvain, 1976).
Breisach, E., ed., *Classical Rhetoric and Medieval Historiography* (Kalamazoo, 1985).
Brock, Sebastian, 'Aspects of translation technique in antiquity', *Greek, Roman and Byzantine Studies*, 20 (1979), 69–87.
Brown, Malcolm, ed., *Plato's Meno, Text and Essays* (New York, 1971).
Brown, Peter, *Religion and Society in the Age of St. Augustine* (London, 1972).
Society and the Holy in Late Antiquity (London, 1982).
The Cult of Saints: Its Rise and Function in Late Christianity (London, 1981).
'Eastern and western Christianity in late antiquity: a parting of the ways', *Studies in Church History*, 13 (1976), 1–24.
Relics and Social Status in the Age of Gregory of Tours (Reading, 1977).

Augustine of Hippo, A Biography (London, 1967).

Calvo, Francesco, *Cercare l'uomo, Socrate, Platone, Aristotele* (Genoa, 1989).

Cameron, Averil, 'The last days of the Academy at Athens', *Proceedings of the Cambridge Philological Society*, 196 (1969), 7–29.

Chadwick, Henry, *Boethius, The Consolations of Music, Logic, Theology and Philosophy* (Oxford, 1981).

Chadwick, W. Owen, *John Cassian: A Study in Primitive Monasticism*, 2nd edn (Cambridge, 1968).

Chaix-Ruy, Jules, *Saint Augustin: temps et histoire* (Paris, 1956).

Chausserie-Laprée, *L'Expression narrative chez les historiens latins, histoire d'un style* (Paris, 1969).

Cornford, F. M., *Principium Sapientiae* (Cambridge, 1952).

Courcelle, Pierre, *Connais-toi toi-même: de Socrate à St. Bernard*, 3 vols. (Paris, 1974–5).

Late Latin Writers and their Greek Sources (Cambridge, Mass., 1969).

Recherches sur les Confessions de Saint Augustin (Paris, 1950, revd 1968).

Delehaye, Hippolyte, *Les passions des martyrs et les genres littéraires*, 2nd revd edn (Brussels, 1966).

Les legendes hagiographiques (Brussels, 1905).

Dillon, J., *The Middle Platonists* (London, 1977).

Dodds, E. R., *Pagan and Christian in a World of Anxiety* (Cambridge, 1965).

Dover, K., 'Thucydides "as history" and "as literature"', *History and Theory*, 22 (1983), 51–63.

Fox, Robin Lane, *Pagans and Christians* (Harmondsworth, 1986).

Hadot, Pierre, *Porphyre et Victorinus* (Paris, 1968).

Hadot, P., ed., *Marius Victorinus: traités théologiques sur la trinité*, SC 68 (Paris, 1960).

Hamlyn, D. W. 'Aristotle's account of *aesthesis* in the *De Anima*', *Classical Quarterly*, ns 9 (1959), 6–16.

Henry, P., *Saint Augustine on Personality* (New York, 1960).

Huber, Carlo, *Anamnesis bei Plato* (Munich, 1964).

Huddlestun, B., 'St. Augustine and Aristotle on time and history' in J. K. Ryan, ed., *Heirs and Ancestors, Studies in Philosophy and the History of Philosophy*, 6 (Washington, D.C., 1973), 279–91.

Ivánka, von, E., *Plato Christianus, Übernahme und Umgestaltung des Platonismus durch die Väter* (Einsiedeln, 1964).

Kahn, C. H., 'Sensation and consciousness in Aristotle's psychology' *Archiv für Geschichte der Philosophie*, 18 (1966), 44–70.

Lefèvre, C., *Sur l'évolution d'Aristote en psychologie* (Louvain, 1972).

Lesher, J., 'The role of *nous* in Aristotle's *Posterior Analytics*', *Phronesis*, 18 (1973), 44–68.

Lloyd, G. E. R., *Magic, Reason and Experience, Studies in the Origins and Development of Greek Science* (Cambridge, 1979).

Lloyd, G. E. R. and G. E. L. Owen eds., *Aristotle on Mind and the Senses, proceedings of the seventh symposium Aristotelicum* (Cambridge, 1978).

Mansion, A., 'L'immortalité de l'âme et de l'intellect d'aprés Aristote', *Revue Philosophique* (Louvain) 51 (1953), 456–65.

Markus, R. A., 'Augustine', chs. 21–27 in H. A. Armstrong, ed., *The Cambridge History of Later Greek and Early Medieval Philosophy* (Cambridge, 1967).

'Vie monastique et ascetisme chez Saint Augustin' in *Atti, Congresso internazionale su S. Agostino nel XVI centenario della conversione* (Rome, 1987), 119–25.

Conversion and Disenchantment in Augustine's Spiritual Career (Villanova, 1985).

'Imago' and 'similitudo' in Augustine', *Revue des Etudes Augustiniennes*, 10 (1964), 125–43.

Marrou, H.-I., *L'ambivalence du temps et de l'histoire chez Saint Augustin* (Paris, 1950).

Saint Augustin et la fin de la culture antique (Paris, 1949).

Moline, Jon, *Plato's Theory of Understanding*, (Madison, Wisconsin, 1981).

Momigliano, Arnaldo, *Essays in Ancient and Modern Historiography* (Middletown, Connecticut, 1977).

Momigliano, A. ed., *The Conflict Between Paganism and Christianity in the Fourth Century* (Oxford, 1963).

Moravcsik, J. M., 'Recollecting the theory of forms', in W. H. Werkmeister, ed., *Facets of Plato's Philosophy, Phronesis*, supplement 2 (Assen, 1976), 1–20.

'Understanding and knowledge in Plato's philosophy', *Neue Hefte für Philosophie*, 15–16 (1978), 53–69.

Muckle, J. T., 'The doctrine of St. Gregory of Nyssa on Man as the Image of God', *Mediaeval Studies*, 7 (1945), 55–84.

Nussbaum, Martha C., *The Fragility of Goodness, Luck and Ethics in Greek Tragedy and Philosophy* (Cambridge, 1986).

Logic, Science and Dialectic: Collected Papers on Ancient Greek Philosophy (London, 1986).

O'Meara, D. J., ed., *Neoplatonism and Christian Thought* (Albany, New York, 1982).

Owen, G. E. L. 'Tithenai ta phainomena', in S. Mansion ed., *Aristote et les problèmes de méthode* (Louvain, 1961), 83–103.

'Logic and metaphysics in some earlier works of Aristotle', in I. Düring and G. E.L. Owen, eds., *Aristotle and Plato in the Mid-Fourth Century* (Göteborg, 1960), 163–90.

Pépin, J., 'Une nouvelle source de S. Augustin: le zētēma de Porphyre sur l'union de l'âme et du corps', *Revue des Etudes Augustiniennes*, 66 (1964), 53–107.

Quinn, John M., 'The concept of time in St Augustine', in John K. Ryan, ed., *Studies in Philosophy and the History of Philosophy*, 4 (Washington, D.C., 1969), 75–127.

Rorty, Amelie, ed., *Essays on Aristotle's Ethics* (Berkeley, 1980).

Sambursky, S. and S. Pines, *The Concept of Time in Late Neoplatonism* (Jerusalem, 1971).

Schofield, Malcolm, M. Burnyeat, J. Barnes, eds., *Doubt and Dogmatism: Studies in Hellenistic Epistemology* (Oxford, 1980).

Schofield, M. and M. Nussbaum, eds., *Language and Logos, Studies in Ancient Greek Philosophy presented to G. E. L. Owen* (Cambridge, 1982).

Scolnicov, S., 'Three aspects of Plato's philosophy of learning and instruction', *Paideia, special Plato issue* (1976), 50–62.

Sorabji, Richard, *Time, Creation and the Continuum: Theories in Antiquity and the Early Middle Ages* (London, 1983).

'Body and soul in Aristotle', *Philosophy*, 49 (1974).

Necessity, Cause and Blame: Perspectives on Aristotle's Theory (London, 1980).

TeSelle, E., 'Porphyry and Augustine', *Augustinian Studies*, 5 (1974), 113–47.

Vlastos, G., 'Degrees of reality in Plato' in R. Bambrough, ed., *New Essays on Plato and Aristotle* (London, 1965), 1–20.

Vlastos, Gregory, ed., *Plato: A Collection of Critical Essays*, 2 vols. (New York, 1971).

de Vogel, Cornelia, 'The concept of personality in Greek and Christian thought', *Studies in Philosophy and the History of Philosophy*, 2 (Washington, D.C., 1963), 20–60.

Wilkinson, L. P., 'Cicero and the relationship of oratory to literature', in E. J. Kenney, ed., *The Cambridge History of Classical Literature* vol. 2: The Late Republic (Cambridge, 1982), 56–93.

Wilmart, André, 'La tradition des grands ouvrages de Saint Augustin', *Miscellanea Agostiniana*, testi et studi, II (Rome, 1931).

MEDIEVAL AND RENAISSANCE

Adams, Marilyn McCord, *William of Ockham* (Notre Dame, 1987).

'Intuitive cognition, certainty and skepticism in William of Ockham', *Traditio*, 26 (1970), 389–98.

Alféri, Pierre, *Guillaume d'Ockham, le singulier* (Paris, 1989).

Auerbach, E., 'Figura' in *Scenes from the Drama of European Literature* (New York, 1959).

Baron, Hans, 'The Querelle of ancients and moderns as a problem for Renaissance scholarship', *Journal of the History of Ideas*, 20 (1959), 3–22.

Baron, H., *The Crisis of the Early Italian Renaissance*, 2 vols. (Princeton, 1955).

Bäuml, Franz, 'Varieties and consequences of medieval literacy and illiteracy', *Speculum*, 55 (1980), 237–65.

Beer, Jeanette, *Narrative Conventions of Truth in the Middle Ages* (Geneva, 1981).

Benson, R., G. Constable, C. Lanham, eds., *Renaissance and Renewal in the Twelfth Century* (Cambridge, Mass., 1982).

Berubé, Camille, *La connaissance de l'individuel au moyen âge* (Paris/Montreal, 1964).

Biard, Joël, *Logique et théorie du signe au xive siècle* (Paris, 1989).

Black, Robert, 'Ancients and moderns in the Renaissance, rhetoric and history in Accolti's Dialogues on the preeminence of men of his own times', *Journal of the History of Ideas*, 43 (1982), 3–32.

Benedetto Accolti and the Florentine Renaissance (Cambridge, 1985).

Booth, Edward, *Aristotelian Aporetic, Ontology in Islamic and Christian Thinkers* (Cambridge, 1983).

Bonner, Gerald, ed., *Famulus Christi: Essays in Commemoration of the Thirteenth Centenary of the Birth of the Venerable Bede* (London, 1976).

Bourdé, Guy and Hervé Martin, *Les Ecoles Historiques* (Paris, 1983).

Bredero, Adriaan, *Etudes sur la Vita Prima de Saint Bernard* (Rome, 1960).

Bredero, A., 'Cluny and Cîteaux au xii^{e}s., les origines de la controverse', *Studi Medievali*, 3rd ser., 12, i (1971), 135–75.

Brémond, Claude, J. LeGoff and J.-Cl. Schmitt, *L'Exemplum* (Typologie des sources du moyen age occidental, 40) (Turnhout, 1982).

Bultot, Robert, *Christianisme et valeurs humains: la doctrine du mépris du monde en occident de S. Ambroise à Innocent II*, 4 vols. (Louvain, 1963–4).

Burke, Peter, *Tradition and Innovation in Renaissance Italy* (London, 1974).

Bursill-Hall, G. L., *Speculative Grammars of the Middle Ages* (The Hague/Paris, 1971).

Buytaert, E. M., ed., *Ph. Boehner, Collected Articles on Ockham* (St Bonaventure, N.Y., 1958).

Bynum, Caroline W., *Jesus as Mother, Studies in the Spirituality of the High Middle Ages* (Berkeley, 1982).

Callus, D. A., 'Introduction of Aristotelian learning to Oxford', *Proceedings of the British Academy*, 29 (1943), 229–81.

'Gundissalinus' *De Anima* and the problem of substantial form', *The New Scholasticism*, 13 (1939), 338–55.

Chenu, M.-D., *Nature, Man and Society in the Twelfth Century*, trans. J. Taylor and L. K. Little (Chicago, 1968).

Chatillon, J., 'L'influence de S. Bernard sur la pensée scholastique au xiie et au xiiie s.', in *Saint Bernard Théologien, Analecta S.O. Cist.* 3–4 (1953), 284–7.

Clanchy, Michael, *From Memory to Written Record, England 1066–1307* (London, 1979).

'Remembering the past and the Good Old Law', *History*, 55 (1970), 177–88.

Classen, Peter, ed., *Recht und Schrift im Mittelalter* (Vorträge und Forschungen, Konstanzer Arbeitskreis fur Mittelalterliche Geschichte, xxiii) (Sigmaringen, 1977).

Clemoes, Peter and K. Hughes, eds., *England Before the Conquest, Studies Presented to Dorothy Whitelock* (Cambridge, 1971).

Cochrane, Eric, *Historians and Historiography in the Italian Renaissance* (Chicago, 1981).

Coleman, Janet, '*Dominium* in 13th and 14th-century political thought and its 17th-century heirs: John of Paris and Locke', *Political Studies*, 33 (1985), 73–100.

'The *Owl and the Nightingale* and papal theories of marriage', *Journal of Ecclesiastical History*, 38 (1987), 517–68.

'The relation between Ockham's intuitive knowledge and his political science', *Théologie et Droit dans la Science politique de l'Etat Moderne* (Table Ronde du CNRS, L'Ecole française de Rome, 1987).

Piers Plowman and the Moderni (Rome, 1981).
English Literature in History: 1350–1400, Medieval Readers and Writers (London, 1981).
'The two jurisdictions: theological and legal justifications of Church property in the 13th century', *The Church and Its Wealth*, ed. W. Shiels and D. Wood, *Studies in Church History*, 23 (1987), 75–110.
'English Culture in the Fourteenth Century', in Piero Boitani ed., *Chaucer and the Italian Trecento* (Cambridge, 1983), 33–63.
'Property and Poverty', in J. H. Burns ed., *The Cambridge History of Medieval Political Thought* (Cambridge, 1988), 607–48.
'Late scholastic *memoria et reminiscentia*; its uses and abuses', in P. Boitani and A. Torti, eds., *Intellectuals and Writers in Fourteenth-Century Europe* (Tübingen, 1986).
Colish, Marcia, *The Mirror of Language, A Study in the Medieval Theory of Language* (New Haven, 1968).
Constable, Giles, *Cluniac Studies* (Variorum reprints, London, 1980).
'Monastic legislation at Cluny in the eleventh and twelfth centuries', *Proceedings of the 4th International Congress of Medieval Canon Law*, Toronto 1972, (Vatican City, 1976), 151–62.
'The monastic policy of Peter the Venerable', in *Pierre Abélard, Pierre le Vénérable, les courants philosophiques, littéraires et artistiques en occident au milieu du xiie s*, Colloque international, Abbaye de Cluny, 1972 (Paris, 1975), 119–38.
Courtenay, William J., 'Nominalism and late medieval religion', in C. Trinkaus and H. A. Oberman, eds., *The Pursuit of Holiness in Late Medieval and Renaissance Religion* (Leiden, 1974), 26–59.
Adam Wodeham (Leiden, 1978).
'Nominalism and late medieval thought, a bibliographical essay', *Theological Studies*, 33 (1972), 716–34.
'The role of English thought in the transformation of university education in the late Middle Ages', in J. A. Kittleson, ed., *Rebirth, Reform and Resilience: Universities in Transition 1300–1700* (Columbus, Ohio, 1981).
'*Antiqui* and *Moderni* in late medieval thought', in *Ancients and Moderns*, a symposium, *Journal of the History of Ideas*, 48 (1987), 3–10.
'John of Mirecourt and Gregory of Rimini on whether God can undo the past', *Recherches de Théologie ancienne et médiévale*, 39 (1972), 224–56, and 40 (1973), 147–74.
'The reception of Ockham's thought at the University of Paris', in Z. Kałuza and P. Vignaux, eds., *Preuve et Raisons à l'université de Paris: logique, ontologie et théologie au XIVe siècle* (Paris, 1984), 43–64.
Courtenay, W. J. and K. Tachau, 'Ockham, Ockhamists and the English-German Nation at Paris, 1339–1341', *History of Universities*, 2 (1982), 53–96.
Dagens, C., *Saint Grégoire le Grand: culture et expérience chrétiennes* (Paris, 1977).
Damiata, M., *Guighelmo d'Ockham: povertà e potere*, vol. I: *Il problema della povertà evangelica e francescana nel sec. xiii e xiv. Origine del pensiero politico di*

G. d'Ockham. vol. II: *Il potere, come servizio. Dal 'principatus dominativus' al 'principatus ministrativus'* (Florence, 1978–9).

Davis, R. H. C. and J. M. Wallace-Hadrill, eds., *The Writing of History in the Middle Ages* (Oxford, 1981).

Day, Sebastian, *Intuitive Cognition, A Key to the Significance of the Late Scholastics* (St Bonaventure, N.Y., 1947).

Déchanet, J., *Guillaume de Saint Thierry, aux sources d'une pensée* (Paris, 1978).

De Bruyne, E., *Etudes d'esthétique médiévale* (Bruges, 1946).

Deluz, Christiane, 'Indifference au temps dans les récits de pélérinage (du xiie au xive siecle)?', *Annales de Bretagne et des Pays de l'Ouest*, 83 (1976), 2, 303–13.

De Rijk, L. M., *Logica Modernorum*, 2 vols. (Amsterdam, 1962–7).

van Dijk, P. and J. H. Walker, *The Origins of the Modern Roman Liturgy, The Liturgy of the Papal Court and the Franciscan Order in the Thirteenth Century* (London, 1960).

Dronke, Peter, ed., *A History of Twelfth-Century Western Philosophy* (Cambridge, 1988).

Duby, Georges, *Saint Bernard, L'Art Cistercien* (Paris, 1976).

Evans, G. R., *Anselm and a New Generation* (Oxford, 1980).

The Mind of St Bernard of Clairvaux (Oxford, 1983).

Fay, Thomas, '*Imago Dei*: Augustine's metaphysics of Man', *Antonianum*, 2–3 (1974), 173–97.

Flint, Valerie, 'The school of Laon: a reconsideration', *Recherches de Théologie ancienne et médiévale*, 43 (1976), 89–110.

Folz, Robert, 'Pierre le Vénérable et la liturgie', in *Pierre Abélard, Pierre le Vénérable* (Paris, 1975), 143–64.

Francastel, Pierre, *Peinture et Societé, Naissance et destruction d'un espace plastique. De la Renaissance au Cubisme* (Paris, 1951).

Fredborg, K., 'Petrus Helias on rhetoric', *Cahiers de l'institut du Moyen-Age Grec et Latin de Copenhague*, 13 (1974), 31–41.

Freeman, Ann, 'Carolingian orthodoxy and the fate of the *Libri Carolini*', *Viator*, 16 (1985), 65–108.

Fortin, E. L., 'Saint Augustin et la doctrine néo-platonicienne de l'âme', *Augustinus Magister*, 3 vols. (Paris, 1954), III, 371–80.

Fuchs, Oswald, *The Psychology of Habit according to William of Ockham* (St. Bonaventure, N.Y., 1952).

Fussner, F. S., *The Historical Revolution: English Historical Writing and Thought 1580–1640* (London, 1962).

Gál, G., 'Adam Wodeham's Question on the 'complexe significabile' as the immediate object of scientific knowledge', *Franciscan Studies*, 37 (1977), 66–102.

Gauthier, Léon, *Ibn Rochd (Averroés)* (Paris, 1948).

Genet, Jean-Philippe, 'Droit et histoire en Angleterre: la préhistoire de la "revolution historique"', in *L'Historiographie en occident du ve au xve s.*, *Annales de Bretagne et des Pays de l'Ouest*, 87 (1980), 319–66.

de Ghellinck, J., *Le mouvement théologique de xiie s.* (Bruges, 1948).

Ghisalberti, A., 'L'intuizione in Ockham,', *Revista di filosofia neo-scolastica*, 70 (1978), 207–26.

Gibson, Margaret, 'The "opuscula sacra"', in M. Gibson, ed., *Boethius, His Life, Thought and Influence* (Oxford, 1981).

Gilbert, N. W., 'Ockham, Wyfclif and the "via moderna"', in W. Zimmermann, ed., *Antiqui und Moderni* (Miscellanea Mediaevalia 9) (Berlin, 1974), 85–125.

Gilissen, John, *La Coutume* (Typologie des sources du moyen-âge occidental, 41) (Turnhout, 1982).

Gilson, Etienne, *Jean Duns Scot, introduction à ses positions fondamentales* (Paris, 1952).

'*Regio dissimilitudinis* de Platon à Saint Bernard de Clairvaux', *Mediaeval Studies*, 9 (1947).

'Les sources greco-arabes de l'augustinisme avicennisant', *AHDLMA*, 4 (1929–30), 5–149.

Glorieux, P., *Répertoire des maîtres en théologie de Paris au xiiiᵉ s.* (Paris, 1934).

Goichon, A.-M., *La philosophie d'Avicenne et son influence en Europe médiévale*, 2nd edn. (Paris, 1951).

Gössmann, Elisabeth, *Antiqui und Moderni im Mittelalter* (Paderborn, 1974).

Gramain, Monique, 'Memoires paysannes, des exemples bas languedociens aux xiiiᵉ et xivᵉ siecles', *Annales de Bretagne et des Pays de l'Ouest*, 83 (1976), 2, 315–24.

Gransden, Antonia, *Historical Writing in England, 550–c. 1307*, vol. I (London, 1974) and vol II. *c. 1307–early sixteenth century* (London, 1982).

Gregory, Tullio, *Anima Mundi, la filosofia di Guglielmo di Conches e la scuola di Chartres* (Florence, 1955).

Guenée, Bernard, 'Les genres historiques au Moyen Age', *Annales, E.S.C.*, 28 (1973), 997–1016.

Histoire et culture historique dans l'occident médiéval (Paris, 1980).

Guenée, B., ed., *Le métier d'historien au Moyen Age. Etudes sur l'historiographie médiévale* (Paris, 1977).

Gy, P. M., 'Les tropes dans l'histoire de la liturgie et de la théologie', in G. Iversen, ed., *Research on Tropes* (Stockholm, 1983).

Hajdu, H., *Das Mnemotechnische Schriftum des Mittelalters* (Vienna/Leipzig, 1936).

Hallinger, K., *Gorze-Kluny* (Studia Anselmiana, 22–5), 2 vols. (Rome, 1950–1).

Harvey, E. Ruth, *The Inward Wits, Psychological Theory in the Middle Ages and the Renaissance* (London, 1975).

Herrin, Judith, *The Formation of Christendom* (Oxford, 1987).

Howell, W. S., *The Rhetoric of Charlemagne and Alcuin* (Princeton, 1941).

Hudson, Ann and Michael Wilks, eds., *From Ockham to Wyclif, Studies in Church History*, subsidia 5 (Oxford, 1987).

Hunt, Noreen, ed., *Cluniac Monasticism in the Central Middle Ages* (London, 1971).

Hunt, R. W., 'Hugutio and Petrus Helias', *Medieval and Renaissance Studies*, 2 (1950), 174–8.

Hutton, Patrick, 'The art of memory', *Journal of the History of Ideas*, 48 (1987), 371–92.

Inciarte, F., 'Die Suppositionstheorie und die Anfänge der extensionalen Semantik', in W. Zimmermann, ed., *Antiqui und Moderni*, (Miscellanea Mediaevalia 9) (Berlin, 1974), 126–41.

Irvine, Martin, 'Bede the grammarian and the scope of grammatical studies in 8th-century Northumbria', *Anglo-Saxon England*, 15 (1986), 15–44.

von Ivánka, E., 'Der *apex mentis*', in W. Beierwaltes, ed., *Platonismus in der Philosophie des Mittelalters* (Darmstadt, 1969), 140–6.

'*Apex mentis*. Wanderung and Wandlung eines stoischen Terminus', *Zeitschrift für Katholische Theologie*, 72 (1950), 129–72.

Jacobi, Klaus, *Die Modalbegriffe in den Logischen Schriften des Wilhelm von Shyreswood und in anderen Kompendien des 12. und 13. Jahrhunderts* (Leiden/Koln, 1980).

Javelet, R., *Image et ressemblance du 12e s. de S. Anselme à Alain de Lille* (Paris, 1967).

Jolivet, Jean, *Arts du Langage et théologie chez Abélard* (Paris, 1969).

Kaczmarek, L., *Modi significandi und ihre Destruktionen: zwei Texte zur scholastischen Sprachtheorie im 14. Jahrhundert* (Münster, 1980).

Kelley, Donald, *The Foundations of Modern Historical Scholarship* (New York, 1970).

Knowles, David, 'Cistercians and Cluniacs', in *The Historian and Character* (Cambridge, 1963).

The Monastic Order in England from the times of St. Dunstan to the Fourth Lateran Council, 2nd edn (Cambridge, 1963).

'The primitive Cistercian documents', in *Great Historical Enterprises: Problems in Monastic History* (London, 1963), 197–222.

Kretzmann, Norman, Anthony Kenny, Jan Pinborg, eds., *The Cambridge History of Later Medieval Philosophy* (Cambridge, 1982).

Lackner, Bede, 'The liturgy of early Cîteaux', in *Studies in Medieval Cistercian History presented to Jeremiah F. O'Sullivan* (Spencer, Mass., 1971), 1–34.

Laclotte, M. and D. Thiébaut, *L'Ecole d'Avignon* (Paris, 1983).

Lacroix, Benoît, *L'Historien au Moyen Age* (Paris/Montreal, 1971).

Landfester, R., *Historia Magistra Vitae, Untersuchungen zur humanistischen Geschichtslehre des 14. bis 16. Jahrhunderts* (Geneva, 1972).

Lapidge, Michael and Helmut Gneuss, eds., *Learning and Literature in Anglo-Saxon England: Studies presented to Peter Clemoes on the Occasion of his 65th Birthday* (Cambridge, 1985).

Lapidge, M., 'The school of Theodore and Hadrian', *Anglo-Saxon England*, 15 (1986), 45–72.

Law, Vivien, *The Insular Latin Grammarians*, (Woodbridge and Totowa, New Jersey, 1982).

Leclercq, Jean, 'Pour une histoire de la vie à Cluny', (I), *Revue d'Histoire Ecclesiastique*, 57 (1962), 385–408; (II) 783–812.

'Ecrits monastiques sur la Bible aux xi[3] – xiiie s', *Mediaeval Studies*, 15 (1953), 95–106.

La spiritualité de Pierre de Celle (1115–82) (Paris, 1946).

La vie parfaite; points de vue sur l'essence de la vie religieuse (Paris/Turnhout, 1948).

'Les prologues de S. Bernard et sa psychologie d'auteur', *Cahiers de civilisation médiévale*, 1 (1958), 425–36.

The Love of Learning and the Desire for God, trans. C. Misrahi, 2nd revd edn. (London, 1974).

Monks and Love in Twelfth-Century France: Psycho-Historical Essays (Oxford, 1979).

'Lettres de S. Bernard: histoire ou littérature?', *Studi medievali*, 3rd ser., 12 (1971), 1–74.

Etudes sur S. Bernard et le texte de ses écrits (Rome, 1953).

Leff, Gordon, *William of Ockham, The Metamorphosis of Scholastic Discourse* (Manchester, 1975).

LeGoff, Jacques, *Pour un Autre Moyen Age* (Paris, 1977).

LeGoff, J. and P. Nora, *Faire de l'histoire, nouveaux problèmes, nouvelles approches*, 2 vols. (Paris, 1974).

Lekai, Louis J., *The Cistercians, Ideals and Reality* (Kent State, 1977).

Levao, Ronald, *Renaissance Minds and their Fictions* (Berkeley, 1985).

Lottin, O., *Psychologie et Morale aux xiie et xiiie s.*, 6 vols. (Gembloux, 1928–60).

de Lubac, Henri, *Exegèse médévale, les quatre sens de l'écriture*, 2 vols. (Paris, 1959).

Luciani, E., *Les confessions de S. Augustin dans les lettres de Petrarque* (Paris, 1982).

Luscombe, David, *The School of Peter Abelard* (Cambridge, 1969).

Mahoney, E. P., 'Themistius and the agent intellect in James of Viterbo and other thirteenth century philosophers (St Thomas, Siger of Brabant, Henry Bate)', *Augustiniana*, 23 (1973), 422–61.

Maier, Anneliese, 'Das Problem des *Species sensibiles in medio* und die neue Naturphilosophie des 14. Jahrhunderts' in *Ausgehendes Mittelalters*, vol. 2 (Rome, 1967), 419–51.

Maierú, Alfonso, ed., *English Logic in Italy in the 14th and 15th centuries*, Acts of the fifth European symposium on medieval logic and semantics, 1980 (quinto simposio Europeo sulla logica e la semantica nel medioevo) (Rome, 1981).

Marenbon, John, *From the Circle of Alcuin to the School of Auxerre, Logic, Theology and Philosophy in the Early Middle Ages* (Cambridge, 1981).

Markus, R. A., 'Gregory the Great and a papal missionary strategy', in G. C. Cuming, ed., *The Mission of the Church and the Propogation of the Faith, Studies in Church History*, 6 (Cambridge, 1970).

Marsh, David, *The Quattrocento Dialogue, Classical Tradition and Humanist Innovation* (Cambridge, Mass., 1980).

Mazza, Mario, *Storia e ideologia in Tito Livio* (Catania, 1966).

McGinn, Bernard, *The Golden Chain, A Study in the Theological Anthropology of Isaac of Stella* (Cistercian Studies) (Washington, D.C., 1972).

McGrade, Arthur, S., 'Ockham and the birth of individual rights', in B. Tierney and P. Linehan, eds., *Authority and Power, Studies on Medieval Law and Government Presented to Walter Ullmann on his Seventieth Birthday* (Cambridge, 1980), 149–165.

The Political Thought of William of Ockham (Cambridge, 1974).

McGrath, Alister, *The Intellectual Origins of the European Reformation* (Oxford, 1987).

McKisack, May, *Medieval History in the Tudor Age* (Oxford, 1971).

Meier, Christel, 'Vergessen, Erinnern, Gedächtnis im Gott-Mensch-Bezug. Zu einem Grenzbereich der Allegorese bei Hildegard von Bingen und anderen Autoren des Mittelalters', in H. Fromm, W. Harms and U. Ruberg, eds., *Verbum et Signum, Festschrift für F. Ohly* (Beiträge zur mediavistischen Bedeutungsforschung) (Munich, 1975), 143–94.

Mews, Constant, 'Man's knowledge of God according to Peter Abelard', in C. Wenin, ed., *L'Homme et son Univers en Moyen Age*, 2 vols. (Louvian-la-Neuve, 1986), 419–26.

'On dating the works of Peter Abelard', *AHDLMA*, 52 (1985), 73–134.

Meyvaert, Paul, *Benedict, Gregory, Bede and Others* (Variorum, London, 1977).

Michaud-Quantin, Pierre, 'La classification des puisssances de l'âme au xiie s.', *Revue de moyen-âge latin*, 5 (1949), 15–34.

'Une division "augustinienne" des puissances de l'âme au moyen âge', *Revue des Etudes Augustiniennes*, 3 (1957), 235–48.

'Les 'Platonici' dans la psychologie de S. Albert le Grand', *Recherches de Théologie ancienne et médiévale*, 23 (1956), 194–207.

Michaud-Quantin, P., and M. Lemoine, *Etudes sur le vocabulaire philosophique du Moyen Age* (Rome, 1970).

Miethke, Jürgen, 'Marsilius und Ockham, Publikum und Leser ihrer politischen Schriften im späteren Mittelalter', *Medioevo, rivista di storia della filosofia medievale*, 6 (1980), 543–67.

Ockhams Weg zur Sozialphilosophie (Berlin, 1969).

Milsom, S. F. C., *The Legal Framework of English Feudalism* (The Maitland Lectures, 1972) (Cambridge, 1976).

Minio-Paluello, Lorenzo, 'Le texte du 'De Anima' d'Aristote: la tradition latine avant 1500', in *Autour d'Aristote; recueil d'études de philosophie ancienne et médiévale offert à Monseigneur A. Mansion* (Louvain, 1955), 217–43.

'Iacobus Veneticus Grecus, canonist and translator of Aristotle', *Traditio*, 8 (1952), 265–304.

Mohrmann, Christine, *Etudes sur le latin des chrétiens*, 3 vols. (Rome, 1961).

Montasani, J., *George of Trebizond, A Biography and A Study of his Rhetoric and Logic* (Leiden, 1976).

Moody, Ernest, *Studies in Medieval Philosophy, Science and Logic, Collected Papers 1933–69* (Berkeley, 1975).

Murphy, James J., *Rhetoric in the Middle Ages* (Berkeley, 1974).

Medieval Eloquence: Studies in the Theory and Practice of Medieval Rhetoric (Berkeley, 1978).

Nardi, Bruno, 'Anima e corporo nel pensiero di San Tommaso (1942)', in *Studi di Filosofia medievale* (Rome, 1960), 163–91.

Soggetto e oggetto del conoscere nella filosofia antica e medievale, 2nd edn (Rome, 1952).

Oberman, Heiko A., *Masters of the Reformation, The Emergence of a New Intellectual Climate in Europe*, trans. D. Martin (Cambridge, 1981).

Oberman, H. A., *The Dawn of the Reformation, Essays in Late Medieval and Early Reformation Thought* (Edinburgh, 1986).

Oberman, H. A., '*Via antiqua* and *via moderna*: late medieval prolegomena to early Reformation thought', *Journal of the History of Ideas*, 48 (1987), 23–40.

The Harvest of medieval Theology, Gabriel Biel and Late Medieval Nominalism, 2nd revd edn (Grand Rapids, Michigan, 1967).

Obertello, Luca, *Severino Boezio: La Consolazione della Filosofia: gli Opuscoli Teologici* (Milan, 1979).

Oexle, Otto G., 'Liturgische *memoria* und historische Errinerung. Zur Frage nach dem Gruppenbewusstsein und dem Wissen der eigenen Geschichte in den mittelalterlichen Gilden', in N. Kamp and J. Wollasch, eds., *Tradition als historische Kraft* (Berlin, 1982), 323–40.

Ohly, Friedrich, 'Der Zeitenraum und das liturgische Zeitengedächtnis' in *Schriften zur Mittelalterlichen Bedeutungsforschung* (Darmstadt, 1977), 254–67.

Palmer, J. J. N., ed., *Froissart: Historian* (Woodbridge, Suffolk, 1981).

Paqué, Ruprecht, *Das Pariser Nominalistenstatut. Zur Entstehung des Realitätsbegriffs der neuzeitlichen Naturwissenschaft* (Berlin, 1970).

Partner, Nancy, *Serious Entertainments: The Writings of History in Twelfth-Century England* (Chicago, 1977).

'Making up lost time: writing on the writing of history', *Speculum*, 61 (1986), 90–117.

Pennington, M. Basil, ed., *One Yet Two: Monastic Tradition East and West* (Kalamazoo, 1976).

Peters, F. E., *Aristoteles Arabus: The Oriental Translations of Commentaries on the Aristotelian Corpus* (Leiden, 1968).

Petersen, Joan M., *The Dialogues of Gregory and Great in Their Late Antique Cultural Background* (Toronto, 1984).

Philips, Mark, 'The disenchanted witness: participation and alienation in Florentine historiography', *Journal of the History of Ideas*, 44 (1983), 191–206.

Pocock, J. G. A., 'The concept of language and the métier d'historien: some considerations on practice', in Anthony Pagden, ed., *The Language of Political Theory in Early-Modern Thought* (Cambridge, 1987), 19–40.

Pranger, M. Burcht, 'Masters of suspence: argumentation and imagination in Anselm, Bernard and Calvin', in *Assays: New Approaches to Medieval and Renaissance Texts*, I (Pittsburgh, 1981), 15–33.

'Anselm's *Brevitas*', *Anselm Studies* II, proceedings of the fifth international St. Anselm conference, ed. J. C. Schnaubelt, T. Losoncy, F. Van Fleteren and J. Frederck (New York, 1988), 477–58.

'*Studium sacrae scripturae*'. Comparaison entre les méthodes dialectiques et méditative dans les oeuvres systematiques et dans la premierè méditation d'Anselme', *Les mutations socio-culturelles au tournant des xie–xii^{e}s.*, *Etudes Anselmiennes*, (Abbaye Notre Dame du Bec, 1982) (Paris, 1984).

'La langue, corps de la théologie médiévale', in H. Hillenaar and E. van der Starre, eds., *Le Roman, le Récit et le Savoir* (Groningen, 1986), 50–67.

Ray, Roger, 'Medieval historiography through the twelfth century: problems and progress of research', *Viator*, 5 (1974), 33–59.

'Bede's *vera lex historiae*', *Speculum*, 55 (1980), 1–21.

Bibliography

Rockinger, Ludwig, *Briefsteller und Formelbücher des elften bis vierzehnten Jahrhunderts*, 2 vols. (Munich, 1863–4, reprinted New York, 1961).

Rohmer, J., 'La théorie de l'abstraction dans l'école franciscaine', *AHDLMA*, 3 (1928), 104–85.

Ryan, J. K. and B. M. Bonansea, eds., *John Duns Scotus, 1265–1965* (Washington, D.C. 1965).

Salmon, P., *L'Office divin au moyen âge, histoire de la formation du breviaire du ix* au *xvi* siècle* (Paris, 1967).

Shiel, J., 'Boethius' commentaries on Aristotle', *Medieval and Renaissance Studies*, 4 (1958), 217–44.

Schmaus, M., *Die Psychologische Trinitätslehre des heiligen Augustinus*, 2nd edn (Münster, 1967).

Schmid, K. and J. Wollasch, eds., *Memoria, der geschichtliche Zeugniswert des liturgischen Gedenkens im Mittelalter* (Munich, 1984).

Schmitt, C. B., Q. Skinner, E. Kessler, J. Kraye, eds., *The Cambridge History of Renaissance Philosophy* (Cambridge, 1988).

Schmitt, Charles B., 'Towards a reassessment of Renaissance Aristotelianism', *History of Science*, 11 (1973), 159–93.

Scholz, Richard, *Unbekannte kirchenpolitische Streitschriften aus der Zeit Ludwigs des Bayern (1327–59)*, 2 vols. (Rome, 1914).

Sigal, P. A., 'Histoire et hagographie: les *miracula* aux xi^e et xii^e s.', *Annales de Bretagne et des Pays de l'Ouest*, 87 (1980), 237–57.

Skinner, Quentin, *The Foundations of Modern Political Thought*, 2 vols. (Cambridge, 1978).

Smalley, Beryl, *English Friars and Antiquity in the early Fourteenth Century* (Oxford, 1960).

Sommerfeldt, John R., ed., *Cistercian ideals and reality* (Kalamazoo, 1978).

Southern, R. W., 'Aspects of the European Tradition of Historical Writing', *Transactions of the Royal Historical Society*, 5th ser., 20 (1970), 173–96; 21 (1971), 159–79; 22 (1972), 159–80.

Stock, Brian, *The Implications of Literacy: Written Language and Models of Interpretation in the Eleventh and Twelfth Centuries* (Princeton, 1983).

Struever, Nancy, *The Language of History in the Renaissance* (Princeton, 1970).

Temps, mémoire, tradition au moyen âge, Actes du xiiie congrès de la societé des historiens médiévistes de l'enseignement supérieur public (Aix-en-Provence, 1983).

Thomson, Rodney, 'Willian of Malmesbury as historian and man of letters', *Journal of Ecclesiastical History*, 29 (1978), 387–413.

Trapp, Damasus, 'Augustinian theology of the fourteenth century: notes on editions, marginalia, opinions and book-lore', *Augustiniana*, 6 (1956), 147–265.

Trinkaus, Charles, *The Poet as Philosopher, Petrarch and the formation of the Renaissance Consciousness* (New Haven, 1979).

'*Antiquitas versus modernitas*: an Italian humanist polemic and its resonsance', *Journal of the History of Ideas*, 48 (1987), 11–21.

Tweedale, Martin, *Abailard on Universals* (Amsterdam, 1976).

Van Steenberghen, Fernand, *Thomas Aquinas and Radical Aristotelianism* (Washington, D.C., 1980).

Aristotle in the West: The origins of Latin Aristotelianism, trans. L. Johnston, 2nd edn (Louvain, 1970).

La philosophie au xiiie s. (Paris/Louvain, 1966).

Vignaux, Paul, 'Structure et sens du *Monologion*', *Revue des sciences philosophiques et théologiques*, 31 (1947).

'Infini, liberté et histoire du salut', in *Deus et homo ad mentem I. Duns Scoti*, Studia Scholastica-Scotistica 5 (Rome, 1952), 495–507.

Nominalisme au xive siècle (Paris, 1948).

Walzer, Richard, 'Arabic transmission of Greek thought to medieval Europe', *Bulletin of the John Rylands Library*, 29 (1945), 3–26.

Ward, John O., 'Classical rhetoric and the writing of history in medieval and renaissance culture', in F. McGregor and N. Wright, eds., *European History and its Historians* (Adelaide, 1977).

Werner, K., *Der Entwicklungsgang der mittelalterlichen Psychologie* (Vienna, 1876).

Wilks, Michael, ed., *The World of John of Salisbury*, (*Studies in Church History*, subsidia 3) (Oxford, 1984).

Wippel, John F., *Metaphysical Themes in Thomas Aquinas* (Washington, D.C., 1984).

Wolfson, Harry A., 'Isaac Israeli on the internal senses', in *Jewish Studies in memory of George A. Kohut* (New York, 1945), 583–98.

Wolfson, H. A., 'The internal senses in Latin, Arabic and Hebrew philosophical texts', *Harvard Theological Review*, 28 (1935), 69–133.

Wood, Diana, *Clement VI, the Pontificate and Ideas of an Avignon Pope* (Cambridge, 1989).

Wootton, David, *Paolo Sarpi, between Renaissance and Enlightenment* (Cambridge, 1983).

Yates, Frances, *The Art of Memory* (London, 1966).

MODERN

Anscombe, G. E. M., 'Memory and the Past', in *Metaphysics and the Philosophy of Mind, collected papers*, vol. 2 (Oxford, 1981), 103–32.

Adorno, Theodor, *Minima Moralia, Reflections from Damaged Life*, trans. E. F. N. Jephcott (London, 1974).

Baddeley, Alan, *Your Memory, A User's Guide* (Harmondsworth, 1983).

The Psychology of Memory (New York, 1976).

Bartlett, F. C., *Remembering. A Study in Experimental and Social Psychology* (Cambridge, 1932).

Bateson, Gregory, *Mind and Nature, A Necessary Unity* (London, 1979).

Beattie, Alan, *History in Peril: May Parents Preserve It* (Centre for Policy Studies London, 1987).

Berlin, Isaiah, 'The concept of scientific history', in *Concepts and Categories* (New York, 1979).

Berlin, I., *Historical Inevitability* (Oxford, 1954).

Berlyne, D. E., *Aesthetics and Psychobiology* (New York, 1971).

Blakemore, Colin, *Mechanics of the Mind* (Cambridge, 1977).

Borges, Jorge Luis, 'Funes, the memorious' (1942), in *Ficciones*, ed. A. Kerrigan (New York, 1962).

Brown, Richard H. and Stanford M. Lyman, eds., *Structures, Consciousness and History* (Cambridge, 1978).

Butterfield, Herbert, *Man on his Past* (Cambridge, 1955).

Collingwood, R. G., *The Idea of History* (Oxford, 1946).

Dilthey, W., *Selected Writings*, ed. and trans. H. P. Rickman (Cambridge, 1976).

Eysenck, Michael W., *Human Memory, Theory, Research and Individual Differences* (Oxford, 1977).

Fodor, Jerry, *The Modularity of Mind: An Essay on Faculty Psychology* (Cambridge, Mass., 1984).

Freud, Sigmund, *The Writings of S. Freud*, 15 vols., ed. J. Strachey (Harmondsworth, 1985).

Gadamer, Hans-Georg, 'The universality of the hermeneutical problem', in *Philosophical Hermeneutics*, ed. and trans. D. Linge (Berkeley, 1976), 3–17.

Gadamer, H.-G., *Wahrheit und Methode: Grundzuge einer philosophischen Hermeneutik* (Tübingen, 1960).

Gellner, Ernest, *Words and Things* (Harmondsworth, 1968 (1959)).

Goody, Jack, *The Logic of Writing and the Organization of Society* (Cambridge, 1986).

The Domestication of the Savage Mind (Cambridge, 1977).

Goody, J. and Ian Watt, eds., *Literacy in Traditional Societies* (Cambridge, 1968).

Graff, Harvey J., *Literacy and Social Development in the West: A Reader* (Cambridge, 1981).

Gregg, Vernon H., *Introduction to Human Memory* (London, 1986).

Halbwachs, Maurice, 'La mémoire collective et le temps', *Cahiers internationaux de Sociologie*, 2 (1947), 3–31.

Les Cadres Sociaux de la Mémoire (Paris, 1952).

Hamilton, Malcolm B., 'The elements of the concept of ideology', *Political Studies*, 35 (1987), 18–38.

Helbling, Hanno, 'Der Mensch im Bild der Geschichte', in *Erfahrung und Denken* (Berlin), 30 (1969), 18–41.

Hempel, Carl, 'Function of general laws in history', *Journal of Philosophy*, 39 (1942), 35–48.

Henle, M., J. Jaynes and J. J. Sullivan, eds., *Historical Conceptions of Psychology* (New York, 1973).

Humphreys, R. Stephen, 'The historian, his documents and the elementary modes of historical thought', *History and Theory*, 19 (1980), 1–20.

Hunter, Ian M. L., *Memory* (Harmondsworth, 1964).

'Lengthy verbatim recall: the roll of text', in A. Ellis, ed., *Progress in the Psychology of Language* (London, 1985), 207–35.

Jacoby, Russell, *Social Amnesia, A Critique of Conformist Psychology from Adler to Laing* (Hassocks, 1975).

Jauss, Hans-Robert, *Toward an Aesthetic of Reception*, trans. T. Bahti (Brighton, 1982).

'Littérature médiévale et théorie des genres', *Poetique*, I (1970), 79–101.

Jaynes, Julian, *The Origins of Consciousness in the Breakdown of the Bicameral Mind* (Harmondsworth, 1982 (1971)).

Jung, C. G., *Memories, Dreams, Reflections*, trans. R. and C. Winston (London, 1963).

Kelley, Donald R., 'Horizons of intellectual history', *Journal of the History of Ideas*, 48 (1987), 143–69.

King, Preston, ed. and introd., *The History of Ideas* (London, 1983).

Kohli-Kunz, Alice, *Errinern und Vergessen. Das Gegenwärtigsein des Vergangenen als Grundproblem historischer Wissenschaft* (Berlin, 1973).

Kosselleck, Reinhart, *Futures Past, on the semantics of historical time*, trans. K. Tribe (Cambridge, Mass., 1985 (1979)).

Lacapra, Dominick, 'Rethinking intellectual history and reading texts', *History and Theory*, 19 (1980), 245–76.

Laslett, Peter, ed., *The Physical Basis of Mind* (Oxford, 1950).

von Leyden, W., *Remembering, A Philosophical Problem* (New York, 1961).

Macdonald, G. F., ed., *Perception and Identity, Essays presented to A. J. Ayer with his Replies to Them* (London, 1979).

Martin, Rex, *Historical Explanation, Re-enactment and Practical Inference* (Ithaca, 1977).

Mauss, Marcel, 'Les techniques du corps' (1936), *Sociologie et Anthropologie* (Paris, 1950), 363–86.

Neisser, Ulric, *Cognitive Psychology* (New York, 1967).

Piaget, Jean, and Bärbel Inhelder, *Memory and Intelligence*, trans. A. J. Pomerans (London, 1973 (1968)).

Popper, Karl, *Objective Knowledge: An Evolutionary Approach*, revd edn (Oxford, 1979).

Plumb, J. H., *The Death of the Past* (London, 1969).

Pribram, K. H., ed., *Brain and Behaviour 3: Memory Mechanisms* (Harmondsworth, 1969).

Rorty, R., J. B. Schneewind and Q. Skinner, eds., *Philosophy in History* (Cambridge, 1984).

Sacks, Oliver, *The Man who Mistook his Wife for a Hat* (London, 1985).

Seamon, John G., *Memory and Cognition, An Introduction* (Oxford, 1980).

Weisberg, Robert W., *Memory, Thought and Behavior* (Oxford, 1980).

White, Hayden, 'Rhetoric and history', in *Theories of History* (Los Angeles, 1978).

Metahistory: The Historical Imagination in 19th-Century Europe (London, 1973).

'The fictions of factual representation', in *The Literature of Fact*, ed. Angus Fletcher (New York, 1976), 21–44.

Wolin, Sheldon, *The Presence of the Past* (Baltimore/London, 1989).

Wollheim, Richard, *The Thread of Life* (Cambridge, 1984).

Young, J. Z., *Programs of the Brain* (Oxford, 1978).

INDEX

Abelard, Peter, 173, 190, 231–2, 233–73, 378, 420, 428, 440, 506, 527–8, 545, 561, 565, 580, 593, 606
  ars disserendi, logic as, 235
  ars sermocinales, logic as, 237
  chimeras, 240, 245 *see also* opinion
  Commentary on Paul's Epistle to Romans, 263, 282
  Dialectica, 235, 238 nn.240, 241, 243
  Historica calamitatum, 316
  history and the past, 242, 243, 254–8, 262–73
  hypothetical necessity (law of nature), 241–2 *see also* Aristotle, natural regularities (presupposed); Ockham, hypothetical necessity
  language, as convention, 239–43, 257, 260, 262, 267, 273, 528 *see also* Boethius
  Logica Ingredientibus, 234, 239, 243–9 *see also* Boethius
  Logica 'nostrorum petitioni sociorum', 238, 241
  nominalism, 236–7, 239 *see also* Nominalism, logical (terminism)
  opinion, 242, 247, 272
  psychology of signification, 243, 244–50 *see also* Boethius
  realists/realism, 245, 258–9
  'school of' Abelard, *Ysagoge in theologiam*, 215, 234
  Sic et Non, 262–71, 288 *see also* history and the past
  status, as common nature, 237, 259–61, 267, 271–2
  Tractatus de Intellectibus, 234, 239, 243–4, 249
  universals, as words, 239–40, 244, 247, 260, 267–8
  voces and *sermones*, 238

see also John of Salisbury; Ockham
Accolti, Benedetto, 558, 561, 581
Aelred of Rievaulx, *De Anima*, 208–15, 223
  cognitive memory and historiography, 214
  compared with Isaac of Stella, 218
  memory, 210, 212–14
  ratio (memory, intellect, will), 210
  sensualis vis, 209–13
  vis spiritualis, 211
  see also Cistercians
Albert the Great, 416–21, 469 *see also* Cicero, mnemotechnics, *ars memoria*
Alcuin, *Dicta albini*, 196–7, 203, 205, 215, 220
Ammirato, Scipio, 585 *see also* Machiavelli
Anonymous ad Cuimnanum, 142 *see also* Ars Grammatica
Anselm of Aosta, St, 155, 157–68, 220, 243, 247, 260, 294–5 (compared with Augustine)
  cogitare and *intelligere* (*ratio*), 167
  Cur Deus Homo, 295
  De Grammatico, 289
  intrinsic natural speech, 296
  locutio, divine and human, 159–67
  memory, 162–7
  Monologion, 158–67
  Proslogion, 166
  verbum mentis, 167
  De Veritate, 166
Anselm of Laon, disciples/school of, 192, 201 (William of St Thierry), 210 (Aelred of Rievaulx), 220
Aquinas, Thomas, St, 32, 234, 252, 327, 386, 412, 413, 414, 419, 420, 421, 422–60, 466, 469, 470, 475, 476, 477, 485, 493–4, 508, 512, 514, 515, 519, 523, 544, 572, 580, 607
  analogy and history, 454–60
  anti-Platonism, 436–40

638

Index